Essays in International Economic Theory

THE THEORY OF COMMERCIAL POLICY
Essays in International Economic Theory

Volume 1

Jagdish Bhagwati

Edited by Robert C. Feenstra

The MIT Press
Cambridge, Massachusetts
London, England

Printed and bound in the United States of America.

Library of Congress Cataloging in Publication Data
Bhagwati, Jagdish N., 1934–
The theory of commercial policy.
(Essays in international economic theory; v. 1)
Includes bibliographies and index.
1. Commercial policy—Addresses, essays, lectures.
I. Feenstra, Robert C. II. Title. III. Series:
Bhagwati, Jagdish N., 1934– . Essays in international economic theory; v. 1.
HF1411.B466 1983 vol. 1 337s [382′.3] 83-858
ISBN 0-262-02196-X

For
PADMA

CONTENTS

Volume 1
The Theory of Commercial Policy

III
Tariffs, Quotas, and Subsidies

IV
Directly Unproductive Profit-Seeking (DUP) Activities: Illegal Trade and Lobbying

Author's Preface

These two volumes contain a selection of my major writings in the theory of international trade since my first note on the theory of immiserizing growth appeared a little over two decades ago in the *Review of Economic Studies* in June 1958.

I have had the pleasure of collaborating with a number of teachers, students, and colleagues over a number of years. My debt to them is considerable. Harry Johnson, with whom I wrote two papers (both in volume 1), and T. N. Srinivasan, with whom I have written several (in both volumes), deserve particular thanks. The former seduced me into international trade at Cambridge, England, where I studied for the Economics Tripos during 1954–1956; the latter has been a close friend and collaborator ever since his return to Delhi in 1964 from his PhD at Yale. In addition, I must list among my colleagues and friends the following coauthors as well: Padma Desai, Koichi Hamada, Bent Hansen, Murray Kemp, V. K. Ramaswami, and Henry Wan, Jr. And my collaborating students have included Richard Brecher, Robert Feenstra, and Earl Grinols.

I am particularly thankful to Robert Feenstra for editing these two volumes with great care and attention to detail. MIT produced in the mid-1950s, when I had the good fortune to spend a year (1956–1957) there, a major generation of trade theorists, among whom were Ronald Jones, Robert Mundell, Jaroslav Vanek, Egon Sohmen, Ronald Findlay, and other important scholars, such as Stephen Hymer and Carlos Diaz Alejandro. I had the additional good fortune during my years at MIT (1968–1980) to oversee a new wave: Richard Brecher (cross-registering from Harvard), Paul Krugman, Gene Grossman, Robert Feenstra, and Earl Grinols, to name several of the leading young trade-theorists today. To have one of them edit these volumes is a great pleasure indeed.

Editor's Preface

These two volumes of Jagdish Bhagwati's essays in the theory of international trade are arranged into broad areas: first, commercial policy; and second, factor mobility. Each volume begins with essays of general interest and is then divided into specific topics. Earlier reprinted articles from *Trade, Tariffs and Growth,* including Bhagwati's widely read survey of international trade, have also been included. Editorial notes and errata are provided at the ends of the essays, where appropriate.

I had the pleasure of reading many of these essays while studying international economics with T. N. Srinivasan and Jagdish Bhagwati at the Massachusetts Institute of Technology. A substantial number of the essays in volume 1 are the result of their fruitful collaboration. Editing these volumes has filled out the gaps in my own reading, and increased my admiration for Bhagwati's significant contribution to trade theory over the past twenty-five years.

I
THE THEORY OF COMMERCIAL POLICY

The Theory and Practice of Commercial Policy: Departures from Unified Exchange Rates

In this study we shall consider the problems of commercial policy in its widest sense, exploring arguments that justify a departure from unified exchange rates in general. Unified exchange rates are defined to mean that (1) all exports occur at the same effective exchange rate as all imports (where the "effective rate" includes tariffs, trade subsidies and premia); and (2) the domestic incentives to produce and consume are not, in turn, distorted (by taxes and subsidies on domestic production, consumption and factor use) away from those provided by the structure of international prices. Thus the relative incentive to produce and consume tradable commodities, as provided by their domestic relative prices, is (identical or) unified with that obtaining internationally.

These questions have assumed considerable policy importance in recent years, especially in relation to the less developed countries. Although their economic performance can least afford to be guided by inefficient policies, it is increasingly becoming obvious that they have been severely impeded by a combination of trade and exchange-rate policies capable of inflicting serious losses from resulting misallocations of scarce resources. I shall thus go on to argue that, while a considerable body of argument can indeed be developed in defense of departures from unified exchange rates, the *de facto* operation of multiple effective rates by many developing countries today is incapable, in general, of rationalization on such grounds, and the likelihood of significant losses resulting from such policies can be empirically indicated. I shall also offer certain observations on the reasons for this state of affairs.

I. UNIFIED EXCHANGE RATES

At the heart of the welfare theory of trade are three basic propositions (see Bhagwati, 1967b):

Proposition (1) The trade situation (the opportunity to trade) is superior to the no-trade situation (the absence of trade opportunity), from the viewpoint of efficient technical possibilities.

Proposition (2) Under perfect competition, free trade will enable the economy to operate with technical efficiency.

Proposition (3) Under perfect competition, free trade will enable the economy to maximize utility, subject to the given constraints, so that, from the viewpoint of utility-based rankings as well, free trade is optimal and superior to no trade.

For Proposition (1), remember that technical efficiency is defined in the usual Paretian sense. Hence Proposition (1) merely states that it is *possible* to get more of one good and no less of the other when the opportunity to trade is available than when it is not.

This is readily seen in Figure 1, similar to Samuelson's illustration, where the price line $CD = EF$ represents the international prices and OAB the production-possibility set for an individual country. If production is set at P and trade is undertaken (as it must be) at the stated international prices, OEF becomes the availability set and EF the availability frontier, the Pareto-efficient locus of available combinations of the two commodities. But if production is set instead at P^*, the availability set is the *largest* possible, at OCD, and CD represents the most efficient Pareto-optimal availability line subject to the domestic and foreign transformation constraints.[1] On the other hand, AB, the production-possibility frontier, represents the efficient availability line in the absence of trade opportunity.

It is thus clear immediately, since CD lies uniformly outside AB (though touching it at P^*), that *any* bundle of commodities which is available by production alone (that is, in the no-trade situation) *can* be improved upon (with one borderline case at P^*) by production at P^* and trade therefrom.

Hence, the opportunity to trade represents for the economy a superior situation than the absence of trade. In other words, the trade situation is superior to the no-trade situation.

Note that this proposition merely states that it is *possible*, if the trade opportunity is exploited in a certain way, to have more of one good and no less of the other(s) under trade than under no trade. The

[1] Note that any shift of production from P^*, and trade therefrom, to production at another point (such as P) and trade from that new point will only *reduce* the availability set open to the economy. Hence, production at P^* represents the most efficient production point from which trade can be conducted.

Figure 1
Trade Situation versus Autarky

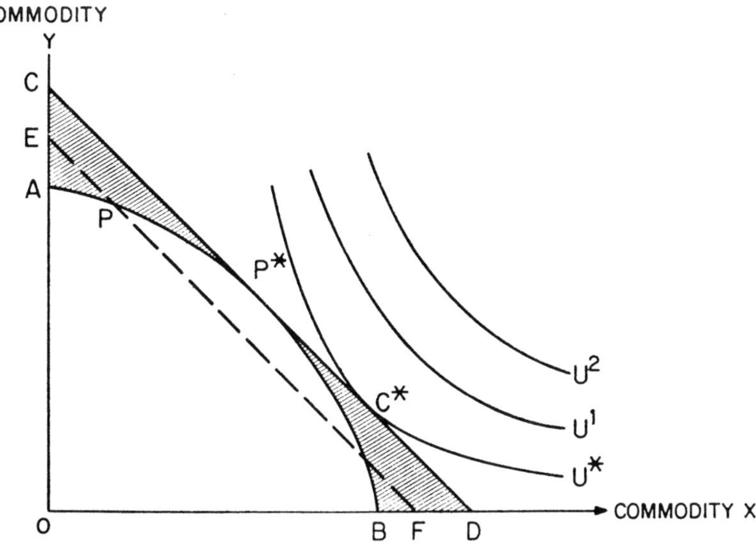

Without trade, APP^*B represents the production-possibility, and hence availability (or consumption-possibility) frontier for an individual country. If unlimited trade is possible at the world price ratio given by CD's slope, the new availability frontier is given by CP^*D, the farthest-out line with slope CD that touches the domestic production-possibility frontier. Any domestic welfare function (of the standard static variety) will be maximized at a point such as C^*, which gives more welfare than any point within APP^*B (save in the singular case where C^* and P^* happen to coincide).

proposition does *not* assert anything as to whether a specific economic system will in fact manage to utilize the trade opportunity in this technically efficient manner. Of course, the proposition that trade could expand the economy's availabilities is hardly surprising once one realizes that the possibility of trade really adds yet another "technological" process of transforming exportables into importables, and this cannot but improve (or, at worst, leave unchanged) the availabilities defined by the *domestic* resource and technological constraints. The proposition is thus clearly not conditional on the properties of the domestic production-possibility set.

This is not the case with Proposition (2), which relates explicitly to whether an actual institutional system will operate with *technical* efficiency. It states that, for a competitive price system, free trade *will* in fact enable the economy to exploit the trade opportunity most effectively and thus operate efficiently (that is, bring production to P^* and trade along CP^*D in Figure 1). The proof of this proposition is straightforward and rests on the fact that with (a) free trade defined as a policy constituting the equalization of foreign and domestic prices, and (b) perfect competition assuring the equalization of domestic prices with the marginal rate of transformation in production (on the production-possibility frontier), the economy must necessarily end up producing and trading efficiently, provided the production possibilities are a convex set. This rules out (as we shall see later) increasing returns leading to concavity. To illustrate: under free trade at price $CD = EF$, the economy *will* produce at P^* and trade along CD, thus operating with technical efficiency.

Note further that Proposition (2) can be readily adapted for institutional frameworks other than that of a competitive price system. Thus, for an economic system which does not use (domestic) prices to guide production, it is conceivable that an alternative way of operating with efficiency would be for planners to follow the rule of *equating foreign prices with the marginal rate of transformation of products in domestic production.*[2] This efficiency rule will ensure the operation of the economy at technical efficiency; in Figure 1, the planners will be guided by the rule to producing at P^* and thus trading along CP^*D. Free trade merely happens to be the policy that enables a competitive price system to implement this efficiency rule.[3]

It is now possible to go beyond questions of technical efficiency and raise the issue of utility-based ranking of free trade and no trade. If we take a well-ordered index of social utility, Proposition (3) follows immediately. Formally, we would be maximizing a function such as

[2] For a country, however, that enjoys monopoly power in trade, the rule modifies to the well-known prescription to equate the marginal terms of trade (that is, the marginal rate of transformation through foreign trade) with the marginal rate of transformation in domestic production. The rule can be obtained more directly by maximizing the availability of one commodity subject to specified level(s) of the other(s), subject further to the constraints imposed by the implicit domestic-transformation function and the foreign reciprocal-demand function. I shall return to this point later, in Chapter II.

[3] Following on this, I have found it useful, in the classroom, to tell my Indian students that even a "Soviet-type" economic system, which may decide to avoid the use of prices to guide domestic allocation of resources, cannot afford to ignore *international* prices, the reason being that they really represent, from the welfare point of view, a "technological" datum. I may also add that the distinction between Propositions (2) and (3), based on the distinction between technical efficiency and utility maximization, is also very useful if one is teaching students living in a "planned" economy. Professor Bent Hansen, who has taught in Cairo for some years, told me some time ago that he has also found it useful to teach free-trade optimality in terms of Propositions (1) and (2) above.

$U = U(X, Y)$, where U stands for social welfare, X and Y for the available commodities, and the function has the standard properties (see Samuelson, 1956), such as

$$\frac{\partial U}{\partial X} > 0, \ \frac{\partial U}{\partial Y} > 0, \ \left|\frac{dX}{dY}\right|_{U = \text{constant}} < 0 \quad \text{and} \quad \left|\frac{d^2X}{dY^2}\right|_{U = \text{constant}} < 0$$

This function would be maximized subject to the implicit domestic-transformation function and the foreign-reciprocal-demand function. It would then be shown that, under free trade, a perfectly competitive system would satisfy the derived maximizing conditions.

For those not anxious to raise questions about the incomparability of different persons' utilities and who are ready to accept a well-ordered index of social utility, this procedure would be entirely satisfactory.[4] But those who, reluctant to go beyond consideration of utility for each (incomparable) individual, wish to base rankings by utility on the criterion of superiority for all income distributions may prefer the approach of comparing utility-possibility loci used by Samuelson [1962] and Kemp [1962]. They argue, quite correctly, that the fact that CD, the availability frontier under free trade, lies uniformly outside (though once touching) AB, the availability frontier under no trade, implies that the utility-possibility locus for the free-trade situation must also lie uniformly outside (though possibly touching) that for the no-trade situation, as illustrated in Figure 2 for a two-person economy. This implies that, under free trade, for *any* utility distribution (except at the point(s) where the two loci touch[5]) achieved under no trade, it is possible (via ideal lump-sum taxes and subsidies) to achieve a higher level for both individuals. And, similarly, under free trade, for *any* utility distribution achieved under restricted trade, it can be shown that it is possible (via ideal lump-sum taxes and subsidies) to achieve a higher level for both individuals. Hence free trade is the optimal policy (for all income distributions).[6]

[4] For those unwilling to assume that *laissez-faire* can be counted on to provide the ethically proper income distribution and yet want to use a social-utility index, Samuelson's (1956) construction of "social-indifference curves" is the appropriate reference.

[5] As Professor Samuelson has pointed out to me in correspondence, the utility-possibility locus under free trade may even *coincide* with the utility-possibility locus under no trade if all individuals are alike and have unitary income elasticities, and if C^* in Figure 1 coincides with P^*.

[6] While the argument developed around the illustrations has assumed trade only in final products, absence of intermediates, and given endowments of primary

Figure 2

Superiority of Free Trade over Autarky, Illustrated through Utility-Possibility Curves

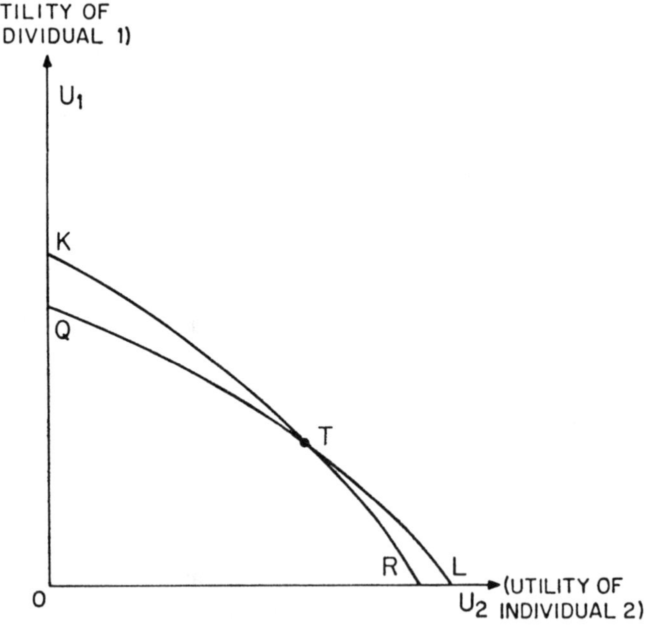

QTR represents the utility-possibility curve, in a two-person economy, corresponding to the no-trade situation. *KTL* represents the utility-possibility curve corresponding to the free-trade situation. *KTL* lies uniformly outside *QTR* (though touching it at *T*), indicating that the free-trade situation is superior (or, at minimum, equivalent) to the no-trade situation from the viewpoint of social welfare.

It follows, from these fundamental insights of the theory of trade and welfare, that economic welfare, derived from the flow of currently available goods and services, will be maximized by the adoption of policies that unify the effective exchange rate, provided suitable monetary and fiscal policies are adopted to maintain Keynesian full employment. Any departures from such a policy would involve (1) trade tariffs, subsidies, and quantitative restrictions, (2) production and consumption taxes and subsidies, (3) taxes and subsidies on factor use, or (4) exchange control combined with overvaluation of the exchange rate, or undervaluation of the exchange rate, any of which policies will result in nonunified effective exchange rates and thus will pull the economy away from the optimal position.

---

factors, the theorem that free trade is the optimal policy is independent of these simplifying assumptions.

The conclusions are so impressive that Graham (1934) could write with eloquence:

> . . . Whether a country is rich or poor, big or little, new or old, with or without high standards of living, agricultural, industrial, or mixed, makes no difference. It is a matter of mathematics, quite independent of environment, that there is an *inherent* gain in the specialization along the lines of *comparative* competence which unshackled trade tends to develop.
>
> There is no possible refutation of this analysis. Advocates of a restrictive commercial policy must, in logic, accept it as a fact and attempt to show that the gain may be outweighed by economic or other considerations of superior importance. . . . The *presumption* is always in favor of free trade, since the gain therefrom is certain, and the loss, if any, dependent upon incidental circumstance. This presumption is rebuttable but it is ever present; and, in this sense, the classical economists were right in insisting that free trade is a ubiquitous and timeless principle. Other things being equal, it will enable people to have more goods of every kind than would otherwise be possible (pp. 58-59).

An economist writing today could not have put the essence of the problem better. But the fact is that the analytical writings since Graham's time have resulted in an overwhelming accumulation of arguments which indeed accept the basic efficiency of specialization in trade but demonstrate the advantages of departure therefrom for "economic or other considerations of superior importance." It is to these arguments, and some novel but (in my judgment) significant ones, that I now turn.

II. JUSTIFIABLE DEPARTURES FROM UNIFIED EXCHANGE RATES

The arguments for departing from unified exchange rates can, in general, be divided into two broad types: (1) those that accept the traditional adoption of the objective function which defines social welfare as a function of the currently available flow of goods and services but point to factors such as externalities, for example, to show that a departure from unified exchange rates is called for; and (2) those that modify the objective function, thereby resulting in different optimality conditions from those satisfied by unified exchange rates.

The former set of arguments can again be classified into (a) those resulting in optimal intervention in the form of tariffs, (b) those calling for optimal intervention in the form of export subsidies, and (c) those leading to optimal intervention in the form of *domestic* tax-cum-subsidies on consumption, production, or factor use. The latter set of arguments, depending on changes in the objective function, are broadly divisible into two classes: (a) those that involve essentially the notion of "dynamic comparative advantage," leading to a conflict between today and tomorrow; and (b) those that invoke objectives, many traditionally (though rather oddly) considered to be "non-economic," such as the collection of revenue, achievement of specified income distribution, maintenance of specified levels of production in industries of "strategic importance," and so on.[7]

A. TRADITIONAL OBJECTIVE FUNCTION

I shall deal successively with the arguments resulting in first-best cases for tariffs, trade subsidies, and domestic tax-cum-subsidies on production, consumption, and factor use. Where it seems useful, I shall also consider whether alternative forms of intervention, though sub-optimal, may still improve welfare over the level reached under unified rates.

[7] Needless to say, some of the non-economic objectives are themselves treated best sometimes as essentially involving a conflict between today and tomorrow. For example, industrialization can be treated *either* as a non-economic objective *or* as an economic policy that is justified by externality arguments which may involve a conflict between income today and income tomorrow. Similarly, revenue collection may be required to raise the savings rate in the interest of growth but may involve loss of current income regardless of how revenue is raised (for, let it be admitted, revenue cannot in practice be raised by lump-sum taxes).

1. Arguments for Tariffs as First-Best Policy

(1) The traditional argument for first-best tariffs relates to the presence of monopoly power in trade. Unified exchange rates, in such a situation, will not lead to a satisfaction of the first-order conditions for a Paretian optimum: the equalization of foreign and domestic prices will not equate the domestic marginal rate of transformation in production and the domestic marginal rate of substitution in consumption with the marginal rate of transformation through foreign trade. On the other hand, the adoption of a suitable tariff (or structure of tariffs) will permit these three marginal rates to be equated, thus leading to optimality. The first-best solution for utility maximization will therefore involve the levy of a suitable tariff (or structure of tariffs, if more than two goods are considered, in which case, because of cross-elasticity terms, some imports and exports may be subsidized).

The optimum tariff, when derived, will vary with the income distribution. Further, and more importantly, if the producers themselves combine to exercise the monopoly power, the need to impose the optimum tariff by policy will be avoided. However, the situation will turn into a sub-optimal one *if* the monopoly is extended also to domestic sales, as would seem natural. Further, these arguments for departing from a unified exchange rate are not to be dismissed as unimportant in practice: countries do possess such monopoly power, for certain lengths of time, although over protracted periods substitution possibilities tend to be considerable. Nor does the possibility of retaliation necessarily rule out the possibility of gain from the imposition of monopoly tariffs. Recent analyses (see Johnson, 1965b) of the question, using a Cournot-type reaction mechanism where countries retaliate on the principle of levying optimum tariffs, have shown that at the end of such a process a country may still be left better off than under a unified exchange rate.[8]

(2) An important variation of this argument, with rather more empirical relevance today, concerns the possibility of discrimination between alternative markets, as distinct from the exercise of monopoly power in a unified foreign market. Typically, trade opportunities present themselves discretely, among different trading blocs that are

[8] If the possibility of tariff retaliation *decreases* when the monopoly power is exercised by a domestic production subsidy to the importable industry, then (even though this would be *ceteris paribus* an inefficient way of exercising the monopoly power in trade) the country might be left better off by levying such a production subsidy-cum-tax rather than by imposing tariffs.

demarcated in varying degrees. If the marginal terms of trade differ from the average terms of trade in two alternative markets, for example, the optimal policy would involve equating the marginal terms of trade in the two markets to the domestic marginal rate of transformation and rate of substitution in consumption and *not* operating at a unified exchange rate. Typically, this is the kind of situation that confronts many developing countries today, as a result especially of the possibility of bilateral-trading arrangements with a large number of potential trading partners (including the Soviet bloc).

(3) An important first-best argument for using tariffs, though transitionally, derives from the manner in which tariff negotiations are conducted. For a country without monopoly power in trade, a unified exchange rate will in general be the optimal policy. Hence the imposition of a tariff will reduce economic welfare. But suppose that the tariff can be used as the lever with which to bargain for a reduction in the tariff of the trading partner. In this case, the net result, if and when *both* tariffs are removed, could be to increase the country's welfare above what it would have been in the absence of the tariff. This possibility also helps to explain the well-known puzzle of the free traders as to why countries insist on reciprocity in tariff cuts if theory can demonstrate that a unilateral cut would be beneficial.[9]

It is interesting to note that Graham was well aware of this argument:

> Protection is at times used as a weapon to punish or prevent foreign discrimination, to force a more liberal trade policy on other nations, to serve as a retaliatory measure against restrictions which, though not discriminatory between foreign nations, are regarded as undue, and to establish a favorable bargaining position for prospective international commercial negotiations. The certain immediate loss to the levying country is not always recognized, but where it is, retaliatory duties are levied in the expectation that a still greater loss will be imposed on the foreign country against which they are specially aimed and that such country will thereby be persuaded to take a tractable attitude . . . , when used for the purposes discussed in this paragraph, the object of the protective measures is not to restrict but to enlarge the freedom of commercial intercourse; it

[9] For an extended discussion of the reasons which can be adduced to explain the demand for reciprocity in tariff negotiations, see Johnson (1965b) and Bhagwati (1967c).

seeks to restrain restraints. The protection is then justified not on its own account but solely as a means of securing freer trade (pp. 85-86).

(4) Finally, if the imposition of quotas will induce an inflow of private investment from foreign firms interested in "sales maximization," for example, then it is conceivable that the loss imposed by protection is outweighed by the advantage gained by the resulting inflow of investment.[10] From the viewpoint of national advantage, therefore, this involves again the case for first-best tariffs. Remember, however, that if the same inflow of investment could be attracted by subsidizing domestic production instead, then (as I shall soon argue) this would be a superior policy since it would permit the same advantage from the resulting inflow of investment while reducing the cost of protection by permitting the consumption of the protected items to occur at international prices.

2. Arguments for Trade Subsidies as First-Best Policy

While arguments in support of tariffs as first-best policy are sufficiently understood, as also those to be shortly developed here in support of domestic subsidy-cum-tax policies as first-best policies, this is *not* the case with export subsidies. Catch hold of any trade theorist and he is certain to rule them out as first-best policies. This discriminatory neglect by analysts is shared by international institutions, such as the GATT, which asymmetrically disapprove of export subsidies more than of tariffs and import restrictions. As a result export subsidization often takes devious forms permitting the customary reconciliation of public morality with private behavior.

Undoubtedly there are many specious arguments in support of export subsidies. Thus, for example, take the following untenable arguments, which are much too common.

(1) It is often argued that export subsidies are good because they increase the volume of world trade. It is not unusual to come across exhortations to "maximize world trade." However, this is clearly a nonsense proposition, though even distinguished economists like Ragnar Frisch (1948) have sometimes fallen unawares into the trap.

[10] Marginal inflow of such investment may be of net benefit, even if there are no externalities, no governmental siphoning-off of profits, and no monopoly power in trade, despite capital earning the value of its marginal product if the marginal return to capital is below the average and there is already some investment from abroad in the country (or if we are dealing with discrete inflows of investment).

There is an optimum degree of trade; one can trade *both* too much and too little.

(2) A superficially more attractive version in which this doctrine turns up, however, is that "it is desirable that a country in balance of payments difficulties should correct its deficit by increasing trade and making fuller use of international specialization, whereas a country resorting to import controls [and import tariffs] would reduce international specialization" (Streeten, 1963, p. 15). Firstly, the optimal method of correcting the balance of payments would be to change the exchange rate and to maintain a unified exchange rate (assuming, of course, that none of the qualifications being considered here are present). Secondly, even if second-best methods are to be used, it does not follow by any obvious means that export subsidization will be superior as a sub-optimal policy to tariff or import restrictions.[11]

(3) It is also sometimes argued that domestic entrepreneurs have less information about foreign markets than about domestic markets and hence export subsidization is called for in order to offset this asymmetry. But this is also a fallacious argument, because the acquisition of information expends real resources, and foreign sales, in principle, should yield enough returns to cover these costs if they are to be privately *and* socially desirable. Unless, therefore, some externality argument is produced, there is no case for an export subsidy merely because of the asymmetry between available information on domestic and foreign markets.

On the other hand, there *are* valid arguments which can make the adoption of export subsidization part of a first-best policy. I shall now

[11] Export subsidies can actually be shown to be inferior if the export subsidies are sufficiently large to reverse the pattern of trade in a two-good model (see for example Bhagwati, 1967b): such export subsidization will be inferior to autarky which, in turn, will be inferior to trade at any level if it is restricted by tariffs or as to quantity.

Of course, the ultimate second-best choice between export subsidies and tariffs and quantitative restrictions would also involve judgments with respect to questions such as, for example, the possibility of retaliation and the revenue problems associated with either policy. Thus, for instance, comparing export subsidies with quantitative restrictions, Streeten (1963, p. 16) has argued that "Export subsidies will tend to be less inflationary than import restrictions. Part of the increase in export earnings will have been matched by extra domestic taxation, thus reducing demand inflation from the improvement in the balance of payments."

But this particular argument is false because, if effective taxation has (automatically) increased in the case of export subsidies, there is no reason why it could not be stepped up (by explicit policy) in the case of import restrictions.

set up three arguments in support of this contention, though not all of them are of equal empirical relevance.

(1) The *private* evaluation of risk with respect to sales abroad may be in excess of the social evaluation, which may be more realistic. The private entrepreneur may, for example, exaggerate the risk of losses from a quota being imposed on his sales in a foreign market, whereas the government may have recourse to relief via representation at GATT and/or intergovernmental negotiations, which is underestimated by the private entrepreneurs in question. In such a case, it is *not* enough merely to provide *information* to private entrepreneurs; the entrepreneurs may continue to have views concerning the risks of (a) insufficient action by the domestic government and (b) inadequate response by the foreign government, either or both of which may diverge from the official views.

(2) It is necessary to invest in cultivating a market and these costs can be significant in international markets for manufactures. Any firm breaking into a foreign market may thus find that, if *other* firms can exploit a market opened up by its own expenditures, the private returns to this activity are less than the actual social returns.[12] This element of *externality* would then justify the grant of an appropriate export subsidy to this (exportable) industry. Note that this argument for an export subsidy depends on (a) an asymmetry of externalities between external and internal markets and (b) the assumption that the firms cannot sell any amount, at a given price, internationally; but neither of these assumptions can be ruled out *a priori*. In fact, the notion of an "infant export industry" makes very good sense if construed in this manner, and thus justifies, where the above argument is valid, the grant of export subsidies.

(3) Externalities of other kinds also can be quite important in practice and may result in the case for an optimum export subsidy. Thus, for example, it is well known to aid recipients that a superior "export performance" is taken nowadays to be a sign of successful economic planning and is productive of smoother, perhaps larger aid flows. Hence, even an otherwise sub-optimal policy of export subsi-

[12] Thus, an Indian firm undertaking initial losses abroad to sell its products in the hope of building up later sales may fear that its Indian rivals will exploit this groundwork. Once the reputation of "Indian supplies" has been established, there is nothing to prevent competitors from cutting into its future sales in this foreign market.

dization, provided it results in a larger inflow of resources on aid terms and with net positive marginal productivity to the economy, may well be optimal.[13] Just as an economy will trade too much under a unified rate when there is monopoly power in trade, the link with aid could mean that a country is trading too little under a unified rate.

3. Arguments for Domestic Tax-cum-Subsidies as First-Best Policy

I now come to the arguments which lead to the case for *domestic* as distinct from foreign-trade instruments as first-best policy. In essence, these arguments invoke two types of phenomena:

(1) The domestic prices may not measure social opportunity costs (as indicated by the marginal rate of transformation in efficient domestic production) and thus involve a breakdown of the equality between the marginal rates of transformation in production with both the domestic marginal rate of substitution in consumption and the marginal rate of transformation through foreign trade, *if a unified exchange rate is adopted.*

(2) Further, the domestic prices may not measure the social rate of substitution in consumption, in which case again a unified exchange rate will result in a nonfulfillment of the first-order conditions for utility maximization because the marginal rate of substitution in consumption will fail to be equated with the two rates of transformation through trade and domestic production.

The former phenomenon may arise owing to (a) externalities in production, (b) monopoly in product markets, or (c) imperfections in the factor market. The latter phenomenon would arise if there were externalities in consumption. In each case, however, it is readily shown that the suitable first-best policy will involve a *domestic* tax-cum-subsidy, aimed at making effective market prices reflect true opportunity costs or ratio of social marginal utilities. Intervention in the form of commercial policy will be sub-optimal, although if appropriately chosen it may result in welfare levels higher than under a unified exchange rate. Thus, for example, if the factor prices are different

[13] Such an externality obtains, even more obviously, with respect to private foreign investment. Acceptance of such investment, even when its net social marginal productivity is not positive, may turn out to be productive of more Western aid and hence be optimal overall. Or take the case of untied aid: it may be wise to spend it sub-optimally at the source of origin, for if it is not spent there this may cut into the future aid flow itself. And so on.

between sectors and represent a genuine distortion, it will be optimal to subsidize the use of the factor by the sector which otherwise has to pay a higher price, thereby eliminating the distortion directly. Similarly, if there is externality such that the market price understates the social-opportunity cost of production, then a tax-cum-subsidy on production which offsets this degree of imperfection will be optimal. In each case, the optimal policy will have to be applied at the point at which the distortion arises; in each case, the policy of a unified exchange rate will be inefficient.

(a) Tax-cum-Subsidies on Production

(1) In the case of production externalities, where the output of a product affects the output of another without the market enabling the producer of the former to appropriate the imputed value of this productivity to himself, the private return to producing this item will fall below its social value. It will be necessary, therefore, to introduce an appropriate tax-cum-subsidy measure on production to correct for this distortion. Meade's classic example of the honey producers profiting without payment from the apple blossoms growing next to the bees is an apt illustration. Apples will have to be subsidized so as to make the private returns to apple growers equal to the social returns. In Figure 3, at the given international prices *FP*, production will be (with nontangency) at P^o, consumption at C^o, and welfare at U^o. An appropriate production tax-cum-subsidy, given the foreign price ratio which is fixed throughout the analysis, will take the economy to production at P^*, to consumption at C^*, and to welfare, at a maximum, at U^*. On the other hand, an export subsidy, which is a sub-optimal policy, is shown at a level that leads to production at P^*, to consumption at C^{ES}, and to utility level at U^{ES}.[14]

[14] Formally, the problem is easily stated. Let the linear homogeneous production functions be

$$X = X(K_x, L_x),$$
$$Y = Y(K_y, L_y, X).$$

Then, for a competitive economy, it can be shown that (1) the economy will operate on the production-possibility curve, that is, with technical efficiency, *but* (2) the price ratio between commodities will diverge from the slope of the production-possibilities curve. The production-possibility set further may cease to be convex, a possibility that is abstracted from in the text.

The reader may note that Kemp (1964, p. 128) has shown why, in the present case, the economy will continue to operate on the efficient production-possibility curve, at points such as P^o and P^*, rather than inefficiently within and off the production-possibility curve.

Figure 3
Externality in Production and Optimality of a Policy of a Tax-cum-Subsidy on Production

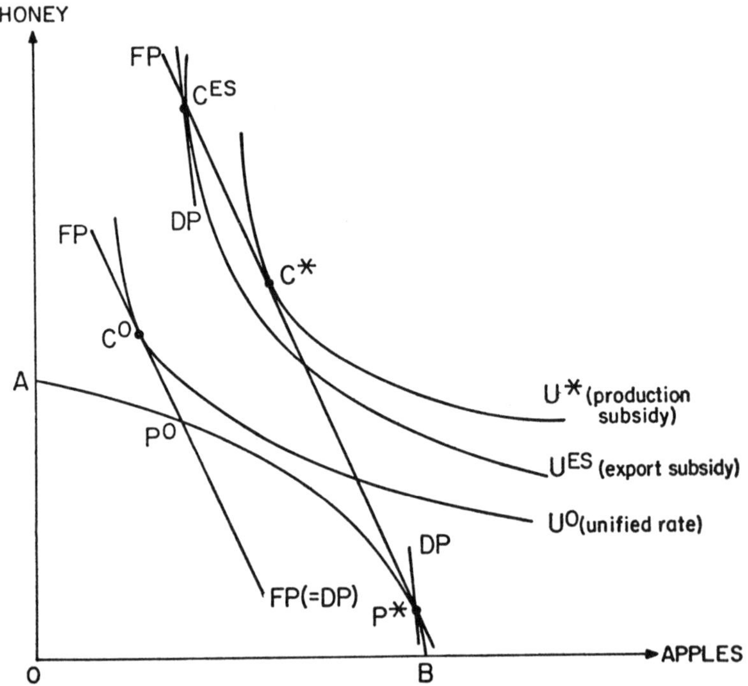

AB is the production-possibility curve between apples and honey. The externality in production, such that the market does not remunerate apple growers for the increment in honey output, results in the nontangency between the commodity price ratio and the production-possibility curve at P^o. With given foreign prices (*FP*) for a small country, a unified rate policy will take welfare level to U^o. A suitable policy of a tax-cum-subsidy on production, in favor of apples, will however lead to optimality, with production at P^*, consumption at C^*, and welfare at U^*: production will be in response to the domestic price ratio for producers that includes the tax-cum-subsidy (*DP*). An export-subsidy policy which takes production to P^* as well, however, will be sub-optimal as it will distort consumption to C^{ES} (at prices including export subsidies *DP*) and thus reduce welfare to U^{ES}.

(2) Where there is monopoly in the domestic sale of output the results are similar. Monopoly will result in a similar divergence of the commodity prices from the social opportunity costs, thus showing up in a domestic distortion. In such a case, the first-best remedial policy is clearly to use tax-cum-subsidy measures to guide production away to a mix where the marginal rate of transformation in domestic production equals the foreign prices at an exchange rate which is other-

wise unified. Under unified-exchange-rate policies, the economy will be in a sub-optimal position and may even be worse off than under autarky. Again, intervention through trade tariffs or subsidies will be sub-optimal; but, at appropriate levels, even such measures may enable an improvement over the welfare level reached under a unified exchange rate.[15]

(b) Tax-cum-Subsidies on Factor Use

Where, however, there are imperfections in factor markets, the optimal policy will be the adoption of tax-cum-subsidy measures with respect to factor use rather than domestic production.

Three major types of imperfections in factor markets need to be distinguished *in principle*, though clearly not all of them are equally important:

(i) There may be a distorting wage differential between activities for the same factor, as alleged for labor between manufacturing and agriculture.

(ii) The wages may be equal between activities *but* may diverge from value of marginal product in an activity, as alleged in agriculture with farming by peasant families.

(iii) The wages may be equal between activities *but* may diverge from the shadow, or optimal, wage for the economy, as is alleged sometimes for the so-called "surplus labor" economies whose optimal wage is supposed to be zero and below the actual wage.

Of these three possible imperfections, only the first has been discussed at length in the literature, though it may be the least consequential in reality. I shall discuss each of the imperfections now, in turn.

(1) The argument related to wage differentials dates back to Manoilesco and was revived recently by Hagen in reference to the observed wage differentials between the urban and the rural sector in several countries. It is pertinent, before analysis is built upon their distorting effects, to consider the circumstances when they may *not* represent a genuine distortion. For instance, they may reflect (a) a utility preference between occupations on the part of the wage-earners,

[15] However, since tariff protection itself may accentuate the domestic monopoly, while free trade with a unified exchange rate may eliminate it altogether, it is possible to argue even in this case that the first-best policy in this eventuality could again be a unified exchange rate.

or (b) a rent (on scarce skills), or (c) a return on investment in human capital (by training), or (d) a return on investment in the cost of movement (from the rural to the urban sector). There is a distortion, however, where the differential is attributable to (e) trade-union intervention, or (f) grounds of prestige based on humanitarianism ("I must pay my man a decent wage") that fix wages at varying levels in different sectors (see Bhagwati and Ramaswami, 1963).

Three other types of explanations may also be discussed: (g) The differential may occur in manufacture, because this is the advancing sector and growing activities inevitably have to pay higher wages to draw labor away from other industries. While this "dynamic" argument appears to provide support for the distorting character of the differential, there are difficulties connected with it. For instance, the fact that a differential has to be maintained to draw labor away may very well be due to the cost of movement. (h) A more substantive argument is that the rural sector affords employment to non-adult members of the family, whereas in the urban sector the adult alone gets employment (owing to institutional reasons, such as factory acts). Hence, to migrate, an adult would need to be compensated for the loss of employment by the non-adult members of his family. If this is the case, there is certainly a market imperfection (assuming that individual preferences rather than collective preferences, expressed in legislation, are relevant) and hence distortion.[16] (i) Finally, even if the differential can be entirely attributed to the cost of movement between the sectors, if the capital market for financing such movement is imperfect and makes such movement more expensive than investment in other activities, as may well be the case, there is still an element of the wage differential which will be "distorting" from the welfare point of view.

Assuming, therefore, that the differential is distorting and, for simplicity, that it can be treated as constant throughout the analysis with the wage rate in one sector a constant multiple of the wage in the other sector, it can be readily shown that (1) the economy will *not* operate on the efficient transformation frontier (for the two sectors will have, in equilibrium, unequal rates of substitution between factors); (2) the commodity price ratio will *not* equal the marginal rate of transformation in domestic production; and (3) the feasible production-possi-

[16] This "distortion," unlike the others, involves a contraction of the labor force as labor moves from one sector to another. Hence, the following analysis does not apply, and a fresh solution incorporating a changing labor supply is called for.

bility set may even cease to be convex. It follows, equally readily, that a unified exchange rate will be a sub-optimal policy and that the first-best optimal policy will be a tax-cum-subsidy policy on factor use that offsets the differential. A little less obviously, if such a first-best policy is ruled out, the second-best policy would be a tax-cum-subsidy on production. Intervention via trade policy would thus be inferior to both these first-best and second-best policies; but, if appropriately set, trade policy may be superior to a unified exchange rate.

Thus, in Figure 4, it is shown that the introduction of a wage differential against commodity X will lead to the decline of welfare from U_f to U_u if a unified exchange rate is being adopted. On the other hand, an appropriate tax-cum-subsidy policy with respect to factor use will offset this distortion and lead the economy back to its *maximal* welfare potential, given the resources and know-how. The *second-best* policy will be an appropriate tax-cum-subsidy on production which, while it cannot eliminate the shrinking-in of the feasible production set, will offset the welfare-reducing nontangency; thus the economy will operate at P_s, C_s, and U_s ($< U_f$ but $> U_u$). In this instance, an export-subsidy policy may improve welfare over the level reached under a unified exchange rate; but it will be inferior to the second-best policy.

Note further that, if there is a parallel and equal differential in the *other* factor (in a two-factor world), then the economy will operate on the most efficient production-possibility curve—for, in this case, both activities will have identical factor price *ratios* and hence the rates of substitution between the factors in both activities will be equalized. However, the distortion in the shape of the *non*tangency will be accentuated. At the other extreme, one could imagine a *reverse* differential—the wage of one factor higher in one sector and of the other factor higher in the other sector—which tended to offset the nontangency effect while accentuating the shrinking-in of the feasible production-possibility set. The latter possibility might even be realistic if the higher interest rates observed in rural areas are not to be attributed entirely to risk—in which case, protection, either through commercial policy or through tax-cum-subsidies on production, would reduce welfare further rather than improve it over that reached under a unified exchange rate, insofar as the nontangency effect is *fully* offset in the relevant range.

(2) The analysis of the alternative possibility, in which the wage is identical between sectors but exceeds marginal product in the

Figure 4

Distorting Wage Differentials and Alternative Policies

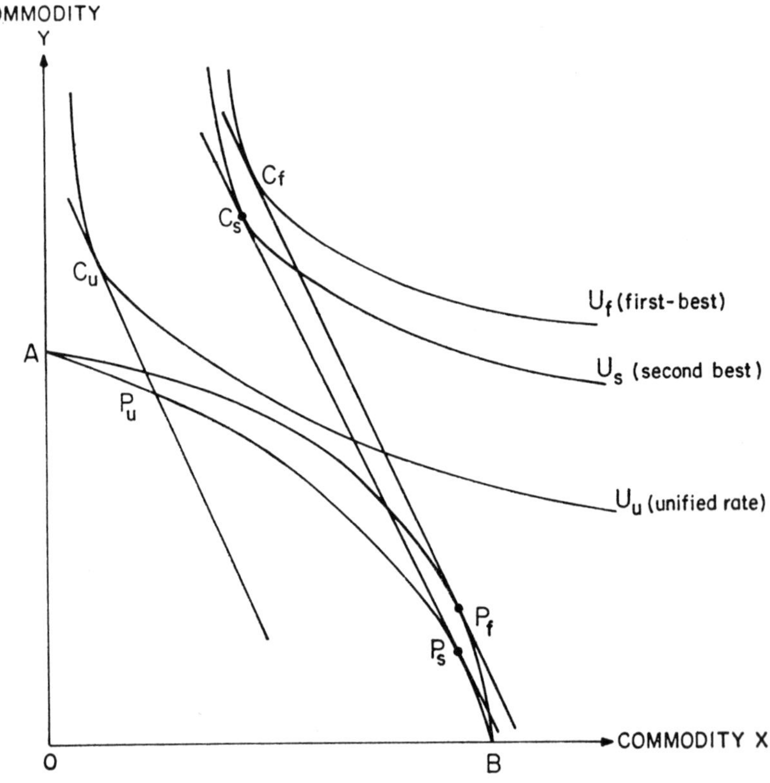

For the case where there is a distorting wage differential operating against commodity X, the diagram illustrates how (1) a factor-subsidy policy which "eliminates" the differential will be the first-best policy, taking welfare level to U_f and enabling production to be at the efficient production-possibility curve at P_f, (2) a unified rate will result in production P_u along a shrunk-in production-possibility curve, with nontangency with the commodity price ratio P_uC_u, and welfare at U_u, and (3) a policy of tax-cum-subsidy on production can, as a second-best solution, take production to P_s on the shrunk-in production-possibility curve and welfare to U_s.

peasant-family sector, is familiar from Arthur Lewis' writings (1959; see also Bhagwati and Ramaswami, 1963). This leads again to inefficient production in two senses: nontangency and shrinking-in of the feasible production-possibility locus. Again, a suitable tax-cum-subsidy on factor use, which equates the marginal products in the different sectors for the same factor, will be the first-best policy.

(3) However, the case where the wage is identical between sectors *but* differs from the shadow or optimal wage is conceptually and

analytically quite different from the preceding two varieties of market imperfection. The following argument shows how, in such a situation, a unified exchange rate may actually worsen the welfare level vis-à-vis autarky and how a departure from unified exchange rates in the form of commercial-policy intervention, and preferably through a domestic tax-cum-subsidy on production, may improve welfare. Clearly, the optimal policy will, in this case, be to eliminate the distortion at the source itself, by means of a suitable tax-cum-subsidy on factor use in *all* sectors.

Figure 5 illustrates the well-known Samuelson relationship between

Figure 5

The Case of Divergence of Actual from Shadow Wage Rates

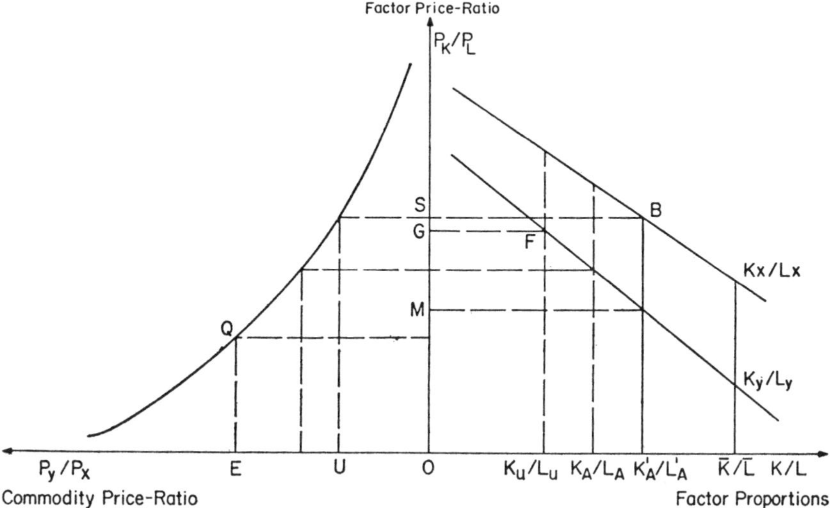

The possibility that free trade may result in loss of welfare in relation to autarky when the shadow wage differs from the actual wage is illustrated in the context of Samuelson's well-known factor-price-equalization diagram. The righthand quadrant shows the factor-use ratios K_x/L_x and K_y/L_y in the two commodities X and Y, at different factor price ratios P_K/P_L. The lefthand quadrant shows the unique relationship between the commodity price ratio P_y/P_x and the factor price ratio P_K/P_L. In the argument in the text, use is made of the well-known proposition that, given any factor endowment ratio for the economy (such as K'_A/L'_A), the feasible factor price ratios are constrained (as at range SM) by the assumption of full employment of factors.

factor prices, commodity prices, and factor intensities for a two-factor (K and L), two-commodity (X and Y) model with linear homogeneous production functions. The given factor endowment ratio is $\bar{K}/\bar{L}$, but, as the real wage of factor L is fixed in terms of X at a level defined by point B, there must be unemployment of factor K. A reduced factor endowment ratio K'_A/L'_A with specialization on X would be a possible point of equilibrium under autarky; however, if demand conditions are not compatible with it, a possible point of equilibrium could be at incomplete specialization with endowment at K_A/L_A, factor price ratio at OS, and commodity price ratio at OU.

Then, under a unified exchange rate, with foreign prices given at OE, a possible position of equilibrium would be at endowment ratio K_u/L_u, complete specialization on producing Y, marginal product in terms of Y given at F, factor price ratio at OG, and marginal product in terms of X at the desired level defined by B through the terms of trade being sufficiently in favor of Y at OE. However, the situation registers a still further decline in employment of K, the factor endowment ratio in employment having gone down from K_A/L_A to K_u/L_u. Thus, the situation under a unified rate shows a reduced level of employment for factor K, with factor L earning the same marginal product as under autarky in terms of X, so that the net result could be deterioration in social welfare. (Note that the result demonstrated is a mere possibility, and that one could equally well envisage the possibility of there being equilibrium established under a unified rate, in this case, at a *higher* level of K/L employment ratio than K_A/L_A).

Further, in this specific eventuality, an import tariff (or preferably still a domestic production tax-cum-subsidy in favor of importables) will lower the effective relative commodity price ratio domestically from OE to OU and restore the economy to the factor endowment ratio K_A/L_A and lead to a higher level of welfare than under the unified exchange rate.

4. First-Best Argument for Tax-cum-Subsidy with Respect to Consumption

If, however, externality obtains with respect to consumption, the optimal form of policy intervention would be tax-cum-subsidies on consumption, for similar reasons as with domestic production tax-cum-subsidies in the case of certain forms of externalities in domestic production, whereas a unified-exchange-rate policy would lead to a sub-optimal situation. Again, any other form of intervention, such as tariffs, trade subsidies, and tax-cum-subsidies on production would be sub-optimal and, hence, even if it manages to improve welfare above the level reached under a unified-exchange-rate policy, would still be inferior to a suitable tax-cum-subsidy on consumption.

While formally this argument is symmetrical with the argument for production externalities, I am not impressed with its empirical significance from the point of view of official policy, even though its philosophical importance is quite considerable. I would rather conclude that, in view of this, together with the interdependence of tastes and the current availability of outputs, it makes more sense perhaps for the economist to stop worrying about utility maximization and to concern himself instead with technical efficiency, where he is on much surer and common ground with other analysts. But I admit that there is scope for endless disagreement on this issue.

B. MODIFIED OBJECTIVE FUNCTIONS

I now come to the range of arguments which depend *essentially* upon departures from the traditional objective function *either* within a static framework *or* by introducing dynamic considerations involving the notion of utility maximization over time. I shall consider the latter set of arguments first, as they seem to me to be of somewhat greater analytical and empirical significance.

1. Arguments Based on Dynamic Considerations

There are broadly four main varieties of argument in this area: (1) those that involve the effect of current policies on the rate of saving and hence on future income via the rate of growth; (2) those relating to investment, both its composition and the inducement to invest; (3) those relating clearly to familiar externalities such as "learning by doing" and investment in the training of skills in infant industries; and (4) those that involve resort to notions that diversification should be preferred to specialization according to what Graham described as the principle of "insurance."

(a) Savings Arguments

There are basically two arguments which may be made in order to justify a departure from a unified exchange rate on grounds that the average savings ratio may increase sufficiently to lead to a higher rate of growth.

(1) One argument that is quite traditional builds on the premise that the average savings ratio is dependent on income distribution,

with fiscal policy subject to serious limitations. Thus, a policy of a unified exchange rate, as opposed to a policy that shifts production to a different mix, may lead to income distribution in favor of those who save less, and hence may result in a lower rate of growth of real income. In this case, there is a conflict between maximizing current income and maximizing the rate of growth; and the optimal policy, if a utility function over time is maximized, could well call for a departure from a unified exchange rate. Note, however, that, in this case, a policy of a tax-cum-subsidy on production would be a *superior* policy to a tariff or trade-subsidy policy because it would achieve the desired shift in production and, hence, in income distribution without inflicting a consumption loss through forcing consumers to consume at distorted prices (different from international prices).

(2) An alternative argument links the capacity to raise savings through fiscal policy to the *pattern* of consumption. A unified exchange rate may lead to the importation and conspicuous consumption of luxury goods which would undermine the capacity to tax. Austerity may be difficult to impose in the presence of conspicuous consumption. Note, however, that this argument strictly requires that the *availability*, rather than importation, of these luxury goods be eliminated or reduced below the levels reached under a unified rate. If importation alone were made more difficult, the incentive to produce or extend the production of these luxury goods would correspondingly increase. Hence, the present argument, where relevant, leads to the case for schemes involving tax-cum-subsidies on consumption and *not* to tariffs as the suitable policy.

(b) Investment Arguments

Then arguments can be developed which call for a suitable departure from unified exchange rate by relating the choice of current policies to the problem of raising the rate of investment.

(1) One argument, familiar from the writings of Hirschman and Myrdal (1955), is that the surest way to raise the rate of investment is to cut down imports of hitherto imported items. Since the potential domestic entrepreneurs will feel sure in such a case of having a domestic market for their output, they will invest. To close the implicit model, one would have to assume that the necessary saving is forthcoming, for example, through fiscal policy. The argument has strong appeal: it seems pointless to worry about the efficiency of investment

unless investment is forthcoming—as the French say, you cannot make ragout unless you have a rabbit. I myself remain skeptical of the wisdom of this prescription, however, even though I agree that one cannot rule it out altogether. It is difficult to see why economic policy cannot be designed to create the necessary incentives to invest while maintaining the framework of comparative advantage. I am afraid that prescriptions to the contrary seem to be based on a willingness to reconcile oneself to inefficient policies rather than a necessity to do so.

(2) Another argument, of some empirical importance, emerges from "structural" models. If one assumes that the economy faces, through all periods, given international prices (which, however, may change between periods), that the rate of saving is capable of being varied freely by fiscal policy, and that investment always matches available savings, then a policy of a unified exchange rate, combined with fiscal policy to peg the savings rate at an optimal rate, will be sufficient to put the economy on an optimal time path, which in fact will be unique and independent of the terminal configuration of availability in a model with a finite time horizon.[17] But suppose, however, that the economy is presented with finite export elasticities at each point of time. In this case, while the State can work out the optimal time path of output on the basis of perfect foresight and there will be shadow prices associated with the solution, there is no reason to think that the market would necessarily operate in such a way as to generate these prices *on its own*. Hence, a suitable policy of a tax-cum-subsidy on production is called for, in order to steer the economy in the direction indicated by the time path. It would be wrong to consider that mere dissemination of the information on shadow prices would be adequate; there is no reason why they should be taken seriously unless they are made effective by actual intervention.

Take the simple example of a Feldman-(Domar, 1957, p. 223)-Mahalanobis (1955) type of model where, at the margin, there is a unit elasticity of demand for exports abroad and, hence, the decision to raise the future rate of investment may require a shift in the allocation of resources towards the capital-goods sector. In this case, if private entrepreneurs underinvest in the capital-goods sector because they do not anticipate correctly the implications of the governmental

[17] Bent Hansen, in his de Vries lectures (1966), has developed this argument with great elegance.

decision to raise investment in the future (in conjunction with the stated assumption with respect to trade possibilities), then the investment rate in the future will be jeopardized. In order to correct this, it may be necessary to adopt a tax-cum-subsidy policy which gives incentive to produce capital goods and to move away from a unified-exchange-rate policy. Note that this argument for departure from a unified exchange rate depends on the divergence in views concerning future demand, arising out of a model which makes optimality conditional upon being able to forecast this well enough. The State is assumed to do the job better, partly because it is considered to be in a position to work out the structural implications of its decision to raise the rate of saving, whereas private entrepreneurs are more likely to have their views as to the future conditioned by the preceding past and thus to miss the significance of impending transformations in the economy which optimality requires. Again, as with all these arguments, the present case for a departure from a unified exchange rate merely outlines a possibility; the probability of such a possibility in reality is a different issue.

(c) Externality Arguments

I now come to the externality arguments, mostly classical, which are the backbone of the case for "infant-industry" protection. Two kinds of arguments need to be distinguished in this area: (1) those which depend on "learning by doing," a notion which is familiar to us since Arrow's seminal work (1962); and (2) those which depend on what I like to describe as "learning by someone else's doing." Arguments of the latter variety are more current in the literature, and I shall develop them first.

There are two major varieties of arguments in this category. First, it is contended that the pioneering entrant into an industry will have to train its labor force but that *other* firms, entering later, could attract this labor force away so that the return to this activity or investment by the firm in training will be imputed to the labor force instead of accruing to the firm itself. Owing to this externality, which is likely to be associated with infant industries (but will be mitigated insofar as long-term contracts can be signed with labor or, alternatively, labor can be underpaid or even explicitly charged for the training it receives, as my colleague Gary Becker has emphasized), a policy of subsidizing the training of labor will be desirable to stimulate entry into the industry. Note again that a domestic production-tax-cum-subsidy policy will be inferior and a tariff policy still worse.

Second, it has been argued by Kemp (1960) that the fact that the acquisition of knowledge by a firm requires investment by it, and that this knowledge cannot be successfully held by the firm so as to enable it to charge other firms for its use, could keep a pioneering firm from entering an industry even though the activity might be socially desirable. As Johnson has lucidly summarized the argument:

> . . . once knowledge of production technique is acquired, it can be applied by others than those who have assumed the cost of acquiring it; the social benefit at least potentially exceeds the private benefit of investment in learning industrial production techniques, and the social use of the results of such learning may even reduce the private reward for undertaking the investment. Where the social benefits of the learning process exceed the private benefits, the most appropriate governmental policy would be to subsidize the learning process itself, through such techniques as financing or sponsoring pilot enterprises on condition that the experience acquired and techniques developed be made available to all would-be producers (1965a, p. 28).

Applied at the level of the firm, this argument therefore results in the recommendation of a suitable subsidy policy because rival firms can learn by the pioneering firm's doing.

However, even the phenomenon of "learning by doing," as discussed by Arrow, results in a departure of the competitive system from Pareto-optimality and, hence, in a prescription for suitable governmental intervention. Recently, in the first dynamic analysis of the "infant-industry" argument, based on Arrow's notions, Bardhan (1966) has analyzed the time profile of the optimal subsidy to production that would be called for in an industry whose production function was modified to incorporate an Arrow-type learning effect. Bardhan modifies the Arrow assumption, that productivity in the industry is a function of the cumulated gross investment, to the alternative assumption that the productivity changes with respect to cumulated *output*, in a Hicks-neutral sense. With such an effect built into the production function of just one industry in a two-industry model, Bardhan shows how the commodity price ratio will no longer equal the social marginal rate of transformation between the two commodities and, hence, that there will follow a case for a suitable production tax-cum-subsidy, the time profile of which he investigates.

Note that the optimal policy would shift to an appropriate tax-cum-subsidy policy with respect to investment in the industry, if the learning effect were to operate, as with Arrow, through cumulated gross investment rather than output. In any case, a tariff policy would be inferior, in either case, because it would additionally incur the consumption cost we discussed earlier. Further, from a formal point of view, the result developed by Bardhan in a dynamic setting is similar to the result which follows when the output of one industry is made a function of output in another industry (rather than to the cumulated output in the same industry). In either case, the market fails and intervention follows.

Finally, the argument could be fully generalized and productivity in all industries could be made a function of the cumulated output, or cumulated labor force for example, in one industry. Thus, Graham argued:

> If, in any given nation, free trade would produce specialization in a highly restricted group of industries it might have a repressive effect upon progress. If, for example, comparative competence, in a certain nation and at a certain period, lies in agricultural rather than manufacturing pursuits it might well happen, under free trade, that there would be much mechanical talent, and perhaps inventive genius, which would never find an opportunity to express itself. The nation and the world would be the poorer for its suppression. This argument was used by the original sponsors of protection in this country, was greatly developed by Frederick List, and, in certain circumstances, is cogent (1934, p. 65).

Graham did add rather shrewdly that "It is possible, moreover, that national specialization in mechanical pursuits might smother latent genius in botanical or zoölogical activities just as specialization in the latter occupations may lead to a waste of mechanical genius." Clearly, Graham had in mind a generalized Arrow-type model, which (as we have just seen) does lead to the case for appropriate governmental intervention. In Graham's problem, the learning effect in all industries depends on the growth of one type of activity (manufacture) through the employment of labor in that activity, so that the appropriate intervention can be shown to be a labor subsidy for labor use in that activity.

Before I conclude the discussion of the externalities which are usually associated with the case for "infant-industry" protection, let me touch on the recent argument of Kaldor (1964) that, if economies of scale obtain in infant industries, subsidization of exports is a superior (second-best) policy to tariff protection, for the latter will restrict markets whereas the former will expand them and permit production at lower unit costs. Quite aside from the fact that Kaldor fails to point out that *domestic*, rather than *trade*, policies would be optimal for infant-industry protection, his argument is invalid as a general proposition. It ignores the fact that export subsidization generally increases the cost of tariff protection still further. This is the case for industries which are not currently competitive with imports, and in which the increasing returns are such that they still permit increasing marginal cost of transformation in production. In such a case export subsidization will be a policy inferior to tariffs and either will be inferior to a suitable domestic policy.

Finally, I might record an interesting argument of Graham's, involving a dynamic externality, which states that the "quality" of the labor force in the future, and hence the level of future total and per capita income, may depend, via the link between current income and birth rates, on the current income distribution and, hence, on the choice between a unified exchange rate and rival policies. It is best to quote him fully on this issue, which involves yet another ground for departure from unified exchange rates:

> Comparative competence in a given employment is sometimes due to the presence of a relatively low grade of labor which shows a special bent for the employment in question. A *laissez-faire* policy may result in so great an extension of this employment as, over a period of years or decades, to exert a marked adverse effect on the average quality of the population. The extension of cotton growing in the United States, for instance, was not only originally dependent upon the presence of Negro labor, which we may perhaps not unjustly assume was of lower average quality than the white population, but it also seems to have tended to increase the ratio of the Negro to the white element in our racial structure. . . .
>
> If, in the long run, through adjustment of birth rates to relative

economic opportunity, the quality of a population tends to adapt itself to the demands which the national industry makes upon it, one might go on to an argument for protection for *any* comparatively incompetent industry provided it could be shown that it would set up a demand for, and possibly evoke a supply of, a larger proportion of high-grade workers than the employments it would, as a result of the protective policy, tend partially to displace. [Graham immediately added:] Put thus, the argument becomes rather far-fetched. The case, indeed, is seldom clear enough to permit the degree of assurance on which discriminatory legislative action should alone be taken. . . . History does show, however, some instances in which the artificial encouragement of trades requiring highly skilled workers and technicians seems to have had beneficial effects on the character both of the population and of the industry of the country concerned (1934, pp. 72-74).

Graham's argument must be treated as valid insofar as it implicitly depends on the *externality* that may obtain because the quality of the labor force is conditional on the environmental advantages which accrue *within* the family and insofar as these advantages can be demonstrated to inhere within certain classes of the population more effectively than in others. It would further require an additional constraint on fiscal policy; for, if it were not imposed, it should be possible (via suitable transfers) to redistribute income to the desired pattern. Further, *trade* policy would again be inferior to *domestic* tax-cum-subsidy policies for bringing about the desired distribution of income.

(d) Diversification and Insurance

Arguments have traditionally been put forth against the specialization that may develop under a unified-exchange-rate policy, on grounds that, as with the principle of insurance, a country ought to diversify its production as well. Note that diversification of production is also supported on "non-economic" grounds such as defense production, in which case the only sensible economic question that arises relates to the optimal and least-cost way in which such a non-economic objective would be fulfilled. Here, however, the prior question is whether such diversification can be supported by reference to purely economic objectives. Let me quote Graham on this issue:

Dispersion of risk is, of course, a fundamental principle of insur-

> ance, and diversification of industry disperses the national risk from vicissitudes peculiar to single industries or groups of industries. The value of insurance depends, of course, upon its cost relative to the risks against which safeguards are feasible. The risks arising from a specialization of the national economic structure are perhaps increasing as the ratio of the value of fixed capital to annual output rises, and the cost of suddenly effecting a considerable alteration in the character of the national production is thereby enhanced. The argument from insurance is probably, therefore, of growing importance (1934, p. 65).

This argument for diversifying production makes sense, however, insofar as it can be argued that private entrepreneurs left to themselves will not secure the necessary dispersion of risk on their own. Once again, therefore, we must appeal to some form of externality. The argument seems to boil down to one discussed earlier, in which the private entrepreneurs will have a different evaluation of the future from the state and the state's evaluation will be more objective. *In principle*, such an externality could work in favor of, or against, increasing the range of production above the level reached under a unified exchange rate. Further, a policy of a tax-cum-subsidy with respect to domestic production will be less expensive than a tariff or trade-subsidy policy in changing the level of diversification to the optimal level, for it will permit consumption to take place at international prices.

2. Arguments within the Static Framework

I now come to those arguments for departure from a unified exchange rate which accept the static framework but depart from the traditional solution because they involve maximization of a social-welfare function which does not depend exclusively on the current flow of goods and services. In the analysis that follows, however, I shall be dealing with the problems posed by the introduction of such additional social objectives as essentially formal maximization problems, with the traditional social-welfare function, but with additional constraints in the form of the added objectives. Thus, the problems will be formally treated as essentially second-best problems with the objective function unchanged from its traditional formulation. This formal treatment stops short of exploring the possible trade-offs between social utility from the flow of goods and services and social utility from achieving more of the additional objective; but the analysis could be extended in that fashion, in principle.

The arguments that I propose to consider involve (1) achievement of a certain income distribution; (2) achievement of specific levels of production in certain activities, on grounds such as defense; (3) achievement of specific levels of employment of a factor of production, such as labor, in certain activities, on grounds such as the "creation of national character"; (4) reduction of import dependence or achievement of "self-sufficiency"; (5) reduction of "domestic availability" of items, such as luxury consumer goods, on grounds of social policy; (6) collection of revenue for state expenditure; and (7) constraints placed on efficiency through aid-tying, amounting to the required achievement of a specific form of aid utilization.[18]

(a) Income Distribution

I have already discussed how, via income distribution, there may arise a conflict between future income and current income, which could call for a departure from unified exchange rates. However, it is possible for the country to be *directly* interested in the actual income distribution that arises thanks to the market, if the fiscal system is incapable of redistributing market-imputed incomes. In this case, rational policy would involve maximizing utility from the currently available flow of goods and services *subject* to certain income distributional constraints being simultaneously satisfied. The second-best solution, in such a case, could involve departure from unified exchange rates. However, in such a case too, tax-cum-subsidies on domestic production would be a superior, and least-cost, way of achieving the desired income-distribution change via shift in production rather than trade-policy measures which would additionally impose a consumption cost.[19]

A similar argument involving possible departure from unified exchange rates arises in practice also because the objective of income distribution takes the form of different regions *within* a country seeking market-imputed incomes which do not fall below certain absolute

[18] It is possible to quibble whether some of these constraints are "political" or "economic." The question would be semantic were it not for the fact that frequently economists are inclined to treat the "political" constraints as "irrational."

[19] It might, of course, be questioned whether a government which cannot tax in order to redistribute income will be able to undertake tax-cum-subsidy policies in order to bring about a different market-imputed distribution of income.

or relative shares. This type of constraint can be even independent of the possibility of income redistribution by fiscal means: the objective of income distribution may, and frequently does, refer to earned incomes. Anyone who has had to advise on economic policy in countries characterized by regional differences of political significance will realize how important a constraint this is in practice.

(b) Specific Levels of Production as Non-Economic Objective

If, for reasons such as defense, production in specific activities is required to be raised *above* the level reached under the optimal unified-exchange-rate policy, then the problem reduces formally to that of second-best maximization subject to the added constraint that production in these activities cannot fall below the stated levels.

Corden (1957) has then shown that a policy of a tax-cum-subsidy on production will be a superior way of obtaining the requisite shift in production than tariff (or export-subsidy) policy, for the now-familiar reason that it will avoid any consumption cost in the process by permitting consumption to occur at international prices.

But a policy of a tax-cum-subsidy on production is not merely superior to a tariff (or export-subsidy) policy; it is also the *optimal* policy under the stated non-economic objective. An adaptation of the diagram used by Corden to demonstrate the superiority of the policy of a tax-cum-subsidy production over tariff policy will serve to demonstrate also its superiority over a factor-subsidy policy by which the use of one (as against both at identical rates, which would be equivalent to a tax-cum-subsidy on production) factor alone may be subsidized in the activity whose expansion to the desired level is sought. The diagram is drawn to illustrate the case in which the production of the importable good is to be raised above the free-trade level but could readily be adapted to the case in which the production of the exportable good instead is to be so raised. Instead of the tariff, we should then be discussing a trade-subsidy policy but the optimal policy would still be a tax-cum-subsidy on production. With production of Y in Figure 6 to be raised at least to P^*, the tax-cum-subsidy on production will be superior to the tariff policy ($U_{ps} > U_t$) whereas a factor-subsidy policy, which leads to a shrinking-in of the production-possibility curve and to a nontangency of the commodity-price line with this shrunken feasible production set, will lead to production at P_{fs}, consumption at C_{fs}, and a still lower level of welfare. Thus, the tax-cum-subsidy on production will be superior even to this alternative method of achieving the same non-economic objective with respect to produc-

Figure 6

Non-Economic Objective Relating to Production Level and Optimal Policy Intervention

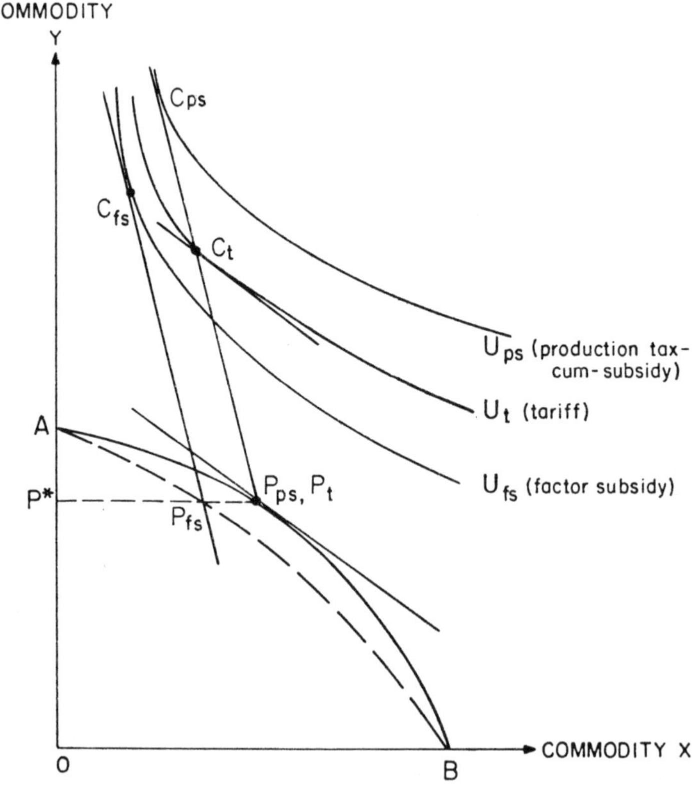

The case where production of commodity *Y* cannot be allowed to fall below *P** and this is a binding constraint, is illustrated. The superiority of a tax-cum-subsidy on production, vis-à-vis the two alternative policies (discriminatory factor-subsidy and tariff) is shown.

tion levels: a straightforward solution to the simple maximizing problem involved demonstrates the optimality of the policy of a production tax-cum-subsidy (see Bhagwati and Srinivasan, 1967).

For the case in which monopoly power is excluded, Bhagwati (1967d) has investigated the question whether, while a domestic tax-cum-subsidy policy with respect to production is optimal, the *sub-optimal* policy of tariffs and trade subsidies will still be superior to autarky as a way of reaching the required production bundle in a least-cost manner. It turns out that, in the case in which the desired production bundle can be reached with a trade tariff (rather than a trade subsidy), a (sub-optimal) trade-tariff policy will *necessarily* be superior to a (sub-optimal) autarkic policy, thus giving the strong ranking of the following three policies: (1) tax-cum-subsidy on domestic production; (2) trade tariff; and (3) autarky. On the other hand, no such strong ranking between the latter two sub-optimal policies is possible when the desired production bundle can be reached only under a trade *subsidy*.

For the case in which there is monopoly power in trade as well, and the required production level lies below the optimum tariff level of production while lying above the level reached under the unified-exchange-rate policy, Corden has further shown that the tariff will be a superior policy—which is readily seen once it is realized that tariffs will improve welfare as they are increased to the optimum tariff level.[20] For the case of variable terms of trade, therefore, the optimal policy will, in general, be a combination of tariffs and tax-cum-subsidies on production.

Finally, Johnson (1960) has shown that, if the analysis admits multiple importable commodities, and the objective is to achieve a specified increase in the aggregate value of production of importables (at given terms of trade) *above* the level reached under a unified exchange rate, the tariff structure will in general involve *differentiated* rates.

(c) Specified Levels of Employment in Certain Activities as Non-Economic Objective

Graham correctly observed that among the reasons cited for protection was the desire to raise *employment of labor* in certain activities above the level reached under unified exchange rates. He noted that the protection of agriculture was cited as necessary on the ground that "the farmer is the 'backbone' of the nation," wryly commenting at the same time that "the assumption that rural activities are superior to those of the city as creators of character cannot be said to be proven."

Where the objective thus defined is to prevent *employment* levels

[20] This last proposition has recently been stated formally, amplified, and shown to require the exclusion of inferior goods, by Bhagwati and Kemp (1967).

of a factor in certain activities from falling below desired magnitudes, rather than the achievement of specific levels of production in these activities, it has been shown by Bhagwati and Srinivasan (1967) that the optimal policy is to subsidize directly the use of that factor in the activity where its employment otherwise would fall below the required level.

In Figure 7, this result is illustrated. Assume that the employment

Figure 7
Non-Economic Objective Relating to Employment in a Sector and Optimal Policy Intervention

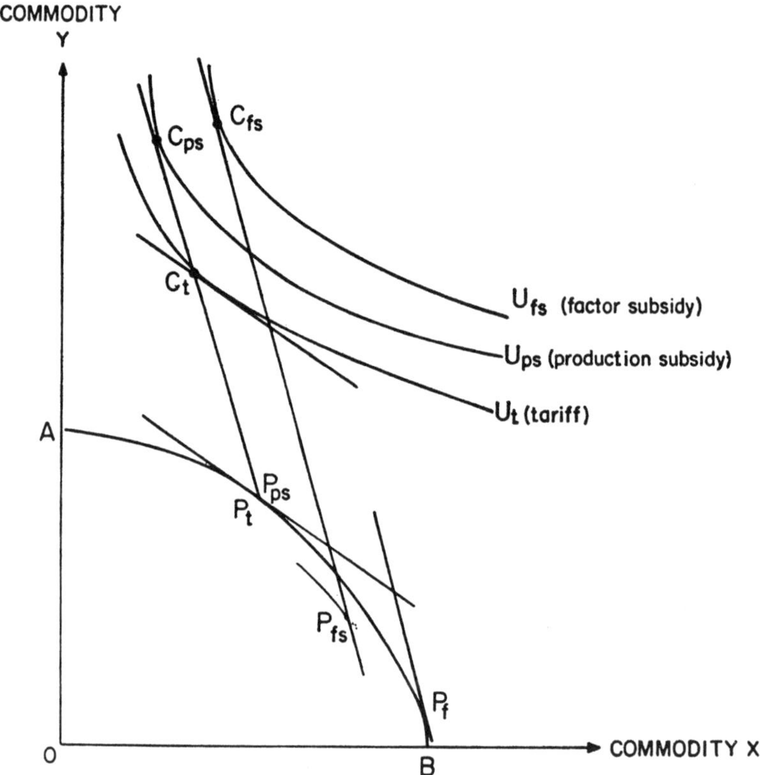

For the case where the employment of factor L in activity Y must not be allowed to fall below pre-specified level L^*, and this is a binding constraint, the factor-subsidy policy takes production to P_{fs}, consumption to C_{fs} and welfare to U_{fs}; a tax-cum-subsidy on production will take production to P_{ps}, consumption to C_{ps} and reduce welfare to U_{ps}; and a tariff policy will add the consumption loss to the level of welfare under a tax-cum-subsidy on production and reduce welfare still further to U_t (while maintaining production at $P_t = P_{ps}$). P_f represents the free trade, or unified rate, level of production at which the employment constraint is not satisfied. Absence of monopoly power in trade is assumed.

of labor in Y can be increased to the required level by shifting production away from the free-trade level at P_f to P_{ps} (or P_t) by a suitable tariff policy or a tax-cum-subsidy on production. This shift is illustrated in the familiar box diagram in Figure 8 by the shift from Q to R, which takes the amount of labor in Y from L_f to the desired level L^*. It should now be obvious that the policy of a tax-cum-subsidy on production will be superior to the tariff policy, as it will avoid the consumption loss associated with tariff intervention. But a still better, and optimal, policy will be a factor-subsidy policy which will subsidize the use of labor in Y (or tax its use in X) and shift equilibrium to S in Figure 8 and to P_{fs} for production, C_{fs} for consumption, and U_{fs} ($U_{ps} > U_t$) for welfare in Figure 7.

Figure 8
Non-Economic Objective Relating to Employment in a Sector and Optimal Policy Intervention

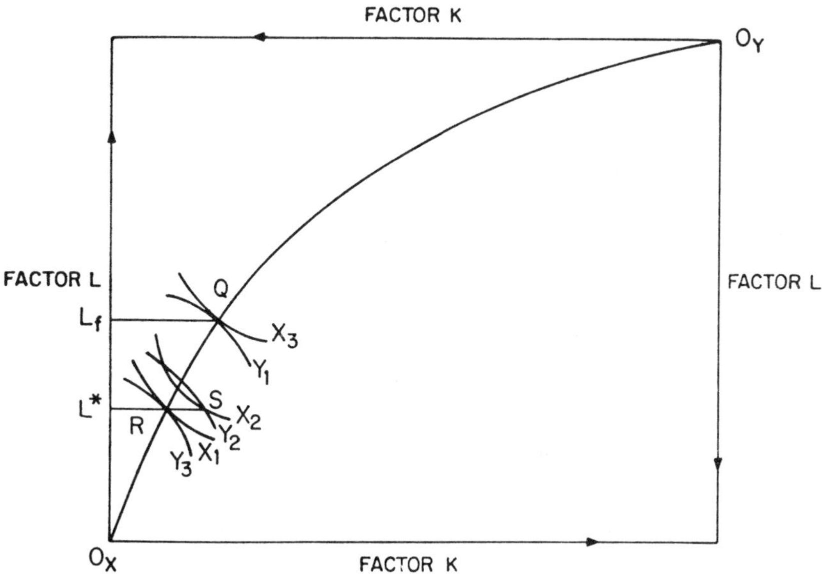

This Edgeworth box-diagram illustrates the same propositions as Figure 7. With point Q corresponding to the free trade level of production P_f in Figure 7, the level of labor employment in activity Y is at L_f, which falls below the pre-specified minimum of L^*. R is the point on the Edgeworth contract curve which corresponds to the tax-cum-subsidy on production taking production to P_{ps} in Figure 7, and S the point off the contract curve that corresponds to the labor-subsidy policy for employment in Y, that takes production to P_{fs} in Figure 7, both points R and S satisfying the constraint that $L \geqq L^*$. Figure 7 illustrates that point S yields higher welfare than point R.

(d) "Self-sufficiency" or Reduction of Imports as Non-Economic Objective

The non-economic objective, on the other hand, may be a reduction in the degree of import dependence and may call for a reduction in the value of imports. For the case in which there is no monopoly power in trade, this objective is identical with the objective of reducing the volume of imports (or exports).

Johnson (1965a) has shown, in this case, that a tariff policy will be superior to a tax-cum-subsidy on production. It can, however, be shown that a tariff policy will be *optimal* in this instance and hence superior to all other policies. This result has been established by Bhagwati and Srinivasan (1967), who have further extended the analysis to the case where the terms of trade are not fixed and have shown that, in this case, the optimal policy will be only a tariff policy.

This conclusion, for the case where the terms of trade are fixed, can be illustrated by adapting Johnson's diagram showing that a tariff policy is superior to a tax-cum-subsidy on production when the objective is self-sufficiency. In Figure 9, it is shown that the same level of utility is reached (and therefore the same loss of welfare incurred) under four alternative policies: a tariff policy that leads to production at P_t and consumption at C_t, a tax-cum-subsidy on production that leads to production at P_{ps} and consumption at C_{ps}, a tax-cum-subsidy on consumption that leads to production at P_{cs} and consumption at C_{cs}, and a tax-cum-subsidy on factors that leads to production at P_{fs} and consumption at C_{fs}. It is readily seen that the level of imports will be least under the tariff policy, though it will not be possible to rank uniquely the other three policies vis-à-vis one another. Since the tariff policy achieves the greatest reduction in imports, given the loss in welfare, it follows that it will achieve a given reduction in the level of imports with the least loss of welfare.

(e) Reduction in Domestic Availability of Certain Commodities as Non-Economic Objective

The non-economic objective may well consist in preventing the domestic availability of certain commodities, whether domestically produced or imported, from exceeding levels defined on social grounds. This is often the case with luxury goods in the social policies of many countries.

Figure 9
Non-Economic Objective Relating to Self-Sufficiency and Optimal Policy Intervention

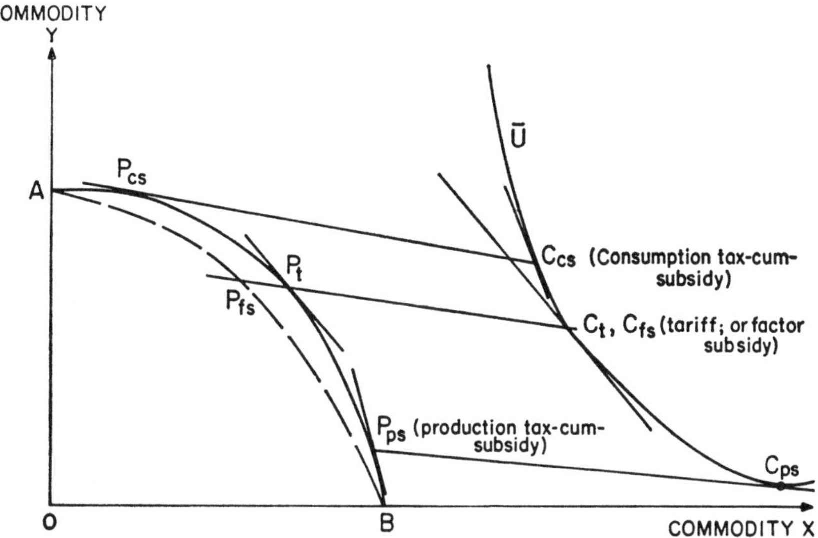

For the case where the non-economic objective is self-sufficiency defined as reduction in the value of imports, this diagram illustrates (for a small country with no monopoly power in trade) that, subject to the same loss of welfare and, hence, relegation to the same social-indifference curve $\bar{U}$, a suitable tariff policy (with production at P_t and consumption at C_t) will produce the largest reduction in imports, as compared with the tax-cum-subsidy on consumption (with production at P_{cs} and consumption at C_{cs}), the tax-cum-subsidy on production (with production at P_{ps} and consumption at C_{ps}) and the factor-subsidy policy (with production at P_{fs} and consumption at C_{fs}).

In this case, the optimal policy has been shown by Bhagwati and Srinivasan (1967) to be a tax-cum-subsidy on consumption when the terms of trade are fixed, whereas, with variable terms of trade, the optimal policy involves a combination of a tariff and the tax-cum-subsidies on consumption.

This is illustrated, for fixed terms of trade, in Figure 10, where $\bar{Y}$ represents the maximum level of Y-availability that is to be permitted and Y_f represents the level that would be reached under free trade. A tax-cum-subsidy on consumption will enable consumption to occur at C_{cs} and welfare to be maximized at U_{cs}, because any alternative policy is easily seen to involve equilibrium consumption to the west or southwest of C_{cs}.

Figure 10

Non-Economic Objective Relating to Consumption in a Sector and Optimal Policy Intervention

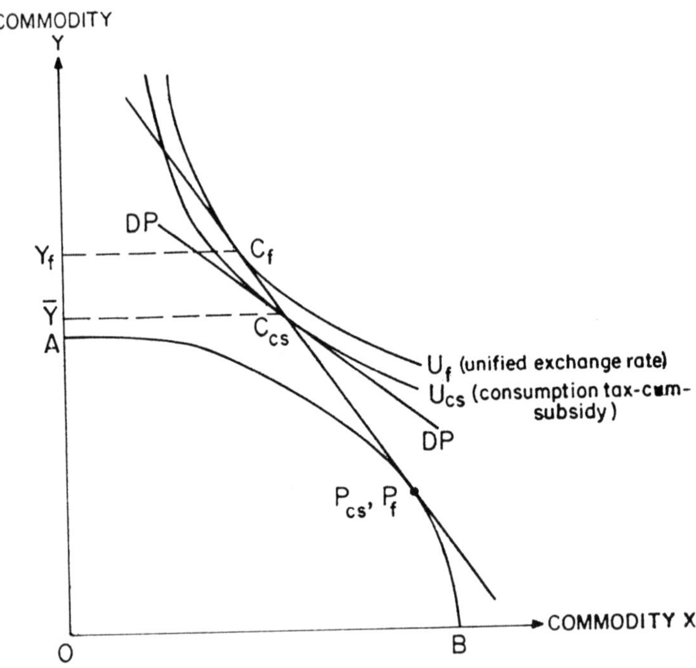

The diagram illustrates the case where, under a unified-rate policy, consumption of commodity Y will be at Y_f, which is in excess of the level $\bar{Y}$, above which the consumption of Y cannot be allowed to rise for non-economic reasons. A suitable tax-cum-subsidy on consumption will shift consumption to C_{cs} and welfare to U_{cs}. This policy will minimize the welfare loss associated with satisfying the consumption constraint, as any other policy will involve consumption along $C_{cs}\bar{Y}$, to the left of C_{cs}, and hence yet lower welfare.

(f) Revenue Collection as Objective

If the possibility of the substitution between leisure and income is admitted, the only nondistorting taxes are lump-sum taxes. So far, however, I have been discussing welfare questions, implicitly or explicitly, on the basis of fixed factor supplies, so that it should always be possible to collect revenue by uniform consumption taxation, for example, without incurring welfare losses.

Suppose, however, that such taxation is not possible—as is alleged by some less developed countries on administrative grounds—and the revenue must be collected by trade taxes alone. If one sticks, in this second-best framework, to the traditional model confined to two commodities and two primary domestic factors, then (since an export tariff is equivalent to an import tariff) the only meaningful question to ask would be in "positive" analysis, such as that investigated by Johnson (1951) in comparing the tariff that gave rise to maximum revenue with the optimum tariff. If one is to ask meaningful questions relating to welfare, one would have to admit the possibility of multiple imports (or exports) and examine the optimal *structure* of tariffs to yield pre-specified revenue, for example.

In fact, Ramaswami and Srinivasan (1967) have recently analyzed this question with considerable elegance, using a three-good model with an exportable good that does not enter into domestic consumption, a nontraded good that is made for home consumption, and an imported consumer good, one primary (domestic) factor (labor) and one wholly imported factor (metal) and no monopoly power in trade. Taking the revenue constraint to be specified as a given money sum and as a fraction of the wage bill, in turn, they have demonstrated the possibility of multiple rates arising in the constrained optimum solution. In the more interesting case in which the revenue is specified as a fraction of the wage bill, for example, it is shown that if the given trade deficit [equal to aid inflow, for example] at world prices is equal to or less than revenue required when the wage rate is at the balanced free-trade level, the optimal policy is to subsidize exports at as high a rate as possible while taxing imports of metal to make exports at the same rate, and to tax imports of the consumer good and of metal to make the good for home use at the higher rate that secures the specified revenue.

(g) Tied Aid

A departure from unified exchange rates may be called for also as a result of the tying of aid leading to a constrained maximization of social welfare. Note here that this may *not* call for explicit state intervention; but it may, in the form of trade or domestic-policy instruments.

Take, for example, the following Models I and II, which are made deliberately simple so as to bring out the essence of the problem.[21] In each case, one designed to show the implications of tying with respect to commodities and the other the implications of tying with

[21] I am thankful to T. N. Srinivasan for showing how these two simplified versions of more complex models designed by me to bring out the same points are sufficient to demonstrate the emergence of multiple rates owing to aid-tying.

respect to source, the possibility of multiple rates arising is demonstrated. The implication is that observed discrepancies between the (best) foreign prices and domestic prices will signify inefficiency with respect to the aid inflow and *not* with respect to the efficiency of allocation of resources, given the constraints on the aid-flow utilization. In Model III, I shall portray a case where the tying is such as to require actual state intervention to support the required outcome. This case will correspond to the analysis of situations where bulk trading, for instance, is carried out in a competitive economy at terms that are incompatible with market conditions except through governmental action in the form of tax-cum-subsidies or trade tariffs and subsidies. In this case as well, the implication will be that the official departure from the unified-rate policy is a result of constrained maximization imposed by aid conditions; it will *not* be that official policies pursued by the *recipient* country are inefficient.

Model I. Assume a single product, no exports, imports of two inputs financed by aid, aid tied to specific purchases of the two inputs, and no domestic factors. Let the production function for output be characterized by diminishing returns along isoquants. The international prices of the inputs are fixed.

The model can then be illustrated in Figure 11. $\overline{K}$ and $\overline{L}$ are the fixed quantities of inputs obtainable under tied aid; AB represents the availability line for these inputs, at the given international prices, *if* aid is not tied. The amount of output produced with tied aid is X as measured at the isoquant passing through $(\overline{K}, \overline{L})$. On the other hand, under untied aid, the optimal solution and equilibrium would be at (K^*, L^*), where the domestic price ratio would equal the international price ratio. At $(\overline{K}, \overline{L})$, however, the price ratio diverges from the international price ratio, signifying a sub-optimal position, one however which a competitive system would reach but which has been caused by the tying of aid rather than by inefficient policies of the recipient country. Multiple rates will thus exist and will signify the inefficiency resulting from the tying of aid.

Model II. Assume the same model as Model I, except that the aid is now tied to sources rather than to commodities. Let then the supply of input K be cheapest from Source I and of input L from Source II. The prices are fixed at either source of supply, as before.

The model can then be illustrated in Figure 12. $A_{II}\, B_{II}$ represents the aid-availability (in terms of possible combinations of K and L) line from Source II, where L is cheaper; $C_I D_I$ the aid-availability line from the other Source I. The total aid-availability line then (in terms of *feasible* combinations of K and L) will be EFG under aid tying, where EF is parallel to AB and FG is parallel to CD and $(OC_I + OA_{II}) = OE$, and $(OD_I + OB_{II}) = OG$. If there were no tying, the possibility curve would be the straight line JFQ. At F, the two inputs are bought at their cheapest sources.

Figure 11

Aid Tied to Commodities and Multiple Exchange Rates

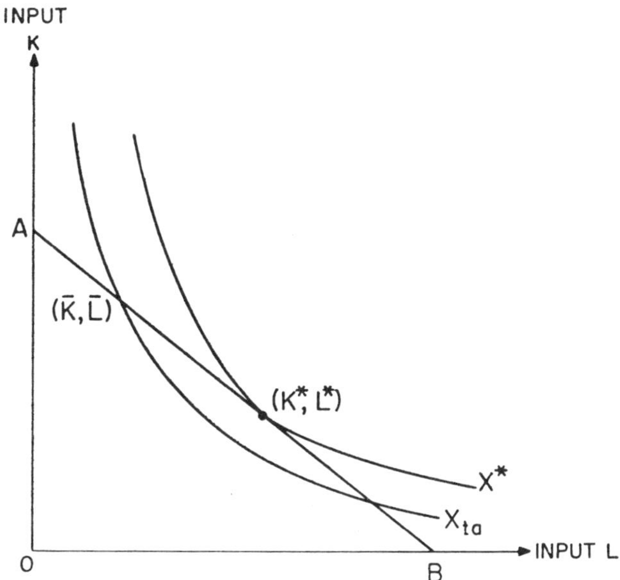

The diagram illustrates the possible emergence of multiple exchange rates when aid is tied by commodity specification. Aid is equal to OB of input L or OA of input K at international prices. The optimal combination of inputs to purchase with the aid would be (K^*, L^*). Thus, aid tied to the bundle $(\bar{K}, \bar{L})$ will result in sub-optimality and also in multiple exchange rates as the domestic price ratio between K and L, given by the tangent to isoquant X_{ta} at $(\bar{K}, \bar{L})$, will diverge from the international price ratio.

Under source-tied aid in this model, then, if the maximal isoquant were to touch EF at P, multiple rates would follow, because the marginal rate of substitution in production would equal the price ratio in Source II and, hence, diverge from the "best" international price ratio JFQ. Output would be sub-optimal in relation to the level possible under untied aid (at P^*); the entire aid from Source I would be used to import K. A similar conclusion, *mutatis mutandis*, would hold for

Figure 12

Aid Tied by Source and Multiple Exchange Rates

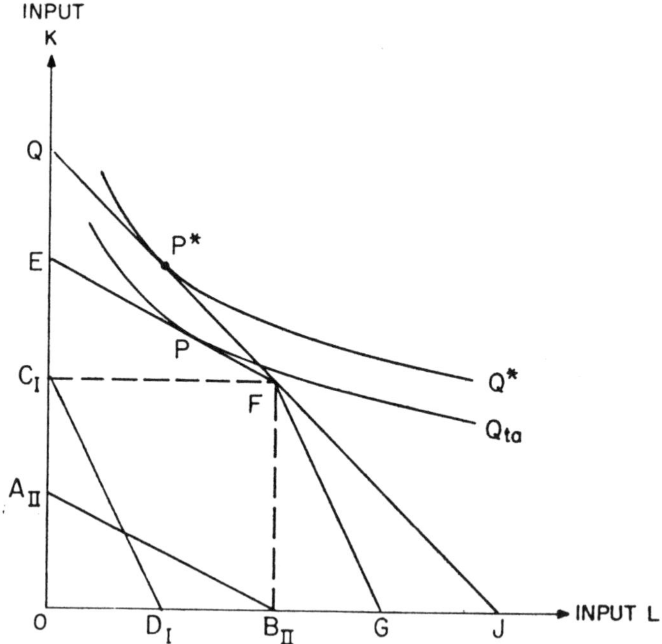

The diagram illustrates the possible emergence of multiple exchange rates when aid is tied by source. *QJ* is the aid-availability line giving alternative combinations of factors *K* and *L* which can be purchased at the *lowest* international prices if aid is untied. *EFG*, however, is the *feasible* total-aid-availability line if aid is tied to source by each country, I and II, with $C_I D_I$ and $A_{II} B_{II}$ the resulting country-aid-availability lines. If, then, the maximal isoquant were to touch *EFG* at a point such as *P*, the domestic price ratio (given by the tangent at *P* to *EF*) will diverge from the true international price ratio (given by *QJ*).

the case where the maximal isoquant were to touch *FG*. If the maximal isoquant were to pass through *F*, however, there would be multiple rates and inefficiency, *unless*, in the borderline case, the slope of the isoquant at *F* equalled *JFQ*.

Model III. I now come to a model which is somewhat more complex, but realistic, with respect to the form of tying employed. Suppose that the so-called "additionality" principle is assumed, so that the recipient country must import specific commodities in full addition to initial imports. (A similar form of additionality with respect to source tying can also be analyzed, by extension of the present analysis.)

Assume, for this problem, that two commodities are producible with domestic resources and the production-possibility curve is a convex set.

Additionality takes the form of requiring that, on top of existing pre-aid imports, the full value of aid must be imported in the specific form of importables. In Figure 13, for example, the country would have produced at P_0 and consumed at C_0, with P_0C_0 being the given price ratio abroad. However, with aid equivalent to E_0F_0 of X-goods or

Figure 13

"Additionality" in Aid-tying and Multiple Exchange Rates

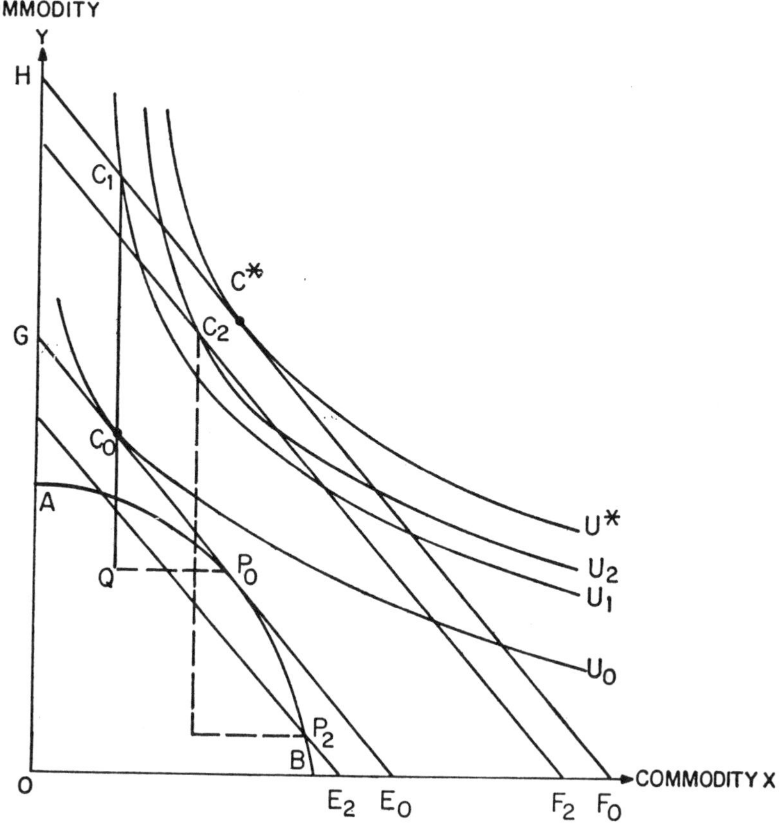

The diagram illustrates the emergence of multiple exchange rates when aid is tied by the "additionality" principle such that the recipient country must import specific commodities in addition to initial imports. AB is the production-possibility curve, in the two-commodity model. With aid equivalent to E_0F_0 of X-goods and C_0P_0 the fixed international price ratio, C^* would be the optimal consumption bundle. With "additionality" in aid, however, this recipient economy must import $(GH + C_0Q)$ of Y-imports. Production continuing at P_0 and consumption shifted to C_1, with a tax-cum-subsidy on consumption, will satisfy the necessary additionality. So will consumption at C_2 and production at P_2, brought about by suitable tax-cum-subsidies on production and consumption. In either case, multiple exchange rates emerge: domestic price ratios will diverge from the international price ratio.

GH of Y-goods, C^* would have been the optimal point of consumption and social welfare would have been at U^*. Suppose, however, that the aid-giver demands that (on the so-called "additionality" principle) the recipient should absorb altogether $(GH + C_0Q)$ amount of imports of Y. In this case, one *possible* equilibrium position, calling for a suitable consumption-tax-cum-subsidy policy, is with consumption at C_1, production continuing at P_0, and with C_1C_0 of Y being absorbed as aid and C_0Q_0 of Y being imported in exchange for P_0Q of X. But a *superior* position is at C_2 with production at P_2, where total imports of Y, under trade and aid, continue to be at the required level, but welfare level has risen to U_2. Clearly, the optimal second-best policy under this form of tied-aid constraint will involve suitable policies of taxes and subsidies on both consumption and production.

In this case, which corresponds in spirit to the more usual analysis of bulk-trading situations, the receipt of aid is *conditional* upon a certain pattern of trade and thus *requires* governmental intervention directly into the competitive system, for the market will not throw up the required pattern of trade on its own. Note, again, that the multiple rates are here the product of aid tying, and the inefficiencies they reflect are *not* to be interpreted as those resulting from inefficient policies of the recipient government.

Further, there may even be a dynamic reason here for departure from a unified exchange rate. It could be argued quite realistically that, even when such tying is not formally imposed, it is often considered to be "wise" to act as though it is, in the interests of *future* aid inflow. Thus, owing to this link between the current pattern of utilization of aid and the future aid inflow, it may be wise to forego some current income through treating the current inflow *as though* it were tied. Policies which thus appear to be inefficient from the current point of view may turn out to be fully rational, in economic terms, if the future is also considered.

C: IMPLICATIONS

In conclusion, we must remember that, with all these arguments for departures from unified exchange rates, official intervention must contend with the questions:

(1) What *form* of departure is optimal (tariffs versus production tax-cum-subsidies, and so forth)?

(2) At what *level* must the policy instruments (trade tariffs, subsidies, and domestic tax-cum-subsidies) be exercised?

(3) Where the policy instrument must be used with respect to different commodities, what is the optimal *structure* thereof (if tariffs are to be levied, for example, to diversify production, what is the optimal tariff structure that will bring this about at least cost)?

(4) If sub-optimal forms of intervention are adopted, at what level and structure must they be exercised to yield, at least, an improvement rather than deterioration in welfare compared to the level reached under a policy of unified exchange rates?

Unless these essential questions are posed, if not answered, it is utopian to expect that the numerous departures from unified exchange rates that we observe will generally yield any greater improvement in welfare than would unified exchange rates. Furthermore, as I shall go on to argue in the next Section, a close look at the reality in many parts of the world reveals forms of governmental departures from unified exchange rates which make little sense indeed from rational points of view.

III. DEPARTURES FROM UNIFIED EXCHANGE RATES IN PRACTICE

The recent cumulation of knowledge about the pattern of departures from unified exchange rates, arising particularly acutely in several less developed countries in Asia and in Latin America from the maintenance of overvalued exchange rates and from a widespread tendency to afford *de facto* protection through quantitative restrictions as soon as domestic production has become available in any and every industry, suggests very strongly that serious losses are accruing from the present policies—when one takes as the reference point a system of "rational" departures from unified rates.

A. PATTERN OF RELUCTANT EXCHANGE-RATE ADJUSTMENTS

At the heart of these inefficiencies is the pattern of exchange-rate adjustments to which many of the less developed countries seem to have become accustomed (with the exception of Latin America, where exchange rates lagging behind wildly rising price levels lead, *de facto*, to identical results). The pattern of reluctant adjustment of exchange rates is familiar enough to analysts of the international economic system, having belied the expectations of the early postwar period which feared competitive depreciations predicated on the interwar experience. The system is not an exclusive prerogative of the less developed countries by any means. But with them the resulting costs are more expensive at the margin; for their economic maneuverability is frequently limited by rising populations and insufficiently growing incomes.

The typical stages in the transition of a less developed country, from one parity to another, may be described as follows:

(1) Balance-of-payments difficulties, under a fixed parity, lead to the establishment and frequently to the more or less permanent continuation of a regime of quantitative restrictions. The result is the establishment of several *ad hoc, de facto* effective tariffs on different activities—a set of multiple import rates. There also comes about a net export rate (equal to parity) that falls below the effective import rates. (They exceed parity by the premium on imports, which may vary between different imports if the exchange markets are effectively segmented.) This export rate not only discriminates against exports

but also compounds the distortions that would arise from a multiplicity of rates on imports.

(2) Gradual shift towards a system of effective export subsidies occurs as the tight balance-of-payments situation and the quantitative restrictions continue, in order to increase export earnings. The effect is to reduce the differential between the export and the import rates, while often leading to multiple rates on exports as well, since official subsidies on exports almost always are discriminatory in practice.

(3) As the import premium continues, while lessened (*ceteris paribus*) by the export subsidization, governments turn gradually (under public criticism) to using tariffs more actively so as to cut into this premium and earn the scarcity profits themselves. The result is that, with both export subsidies and import tariffs being used in this fashion, there comes about a *de facto* devaluation on current visible transactions (extended gradually again to invisibles, such as remittances from settlers abroad and tourist earnings, but practically never to transactions on capital account. The *de facto* devaluation, however, is characterized by numerous rates on imports and exports, and conceals effective export rates on specific commodities that may exceed or fall below their effective import rates, so that numerous distortions remain embedded in the system.

(4) As the realization grows that a *de facto* devaluation has occurred, in an inefficient manner, the way is seen to rationalize the situation by devaluing the rate formally and thereby managing to reduce, if not eliminate, the reliance on export subsidies and import tariffs, though even this is done with considerable reluctance.

(5) Then the process can, and frequently does, start all over again, with the system of quantitative restrictions again taking the brunt of initial adjustment and then gradually being eased by export subsidies and import tariffs.

There are several variations on this general sequence, of course. In place of a freer use of import duties, for example, exchange auctions (as in Brazil) or multiplicity of exchange rates, fixed directly by exchange-control authorities (in many Latin American countries), have been used. Similarly, there are wide variations in the forms of export subsidy and the manner in which selectivity is exercised in granting them. In Pakistan and India, the most important form of export subsidization has been variations of the exchange-retention schemes which were fairly common with respect to dollar-earning exports in the early postwar period. Under these schemes, the exporter becomes entitled to an import license of the value given by a certain proportion of f.o.b. value of exports effected. Since there is a premium on imports, this "import entitlement" becomes effectively an export subsidy whose value can be measured as the rate of entitlement multiplied by the premium. The effective subsidies thus given have varied between activities because the entitlement rates were different between activities and also, much more acutely in the Indian schemes, because the market for sale of the import licenses was segmented according to the different schemes being administered separately for different activities. In the vast bulk of cases, however, the entitlement rate being below unity (100 per cent), the effective rate on exports was *below* the effective rate on imports and hence the degree of differential between export and import rates was reduced but *not* eliminated.[22]

The quite *indiscriminate* multiplicity of export and import rates, as also the continued differential between (higher, average) import rates and (lower, average) export rates which characterizes this pattern of reluctant adjustment in these countries is undoubtedly a source of considerable waste. There is a tendency to consider these sources of waste as not very important, for the reason that some of the recent empirical estimates of Harberger (1959), Johnson (1965c), and others have shown that, if several (rather weak) assumptions are made concerning elasticities of supply and demand, the effects of distortions from sources such as (certain types of) tariffs are but a small percentage of national income.

Undoubtedly these estimates are within a static framework and further ignore (what many economists consider to be very important) sources of inefficiency such as the neglect of cost minimization at any output level because of absence of competition. As economists such as Paul Streeten have rightly emphasized, what is measurable need not be important at all. However, even within the framework used to develop them, these estimates are seriously misleading.

[22] This can be seen readily. Under these schemes, for exports effected, an exporter could earn an import license of e per cent (of f.o.b. value of exports) which, when disposed of at a premium of y per cent in the market, gave rise to a net *ad valorem* subsidy on export value of ey per cent. On the other hand, the *effective* cost (in foreign exchange) for imports (ignoring certain minor complications resulting from the nontransferability of *some* imports) was only y per cent higher than the parity rate. Thus the effective export rate was $(1 + ey)$ while the effective import rate was $(1 + y)$. In cases where the import entitlement was over 100 per cent ($e > 1$), however, the situation was one of *net* export subsidization.

First, there is the psychological point that practically anything divided by national income is likely to look "small." On the other hand, this optical illusion can be readily destroyed in the present instance by turning the estimates around and arguing, more impressively, that an average savings ratio of 15 per cent, combined with a marginal capital/output ratio of 3:1 will yield a growth rate of 5 per cent. Thus, a loss of even 10 per cent of national income will represent a loss that is twice the growth of output that is normally expected per annum for many countries on the average.

Second, it must be emphasized that the estimates presented by these authors are, directly or implicitly (via thinly disguised *guesses* at substitution possibilities for specific countries), strictly hypothetical. Lest any reader may have been bamboozled by the deployment of elementary mathematics and Cobb-Douglas and CES production functions into believing that an inherent property of inefficiency is that it must necessarily be insignificant, I refer you to Figure 14. There I have shown that, by suitable export-subsidization policy, for a country with neither monopoly power in trade nor any domestic imperfections requiring the use of first-best domestic tax-cum-subsidies, the government of that country can inflict a significant loss on its system, *as compared with the optimal level under a unified exchange rate.* Thus, for example, by shifting production to P_E through appropriately subsidizing the export of commodity Y when under a unified exchange rate the economy would have been exporting commodity X instead, the economy can be shifted from real income (measured at international prices) of OD in terms of commodity X to real income of OC, which is exactly *half* the level under the unified rate. And the damage could have been worse, if I had cared to demonstrate it in this example!

Third, it is frequently thought that the cost of inefficient allocative policies is likely to be small for the less developed countries because their economic structures are rigid (as Charles Kindleberger has always emphasized). Two qualifications, however, need to be made to this argument. (1) A less developed country, which is predominantly agricultural, may still have significant substitution possibilities from our present viewpoint: a country or region dependent on rice paddy and jute, for example, would be characterized by strong technological substitution possibilities within existing resources at a point of time and could thus suffer seriously from distorting policies (affecting the relative incentives between the two crops). On the other hand, because

Figure 14

Possibility of Significant Loss of Real Income from Policies Resulting in Misallocation of Resources

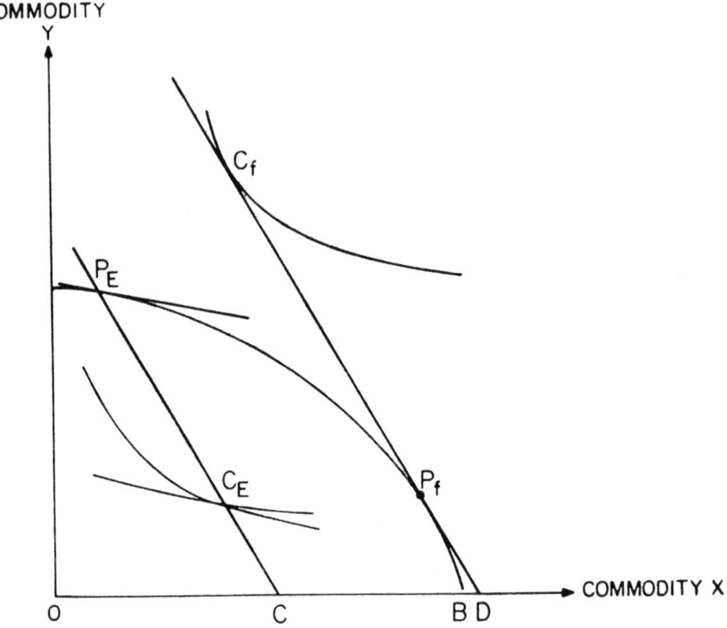

The diagram illustrates how real income can be halved from *OD* to *OC*, measured in *X*-goods, if the policy adopted is changed from a unified rate to an (appropriate) export-subsidization policy.

of the considerable nonmalleability of capital (emphasized by the Cambridge school, led by Mrs. Joan Robinson), the advanced economies with large stocks of physical capital among their existing resources may have very limited substitution possibilities in the short run. (2) Moreover, the proposition that the less developed countries will not suffer seriously from distortions, because of rigid economic structures, must be qualified insofar as a significant augmentation of their resources annually occurs via foreign aid in many cases, and these resources are malleable in a very large degree (despite aid tying by end use) and therefore characterized by considerable substitution possibilities from our point of view. A static view, such as that embodied in the approach of many trade theorists even up to this date, removes this point from their analysis of the problem altogether, but it is none the less a significant point, as much of the waste attaches to the utilization of these incremental malleable resources in these developing countries.

To return to these countries, then, a close look at their vast multiplicity of effective rates, arrived at almost without any clear economic rationale (in many cases purely as a side-result of the method of reluctant adjustment), throws up numerous instances of inefficiencies that leave a clear impression of concealed gross losses.

Thus, for example, recent attempts at evaluating projects at international prices, implying operationally the application of the principle of unified exchange rates, shows that the return to domestic resources employed in these projects, which have absorbed considerable resources, may actually be negative, thus implying that in terms of international opportunity cost these projects have actually led to a *decline* in national income. In a recent study of a major heavy electrical plant, which was one of the few capital-intensive projects of India's Second Five-Year Plan, Ian Little found that the rate of return actually turned out to be negative, at international prices, even though evaluated at *blueprint* efficiency (which, needless to say, is rather a distant goal)!

Closer analyses of the results of export-incentive schemes, as operated in India, have thrown up several other clear examples of waste resulting from the indiscriminate creation of multiple rates. Several products have been exported f.o.b. at low, give-away prices (with domestic incentives compensating for losses), while identical homogeneous items have been imported by yet other user-producers at *higher* international c.i.f. prices, because the effective rates to these different parties on their respective transactions were not unified. Similarly, because export subsidization occasionally exceeded the effective import rate for specific products, incentives were set up to export items on which the cost of inputs (evaluated at c.i.f. cost) would exceed the (f.o.b.) value of export, thus indicating again negative value added at international prices. This may be seen readily in terms of the following logic.

Let P_x stand for unit export price (which, for simplicity, is assumed to be constant), P_m for unit average price of inputs (at c.i.f. value) in exportable production, m_x for the input content per unit exportable, and P_D for the domestic unit price of the exportable commodity.

Then two conditions must be satisfied before export will be effected in this industry under the exchange-retention scheme:

$$P_x\,(1+ey) \geqq P_D \qquad (1)$$

$$\text{and } P_x > P_m \cdot m_x\,(1+y)/(1+ey). \qquad (2)$$

The former condition merely states that the return from unit export must be at least equal to the return from unit sale in the domestic market, else, domestic sale will be preferred to foreign sale. The latter condition further states that the revenue from unit export must exceed the cost of the inputs as given by the premium in the market for foreign exchange.

Now, consistent with these two conditions, we can have $P_x < P_m \cdot m_x$ (that is, negative value added) if $e > 1$, that is, the entitlement rate is greater than 100 per cent. On the other hand, note that, if overinvoicing of exports is practiced, the possibility of negative value added arising, signifying inefficient exportation, increases. In this case, condition (2) now becomes

$$P_x > P_m \cdot m_x \frac{1+y}{1+ey+k\,(ey-\rho)}, \qquad (2a)$$

where k is the proportion of f.o.b. value by which export value is raised by faked declarations incorporating overinvoicing and ρ is the black-market premium on foreign exchange. Thus, in this instance, even if $e < 1$, it would now be possible to have $P_x < P_m \cdot m_x$ *consistent* with conditions (1) and (2a) being satisfied. Since, in India, overinvoicing has been a widespread phenomenon, the incidence of negative value added arising is not to be discounted and instances have been readily found (Bhagwati, 1967a).[23]

Similar results have been found in several other countries—in the Philippines and Pakistan in Asia, in Brazil and Argentina in Latin America, and would undoubtedly come to light in other parts of the world if only one cared to look for them. Such results, after all, only dramatically highlight the wasteful effects of the distortions introduced by departures from unified rates introduced by the institution of exchange-control systems; the *total* losses inflicted by the multiplicity of rates must be larger.[24]

[23] Note that, in this instance, we observe the phenomenon of negative value added (at international prices) *not* because investment in the industry is economically wasteful *per se*, but because (net) export subsidization makes it so. It is perfectly conceivable, therefore, that, with such incentives removed, the industry would show positive returns (at international prices) and might even have *comparative* advantage in production (though *not* for export).

[24] These losses, however, are exaggerated by Anne Kreuger (1966), whose recent application of the same technique of evaluating value added at international prices for Turkey arrives at loss levels that are very large in relation to national income. While the losses from the operation of exchange control in Turkey may be as large as Kreuger thinks, the method of analysis used by her is limited by two

B. INEFFICIENT METHODS OF IMPORT SUBSTITUTION AND EXPORT PROMOTION

While, however, the observable exchange-rate policies of many less developed countries will, in general, lead to sizeable losses thanks to the resulting multiplicity of rates which have no economic rationale, the situation is actually more serious than has been suggested so far. The reason is that the precise method of operation of the quantitative restrictions, the export subsidies, and the investment controls that are frequently the domestic counterpart of this trade regime compound the inefficiencies considerably. While what I now proceed to describe could well be documented by reference to most less developed countries with balance-of-payments difficulties, the main outlines relate to the experience of India over the last decade, for I am well acquainted with its many nuances and well aware of its relevance to experience elsewhere.

The system of quantitative restrictions there not only created a maze of multiple rates with differential effects on incentives, but it was also squarely based on the principle that domestic availability justified exclusion of imports. This principle implied a built-in promise of getting *de facto* protection by the granting of quantitative restrictions as soon as domestic production came into effect (*no matter what the domestic cost of production relative to foreign cost*). This principle of protection, observed in countries as wide apart as Pakistan, Turkey, and Brazil as well, led to a *total* disregard of efficiency in the resulting investments. Where the investments were controlled by licensed entry, the choice among industries was again determined without reference to costs and purely by reference to aggregative notions such as "the need for heavy industry," ignoring the fact that, even if a case could be made for investing in a capital-goods sector on long-term grounds,

factors: (1) it would be inappropriate to assume that the assumption of infinite elasticities of supply and demand internationally can be applied to all processes in Turkey; and (2) similarly, it cannot be implicitly assumed that constant costs obtain once significant shifts in investment and output levels are admitted, as they must be, in making the estimates. Moreover, the estimates in Kreuger's stimulating paper need to be adjusted for (at the very least) some of the kinds of qualifications to the principle of unified exchange rates that were listed in Section II above. Finally, it has been stressed to me by Bela Balassa that *all* tradables should be evaluated at *international* prices, as is clearly the practice of economists, such as Tinbergen and Little, who have used the technique (involving the application of the principle of unified exchange rates) for evaluating and ranking projects by their comparative advantage. If this is not done, then the ranking of projects, as well as the real cost of distortions, measured by the technique of evaluating at international prices, will be distorted.

there were numerous choices *within* the so-called "heavy-industry" complex which, if properly exploited, could yield significant gains in real income.

With the actual pattern of investments thus being determined primarily by effective incentives set up by existing *and* anticipated quantitative restrictions—subject to restrictive licensing, informed in turn by notions that had little in common with the concepts of costs and comparative advantage—the results could hardly be expected to be inviting if one compared the outcome with what *could* be achieved under ideally efficient policies. Even the allocations of foreign exchange and domestic materials *qua* inputs into existing capacities were strictly rationed, by industry, and by firm within industry, and retransfers were made illegal in general, so that the possibility of market-directed shifts in utilization towards more efficient plants or firms were also ruled out (although illegal transfers, within limits, were possible).[25]

A notable casualty of these developments was the Tariff Commission, which had, until these years, played a marked role in giving protection to domestic industries and in following systematically (if not efficiently, from an economic viewpoint) the progress in the cost structure of the protected industries with a view to determining the magnitude and duration of the tariff protection. The Tariff Commission lost touch with the major industrial developments in the country, as few industries applied for tariff protection when the exchange restrictions did the job well enough. More importantly, even where the industries applied for protection to the Commission (mostly as a second line of defense if quotas were to be liberalized), the Commission acted virtually as a tariff-estimating agency whose job apparently was to make the tariff-inclusive landed price of the imports uncompetitive with the domestic prices of produced outputs, estimated on the basis of a "fair price" formula which added a standard rate of return to the costs of (often the least efficient firm's) production. The notion that the Tariff Commission could turn down an application for protection was no longer relevant, as the primary decisions on *that* issue belonged to other more important agencies—the Planning Commission, the

[25] Since allocations of profitable foreign exchange and domestic materials at controlled prices were related under the system to existing capacity, with quotas estimated on a *pro rata* basis, the system also built into itself a distorting incentive to add to capacity even when there was underutilization of existing capacity.

licensing authorities, and the exchange and import controllers. As Lakdawala (1964, p. 109) observed, in his Presidential address to the Indian Economic Association recently:

> In the old Tariff Commission procedure . . . there were checks both on the types of industries protected, and the later behaviour of the firms in the industry. Besides the periodical public inquiries, the annual Report paid attention to questions like prices, costs, quality, consumers' satisfaction, etc., of protected industries. There are no parallel safeguards being observed now.

Nurul Islam has recorded a similar situation in Pakistan, of a Tariff Commission emasculated by the growth of the quota system (somewhat less so than in India, but still sufficiently so) and reduced to a minor role. Let me quote him from a recent study (1967):

> The Tariff Commission examines and suggests tariff rates for one industry at a time as and when the industry concerned applies for protection and the Government refers the case to the Commission for examination. . . . The programming of industries or determination of priorities in the field of industry belongs to different policymaking organizations such as industrial licencing authorities and the Planning Commission. The Tariff Commission is not a party to the process of the formulation of industrial priorities or selection of industrial projects. The Tariff Commission comes into the picture only at a later stage when the industry has already been sanctioned by the appropriate authorities and is functioning for some time.

But if the situation has been so grotesque on the side of imports and investment allocations for import substitution (in the widest sense), it seems to have been equally disturbing with respect to exports. Beginning from a situation of rather large premia on imports and little export incentives, with differentials between the export and import rates ranging upwards of 50 per cent in favor of imports, the system moved away in India towards a more active form of export subsidization which, *ceteris paribus*, narrowed this differential. However, it soon became official policy to grant to any potential exporter who came to the Government sufficient export subsidy to offset whatever loss he said he would have to incur by diverting sale abroad. Thus, a whole range of export incentives was granted through the import-entitlement schemes, tax rebates, and other methods, with a variety of effective incentives and rates, whose major rationale was the decision to increase *any and all* exports by providing all necessary offsets to excess of domestic profitability over foreign prices.[26] Quite aside from the fact that there was practically no way of checking whether the declared unprofitability of sales abroad were genuine (so that large profits must have undoubtedly occurred from merely exaggerating the costs of foreign sale), the principle of comparative advantage was not merely violated by such a system but, in fact, directly contradicted: for, under it, there was a systematic encouragement of the export of uncompetitive items as against the export of competitive ones! How persuasive the principle looked to policymakers, keen to increase exports, and how lucrative its implementation must have been to exporters, could be seen by the growing demands on the part of potential exporters for higher subsidies to offset transport costs when the exportables were made from deep within the land mass of the country![27]

Clearly, the operative principle with the Ministry of International Trade had become: export maximization. Economists frequently worry about educating policymakers that import substitution is not desirable, except when it is shown otherwise—on grounds such as infant industries. It needs, however, to be equally emphasized that all exports or any exports are not desirable either, and that countries can export too much and the wrong things. This is a difficult thing to do when exchange control leads to a differential between export and import rates that *does* call for a corrective export subsidy. In such a case, the economist must support export subsidies but must oppose the absurdly

[26] In fact, at one time the Government was operating a clandestine scheme under which, if the normal cluster of incentives was insufficient to yield adequate subsidy for effecting any specific export, the Government would grant *additional* entitlements on an *ad hoc* basis. The scheme was clandestine because the entitlements were import licenses for dryfruit, which carried a lucrative premium. But it would have been impossible to admit this formally to the IMF because the IMF "did not ask questions" of the Indian Government about the entitlement schemes. Both pretended that the entitlements were not "really" subsidy schemes but were intended to supply scarce materials to export industries which "were earning their imports." This pretense did not make sense if a truck exporter was getting a dryfruit license!

[27] The demands went so far as to claim that subsidies should be made directly a function of the internal transport cost incurred in bringing the product from the hinterland to the nearest port! The economic magnitude of this demand will become clear if it is realized that among those demanding such incentives from a willing Ministry were exporters of bicycles and sewing machines over 1,000 miles from the nearest outlets!

wasteful forms in which they are given, and policymakers often have no patience for such subtleties.[28]

The inventory of the inefficiencies of this system would be incomplete if I did not describe also how it virtually eliminated the cost efficiency which derives from competition by leading to fully sheltered markets for each firm. Quantitative restrictions rigidly eliminated competition from abroad, while licensing eliminated the possibility of domestic entry by rival firms. In either case, the short-sighted thought was to "prevent waste of scarce resources" when there was already domestic capacity in an activity. At the same time, the allocative system for inputs implied that the efficient existing firms could not even outbid scarce materials from rival firms, so that *all* conceivable forms of competition were ruled out. Under such a system, there was little reason indeed for firms to pursue economies in production relentlessly, if at all. It is impossible to quantify these inefficiencies meaningfully; they often take the form of indifference to quality and consumer complaints. It is impossible to believe that the widespread dissatisfaction that one comes across in these countries, among consumers of both finished and intermediate items, with the quality of the domestic items that they are forced by policy to use, stems primarily from the difficulties of "learning by infants" or from what is rather passionately (and sometimes accurately) described as xenophilia. Most certainly, much of it is a product of the featherbedding caused by the system of reluctant adjustment combined with the *de facto* protection of any and every item of domestic production.

If these systems to which the less developed countries seem to have

[28] There are also political reasons why it is difficult to get reforms introduced in this area, once the whole complex of such export subsidies has got under way. (1) Often, the Minister's political reputation depends on his producing a sizeable increase in export earnings, *no matter how*. Thus, for example, when Goa was taken over by India and the Indian statistics thereafter showed a sizeable increment in export earnings, the Minister's reputation went up: Indian exports were beginning to move! Changes in the terms of trade, brought about by external factors, have a similar effect. Michael Michaely tells me that the Israeli Minister responsible for exports once refused to release export figures until somehow the figure was pushed up above the preceding year's level! Perhaps the answer is to abolish all separate Ministries for exports, and to educate politicians *and* international institutions that exports *in themselves* are a poor index of efficiency in economic performance. (2) Equally important is the opposition provided by the beneficiaries of these subsidy schemes, who would find to their definite disadvantage a reform making it impossible to fatten on what are effectively variable-subsidy schemes (largely manipulated by themselves for their own benefit), and who also manage frequently to frighten the Ministry in charge of exports into believing that any reform will "sabotage the export effort."

become attached are so wasteful, the pertinent question is: why is it that they still have so much appeal to policymakers in these countries? It is always worth asking this question, as economists have rightly been careful not to fall behind policymakers in formulating correct answers to practical problems ever since Keynes was anticipated by deficit financing. In this instance, however, I think that the reasons which serve to explain the adoption of these inefficient policies seem to reveal merely how easy it is to get economic policy premised on a false and wasteful basis.

I think that the explanation for the prevailing state of affairs is to be found in two rather broad and similar reasons for loss of faith in the price mechanism: one relating to the foreign-trade sector, and the other to the domestic. Put in a nutshell, few policymakers in these countries seem to believe in the efficacy, not to raise the question of the efficiency, of exchange-rate adjustments, for a variety of reasons, of which perhaps the most important is the notion that the less developed countries have "foreign-exchange bottlenecks," which leads to a modern version of "elasticity pessimism." Moreover, there is an equally blanket premise that the problems faced by the less developed countries relate to growth and transformation, to which the price mechanism has little relevance, that growth is more important than choice (in Peter Wiles' well-known words). I wish to elaborate on each of these themes a little, for unless these views are countered, the possibility of getting the requisite changes away from the kind of systems that I have been describing seems to me to be quite remote.

C. ATTITUDES TOWARD EXCHANGE-RATE CHANGES

A range of hostile attitudes toward exchange-rate changes can be found in these countries.

(1) In India, for example, as also in countries that have inherited the British traditions in the civil service, there seems to have been a carry-over of the distrust and dislike of devaluations, which are viewed practically as affronts to national dignity. Such attitudes, of course, seem very funny in countries which have rarely had the remotest claims to having a prestigious currency (in *any* sense of the term), but they are quite real, as we discovered when pressing for devaluation in India in June 1966.

(2) Much the more important, and general, is the widespread feeling that the development of the less developed countries is being

handicapped by the *bottleneck* posed by foreign exchange. This has led to policy being dictated by the premise that the really important thing is to look for aid, to treat foreign exchange as though it were something apart from other resources, and to treat allocation thereof as something so particularly important as to require a *direct* allocative mechanism as distinct from an amorphous and unpredictable price mechanism.

At the outset, it must be recognized that foreign-exchange bottlenecks can certainly exist and that whether they do is an empirical matter. It would be tedious to insist on this elementary issue were it not for the fact that there is a tendency, emanating from the Chicago school, to regard such phenomena as exchange bottlenecks and disguised unemployment as though they conflicted with logic and sense. It is perfectly conceivable that the possibility of translating savings into investment, for example, may be constrained at the margin by lack of domestic shiftability of capacities combined with limited trade-transformation possibilities, so that it is the limited trade opportunity rather than the capacity to raise *ex ante* savings still further that provides the constraint on raising real investment (cf. Bhagwati, 1962). Indeed, the recent work of Hollis Chenery (1962) in this area indicates that foreign transformation possibilities, rather than the ability to raise *ex ante* savings, may be the real limitation on the capacity to raise real incomes in several less developed countries.

However, it is easy enough to quarrel with the rigid patterns of demand (both intermediate and final) built into his models, and the overly pessimistic estimates of export feasibilities which he is often constrained to accept from the planners in less developed countries. Both of these assumptions must bias Chenery's estimates rather heavily toward his results.

Moreover, one must not forget that foreign-aid flows are frequently considered to be related to the ability to work out plausible *ex ante* gaps of foreign exchange, a practice that dates back to the Marshall Plan. Some of you must have heard the story of how, when the Marshall Plan recipient countries were putting together their *ex ante* gap estimates under the chairmanship of Sir Oliver Franks, the leader of the Turkish delegation caused a stir by announcing that their calculations showed an *ex ante* surplus. When Sir Oliver, with his well-known tact, suggested that there must be a mistake, some signs mixed up somewhere, and perhaps the Turkish delegation would like to adjourn, the offer was strenuously resisted. When, finally, an emissary was despatched from the British delegation to explain how an *ex ante* gap was necessary if Turkey was to be included in the list of claimants, the delegation leader is supposed to have been shattered: "Oh, but we thought that, if you wanted to borrow abroad, you had to show a sound payments position!" Needless to say, the adjournment was accepted and the "arithmetical errors" rectified to arrive at a suitable *ex ante* deficit. The lesson, we will admit, has now been widely learnt.

Further, to many of us who have been engaged in policy debate in our countries, it is clear that: (a) The quantitative restrictions have led to heavy import dependence by encouraging the inflow of private capital for the purpose of assembling finished goods. These set up their own demands for imported components whose c.i.f. costs come very close to the c.i.f. cost of the finished manufactured imports themselves, thus creating a pattern of growth in which each unit value added becomes extremely import-intensive. (b) The claim that, despite willingness to save, investment cannot be raised, wears thin as one sees resources continually used up in providing for consumption rather than investment. Even though it may be impossible to raise investment further in any one period, the allocation of investment *currently* to the capital-goods sector will enable one to raise investment higher in the *next* period. On the other hand, one typically finds the foreign-exchange resources (which are mostly flexible in this respect) being used quite generously for supporting consumption through the creation of still more capacity aimed at increasing overall consumption.

However, regardless of whether it makes empirical sense in any specific country to argue that its investment, or rate of growth, is constrained by the inability to transform commodities through trade at infinitely elastic international prices, it should be seen immediately that this amounts merely to a feasibility constraint. I cannot see any reason at all to deduce from this that exchange-rate adjustments are inferior to the pattern of reluctant adjustments. The existence of a bottleneck merely requires the adoption of optimum tariffs, which amount to a well-defined set of departures from unified exchange rates. Admittedly, an overvalued exchange rate which involves a net import rate exceeding the export rate is formally identical with a suitable tariff rate on a lowered parity (with an adjusted wage-price level). However, the reluctant-adjustment mechanism is *not* in practice equivalent to, but is actually inferior to, an optimal tariff system, for the simple reason that it involves, as I have already argued, a systematic bias toward *indiscriminate* protection (and, in later stages, indiscriminate export subsidization).

Thus, the notion that foreign-exchange bottlenecks imply a decline in the efficacy and efficiency of exchange-rate adjustments is an erroneous one. I am afraid that undue preoccupation with what is not feasible—for instance, "we cannot have X per cent rate of growth because of a foreign-exchange bottleneck"—has led to an irrational neglect of policies even to attain what *is* within grasp.

(3) A related impediment to a freer use of exchange-rate changes, which is common in my part of the world, is worth recording here. It is argued that, under a pegged-exchange-rate system, frequent changes in the exchange rate are difficult, if not impossible. Hence, it is smarter to use import tariffs and export subsidies, which are more readily adjustable than exchange rates.

Note that this argument, when used by policymakers, represents a major triumph in educating them: the recognition of the equivalence between exchange-rate changes and import tariffs plus export subsidies is rare indeed. Arnold Harberger tells the story of a public meeting in Chile where, the preceding speaker having been drowned in hostile jeers for having suggested a devaluation, he was met with thunderous applause for shifting around and recommending instead an equivalent increase in import tariffs to protect domestic manufacture "against foreign competition" and an equivalent increase in export subsidies to carry Chile's manufactures "right into foreign markets."

However, when the equivalence proposition is used instead to *avoid* formal parity changes, it is necessary to point out the limitations of the equivalence in practice:

(1) For full equivalence, the tariffs and export subsidies would have to be extended to *all* transactions, to invisibles and capital-account transactions as well. Short of a parity change itself, this is not something that will be done. In practice, the tariffs and export subsidies remain (at best) confined to visibles and a few invisibles (such as remittances and tourism), thus leading to a "dual" rate system without any economic rationale.

(2) In practice, the tariffs and export subsidies, even on visibles, can end up being selective and discriminatory between items without any economic rationale.

(3) The administrative costs of implementing subsidy and tariff programs via Customs and Revenue authorities are significantly greater in relation to a straightforward change in parity.

(4) The question whether such programs can be implemented without causing widespread corruption and evasion, when the export subsidies and import tariffs rise to high levels in lieu of formal parity changes, is a very pertinent one, and, I am afraid, one to which most experience seems to point to an answer in favor of parity changes.

I think that these are overwhelming arguments in support of formal parity changes as distinct from equivalent measures involving tariff plus export subsidies. However, insofar as it is considered impolitic to resort to frequent parity changes, tariffs and export subsidies ought to be considered as useful second-best methods (superior to quota regimes) of achieving transitions from one parity to another, precisely because they are more freely employed.

D. ATTITUDES TOWARD THE PRICE MECHANISM

The willingness to put up with the inefficiencies from indiscriminate protection through overvalued rates under exchange-control regimes, combined with the often explicit philosophy that "essential" imports are only those of which there is "inadequate" domestic production (thus all production ought to be automatically protected), must be traced also to a general lack of conviction in the capacity of the price mechanism to allocate resources in a situation where (1) major transformations in economic structure may be called for, and (2) capital and entrepreneurship may be in inadequate supply.

But, while these factors explain, they do not really justify the policies adopted. There is no reason why the framework of incentives provided to encourage domestic entrepreneurship should not be reasonably in conformity with comparative advantage instead of being indiscriminate in its incidence. Nor does it seem impossible, or excessively difficult, to exploit the market mechanism so as to push decisions in desired efficient directions, supplementing tardy entrepreneurship (where necessary) with direct investments *in conformity with efficiency.*

The fact is all too obvious that even when less developed countries have bypassed the use of the price mechanism in allocating resources, as with public-sector investments in India, efficiency has been ignored and a wasteful "physical" approach to planning has been readily adopted, leading to production whose profitability again was secured by the system of quantitative restrictions with its automatic extension of effective protection to all production.

Unfortunately, the practices of the donor countries only serve to accentuate some of the difficulties traceable to these attitudes and resulting economic policies. Thus, aid is occasionally tied to projects which suit the interests of the donor's exporters rather than fit into the recipient's economy to greatest advantage: the recipient has sometimes little choice in the matter and is glad to receive whatever he gets. *Economic* irrationality is *not* a unique and exclusive quality of the less developed countries.

IV. CONCLUDING REMARKS

Economists clearly have to keep focussing on these issues of commercial policy (in its widest sense), for they seem to me to have acquired considerable relevance to the prospects of rapid development in the poorer countries of the world. Unless the productivity of investments in these areas increases dramatically, as it surely can (for we have phenomenal waste at the moment), the task of raising the rates of growth of real income to higher levels is going to be awfully difficult.

I remain a mild optimist on the question of getting the necessary changes in attitudes and policies accepted and implemented in the foreseeable future. Philosophies of economic policy often live short lives; and I think the regime of indiscriminate protection and physical planning will soon begin to give way to more sensible policies. Economists merely have to keep the pressure on.

Bibliography

Arrow, Kenneth J."The Economic Implications of Learning by Doing," *Review of Economic Studies*, Vol. 29 (June 1962), pp. 155-173.

Bardhan, Pranab K. "On Optimum Subsidy to a Learning Industry: An Aspect of Infant-Industry Protection," *Mimeographed* (1966).

Bhagwati, Jagdish. "Indian Balance of Payments Policy and Exchange Auctions," *Oxford Economic Papers*, N.S. Vol. 14 (February 1962), pp. 51-68.

——— "The Phenomenon of Negative Value Added Industries," *Mimeographed* (1967[a]).

——— "The Gains from Trade Once Again," *Oxford Economic Papers*, forthcoming.

——— "Trade Liberalization among LDC's, Trade Theory and G.A.T.T. Rules," in J. N. Wolfe, ed., *Value, Capital and Growth, Hicks Festschrift Volume* (Edinburgh: Edinburgh University Press, 1968).

——— "Non-Economic Objectives and the Efficiency Properties of Trade," *Journal of Political Economy*, forthcoming.

——— and Kemp, Murray C. "Ranking of Tariffs under Monopoly Power in Trade," forthcoming.

——— and Ramaswami, Vangal K. "Domestic Distortions, Tariffs and the Theory of Optimum Subsidy," *Journal of Political Economy*, Vol. 71 (February 1963), pp. 44-50.

——— and Srinivasan, Thirukodikaval N. "Non-Economic Objectives and Optimal Policy Intervention," *Mimeographed* (1967).

Chenery, Hollis B. and Bruno, Michael. "Development Alternatives in an Open Economy: The Case of Israel," *Economic Journal*, Vol. 72 (March 1962), pp. 79-103.

Cordon, W. Max. "Tariffs, Subsidies and the Terms of Trade," *Economica*, N.S. Vol. 24 (August 1957), pp. 235-242.

Domar, Evsey D. "A Soviet Model of Growth," *Essays in the Theory of Economic Growth* (New York: Oxford University Press, 1957), pp. 223-261.

Frisch, Ragnar. "Outline of a System of Multicompensatory Trade," *Review of Economics and Statistics*, Vol. 30 (November 1948), pp. 265-271.

Graham, Frank D. *Protective Tariffs* (New York: Harper & Brothers, 1934).

Hansen, Bent. *Fiscal and Monetary Planning* (Rotterdam: De Vries Lectures, 1966).

Harberger, Arnold C. "Using the Resources at Hand More Effectively," *American Economic Review Papers and Proceedings*, Vol. XLIX (May 1959), pp. 134-146.

Islam, Nurul. "Comparative Costs, Factor Proportions and Industrial Efficiency in Pakistan," *Pakistan Development Review*, Vol. VII (Summer 1967), pp. 212-246.

Johnson, Harry G. "Optimum Welfare and Maximum Revenue Tariffs," *Review of Economic Studies*, Vol. 19 (No. 1, 1951), pp. 28-35.

——— *International Trade and Economic Growth* (London: Allen & Unwin, 1958).

——— "The Cost of Protection and the Scientific Tariff," *Journal of Political Economy*, Vol. 68 (August 1960), pp. 327-345.

——— "Optimal Trade Intervention in the Presence of Domestic Distortions," in Robert E. Baldwin *et al., Trade, Growth, and the Balance of Payments* (Chicago: Rand McNally & Company; and Amsterdam: North-Holland Publishing Company, 1965 [a]), pp. 3-34.

——— "An Economic Theory of Protectionism, Tariff Bargaining, and the Formation of Customs Unions," *Journal of Political Economy*, Vol. 73 (June 1965 [b]), pp. 256-283.

——— "The Costs of Protection and Self-Sufficiency," *Quarterly Journal of Economics*, Vol. 79 (August 1965 [c]), pp. 356-372.

Kaldor, Nicholas. "Dual Exchange Rates and Economic Development," *Essays on Economic Policy*, Vol. II, Chapter 19 (London: Duckworth, 1964).

Kemp, Murray C. "The Mill-Bastable Infant-Industry Dogma," *Journal of Political Economy*, Vol. 68 (February 1960), pp. 65-67.

——— "The Gain from International Trade," *Economic Journal*, Vol. 72 (December 1962), pp. 803-819.

——— *The Pure Theory of International Trade* (Englewood Cliffs, New Jersey: Prentice-Hall, 1964).

Krueger, Anne O. "Some Economic Costs of Exchange Control: The Turkish Case," *Journal of Political Economy*, Vol. 74 (October 1966), pp. 466-480.

Lakdawala, Dansukhlal T. "Aspects of Trade Policy in India," *Indian Economic Journal*, Vol. 12 (October-December 1964), pp. 89-110.

Lewis, W. Arthur. "Economic Development with Unlimited Supplies of Labour," *Manchester School*, Vol. XXII (May 1954), pp. 139-191.

Mahalanobis, P. "The Approach of Operational Research to Planning in India," *Sankhya, The Indian Journal of Statistics*, Vol. 16 (December 1955), pp. 3-130.

Myrdal, Gunnar. *An International Economy* (New York: Harper, 1956).

Ramaswami, Vangal K. and Srinivasan, Thirukodikaval N. "Optimal Subsidies and Tariffs When Some Factors are Traded," *Mimeographed* (1967).

Samuelson, Paul A. "Social Indifference Curves," *Quarterly Journal of Economics*, Vol. 70 (February 1956), pp. 1-22.

——— "The Gains from International Trade Once Again," *Economic Journal*, Vol. 72 (December 1962), pp. 820-829.

Streeten, Paul. "The Case for Export Subsidies," *AICC Economic Review* (New Delhi, India), Vol. 14 (April 1, 1963), pp. 15-16.

Editor's Notes

The stages of exchange-rate adjustments developed in section III of this essay have been extended and applied to country experiences in the National Bureau of Economic Research Study on Foreign Trade Regimes and Economic Development, directed by Jagdish N. Bhagwati and Anne O. Krueger. See these summary volumes: J. N. Bhagwati, *Anatomy and Consequences of Exchange Control Regimes*, Cambridge, MA: Ballinger, 1978; and A. O. Krueger, *Liberalization Attempts and Consequences*, Cambridge, MA: Ballinger, 1978.

The question of the optimal trade and payments strategy for developing countries has been further considered in J. N. Bhagwati and A. O. Krueger, "Exchange Control, Liberalization, and Economic Development," *American Economic Review* (May 1973): 419–427; and J. N. Bhagwati and T. N. Srinivasan, "Trade Policy and Development," in R. Dornbusch and J. A. Frenkel, eds., *International Economic Policy: Theory and Evidence*, Baltimore: Johns Hopkins, 1979, chapter 1, pp. 1–35.

Reprinted from:
Trade, Balance of Payments, and Growth
North-Holland Publishing Company

THE GENERALIZED THEORY OF DISTORTIONS AND WELFARE

Jagdish N. BHAGWATI

The theory of trade and welfare [1] has recently developed independently in seven areas that have apparently little analytical relationship among themselves:

1. The Suboptimality of Laissez-Faire Under Market Imperfections: It has been shown that, when market imperfections exist, laissez-faire (otherwise described as "a policy of unified exchange rates" [5]) will not be the optimal policy. Among the market imperfections for which the suboptimality of laissez-faire has been demonstrated are four key types: (i) factor market imperfection, a wage differential between sectors; [2] (ii) product market imperfection, a production externality; [3] (iii) consumption imperfection, a

[1] This paper is the result of thinking and research over a period of many years, originating in my 1958 paper on immiserizing growth [1] and developing considerably since my joint paper with the late V.K. Ramaswami in 1963 [2] on domestic distortions. Since 1965, T.N. Srinivasan and I have collaborated on research in related matters, pertaining to the theory of optimal policy intervention when noneconomic objectives are present [7], a subject pioneered by Max Corden's brilliant work [12]. In many ways, therefore, this paper has grown out of the ferment of ideas in Delhi during 1963–1968, when Srinivasan, Ramaswami, and I happened to work together and independently on the diverse subjects which are brought together in this paper. The work of others, particularly Murray Kemp [23], [24] and Harry Johnson [18], has also contributed to the development of my thinking. The influence of Meade's work must also be acknowledged.

[2] I assume here that the wage differential is "distortionary" and cannot be attributed to legitimate economic grounds, such as disutility in occupations where the higher wage is charged. For a detailed discussion, see Fishlow and David [13] and Bhagwati and Ramaswami [2].

[3] See Kemp [21], Chapter 11, for a fuller discussion of alternative types of production externalities. I have in mind here the case of a "pure" production externality of the Meade variety, as set out in footnote 10 later.

consumption externality;[4] and (iv) trade imperfection, monopoly power in trade.[5]

2. Immiserizing Growth: Examples have been produced where a country, after growth (in factor supplies and/or technological know-how), becomes worse off, phenomena described as *immiserizing growth*. I produced an example of such a phenomenon in 1958 [1] (as also did Harry Johnson independently at the time) where growth led to such a deterioration in the country's terms of trade that the loss from the worsened terms of trade outweighed the primary gain from growth. Subsequently, Johnson [19] produced another example of immiserization, in which the country had no ability to influence her terms of trade but there was a tariff (which is necessarily welfare reducing in view of the assumed absence of monopoly power in trade) in both the pregrowth and the postgrowth situations, and growth impoverished the country in certain cases. I later produced yet other examples of immiserizing growth [6], one in which there was a wage differential in the factor market, and another in which the country had monopoly power in trade (as in my original 1958 example), but the country had an optimum tariff (before growth) which became suboptimal after growth.

3. Ranking of Alternative Policies under Market Imperfections: For the four major imperfections described earlier, the optimal policy intervention has been analyzed by several economists. Hagen [16] has argued that the optimal policy for the case of the wage differential would be a factor tax-cum-subsidy. For the production externality, Bhagwati and Ramaswami [2] have shown that the optimal policy intervention is a production tax-cum-subsidy. For the consumption externality case, it follows from the general arguments in Bhagwati and Ramaswami [2] that a consumption tax-cum-subsidy ought to be used. Finally, for the case of monopoly power in trade, it has been known since the time of Mill and has been demonstrated rigorously by (among others) Graaff [14] and Johnson [17] that a tariff is the optimal policy. Recent work of Bhagwati, Ramaswami, and Srinivasan [8] has then extended the analysis, for each market imperfection, to the ranking of *all* alternative policies: the tariff (trade subsidy) policy, the production tax-cum-subsidy policy, the consumption tax-cum-subsidy policy, and the factor tax-cum-subsidy policy.[6]

[4] Instead of a consumption externality, one could assume a situation in which sellers charge a uniform premium on a commodity's import and production price.

[5] The precise sense in which monopoly power in trade represents a market imperfection, in the trade sector, is that foreign prices will not equal the marginal, foreign rate of transformation (as discussed later in the text).

[6] Since the production tax-cum-subsidy policy is equivalent to a tax-cum-subsidy

4. Ranking of Tariffs: Yet another area of research in trade and welfare has raised the question of ranking policies that constitute impediments themselves to the attainment of optimality. Thus, for example, Kemp [22] has analyzed, for a country without monopoly power in trade (and no other imperfections), the question as to whether a higher tariff is worse than a lower tariff. Similarly, Bhagwati and Kemp [10] have analysed the problem for tariffs around the optimal tariff for a country *with* monopoly power in trade.

5. Ranking of Free Trade and Autarky: A number of trade theorists have compared free trade with autarky, when there were market imperfections such as wage differentials (Hagen [16]) and production externality (Haberler [15]), to deduce that free trade was no longer necessarily superior to self-sufficiency. Melvin [26] and Kemp [23] have recently considered the comparison between free trade and autarky when there are commodity taxes.

6. Ranking of Restricted Trade and Autarky: Aside from the case in which trade is tariff restricted (wherein the comparison between restricted trade and autarky becomes the comparison of tariffs discussed in item 4) Bhagwati [4] has considered the ranking of other policies (e.g., production tax-cum-subsidies) that restrict trade and autarky.

7. Noneconomic Objectives and Ranking of Policies: Finally, a number of economists have addressed themselves to the question of optimal policy intervention when the values of different variables are constrained, as noneconomic objectives, so that full optimality is unattainable. Four key types of noneconomic objectives have been analyzed. Corden [12] has shown that a production tax-cum-subsidy is optimal where the constrained variable is production (for reasons such as defense production). Johnson [18] has shown a tariff to be optimal when imports are constrained instead (in the interest of "self-sufficiency"). Bhagwati and Srinivasan [7] have demonstrated that a factor tax-cum-subsidy is optimal when the constrained variable is employment of a factor in an activity (i.e., in the interest of "national character") and a consumption tax-cum-subsidy when the constrained variable is domestic availability of consumption (i.e., to restrict "luxury consumption"). Bhagwati and Srinivasan have also extended the analysis to the ranking of *all* policy instruments for a number of these noneconomic objectives.

This paper is aimed at putting these diverse analyses into a common

given to *all* factors (used in production) of an equivalent and uniform magnitude, the factor tax-cum-subsidy policy referred to in this paper relates to a tax-cum-subsidy policy that applies in a *discriminatory* fashion between or among factors.

analytical framework. This results in the logical unification of a number of interesting and important results, leading in turn to fresh insights while also enabling us to derive remarkable "duality" relationships between the analysis of policy rankings under market imperfections and policy rankings to achieve noneconomic objectives.

4.1. Alternative Types of Distortions

It can be readily shown, in fact, that the diverse results reviewed so far belong to what might aptly be described as the theory of distortions and welfare.

The theory of distortions is built around the central theorem of trade and welfare: that laissez-faire is Pareto optimal for a perfectly competitive system with no monopoly power in trade. [7] Ruling out the phenomenon of diminishing cost of transformation between any pair of commodities (i.e., the concavity of the production possibility set in the familiar, two-commodity system), [8] the Pareto optimality of the laissez-faire policy follows quite simply from the fact that the economic system will operate with technical efficiency (i.e., on the "best" production possibility curve, if we think again of two commodities for simplicity). The economic system will also satisfy further the (first-order) conditions for an economic maximum: DRT = FRT = DRS (where DRT represents the marginal rate of transformation in domestic production, FRT represents marginal foreign rate of transformation, and DRS represents the marginal rate of substitution in consumption). [9]

[7] The classic proof of this proposition is in Samuelson [28]. For later treatments, see Samuelson [29], Kemp [22] and Bhagwati [4] and [5].

[8] The phenomenon of diminishing marginal cost of transformation can arise either because of increasing returns [21, Ch. 8] (which is a purely technological phenomenon) or because of factor market imperfection in the shape of a wage differential [2] [13] [20]. The phenomenon has to be ruled out so as to eliminate certain well-known difficulties that it raises (requiring in particular the distinction between global and local maxima [30] and attention to second-order conditions and possibilities of inefficient specialization [27]).

[9] Equalities have been used in stating the first-order conditions, for each pair of commodities, so as to preserve simplicity; they imply, of course, incomplete specialization in production and consumption. Inequalities can be introduced easily, but nothing essential would be gained by way of additional insights. The simplifying assumption of a two-commodity system will also be used through the rest of the paper; this does not critically affect the analysis, although problems associated with devising optimum policy *structures* (e.g., the optimal tariff structure [14] in the case of monopoly power in in trade) are naturally not raised in consequence.

The theory of distortions is then concerned with the following four pathologies which may characterize, singly or in combination, the economic system:

Distortion 1: FRT ≠ DRT = DRS

Distortion 2: DRT ≠ DRS = FRT

Distortion 3: DRS ≠ DRT = FRT

Distortion 4: Nonoperation on the efficient production possibility curve.

"Endogenous" Distortions

These distortions (implying departures from full optimality) may arise when the economy is characterised by *market imperfections* under a policy of laissez-faire. Thus, the presence of national monopoly power in trade will lead to Distortion 1, because foreign prices will not equal FRT. The case of the Meade type of production externality [10] leads to Distortion 2. Distortion 3 will follow when sellers of the importable commodity, for example, charge a uniform premium on imported as well as home-produced supplies. Distortion 4 follows when there is a factor market imperfection resulting from a wage differential, for a factor, between the different activities. [11] In these cases, therefore, the resulting distortions (arising from the market imperfections) are appropriately described as "endogenous" distortions.

"Policy-Imposed" Distortions

On the other hand, the four varieties of distortions listed earlier may be the result of economic policies, as distinct from endogenous phenomena such as market imperfections. Thus, Distortion 1 will arise for a country with no monopoly power in trade if the country has a tariff; it will also arise for a country with monopoly power in trade if the tariff is less or greater than the optimal tariff. Distortion 2 will follow if the government imposes a production tax-cum-subsidy. Distortion 3 will be the consequence similarly of a consumption tax-cum-subsidy policy. Finally, the adoption of a factor

[10] This externality can be formally stated as follows [21, p. 128]: For linearly homogeneous production functions $x = x(K_x, L_x)$, $y = y(K_y, L_y, x)$ it can be shown that, with y entrepreneurs not having to pay for their "input" of x, the economy will be characterised by Distortion 2.

[11] A constant wage differential will also lead to Distortion 2; in this instance, we have a case of two distortions occurring at the same time. In fact, the wage differential case leads also to the possibility of a concave production possibility set, as we have already noted; furthermore, as Bhagwati and Srinivasan [11] have shown, the response of production to relative commodity price change also becomes unpredictable, a question, however, of no welfare significance in the context of this paper.

tax-cum-subsidy policy will result in Distortion 4.[12] These are instances therefore of "policy-imposed" distortions.

But as soon as we probe the reasons for the existence of such policy-imposed distortions, two alternative interpretations are possible. Either we can consider these policies as *autonomous* (i.e., a tariff, which leads to Distortion 1, may for example be a historic accident), or we may consider these policies as *instrumental* (a tariff, leading to Distortion 1, may be the policy instrument used in order to reduce imports) – as in the case of the theory of noneconomic objectives when Distortion 1 is created through the deployment of a tariff when the objective is to reduce imports in the interest of "self-sufficiency".

We thus have altogether three sets of "causes" for the four varieties of distortions that can be distinguished: *endogenous*; *autonomous, policy-imposed*; and *instrumental, policy-imposed*. The entire literature that I reviewed earlier can then be given its logical coherence and unity around these alternative classes and causes of distortions.

Before formulating the general theory of distortions and generalizing the theorems discussed in the introduction into other areas, it would be useful to underline the precise manner in which these theorems relate to the different varieties of distortions that we have distinguished so far.

1. The theorems on the suboptimality of different market imperfections clearly relate to the theory of endogenous distortions. Within a static welfare context, they demonstrate that these market imperfections result in the different types of Distortions 1–4, thus resulting in the breakdown of the Pareto optimality of laissez-faire in these cases.

2. The theorems on immiserizing growth, on the other hand, relate to the comparative statics of welfare when distortions are present. The theorems developed in this literature involve cases in which growth takes place under given distortions, either endogenous or policy imposed, and the primary improvement in welfare (which would have accrued if fully optimal policies were followed both before and after growth) is outweighed by the accentuation of the loss from the distortion in the postgrowth situation [6].

Thus, in the original Bhagwati example of immiserizing growth, the assumed free trade and hence failure to impose an optimum tariff (to exploit the monopoly power in trade) in both the pregrowth and the postgrowth situations involves welfare-reducing "distortionary" policies in both situa-

[12] A constant rate of factor tax-cum-subsidy will also produce Distortion 2, as in the case of a constant wage differential. However, as we shall see later, a variable factor tax-cum-subsidy policy can be devised which produces *only* Distortion 4.

tions. Immiserization occurs therefore because the gain, which would necessarily accrue from growth if the optimal tariff were imposed in both situations, is smaller than the incremental loss arising from the accentuation (if any) in the postgrowth situation of the welfare loss resulting from the "distortionary" free-trade policy (implying an endogenous Distortion 1 in this instance) in both situations.

Harry Johnson's example of immiserization where the country has no monopoly power in trade but a tariff (which thus constitutes an autonomous policy-imposed Distortion 1) in both the pregrowth and the postgrowth situations, is to be explained in terms of the same logic. In the absence of monopoly power in trade, the tariff is necessarily "distortionary" and, compared with the fully optimal free-trade policy, causes a loss of welfare in each situation. If the growth were to occur with free trade, there would necessarily be an increment in welfare. However, since growth occurs under a tariff, there arises the possibility that the loss from the tariff may be accentuated after growth, and that this incremental loss may outweigh the gain (that would occur under the optimal, free-trade policy), thus resulting in immiserization. Thus, the policy-imposed distortion (i.e., the tariff) generates the possibility of immiserizing growth.

3. The theorems that rank alternative policies under market imperfections are addressed to a different range of questions. They relate to endogenous distortions, of each of the four varieties we have distinguished, and then seek to rank the different, available policy instruments (extending to the full complement: production, consumption, trade, and factor tax-cum-subsidies) in relation to one another and vis-a-vis laissez-faire itself. The problem has been posed in this fashion by Bhagwati, Ramaswami, and Srinivasan [8] in their recent work.

4. The theorems of Kemp [22] and Bhagwati and Kemp [10], which rank tariffs in relation to one another, however, belong to a yet different genre. They relate to policy-imposed distortions, autonomous in the sense defined in this paper, and aim at ranking different levels at which policy may impose the specified distortion (e.g., Distortion 1 in the cases in which tariffs are ranked).

5. The ranking of free trade and autarky under situations involving market imperfections or taxes involves, on the other hand, a comparison of essentially two levels (the zero tariff level and the prohibitive tariff level) at which a policy-imposed distortion (the tariff) is used, in a situation which is itself characterized by another distortion (either endogenous, such as the wage differential in Hagen [16], or policy-imposed, such as a tax on consumption of a commodity).

6. The ranking of a situation with trade restricted by a nontariff policy with a situation of autarky (with therefore an implicit, prohibitive tariff) involves an altogether different type of comparison: of one distortion with another, both autonomous policy-imposed in Bhagwati's analysis [4].
7. The theory of noneconomic objectives [7], on the other hand, relates to the optimal nature of intervention and the ranking of alternative policies, when certain variables are precluded from specified ranges of values in the interest of "noneconomic" objectives. It is therefore, from an analytical point of view, a theory of how optimally (i.e., at minimum cost) to *introduce* distortions in the economic system, when the attainment of the full optimum is precluded by the noneconomic-objective constraints and also of what the relative costs of alternative policies or methods of introducing such distortions, in pursuit of the noneconomic objectives, are. It is thus a theory pertaining to the ranking of instrumental, policy-imposed distortions, with each distortion being defined under a common set of economic and noneconomic constraints.

It is clear, therefore, that these diverse theorems relate to different types of distortions and raise a number of diverse questions relating thereto. But as soon as we grasp this central fact, it is possible to unify and extend the entire body of this literature and thus to develop a general theory of distortions and welfare.

4.2. Distortions and Welfare: General Theory

This generalized theory of distortions and welfare can be developed in terms of seven central propositions.

Proposition 1:
There are four principal types of distortions:

1. FRT ≠ DRT = DRS;
2. DRT ≠ DRS = FRT;
3. DRS ≠ DRT = FRT; and
4. Nonoperation on the efficient production possibility curve.

These, in turn, can be caused by factors that are:

1. Endogenous;
2. Autonomous, policy-imposed; and
3. Instrumental, policy-imposed.

This proposition is merely a recapitulation of the concepts and analysis developed in the preceding section and requires no further comment. Note merely, by way of reemphasis, that in each of the (4 × 3 = 12) distortionary situations, the economic system departs from full Pareto optimality.

Proposition 2:

i. Optimal policy intervention, in the presence of distortions, involves a tax-cum-subsidy policy addressed directly to offsetting the source of the distortions, when the causes are endogenous or autonomous, policy-imposed. Dual to (i) is the theorem that:

ii. When distortions have to be introduced into the economy, because the values of certain variables (e.g., production or employment of a factor in an activity) have to be constrained, the optimal (or least-cost) method of doing this is to choose that policy intervention that creates the distortion affecting directly the constrained variable.

These two propositions, which constitute a remarkable duality of theorems, extend between themselves to all the classes of Distortions 1 to 4 and their three possible causes, endogenous, autonomous policy-imposed, and instrumental policy-imposed. Furthermore, each proposition is readily derived from the theorems on market imperfections and on noneconomic objectives.

Proposition 2(i) was formulated, in essentially similar form, by Bhagwati and Ramaswami [2] and later by Johnson [18], for the case of endogenous distortions. For Distortion 1, resulting from monopoly power in trade under laissez-faire, it is well known that the optimal policy intervention is a tariff. For Distortion 2, Bhagwati and Ramaswami showed that the optimal policy was a production tax-cum-subsidy. For Distortion 3, correspondingly, the optimal policy is a consumption tax-cum-subsidy. Finally, when a wage differential causes Distortion 4, Hagen [16] showed that the optimal intervention was through a factor tax-cum-subsidy. In each instance, therefore, the policy required is one that directly attacks the source of the distortion.

It follows equally, and trivially, that if these distortions are autonomous policy-imposed, the optimal intervention is to eliminate the policy itself: hence, again the optimal policy intervention is addressed to the source of the distortion itself. Thus, with a suboptimal tariff leading to Distortion 1, the optimal policy is to change the tariff to an optimal level (equal to zero, if there is no monopoly power in trade). Similarly, if a consumption tax-cum-subsidy causes Distortion 3, the optimal policy is to offset it with an equivalent consumption tax-cum-subsidy (which leaves zero net consumption tax-cum-subsidy and thus restores full optimality).

But the extension of these results, via the "dual" Proposition 2(ii), to the class of instrumental, policy-imposed distortions, is far from trivial. And the duality is remarkable. Corden [12] has shown that the optimal policy, if the binding noneconomic constraint relates to production, is a *production* tax-cum-subsidy. Johnson [18] has demonstrated that the optimal policy, if the binding noneconomic constraint relates to import (export) level, is a *tariff or trade subsidy*. Bhagwati and Srinivasan [7] have extended the analysis to show that, if the binding noneconomic constraint relates to the level of employment of a factor of production in a sector, the optimal policy is to use a *factor* tax-cum-subsidy that directly taxes (subsidises) the employment of the factor in the sector where its employment level must be lowered (raised) to the constrained level. [13] They have also demonstrated that the optimal policy for raising (lowering) consumption to a constrained level is a *consumption* tax-cum-subsidy policy.

To put it somewhat differently, a trade-level noneconomic objective is achieved at least cost by introducing a policy-imposed Distortion 1 via a trade tariff or subsidy; a production noneconomic objective by introducing a policy-imposed Distortion 2 via a production tax-cum-subsidy; a consumption noneconomic objective by introducing a policy-imposed Distortion 3 via a consumption tax-cum-subsidy; and a factor-employment (in a sector) noneconomic objective by introducing a policy-imposed Distortion 4 via a factor tax-cum-subsidy.

Proposition 3:

i. For each distortion, whether endogenous or autonomous, policy-imposed, in origin, it is possible to analyse the welfare ranking of all alternative policies, from the (first best) optimal to the second best and so on.

ii. a. When distortions have to be introduced into the economy, because the values of certain variables have to be constrained (e.g., production or employment of a factor in an activity), the policy interventions that do this may similarly be welfare ranked. b. The ranking of these policies is further completely symmetrical with that under the "corresponding" class of endogenous or autonomous policy-imposed distortions (e.g., the ranking of policies for production externality, an endogenous Distortion 2, is identical with the ranking of policies when production is constrained as a noneconomic objective).

Since there are four different types of policies (factor, production,

[13] Unlike the case of a *constant* wage differential, which also leads to Distortion 2 in addition to Distortion 4, we can devise [7] a variable tax-cum-subsidy that satisfies the constraint on factor employment while creating *only* Distortion 4.

consumption, and trade tax-cum-subsidies), the propositions listed here are aimed at ranking *all* of them for each of the (twelve) varieties of distortions and establishing "duality" relations of the kind we discovered for optimal policies alone in Proposition 2(ii).

Bhagwati, Ramaswami, and Srinivasan [8] have recently analyzed the welfare ranking of all policies for endogenous distortions and establishing the following rankings: [14]

Distortion 1: FRT ≠ DRT = DRS

This is the case of monopoly power in trade. The ranking of policies then is

i. First best: tariff;
ii. Second best: either production tax-cum-subsidy or factor tax-cum-subsidy (all policies are superior to laissez-faire but cannot be ranked uniquely vis-à-vis one another). [15]

Distortion 2: DRT ≠ DRS = FRT

This is the case of a pure production externality. The ranking of policies then is

i. First best: production tax-cum-subsidy;
ii. Second best: either tariff (trade subsidy) or factor tax-cum-subsidy

[14] Their argument is summarised as follows: They use the notation [8]: C_i, X_i denote the consumption and domestic output respectively of commodity *i*, where $i = 1, 2$. Also, P_c denotes the ratio of the price of the first to that of the second commodity confronting consumers (DRS); P_t denotes DRT $= dX_2/dX_1$; and P_f denotes the ratio of the world price of the first commodity to that of the second commodity, i.e., the *average* terms of trade. The marginal terms of trade FRT $= pf$ only in the special case in which national monopoly power does not exist.

The welfare function $U(C_1, C_2)$ and the production functions are assumed to be differentiable as required. The U_i denotes the marginal utility of commodity $i (i = 1,2)$. It is assumed throughout the analysis that under laissez-faire there is nonspecialisation in consumption and production, and that some trade takes place. Then, the following expression, for the change in welfare when there is an infinitesimal movement away from laissez-faire equilibrium, is derived:

$$dU = U_2[dX_1(p_f - p_t) + (X_1 - C_1)dp_f + (p_c - p_f)dC_1$$

If one uses this expression, the different distortions are easily analyzed for alternate policy rankings. Thus, in the case in which DRT ≠ FRT = DRS, which is Distortion 2 in the text just following, the expression reduces to $dU = U_2[dX_1(P_f - P_t)]$ because $P_c = P_f$, $dp_f = 0$ and $p_f \neq p_t$. It follows that either a tariff (trade subsidy) or a factor tax-cum-subsidy that increases (reduces) X_1, if $p_f > p_t$ ($p_f < p_t$), will increase welfare.

[15] For finite tax-cum-subsidies, however, the production tax-cum-subsidy will be superior to the factor tax-cum-subsidy.

(both policies are superior to laissez-faire but cannot be ranked uniquely vis-à-vis each other);

iii. Consumption tax-cum-subsidy will not help.[16]

Distortion 3: DRS ≠ DRT = FRT

This is the case in which, for example, the sellers of a commodity charge a uniform premium to buyers over the cost of supplies, whether imported or domestically produced. The ranking of policies then is

i. First best: consumption tax-cum-subdidy;

ii. Second best: tariff;

iii. Production or factor tax-cum-subsidy will not help.[17]

Distortion 4: Nonoperation on the efficient production possibility curve

This is the case in which there is a wage differential, a factor market imperfection. In this case, the ranking of policies is

i. First best: factor tax-cum-subsidy;

ii. Second best: production tax-cum-subsidy;

iii. Third best: tariff (trade subsidy);

iv. Consumption tax-cum-subsidy will not help.[18]

It is clear that the extension of these rankings to the corresponding cases where the distortions are autonomous policy-imposed (e.g., Distortion 2 resulting from the autonomous levy of a governmental tax, or Distortion 4 resulting from the grant of a governmental subsidy on employment of a factor in one activity) is total and trivial. It is interesting and remarkable, however, that these rankings carry over also to the class of instrumental, policy-imposed distortions.

Thus, for the case of noneconomic objectives, Bhagwati and Srinivasan [7] have provided the basis for analyzing the rankings of different policies, which I now proceed to develop fully:

Trade-level as a Constraint: The ranking of policies in this case is

i. First best: tariff;

[16] This conclusion holds for infinitesimal tax-cum-subsidy. A finite consumption tax-cum-subsidy will actually be worse than laissez-faire in this instance, as it will impose a "consumption loss" on the economy, over and above the loss it is already suffering from the endogenous Distortion 2.

[17] This conclusion again holds only for infinitesimal tax-cum-subsidies on production or factor use. For finite tax-cum-susidies, these policies will necessarily be worse than laissez-faire (unless inferior goods are present).

[18] Again, this conclusion concerning the consumption tax-cum-subsidy must be read in the same sense as in footnote 16.

ii. Second best: either production tax-cum-subsidy or factor tax-cum-subsidy or consumption tax-cum-subsidy (these policies cannot be ranked vis-à-vis one another).[19]

Note the complete symmetry with the rankings under Distortion 1 earlier.

Production level as a Constraint: The ranking of policies in this case is

i. First best: production tax-cum-subsidy;
ii. Second best: either tariff (trade subsidy) or factor tax-cum-subsidy (these policies cannot be ranked vis-à-vis each other);
iii. Consumption tax-cum-subsidy will not help.[20]

Note again the complete symmetry with the rankings under Distortion 2.

Consumption level as a Constraint: The ranking of policies in this case is

i. First best: consumption tax-cum-subsidy;
ii. Second best: tariff;
iii. Production or factor tax-cum-subsidy will not help.[21]

Again, the symmetry with the ranking under Distortion 3 is total.

Factor Employment (in a Sector) as a Constraint: The ranking of policies in this case is

i. First best: factor tax-cum-subsidy;
ii. Second best: production tax-cum-subsidy;
iii. Third best: tariff (trade subsidy);
iv. Consumption tax-cum-subsidy will not help.[22]

In this final case as well, the symmetry with the corresponding Distortion 4 is complete.

Thus, the duality of the policy rankings, for endogenous and autonomous policy-imposed distortions on the one hand and instrumental policy-imposed distortions on the other hand, is altogether complete and remarkable.

Proposition 4:

For each kind of distortion, growth may be immiserizing.

For endogenous and autonomous policy-imposed distortions, belonging to

[19] For finite tax-cum-subsidies, however, the factor tax-cum-subsidy policy will be inferior to the production tax-cum-subsidy policy, as Bhagwati and Srinivasan [7] have demonstrated.

[20] This statement must again be read in the same sense as in footnote 16 and footnote 18 earlier.

[21] This statement must be construed in the same sense as in footnote 17.

[22] This statement must be interpreted again in the same sense as in footnotes 16, 18, and 20 earlier.

each of the varieties 1 to 4 that we have distinguished, this proposition has already been demonstrated by Bhagwati [6].

Thus, for example, where Distortion 1 obtains endogenously under laissez-faire because of monopoly power in trade, Bhagwati's 1958 analysis [1] demonstrates the possibility of immiserization. Where Distortions 2 and 4 obtain simultaneously as a result of an endogenous wage differential, the same possibility has again been demonstrated by Bhagwati [6]. Johnson's demonstration [19] of immiserization, when a country has no monopoly power in trade but a tariff, illustrates Proposition 2 for the case of an autonomous policy-imposed Distortion 1.

Note again that the underlying reason for immiserizing growth is that the growth takes place in the presence of a distortion. This distortion produces a loss of welfare from the fully optimal welfare level. Thus, if there is an accentuation in this loss of welfare, when growth has occurred and the distortion has continued, this incremental loss could outweigh the gain that would have accrued if fully optimal policies had been followed in the pregrowth and postgrowth situations [6]. It also follows that such immiserizing growth would be impossible if fully optimal policies were followed in each situation, i.e., if the distortions resulting from the endogenous and policy-imposed causes were offset by optimal policy intervention, as discussed under Proposition 2(i) earlier. [23]

But so far we have discussed only distortions resulting from endogenous and policy-imposed, autonomous factors. However, Proposition 4 applies equally, and can be generalized, to *instrumental* policy-imposed distortions as well.

In complete symmetry with the endogenous and autonomous policy-imposed distortions, the phenomenon of immiserizing growth will be precluded when the constrained variable (e.g., production in the case of a production objective) is attained (in the pregrowth and the postgrowth situations) by optimal policy. On the other hand, immiserization becomes possible as soon as any of the second-best (or third best) policies is adopted to constrain the variable (to a preassigned value in both the pregrowth and postgrowth situations).

This generalization of the theory of immiserizing growth is readily illustrated with reference to production as the constrained variable. Remember that a production tax-cum-subsidy is the optimal policy in this case and a

[23] For phenomena of immiserizing growth arising from reasons other than distortions, see Melvin [25] and Bhagwati [9].

tariff a second best policy. Figure 4.1a then illustrates how it is impossible, after growth, to become "worse off" if the production level of a commodity is constrained to the required level by a suitable production tax-cum-subsidy policy. The y production is constrained to level $\bar{y}$; the production possibility curve shifts out from AB to $A'B'$. With a suitable production tax-cum-subsidy used in both the pregrowth and the postgrowth situations, to constrain y production to $\bar{y}$, it is clear that it is impossible to worsen welfare after growth. Figure 4.1b illustrates, however, the possibility of immiserizing growth when the suboptimal tariff policy is followed instead in each case to constrain y output to level $\bar{y}$. Note that this demonstration, where the welfare level reduces after growth to U' from U, does not require the assumption of inferior goods.

Similar illustrations could be provided for the other three cases, where consumption, factor employment in a sector, and trade-level are constrained. In each case, only the pursuit of a suboptimal policy to achieve the specified noneconomic objective could lead to immiserization.

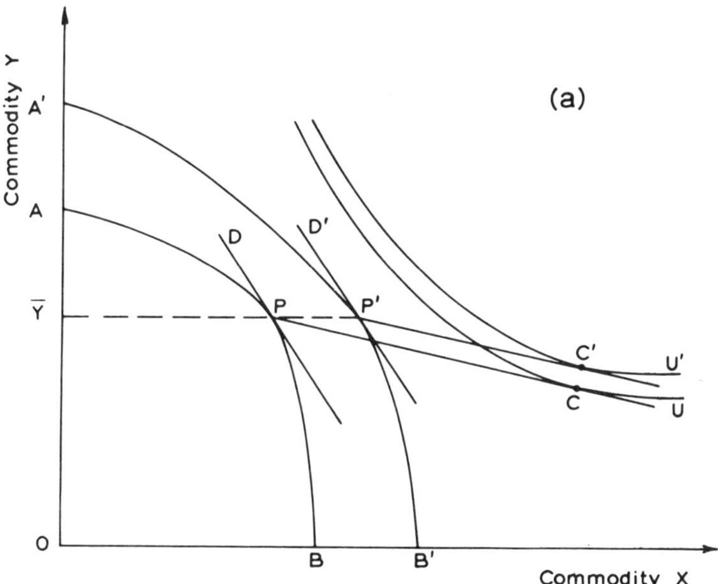

Figure 4.1a. AB is the pregrowth production possibility curve; $A'B'$ the postgrowth production possibility curve. The international price ratio is given at $PC = P'C'$. Production of y is constrained to level $\bar{y}$. A suitable production tax-cum-subsidy takes production, before growth, to P at domestic, producer price ratio DP. After growth, a suitable production tax-cum-subsidy takes producer price ratio to $D'P'$ and production to P'. Welfare level has increased, after growth, to U' ($> U$).

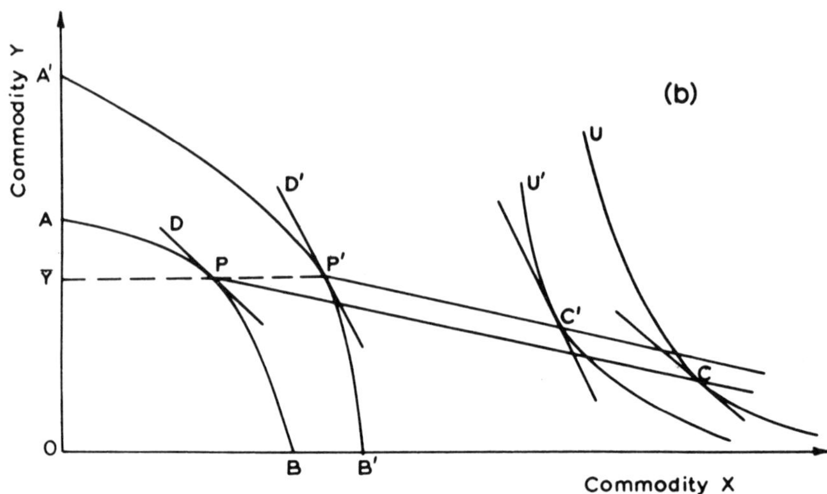

Figure 4.1b. The production possibility curve shifts, after growth, from AB to $A'B'$. In each case, the production of y is constrained to $\bar{y}$ by a tariff. In the pregrowth case, this tariff leads to production at P (with domestic price ratio DP), consumption at C and welfare at U. After growth, production is at P', consumption at C', and welfare has reduced to U' ($< U$), implying immiserizing growth.

Proposition 5:

Reductions in the "degree" of (an only) distortion are successively welfare increasing until the distortion is fully eliminated.

This theorem holds whether we take endogenous or policy-imposed distortions. However, it needs to be qualified, so as to exclude inferior goods for all cases except where a *consumption* tax-cum-subsidy is relevant.

For autonomous, policy-imposed Distortion 1, the Kemp [22] and Bhagwati–Kemp [10] theorems are special cases of Proposition 5: Each further requires the exclusion of inferior goods and attendant multiple equilibria if the possibility of the competitive system "choosing" an inferior-welfare equilibrium under the lower degree of distortion is to be ruled out. [24] In point of fact, identical propositions could be derived for alternative forms of autonomous policy-imposed distortions, factor tax-cum-subsidy, production tax-cum-subsidy, and consumption tax-cum-subsidy. [25]

[24] On this, see Bhagwati [4], Kemp [23], and Bhagwati–Kemp [10].

[25] For the consumption tax-cum-subsidy, the complication arising from inferior goods is not relevant.

Similarly, we can argue that reduction in the degree of each market imperfection will cause a reduction in the degree of its consequent distortion and thus raise welfare. Thus, for example, a reduction in the degree of production externality will reduce the degree of Distortion 2 and increase the level of welfare. [26]

Finally, identical conclusions apply if we reduce the degree of "required" distortion, of the instrumental policy-imposed type, by relaxing the binding constraint on the "noneconomic"-objective variable. Thus, marginally relaxing the constraint on production will suffice to improve welfare. As is clear from Figure 4.2a, the relaxation of the constraint on y production, from $\bar{y}$ to $\bar{y}_n$, will necessarily improve welfare by shifting the "availability line" outwards – if, in each case, the policy adopted is a production tax-cum-subsidy policy.

If, however, as Figure 4.2b illustrates, a (suboptimal) tariff policy is

[26] Note again the *caveat* regarding inferior goods. This will not apply, however, where the consumption distortion is reduced.

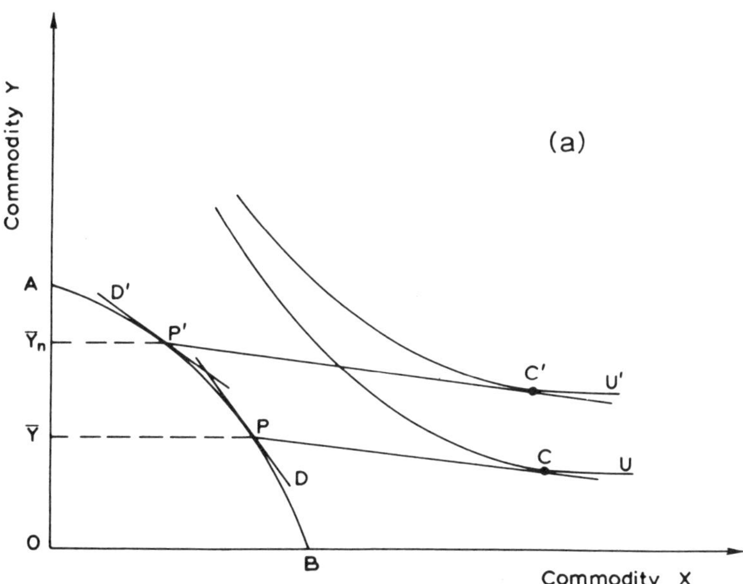

Figure 4.2a. With AB as the production possibility curve, $\bar{y}$ and $\bar{y}_n$ are the successive noneconomic constraints on y production, which are met by use of a suitable production subsidy policy in each case. For $\bar{y}$, production then is at P, consumption at C and welfare level at U. For $\bar{y}_n$, a relaxation in the constraint, production shifts to P' (with producer price ratio at $D'P'$ now), consumption to C', and welfare has increased to U' ($> U$).

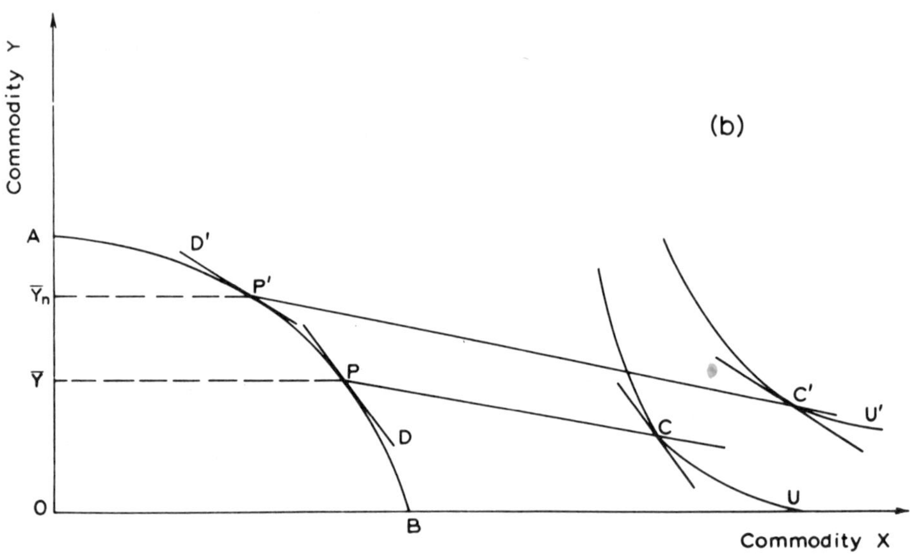

Figure 4.2b. With production of y-commodity constrained successively at $\bar{y}$ and $\bar{y}_n$, a tariff used for that purpose, and production possibility curve AB, the production for $\bar{y}$ constraint is at P, consumption at C and welfare at U. Relaxation in the constraint to $\bar{y}_n$ leads to production at P' and consumption at C' (at price $D'P'$) and welfare increases to U' ($> U$).

followed instead, to constrain y-production to the required level, the result of a relaxation in the constraint is identical; the only qualification is relating to that arising from inferior goods. Further, an identical conclusion holds, as in the case of a production tax-cum-subsidy, for the case of a factor tax-cum-subsidy instead.

Thus, Proposition 5 applies in the case of instrumental policy-imposed distortions, no matter *which* policy is considered (in other words, no matter which distortion is introduced in pursuit of the specific noneconomic objective).

Proposition 6:

Reductions in the "degree" of a distortion will not necessarily be welfare increasing if there is another distortion in the system.

This proposition is readily established for endogenous or autonomous policy-imposed distortions.

Let us first consider a case in which reductions in one distortion *do* lead to improvement in welfare despite the presence of another distortion in the system. Thus, consider the case in which a production externality, an endogenous Distortion 2 where DRT ≠ DRS = FRT, is combined with a consumption tax-cum-subsidy, an autonomous policy-imposed Distortion 3 where DRS ≠ FRT = DRT, but there is no monopoly power in trade. Assume further that the two distortions combine so as to yield altogether the initial situation where DRT ≠ DRS ≠ FRT (so that they are not mutually offsetting as far as one inequality is concerned). In this case, successive reductions in the consumption tax-cum-subsidy will necessarily be welfare increasing, given the production externality; and successive reductions in the production externality will improve welfare (except for the complication introduced by inferior goods).[27]

Next, however, consider the case where there is a production externality (endogenous, DRT ≠ DRS = FRT) combined with a tariff without monopoly power in trade (autonomous policy-imposed FRT ≠ DRS = DRT) and assume that the resulting initial situation is characterized by FRT ≠ DRT ≠ DRS. In this case, successive reductions in the tariff will not necessarily improve welfare steadily, if at all, and the gains may turn into losses.[28] The theorems on the possible inferiority of free trade (i.e., zero tariff) to no trade (i.e., prohibitive tariff) when there is a production externality [15] or a wage differential [2] [16] are only special cases of this general theorem that illustrates Proposition 6.

It is interesting to note further that this theorem can with equal insight be analyzed in terms of Proposition 4 if we recognize that, if optimal policies are followed in *both* the autarkic and the trading "situations", the trade situation must necessarily enable the economy to be "better off" – as is obvious to trade theorists familiar with the Baldwin-envelope technique. If then there is a distortion common to both situations, as with an endogenous wage differential or production externality or with an autonomous policy-imposed production tax-cum-subsidy, the transition to the (free) trading situation may well be immiserizing (i.e., therefore, free trade inferior to autarky) if the loss from this distortion is accentuated and outweighs the primary gain from the shift to (free) trade itself.

[27] These conclusions can also be derived by reference to the Bhagwati-Ramaswami-Srinivasan [8] formula, in footnote 14, which reduces for this case to $dU = U_2[dX_1(p_f - p_t) + (p_c - p_f)dC_1]$.

[28] This is seen again by examining the Bhagwati-Ramaswami-Srinivasan formula which reduces, in this instance, to $dU = U_2[dX_1(p_f - p_t) + (p_c - p_f)dC_1]$. It is clear then that a reduction in the tariff, by affecting both X_1 and C_1 may worsen rather than improve welfare; and that the welfare effect of successive tariff changes need not be unidirectional.

Proposition 7:

Distortions cannot be ranked (uniquely) vis-à-vis one another.

This is a readily apparent proposition and applies clearly to all the classes of distortions we have discussed.

Bhagwati's demonstration [4] that Kemp's theorem [22] of the superiority of tariff-restricted trade over no trade will not extend to cases where the trade is restricted instead by policies such as consumption and production tax-cum-subsidies becomes intuitively obvious as soon as it is seen that it falls into the class of theorems belonging to Proposition 7. For, in this instance, two distortions are being compared: (i) a consumption tax-cum-subsidy leading to Distortion 3, DRS ≠ DRT = FRT, with a situation of autarky and hence implicit prohibitive tariff, thus involving Distortion 1, FRT ≠ DRT = DRS; and (ii) a production tax-cum-subsidy leading to Distortion 2, DRT = DRS = FRT, with autarky involving Distortion 1, FRT ≠ DRT = DRS. In principle, of course, the demonstration of impossibility of unique ranking between autarky and restricted trade could be carried equally into the case where trade-restriction occurs via use of a factor tax-cum-subsidy involving Distortion 4 along with 2.

4.3. Concluding Remarks

We have thus succeeded in unifying a considerable body of literature on the welfare economics of trade into a series of major propositions that constitute a generalized theory of distortions and welfare. Aside from the intrinsic elegance of such unification, this has resulted in a number of insights into, and extensions of, the theorems to date in this significant area of economic policy.

References

[1] Bhagwati, J. "Immiserizing Growth: A Geometrical Note." *Review of Economic Studies*, 25 (June 1958).

[2] Bhagwati, J., and Ramaswami, V.K. "Domestic Distortions, Tariffs and the Theory of Optimum Subsidy." *Journal of Political Economy*, 71 (February 1963).

[3] Bhagwati, J. "Non-Economic Objectives and the Efficiency Properties of Trade." *Journal of Political Economy*, 76 (October 1968).

[4] Bhagwati, J. "Gains from Trade Once Again." *Oxford Economic Papers*, 20 (July 1968).

[5] Bhagwati, J. *The Theory and Practice of Commercial Policy*. Frank Graham

Memorial Lecture (1967), Special Papers in International Economics No. 8, Princeton University, 1968.

[6] Bhagwati, J. "Distortions and Immiserizing Growth: A Generalization," *Review of Economic Studies*, 35 (November 1968).

[7] Bhagwati, J. and Srinivasan, T.N. "Optimal Intervention to Achieve Non-Economic Objectives." *Review of Economic Studies,* 36 (January 1969).

[8] Bhagwati, J., Ramaswami, V.K. and Srinivasan, T.N. "Domestic Distortions, Tariffs and the Theory of Optimum Subsidy: Some Further Results." *Journal of Political Economy*, 77 (November/December 1969).

[9] Bhagwati, J., "Optimal Policies and Immiserizing Growth." *American Economic Review*, 59 (December 1969).

[10] Bhagwati, J. and Kemp, M.C. "Ranking of Tariffs under Monopoly Power in Trade." *Quarterly Journal of Economics*, 83 (May 1969).

[11] Bhagwati, J. and Srinivasan, T.N. "The Theory of Wage Differentials: Production Response and Factor Price Equalisation", *Journal of International Economics*, 1 (February 1971).

[12] Corden, W.M. "Tariffs, Subsidies and the Terms of Trade." *Economica*, 24 (August 1957).

[13] Fishlow, A. and David, P. "Optimal Resource Allocation in an Imperfect Market Setting." *Journal of Political Economy*, 69 (December 1961).

[14] Graaff, J. "On Optimum Tariff Structures." *Review of Economic Studies*, 17 (1949–1950).

[15] Haberler, G. "Some Problems in the Pure Theory of International Trade," *Economic Journal,* 30 (June 1950).

[16] Hagen, E. "An Economic Justification of Protectionism," *Quarterly Journal of Economics*, 72 (November 1958).

[17] Johnson, H.G. *International Trade and Economic Growth*, London: George Allen and Unwin Ltd, 1958.

[18] Johnson, H.G. "Optimal Trade Intervention in the Presence of Domestic Distortions." in R.E. Caves, H.G. Johnson and P.B. Kenen (eds.), *Trade, Growth and the Balance of Payments*, Amsterdam: North-Holland Publishing Company, 1965.

[19] Johnson, H.G. "The Possibility of Income Losses from Increased Efficiency or Factor Accumulation in the Presence of Tariffs." *Economic Journal*, 77 (March 1967).

[20] Johnson, H.G. "Factor Market Distortions and the Shape of the Transformation Curve." *Econometrica*, 34 (July 1966).

[21] Kemp, M.C. *The Pure Theory of International Trade.* Englewood Cliffs, N. J.: Prentice-Hall, 1964.

[22] Kemp, M.C. "The Gain from International Trade." *Economic Journal*, 72 (December 1962).

[23] Kemp, M.C. "Some Issues in the Analysis of Trade Gains." *Oxford Economic Papers*, 20 (July 1968).

[24] Kemp, M.C. and Negishi, T. "Domestic Distortions, Tariffs and the Theory of Optimum Subsidy," *Journal of Political Economy*, 77 (November/December 1969).

[25] Melvin, J. "Demand Conditions and Immiserizing Growth." *American Economic Review*, 59 (September 1969).

[26] Melvin, J. "Commodity Taxation as a Determinant of Trade." University of Western Ontario, *mimeographed*, 1968.
[27] Matthews R.C.O. "Reciprocal Demand and Increasing Returns." *Review of Economic Studies*, 17 (1949–1950).
[28] Samuelson, P.A. "The Gains from International Trade." *Canadian Journal of Economics and Political Science*, 5 (May 1939).
[29] Samuelson, P.A. "The Gains from International Trade Once Again." *Economic Journal*, 72 (December 1962).
[30] Tinbergen, J. *International Economic Cooperation*, Amsterdam: North-Holland Publishing Company, 1946.

Erratum

Page 83, line 5: "*AP*" should read "*AB*".

II
GROWTH AND WELFARE

INTERNATIONAL TRADE AND ECONOMIC EXPANSION

By JAGDISH BHAGWATI*

The recent literature on the effects of economic expansion on international trade has been concerned with two principal problems: the impact of the expansion on the terms of trade; and the resultant change in the welfare of the trading nations. The solutions offered, however, are not fully satisfactory. Thus H. G. Johnson [5] and W. M. Corden [3], who attempt to tackle the first problem, succeed only in establishing the *direction*, as distinct from the *extent*, of the consequential shift in the terms of trade. In so far as the full impact of the expansion on the terms of trade must be known prior to determining the change in the welfare of the countries involved, it is not surprising that the second problem has received scant attention.[1]

It is intended in this paper to resolve principally the problem of bringing the different factors that affect the terms of trade into a single formula to determine the extent of the shift in the terms of trade consequent upon economic expansion. The analysis is further rendered geometrically by translating the usual textbook back-to-back partial diagram, depicting international trade equilibrium in a single commodity, into a general equilibrium framework. The argument is then extended, in a brief section, to the welfare effects of the expansion. To the gain from growth must be added the gain or loss from the resultant shift, if any, in the terms of trade; conditions are derived to determine whether the growing country will experience a net gain or loss from the expansion. The final section of the paper is concerned with the concept of the "output elasticity of supply" (to be used in the paper) and the analytical methods that can be employed to investigate the output elasticity of supply of different activities under specified varieties of expansion.

I. *Formula to Determine Change in the Terms of Trade*

The model used here is the familiar two-country (I and II), two-commodity (X and Y), "real" model with continuous full employment of all factors. Transport costs and intercountry factor movements are ab-

* The author holds a studentship at Nuffield College, Oxford. This paper was read at Roy Harrod and Donald MacDougall's seminar on international economics at Oxford.

[1] It should be mentioned, however, that Johnson [5] has an excellent analysis of this problem in the context of a model of complete specialization, although the concern of the article is principally to evolve a criterion to determine the impact of expansion on the terms of trade.

sent. To simplify the analysis, economic expansion, defined as the country's capacity to produce extra output at constant relative commodity prices, is confined to country I. We wish to determine the consequent impact on I's commodity terms of trade. The analysis is conducted in terms of I's importable good (Y); it is one of the advantages of our two-good model that the analysis can be couched entirely in terms of one good and yet will hold generally.

The total impact on the terms of trade of country I as a result of the expansion is compounded of six effects:

1. *Change in the Output of Y due to Economic Expansion.* The change in the output of importables (Y) in country I, at constant relative commodity prices, as a result of the economic expansion, is given by:

$$\frac{\delta Y}{\delta K}\cdot dK = Y\cdot E_{SY}\cdot \overline{K} \tag{1}$$

where Y is the domestic production of importables in I prior to the expansion; K is I's productive capacity which is assumed to be kept fully employed and is measured by the value, in terms of exportables (X), of the output the country would produce at the initial terms of trade;

$$\overline{K}=\frac{dK}{K}; \text{and } E_{SY}=\frac{K}{Y}\cdot\frac{\delta Y}{\delta K}$$

is the output elasticity of supply of importables at constant relative commodity prices. This represents, therefore, the change in the domestic production of importables directly as a result of expansion, at constant terms of trade. If (1) is positive, the supply of Y is increased; if it is negative, the supply of Y is reduced.[2]

2. *Change in the Demand for Y due to Economic Expansion.* We must now consider the change in the demand for importables, at constant relative commodity prices, as a direct result of the expansion. This is given by:

$$\frac{\delta C}{\delta K}\cdot dK = C\cdot E_{DY}\cdot \overline{K} \tag{2}$$

where C is the pre-expansion consumption of importables (Y) in I and

$$E_{DY}=\frac{K}{C}\cdot\frac{\delta C}{\delta K}$$

is the output elasticity of demand for importables at constant relative

[2] Formula (1) may be negative under certain circumstances. This possibility is outlined again in Section III and is actually demonstrated, in the context of our highly simplified model, in Section IV. Also see Bhagwati [1].

commodity prices.[3] If (2) is positive, there is an increase in the demand for Y; if it is negative, the demand for Y is decreased.

It follows that the net change in the demand for imports, at constant terms of trade, will be given by [(1)−(2)]. If this expression is positive, there is a net decrease in I's demand for imports at the pre-expansion terms of trade and hence the terms of trade will tend to improve for I (unless II's offer curve is infinitely elastic); if the expression is negative, there is a net increase in I's demand for imports and the terms of trade will tend to deteriorate for I.[4] In order to determine the extent of the shift in the terms of trade which will be necessary to restore equilibrium, however, we must introduce the following four factors, three domestic and one foreign. Each of them measures one aspect of the changes in the supply of and demand for importables induced by a shift in the terms of trade.

3. *Change in the Demand for Y due to Price Shift.* The change in the demand for Y due to the shift in the terms of trade may be measured by the following expression:

$$\frac{\delta C}{\delta p}\cdot dp = -\frac{C}{p}\cdot\epsilon\cdot dp \tag{3}$$

where p is the terms of trade, measured as the number of units of exportables required to buy a unit of importables; and

$$\epsilon = -\frac{p}{C}\cdot\frac{\delta C}{\delta p}$$

is the income-compensated or constant-utility demand-elasticity for importables (Y), representing movement *along* the indifference curve in response to the price-shift. If (3) is positive, there is an increase in the demand for Y; if it is negative, there is a reduction in the demand for Y. The demand for Y will be negatively correlated with changes in the price of Y relative to the price of X.[5]

4. *Change in the Supply of Y due to Price Shift.* The change in the domestic supply of Y due to the shift in the terms of trade is:

$$\frac{\delta Y}{\delta p}\cdot dp = \frac{Y}{p}\cdot\sigma\cdot dp \tag{4}$$

where

$$\sigma = \frac{p}{Y}\cdot\frac{\delta Y}{\delta p}$$

[3] Output elasticity of demand is used in preference to income elasticity to describe the behavior of aggregate consumption as aggregate income rises, to include the effects of population changes, growth of per capita incomes, and resultant changes in income distribution.

[4] This is, in effect, Johnson's [5] central argument.

[5] This is so because we normally assume, for well-known reasons, that the substitution effect, with which (3) is concerned, is negative.

is the supply-elasticity of importables based on movement along the transformation curve in response to the price-shift. When (4) is positive, the supply of Y is increased; when it is negative, it is decreased. The supply of Y will normally be positively correlated with changes in the price of Y relative to the price of X.[6]

5. *Change in the Demand for Y due to Change in Real Income resulting from Shift in the Terms of Trade.* A change in the terms of trade leads to a consequent change in real income. This income change is approximated here by the usual method employed widely in the theory of international trade and based on the theory of value, namely, by the difference in the cost of the initial quantity of imports. The resultant change in the demand for Y is:

$$-\frac{\delta C}{\delta K}\cdot M\cdot dp = -\frac{C}{K}\cdot M\cdot E_{DY}'\cdot dp \tag{5}$$

where $M \equiv C - Y$ is the quantity of initial imports; and

$$E_{DY}' = \frac{K}{C}\cdot\frac{\delta C}{\delta K}$$

is the elasticity of demand for Y with respect to a change in income resulting from changed terms of trade. If (5) is positive, there is an increase in the demand for Y; if it is negative, there is a reduction in the demand for Y.

6. *Change in the Supply of Y by Country II due to Price Change.* As a result of the shift in the terms of trade, the supply of Y by II to I changes. This is given by:

$$\frac{\delta S_m}{\delta p}\cdot dp = \frac{M}{p}\cdot r_m\cdot dp \tag{6}$$

where $S_m \equiv M$ and

$$r_m = \frac{p}{M}\cdot\frac{\delta S_m}{\delta p}$$

is the *total* elasticity of II's supply of its exports (commodity Y) to I, in response to a shift in the terms of trade. II's supply of Y to I increases or decreases according as (6) is positive or negative.[7]

The total impact on the terms of trade is then derived from the simple proposition that, in equilibrium, the excess demand for Y should be zero. Thus we can collect all the effects into two groups: those on the

[6] This holds again because we normally assume that the transformation curve is a convex set.

[7] The elasticity r_m will be negative, for instance, when the exports of I are Giffen goods in II; though this is by no means a necessary condition for r_m to be negative.

supply side, [(1)+(4)+(6)]; and those on the demand side,[(2)+(3) +(5)]. We subtract the latter from the former and set the expression equal to zero. Solving for dp, we get the magnitude of the shift in the terms of trade consequent upon economic expansion:

$$(7)\qquad dp = \frac{(C\cdot E_{DY} - Y\cdot E_{SY})\cdot \overline{K}}{\left[\dfrac{Y}{p}\cdot\sigma + \dfrac{M}{p}\cdot r_m + \dfrac{C}{p}\cdot\epsilon + \dfrac{C}{K}\cdot M\cdot E_{DY}'\right]},$$

which may be rewirtten as:

$$(8)\qquad dp = \frac{p\cdot dM}{M\left[\dfrac{Y}{M}\cdot\sigma + r_m + \dfrac{C}{M}\cdot\epsilon + p\cdot\dfrac{C}{K}\cdot E_{DY}'\right]},$$

provided it is remembered that dM refers to the income effect of expansion on imports at constant terms of trade.

We have thus succeeded in bringing together into a single formula, and thereby establishing the relative significance of, the different factors (elasticities) which simultaneously determine the impact of expansion on the international commodity terms of trade. The analysis can be readily extended to the case of simultaneous growth in *both* countries. This can be done by replacing

$$\left[\frac{M}{p}\cdot r_m\cdot dp\right]$$

by an elaborate expression derived by extending to country II an analysis exactly analogous to that we have applied to country I.[8]

Some interesting results follow from our analysis. Thus in order for the terms of trade to turn adverse to the growing country it is not sufficient that the income effects of the expansion should be unfavorable and should create an increased demand for imports (that is, $C.E_{DY} > Y.E_{SY}$). It is also necessary that the expression

$$\left[\frac{Y}{M}\cdot\sigma + r_m + \frac{C}{M}\cdot\epsilon + p\cdot\frac{C}{K}\cdot E_{DY}'\right],$$

which constitutes the denominator in (8), should be positive. Since both σ and ϵ are normally positive, and since E_{DY}' is also positive (unless either the commodity Y is an inferior good in the strict Hicksian sense or the expansion is accompanied by a redistribution of income biased strongly against the consumption of Y), it follows that r_m will have to be not merely negative but also sufficiently large in magnitude

[8] Nothing substantive is gained by carrying out this exercise.

in order that the entire expression should be negative. The converse is also true: where the income effects are favorable and lead to a reduction in the demand for imports, the terms of trade may still worsen for the growing country I if the total elasticity of II's supply of its exports (Y) to I is sufficiently large and negative to make the denominator in (8) negative. These conclusions are, no doubt, intuitively plausible, which is perhaps an advantage; what is chiefly claimed is that the precise relation in which the different operative factors stand vis-à-vis one another, which has been attempted here, lends a needed element of rigorousness to these qualitative results. Besides, it enables us to investigate more satisfactorily the related problem of the impact of economic expansion on the welfare of the growing country (Section III).

II. *Geometrical Analysis*

Using the familiar partial equilibrium back-to-back diagram determining the flow of exports of a single commodity from one country to another, we propose now to: (1) show how this partial diagram can be transformed into a general equilibrium diagram; and (2) relate the diagram to, and thereby illustrate, the argument algebraically presented in Section I.

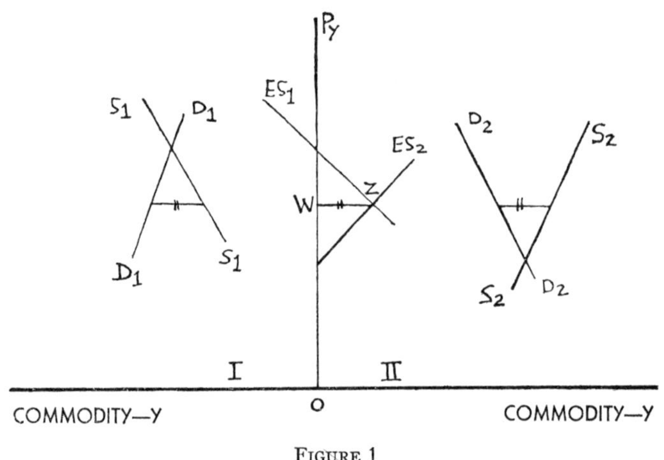

FIGURE 1

Figure 1 shows the usual partial equilibrium diagram for depicting international trade equilibrium in a two-country model. Transport costs are assumed to be zero. D_1D_1, S_1S_1 and D_2D_2, S_2S_2 are the domestic demand and supply curves of countries I and II respectively. ES_1 and ES_2 are the excess-supply functions, as Samuelson [11] calls them, of I and II respectively. Equilibrium is at Z where the exports of Y from II match the imports of Y into I; the equilibrium price of Y is OW.

Now this diagram can be readily converted into a general equilibrium diagram in the following fashion. Relabel the vertical axis $p = p_y/p_x$, the terms of trade, instead of p_y, the price of Y. Further, instead of regarding D_1D_1, D_2D_2, S_1S_1 and S_2S_2 as partial curves,[9] treat them as general equilibrium or total curves. Thus S_1S_1 and S_2S_2 now represent schedules of varying supply of Y as the change in the terms of trade shifts production along the transformation curve. The reinterpretation of D_1D_1 and D_2D_2 is slightly more involved as the schedules are now compounded of two effects: (1) the shift in the demand for Y caused by the real-income change resulting from the change in the terms of trade; and (2) the change in the demand for Y as the change in the terms of trade shifts consumption along the indifference curve (i.e., the substitution effect).

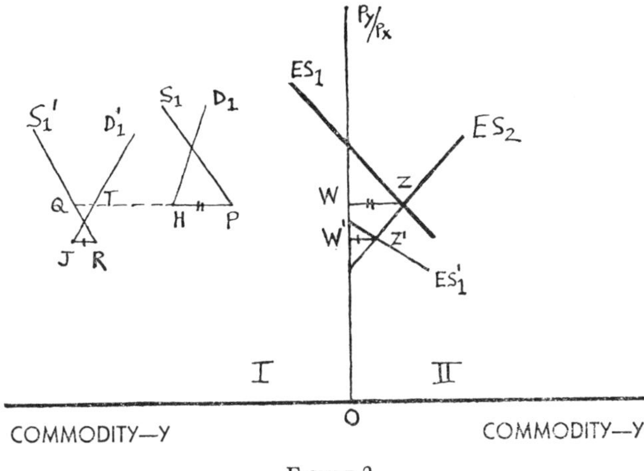

FIGURE 2

The reader may still doubt whether the transformation of the partial into a general equilibrium diagram has been accomplished. Equilibrium in the diagram, as now interpreted, is still in the Y market. What about the X-market? The answer is straightforward. As argued before, it is one of the advantages of a two-good model, such as the one employed here, that the argument can be couched entirely in terms of one good. Equilibrium in the Y-market implies equilibrium in the X-market as well.

We have thus accomplished our first task of transforming the partial into a general equilibrium diagram. We can now proceed to derive geometrically the argument and result of Section I. In Figure 2 we assume that, as a result of economic expansion, S_1S_1 and D_1D_1 shift to $S_1'S_1'$ and $D_1'D_1'$ respectively. ES_1 correspondingly shifts to ES_1' and the new

[9] See an interesting note by Hicks [4] on how the Marshallian supply curve, corresponding to Marshall's demand curve, should be derived.

equilibrium terms of trade are at OW'. Country II now exports $W'Z'$ of Y and I imports JR $(=W'Z')$ of Y. The total impact on imports and exports can then be analyzed as follows:

1. *Total Effect on Demand for Y in I.* (a) The movement from H to T is the income effect of expansion, measured by (2) in Section I. (b) The movement from T to J is compounded of the income effect on consumption of Y due to the shift in the terms of trade and the substitution effect on consumption of Y due to the same shift. It is measured therefore by (5) and (3) in Section I. (c) The movement from H to J, representing the total effect on the demand for Y in I, is thus measured by [(2)+(3)+(5)].

2. *Total Effect on Supply of Y in I.* (a) The movement from P to Q is the income effect on production of the expansion, measured by (1). (b) The movement from Q to R is the substitution effect on production of Y due to the shift in the terms of trade and is measured by (4). (c) The movement from P to R, representing the total effect on the supply of Y in I, is thus measured by [(1)+(4)].

3. *The Net Effect on the Excess Supply of Y in I.* This is then given by: (1)+(4)−[(2)+(3)+(5)]. This corresponds to the difference between HP $(=WZ)$, the old volume of imports, and JR $(=W'Z')$ the new volume of imports. If the expression is positive, there is a net reduction in the demand for imports into I; if it is negative, there is a net increase.

4. *The Net Effect on the Excess Supply of Y in II.* This is similarly given by (6). It corresponds to the difference between WZ and $W'Z'$. If it is positive, there is a net increase in the supply of imports to I; if it is negative, there is a net decrease.

The formula for determining the shift in the terms of trade is now easily derived. In equilibrium, the net changes in the excess supplies of Y in I and II must match each other and also add up to zero:

$$(1) + (4) - [(2) + (3) + (5)] + (6) = 0.$$

Solving the above for dp, we can derive formula (7). The geometrical construction not only represents the transformation of a useful diagram of partial analysis into a general equilibrium framework but also serves the purpose of deriving the results of Section I visually. There is an additional advantage that follows from our transformation; this is a direct result of Samuelson's ingenious use of this diagram (in a partial framework) to convert the international trade problem involved into a maximum problem, thereby enabling the anlayst "to make rigorous predictions as to the qualitative direction in which the variables of the system will change when some change is made in the data of the problem" [11, p. 299] and to derive generalized reciprocity relations.

III. *Expansion and Economic Welfare*

Having derived an expression to measure the precise impact of expansion on the commodity terms of trade, we can now analyze the net effect of expansion on the welfare of the growing country. Economic expansion, while increasing output, might lead to a deterioration in the terms of trade and a corresponding reduction in the growth in real income of the country experiencing the expansion. Where expansion leads to deterioration in the country's commodity terms of trade, there are three possible outcomes for the country's economic welfare:[10] net gain, no gain, or actual loss. We propose now to investigate the conditions under which these possibilities will respectively materialize.

Let dK denote the gain in real income that results from growth of output, at constant relative commodity prices. From this we must subtract the loss of real income that arises from the attendant deterioration in the terms of trade by approximating this loss with the familiar expression: $M.dp$. Using formula (8), we can say that the growing country, I, will, as a result of growth, experience net gain, make neither gain nor loss, or actually suffer immiserizing growth according as:

$$dK \gtreqless \frac{p \cdot dM}{\left[\frac{Y}{M} \cdot \sigma + r_m + \frac{C}{M} \cdot \epsilon + p \cdot \frac{\delta C}{\delta K}\right]}$$

which simplifies to:

$$\left[\frac{Y}{M} \cdot \sigma + \frac{C}{M} \cdot \epsilon + y\right] \gtreqless - r_m \tag{9}$$

where $y = p.(\delta Y/\delta K)$ and it is assumed that $E_{DY}' = E_{DY}$, so that a change in real income due to a reduction of import prices has the same effect on the demand for importables as a change in real income due to growth.[11]

It may be of interest to note that, since ϵ and σ are necessarily positive,[12] the possibility that growth might be immiserizing would arise only if either the demand for the growing country's exports is inelastic (r_m is negative) or growth actually reduces the domestic production of importables at constant relative commodity prices (y is negative). (Neither of these conditions, it should be noticed, is sufficient for im-

[10] The analysis outlined here is subject to all the familiar caveats attending on discussions of social welfare.

[11] For a similar assumption, see Bhagwati [1]. For further observations and an able discussion of related issues, see Johnson [7].

[12] This argument is again based on the assumption of convex indifference and transformation curves, convexity being defined in the strict mathematical sense.

miserizing growth to occur.[13]) Although, as indicated in Section I, y will normally be positive, it is possible to postulate assumptions under which it will be negative; this possibility is demonstrated in Section IV where the concept of the output elasticity of supply is further explored.

IV. *Increased Factor Supply and Output Elasticity of Supply*

Our formulae for determining the change in the terms of trade and the impact of growth on the welfare of the growing country draw upon elasticity concepts that are familiar to economists from the modern theory of value.[14] The concepts of output elasticity of supply and of demand (at constant relative commodity prices), E_{SY} and E_{DY}, however, are fairly recent concepts although they have already been widely used [2] [3] [5] [6]. They would appear far more familiar if they were described as yielding respectively Engel's curves of production and consumption of the commodity in question. Whereas, however, Engel's curves of consumption are respectable in the literature, those for production are still a sufficiently rare phenomenon to justify a sketch of the analytical techniques by which they may be derived. Of the two major sources of economic growth, namely expansion of factor supply and technical progress, the former is analyzed in our simple model, and the output elasticities of supply of the two activities X and Y implied thereby are investigated.

Let a and b be the amounts of the two factors employed in industry X and a', b' the amounts employed in industry Y. The prices, p_x and p_y of X and Y respectively, are assumed to be constant throughout the analysis. $a+a'=A$ and $b+b'=B$ where A and B are the total factor endowment enjoying full employment. It is assumed that B is constant. Therefore, $db+db'=0$. A is assumed to change infinitesimally so that $da+da'=dA$. The production functions are assumed to be linear and homogeneous and remain unchanged throughout the analysis. We can now proceed to analyze the impact of the change in A on the output of Y as follows:

From equilibrium conditions, we have

$$p_x \cdot \frac{\delta X}{\delta a} = p_y \cdot \frac{\delta Y}{\delta a'} = \Pi_a$$

$$p_x \cdot \frac{\delta X}{\delta b} = p_y \cdot \frac{\delta Y}{\delta b'} = \Pi_b$$

[13] This is best seen by rewriting the criterion thus:

$$\left(\frac{Y}{M} \cdot \sigma + \frac{C}{M} \cdot \epsilon + y + r_m \right) < 0$$

For further discussion of the economic implications of this criterion, see Bhagwati [1].

[14] Our substitution elasticities are not identical with, though similar to, the elasticities of substitution in the literature. See Morrissett [8].

Differentiating these, with p_x and p_y constant, and then using the relations $da+da'=dA$ and $db+db'=0$, we get:

$$(10)\quad \left(p_y\cdot\frac{\delta^2 Y}{\delta a'^2}+p_x\cdot\frac{\delta^2 X}{\delta a^2}\right)\cdot da'+\left(p_y\cdot\frac{\delta^2 Y}{\delta a'\delta b'}+p_x\cdot\frac{\delta^2 X}{\delta a\delta b}\right)db' = p_x\cdot\frac{\delta^2 X}{\delta a^2}\cdot dA$$

$$(11)\quad \left(p_y\cdot\frac{\delta^2 Y}{\delta a'\delta b'}+p_x\cdot\frac{\delta^2 X}{\delta a\delta b}\right)\cdot da'+\left(p_y\cdot\frac{\delta^2 Y}{\delta b'^2}+p_x\cdot\frac{\delta^2 X}{\delta b^2}\right)\cdot db' = p_x\cdot\frac{\delta^2 X}{\delta a\delta b}\, dA$$

Using equations (10) and (11) and the identity

$$p_y\cdot\frac{dY}{dA}=\Pi_a\frac{da'}{dA}+\Pi_b\frac{db'}{dA}$$

and choosing units such that all prices are equal to unity, we arrive at the following formula:[15]

$$(12)\qquad dY=\frac{b\cdot Y}{(a'b-ab')}\cdot dA.$$

Some interesting conclusions emerge from this formula. First, the formula has the property that the output elasticity of supply of Y (as also X) is independent of the scale of the two activities, X and Y, and depends exclusively on the factor proportions in the two activities. This is easily demonstrated by rewriting the formula thus:[16]

[15] Since the change in A is assumed to be infinitesimal, formula (12) can be derived much more readily by using the Samuelson theorem [12] that the relationship between commodity and factor price ratios is unique under the conditions postulated. J. Black informs me that the following alternative proof is available, if the Samuelson theorem is used: Assume, by choice of units, that all prices equal unity.

$$da+da'=dA\cdot\quad da'=\frac{a'}{(a'+b')}\cdot dY.$$

Similarly,

$$dY=\frac{(a'+b')}{b'}\cdot db'=-\frac{(a'+b')}{b'}\cdot\frac{b}{(a+b)}\cdot dX\cdot(db=-db').$$

Therefore,

$$da=\frac{a}{(a+b)}\cdot dX=-\frac{ab'}{b(a'+b')}\cdot dY.$$

Therefore,

$$dA=da+da'=-\frac{ab'}{b(a'+b')}\cdot dY+\frac{a'}{(a'+b')}\cdot dY.$$

Therefore,

$$dY=\frac{b(a'+b')}{(a'b-ab')}\cdot dA=\frac{b\cdot Y}{(a'b-ab')}\cdot dA.$$

The analytical method employed in the text, however, is more general and can be used for other similar problems where nothing comparable to the Samuelson theorem is available.

[16] This property is geometrically demonstrated in a different context by Mundell [9].

$$dY = \frac{1 + \frac{a'}{b'}}{\left(\frac{a'}{b'} - \frac{a}{b}\right)} \cdot dA \tag{13}$$

Further, the familiar Rybczynski [10] proposition that the output of the B-intensive industry will contract, under the assumptions made here, when the supply of A increases, at constant relative commodity prices, follows quite readily from (12). If Y is B-intensive, it follows that

$$\frac{a'}{b'} < \frac{a}{b}$$

and thus $a'b < ab'$. Under our assumptions, therefore, it can be established that dY/dA is negative if Y is B-intensive. It follows then that E_{SY} (and y) may be negative, indicating that the domestic output of importables declines absolutely, at constant terms of trade, as a result of the expansion.

The analytical technique outlined above is perfectly general and can be utilized for determining the output elasticities of supply under other types of expansion as well, such as neutral technical progress in an activity. It would thus be feasible to undertake an interesting taxonomic exercise: to consider different varieties of expansion and investigate the output elasticities of supply (and of demand) implied by them; and to relate them with different values for the substitution elasticities to discover the full impact on the terms of trade of expansion under different circumstances. Such an analysis, however, cannot be attempted here as the task would take us far afield.[17]

References

1. J. Bhagwati, "Immiserizing Growth: A Geometrical Note," *Rev. Econ. Stud.*, June 1958, *25* (3), 201–5.
2. J. Black, "Economic Expansion and International Trade: A Marshallian Approach," *Rev. Econ. Stud.*, 1955–56, *23* (3), 204–12.
3. W. M. Corden, "Economic Expansion and International Trade: A Geometric Approach," *Oxford Econ. Papers*, June 1956, *8*, 223–28.
4. J. R. Hicks, "A Note on the Elasticity of Supply," *Rev. Econ. Stud.*, 1934–35, *2*, 31–37.
5. H. G. Johnson, "Economic Expansion and International Trade," *Manchester School Econ. Soc. Stud.*, May 1955, *23*, 95–112.
6. ———, "A Mathematical Note on Immiserizing Growth," *Unpublished Manuscript*, 1956.

[17] See Johnson [5] for a very able taxonomic exercise of this nature.

7. ———, "The Transfer Problem and Exchange Stability," *Jour. Pol. Econ.*, June 1956, *64*, 212–25.
8. I. Morrissett, "Some Recent Uses of Elasticity of Substitution—A Survey," *Econometrica*, Jan. 1953, *21*, 41–62.
9. R. A. Mundell, "International Trade and Factor Mobility," *Am. Econ Rev.*, June 1957, *47*, 321–35.
10. T. Rybczynski, "Factor Endowments and Relative Commodity Prices," *Economica*, Nov. 1955, *22*, 336–41.
11. P. A. Samuelson, "Spatial Price Equilibrium and Linear Programming," *Am. Econ. Rev.*, June 1952, *42*, 283–303.
12. ———, "Prices of Factors and Goods in General Equilibrium," *Rev. Econ. Stud.*, 1953–54, *21* (1), 1–21.

IMMISERIZING GROWTH: A GEOMETRICAL NOTE

The effect of economic expansion on international trade has been receiving increasing attention from economic theorists since the publication of Professor Hicks' stimulating analysis of the "dollar problem".[1] It has, however, been insufficiently realised that, under certain circumstances, economic expansion may harm the growing country itself.[2] Economic expansion increases *output* which, however, might lead to a sufficient deterioration in the terms of trade to offset the beneficial effect of expansion and reduce the *real income* of the growing country. It is the purpose of this note to formulate the conditions under which immiserizing growth will occur. Section I sets out the analysis geometrically and arrives at the criterion for immiserizing growth. Section II discusses some of the implications of this criterion.

I

In the ensuing analysis we assume the traditional two-country, two commodity "real" model where full-employment always obtains. We also assume, to simplify the analysis, that growth is confined to a single country so that the other country (i.e., the rest-of-the-world) is not experiencing any growth in *output*; this assumption enables us to assume the offer curve of the rest-of-the-world as "given" during the course of our analysis. Finally, we simplify the problem by beginning with an investigation of the conditions under which growth would leave the country just as well off as before, and then determining whether the equilibrium actually realised would involve still less favourable terms of trade; this approach has the convenience of avoiding the need for an explicit analysis of the income effect of growth.

Consider now Fig. (1) which represents the growing economy. C_0 is the pre-expansion consumption point, P_0 the pre-expansion production point, P_0C_0 the pre-expansion terms of trade or price-line, C_0R_0 the imports of Y into the country and R_0P_0 the exports of X from the country. The production-possibility curve tangential to P_0C_0 has not been drawn in to avoid cluttering up the diagram; the indifference curve through C_0 is tangential to P_0C_0 at C_0 and has been drawn partially. Consider now growth which pushes the production-possibility curve outwards and which, at *constant terms of trade*, would bring production from P_0 to P_1'. Now assume that the terms of trade are changed just enough to offset

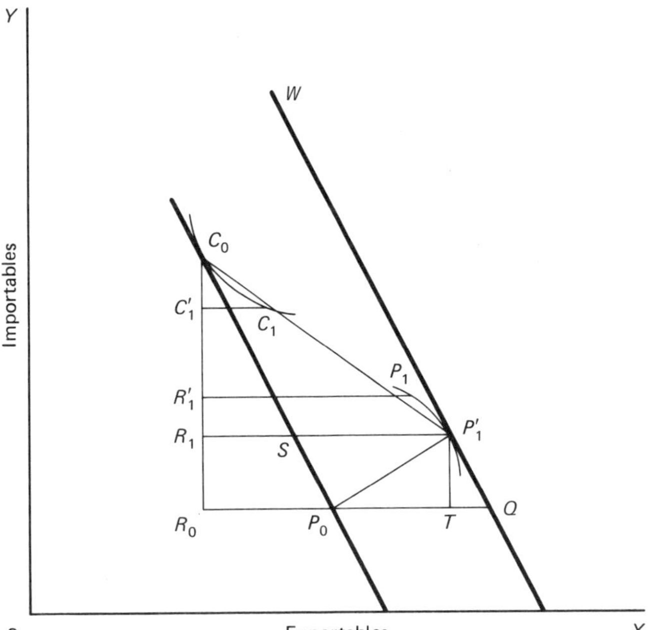

Figure 1

indifference and the *new* production-possibility curve. We later assume, legitimately for infinitesimal changes, that C_1P_1 coincides with C_0P_1'.

The combined effect of the expansion and the compensating adjustment of the terms of trade is to reduce the demand for imports from C_0R_0 to $C_1'R_1'$. This reduction can be analysed into the sum of three effects:

(1) *The increase in production of importables due to the economic expansion*: This increase (R_0R_1 in the diagram) may be analysed as follows. Let p_0 and p_1 be the original and the *zero-gain* prices respectively, measured as the number of units of exportables required to buy a unit of importables. Then the change in total output, valued at *initial* prices, is:

$$P_0T + TQ = P_0Q = SP_1'$$

And

$$SP_1' = \frac{P_1'R_1 - R_1S}{C_0R_1} \cdot C_0R_1 = (p_1 - p_0) \cdot C_0R_1$$

The change in the production of importables is:

$$R_0R_1 = P_1'T = \frac{\delta Y}{\delta K} \cdot P_0Q = \frac{\delta Y}{\delta K} \cdot SP_1'$$

where K is defined to be the country's productive capacity which is assumed to be kept fully employed and is measured by the value in terms of exportables of the output the country would produce at the initial terms of trade and Y is the domestic output of importables. Then,

$$R_0R_1 = C_0R_1 \cdot \frac{\delta Y}{\delta K} \cdot (p_1 - p_0)$$

Since we have assumed the changes to be infinitesimal, it follows that we can assume $C_0R_1 = C_0R_0$, the initial volume of imports, so that

$$R_0R_1 = M \cdot \frac{\delta Y}{\delta K} \cdot dp \quad (S_m \equiv M) \tag{1}$$

where M is the quantity of imports.

This shows the change in the production of importables due to the economic expansion itself. The expression is normally positive, indicating that the output of importables increases, consequent on economic expansion, at constant terms of trade. It should be noted here, however, that, as argued in Section II, the output of importables may actually contract due to the expansion.

(2) *The decrease in consumption of importables due to the price-change*: The price-change (from p_0 to p_1) shifts consumption *along* the indifference curve to C_1. The consumption of importables is then reduced by:

$$C_0C_1' = -\frac{\delta C}{\delta p} \cdot dp \tag{2}$$

where C is the total demand for importables.

(3) *The increase in production of importables due to the price-change*: The price-change shifts production *along* the production-possibility curve to P_1. The production of importables is then increased by:

$$R_1R_1' = \frac{\delta Y}{\delta p} \cdot dp \tag{3}$$

The total decrease in the domestic demand for *imports*[3] is the sum of the three effects (1), (2) and (3):

$$\left(M \cdot \frac{\delta Y}{\delta K} + \frac{\delta Y}{\delta p} - \frac{\delta C}{\delta p}\right) \cdot dp \tag{4}$$

This expression measures the decrease in demand for imports when the effect of growth on real income is exactly offset by an adverse movement of the terms of trade. In the abnormal case where output of importables *falls* as a result of growth, the expression may be negative, indicating an *increase* in the demand for imports.

Whether the country will actually be made worse off or not depends on what would happen to the quantity of imports supplied if the terms of trade were adjusted as assumed. The change in imports supplied as a result of such a price change is:

$$\frac{\delta S_m}{\delta p} \cdot dp \tag{5}$$

The sum of (4) and (5) constitutes the excess supply of imports at the zero-gain terms of trade: if it is positive, the terms of trade will not move against the growing country enough to deprive it of all gain from growth; but if it is negative, the price of imports will have to rise still further to preserve equilibrium, and the growing country will actually be made worse off by growth.

The economic meaning of this criterion for immiserizing growth will be considered in the next section; for this purpose a neater formulation of the criterion is desirable, and this can be derived by subjecting it to some algebraic manipulation.

Multiplying (4) and (5) by $p/M \cdot dp$, we get our criterion for immiserizing growth as:

$$\left(\frac{C}{M} \cdot \epsilon + \frac{Y}{M} \cdot \sigma + y + r_m\right) < 0 \tag{6}$$

which may be written as:

$$\left(\frac{C}{M} \cdot \epsilon + \frac{Y}{M} \cdot \sigma + y\right) < -r_m \tag{7}$$

where

$$\epsilon = -\frac{p}{C} \cdot \frac{\delta C}{\delta p}, \qquad r_m = \frac{p}{M} \cdot \frac{\delta S_m}{\delta p} \quad (S_m \equiv M)$$

$$\sigma = \frac{p}{Y} \cdot \frac{\delta Y}{\delta p} \qquad \text{and} \qquad y = p \cdot \frac{\delta Y}{\delta K}$$

This criterion is also expressible in the alternative equivalent form:

$$\left(\frac{C}{M} \cdot \epsilon + \frac{Y}{M} \cdot \sigma + y\right) < 1 - \eta_x \tag{8}$$

where $\eta_x = (p/X^0) \cdot (\delta X^0/\delta p)$ and X^0 is the quantity of exports. This follows from the fact that η_x and r_m are the *total* elasticities of the rest-of-the-world's offer curve; η_x being the elasticity of the rest-of-the-world's demand for imports (into the rest-of-the-world) in response to an infinitesimal change in the terms of trade and r_m being the elasticity of the rest-of-the-world's supply of (its) exports (to the growing country) in response to an infinitesimal shift in the terms of trade. It is a well-known proposition in the theory of international trade that $\eta_x - r_m = 1$; hence, $1 - \eta_x = -r_m$.

II

What are the implications of the criterion that we have derived in Section I? It will be remembered that $\sigma = (p/Y) \cdot (\delta Y/\delta p)$ and is thus necessarily positive and $\epsilon = -(p/C) \cdot (\delta C/\delta p)$ which again, being the constant-utility or expenditure-compensated demand-elasticity with respect to a change in the price of importables, is necessarily positive.[4] We can see from (6), (7) or (8) that the *possibility* of immiserizing growth is increased if:

(i) Y/M, the ratio of domestic production to import of importables is small. Since $C/M = 1 + (Y/M)$, it follows that C/M will also be small when Y/M is small;

(ii) ϵ, the constant-utility demand-elasticity for importables with respect to a change in the price of importables, is small; this would depend on the substitution effect against importables being negligible when the price of importables rises; and

(iii) σ, the elasticity in supply of importables when production shifts along the production-possibility curve in response to a change in the price of importables, is small.

These are, neither singly nor in combination, sufficient conditions for immiserizing growth. In fact, the *possibility* of immiserizing growth arises only when, with these conditions favourably fulfilled, either or both of the following crucial conditions are fulfilled:

(a) the offer of the rest-of-the-world is inelastic, (i.e., r_m is negative, which may be for the *extreme,* and by no means necessary, reason that the growing country's exports are Giffen goods abroad); and

(b) growth actually reduces the domestic production of importables at constant relative commodity prices (i.e., y is negative).

Stringent as the latter condition may appear at first sight, recent analyses have shown that it is feasible under relatively simple assumptions. Thus the Rybczynski proposition states that under a two-commodity, two-factor model where, say, labour and land being the factors, one good is labour-intensive and the other land-intensive, if labour (land) increases in supply, then the output of the land-intensive (labour-intensive) industry must actually contract if the relative commodity prices are maintained constant.[5] Professor Johnson has recently advanced the proposition that under neutral technical progress in one industry, the technology of the other and the total factor endowment remaining unchanged, the output of the other industry must actually fall under constant relative commodity prices.[6] It may be of interest to note that under biased progress as well it is possible to establish conditions under which the output of the non-innovating industry will contract.[7]

I wish to thank Professor Harry Johnson for his generous assistance and encouragement in the writing of this paper. My thanks are also due to Sir Donald MacDougall and J. Black for helpful comments. The responsibility for any errors that remain is entirely mine.

1. J. R. Hicks, "An Inaugural Lecture," *Oxford Economic Papers,* N.S. Vol. 5, No. 2 (June, 1953). The following are of interest: H. G. Johnson, "Economic Expansion and International Trade," *The Manchester School of Economic and Social Studies,* May, 1955; E. J. Mishan, "The Long-Run Dollar Problem: A Comment," *Oxford Economic Papers,* N.S. Vol. 7, No. 2 (June, 1955); and W. M. Corden, "Economic Expansion and International Trade: A Geometric Approach," *Oxford Economic Papers,* N.S. Vol. 8, No. 2 (June, 1956).

2. Exception must be made, however, in the case of Professor Johnson, "Equilibrium Growth in An Expanding Economy," *The Canadian Journal of Economics and Political Science,* Vol. XIX, No. 4, (Nov., 1953), p. 495; and also his *Manchester School,* May 1955, article. It should also be mentioned that Prof. Johnson has independently worked out mathematically, in an unpublished note, a criterion for immiserizing growth which confirms the results derived geometrically in this note.

3. As distinguished from *importables.*

4. This argument obviously rests on the assumption of "well-behaved" (convex) indifference curves and (concave) transformation curves, concavity being defined with reference to the origin and *not* in the strict mathematical sense.

5. Rybczynski, "Factor Endowments and Relative Commodity Prices," *Economica,* Nov., 1955. Linear homogeneity of the production functions and diminishing returns are *sufficient* conditions for the proposition to hold. The strong Samuelson notion of factor-intensity is not necessary.

6. Johnson, *Manchester School, op. cit.* Diminishing returns are *sufficient* for this proposition to hold. The proposition can be readily extended to more than two goods and factors.

7. The conditions under which this result will obtain can be established for specified production functions.

Distortions and Immiserizing Growth: a Generalization

In an earlier note in this *Review* I had analyzed the case of " immiserizing growth ", where growth (due to technical progress and/or factor accumulation) leads to a sufficiently acute deterioration in the terms of trade which imposes a loss of real income outweighing the primary gain in real income due to the growth itself.[1] Recently, Harry Johnson has shown that the phenomenon of immiserizing growth, involving reduction in social welfare below the initial pre-growth level, can arise also in the case of a small country without any monopoly power in trade if technical progress occurs in a *tariff-protected* import-competing industry or if the factor in whose use this industry is intensive is augmented.[2]

In point of fact, both these cases belong to a *general* class of immiserizing-growth phenomena which can arise in the presence of distortions. In the traditional case where gains from growth are out-weighed by the loss from worsened terms of trade, the distortion is foreign: the average terms of trade differ from the marginal terms of trade. In the tariff situation for a small country, analyzed by Johnson now, the distortion is policy-imposed: the tariff results in sub-optimality. In either case, the essential point is that the gain which would accrue from growth, *if optimal policies were followed*, is outweighed by the incremental loss of real income which the distortion imposes in the post-growth situation vis-à-vis the pre-growth situation. Thus, the phenomenon of immiserizing growth can occur in principle, whenever distortions obtain in an economic system.

I. DISTORTIONARY WAGE DIFFERENTIALS

Take, for example, the case of distortionary wage differentials in the traditional two-factor, two-commodity model of trade theory. It is known that such a differential will result in (i) a shrinking-in of the feasible production possibility curve and (ii) a non-tangency between the commodity price-ratio and the feasible production possibility curve.[3] Suppose that this differential operates against commodity X in Figure 1 where the case of a small country with no monopoly power in trade is depicted. AB is the shrunk-in, feasible production possibility curve. P_0C_0, parallel to P_nC_n, is the fixed international price ratio. In the initial situation, P_0 is the production bundle and C_0 the consumption bundle. Next, assume that neutral technical progress takes place in industry Y.

It can then be shown, as is done below, that the output of X will fall and that of Y will increase. If, then, the production bundle shifts to a point such as P_n, to the left of P_0C_0, the availability line will become P_nC_n, consumption will be at C_n and social welfare will have been reduced ($U_n < U_0$).

That the output of X will fall and of Y will increase at constant commodity price ratio when there is neutral technical progress in industry Y in the Hicksian sense, is easily

1 See Bhagwati [1]. This case was also noted independently by Harry Johnson.

2 See Johnson [5].

3 These propositions have been discussed by Hagen [4]. The conditions under which the wage differential will be distortionary, as also the possibility of the feasible production curve losing convexity, are discussed in Bhagwati and Ramaswami [2].

demonstrated by the use of the Findlay-Grubert technique.[1] For a commodity price-ratio implying the exchange of $\overline{X}$ for $\overline{Y}$, the factor price-ratio faced by X-entrepreneurs is RT and by $\overline{Y}$-entrepreneurs is RS in Figure 2. Factor L is thus more expensive to X-entrepreneurs by proportion ST/OT. With neutral technical progress in the Y-industry, the

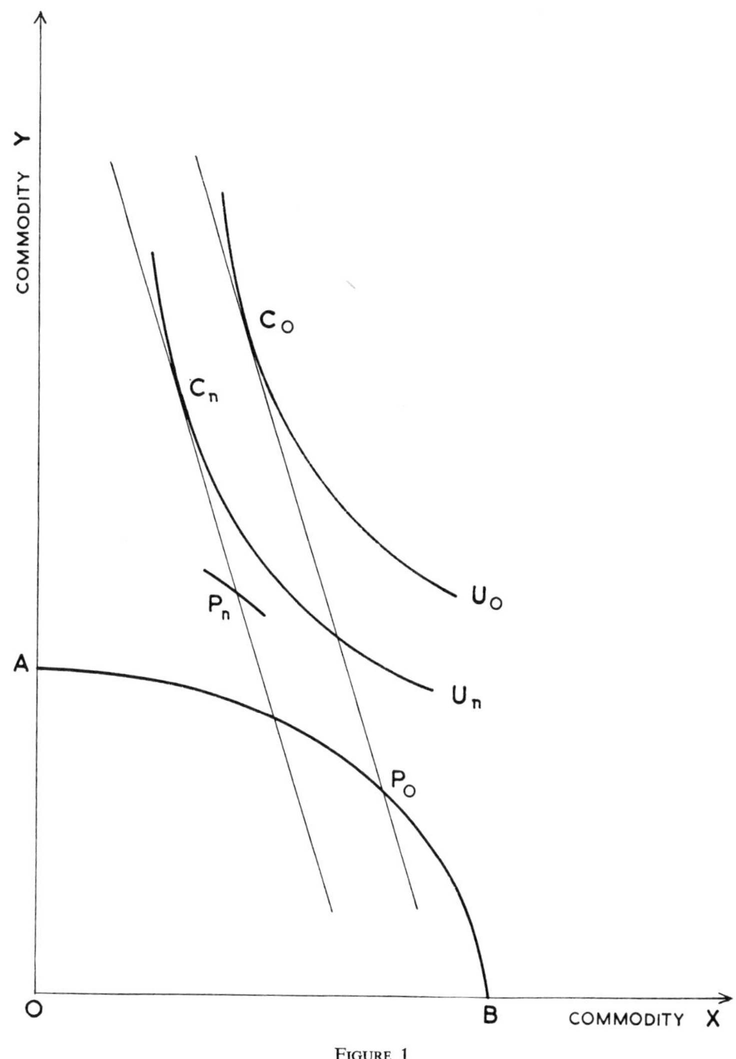

FIGURE 1

output level $\overline{Y}$ can be reached by isoquant $\overline{Y}_n$ and, if the factor price-ratio were to continue to be $R'S' = RS$, then the factor proportion in Y would be given at M, equal to that at K.

[1] The same result would hold for augmentation of the factor L in which industry Y is assumed to be intensive, or for labour saving technical progress in industry Y. See Findlay and Grubert [3].

However, as is seen from $R'T'$ and $R'S'$, it is not possible for the commodity price-ratio to remain unchanged and also for the techniques and factor price-ratios not to change. It is seen readily that the new equilibrium will be reached at K/L ratios for X and Y which are both greater than in the initial equilibrium, if the commodity price-ratio is to remain

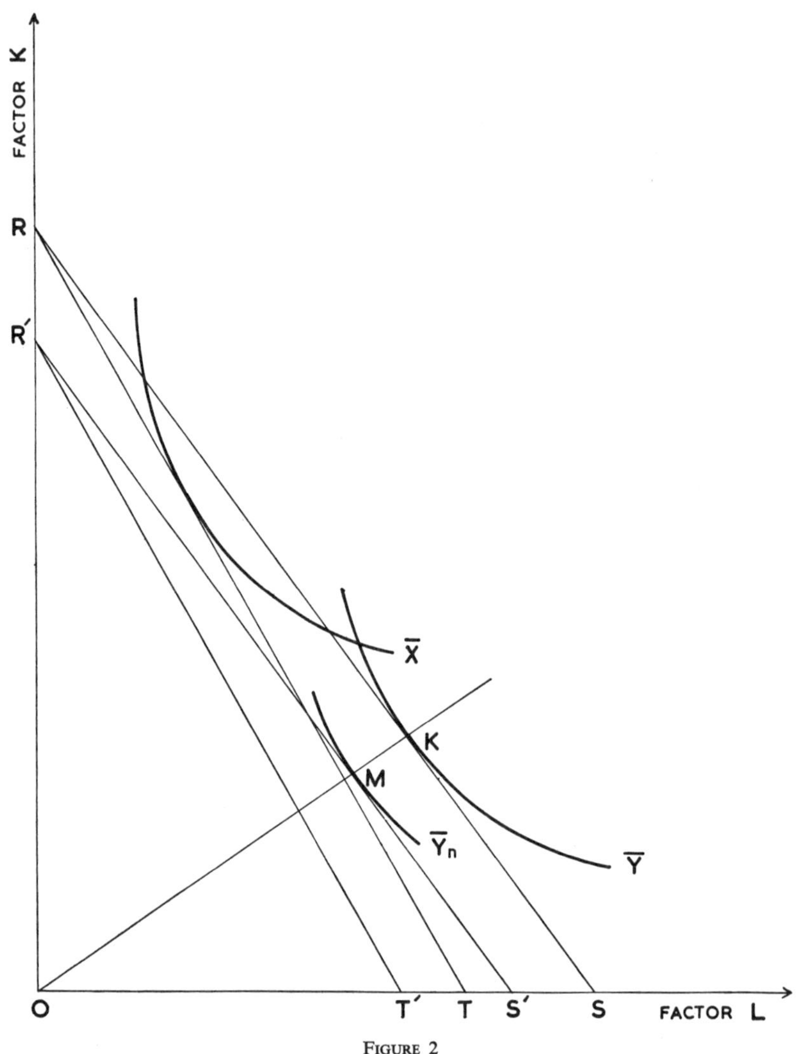

FIGURE 2

unchanged and the factor price differential between the two activities is also to be maintained. This increment in the K/L ratios in X and Y could be readily illustrated by sketching in a new point R'' on the vertical axis, with two lines from it, one tangent to $\overline{X}$ and meeting the horizontal axis at point T'', and the other tangent to $\overline{Y}_n$ and meeting the horizontal axis at point S'', such that the ratio OS''/OT'' is the same as the ratio OS/OT. But, then, with total amounts of fully employed K and L given, and X being K-intensive, this implies that the output of X will fall and that of Y rise. If the loss in X-output is large enough, P_n may well lie (in Figure 1) to the left of P_0C_0.

Thus, the possibility of immiserizing growth may arise also when there is a domestic distortion resulting from a wage differential.

II. TARIFFS AND MONOPOLY POWER IN TRADE

I have already noted that the possibility of immiserizing growth has earlier been demonstrated in the cases where (1) for a country, with monopoly power in trade, growth

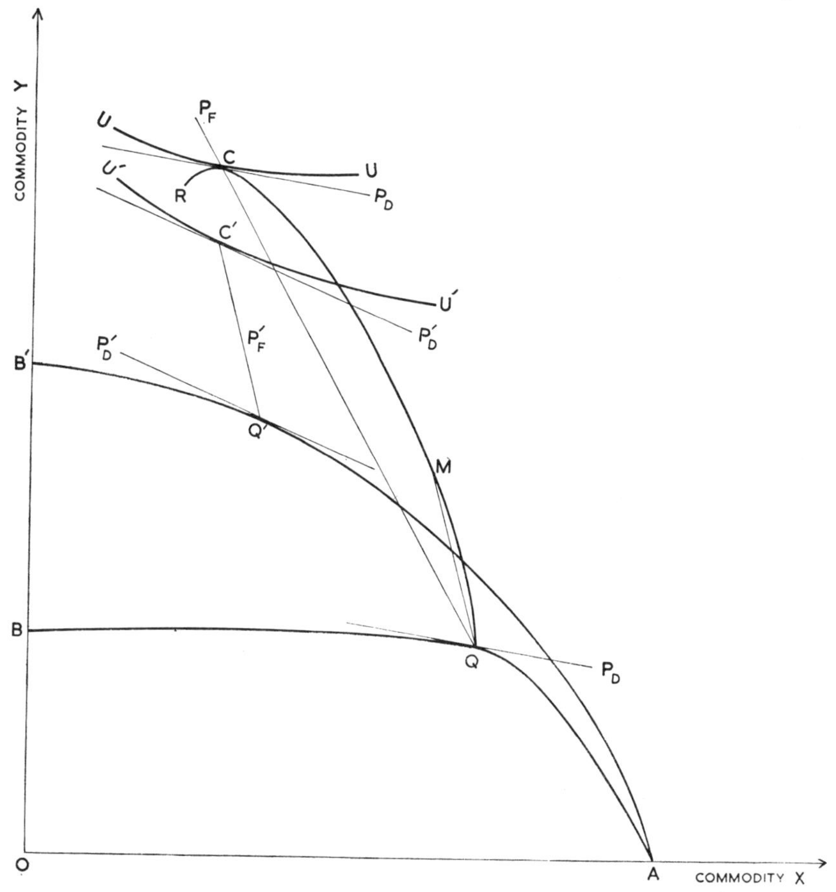

FIGURE 3

occurs under a zero tariff and (2) for a country, with no monopoly power in trade, growth occurs under a positive tariff.[1] Both these propositions, however, can be generalized and the phenomenon of immiserizing growth shown to be possible when, for a country with monopoly power in trade, growth occurs under a positive tariff.

[1] See Bhagwati [1] and Johnson [5] respectively. Note also that the second case would equally hold for a production tax-cum-subsidy policy, as distinct from a tariff policy.

Immiserizing growth will be possible, in this case, if the tariff is sub-optimal in both the pre-growth and the post-growth situations, or if it is optimal in the former but sub-optimal in the latter situation. Clearly, however, it cannot arise when the tariff is optimal in both situations or only in the latter.

Take, for example, the case where there is monopoly power in trade and the economy has acquired an optimum tariff. In such a case if finite growth occurs, the specific tariff which was optimal in the initial situation will, in general, become sub-optimal in the new situation. And the loss from the sub-optimality of the tariff may out-weigh the gain that would accrue from growth (as measured at optimal levels in both situations). This possibility is illustrated in Figure 3.

AQB is the pre-growth production possibility curve, $QMCR$ the given foreign reciprocal demand curve, QC the international price-ratio (P_F), and P_D the domestic price-ratio under an optimum tariff. $AQ'B'$ is the post-growth production possibility curve and $Q'C'$ the new international price ratio (P'_F)—which yields a volume of trade, with production Q' and consumption C' at domestic price-ratio P'_D, that is consistent with the foreign reciprocal demand curve, as seen by reference to QM. Note that, with the tariff rate assumed to be unchanged in post-growth situation, $P'_D = P'_F(1+t_m)$ and $P_D = P_F(1+t_m)$, at identical t_m and with the relative price defined as the price of the importable divided by the price of the exportable. The resulting welfare levels show that $U' < U$, which implies immiserizing growth.[1]

Note further that this case does not depend on "freakish" phenomena such as inferiority of either good in social consumption; it does however require that the growth be ultra-biased against the production of the exportable commodity X, such that the output of X falls at constant commodity price-ratio. Thus, the case can arise when there is: (i) neutral technical progress in the importable industry, or (ii) the factor in which the importable industry is intensive increases, or (iii) biased technical progress occurs in the importable industry, with the bias in favour of (i.e. increasing the relative use of) the factor in which the exportable industry is intensive.[2]

Massachusetts Institute of Technology
and
Delhi School of Economics.

JAGDISH N. BHAGWATI

REFERENCES

[1] Bhagwati, J. "Immiserizing Growth: a Geometrical Note", *Review of Economic Studies*, **25** (June 1958).

[2] Bhagwati, J., and Ramaswami, V. K. "Domestic Distortions, Tariffs and the Theory of Optimum Subsidy", *Journal of Political Economy* (February 1963).

[3] Findlay, R., and Grubert, H. "Factor Intensity, Technological Progress, and the Terms of Trade", *Oxford Economic Papers*, **11** (February 1959).

[4] Hagen, E. "An Economic Justification of Protectionism", *Quarterly Journal of Economics* (November 1958).

[5] Johnson, H. G. "The Possibility of Income Losses from Increased Efficiency or Factor Accumulation in the Presence of Tariffs", *Economic Journal*, **77** (March 1967).

1 It may be stressed that immiserizing growth would necessarily be precluded if the post-growth tariff was changed to the optimal level. The economy would then, in figure 3, be able to operate on the necessarily-superior envelope of consumption possibilities generated by the unchanged foreign reciprocal demand curve and the improved domestic production possibilities.

2 Cf. Findlay and Grubert [3].

THE THEORY OF IMMISERIZING GROWTH: FURTHER APPLICATIONS

In this paper, I consider two applications of the theory of immiserizing growth (Bhagwati, 1968).

In Section I, I examine mainly the paradox of a reduction in the welfare of a 'small' country, with a domestic distortion in production, when its terms of trade improve exogenously. This, and related, paradoxes are seen to be nothing but special cases of the general theory of immiserizing growth.

In Section II, I examine the paradox of a reduction in the welfare of a country following a tariff-induced inflow of capital. This paradox again follows from the theory of immiserizing growth; besides, it is clearly of immediate and direct relevance to policymaking.

I. Wage Differentials, Terms of Trade Improvement, and Immiserizing Growth

Batra and Pattanaik (1970) have produced recently the paradoxical proposition that an exogenous improvement in the terms of trade can worsen, rather than improve, welfare if a country has a distortionary wage differential. Batra and Scully (1971) have now added yet another paradox to the theory of trade and welfare in showing that immiserizing growth can occur, *despite endogenous-growth-induced improvement in the terms of trade,* if wage differentials are present. It is easy to provide the underlying rationale for these two paradoxes by drawing on recent insights into the theory of immiserizing growth.[1]

Batra-Pattanaik Paradox

Let me first examine the Batra-Pattanaik (1970) paradox. It can easily be shown that this paradox is, paradoxically enough, yet another instance of the generalised theory of immiserizing growth.

This theory (Bhagwati, 1968) states that if growth takes place in a country characterised by (a distortion and hence by) a sub-optimal policy, then immiserizing growth can ensue; conversely, growth cannot be immiserizing if optimal policies are pursued (before and after growth). Growth can only improve welfare if optimal policies are pursued; however, if sub-optimal policies are followed before and after growth, immiserizing growth will ensue if the primary gain from growth, measured as the gain which would accrue if optimal policies were followed, is outweighed by the *incremental* loss that could arise from the pursuit instead of sub-optimal policies.

As Batra and Scully have noted, I have used this theory elsewhere (Bhagwati, 1968) to show that in the presence of a wage differential, immiserizing growth can occur for a country with *given* terms of trade and *laissez-faire* as its economic policy. The reason is that *laissez-faire* is a sub-optimal policy when a distortionary wage-differential is present, as argued by Hagen (1958) in a classic paper.

But I have also noted elsewhere (Bhagwati, 1971) that the theory of immiserizing growth can be used to illuminate, and prove, other propositions of trade theory where no growth, in an obvious sense, is involved. Thus, the classic propositions of Gottfried Haberler (1950), which compare free trade (i.e. *laissez-faire*) with no trade (i.e. autarky) and demonstrate that the two policies cannot be ranked uniquely if production externalities or factor-price rigidities are present, can be readily seen to be examples of the theory of immiserizing growth. This is because, as Baldwin (1948) has shown, the free-trade-situation availability locus lies uniformly outside (except for overlaps) the production possibility curve which is, of course, the no-trade-situation availability locus. Thus, the no-trade and free-trade policies are conceptually the same as pre-growth and post-growth situations. Hence, if a distortion is present in the two situations, so that the two situations are sub-optimal, immiserizing growth can follow: that is to say, free trade can be inferior to no trade.

The Batra-Pattanaik paradox also falls into place in a similar fashion. The exogenous improvement in the terms of trade implies an outward shift of the Baldwin availabilities locus, implying 'growth'; the presence of the distortionary wage differential implies that this 'growth' is occurring in the presence of sub-optimal policies. Hence 'immiserizing growth' can occur: that is to say, an exogenous improvement in the terms of trade can worsen welfare.

Batra-Scully Paradox

The Batra-Scully proposition involves a paradox within a world of paradoxes. While it has been shown (Bhagwati, 1968) that the presence of wage differentials in a 'small' country can lead to immiserizing growth, they demonstrate that such immiseration can arise even when, for a 'large' country, the terms of trade have *improved* as a result of this growth.

The Batra-Scully paradox is, however, similar to my other demonstration (Bhagwati, 1968) of the possibility of immiserizing growth when, for a large country, the pre-growth optimal tariff is kept unchanged after growth and ceases to be optimal in the post-growth situation. In the

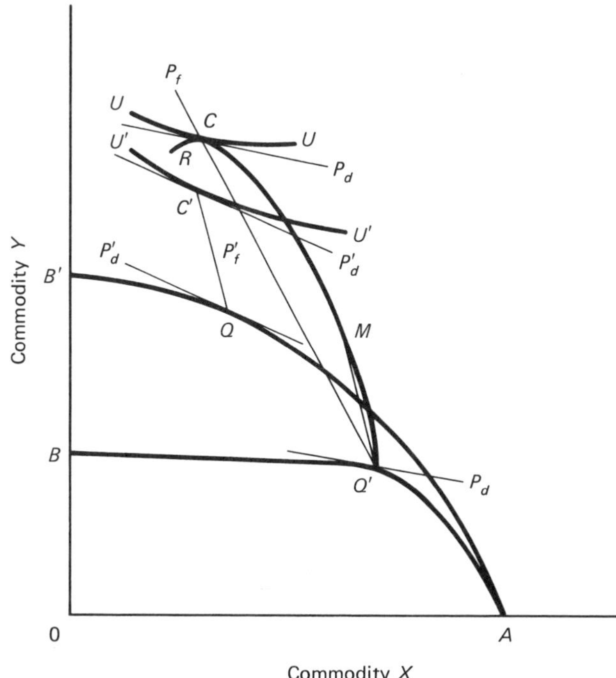

Figure 1

geometrical illustration (Figure 2, Bhagwati, 1968) of this possibility, reproduced here as Figure 1 for convenience, the terms of trade actually improved in the post-growth situation and yet growth was immiserizing;[2] however, the paradoxical phenomenon of improvement in the terms of trade was neither noted nor explained.

And yet this paradox is readily resolved. When the growth occurs and the tariff (which is optimal in the initial, pre-growth situation) is kept unchanged, the tariff ceases in general to be optimal.[3] Hence the loss from this sub-optimal policy can outweigh the gain from growth (measured as when an optimal tariff were levied in the post-growth situation as well). That this can happen when the terms of trade improve is, in turn, seen as follows. If the growth is heavily biased in favour of the importable good,[4] then the marginal rate of domestic transformation improves in favour of the importable good thus implying that the optimal tariff should be increased. Since it is not, there is a loss of welfare which outweighs, when large enough, the gain from growth. At the same time, given the foreign offer curve facing the country and the country's unchanged tariff, the growth (which is, in the illustration, ultra-biased in favour of the importable good and hence shrinks the country's own offer curve) will improve the terms of trade. Hence the phenomenon of terms-of-trade improvement can arise simultaneously with the phenomenon of immiserizing growth.

The Batra-Scully paradox is to be explained in similar terms. Their analysis is for a large country with *laissez-faire and* with distortionary wage differential: hence they are comparing the pre-growth and the post-growth situations which are both characterised, in general, by sub-optimality arising from *two* distortions: failure to offset the wage differential and failure to pursue a policy designed to exploit the country's largeness (i.e. its monopoly power in trade). Hence immiserizing growth is possible. At the same time, growth may shrink the country's offer curve, causing the terms of trade to improve. Hence arises the possibility illustrated in Figure 2, where the production possibility curve shifts with growth from *AB* to *EF*, the initial terms of trade are *PC*, the initial welfare level at *U*, and the new equilibrium is at improved terms of trade P_gC_g but at reduced welfare level U_g, implying immiserizing growth.[5]

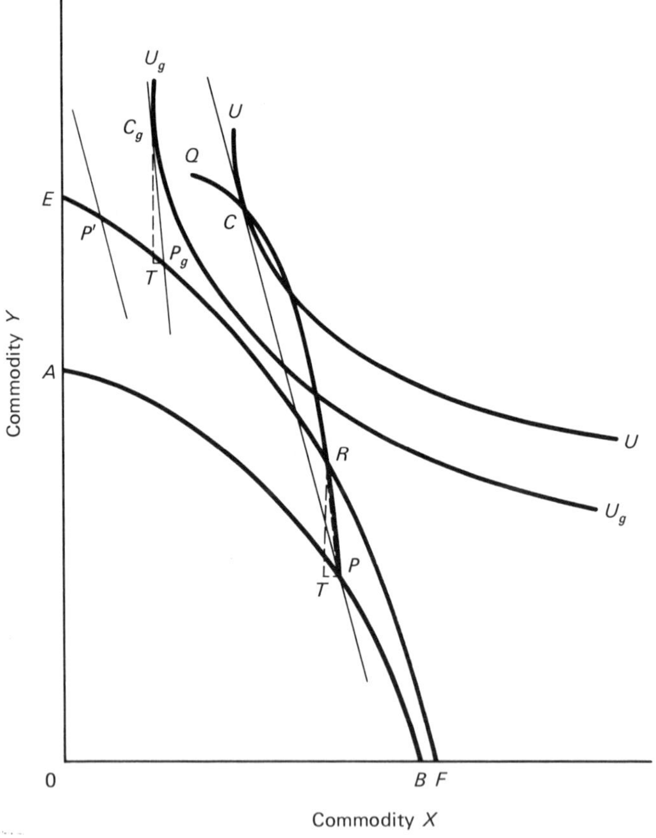

Figure 2

II. Tariff-Induced Capital Inflow and Immiseration

The second application of the theory of immiserizing growth arises from Harry Johnson's (1967) demonstration that a 'small' country, growing subject to a constant tariff, can experience immiserizing growth. His analysis clearly points to the possibility of immiseration following from a tariff-induced inflow of capital. However, the analysis cannot be carried over identically and fully as Tan (1969), in his subsequent examination of the conditions for Johnson's possibility to occur, has implied.[6]

Johnson's analysis relates to a comparison of the pre-growth and post-growth situations, both subject to a given tariff. On the other hand, the analysis of tariff-induced capital inflow and (resulting) immiseration requires a comparison of the free-trade situation with the tariff-inclusive, post-growth (*via*-capital-influx) situation. I now explore this particular comparison and discuss the conditions under which immiseration will follow.

Johnson's Paradox

In Johnson's paradox, illustrated in Figure 3, the pre-growth tariff-inclusive production is at P_t, the given international price-line is $C_tP_t \parallel C_t'P_t'$, the pre-growth consumption is at C_t and welfare is at U_t. With capital

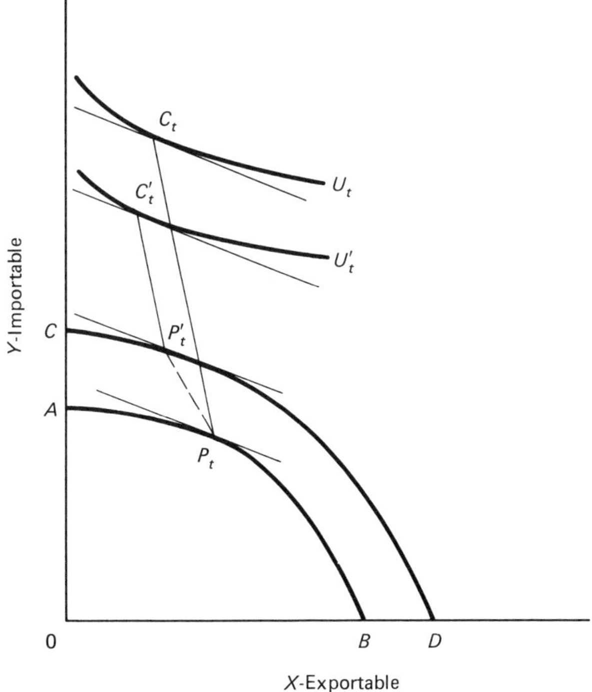

Figure 3

accumulation, the production possibility curve shifts from AB to CD, production to P_t', consumption to C_t' and welfare is reduced to U_t' ($<U_t$). It is clear that a necessary and sufficient condition for such immiseration is that the Rybczynski-line P_tP_t' be less steep than the international price-ratio P_tC_t; a necessary condition for such immiseration is that the output of the exportable good must fall at constant, tariff-inclusive prices (i.e. growth should be ultra-biased in favour of the importable good).

Tariff-Induced Capital Inflow

When, however, we wish to examine the conditions under which the possibility of immiseration will emerge if we have a tariff-induced capital inflow, we have the following four welfare elements in the transition from an initial free-trade situation to the tariff-and-capital-inflow-inclusive situation:

(i) The tariff imposes a production cost by distorting the prices faced by producers.

(ii) The capital influx implies 'growth', at constant tariff-inclusive domestic prices faced by producers, which may imply a welfare gain or a welfare loss.

(iii) The tariff imposes a consumption cost by distorting the prices faced by consumers; and

(iv) The tariff-induced capital influx earns a reward which must be reckoned as a cost and hence a welfare loss to the tariff-imposing country.

These elements are illustrated in Figure 4. The initial free-trade equilibrium with production possibility curve AB and the fixed international price-line P_fC_f, is characterised by production at P_f, consumption at C_f and welfare at U_f. The tariff-plus-capital-influx equilibrium is, with the foreign-capital-augmented production possibility curve CD, at P_t, C_t^4 and U_t^4 ($<U_f$) and shows, in consequence, immiseration. The transition from U_f to U_t^4 can be built up through the four elements we have already distinguished:

(i) The tariff shifts production from P_f to P_t' along AB, leading to a decline in welfare from U_f to U_t^1; this is the result of the production distortion.

(ii) The influx of foreign capital shifts production, at tariff-inclusive prices, from P_t' to P_t and therefore welfare from U_t^1 to U_t^2; this welfare-shift, *identical* with the one underlying the Johnson paradox (which involves immiserizing growth under a given tariff), may be positive (as in Figure 4) or negative (as in the Johnson paradox).

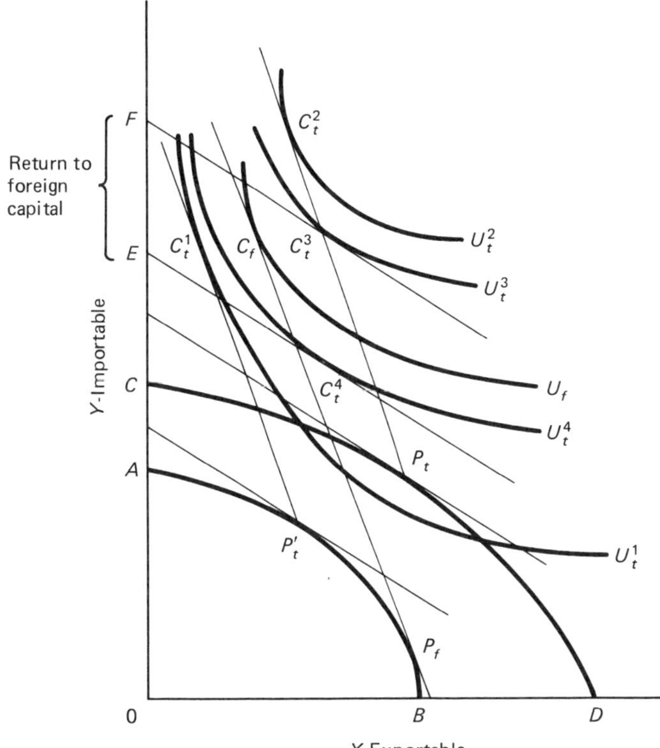

Figure 4

(iii) Consumption must also be shifted because it will occur at tariff-inclusive prices; this reduces the economy from U_t^2 to U_t^3; and finally

(iv) The return to the foreign capital inflow, measured at *EF* amount of *Y*-goods in domestic prices,[7] will reduce the economy still further to U_t^4.[8]

It is clear, therefore, that the tariff-induced-capital-inflow immiseration requires far less stringent conditions than the Johnson case. The latter must rely entirely on effect (ii) being negative, this being a necessary and sufficient condition for the immiserizing phenomenon. On the other hand, in the present case, effects (i), (iii) and (iv) being necessarily negative, effect (ii) can be positive and yet be compatible with immiseration, as is in fact depicted in Figure 4. It should be possible to set down formally the necessary and sufficient conditions for immiseration in this case; but this has not been attempted here.

Thanks are due to the National Science Foundation for research support. Thanks are due to Michael Connolly for helpful comments.

1. The substance of the following argument is now summarised in Batra-Scully (1971).

2. Thus, in Figure 1, *AB* is the pre-growth production possibility curve, *AB′* the post-growth production possibility curve, *QMCR* the super-imposed foreign offer curve facing the country, the post-growth equilibrium shows lower welfare level implying immiserzing growth ($U > U'$) and the terms of trade have improved after growth (from *QC* to *QM* = *Q′C′*).

3. Note that the foreign offer curve facing the growing country is taken, as always, to be given in the analysis.

4. In Figure 1, the growth is ultra-biased in favour of the importable good so that, at constant commodity prices, growth actually reduces the output of the exportable good.

5. P′ shows the production point after growth if terms of trade were held constant, implying that growth is ultra-biased in favour of the importable commodity *Y*; and *PRCQ* is the given foreign offer curve, with P_gC_g parallel and equal in length to *PR*, implying that the illustrated post-growth equilibrium is consistent with the given foreign offer curve.

6. Bertrand and Flatters (1971) also have, subsequent to Tan's work, explored the conditions for Johnson's paradox to occur when capital accumulation is responsible for the growth. Bhagwati (1968) has provided the general theory of immiserizing growth which reduces Johnson's and other earlier (Bhagwati, 1958) paradoxes to special cases.

7. While capital will earn the value of its marginal product, the return would have to be modified by phenomena such as corporation taxes. We must therefore take the *net* return into account.

8. An alternative way to get from U_f to U_t^4 would be to (i) go from U_f to U_f^* on assumption that capital has come in but that we are still in free trade; this would be done by putting the international price-line tangent to *CD* and then tangent, in turn, to U_f^* this is necessarily a welfare gain; (ii) go from U_f^* to U_t^2, which would be the production loss associated with the tariff, but now taken at *CD*; (iii) go from U_t^2 to U_t^3, which is the consumption loss; and (iv) go finally from U_t^3 to U_t^4, which would be the loss from netting out the reward to foreign capital.

References

1. R. Baldwin, 'Equilibrium in International Trade: A Diagrammatic Analysis', *Quarterly Journal of Economics*, Vol. 62, No. 5 (November, 1948), pp. 748–62.

2. R. Batra and P. Pattanaik, 'Domestic Distortions and the Gains from Trade', *Economic Journal*, Vol. 80, No. 319 (September, 1970) pp. 638–49.

3. R. Batra and G. Scully, 'The Theory of Wage Differentials: Welfare and Immiserizing Growth', *Journal of International Economics*, Vol. 1, No. 2 (May, 1971), pp. 241–7.

4. T. Bertrand and F. Flatters, 'Tariffs, Capital Accumulation and Immiserizing Growth', *Journal of International Economics*, Vol. 1, No. 4 (November, 1971), pp. 453–60.

5. J. Bhagwati, 'Immiserizing Growth: A Geometric Note', *Review of Economic Studies*, Vol. 25, No. 68 (June, 1958), pp. 201–5.

6. J. Bhagwati, 'Distortions and Immiserizing Growth: A Generalization', *Review of Economic Studies*, Vol. 35, No. 104 (October, 1968), pp. 481–5.

7. E. Hagen, 'An Economic Justification of Protectionism', *Quarterly Journal of Economics*, Vol. 72, No. 4 (November, 1958), pp. 496–514.

8. H.G. Johnson, 'The Possibility of Income Losses from Increased Efficiency or Factor Accumulation in the Presence of Tariffs', *Economic Journal*, Vol. 77, No. 305 (March, 1967), pp. 151–4.

9. A.H. Tan, 'Immiserizing Tariff-induced Capital Accumulation and Technical Change', *Malayan Economic Review*, 1969.

Editor's Note

The problem of when a tariff-induced capital inflow will lead to immiserization, raised in section II of this paper, has been resolved by R. A. Brecher and C. F. Diaz Alejandro, "Tariffs, Foreign Capital, and Immiserization," *Journal of International Economics* 7 (1977): 317–322.

Optimal Policies and Immiserizing Growth

By Jagdish N. Bhagwati*

In 1958, I analysed the paradoxical case of "immiserizing growth" [2] where a country, with monopoly power in trade, found that the growth-induced deterioration in its terms of trade implied a sufficiently large loss of welfare to outweigh the primary gain from growth.[1] An obvious corollary of this proposition was that, if the country imposed an optimum tariff (either in both the pre-growth and the post-growth situations, or in the latter situation alone), this paradox would be eliminated.

James Melvin, in an interesting note [5], has now produced yet another analysis of immiserizing growth, where demand differences of the factor-intensity-reversals type are combined with international identity of production possibilities and growth therein to yield immiserization (for one of the two countries) which *cannot* be eliminated by the imposition of an optimum tariff (by the country experiencing immiserizing growth).[2]

This paradox, in a world of paradoxes, is however readily resolved. It can be easily shown that the Bhagwati and Melvin examples of immiserizing growth belong to two quite different *generic* types; and that each, in turn, can be generalized to a different family of immiserizing growth possibilities. The former type can be eliminated by the introduction of optimal policies; the latter cannot.

I. *Distortions and Immiserizing Growth*

The original Bhagwati immiserizing growth phenomenon belongs to the class of cases where a welfare-reducing *distortion* in the economy is the cause of the immiseration. The essential point involved is that the " . . . gain which would accrue from growth, *if optimal policies were followed*, is outweighed by the incremental loss of real income which the distortion imposes in the post-growth situation vis-à-vis the pre-growth situation" [3, p. 481].

The original Bhagwati example is traditionally analysed in terms of the (primary) gains from growth (at constant terms of trade) being outweighed by the (secondary) loss from worsened terms of trade [2]. A more insightful way of looking at this case, however, is to argue that the assumed free trade and hence failure to impose an optimum tariff (to exploit monopoly power in trade) in both the pre-growth and post-growth situations involves welfare reducing, "distortionary" policies in both these situations. Immiseration then occurs because the gain, which would necessarily accrue from growth if the optimal tariff were imposed in both situations, is smaller than the incremental loss arising from the accentuation (if any) in the post-growth situation of the welfare loss resulting from the distortionary free-trade policy in each situation.

Harry Johnson's [4] further example of immiserizing growth where the country has no monopoly power in trade but imposes a tariff which applies to both the pre-growth and the post-growth situations, is to be explained in terms of the same logic. In the absence of monopoly power in trade, the tariff is necessarily distortionary and, compared with the fully optimal free-trade policy, causes a loss of welfare in each situation. If the growth were to occur with free trade, there would necessarily be an increment in welfare. However, since growth occurs under a tariff, there arises the possibility that the loss from the tariff may be accentuated after growth, and that this incremental loss may outweigh the gain (that would occur under the optimal, free-trade policy), thus resulting in immiseration. Thus,

* The author is professor of economics at the Massachusetts Institute of Technology. Thanks are due to Peter Kenen for helpful comments.

[1] This possibility was also noted and analysed independently by Harry Johnson.

[2] Melvin's geometric analysis uses a case where each country's offer curve, if drawn, would be less than infinitely elastic, thus implying monopoly power in trade for the *other* country.

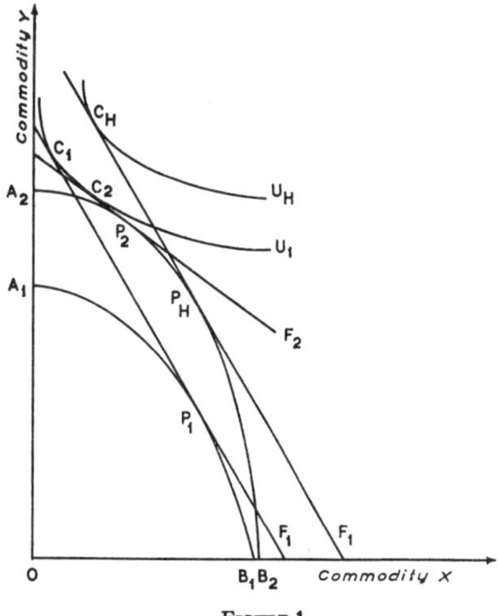

FIGURE 1

the policy-imposed distortion (i.e. the tariff) generates the possibility of immiserizing growth.[3]

I have subsequently produced two more examples of immiserizing growth [3], to underline and illustrate the general proposition that immiserizing growth can arise under *any* kind of distortion, whether endogenous or policy-imposed: first, where the endogenous distortion involves an imperfect factor market, taking the shape of a distortionary wage differential; and second, where the endogenous distortion is foreign, involving monopoly power in trade, and where the country has an optimal tariff in the pre-growth situation.

From the general theory of immiserizing growth, arising from distortions, it is furthermore clear that the removal of a policy-imposed distortion (e.g. removal of the tariff in Johnson's case), or optimal policy intervention to eliminate the welfare-reducing effects of the distortion (e.g. the adoption of a suitable, optimal tariff policy in the original Bhagwati case, or the adoption of a suitable factor-use tax-cum-subsidy policy in the case involving a distortionary wage differential) will eliminate the possibility of immiserizing growth altogether: immiserizing growth can occur only insofar as there is a loss involved in departing from full optimality *and* insofar as such a loss *increases* in the post-growth situation.

II. *Exogenous Reduction in Gains from Trade and Immiserizing Growth*

Consider, however, the case where growth in one country is simultaneously accompanied by growth elsewhere (i.e. the rest of the world). As soon as we change the scenario thus, we are landed with the distinct, and quite unparadoxical, possibility that the primary gain from growth, defined at an *unchanged* foreign offer curve facing one country, and, assuming that optimal policies are followed in the pre-growth and post-growth situations, would be outweighed by the reduction in gain from trade brought about by the *shift* in the foreign offer curve facing the country (resulting from growth abroad). It is clear in such an eventuality that the resulting immiseration accrues really from the fact of an *exogenous* reduction in the gains from trade, obtaining despite the pursuit of optimal policies.

Such a possibility is illustrated most simply with respect to a country with neither monopoly power in trade nor domestic distortions. Remember that, for such a country, free trade is clearly the optimal policy. In Figure 1, the pre-growth situation is depicted by the production possibility curve A_1B_1, the free-trade production and consumption levels by P_1 and C_1, respectively, the given foreign price by F_1, and the welfare level by U_1. If growth were to take place at a *constant* foreign offer (i.e. at constant F_1), then the optimal free-trade policy will imply improvement in welfare at hypothetical level U_H, the post-growth production possibility curve being A_2B_2. However, if we now also assume that the foreign offer curve shifts from F_1 to F_2, production and consumption in the post-growth equilibrium will shift to P_2 and C_2, respectively, and the welfare level will reduce to U_1.[4] The gains from trade will have re-

[3] Augustine Tan [6] has produced an alternative analysis of this case, subsequent to Johnson's paper.

[4] This example would be relevant if the rest-of-the-world was a Ricardian economy and its production pos-

duced to wipe out the primary gain from growth (at an unchanged foreign offer curve). This is the borderline case. If the foreign offer had deteriorated any further, the post-growth equilibrium would have shown immiseration.

This analysis could be readily extended to the case where a country has monopoly power in trade in both the pre-growth and post-growth situations. Immiserizing growth for a country would occur, in this instance, if the primary gain in growth, at *unchanged* foreign offer curve and assuming optimal policies before and after growth, were outweighed by the reduction in the gains from trade resulting from a *shift* in the foreign offer curve.[5] This could be illustrated simply by the use of the Baldwin-envelope technique.

The following observations may then be made about this class of immiserizing growth possibilities.

(1) Since the primary cause of the immiseration is the reduction in the gains from trade resulting from shifts in the foreign offer curve facing the country, even though optimal policies are being followed before and after growth, there is no possibility of devising policies to escape such immiseration. By contrast, the earlier class of immiserizing growth possibilities (Section I) arose precisely from the failure to pursue optimal policies and hence optimal policies could eliminate the immiserizing-growth paradox.

(2) It also follows that any number of such immiseration possibilities could be devised: aside from Melvin's example, we have another case in Figure 1. The required shift in the foreign offer curve may further be brought about by shifts in demand or in production abroad. While, therefore, demand differences play a key role in Melvin's specific example, they are not central to the argument leading to immiserizing growth in this general class of cases.

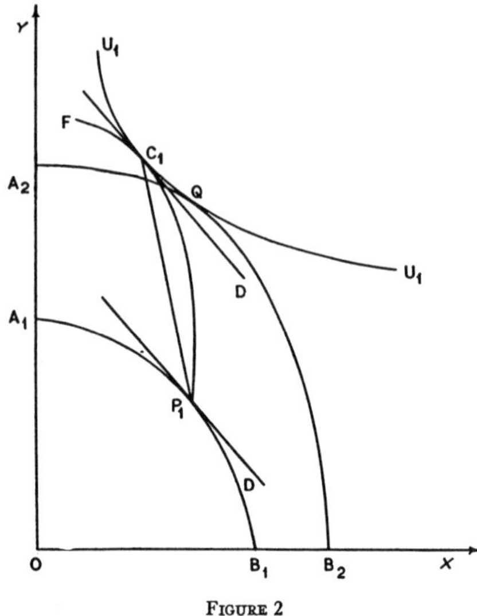

FIGURE 2

(3) The possibility of immiseration would obtain in this class, even if we were to assume that the pre-growth situation was characterised by sub-optimality. In such a case, the reduction in the gains from trade, required to produce immiseration, would merely have to be larger than in the case where the initial pre-growth situation is optimal and hence characterised by a higher welfare level. Melvin's example relates to this kind of comparison: free trade, which is sub-optimal in view of monopoly power in trade, before growth; and an optimal policy after growth. In principle, one could also compare sub-optimal policies both before and after growth and equally well emerge with immiseration.

(4) Finally, note that growth can be immiserizing only insofar as the primary gain from growth is outweighed by the (exogenously) reduced gains from trade. Two corollaries follow immediately. (i) A shift in the foreign offer curve, which increases the gains from trade, cannot lead to immiseration. (ii) The primary gain from growth itself may

sibility curve shifted outwards with bias in favour of the importable commodity. We would further have to assume that our country was operating on the straight line segment of the foreign offer curve from the rest-of-the-world.

[5] The reduction in the gains from trade would have to be measured after the imposition of an optimal tariff relevant to the shifted, foreign offer curve.

be large enough to exceed and dominate the maximum feasible (exogenous) reduction in the gains from trade, thus ruling out immiseration altogether. This is illustrated, for a country with monopoly power in trade, in Figure 2. Before trade, the production possibility curve is A_1B_1. The foreign offer curve facing the country is P_1C_1F and is superimposed on A_1B_1 using Baldwin's technique [1]. Note that the origin of the foreign offer curve now is P_1 (and the offer curve is effectively in the left-hand or fourth quadrant). Figure 2 portrays an optimum tariff policy, with consumption at tariff-inclusive prices at C_1. The resulting welfare level is marked U_1. If then growth were to shift the production possibility curve out to A_2B_2, making it tangential at Q to the pre-growth utility curve, it would be impossible for the country to become worse off than before growth. Indeed, unless gains from trade were to be reduced to zero, the country would become better off than before growth. The possibility of immiserizing growth therefore will arise only insofar as growth is less than that defined by the shift of the production possibility curve to A_2B_2: this is the growth level which implies a primary gain from growth equal to the gains from trade before growth.

References

[1] R. E. Baldwin, "The New Welfare Economics and Gains in International Trade," *Quart. J. Econ.* Feb. 1952, *66*, 91–101.

[2] J. Bhagwati, "Immiserizing Growth: A Geometric Note," *Rev. Econ. Stud.*, June 1958, *25*, 201–5.

[3] ———, "Distortions and Immiserizing Growth: A Generalization," *Rev. Econ. Stud.*, Oct. 1968, *35*, 481–85.

[4] H. G. Johnson, "The Possibility of Income Losses from Increased Efficiency or Factor Accumulation in the Presence of Tariffs," *Econ. J.*, Mar. 1967, *77*, 151–54.

[5] J. R. Melvin, "Demand Conditions and Immiserizing Growth," *Amer. Econ. Rev.*, Sept. 1969, *59*, 604–6.

[6] A. H. Tan, "Immiserizing Tariff-Induced Capital Accumulation and Technical Change," *Malayan Econ. Rev.*, forthcoming.

Immiserizing Growth and Negative Shadow Factor Prices: A Comment on Aumann and Peleg

In Aumann and Peleg (1974, p. 209) the following is stated (my italics): "David Gale (1974) constructs an example of a pure exchange economy with 3 traders in which two of the traders, by exchanging goods among themselves only, can affect prices in the entire economy in such a way so that *both* will benefit (and so necessarily, the third trader will lose). . . . In this note, we discuss a *related phenomenon which at first glance is even more striking* but which is even simpler to prove. In a 2-trader, 2-commodity market, *it is possible for a trader simply to discard some of his initial bundle and to gain from this act*—at the expense of the other trader of course."

It should interest readers to know that the (italicized) proposition advanced by Aumann and Peleg was proved in a more general fashion in Bhagwati (1958) in the *Review of Economic Studies* and is known among economic theorists as a theorem on immiserizing growth. Bhagwati (1958) demonstrated that augmentation of resources or technical change could immiserize a country—and therefore, of course, symmetrically a loss of resources could benefit a country—in free trade because the growth-induced deterioration in the terms of trade could outweigh the primary gain from the growth. Bhagwati (1958) established the conditions for such an outcome *and* showed that the paradox of immiserizing growth was compatible with Walras stability—a matter not investigated by Aumann and Peleg explicitly.[1]

The underlying rationale for this paradox has been developed as the *general theory,* of immiserizing growth in Bhagwati (1968). It is shown there that growth *in the presence of a distortion* can be immiserizing. For the loss imposed by a distortion may be accentuated in the post-growth situation. In the Bhagwati (1958) example and the subsequent Aumann-Peleg (1974) example, the distortion is simply the failure to exercise the economic agent's monopoly power; free trade is *not* an optimal policy when the terms of trade are not fixed.

Trade theorists have considered many such examples of immiserizing growth. For example, Johnson (1967) has shown how growth may be immiserizing for a "small" country with fixed terms of trade but a "distortionary" tariff in place.

Finally, the "dual" counterpart of immiserizing growth is the concept of "negative shadow factor prices," developed in Srinivasan and Bhagwati (1978) and Bhagwati, Srinivasan, and Wan (1978). This concept has been widely used in trade-theoretic and public-finance-theoretic literature and applies to "highly distorted" situations where the withdrawal of resources (as in Aumann-Peleg) from "productive" use leads to welfare improvement rather than to welfare loss.[2]

I am thankful to Kenneth Arrow for drawing my attention to the Aumann-Peleg paper. Arrow's unfamiliarity with the theory of immiserizing growth, as also the evident lack of such familiarity on the part of many mathematical economists, suggested the necessity of writing this brief note. Research support by the National Science Foundation is acknowledged.

1. Besides, Aumann and Peleg use an exchange model, whereas Bhagwati allows for substitution in both production and consumption.

2. I do not go here into Gale's (1974) proposition, which involves more than two agents. That "transfer problem" has been independently analyzed, with focus on the immiserization of the transferee consistent with Walras stability (as always specified), in Brecher and Bhagwati (1981). The three-agent analysis, and its paradoxes, do have a functional relation to the theory of immiserizing growth; this is the subject of a major paper by Bhagwati, Brecher, and Hatta (1982).

References

Aumann, R.J., and B. Peleg, 1974, "A Note on Gale's Example," *Journal of Mathematical Economics* 1: 209–211.

Bhagwati, Jagdish N., 1958, "Immiserizing Growth: A Geometrical Note," *Review of Economic Studies* 25: 201–205.

Bhagwati, Jagdish N., 1968, "Distortions and Immiserizing Growth: A Generalization," *Review of Economic Studies* 35: 481–485.

Bhagwati, Jagdish N., Richard Brecher, and Tatsuo Hatta, 1982, "The Generalized Theory of Transfers and Welfare," *American Economic Review* (1983).

Bhagwati, Jagdish N., T. N. Srinivasan, and Henry Wan, Jr., 1978, "Value Subtracted, Negative Shadow Prices of Factors in Project Evaluation, and Immiserizing Growth: Three Paradoxes in the Presence of Trade Distortions," *Economic Journal* 88: 121–125.

Brecher, Richard, and Jagdish N. Bhagwati, 1981, "Foreign Ownership and the Theory of Trade and Welfare," *Journal of Political Economy* 89 (3): 497–511.

Gale, David, 1974, "Exchange Equilibrium and Coalitions: An Example," *Journal of Mathematical Economics* 1: 63–66.

Johnson, Harry G., 1967, "The Possibility of Income Losses from Increased Efficiency or Factor Accumulation in the Presence of Tariffs," *Economic Journal* 77: 151–154.

Srinivasan, T. N., and Jagdish N. Bhagwati, 1978, "Shadow Prices for Project Selection in the Presence of Distortions: Effective Rates of Protection and Domestic Resource Costs," *Journal of Political Economy* 86 (2): 97–116.

Editor's Note

The relation between contributions to the theory of immiserizing growth in the mathematical-economic literature [stemming from Aumann and Peleg's (1974) note] and in the trade-theoretic literature [stemming from Bhagwati (1958), essay 4 in this volume], has been explored in J. N. Bhagwati, R. A. Brecher, and T. Hatta, "A Tale of Two Literatures: The Paradoxes of Immiserizing Growth, Immiserized Transfer-Recipient and Enriched Transfer-Donor," November 1982 (manuscript).

TRADE AND WELFARE IN A STEADY STATE*

T. N. SRINIVASAN and JAGDISH N. BHAGWATI

1. Introduction

The question of deadweight loss from free trade in growing economies has been raised in recent theoretical literature largely because of several demonstrations (by Bertrand (1975), Deardorff (1973), Johnson (1971, 1972), Smith (1976, 1977, 1979), Stiglitz (1970) and Togan (1975)) that shift from autarky to free trade, in the presence of constant savings ratios, could lower the per capita steady state consumption permanently.

There are really two quite different points involved here. If one considers an arbitrarily-fixed savings ratio, and then compares free trade with autarky by reference to an explicit intertemporal social utility function, it should be obvious to anyone tutored in the theory of trade and welfare that free trade may be dominated by autarky: since the savings ratio is not allowed to be determined optimally, we have here a case of a growing economy subject to a "domestic" distortion and hence free trade may well be immiserizing.[1]

* The views expressed in this paper are personal and not necessarily those of the institutions to which we are affiliated. Thanks are due to the National Science Foundation (Grants No. SOC77-07188 and SOC79-07541) for supporting Bhagwati's research on this paper. The comments of Alan Deardorff and Alasdair Smith on an earlier draft are gratefully acknowledged. Since Egon Sohmen's major work was in international economics and his last major interest was in welfare economics, we hope this paper is a fitting tribute to his memory since it spans both these fields.

[1] That savings may not be subject to fiscal policy and hence may be market-share-determined, resulting in a second-best choice of technique, has been noted also in the developmental-planning literature by Bator, Eckstein, Galenson-Leibenstein, Sen and others. In trade-theoretic literature, we should include the recent papers on the effect of transition to free trade on the savings rate, as determined by market-determined shares in income of two factors of production; see Pattanaik (1974) and Okuguchi (1977). The general proposition that free trade may be immiserizing in the presence of distortions has been known since Haberler (1950) and its relationship to the theory of immiserizing growth is formally demonstrated in Bhagwati (1971).

Flexible Exchange Rates and the Balance of Payments, edited by John S. Chipman and Charles P. Kindleberger

Suppose however that the savings rate is not so pre-fixed but can be chosen optimally. If then we are considering steady states, under free trade and under autarky, for a small open economy, could we argue that there could be a deadweight loss under free trade? Recent writings on *Unequal Exchange* by Emmanuel (1972) and, more directly on the subject, by Mainwaring (1974, 1976, 1977) and Metcalfe-Steedman (1974), suggest that they do contend this to be the case. This would appear to be an invalid claim; and indeed it is so.

Samuelson (1975) has addressed this issue, utilizing a neo-Ricardian time-phased model, and developed a number of interesting propositions relevant to such a model. From the perspective of our present interest, however, he demonstrates three propositions of special interest: (i) the transition from a zero-profit to a cum-profit equilibrium steady state can be attended by trade-pattern reversal; (ii) a cum-profit steady state could imply that "*every person* could end up consuming less until the end of time than he might consume in the zero-profit steady state" (p. 310); and (iii) "even though a cum-profit equilibrium involves *permanently* less of *all* goods than in a zero-profit equilibrium, that does not necessarily imply that the cum-profit equilibrium is non-Pareto-optimal (Pareto-inefficient), for the reason that . . . in going from the cum-profit to the zero-profit steady-state equilibrium, we must traverse a *transient*, non-steady-state path, which may *necessarily involve worsening the consumption of some periods in tradeoff for bettering the consumptions of some later periods*" (page 310).[2]

We now proceed to establish these important results for the Heckscher–Ohlin–Samuelson (HOS) model of trade theory, essentially demonstrating that the Samuelson time-phased model is *not* essential to obtain these results. Moreover, since the Samuelson paper, already a classic in view of its careful treatment of the recent "radical" critiques of the case for free trade, is exceptionally difficult to master, a demonstration of his results in a more familiar trade-theoretic model ought to have a definite pedagogic value. We should also add that our analysis will overlap, at many points, the valuable contributions of many of the authors cited earlier; however, its major thrust, organization and insights are substantially different in view of its being designed to investigate the robustness of the Samuelson results in the HOS model.[3]

2. Optimal growth under autarky

Let us begin with the two-sector optimal growth problem under autarky. The objective is to maximize $\int_0^\infty e^{-\rho t}u(c_t)\,dt$ where $u(c_t)$ is the utility of per capita consumption at time t and $\rho > 0$ is the pure rate of time preference. Population

[2] For "may," read "will."

[3] In addition, our analysis differs from the earlier analysis in its characterization of the steady states.

is assumed to grow at a constant exponential rate $n > 0$ and labor force is assumed to be the same as population, so that per capita values of variables are equivalent to the values of the same variables per unit of labor force. Initial labor force is set at unity by choice of units.

Since our interest is mainly in steady states, let us immediately note that in such a state of balanced growth all the relevant variables (consumption, capital stock in the aggregate as well as in each sector, employment in each sector) grow at the same rate as population. As such we can write:

$$c = l_C f_C(k_C) \tag{1}$$

$$nk = (1 - l_C) f_I(k_I) \tag{2}$$

$$l_C k_C + (1 - l_C) k_I = k \tag{3}$$

where $f_i(k_i)$ $(i = C, I)$ represent the average product of labor in the production of good i with capital-labor ratio being k_i, and l_i is the proportion of labor force employed in sector i.[4] The three equations state respectively that (1) per capita consumption equals per capita output of consumer goods; (2) the gross investment needed to maintain the aggregate capital-labor ratio at k equals the output of investment goods per capita;[5] (3) and the aggregate capital-labor ratio is the weighted average of the sectoral ratios, the weights being the sectoral employment proportions.

Equations (1)–(3) hold for any steady state and they involve five unknowns: (c, l_C, k_C, k, k_I). However, since a necessary condition of optimality is static efficiency in production, the marginal rate of factor substitution in production must be the same in the two sectors. That is,

$$(f_I - k_I f_I')/f_I' = (f_C - k_C f_C')/f_C'. \tag{4}$$

Finally, intertemporal optimization (i.e., maximization of the utility integral) implies that the rate of change of marginal utility of consumption at any t equals the difference between $n + \rho$ and the own rate of interest on capital, i.e.,

$$\frac{d}{dt} u'(c) = n + p - f_I'. \tag{5}$$

Since, in a steady state, c is constant, we can further write (5) as:

$$f_I'(k_I) = n + \rho. \tag{5'}$$

If we assume now that the Inada conditions hold, (5′) determines k_I uniquely. Given k_I (4) determines k_C uniquely. Then (2) and (3) together determine l_C and k uniquely. Finally (1) determines c uniquely.

Now, it is well known that an optimal path can be shown to exist (starting

[4] We are assuming constant-returns-to-scale production functions with strictly concave average-product functions, f_i.

[5] We use the phrases "investment goods" and "capital goods" interchangeably in this paper.

from any initial capital endowment) that converges to the above steady state, as long as the consumer-goods sector is capital-intensive relative to the capital-goods sector at all factor-price ratios. Even without this capital-intensity condition, alternative sufficient conditions for such convergence are also known. (See Drandakis (1963), Haque (1970), Srinivasan (1964) and Uzawa (1963, 1964) for analyses of equilibrium as well as optimal growth in a two-sector model.) However, because our interest is limited to steady states, we will not go further into the convergence issue here and will proceed instead with the steady-state analysis.

Let us then denote the steady-state values of the variables from now on with an asterisk and a superscript A to denote autarky. It can be shown, using (1)–(5), that c^{*A} reaches a maximum at $\rho = 0$. That $\rho = 0$ corresponds to the so-called "Golden Rule" steady state is then seen as follows. With the price of consumption goods in terms of investment goods defined as $p^{*A} \equiv f_I'/f_C'$, the share of investment goods in national income is

$$\frac{(1 - l_C^{*A})f_I}{p^{*A}l_C^{*A}f_C + (1 - l_C^{*A})f_I}$$

and the competitive share of profits in income is

$$\frac{k^{*A}f_I'}{p^{*A}l_C^{*A}f_C + (1 - l_C^{*A})f_I}.$$

The ratio of the former to the latter, given (1)–(5), is then $(n + \rho)/n$ and therefore exceeds unity for $\rho > 0$, $n > 0$. Thus, at $\rho = 0$, this ratio becomes unity so that the profit share and the investment share become equal, thus establishing that $\rho = 0$ results in the "Golden Rule" steady state.[6]

It is seen that in this model, the profit rate is the same as the own rate of return to capital; and this equals $f_1'(k_I) = n + \rho$, as stated in (5′). Now, Samuelson (1975) did not consider population growth. Thus for his model $n = 0$ and hence the profit rate of his model could be identified with ρ. Hence, $\rho = 0$ corresponds to the zero-profit steady state and $\rho > 0$ to the cum-profit steady state. The equivalence of our neoclassical model results to his neo-Ricardian model results should then become transparent.

It is also clear that moving from a steady state with $\rho = \rho_1 > 0$ to a steady state with $\rho = \rho_2 > \rho_1$ involves a loss in steady-state consumption. But clearly this is no deadweight loss. For suppose the economy is in a steady state corresponding to $\rho = \rho_1$, and now ρ is increased to ρ_2. Given the fact that the

[6] Since the utility integral as stated does not have a maximum for $\rho \leqslant 0$, the steady state for $\rho = 0$ is the path to which an optimal path under the "overtaking" criterion will converge, again under suitable sufficient conditions. (See Weizsäcker (1965) for definition of the "overtaking" criterion.)

economy now maximizes a utility integral with $\rho = \rho_2$ and an initial capital endowment corresponding to a steady state with $\rho = \rho_1$, the new *optimal* path that converges to a steady state with $\rho = \rho_2$ is intertemporally efficient while the steady-state path with $\rho = \rho_1$ continues to be feasible. As such, even though the asymptotic (or steady-state) per capita consumption associated with the optimal path with $\rho = \rho_2$ is less than that along the feasible steady-state path with $\rho = \rho_1$, the fact of intertemporal efficiency that follows from optimality ensures that the asymptotic loss in per capita consumption must have been more than offset by larger consumption earlier on.

Finally, an interesting characterization of steady states is obtained by deriving the labor cost of producing a unit of consumer good (p_C) and a unit of capital good (p_I) in any steady state (i.e., constant k_C and k_I), and then observing that the optimal steady state is one in which these socially necessary labor costs, labor being the only primary input in the system, are minimized. In other words, given k_C, k_I and the profit rate $n + \rho$, clearly

$$p_C = \frac{1}{f_C(k_C)} + \frac{k_C p_I (n + p)}{f_C(k_C)},$$

the first term representing the direct labor per unit of output of consumer goods and the second term representing capital (or indirect or congealed-labor) costs. The second term is seen to be the product of the value of capital per unit of output i.e., $p_I k_C / f_C(k_C)$ times the profit rate. Similarly

$$p_I = \frac{1}{f_I(k_I)} + \frac{k_I p_I}{f_I(k_I)}(n + \rho).$$

The value of k_I that minimizes p_I is given by $f_I'(k_I^*) = n + \rho$, and the value of k_C that minimizes p_C, given $k_I = k_I^*$, is given by

$$\frac{f_C}{f_C'} - k_C^* = \frac{f_I}{f_I'} - k_I^*:$$

thus proving our assertion.

3. Optimal growth under free trade

Consider now the same intertemporal optimization model in the context of free trade at given international price p^{*T} of the consumer good in terms of the capital good.

It is clear that as long as the country has no influence over p^{*T}, in the optimization exercise the production choice (i.e., the pattern of production at any time point) could be determined by maximizing income, i.e., the value of output given p^{*T}. The consumption choice then becomes one of determining the optimum savings (and investment) out of this income. Thus the two-sector optimization problem collapses into a one-sector one, in which the income per capita $g(k)$ is first determined by maximizing $p^{*T}l_C f_C + (1 - l_C)f_I$ subject to $l_C k_C + (1 - l_C)k_I = k$. Then, with $g(k)$ as the "production" function, the utility integral $\int_0^\infty e^{-\rho t}u(c_t)\,dt$ is maximized subject to

$$\dot{k} = g(k) - p^{*T}c - nk \qquad (k_0 \text{ given}) \tag{6}$$

Now, the maximization that leads to $g(k)$, given p^{*T}, has the following simple solution. Assume $k_C \geqslant k_I$ for all wage-rental ratios. Then there exist $(\underline{k}, \bar{k})$ such that the economy specializes in the production of the capital good if $k \leqslant \underline{k}$ so that $g(k) = f_I(k)$ for $k \leqslant \underline{k}$. For $\underline{k} < k < \bar{k}$, the economy is incompletely specialized with

$$g(k) = p^{*T}l_C f_C(\bar{k}) + (1 - l_C)f_I(\underline{k}) \tag{7}$$

and

$$k = l_C\bar{k} + (1 - l_C)\underline{k}. \tag{8}$$

For $k \geqslant \bar{k}$, the economy is specialized in the production of the consumption good with $g(k) = p^{*T}f_C(k)$. The values of $\underline{k}$ and $\bar{k}$ are determined by:

$$p^{*T} = \frac{f_I'(\underline{k})}{f_C'(\bar{k})} \qquad \text{and} \qquad (f_C - \bar{k}f_C')/f_C' = (f_I - \underline{k}f_I')/f_I'. \tag{9}$$

Analogous regions of specialization can be derived if $k_C < k_I$.

It is clear that $g(k)$ is an increasing function of k and strictly concave for values of k outside $(\underline{k}, \bar{k})$. Within this region of incomplete specialization, $g(k)$ is linear in k with $g'(k) = f_I'(\underline{k})$.

Turning now to the determination of the optimum consumption path, starting from k_0, it is known from one-sector optimal growth theory (see Koopmans, 1966) that this path converges to a steady state with $k = k^{*T}$ given by $g'(k^{*T}) = n + \rho$. Now (for the case $k_C > k_I$), as long as $f_I'(\underline{k}) \neq n + \rho$, such a k^* is unique. Thus, if $f_I'(\underline{k}) > (<) n + \rho$, an economy starting from *any* k_0 will converge to a steady state with $k^* > \bar{k}(k^* < \underline{k})$ in which it specializes in the production of the consumption (capital) good.

If $f_I'(\underline{k}) = n + \rho$, any k^{*T} in $(\underline{k}, \bar{k})$ could be a steady-state capital stock and the dynamic behavior of the economy depends on the initial capital stock. If $k_0 \leqslant \underline{k}(\geqslant \bar{k})$ it converges to a steady state with $k^{*T} = \underline{k}(\bar{k})$. If $\underline{k} < k_0 < \bar{k}$, it remains in the steady state with $k = k_0$. The modifications in this analysis for $k_C < k_I$ are straightforward.

We saw earlier in (5′) that the steady state to which the optimal path under autarky converges[7] is characterized by $f_I' = n + \rho$. We noted above that *incomplete specialization* under free trade in a steady state can occur only if $f_I'(\underline{k}) = n + \rho$ and $\underline{k} < k_0 < \bar{k}$. The first of these conditions implies that the free-trade price of the consumer good p^{*T} equals its autarky price. It is, therefore, not a very interesting case.

Now, specialization in the steady state in the consumption (capital) good under free trade implies that:

$$f_I'(\underline{k}) > (<)(n + \rho). \tag{10}$$

This inequality implies that k^{*A}_I (the autarky steady-state value of k_I) is greater (less) than $\underline{k}$. Since both pairs $(\underline{k}, \bar{k})$, (k^{*A}_I, k^{*A}_C) are such that the marginal rates of factor substitution are the same in the production of either good, this in turn means, given our assumption that $k_C > k_I$ for all wage-rental ratios, that:

$$p^{*T} = \frac{f_I'(\underline{k})}{f_C'(\bar{k})} > (<) \frac{f_I'(k^{*A}_I)}{f_C'(k^{*A}_C)} \equiv p^{*A}$$

$$= \text{the autarky price of the consumer good.} \tag{11}$$

The modifications for the case where $k_I > k_C$ are straightforward. Thus, given an international price for the consumer good that exceeds its autarky price, the economy will specialize in the production of the consumer good in the steady state and export part of the output to import the needed investment goods. Similarly it can be shown that if the international price of the consumer good is less than its autarky price, the economy will specialize in the production of the investment good in the steady state.

It can be seen again that when the economy specializes in either good, the total labor cost (direct and indirect) of producing a unit thereof is indeed minimized. Thus, consider the case of specialization in the consumption good and let p_L^C and p_L^I denote the direct and indirect labor cost, indirect labor being charged interest at the profit rate $n + \rho$. Then, by definition, using the fact that a unit of imported investment good costs $1/p^{*T}$ in terms of consumption-good exports, we get:

$$f_C(k_C)p_L^C = 1 + k_C(n + \rho)p_L^C/p^{*T} \quad \text{and} \quad p_L^I = p_L^C/p^{*T}. \tag{12}$$

Solving for p_L^C, we get

$$p_L^C = \frac{1}{f_C(k_C) - k_C(n + \rho)/p^{*T}},$$

[7] We noted earlier that convergence in the autarky case requires some additional assumptions (one sufficient condition is that $k_C > k_I$ for all wage-rental ratios). But, this is not necessary in the free-trade case since it is reduced to a one-sector optimization problem.

and this is minimized by setting $p^{*T}f'_C(k_C^{*T}) = n + \rho$. From the fact that the autarky price of the consumption good is less than p^{*T}, it can be shown that p_L^I will be less than its minimal domestic cost of production $1/[f_I(k_I^*) - (n + \rho) k_I^*]$.

Before we proceed to a discussion of the effect of changes in ρ, let us briefly note that the fact that the economy is (except in the case when the autarky price ratio equals the international price ratio) specialized in the steady state (to which it converges) does not mean that it will be specialized, or even that it will be specialized in the same good as in the steady state, throughout its time path. The actual pattern of specialization, complete or incomplete, will depend on the initial capital-labor ratio as well as its time path.[8]

4. Variations in ρ : Trade-pattern reversals

Let us now turn to variations in ρ. For simplicity, let us assume first that the capital good is capital-intensive at all factor-price ratios. In Figure 1, in the first quadrant, the curves $k_C(w)$, $k_I(w)$ are obtained by equating the marginal rate of substitution of labor and capital $f_i - k_i f_i'/f_i'$ $(i = C, I)$ to the wage-rental ratio w. In the second quadrant, the marginal-product-of-capital curve for the capital-good industry is plotted. In the fourth quadrant, the relative cost of production of the consumption good in terms of the capital good (i.e., f_I'/f_C') is plotted as a function of the wage-rental ratio w. The autarky steady state is easily shown in this diagram. Given ρ, say ρ^1, we read from the second quadrant the autarky steady-state capital-labor ratio k_I^{*1} by equating f_I' to $n + \rho^1$. Given k_I^{*1}, we read from the first quadrant the corresponding values of w_1 and k_C^{*1}. Given w_1, we read from the fourth quadrant the autarky price p^{*1}. Given the capital-intensity assumption, that $k_C(w) < k_I(w)$ for all w, p^* decreases as ρ increases.

Then, start from a $\rho(=\rho^1)$ such that $p^{*1} > p^{*T}$ so that the economy specializes in investment goods under free trade, given the international price ratio p^{*T}. Now let ρ increase to ρ^2 while the international price ratio p^{*T} is constant. Since the autarky price p^* decreases as ρ increases, it may soon equal p^{*T} and then become less than p^{*T}. As it does so, under free trade the economy passes from specialization in the production of the capital good at ρ^1 to incomplete specialization at ρ^T and then to specialization in the consumption good at ρ^2. Thus the pattern of specialization can get reversed as ρ increases!

[8] The results that the economy is specialized and that direct and indirect labor costs per unit of output are minimized are the consequences of the fact that the neoclassical economy with a single exponentially growing primary factor, is equivalent in a steady state to a static Ricardian economy to which nonsubstitution theorems, etc., apply.

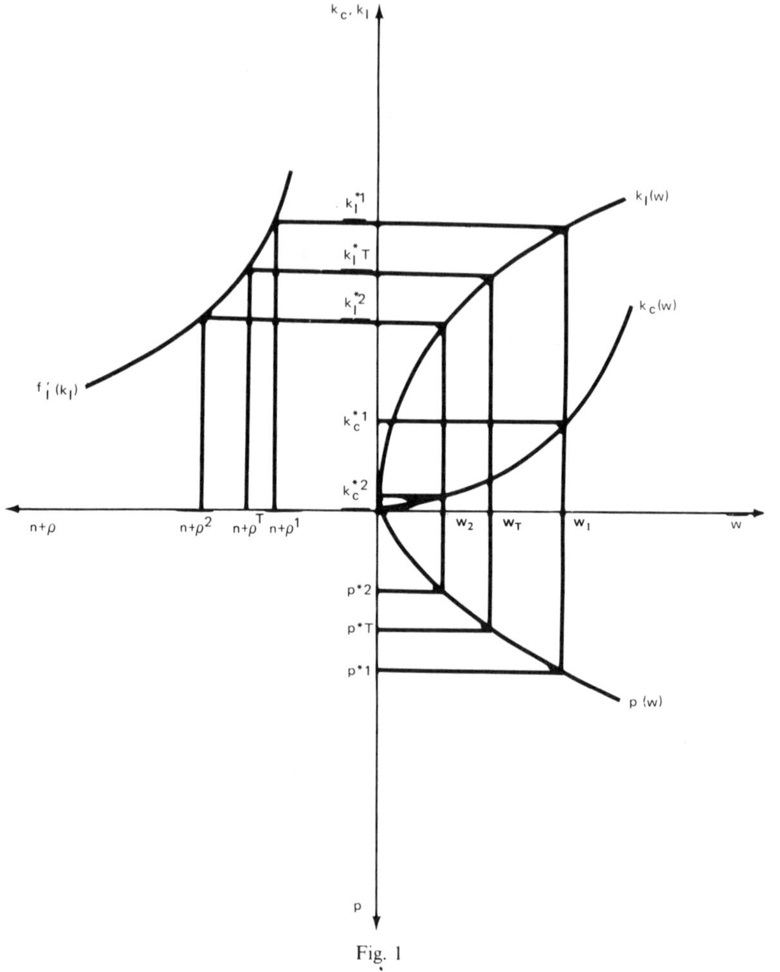

Fig. 1

But regardless of the pattern of specialization, the steady-state per capita consumption c^{*T} [which equals $[f_I(k_I^{*T}) - n\ k_I^{*T}]/p^{*T}$ if the economy is specialized in the capital good and $[p^{*T}f_C(k_C{}^{*T}) - n\ k_C^{*T}]/p^{*T}$ if the economy is specialized in the consumption good] *always* decreases as ρ increases. But, we may re-emphasize, this does *not* mean that there is any deadweight loss. Since the time path that maximizes the utility integral given each ρ is intertemporally efficient, moving from one value of ρ to another cannot involve a deadweight loss, even though the steady-state per capita consumption associated with a given ρ is less than that associated with a smaller ρ.

5. Free trade versus autarky: deadweight loss et al.

We noted above that moving from one value of ρ (say, zero) to a higher value of ρ (say a positive value) will involve a loss in steady-state per capita consumption, be it under autarky or under free trade. In addition, under free trade such a movement may also involve the reversal of the steady-state trade pattern. The final issue we now address is the implication of opening the economy to free trade with *unchanged* ρ from a steady state under autarky.

First consider the case when $\rho = 0$. It can be shown that the steady-state per capita consumption under free trade will always exceed (equal) that under autarky as long as the economy is completely (incompletely) specialized. Suppose the economy is specialized in the capital good. This implies that the free-trade *aggregate* capital-labor ratio (and, hence the capital-labor ratio in the production of the capital good) equals the capital-labor ratio in the production of the capital good under autarky. This is so because the own rate of interest on capital is the same value, n, in both cases. Thus we can denote by k_I^* this common capital-labor ratio; and it is given by $f_I'(k_I^*) = n$. Now the two steady-state consumptions are given by

$$c^{*T} = \frac{f_I(k_I^*) - nk_I^*}{p^{*T}} \tag{13}$$

and

$$c^{*A} = \frac{f_C(f_I(k_I^*) - nk_I^*)}{[f_I(k_I^*) - nk_I^* + nk_C]} = \frac{f_I(k_I^*) - nk_I^*}{p^{*A}}. \tag{14}$$

But specialization in the capital good under free trade implies $p^{*T} < p^{*A}$. Hence $c^{*T} > c^{*A}$.

The situation is more complex, however, for $\rho > 0$. Denote by $p^{*A}(\rho)$ the autarky price of the consumption good. Starting from $p^{*T} < p^{*A}(0)$ as above, by continuity of $p^{*A}(\rho)$ as a function of ρ, we know $p^{*T} < p^{*A}(\rho)$ in some neighborhood to the right of zero for ρ. In this neighborhood, the economy will continue to be specialized in the capital good under free trade and, as such, the aggregate capital-labor ratio $k^{*T}(\equiv k_I^{*T})$ under free trade will equal k_I^{*A} where $f_I'(k_I^{*A}) = n + \rho$. Denoting $k_I^{*A}(\rho)$ as $k_I^*(\rho)$, we then get:

$$c^{*T}(\rho) = \frac{f_I(k_I^*(\rho)) - nk_I^*(\rho)}{p^{*T}} \tag{15}$$

and

$$c^{*A}(\rho) = \frac{[f_I(k_I^*(\rho)) - nk_I^*(\rho)]f_C(k_C^*(\rho))}{f_I(k_I^*(\rho)) - nk_I^*(\rho) + nk_C^*(\rho)}. \tag{16}$$

It follows from (15)–(16) that Sign $c^{*T}(\rho) - c^{*A}(\rho) = \text{Sign } h(\rho)$, where

$$h(\rho) = f_I(k_I^*(\rho)) - nk_I^*(\rho) + nk_C^*(\rho) - p^{*T}f_C(k_C^*(\rho)). \tag{17}$$

As argued above, $h(0) = c^{*T}(0) - c^{*A}(0) > 0$. Differentiating $h(\rho)$ with respect to ρ in a neighborhood of 0 in which there is specialization in the capital good under free trade, we get:

$$h'(\rho) = (f_I' - n)\frac{dk_I^*}{d\rho} + (n - p^{*T}f_C')\frac{dk_C^*}{d\rho}. \tag{18}$$

Clearly,

$$\frac{dk_I^*}{d\rho} < 0, \qquad \frac{dk_C^*}{d\rho} < 0, \qquad (f_I' - n) = \rho > 0,$$

and

$$n - p^{*T}f_C' = \frac{np^{*A}(\rho) - (n + \rho)p^{*T}}{p^{*A}(\rho).}.$$

Now at $\rho = 0$, $n - p^{*T}f_C' > 0$ since by assumption $p^{*A}(0) > p^{*T}$; and hence from (18) it follows that: $h'(0) < 0$. Thus $h(\rho)$ decreases in a neighborhood of $\rho = 0$ from a positive value at $\rho = 0$. The question is whether it can decrease sufficiently to make $h(\rho)$ change sign at some positive ρ. There is nothing in our analysis to preclude this possibility. It is thus possible that, even though the steady-state consumption under free trade exceeds that under autarky for $\rho = 0$ (corresponding to the Samuelsonian zero-profit case), the autarky steady state may have higher per capita consumption for a positive ρ (corresponding to the cum-profit) situation, as illustrated in Figure 2.

It is important finally to realize that the above conclusion does not imply a deadweight loss in moving to free trade for the same reason that there is no deadweight loss in moving down either the free-trade or autarky curve in Figure 2. That is, starting from an autarky steady state with a given ρ, opening trade and then choosing an optimal path can eventually end up in per capita consumption being lower than what would have continued had the economy chosen to remain under autarky, as at $\hat{\rho}$ in Figure 2. But the very fact that such a free-trade steady state is an asymptote of an optimal path implies that along the optimal path (which, because of its optimality, is intertemporally efficient) consumption must have stayed above the autarky level for some length of time. Finally, it is easy to see from Figure 2 that, even if the two curves did *not* cross,

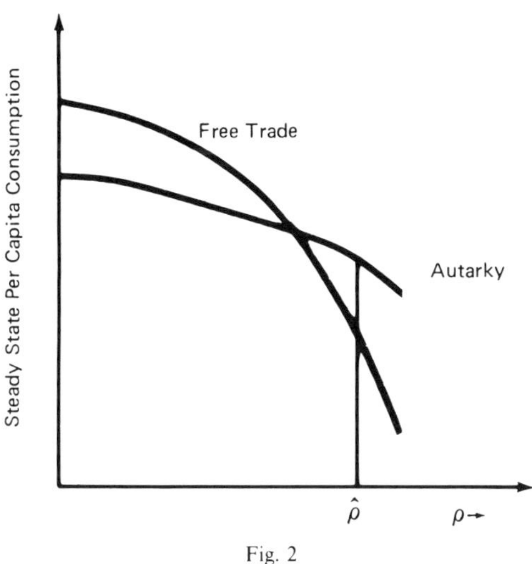

Fig. 2

it is possible that the autarky steady-state consumption for $\rho = 0$ may exceed the free-trade steady-state value for some $\rho > 0$. But, once again, this outcome does not imply that a deadweight loss characterizes the free-trade steady state with its lower per capita consumption.

References

Bertrand, Trent, 1975, "The Gains from Trade: Steady-State Solutions in an Open Economy," *Quarterly Journal of Economics* 89, November, 556–568.

Bhagwati, Jagdish, 1971, "The Generalized Theory of Distortions and Welfare." In Jagdish Bhagwati, Robert A. Mundell, Ronald W. Jones, and Jaroslav Vanek, eds., *Trade, Balance of Payments and Growth: Papers in International Economics in Honor of Charles P. Kindleberger* (Amsterdam: North-Holland), pp. 69–90.

Deardorff, Alan V., 1973, "The Gains from Trade in and out of Steady-State Growth," *Oxford Economic Papers*, N.S. 25, July, 173–191.

Deardorff, Alan V., 1974, "Trade Reversals and Growth Stability,"*Journal of International Economics* 4, April, 83–90.

Drandakis, Emanuel, 1963, "Factor Substitution in the Two-Sector Growth Model," *Review of Economic Studies* 30, October, 217–228.

Emmanuel, Arghiri, 1972, *Unequal Exchange: A Study of the Imperialism of Trade* (New York: Monthly Review Press).

Haberler, Gottfried, 1950, "Some Problems in the Pure Theory of International Trade," *Economic Journal* 60, June, 223–240.

Haque, Wahidul, 1970, "Skeptical Notes on Uzawa's Optimal Growth in a Two-Sector Model of Capital Accumulation, and a Precise Characterization of the Optimal Path,"*Review of Economic Studies* 37, July, 377–394.

Johnson, Harry G., 1971, "Trade and Growth: A Geometrical Exposition," *Journal of International Economics* 1, February, 83–102.

Johnson, Harry G., 1972, "Trade and Growth: A Correction," *Journal of International Economics* 2, February, 87–88.

Koopmans, Tjalling C., 1966, "On the Concept of Optimal Economic Growth." In *The Econometric Approach to Development Planning* (Amsterdam: North-Holland), pp. 225–287.

Mainwaring, Lynn, 1974 "A Neo-Ricardian Analysis of International Trade," *Kyklos* 27, Fasc. 3, 537–553.

Mainwaring, Lynn, 1976, "The Correction of Neo-Ricardian Trade Losses," *Economia Internazionale* 29, February–March, 92–99.

Mainwaring, Lynn, 1977, "Time Phased Systems and the Gain From Trade: Paradox Loss: Paradox Regained," mimeographed manuscript (Cardiff: University College, Department of Economics).

Metcalfe, John S., and Steedman, Ian, 1974, "A Note on the Gain from Trade," *Economic Record* 50, December, 581–595.

Okuguchi, Koji, 1977, "Trade, Savings and a Nontraded Good," *Journal of International Economics*, November, 379–384.

Pattanaik, Prasanta K., 1974, "Trade, Distribution and Saving," *Journal of International Economics* 4, April, 77–82.

Samuelson, Paul A.. 1975, "Trade Pattern Reversals in Time-Phased Ricardian Systems and Intertemporal Efficiency," *Journal of International Economics* 5, November, 309–364.

Smith, M. Alasdair M., 1976, "Trade, Growth and Consumption in Alternative Models of Capital Accumulation," *Journal of International Economics* 6, November, 385–388.

Smith, M. Alasdair M., 1977, "Capital Accumulation in the Open Two-Sector Economy, " *Economic Journal* 87, November, 273–282.

Smith, M. Alasdair M., 1979, "Intertemporal Gains from Trade," *Journal of International Economics* 9, May, 239–248.

Stiglitz, Joseph, 1970, "Factor Price Equalization in a Dynamic Economy," *Journal of Political Economy* 78, May–June, 456–488.

Srinivasan, T. N., 1964, "Optimal Savings in a Two-Sector Model of Growth," *Econometrica* 32, July, 358–373.

Togan, Sübidey, 1975, "The Gains from International Trade in the Context of a Growing Economy," *Journal of International Economics* 5, August, 229–238.

Uzawa, Hirofumi, 1961, "On a Two-Sector Model of Economic Growth, I," *Review of Economic Studies* 29, October, 40–47.

Uzawa, Hirofumi, 1963, " On a Two-Sector Model of Economic Growth, II," *Review of Economic Studies* 30, June, 105–118.

Uzawa, Hirofumi, 1964, "Optimal Growth in a Two-Sector Model of Capital Accumulation," *Review of Economic Studies* 31, January, 1–24.

Weizsäcker, C. Christian von, 1965, "Existence of Optimal Programs of Accumulation for an Infinite Time Horizon," *Review of Economic Studies* 32, April, 85–104.

III
TARIFFS, QUOTAS, AND SUBSIDIES

PROTECTION, REAL WAGES AND REAL INCOMES[1]

1. In a recent article in this Journal[2] on "Protection and Real Wages: A Restatement," Mr. Lancaster has re-examined the famous Stolper–Samuelson theorem and concluded:

> "This paper does not deny that protection will raise the real wage of one of the factors, but shows that no general statement about which of the factors this will be can be deduced from the relative 'scarcity' of the factors in the Stolper–Samuelson sense.
>
> "Although the Stolper–Samuelson theorem 'Protection raises the real wage of the scarce factor' is shown to be an incorrect generalisation, a restatement in the form 'Protection raises the real wage of the factor in which the imported good is relatively more intensive' has general validity."

It is proposed in Section I of this paper to review systematically the original Stolper–Samuelson contribution, therewith to advance a critique (distinct from Mr. Lancaster's criticism, which is not accepted), of the Stolper–Samuelson formulation of the theorem and then to restate the theorem: this restatement being considered to be the only true and general statement about the effect of protection (prohibitive or otherwise) on real wages of factors in the context of the basic Stolper–Samuelson model. The logical truth of the restated theorem is briefly analysed then in the context of alternative models. Section II proceeds to extend the scope of the discussion with the argument that, with a non-prohibitive tariff, a sharp distinction must be drawn between the impact on the real wage of a factor and the effect on its real income; some implications of this distinction are then analysed.

I. Protection and Real Wages

2. In the following analysis, we shall take the *basic* Stolper–Samuelson model to mean that the protecting country has two factors, two commodities enjoying different factor intensities, linear and homogeneous production functions subject to diminishing returns (along isoquants) and incomplete specialisation in production. Full employment of factors, pure competition and perfect mobility of factors are also assumed.

Founded on this model, we have three alternative formulations of the theorem concerning the impact of protection on the real wages of factors:

(1) *Restrictive Stolper–Samuelson Theorem.* "International trade necessarily lowers the real wage of the scarce factor expressed in terms of

[1] This paper was read to the Nuffield Economics Society. My thanks are due to Professor Hicks and J. Black for substantial help with the exposition of the paper. I am also happy to record my heavy indebtedness to Professor Harry Johnson, who has been generous with suggestions that have led to numerous improvements in the paper.

[2] Economic Journal, June 1957, pp. 199–210. The following quotation is from p. 199.

any good." [1] This formulation restricts itself to the comparison of the free-trade real wage with the self-sufficiency real wage of the scarce factor. The comparison is confined to the case of a prohibitive tariff and excludes non-prohibitive protection. The theorem can be re-written as follows: prohibitive protection necessarily raises the real wage of the scarce factor.

(2) *General Stolper–Samuelson Theorem.* Protection raises the real wage of the scarce factor.[2] This formulation is clearly intended to be more general and includes non-prohibitive tariffs as well. To emphasise this, we may rewrite it thus: protection (prohibitive or otherwise) necessarily raises the real wage of the scarce factor.

(3) *Stolper–Samuelson–Metzler–Lancaster Theorem.* "Protection [prohibitive or otherwise] raises the real wage of the factor in which the imported good is relatively more intensive." [3]

In the ensuing analysis any reference to "the Stolper–Samuelson theorems" should be taken to relate to the initial two formulations alone; reference to the last formulation will always be by its full title.

3. We can begin by setting out the basic elements in the argument leading to the twin formulations of the Stolper–Samuelson theorem:

(1) protection increases the internal relative price of the importable good:

(2) an increase in the relative price of a good increases the real wage of the factor used intensively in its production;

(3) the importable good is intensive in the use of the scarce factor.

Therefore,

(4) protection raises the real wage of the scarce factor.

These arguments must each be closely examined.

4. Concerning argument (1), we must distinguish between prohibitive and non-prohibitive protection:

(i) Protection will necessarily raise the relative price of the im-

[1] Stolper and Samuelson, "Protection and Real Wages," *Readings in the Theory of International Trade* (A.E.A., Blakiston Co., 1949), p. 346.

[2] The actual formulation of the general Stolper–Samuelson theorem is from Lancaster, *op. cit.*, p. 199. While the bulk of their analysis relates explicitly to the restrictive formulation, there are several indications that Stolper and Samuelson had in mind the general formulation as well: (1) a large number of quotations they cite from other authors to outline the problem refer to tariffs in general rather than to tariffs of a prohibitive nature alone; (2) they feel it necessary to assume that "the country in question is relatively small and has no influence on the terms of trade. Thus any gain to the country through monopolistic or monopsonistic behaviour is excluded" (*op. cit.*, p. 344); this assumption is quite superfluous, as we shall later see, if we wish to sustain only the restrictive formulation of the theorem; and (3) the title chosen for the article is not "International Trade and Real Wages" but "Protection and Real Wages." Lancaster, *op. cit.*, p. 201, also construes the Stolper–Samuelson theorem in its general form; thus witness his argument that "Protection will cause a movement in the *general direction* $Q'Q$, away from the free-trade point towards the self-sufficiency point" (my italics).

[3] Lancaster, *op. cit.*, p. 199. This theorem has been given its stated name on grounds which are made explicit later.

portable good when the tariff is prohibitive; the free-trade relative price of the importable good is lower than under self-sufficiency.[1]

(ii) Non-prohibitive protection may either raise, leave unchanged or lower the internal relative price of the importable good. Metzler has demonstrated that this last " perverse " possibility will occur, in the context of our present model, when the elasticity of foreign demand for imports (η_x) is less than the domestic marginal propensity to consume exportable goods (c).[2] It follows, then, that if imports are not inferior goods in the protecting country's consumption this case requires inelastic foreign demand; and we can ensure that the internal relative price of the importable good always rises with the imposition of a tariff by assuming *either* elastic foreign demand (sometimes done in the form of assuming a small country) *or* a big enough tariff (in the limit, a prohibitive tariff) for demand to be elastic.

5. Argument (2) follows necessarily from the basic Stolper–Samuelson model. To show this simply, we should recall the technological features of the model employed by Samuelson some years later in this JOURNAL[3] to demonstrate factor-price equalisation: these features are identical with those of the Stolper–Samuelson model in all respects. We propose thus to avoid altogether the use of the box-diagram and work instead with the unique relationships that Samuelson derived in these later articles between commodity price-ratios, factor price-ratios and factor proportions in the two industries in a country, from the given assumptions concerning technology alone. These are summarised in Fig. 1, which is reproduced, with slight changes, from Samuelson's 1949 article.[4]

Let L_C and L_F represent the labour employed in producing clothing and food respectively; T_C and T_F being the quantities of land so employed.

[1] This is true except in a *limiting* case where the terms of trade will not change with trade. This case, however, can be ruled out, in the context of the model used here, by assuming that the community indifference curves (used here without any welfare connotation) are strictly convex. This limiting case will henceforward be ignored.

[2] Metzler, " Tariffs, the Terms of Trade and the Distribution of National Income," *Journal of Political Economy*, February 1949, pp. 1–29. It should be emphasised that the Metzler formula for determining the impact of protection on the internal commodity price-ratio relates to the case where the initial situation is that of free-trade. Where, however, the initial situation itself has a tariff and the impact of *increased* protection is the subject of analysis, the " perverse " possibility mentioned in the text will occur, as argued in Section II, when a slightly altered condition is fulfilled. The discussion in Section I, however, is confined to initial situations of free trade, as with Stolper and Samuelson, Metzler and Lancaster.

[3] " International Trade and the Equalisation of Factor Prices," ECONOMIC JOURNAL, June 1948, pp. 163–84; and " International Factor-Price Equalisation Once Again," ECONOMIC JOURNAL, June 1949, pp. 181–97.

[4] This diagram is to be found on p. 188 of Samuelson's 1949 ECONOMIC JOURNAL article, *op. cit.* Full exploration of this diagram is to be found in an excellent article by Professor Johnson, " Factor Endowments, International Trade and Factor Prices," *Manchester School*, September 1957, pp. 270–83. Professor Johnson, however, works with a slightly adapted diagram, to be found in Harrod, " Factor-price Relations Under Free Trade," ECONOMIC JOURNAL, June 1958, pp. 245–55. On grounds of economy, the discussion of this well-known diagram has been kept brief in this paper.

W/R represents the ratio of wages to rents; L/T the factor endowment ratio of the country; and P_F/P_C the price of food over the price of clothing. Clothing is the labour-intensive industry, food the land-intensive industry, at all relevant factor price-ratios. ($L_C/T_C > L_F/T_F$ at all relevant W/R.)[1] As wages fall relatively to rents, the price of food is shown to rise relatively to that of clothing in a monotonic fashion. The factor endowment ratio of the country (L/T) fixes the range of the diagram which is relevant. This is a purely technology-determined diagram, and demand conditions are totally absent from it.

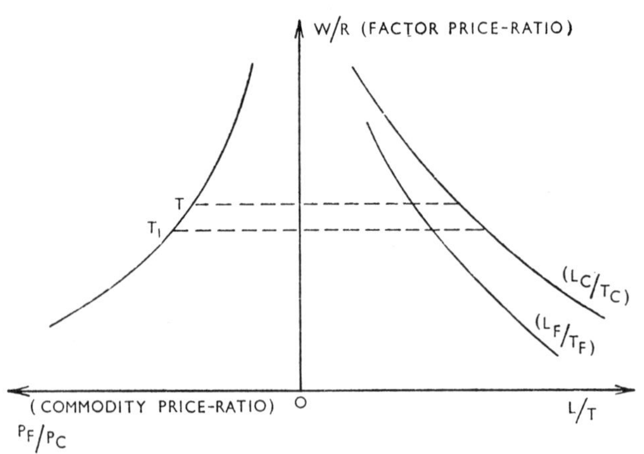

Fig. 1

T being any given commodity price-ratio (P_F/F_C), change it to T_1 such that the relative price of food rises. With it, the labour-to-land ratios in both food and clothing will rise. The marginal physical product of land in both products will thus rise and of labour fall, so that the real wage of land will be unambiguously increased and of labour decreased. Increase in the relative price of food thus increases the real wage of land, the factor intensively employed in its production; and reduces the real wage of labour, the factor intensively used in producing clothing (whose relative price has fallen).

This argument, it should be noted, rests on the assumption, part of the basic Stolper–Samuelson model, that the rise of the relative price of food does not go so far as to make the country specialise completely on food, in so far as the fall in the real wage of labour is concerned; for, once the country is specialised completely, further increases in the relative price of food will raise the real wage of *both* labour and land, which is destructive of the full validity of argument (2).

Given the basic Stolper–Samuelson model, therefore, an increase (de-

[1] Although the factor-intensities of the commodities may be reversible, they *cannot* reverse for a country with a *given* factor endowment. At the present stage of our argument, therefore, we do not need to make the strong assumption that factor-intensities are non-reversible at *all* factor price-ratios.

crease) in the relative price of a good will necessarily increase (decrease) the real wage of the factor intensively used in its production.

6. Argument (3) that the importable good is intensive in the use of the scarce factor is really the well-known Heckscher–Ohlin theorem. The crucial question that it raises is: does the Heckscher–Ohlin theorem follow from the basic Stolper–Samuelson model? To answer this question, we should first have to define "factor scarcity." We may choose from three alternative definitions of factor scarcity:

> *A. Lancaster Definition.* A country's scarce factor is that which is used more intensively in the production of the importable good. This definition may be described as tautological, since it turns the Heckscher–Ohlin theorem into a valid proposition by *definition.* It may also be described as an internal definition, since it excludes any comparison with the foreign country. It has been suggested by Lancaster.[1]
>
> *B. Heckscher–Ohlin Definition.* A country's scarce factor is that whose relative price is higher than abroad under self-sufficiency. This may also be described as a price definition, since the country's scarce factor is that factor which is more expensive prior to trade than abroad. This definition has been used by Heckscher and Ohlin.[2]
>
> *C. Leontief Definition.* A country's scarce factor is that of which there are fewer physical units per unit of the other factor than abroad. This may also be described as a physical definition, since it defines scarcity with reference to the relative physical quantities of factors.[3]

Using each of these definitions in turn, let us analyse the Heckscher–Ohlin theorem.

> *A*: If the Lancaster definition of factor scarcity is used, then the Heckscher–Ohlin theorem holds by definition.
>
> *B*: If the Heckscher–Ohlin definition of factor scarcity is used then the further assumptions of international identity of production functions and non-reversibility of factor-intensities of commodites between the

[1] Lancaster, *op. cit.*, p. 208, argues that "the only acceptable definition" of a scarce factor is that which defines it as the factor "which is used more intensively in the good of which more is produced in isolation than in trade." It is of some interest to note that tariffs designed to influence distribution are probably set with reference to such internal criteria: to raise the real wage of labour, for instance, tariffs are imposed on labour-intensive industries rather than on products of industries using a factor which is scarcer at home than abroad; with the possible exception of the pauper-labour argument for such tariffs.

[2] For a convincing attribution of the authorship of this definition of factor scarcity to Heckscher and Ohlin, see a masterly article by R. Jones, "Factor Proportions and the Heckscher–Ohlin Theorem," *Review of Economic Studies*, 1956–57, pp. 1–10. The definition may be also illustrated in terms of Fig. 1: country *A* is labour-abundant and country *B* land-abundant if, under self-sufficiency, $(W/R)_A < (W/R)_B$.

[3] W. Leontief, "Domestic Production and Foreign Trade: The American Capital Position Re-examined," *Proceedings of the American Philosophical Society*, September 28, 1953; reprinted in *Economia Internazionale*, February 1954. Again, country *A* is labour-abundant and country *B* land-abundant if, under self-sufficiency, $(L/T)_A > (L/T)_B$.

two countries will suffice to ensure the full validity of the Heckscher–Ohlin theorem.[1]

C: If the Leontief definition of factor scarcity is used, then the threefold assumptions of non-reversibilities of factor-intensities of commodities between the trading countries and the international identity of both production functions and tastes will ensure the validity of the Heckscher–Ohlin theorem.[2]

7. We can now sum up on the Stolper–Samuelson formulations as follows:[3]

A. (1) The restrictive Stolper–Samuelson theorem is logically true if we use: (*a*) the basic Stolper–Samuelson model, and (*b*) the Lancaster definition of factor scarcity.

(2) The general Stolper–Samuelson theorem is logically true if we use the further assumption that the elasticity of foreign demand is greater than the marginal propensity to consume exportable goods ($n_x > c$).

B. (1) The restrictive Stolper–Samuelson theorem is logically true if we use: (*a*) the basic Stolper–Samuelson model, (*b*) the Heckscher–Ohlin definition of factor scarcity, (*c*) the assumption of international identity of production functions, and (*d*) the assumption of non-reversibility of factor-intensities of commodities between the countries.

(2) The general Stolper–Samuelson theorem is logically true if we use the further assumption that $n_x > c$.

C. (1) The restrictive Stolper–Samuelson theorem is logically true if we use: (*a*) the basic Stolper–Samuelson model, (*b*) the Leontief definition of factor scarcity, (*c*) the assumption of international identity of production functions, (*d*) the assumption of non-reversibility of factor-

[1] This can be seen readily from Fig. 1. If $(W/R)_A < (W/R)_B$ and production functions with non-reversible factor-intensities are common between the countries, then we can see that $(P_F/P_C)_A > (P_F/P_C)_B$ under self-sufficiency and the labour-abundant country *A* will necessarily export the labour-intensive commodity, clothing. We could, of course, specify what appears to be a less restrictive condition than that set out in the text: for instance, we could sustain the Heckscher–Ohlin theorem by assuming merely that, instead of identical production functions between countries, the differences in the production functions are not large enough to outweigh the effect of differences in factor scarcity on the pre-trade commodity price-ratios. We have preferred to use the strong condition (identity of tastes) instead of the weak one on the ground that the use of the latter seems to be bad methodology, amounting to the argument that the Heckscher–Ohlin definition of factor scarcity will suffice to sustain the Heckscher–Ohlin theorem if other factors do not work to invalidate it.

[2] The Heckscher–Ohlin theorem would not hold as a logically true proposition in this case unless we also postulate now international identity of tastes (or the weak postulate that differences in tastes between countries do not affect the issue). This follows from the fact that while, with identical production functions, country *A* will show a bias towards the production of the labour-intensive commodity, clothing, by virtue of her physical abundance in labour, this bias in production may be more than offset by a bias in *A* towards the *consumption* of clothing: such that, in self-sufficiency, we find that $(P_F/P_C)_A < (P_F/P_C)_B$ and country *A*, although physically abundant in labour, would export the land-intensive commodity, food.

[3] The phrase "logically true" in the following statements is used in the strict mathematical sense: "A statement that is true in every logically possible case is said to be *logically true*" (Kemeny, Snell and Thompson, *Introduction to Finite Mathematics* (Prentice-Hall, 1957), p. 19

intensities of commodities between countries, and (*e*) the assumption of international identity of tastes.

(2) The general Stolper–Samuelson theorem is logically true if we use the further assumption that $n_x > c$.

A tree-diagram, based on this analysis, is presented in Table I.

8. We are now in a position to decide whether Stolper and Samuelson derived their theorems logically. Aside from their basic model:

(1) they adopt, though without complete clarity, the Heckscher–Ohlin definition of factor scarcity and the postulate concerning the non-reversibility of factor-intensities; and, quite explicitly, the assumption of international identity of production functions: [1] this establishes the restictive Stolper–Samuelson theorem as logically true (B(1));

(2) they further assume that " the country in question is relatively small and has no influence on the terms of trade "; [2] this establishes the general Stolper–Samuelson theorem as logically true (B(2)).

9. No critique of the Stolper–Samuelson formulations can thus be founded on the argument that they are not logically true, given the premises. What we could say, however, is that the theorem should be founded as closely as possible on the *basic* Stolper–Samuelson model alone; and

(1) that, if we use the Heckscher–Ohlin definition of factor scarcity, the assumptions that we find ourselves making about the international identity of production functions and the non-reversibility of factor-intensities to sustain the twin formulations of the Stolper–Samuelson theorem are, on this criterion, *restrictive*; and

(2) that, if we use the Leontief definition of factor scarcity (as we should probably want to since it is, in a sense, the most " objective " definition we could adopt in this context), we discover ourselves adopting the threefold restrictive assumptions (C(1)) of international identity of production functions and tastes plus the non-reversibility of factor-intensities of commodities, to sustain the Stolper–Samuelson formulations.[3]

10. It will be remembered, however, that these restrictive assumptions were made only because we wished to use argument (3) concerning the validity of the Heckscher–Ohlin theorem.[4] This may also be seen indirectly from

[1] Stolper and Samuelson, *op. cit.*, pp. 335–40. Some of the argument is, of course, obscure in view of the pioneering nature of the article: a sympathetic interpretation, therefore, is called for. Metzler, *op. cit.*, p. 5, also adopts the Heckscher–Ohlin definition of factor scarcity in discussing the Stolper–Samuelson theorem.

[2] Stolper and Samuelson, *op. cit.*, p. 346.

[3] The additional restrictive assumption that $\eta_x > c$ has not been listed here because we wish at this stage to concentrate on only those restrictive assumptions which are made to sustain argument (3).

[4] It is important to remember that these assumptions are restrictive only in so far as we wish to found our theorem exclusively on the basic Stolper–Samuelson model.

TABLE I

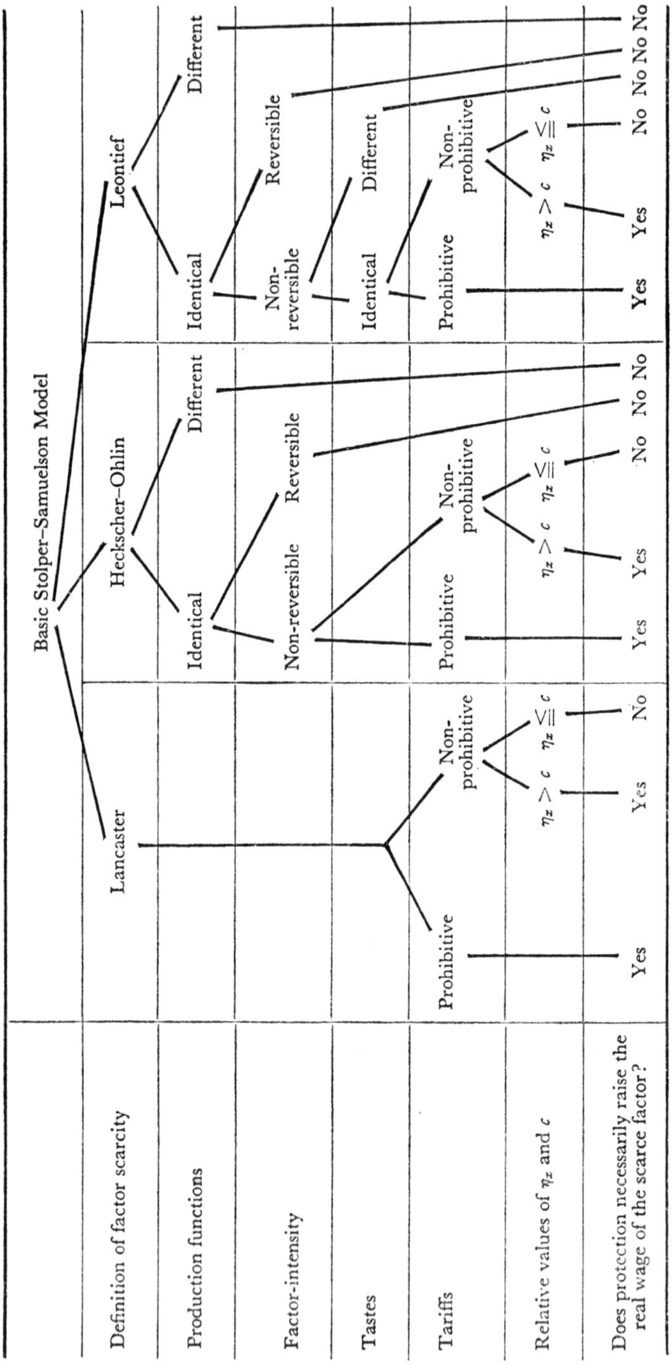

	Basic Stolper–Samuelson Model													
Definition of factor scarcity	Lancaster			Heckscher–Ohlin					Leontief					
Production functions				Identical				Different	Identical					Different
Factor-intensity				Non-reversible			Reversible		Non-reversible				Reversible	
Tastes									Identical			Different		
Tariffs	Prohibitive	Non-prohibitive		Prohibitive	Non-prohibitive				Prohibitive	Non-prohibitive				
Relative values of η_x and c		$\eta_x > c$	$\eta_x \leqq c$		$\eta_x > c$	$\eta_x \leqq c$				$\eta_x > c$	$\eta_x \leqq c$			
Does protection necessarily raise the real wage of the scarce factor?	Yes	Yes	No	Yes	Yes	No	No	No	Yes	Yes	No	No	No	No

the fact that, if we use the Lancaster definition of factor scarcity, no such restrictive assumptions are necessary (A(1)): for the Heckscher–Ohlin theorem has been rendered valid by definition!

The suggestion follows readily from these considerations that we should reformulate our theorem in terms of arguments (1) and (2) alone, while eliminating the use of the troublesome argument (3). This can be done readily: protection (prohibitive or otherwise) raises the real wage of the factor intensively employed in the production of the importable good. This theorem is logically true if we use: (*a*) the basic Stolper–Samuelson model, and (*b*) the assumption that $n_x > c$.

This theorem has been described as the Stolper–Samuelson–Metzler–Lancaster theorem on the following grounds:

(1) It is *implicit* in the Stolper–Samuelson argument, towards the end of their paper: " It does not follow that our results stand and fall with the Heckscher–Ohlin theorem. Our analysis neglected the other country completely. If factors of production are not comparable between countries, or if production functions differ, nevertheless, so long as the country has only two factors, international trade would necessarily affect the real wage of a factor in the same direction as its relative remuneration." [1]

(2) Metzler *explicitly* states it as " the Stolper–Samuelson conclusion that tariffs benefit the factors of production which are required in relatively large amounts in the industries competing with imports." [2]

(3) Lancaster advances this formulation directly as an *alternative* to the Stolper–Samuelson formulations considered above on the ground that it is more general than the latter.

11. Whereas, however, Lancaster's observation that the Stolper–Samuelson formulations are "non-universal" (restrictive) is well taken, the argument by which he supports it is erroneous and different from that set out in this paper. Lancaster proceeds by establishing, with the aid of a highly ingenious model, the proposition that, in the context of the basic Stolper–Samuelson model combined with the assumption of a small country facing fixed terms of trade, differences in demand conditions (" which good is the wage-good ") will affect the composition of a country's foreign trade. On this proposition he founds the following critique:

" The non-universality of the [Stolper–Samuelson] theorem is due to incorrect formulation: if the scarce factor is defined as that which is used more intensively in the good of which more is produced in isolation

[1] Stolper and Samuelson, *op. cit.*, pp. 355–6. Homogeneity of factors between countries has not been listed separately as an assumption in this paper because it is believed that this is implicit in both the Heckscher–Ohlin and the Leontief definitions of factor scarcity.

[2] Metzler, *op. cit.*, p. 13. Metzler, of course, does not state it as a rival formulation, but it is abundantly clear that he is aware that this formulation is implicit in the general Stolper–Samuelson theorem.

> than in trade (the only acceptable definition), then the previous analysis has shown that different wage-goods may make for different factor scarcities. In this sense, the Stolper–Samuelson formulation is meaningless, since the phrases ' real wages . . . in terms of any good ' and ' scarce factor ' represent incompatible concepts." [1]

The following comments on Lancaster's critique seem warranted here, in view of our preceding analysis.

To begin with, it is difficult to understand what Lancaster means by the statement that " the previous analysis has shown that different wage-goods may make for different factor scarcities. In this sense, the Stolper–Samuelson formulation is meaningless, since the phrases ' real wages . . . in terms of any good ' and ' scarce factor ' represent incompatible concepts." Which good will be imported into a country will depend in our model on the pre-trade commodity price-ratios in the trading countries; these price-ratios are determined by domestic supply and demand; and domestic demand is affected by " which good is the wage-good." If the scarce factor is defined tautologously as that which is used intensively in the importable good it follows then, from elementary considerations, that " different wage-goods may make for different factor scarcities." But surely, how can this render the Stolper–Samuelson formulations *meaningless* or make ' real wages . . . in terms of any good ' and ' scarce factor ' *incompatible* concepts? And, more pertinently, why should this make the Stolper–Samuelson formulation " non-universal "?

Indeed, if the tautologous definition of factor scarcity is adopted, as Lancaster suggests, then the general Stolper–Samuelson theorem and the Stolper–Samuelson–Metzler–Lancaster theorem are *identical*: the phrases " scarce factor " and " factor intensively employed in the importable good " can be used interchangeably. Lancaster cannot, therefore, claim one formulation to be " non-universal " and the other to be " universally true ": on his own definition of factor scarcity, the two formulations come to the same thing!

To be sure, Lancaster's critique would be valid (though, as we have shown, incomplete) only if the physical, Leontief definition of factor scarcity were proven to have been adopted by Stolper and Samuelson, and were adopted by Lancaster as well; as formulated, however, the criticism is merely erroneous.[2] In failing to investigate precisely what Stolper and Samuelson assumed by way of their definition of factor scarcity, Lancaster has further by-passed the only legitimate critique that can be sustained against the actual formulation of the theorem by Stolper and Samuelson: namely, that advanced in this paper.

[1] Lancaster, *op. cit.*, p. 208.

[2] Lancaster has pointed out to me, in private communication, that he really had in mind the physical definition of factor scarcity, despite the printed commitment to the tautologous definition: the tenor of the argument on p. 209, *op. cit.*, seems to suggest this, although it follows upon the formulation of the tautologous definition. None of the criticism advanced here should obscure that fact that Lancaster has handled his model with admirable expertise.

12. Our task is yet incomplete. Even the Stolper–Samuelson–Metzler–Lancaster formulation does not found the theorem completely and solely on the basic model. We must still make the restrictive assumption that $\eta_x > c$. We should, however, clearly want to go the whole way and remove all restrictive assumptions and restate the theorem to include the entire matrix of possibilities: such that the theorem is logically true, given only the basic Stolper–Samuelson model. This formulation is: [1]

Protection (prohibitive or otherwise) will raise, reduce or leave unchanged the real wage of the factor intensively employed in the production of a good according as protection raises, lowers or leaves unchanged the internal relative price of that good.

This is really the fundamental theorem that Stolper and Samuelson contributed to our knowedge of the properties of the basic model they were using. Given the basic model, our formulation is logically true for all possible cases.

13. It should perhaps be emphasised that the preceding analysis has been centred entirely on the problem of analysing the impact of protection on real wages of factors in the context of the basic model employed by Stolper and Samuelson. It should be possible, of course, to analyse the problem afresh in terms of models employing alternative assumptions. This, however, would be mostly destructive of the full validity of our theorem.

If we allow for complete specialisation with trade, for instance, we can claim only that protection will raise, lower or leave unchanged the real wage of the factor in which the *exportable* good is postulated to be intensive according as protection raises, lowers or leaves unchanged the internal relative price of the exportable good. But we cannot extend the theorem to the factor postulated to be used intensively in the production, if any, of the importable good because any increase in the internal relative price of the exportable good after complete specialisation must raise the real wage of *both* factors.

However, if we allow the optimum factor-proportions within industries, at given factor price-ratios, to change with scale, our theorem will continue to be logically true and the real wage of the factor intensively employed in a good will rise, fall or be unchanged according as the internal relative price of that good rises, falls or is unchanged with the imposition of protection.[2]

[1] This formulation stems directly from argument (2), which is founded exclusively, as the reader will remember, on the basic Stolper–Samuelson model.

[2] An apparent exception to this proposition may be investigated. Where the optimum factor-ratio changes with scale, at given factor price-ratios, it may happen, for instance, that if the production of labour-intensive importables expands, a higher proportion of labour is released than is needed in import-substitution, even though importables are *on average* more labour-intensive. In this case, increase in the production of importables will lead to a *rise* in the labour-to-land ratios, and hence *reduce* the real wage of labour. This case, however, does not constitute an exception to our theorem, because such technology involves a concave production frontier, so that increase in the production of importables occurs when the price of importables *falls* (and not rises). Hence the logical truth of our proposition, even when we allow for changing optimum factor-ratios with scale.

On the other hand, if we allow for changing returns to scale in either or both of the two activities, clearly it becomes impossible to maintain that our theorem will be logically true.

II. Protection and Real Incomes

14. Our analysis has so far been concerned with the original Stolper–Samuelson problem of discovering the impact of protection on the *real wage* earned by factors in employment. It seems useful, however, to emphasise that if we are interested in finding out the net change in the *real income* of the factors it is only in the case of a prohibitive tariff that a complete identity obtains between change in real wage and change in the real income of a factor. Where the tariff is non-prohibitive, the complication arises from the revenue earned by the Government. If this revenue is assumed to be redistributed to the owners of factors according to some formula, factors will derive incomes *both* from the real wage in employment and from the redistributed proceeds of the tariff-revenue.

Hence arises the interesting possibility that the factor whose real wage has been damaged by protection may still find its real income improved if the formula for the redistribution of the tariff-revenue is heavily biased in its favour. Since this possibility constitutes a qualification to the generally accepted implication of the Stolper–Samuelson analysis, it should be of some interest to delimit the conditions under which it may occur.

To begin with, this possibility of over-compensating the damaged factor *from the tariff-revenue* clearly cannot arise unless the real income of the country as a whole is improved by protection. We know from the preceding analysis that where the real wage of one factor is reduced, that of the other necessarily rises; hence, if protection did not bring some gain to the country as a whole, it should be impossible to overcompensate the factor with the damaged real wage (from tariff-revenues). To rephrase the proposition, then, accrual of gain to the protecting country from the imposition of protection is a necessary, though not sufficient, condition for the possibility of overcompensating the factor with the damaged real wage.[1]

In the following brief analysis we seek to relate this proposition to Metzler's formula for determining the impact of protection on the internal commodity price-ratio: partly to establish link with Metzler's pioneering analysis in this field and largely because it enables us to define, and distinguish between, situations in which the factor with the damaged real wage will be export-intensive (intensively used in exportables) and those where it will be import-intensive. The discussion is then briefly extended to the

[1] That is to say, whereas the country must have gained from protection before the damaged factor can be overcompensated from the tariff-revenues (necessary condition), this gain must be large enough to permit overcompensation (sufficient condition).

case where the initial situation is that of a tariff instead of free-trade and the effect of an *increase* in protection is the subject of inquiry.

15. In Fig. 2 let O_b be the foreign reciprocal demand curve facing country A. F is the free-trade point, OF yielding the corresponding terms of trade. I_a' is the trade-indifference curve of A passing through F at a tangent to OF and intersecting O_b at U. Its postulated curvature derives from

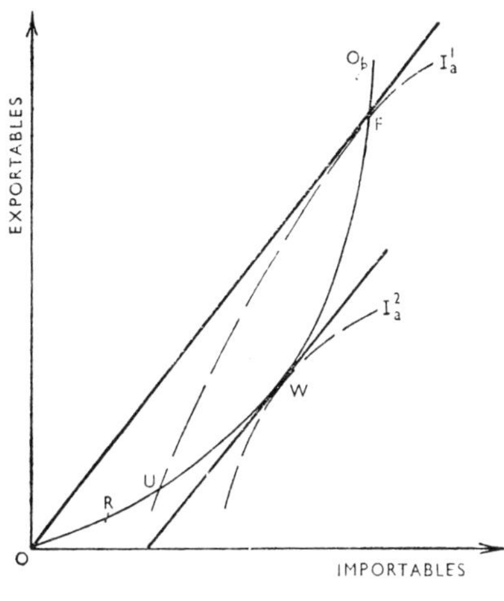

FIG. 2

the assumption of strict convexity of the production frontier and community indifference curves.

(1) Assume that the tariff-added offer curve of country A intersects O_b at U. The internal relative price of the importable good is then given by the slope of the trade-indifference curve I_a' at U, which is clearly, by virtue of the postulated curvature of I_a', greater than at F. We can deduce, therefore, that protection can leave the real income of the country unchanged only if the internal relative price of the importable good rises from the free-trade level with the imposition of protection (in turn, only if $\eta_x > c$).

(2) Similarly, by considering points on O_b to the left of U such as R, we can argue that protection can reduce the real income of the country only if the internal relative price of the importable good rises with protection (in turn, only if $\eta_x > c$).

(3) However, protection can increase the real income of the country whether the internal relative price of the importable good rises, is unchanged (W) or falls with the imposition of protection (in turn, whether $\eta_x \gtreqless c$).

Thus, where $\eta_x \leqq c$, the real income of the country will necessarily improve with the imposition of a tariff; whereas if $\eta_x > c$, the real income may rise, fall or be unchanged.

16. Where the comparison is confined to the real income and real wage of the factors in an initial free-trade position and after the imposition of a tariff, we can then conclude as follows:

> (1) the export-intensive factor will necessarily become better off and it may be possible to overcompensate the import-intensive factor if $\eta_x < c$; [1]
>
> (2) neither factor will become worse off and at least one better off if $\eta_x = c$; [2] and
>
> (3) the import-intensive factor will necessarily become better off and it may be possible to overcompensate the export-intensive factor if two conditions obtain: (i) $\eta_x > c$, and (ii) the tariff is small enough to yield some gain to the country.

If we assume that importables are not inferior goods in the protecting country, it is clear, then, that inelastic foreign demand ($\eta_x < 1$) is a necessary, though not a sufficient, condition for the emergence of the possibility of overcompensating the import-intensive factor. Where, however, foreign demand is elastic and importables are not inferior goods, the export-intensive factor will necessarily find its real wage reduced by protection; and, for the possibility of overcompensating it to arise, it will be necessary, though not sufficient, that the tariff be small enough to make the country better off than under free-trade.

17. If, however, we wish to compare the real incomes and wages of factors in an initial situation of a tariff and after *increase* in the tariff, the analysis must be somewhat modified.

To begin with, the Metzler formula must be altered so as to read: the internal relative price of the importable good will rise, be unchanged or fall according as $\eta_x \gtreqless \dfrac{1 - c'(1+t)}{1 - c't}$ where t is the initial tariff-rate and $c' = (1 - c)$ is the domestic marginal propensity to consume importables.[3]

[1] When $\eta_x < c$ we know now that: (1) the internal relative price of the importable good falls, thus increasing the real wage of the export-intensive factor and reducing that of the import-intensive factor; and (2) the country must have become better off. Hence the proposition in the text.

[2] Where $\eta_x = c$, we know that: (1) the internal relative price of the importable good is unchanged, thus leaving unchanged the real wages of both factors; and (2) the real income of the country must increase. Hence the proposition in the text.

[3] This formula is derived from the following analysis, furnished by Professor Johnson and replacing my earlier, unsatisfactory attempt.

Symbols: Let p be the *external* terms of trade, measured as the price of the importable good over the price of the exportable good, t the initial tariff rate and $\pi = p(1 + t)$ the *internal* terms of trade. c' is the marginal propensity to consume importables, at the initial terms of trade. C is the initial

It will be seen that where the initial situation is that of free-trade, t will be zero and the formula will reduce to the well-known Metzler formula.

Secondly, the impact on the real income of the country will not bear the same relationship to the shifts in the internal commodity price-ratio as in the previous analysis with the free-trade initial situation. It can be demonstrated, by a geometrical argument analogous to that used earlier, that although the internal relative price of the importable good must still rise for the country to be as well off as prior to the increased tariff, both reduction and increase in the real income of the country are now consistent with any shift in this price.

Thirdly, arguing from the optimum tariff theory, we can claim that the real income of the country will improve with increased protection if two conditions obtain: (i) the pre-increase tariff rate is less than the optimum tariff rate $t < \frac{1}{\eta_x - 1}$; and (ii) *either* the post-increase tariff rate is also less than the optimum tariff rate *or*, if it exceeds the optimum tariff rate, it is small enough to leave some gain in real income to the country from the increase in tariff.

---

domestic consumption of importables, Y their production and $M \equiv C - Y$ the initial quantity of imports. $r_m = (\eta_x - 1) = \frac{p}{M} \cdot \frac{\delta Sm}{\delta p}$ $(Sm \equiv M)$ is the elasticity of foreign supply of importables; and $R = tpM$ is the tariff revenue.

Analysis: The simplest approach to the problem is to assume the internal terms of trade to be constant and to investigate the excess demand for importables when t changes. If the excess demand is positive, the internal terms of trade will rise to restore equilibrium; if negative, they will fall: assuming, of course, that we have " well-behaved " substitution elasticities in production and consumption.

Now, $R = tpM = \frac{t}{1+t}\pi \,.\, M$. With π constant, we have $\frac{dp}{dt} = -\frac{p}{(1+t)}$. The shift in the demand for imports due to the change in the tariff is then given by:

$$\frac{dC}{dt} = c'\frac{dR}{dt} = c'\pi\left\{\frac{1}{(1+t)^2}M + \frac{t}{(1+t)}\cdot\frac{dM}{dt}\right\}$$

The shift in the supply of imports is given by:

$$\frac{dM}{dp}\cdot\frac{dp}{dt} = \frac{M}{p}\cdot r_m\cdot\frac{dp}{dt} = -\frac{M}{(1+t)}\cdot r_m$$

The excess demand for importables is then given by:

$$\left(\frac{dC}{dt} - \frac{dM}{dt}\right)$$

$$= \frac{c'\pi}{(1+t)^2}\cdot M + \left\{\frac{c'\pi t}{(1+t)} - 1\right\}\left\{\frac{-M}{(1+t)}\right\} r_m$$

$$= \frac{M}{(1+t)}\{c'p + (1 - c'pt)r_m\}$$

Substituting $r_m = \eta_x - 1$, assuming p to be unity initially by choice of units and simplifying, we arrive at the formula that the excess demand for importables will be positive, zero or negative according as:

$$\eta_x \gtreqless \frac{1 - c'(1+t)}{1 - c't}$$

It will be seen that this formula reduces to the Metzler formula when t is zero.

These considerations lead to the following conclusions:[1]

(1) The export-intensive factor will necessarily become better off and it may be possible to overcompensate the import-intensive factor from *increased* tariff-revenues when three conditions obtain: (i) $\eta_x < \frac{1 - c'(1+t)}{1 - c't}$; (ii) $t < \frac{1}{\eta_x - 1}$; and (iii) *either* the post-increase tariff rate is also less than the optimum tariff rate *or*, if it exceeds the optimum tariff, it is still small enough to leave some gain in real income to the country from the increase in the tariff.

(2) The import-intensive factor will necessarily become better off and it may be possible to overcompensate the export-intensive factor from *increased* tariff-revenues when three conditions obtain: (i) $\eta_x > \frac{1 - c'(1+t)}{1 - c't}$; (ii) $t < \frac{1}{\eta_x - 1}$; and (iii) *either* the post-increase tariff rate is also less than the optimum tariff *or*, if it exceeds the optimum tariff, it is still small enough to leave some gain in real income to the country from the increase in protection.

(3) Where, however, $\eta_x = \frac{1 - c'(1+t)}{1 - c't}$, the real wage of neither factor changes with the increase in protection. It follows, therefore, that the real income of both factors will increase, decrease or remain unchanged according as the increase in tariff raises, lowers or leaves unchanged the real income of the country: assuming, of course, that the tariff-revenues are divided among the factors in a given proportion.

18. In conclusion, it should be re-emphasised that the brief discussion presented here has been concerned only with the limited task of exploring some of the implications of the proposition that accrual of gain to the protecting country from the imposition of protection is a necessary, though not sufficient, condition for the emergence of the possibility of overcompensating, from tariff-revenues, the factor with the damaged real wage. It is planned to present a rigorous analysis of the sufficient conditions for the emergence of this possibility in a subsequent article.[2]

JAGDISH BHAGWATI

Nuffield College,
Oxford.

[1] The first two propositions that follow assume that the factor stated to become necessarily better off continues to receive *at least* the same revenue as in the initial situation; this assumption being made explicit by the use of the phrase " from *increased* tariff-revenues." This assumption is needed because otherwise improvement merely in the real wage of a factor due to increased protection could be offset by an accompanying unfavourable distribution of tariff-revenues to the factor after the increase in the tariff.

[2] This calls for a rigorous analysis of distribution and demand, so that factor earnings and income subsidies from tariff-revenues could be related to real incomes of factors. Such analysis would preclude us from taking as given, as we have done here, the set of community indifference curves: this practice has been adopted in the present paper for strictly pedagogic reasons.

A GENERALIZED THEORY OF THE EFFECTS OF TARIFFS ON THE TERMS OF TRADE[1]

By J. BHAGWATI and H. G. JOHNSON

TRADITIONAL analysis of the effect of a tariff on the terms of trade of the protecting country draws a distinction between two cases: (1) where the tariff revenue is spent by the government; and (2) where the tariff revenue is redistributed as an income subsidy to the private sector. In both cases the conclusion reached is that the terms of trade of the protecting country will improve or deteriorate according as the country's elasticity of demand for imports is greater or less than the marginal propensity to consume importables (of the government or the private sector, as the case may be). By splitting the elasticity of demand for imports into the sum of the compensated elasticity of demand for imports and the private sector's marginal propensity to consume importables, it can further be shown (on the usual assumption of convex indifference and transformation curves) that the terms of trade must improve if the private sector spends the tariff revenue; and that, if the government spends the tariff revenue, the terms of trade can only deteriorate if the government's marginal propensity to consume importables exceeds the private sector's marginal propensity to consume importables by more than the private compensated elasticity of demand for imports. Normally, the terms of trade will not improve sufficiently to offset the effect of the tariff in raising the domestic price of importables; but the tariff will reduce the domestic price of importables if the marginal propensity to consume exportables of whichever sector spends the tariff revenue is greater than the foreign elasticity of demand for exportables.

This analysis, however, is founded on four restrictive postulates:

(1) *Initial free trade.* It is assumed that there is no tariff in effect in the initial situation; hence the analysis does not apply to the case of an increase in an existing tariff rate.

(2) *Independence of consumer taste and government expenditure.* Where the government spends the tariff revenue, it is assumed that the amount of government expenditure—either the total, or the amount spent on particular commodities—does not affect the way in which the private sector divides its expenditure between importables and exportables; hence the

[1] The major part of the work on this paper was done at the University of Chicago; the final draft was prepared at the Institute for Economic Research, Queen's University, Kingston, Ontario. We are grateful to the Institute for extending to us the use of its facilities.

4520.3 Q

analysis does not apply to the case of dependence of consumer taste on the amount of government expenditure.

(3) *Aggregation of the private sector.* It is assumed that the private sector can be treated as a homogeneous unit with respect to its demand for imports; this ignores the effects of a change in the domestic price of importables in redistributing real income (*a*) between consumers with different tastes, and (*b*) between owners of different collections of factors of production, as well as the influence (in case (2)) of the way in which the redistributed tariff revenue is allocated among private consumers.

(4) *Inelastic supply of factors.* In dealing with the effects of a change in the domestic price of importables on domestic production, it is assumed that the supply of resources is given; hence the analysis does not take account of the effects on import demand of changes in factor supplies consequential on the change in the tariff rate.

In this paper we generalize the theory of tariffs by examining the effect of an increase in the tariff rate when these restrictive assumptions do not hold.[1] We distinguish three major cases: (1) where the government spends the tariff revenue and private demand is independent of government expenditure; (2) where the proceeds of the tariff are consumed by the private sector; (3) where the government spends the tariff revenue and the amount of government expenditure influences the private sector's demand for imports. Section I analyses the first two (the traditional) cases, abandoning the restriction of initial free trade. Section II analyses the third case, abandoning the second restriction of independence of private demand and government expenditure. Section III abandons the third restriction and incorporates the effects of disaggregating consumption demand and factor ownership in the analysis of the three cases. Section IV abandons the fourth restriction and extends the analysis to include the effects of variable supplies of factors. These four sections are concerned with the effect of the tariff increase on the terms of trade; in Section V we analyse the effect of the tariff increase on the domestic price of importables.

Throughout the analysis we assume that only two goods are produced and consumed, 'exportables' and 'importables'; in analysing case (3),

[1] For the traditional analysis, reference may be made to A. P. Lerner, 'The Symmetry Between Import and Export Taxes,' *Economica*, N.S., vol. iii, no. 11 (Aug. 1936), pp. 306–13; L. Metzler, 'Tariffs, the Terms of Trade and the Distribution of National Income', *Journal of Political Economy*, vol. lvii, no. 1 (Feb. 1949), pp. 1–29; and R. E. Baldwin, 'The Effect of Tariffs on International and Domestic Prices', *Quarterly Journal of Economics*, vol. lxxiv, no. 1 (Feb. 1960), pp. 65–78. In a later supplement to his classic paper, op. cit., Lloyd Metzler recognized explicitly the dependence of the analysis developed by him, of the effect of tariffs on domestic prices, on the assumption of initial free trade; see his 'Tariffs, International Demand, and Domestic Prices', *Journal of Political Economy*, vol. lvii, no. 4 (Aug. 1949), pp. 345–51.

however, we assume that the amount of government expenditure enters consumers' utility functions as a third consumption good. In dropping restrictions (3) and (4) we assume that income is shared between two individuals, each of whom owns a collection of productive factors and earns an income from the sale of their services; and that each good is produced in a linear homogeneous production function employing two factors, labour and capital, whose earnings are wages and rent respectively, these factors being employed in different ratios in the two industries. Markets for goods and factors are assumed to be perfectly competitive. In analysing the effect of the tariff increase in the various cases, we employ the simplifying device of assuming the conditions for stability in the international market; this permits the effect of the tariff on the terms of trade to be inferred from its effect on the excess demand for imports at the initial terms of trade, and its effect on the domestic price of importables to be inferred from its effect on the excess demand for imports at the initial domestic price of imports.

We employ the following mathematical symbols throughout the article; other symbols are defined when they appear in the argument:

p, the international price of the importable good in terms of the exportable good (the terms of trade); by choice of units, p is initially made equal to unity;

t, the tariff rate, defined as a proportion of the international price of importables;

π, the domestic price of importables in terms of exportables; $\pi = (1+t)p$; because p is initially unity $d\pi/dt$ in the mathematical development below is equal to unity;

P, the quantity of importables produced domestically;

Q, the quantity of exportables produced domestically;

Y, the amount of earned income: $Y = \pi P+Q$;

C, the quantity of importables consumed out of private income; private income is equal to earned income where the government spends the tariff revenue (cases (1) and (3)), and to earned income plus tariff proceeds where the latter are redistributed to the private sector (case (2));

M_1, the quantity of importables imported for private consumption: $M_1 = C-P$;

M_2, the quantity of importables consumed by the government out of tariff revenue; this quantity must obviously be imported, and it simplifies matters to assume that the government buys its importables abroad at the world market price;

M, the total quantity of imports: $M = M_1+M_2$;

R, the tariff revenue: $R = tpM_1$;

c, the private sector's marginal propensity to spend on importables at the domestic price of importables; the private sector's marginal propensity to consume importables is c/π;

g, the government's marginal propensity to spend tariff revenue on imports at the international price of imports; the government's marginal propensity to consume imports is $g/p = g$;

ξ, the domestic price elasticity of private demand for imports, tariff revenue being held constant where it affects private demand [cases (2) and (3)]; $\xi = -\dfrac{\pi}{M_1}\dfrac{\delta M_1}{\delta \pi}$;

η, the price elasticity of private demand for importables, earned income and tariff revenue being held constant; $\eta = -\dfrac{\pi}{C}\dfrac{\delta C}{\delta \pi}$;

η', the compensated elasticity of private demand for importables; $\eta' = \eta - c$;

ϵ, the elasticity of domestic supply of importables with given supplies of factors of production; $\epsilon = \dfrac{\pi}{P}\dfrac{\delta P}{\delta \pi}$;

ξ', the compensated elasticity of private demand for imports:

$$\xi' = \frac{C}{M_1}\eta' + \frac{P}{M_1}\epsilon = \xi - c.$$

Barred symbols denote initial magnitudes of the variables when these might be confused with the functional relationships that determine them. The main equations in the mathematical argument have been numbered; the formulae derived have also been assigned roman numerals.

I. The Effect of an Increase in the Tariff on the Terms of Trade: cases (1) and (2)

An increase in the tariff rate will cause an improvement or a deterioration in the terms of trade according as it gives rise to a negative or a positive world excess demand for importables at the initial international price of imports. Since the quantity of imports supplied by the rest of the world at the initial terms of trade is unchanged by the increase in the tariff, the change in the world excess demand for importables resulting from the tariff increase is equal to the change in the tariff-increasing country's demand for imports. On the usual assumptions that the private sector can be treated as an aggregate and that factor supplies are inelastic, this change, in cases (1) and (2), is the net result of two effects of the tariff increase:

(i) the effect of the increase in the domestic price of importables due to the tariff increase on the quantity of imports privately demanded;

(ii) the effect of the change in the amount of tariff revenue due to the increase in the tariff and the consequential change in the quantity of imports privately demanded under (1) above, on the quantity of imports demanded by the government or the private sector, whichever spends the tariff revenue.

(1) The change in the quantity of imports privately demanded is determined by the elasticity of private demand for imports; this change, which we denote by $\delta M_1/\delta t$ because the tariff increase also affects private demand for imports in other ways in case (2) and other cases considered below, is:

$$\frac{\delta M_1}{\delta t}=\frac{\delta M_1}{\delta \pi}\frac{d\pi}{dt}=-\frac{\bar{M}_1}{\pi}\xi.$$

The change in the quantity of imports demanded due to the increase in the domestic price of importables is actually the net result of three effects of the increase in the domestic price of importables:

(i) the change in private consumption of importables due to the increase in the price of importables, determined by the price elasticity of private demand for importables; this change is:

$$\frac{\delta C}{\delta \pi}\frac{d\pi}{dt}=-\frac{\bar{C}}{\pi}\eta;$$

(ii) the change in private consumption of importables due to the increase in income earned in domestic production resulting from the increased domestic price of importables, determined[1] by the initial amount of domestic production of importables and the marginal propensity to consume importables; this change is:

$$\frac{\delta C}{\delta Y}\frac{\delta Y}{\delta \pi}\frac{d\pi}{dt}=\frac{c}{\pi}\bar{P};$$

(iii) the increase in domestic production of importables in response to the increase in their domestic price, determined by the elasticity of domestic supply of importables; this change is:

$$\frac{dP}{d\pi}\frac{d\pi}{dt}=\frac{\bar{P}}{\pi}\epsilon.$$

The net result of these three effects is:

$$\begin{aligned}\frac{\delta M_1}{\delta t}&=-\frac{\bar{M}_1}{\pi}\left(\frac{\bar{C}}{\bar{M}_1}\eta-\frac{\bar{P}}{\bar{M}_1}c+\frac{\bar{P}}{\bar{M}_1}\epsilon\right)\\&=-\frac{\bar{M}_1}{\pi}\left(\frac{\bar{C}}{\bar{M}_1}\eta'+\frac{\bar{P}}{\bar{M}_1}\epsilon+c\right)\\&=-\frac{\bar{M}_1}{\pi}(\xi'+c).\end{aligned} \tag{1}$$

[1] The effect on the value of output of the increase in production of importables (analysed under (iii) above) and the associated reduction in the production of exportables induced by the increase in the domestic price of importables can be ignored, since maximization of the value of output under competition implies that the effect of small departures of production from the equilibrium quantities is of the second order of smalls.

(2) (*a*) Where the government spends the tariff revenue, the change in the quantity of imports it demands will be determined by the change in the tariff revenue from private imports and the government's marginal propensity to consume importables; this change is:

$$\frac{dM_2}{dt} = g\frac{dR}{dt} = g\left(t\frac{\partial M_1}{\partial t}+\bar{M}_1\right) = g\bar{M}_1\left(1-\frac{t}{\pi}\xi\right). \tag{2 a}$$

(*b*) Where the tariff revenue is redistributed to the private sector the change in the quantity of imports privately demanded will be determined by the change in the tariff revenue and the marginal propensity to consume importables of the private sector; but the change in the tariff revenue in this case is not simply the change in tariff revenue due to the change in private imports analysed under (1) above, but the product of that change and the sum of a series which is determined by the marginal propensity to consume imports of the private sector. The initial change in the tariff revenue due to the increase in the tariff rate and its effect on the quantity of imports privately demanded will change private expenditure on imports by a fraction of itself approximately equal to c, of which c/π will represent a change in the quantity of imports demanded and ct/π a further change in tariff revenue, which will lead to further changes of c^2t/π^2 in the quantity of imports demanded and c^2t^2/π^2 in tariff revenue, and so on. Hence the total change in redistributed tariff revenue will be:

$$\frac{dR}{dt} = \left(1+\frac{ct}{\pi}+\frac{c^2t^2}{\pi^2}+\ldots\right)\frac{\delta R}{\delta t} = \frac{\pi}{1+(1-c)t}\frac{\delta R}{\delta t},$$

where

$$\frac{\partial R}{\partial t} = \frac{\delta}{\delta t}(tM_1) = \bar{M}_1\left(1-\frac{t}{\pi}\xi\right);$$

and the change in the quantity of imports demanded due to the effect of the tariff change on the amount of redistributed tariff revenue will be:

$$\frac{\partial C}{\partial R}\frac{dR}{dt} = \frac{c}{\pi}\frac{\pi}{1+(1-c)t}\frac{\partial R}{\partial t} = \frac{c\bar{M}_1}{1+(1-c)t}\left(1-\frac{t}{\pi}\xi\right). \tag{2 b}$$

In *case (1)* the total effect of the tariff increase on the world excess demand for importables is [the sum of equations (1) and (2 a)]:[1]

$$\begin{aligned}\frac{dM}{dt} &= -\frac{\bar{M}_1}{\pi}\xi+g\bar{M}_1\left(1-\frac{t}{\pi}\xi\right)\\ &= \bar{M}_1\left(g-\frac{1+gt}{\pi}\xi\right)\\ &= \bar{M}_1\left(g-(1+gt)\frac{c}{\pi}-\frac{1+gt}{\pi}\xi'\right).\end{aligned} \tag{3 I}$$

[1] This result can be obtained directly by differentiating the basic equation for this case, $M \equiv M_1+M_2 = M_1(\pi)+M_2(R)$, where $R = tM_1$ and $dM_2/dR = g$.

If initially there is free trade, this reduces to $dM/dt = \bar{M}_1(g-c-\xi')$, which yields the traditional conclusion that world excess demand for importables at the initial world price will be negative and the terms of trade turn in the country's favour unless the government's marginal propensity to consume importables exceeds the private sector's marginal propensity to consume importables by more than the private sector's compensated elasticity of demand for imports. This in turn requires that the government have a stronger marginal preference for importables than the private sector (a higher marginal propensity to spend on them at the same price) and that the private compensated elasticity of demand for imports be less than unity (assuming that imports are not inferior in private consumption, and that the government, having no initial revenue, cannot have a marginal propensity to spend on importables greater than unity). *If there is a tariff in effect, it remains true that the government must have a higher marginal propensity to consume importables than the private sector for the terms of trade to deteriorate; but since the tariff makes the real cost of importables to the consumer higher than to the government* (assuming that the latter chooses rationally on the basis of world and not domestic prices), *this does not necessarily imply that the government has the stronger marginal preference for importables* (in the sense defined above). *In the general case, also, the terms of trade can deteriorate even if the private compensated elasticity of demand for imports exceeds unity*; this could occur if the government's marginal propensity to consume importables (though higher than the private) were sufficiently low or the tariff rate sufficiently high to offset a compensated elasticity above unity, or if importables were inferior goods to the government at the income level represented by the initial tariff revenue.

In *case (2)* the total effect of the tariff increase on the world excess demand for importables is [the sum of equations (1) and (2 b)]:[1]

$$\frac{dM}{dt} = -\frac{\bar{M}_1}{\pi}\xi + \frac{c\bar{M}_1}{1+(1-c)t}\left(1-\frac{t}{\pi}\xi\right)$$

$$= \frac{\bar{M}_1}{1+(1-c)t}(c-\xi)$$

$$= -\frac{\bar{M}_1\xi'}{1+(1-c)t}. \qquad (4)\ \mathrm{II}$$

It follows that world excess demand for importables at the initial world price must be negative and the terms of trade must be improved following an increase in the tariff rate; hence *the result of a tariff increase in case (2) is the same, whether the tariff increase is imposed on an initial free-trade situation*

[1] This result can be obtained directly by differentiating the basic equation for this case, $M \equiv M_1 = M_1(\pi, R)$ where $\delta M_1/\delta R = c/1+t$ and $R = tM_1$.

or on an existing tariff. This is only what one would expect, since redistribution of tariff proceeds reduces the effect of a tariff increase on the demand for imports to a pure substitution effect.

II. The Effect of an Increase in the Tariff on the Terms of Trade: case (3), Dependence

In the preceding section we have analysed the two traditional cases, (1) where the government spends the tariff revenue, and (2) where the tariff revenue is redistributed to the private sector. In analysing the latter case we have assumed that the tariff proceeds are redistributed in the form of an income subsidy, which is spent by the private sector in the same way as would be an increment in earned income.[1] But it would make no difference to the final result if it were assumed that the tariff proceeds were distributed in kind instead of in cash—that the government used the tariff revenue to purchase some collection of exportables and importables and distributed that collection to the public. For the public would merely adjust its purchases from its earned income to obtain the same total consumption of each good as it would have chosen if the tariff proceeds had been redistributed in cash. A subsidy in kind can only produce a different consumption pattern than a cash subsidy if the amount of a particular good distributed in kind is larger than the total that would have been purchased out of the subsidy-recipient's own income plus the cash subsidy, and this possibility is excluded in the present case by the fact that the amount of goods the government can distribute in kind is restricted by the amount of tariff proceeds it collects.

In analysing the former case we have made the traditional assumption that the behaviour of the private sector is unaffected by the expenditure of the tariff revenue by the government—that private-sector tastes are independent of government consumption. The case of dependence of private tastes on government consumption has recently been examined by Robert Baldwin, who reaches the rather surprising conclusion that the results in the dependence case are the same as in the income-subsidy case. This conclusion is understandable, however, once it is realized that Baldwin identifies the general case of dependence with the special case in which consumers regard government purchases as equivalent to an addition to their own private consumption of the goods concerned. In fact, in his theoretical analysis, Baldwin explicitly treats government consumption as the provision of benefits in kind to consumers, which means that the government in effect is not consuming the tariff proceeds on its own behalf but is redistributing them in kind; and, as we have just argued,

[1] This income-subsidy assumption is to be found in J. E. Meade, *A Geometry of International Trade* (London: Allen & Unwin, 1952), chap. vi. Metzler, op. cit., assumes, however, a reduction in an existing income tax by this amount, which reduces to the same thing.

this should have the same effect as redistributing them through income subsidies.[1]

The more interesting general problem of dependence arises when the government uses the tariff proceeds for its own consumption, *and* the amount of some or all of the governmental services provided by this consumption influences the relative quantities of commodities purchased by the private sector from its earned income in a way not necessarily identifiable with the influence of a direct governmental subsidy in cash or kind. This is a more realistic case than that traditionally analysed [our case (1)] and a more general case than that analysed by Baldwin. One would expect that an increase in state expenditure on, say, police services would lead to a reduction in the amount of private expenditure on fire-arms, locks and bolts, and bodyguards, but not that the effects of the two changes on demand would exactly offset one another, since the government provides services in a different form than they would be privately provided. Similarly, the government provides collective goods which would not be privately provided if consumers had the spending of their tax contributions, and which influence the pattern of private demand.

Technically, dependence implies that the amount of some or all of the service provided by government enters the utility function of the private sector in a significant way (i.e. its substitute-complement relationship with commodities privately consumed varies between commodities) so that the private sector's demands for goods become functions of the total or of some component of the amount of government consumption. In so far as the composition of governmental services depends on the relative prices of commodities purchased by the government, the equilibrium of the economy will vary with the nature of the dependence of private demands on the amounts of governmental services provided; but for the present analysis, which is concerned with the effect of a tariff increase on the excess demand for importables at the given initial world price of importables and assumes that the government chooses on the basis of this price, private demands can be assumed to depend only on the total amount of governmental expenditure, since this will determine the amounts of the separate types of government service provided.[2]

[1] R. E. Baldwin, op. cit., especially pp. 69–71. In note 5 to p. 67, Baldwin interprets 'dependence' in the broader sense in which we discuss it: 'However, as long as the consumption by the government furnishes some utility to the private sector, it is possible for this public consumption to change the civilian offer curve of exports for imports.' But in his analysis he gives it the narrow interpretation discussed here. We are indebted to Mr. Baldwin for correspondence and personal discussion which removed a misunderstanding of his argument on our part.

[2] Our problem here is analytically similar to that faced by J. R. Hicks in his analysis of the effects of a change in wants, in chap. xvii, especially pp. 162–4, of *A Revision of Demand Theory* (Oxford: At the Clarendon Press, 1956).

Dependence means that, in addition to the price effect on private demand for imports and the revenue effect on governmental demand for imports analysed under case (1), the tariff increase will have a dependence effect on private demand for imports through its effect on the amount of government revenue and consumption. This effect will be:

$$\frac{\delta C}{\delta R}\frac{dR}{dt} = \frac{b}{\pi}\left(t\frac{dM_1}{dt}+\bar{M}_1\right), \tag{5}$$

where b, the change in private expenditure on importables associated with a unit change in government expenditure, will be positive or negative according as imports are complementary or substitutary with government expenditure in private consumption. The total change in private demand for imports is now [the sum of equations (1) and (5)]:

$$\frac{dM_1}{dt} = -\frac{\bar{M}_1}{\pi}\xi+\frac{b}{\pi}\left(t\frac{dM_1}{dt}+\bar{M}_1\right) = \frac{(b-\xi)\bar{M}_1}{1+(1-b)t}, \tag{6}$$

and the resulting change in government demand for imports is:

$$\frac{dM_2}{dt} = g\left(\frac{t(b-\xi)\bar{M}_1}{1+(1-b)t}+\bar{M}_1\right) = \frac{(\pi-t\xi)g}{1+(1-b)t}\bar{M}_1; \tag{7}$$

hence the total change in world excess demand for importables is [the sum of equations (6) and (7)]:[1]

$$\frac{dM}{dt} = \frac{\bar{M}_1}{1+(1-b)t}\{b+g\pi-(1+gt)\xi\}$$

$$= \frac{\bar{M}_1}{1+(1-b)t}\{b+g\pi-(1+gt)c-(1+gt)\xi'\}. \tag{8) III}$$

If initially there is free trade, this formula reduces to $\bar{M}_1(b+g-c-\xi')$. In contrast to the case of independence [case (1) above], *world excess demand for importables at the initial world price can be positive and the terms of trade deteriorate even if the private sector has a higher marginal propensity to consume importables than the government and the private compensated elasticity of demand for imports exceeds unity; this result can occur if government services are sufficiently strongly complementary with importables in private-sector consumption.* The same conclusion holds *a fortiori* for the case of an existing tariff.[2]

[1] This result can be obtained directly by differentiating the basic equation for this case, $M \equiv M_1+M_2 = M_1(\pi, R)+M_2(R)$, where $\delta M_1/\delta R = b/\pi$, $\delta M_2/\delta R = g$, and $R = tM_1$; it is necessary first to solve for dM_1/dt by differentiating M_1 alone. It should be noted that the stability of equilibrium requires that the denominator in this and similar expressions presented subsequently for cases (2) and (3) must be positive; this is assumed without further comment in the argument of the rest of this article.

[2] It should be noticed that if consumers treat government consumption as equivalent to personal consumption of the commodities concerned (the Baldwin case), with initial free trade $b = c-g$ and the formula is identical with that given earlier for case (2). With a tariff initially in effect the formulae are different because we have assumed that the government does not pay tariff revenue to itself on its imports.

III. The Effect of an Increase in the Tariff on the Terms of Trade: Disaggregation of the Private Sector

In the previous two sections we have analysed the effect of an increase in the tariff rate in our three cases on the assumption that the private sector could be regarded as a homogeneous unit. Abandonment of this assumption introduces three complications:

(1) In so far as consumers consume exportables and importables in differing proportions, as a result of either taste or income differences, a change in the domestic price of importables alters the distribution of real income between them.

(2) In so far as consumers own factors of production in different proportions, a change in the domestic price of importables, by altering the relative prices of factors of production, alters the distribution of earned income between them.

(3) Where the tariff proceeds are redistributed to the private sector and the marginal propensities of consumers to consume importables differ, as a result of either taste or income differences, the way in which the tariff proceeds are divided among consumers will influence the effect of redistribution on the demand for importables.

To develop the analysis of the disaggregated case we assume that the private sector consists of two typical consumers, each of whom derives his earned income from the ownership of a collection of factors used in production. We begin with case (1); once the results for this case have been developed, the modifications required for the other cases are minor. The problem in case (1) is to disaggregate the elasticity of private demand for imports.

It has been shown elsewhere by one of the present writers that the income earned by a factor owner at any particular domestic price ratio between exportables and importables can be equated with the sum of the real values of the quantities (one of which may be negative) of the two commodities which would be produced with his factors at that price ratio.[1] Accordingly, let the earned incomes of the two factor owners at the initial domestic price of importables be:

$$Y_1 = \pi P_1 + Q_1 \tag{9a}$$

and

$$Y_2 = \pi P_2 + Q_2, \tag{9b}$$

where Y represents income and P and Q quantities of importables and exportables produced, and subscripts 1 and 2 denote the two individuals. We now write the total private-sector demand for importables as the sum

[1] H. G. Johnson, 'International Trade, Income Distribution, and the Offer Curve', *Manchester School of Economic and Social Studies*, vol. xxvii, no. 3 (Sept. 1959), pp. 241–60.

of the demands of the two individuals, each of which depends on the domestic price of importables and the individual's income:[1]

$$C \equiv C_1+C_2 = C_1(\pi, Y_1)+C_2(\pi, Y_2).$$

Differentiating by π, we obtain:[2]

$$\frac{dC}{d\pi} = \frac{\partial C_1}{\partial Y_1}\bar{P}_1+\frac{\partial C_1}{\partial \pi}+\frac{\partial C_2}{\partial Y_2}\bar{P}_2+\frac{\partial C_2}{\partial \pi}$$

$$= \frac{c_1}{\pi}\bar{P}_1-\frac{\bar{C}_1}{\pi}\eta_1+\frac{c_2}{\pi}\bar{P}_2-\frac{\bar{C}_2}{\pi}\eta_2$$

$$= -\frac{\bar{C}_1}{\pi}\eta_1'-\frac{\bar{C}_2}{\pi}\eta_2'-\frac{c_1}{\pi}(\bar{C}_1-\bar{P}_1)-\frac{c_2}{\pi}(\bar{C}_2-\bar{P}_2), \tag{10a}$$

where c_1 and c_2 are the marginal propensities to spend on importables of the two individuals, η_1 and η_2 are the price elasticities of their demands for importables from their initial incomes, and η_1' $(=\eta_1-c_1)$ and η_2' $(=\eta_2-c_2)$ are their compensated price elasticities of demand for importables.

The two terms on the right-hand side of the above expression represent the net income effects of the increased price of imports on the demands of the two individuals; the terms in parentheses are the net income-losses themselves. Unless the excess of initial consumption over the amount of importables the individual's factors would produce bears the same ratio to the initial amount of income for each individual, the price increase will alter the relative real incomes of the individuals; that individual will gain relatively who initially spent the smaller proportion of his income on importables, factors being owned in equal ratios by the two individuals, or who possesses the higher proportion of factors used relatively intensively in the importable-good industry, initial consumption proportions being equal. If tastes, incomes, or factor-ownership ratios differ considerably, it is even possible that one individual's consumption of importables will be less than the amount of importables produced by his factors, so that that individual gains real income as a result of the increase in the price of imports; this must be true in the extreme case in which each individual owns the whole supply of one factor, since in that case the individual's income will comprise a negative quantity of the good which uses intensively the factor he does not own. If conditions are such that one individual gains real income, and his marginal propensity to spend on importables is higher

[1] For the analysis of case (2), demands depend on the sum of earned income and the amount of redistributed tariff proceeds received; but the latter is assumed constant in deriving the elasticities of consumption demand and the elasticity of import demand.

[2] For each individual $\delta Y/\delta\pi = P$, since the effect on the real value of his income of changes in the relative amounts of the two goods produced by his factors induced by the change in π can be neglected for small changes.

than that of the other individual, the aggregate income effect on demand for importables may be positive rather than negative; the individual gaining real income must have the higher marginal propensity to spend on importables for this to happen, since the other individual must be consuming both the excess of this individual's production of importables over his consumption and the country's imports from the rest of the world ($\bar{C}_1-\bar{P}_1 = \bar{M}_1+\bar{P}_2-\bar{C}_2$). If the aggregate income effect on demand for imports is positive it may outweigh the negative effects of the compensated elasticities, so that the aggregate effect of an increase in the price of importables is to increase the quantity of imports demanded.

This possibility can be shown by re-writing $dC/d\pi$ in the form

$$\frac{dC}{d\pi} = -\frac{\bar{C}_1}{\pi}\eta_1' - \frac{\bar{C}_2}{\pi}\eta_2' - \left(\frac{c_2}{\pi}-\frac{c_1}{\pi}\right)(\bar{C}_2-\bar{P}_2) - \frac{c_1}{\pi}\bar{M}_1. \quad (10\,\text{b})$$

If individual 2 has the higher marginal propensity to consume importables and his factors produce more importables than he consumes, the second-to-last term on the right will be positive. The quantity of importables demanded will increase when the price of importables rises if

$$(c_2-c_1)(\bar{C}_2-\bar{P}_2) > \bar{C}_1\eta_1'+\bar{C}_2\eta_2'+c_1\bar{M}_1.$$

The total change in private demand for imports resulting from an increase in the domestic price of importables is the difference between the change in consumption demand and the increase in domestic production. Hence the disaggregated elasticity of private demand for imports is:

$$\begin{aligned}\xi &= \left(\frac{\bar{P}}{\bar{M}_1}\epsilon + \frac{\bar{C}_1}{\bar{M}_1}\eta_1' + \frac{\bar{C}_2}{\bar{M}_1}\eta_2' + c_1 + (c_2-c_1)\frac{\bar{C}_2-\bar{P}_2}{\bar{M}_1}\right)\\ &= \{\xi'+c_1+(c_2-c_1)m_2\}, \quad (11)\end{aligned}$$

where $m_2 = (\bar{C}_2-\bar{P}_2)/\bar{M}_1$ is the proportion of the country's imports consumed, net, by individual 2. If m_2 is negative, individual 2 is a 'net supplier' of importables to the economy. For convenience we shall assume in what follows that individual 2 has the higher marginal propensity to consume importables ($c_2 > c_1$).

The formula for the effect of an increase in the tariff rate in the *disaggregated case* (*1*) is readily obtained by substituting the expression for the disaggregated elasticity of private demand for imports just derived into the formula [equation (3)] given in Section I above. The resulting formula is:

$$\frac{dM}{dt} = \bar{M}_1\left(g-(1+gt)\frac{c_1}{\pi} - \frac{1+gt}{\pi}(c_2-c_1)m_2 - \frac{1+gt}{\pi}\xi'\right). \quad (12)\ \text{IV}$$

In the initial free-trade case this reduces to

$$\frac{dM}{dt} = \bar{M}_1\{g-c_1-(c_2-c_1)m_2-\xi'\}.$$

The chief modification to the preceding analysis of case (1) introduced by disaggregation which emerges from this formula is that *it is not necessary for the government to have a higher marginal propensity to consume importables than the private sector for the tariff increase to give rise to a positive excess demand for importables in the world market* and so necessitate a deterioration in the terms of trade. *Such a deterioration can occur even though the government has a lower marginal propensity to consume importables from an increment of tariff revenue than does either individual from an increment in his income,* if the individual with the higher marginal propensity to consume importables is a net supplier of importables to the economy (m_2 is negative in the above formula). Similarly, even in the case of initial free trade a deterioration of the terms of trade does not require an inelastic compensated private demand for imports.

To obtain the formula for the effect of the tariff increase in the *disaggregated case* (*2*) from the formula given [equation (4)] for the aggregated case (2) in Section I, it is necessary both to substitute the disaggregated expression for the aggregate elasticity of private demand for imports and to replace the single marginal propensity to consume importables used in analysing the effect of the change in the amount of redistributed tariff proceeds by an average of the marginal propensities of the two individuals, weighted by the proportions in which they share in the redistributed tariff proceeds. The resulting formula is:

$$\frac{dM}{dt} = \frac{\bar{M}_1}{1+(1-\bar{c})t}(\bar{c}-\xi) = \frac{\bar{M}_1}{1+(1-\bar{c})t}\{(c_2-c_1)(s_2-m_2)-\xi'\}, \quad (13)\text{ V}$$

where s_2 is the share of individual 2 in marginal redistributed tariff proceeds, and $\bar{c}$ [$= c_1+s_2(c_2-c_1)$] is the weighted average marginal propensity to spend redistributed tariff proceeds on importables. This formula shows that, in contrast to the aggregated case (2), *in the disaggregated case* (*2*) *the tariff increase does not necessarily produce a negative world excess demand for importables* and turn the terms of trade in the tariff-increasing country's favour. *The reverse is possible if the share in the redistributed tariff proceeds of the individual with the higher marginal propensity to consume importables is larger than the proportion of the initial quantity of imports he consumes.* This will be the case, for example, if tariff proceeds are redistributed in proportion to income and (for reasons discussed above) the quantity of imports he consumes is smaller in relation to his income than is the quantity consumed by the other individual in relation to the latter's income—so that this individual is overcompensated for the income effect of the increased domestic price of importables. It should be noticed also that, since the individual with the higher marginal propensity to consume importables may be a net supplier of importables to the economy (m_2

negative) there may be *no* way of allocating the marginal change in tariff proceeds between the two individuals which would compensate both of them exactly for the income effect of the tariff increase.

To obtain the formula for the effect of the tariff increase in the *disaggregated case* (3) from the formula [equation (8)] given for the aggregated case (3) in Section II above, it is necessary to substitute the disaggregated expression for the elasticity of private demand for importables in that formula and to rewrite the dependence effect as the sum of the dependence effects on the two individuals (which may be of different magnitudes and opposite signs). The resulting formula is:

$$dM/dt = \frac{\bar{M}_1}{1+(1-b_1-b_2)t}\{b_1+b_2+g\pi-(1+gt)c_1-(1+gt)(c_2-c_1)m_2-(1+gt)\xi'\}. \quad (14)\text{ VI}$$

The main modification introduced by disaggregation arises from the possibility that the individual with the higher marginal propensity to consume importables will gain real income from the increase in the domestic price of importables; the nature of this modification has already been discussed in connexion with the disaggregated case (1).

IV. The Effect of an Increase in the Tariff on the Terms of Trade: Variable Supplies of Factors of Production

In the preceding sections we have successively relaxed three of the assumptions of the traditional analysis of the effect of a tariff on the terms of trade—the assumptions of initial free trade, independence of private from government consumption, and homogeneity of the private sector. We must now relax the fourth assumption, constancy of supplies of factors of production. The analysis of the effects of a tariff when factor supplies are variable is the subject of a paper by Murray C. Kemp, which we have been privileged to read and which suggested the inclusion of the present section of this article to us. We gratefully acknowledge his priority, and also our indebtedness to R. W. Jones, who has since produced a broader study of variability of factor supplies in international trade;[1] our own analysis takes a slightly different form from theirs, better adapted to the general purpose of this article.

For simplicity of analysis we shall assume that only the quantity of labour is variable. This assumption has some economic justification,

[1] M. C. Kemp, 'Tariffs, Protection, and the Distribution of National Income', and R. W. Jones, 'General Equilibrium with Variable Labor Supply'; these two papers are to be merged in a forthcoming joint article, 'Variable Labour Supply and the Theory of International Trade'.

inasmuch as we may assume that the quantity of labour available for employment from a given total stock depends on the relative attractiveness at the margin of the real consumption obtainable by offering labour and of the leisure obtained by not offering it, to the owner of labour, while the total stock of capital, having no alternative utility-yielding use, is always available for employment. The real consumption enjoyed with the employment of a given quantity of labour depends on the quantity of labour employed, the quantity of capital owned, the real wage rate and real rent rate measured in terms of exportable goods, and the relative price of importables; but the real wage and real rent rates are linked through the technology of the economy to the relative price of importables, so that the latter determines the former. In cases (2) and (3), though in different ways, real consumption also depends on the amount of tariff revenue.

With leisure as the alternative to labour the quantity of labour supplied will decrease with an increase in the amount of real income that could be enjoyed with the employment of the initial amount of labour, since some (but not all, barring inferiority of real consumption) of the potential increase in real consumption will be consumed in the form of leisure. The real consumption enjoyable from the employment of the initial amount of labour remaining constant, an increase in the real wage rate will generally, but not always, increase the quantity of labour supplied. Such a 'compensated' increase in the real wage-rate has two effects: it raises the price of labour (the cost of leisure) in terms of goods, and so induces a substitution of labour, and the real consumption it makes possible, for leisure—an increase in the quantity of labour supplied; but it also reduces the relative price of the commodity in whose production labour is used relatively unintensively. If this commodity is substitutary with leisure, the effect is again to induce an increase in the quantity of labour supplied; but if it is complementary with leisure, the effect is to induce a decrease in the quantity of labour supplied, and this effect may be strong enough to outweigh the general tendency to substitute real consumption for leisure, and so reduce the quantity of labour supplied. This possibility we shall describe as one of strong complementarity of leisure and the capital-intensive good in consumption.

With this background, we can proceed to the analysis of the effect of a tariff increase in our three aggregative cases.

The increase in the domestic price of importables resulting from the tariff increase has two effects on the quantity of labour supplied:

(*a*) The loss of real income due to the increase in the price of importables increases the quantity of labour supplied. The loss of real income due to the increased price of importables is approximately equal to the increased cost of the initial volume of private imports, and the change in the quantity of labour supplied for this reason is therefore:

$$\frac{\partial L}{\partial Y'}\frac{\partial Y'}{\partial \pi}\frac{d\pi}{dt} = (-l)(-\bar{M}_1) = \bar{M}_1 l, \tag{15a}$$

where Y' represents real income and l represents the marginal propensity to consume leisure when potential real income increases; l must be positive and smaller than $1/w$ (w being the real wage-rate) on the assumption that neither leisure nor real consumption is inferior.

(*b*) The change in the relative price of labour due to the change in the relative price of importables alters the quantity of labour supplied, the direction and extent of the change being determined by the elasticity of the real wage rate with respect to the price of importables and the elasticity of supply of labour with respect to the real wage-rate. The change in the quantity of labour supplied is:

$$\frac{\partial L}{\partial w}\frac{\partial w}{\partial \pi}\frac{d\pi}{dt} = \frac{\bar{L}}{\pi}\lambda e_w, \tag{15b}$$

where $\lambda \{= (w/L)\partial L/\partial w\}$ is the compensated elasticity of supply of labour, and is positive unless there is strong complementarity between the capital-intensive commodity and leisure, and $e_w \{= (\pi/w)\partial w/\partial \pi\}$ is the elasticity of the real wage-rate with respect to the price of importables. Since a rise in the price of importables will raise or lower the real wage-rate according as labour is used relatively intensively in the importable-goods or the exportable-goods industry, e_w will be positive or negative according as the importable-goods industry is labour-intensive or capital-intensive.

The change in the quantity of labour initially supplied due to these two effects of the increased domestic price of importables resulting from the tariff increase is therefore:

$$\frac{\partial L}{\partial t} = \frac{\partial L}{\partial \pi}\frac{d\pi}{dt} = \frac{\bar{L}}{\pi}\lambda e_w + \bar{M}_1 l. \tag{16}$$

This change in the quantity of labour supplied due to the increase in the domestic price of importables has two effects on the quantity of imports demanded (in addition to those analysed in Section I):

(1) The change in the quantity of labour supplied changes the amount of income earned by the private sector and so changes the quantity of importables demanded. The change in earned income is approximately equal to the wage rate multiplied by the change in the quantity of labour supplied, and the change in the quantity of imports demanded due to a change in earned income is determined by the marginal propensity to consume importables. Hence the change in the quantity of importables

4520.3 R

demanded due to the effect of the tariff increase on the domestic price of importables is:

$$\frac{\partial C}{\partial L}\frac{\partial L}{\partial t} = \frac{cw}{\pi}\left(\frac{\bar{L}}{\pi}\lambda e_w + \bar{M}_1 l\right). \tag{17 a}$$

(2) The change in the quantity of labour supplied changes the amount of importables domestically produced. This change can be deduced from one of the established propositions of the theory of international trade and economic growth, according to which an increase in the quantity of one factor at a given domestic price ratio must be absorbed by transferring both factors out of the industry which uses that factor unintensively into the other industry, where they are combined with the new quantities of the increased factor in the more intensive ratio optimal in that industry; and conversely for a decrease in the quantity of a factor.[1] The changes in the outputs of the two industries, per unit change in the total amount of a factor supplied, are determined by the factor ratios in the two industries and the average output per unit of the factor whose supply is altered in the relevant industry.[2]

It follows from this principle that the change in the output of importables due to a change in the quantity of labour supplied must be greater absolutely than the change in national income due to the same cause, so that the effect on importable goods production dominates the net effect on imports demanded of a change in the quantity of labour supplied. Also, the change in the domestic output of importable goods due to an increase in the quantity of labour supplied must be of the same sign as the change in the real wage-rate due to an increase in the domestic price of importable goods. If labour is used intensively in importable-goods production, an increase in the domestic price of importables must increase the real wage-rate, and an increase in the quantity of labour must be absorbed by an expansion of production of importables at the expense of exportables; conversely, if labour is used intensively in the production of exportables, an increase in the domestic price of importables must lower the real wage-rate and an increase in the quantity of labour supplied must increase the domestic

[1] This proposition is originally due to T. M. Rybczynski, 'Factor Endowment and Relative Commodity Prices', *Economica*, N.S., vol. xxii, no. 88 (Nov. 1955), pp. 336–41. For a recent statement, see J. Bhagwati and H. G. Johnson, 'Notes on Some Controversies in the Theory of International Trade', *Economic Journal*, vol. lxx, no. 277 (Mar. 1960), pp. 74–93, especially p. 82.

[2] Let k_1 and $k_2 (< k_1)$ be the capital: labour ratios in the capital-intensive and labour-intensive industries, and a_1 and a_2 be the average products of labour in those industries. The movement of a unit of labour from the former to the latter industry releases $(k_1 - k_2)$ units of capital, which will permit the employment of an additional $(k_1 - k_2)/k_2$ units of labour in the labour-intensive industry: hence employment of an additional unit of labour in the latter industry requires a transfer of $k_2/(k_1 - k_2)$ labour units (together with the capital employed with them in the capital-intensive industry). Output in the capital-intensive industry, therefore, must fall by $k_2 a_1/(k_1 - k_2)$, and output in the labour-intensive industry rise by $a_2\{1 + k_2/(k_1 - k_2)\} = k_1 a_2/(k_1 - k_2)$ when the labour supply increases by one unit.

production of exportables at the expense of importables. Accordingly, the change in the domestic production of importable goods due to the tariff increase is:

$$\frac{\partial P}{\partial L}\frac{\partial L}{\partial t} = \rho\left(\frac{\bar{L}}{\pi}\lambda e_w + \bar{M}_1 l\right), \tag{17b}$$

where ρ, the change in the quantity of importables domestically produced due to an increase in the quantity of labour supplied, must have the same sign as e_w and exceed w in absolute magnitude.[1]

The net change in the quantity of importables demanded by the private sector due to the change in the quantity of labour supplied resulting from the effect of the tariff increase on the real wage-rate is therefore [the difference between (17a) and (17b)]:

$$\frac{\partial M_1}{\partial L}\frac{\partial L}{\partial t} = \left(\frac{cw}{\pi} - \rho\right)\left(\frac{\bar{L}}{\pi}\lambda e_w + \bar{M}_1 l\right). \tag{18}$$

To allow for variability of the quantity of labour supplied in response to the increase in the domestic price of importables resulting from the tariff increase in deriving the formulae for the effect of the tariff increase on the world excess demand for importables, it is necessary to include the expression just derived in reckoning the effect of the tariff increase on the quantity of importables privately demanded. This entails adding the expression

$$-\frac{\pi}{\bar{M}_1}\frac{\partial M_1}{\partial L}\frac{\partial L}{\partial t} = (\rho\pi - cw)\left(\frac{\bar{L}}{\pi\bar{M}_1}\lambda e_w + l\right), \tag{19}$$

to the elasticity of private demand for imports in the formulae derived in Sections I and II. In this expression $(\rho\pi - cw)$ must have the same sign as ρ, because ρ exceeds w in absolute magnitude and c, the marginal propensity to consume importables, is assumed to be less than unity and therefore less than π.

In *case (1)*, where the government spends the tariff revenue and the preferences of the private sector are independent of the amount of government expenditure, this is the only adjustment required. In *case (2)*, however, the change in the amount of tariff revenue redistributed due to the tariff increase will alter the real income obtainable with the employment of the initial quantity of labour supplied and so alter the quantity of labour supplied. The change in the amount of importables demanded resulting for this reason from the increase in the tariff rate will be:

$$\frac{\partial M_1}{\partial L}\frac{\partial L}{\partial Y'}\frac{dR}{dt} = \left(\rho - \frac{cw}{\pi}\right)l\frac{dR}{dt}. \tag{20}$$

In *case (3)* the quantity of labour supplied will depend on the amount of

[1] It follows from n. 2, p. 242, that $\rho = k_x a_m/(k_x - k_m)$, where the subscripts x and m refer to the exportable-goods and importable-goods industries respectively.

government services if leisure is substitutary or complementary with government services; in this case the change in tariff revenue due to the tariff increase will change the quantity of imports demanded through its effects on the quantity of labour supplied by the amount

$$\frac{\partial M_1}{\partial L}\frac{\partial L}{\partial R}\frac{dR}{dt} = \left(\frac{cw}{\pi}-\rho\right)\alpha\frac{dR}{dt}, \tag{21}$$

where α is the change in the quantity of labour supplied due to a unit increase in government expenditure, and may be positive or negative.

In the *aggregated case* (*1*) with variable labour supply, the effect of the tariff increase on the world excess demand for importables is[1] [derived from (3) and (19)]:

$$\frac{dM}{dt} = \bar{M}_1\left\{g-(1+gt)\frac{c}{\pi}-\frac{(1+gt)}{\pi}\xi'-\frac{(1+gt)}{\pi}(\rho\pi-cw)\left(\frac{\bar{L}}{\pi\bar{M}_1}\lambda e_w+l\right)\right\}. \tag{22) VII}$$

If the elasticity of supply of labour λ is positive, and ρ is also positive, implying that importable-goods production is labour-intensive, the last term within the brackets must be positive, so that all the terms except g have a negative sign, and the traditional conclusion that an adverse movement of the terms of trade requires a governmental marginal propensity to consume importables greater than the private marginal propensity to consume them continues to hold. But if the elasticity of supply of labour λ is positive and ρ is negative, implying that exportable-goods production is labour-intensive, it is possible for the last term to be negative (in spite of the fact that the first half of it must be positive owing to the identity of signs of ρ and e_w), so that the traditional condition is not necessary in this case. If the elasticity of supply of labour λ is negative and ρ is also negative —implying that importables are capital-intensive in production and strongly complementary with leisure in consumption—the last term must be negative, so that the influence of variability of the labour supply is to increase the world excess demand for importables, and the traditional condition is not necessary for the terms of trade to turn against the country. Similarly, if the elasticity of supply of labour λ is negative and ρ is positive— exportables are capital-intensive in production and strongly complementary with leisure in consumption—the last term may be negative on balance, and again the traditional condition is not necessary for the terms of trade to turn against the country.

In the *aggregated case* (*2*), with variable labour supply, the effect of the

[1] This result is obtained, as explained above, by adding the expression for the effect of the tariff increase, via the labour supply, on the demand for importables to the elasticity of private demand for imports in the formula previously derived for the aggregated case with constant labour supply.

tariff increase on world excess demand for importables is [the sum of (4), (18), and (20)]:

$$\frac{dM_1}{dt} = \frac{\partial M_1}{\partial t} + \left(\frac{cw}{\pi} - \rho\right)\frac{\partial L}{\partial t} + \left(\frac{c}{\pi}\right)\frac{dR}{dt} + \left(\rho - \frac{cw}{\pi}\right)l\frac{dR}{dt}$$

$$= -\frac{\bar{M}_1}{\pi}\left\{\xi + (\rho\pi - cw)\left(\frac{\bar{L}}{\pi\bar{M}_1}\lambda e_w + l\right)\right\} + \left\{\frac{c}{\pi} + \left(\rho - \frac{cw}{\pi}\right)l\right\}\left(\bar{M}_1 + t\frac{dM_1}{dt}\right)$$

$$= \frac{\bar{M}_1}{1 + \{1 - c - (\rho\pi - cw)l\}t}\left(-\xi' - (\rho\pi - cw)\frac{\bar{L}}{\pi\bar{M}_1}\lambda e_w\right). \qquad (23)\ \text{VIII}$$

Since $(\rho\pi - cw)(\bar{L}/\pi\bar{M}_1)e_w$ must be positive, the tariff increase cannot turn the terms of trade against the country if the supply of labour is positively elastic with respect to the real wage rate (λ is positive). If the supply of labour is negatively elastic (strong complementarity of the capital-intensive commodity, whichever it is, with leisure in consumption) the terms of trade may turn against the country. Thus variability of the labour supply can reverse the traditional conclusion in the exceptional case of a negative elasticity of supply of labour.

In the *aggregated case (3)*, with variable labour supply, the change in the amount of imports privately demanded due to the tariff increase is:

$$\frac{dM_1}{dt} = \frac{\partial M_1}{\partial t} + \left(\frac{cw}{\pi} - \rho\right)\left(\frac{\partial L}{\partial t}\right) + \left\{\frac{b}{\pi} + \left(\frac{cw}{\pi} - \rho\right)\alpha\right\}\frac{dR}{dt}$$

$$= \frac{b - \xi - (\xi\pi - cw)\{\alpha + (\bar{L}/\pi\bar{M}_1)\lambda e_w + l\}}{1 + \{1 - b + (\rho\pi - cw)\alpha\}t}\bar{M}_1; \qquad (24\text{ a})$$

the change in the amount of imports demanded by the government is:

$$\frac{dM_2}{dt} = g\left(\bar{M}_1 + t\frac{dM_1}{dt}\right) = \frac{\pi - t\xi - t(\rho\pi - cw)\{(\bar{L}/\pi\bar{M}_1)\lambda e_w + l\}}{1 + \{1 - b + (\rho\pi - cw)\alpha\}t}g\bar{M}_1; \qquad (24\text{ b})$$

and the change in the total quantity of imports demanded, and the world excess demand for importables, is consequently [the sum of (24 a) and (24 b)]:

$$\frac{dM}{dt} = \frac{\pi g + b - (1+gt)\xi' - (1+gt)c - (1+gt)(\rho\pi - cw)\{(\bar{L}/\pi\bar{M}_1)\lambda e_w + l) - (\rho\pi - cw)\alpha}{1 + \{1 - b + (\rho\pi - cw)\alpha\}t}\bar{M}_1. \qquad (25)\ \text{IX}$$

In the case of initial free trade, which we shall consider for simplicity, this reduces to:

$$\frac{dM}{dt} = \left[g + b - \xi' - c - (\rho\pi - cw)\left(\frac{\bar{L}}{\bar{M}_1}\lambda e_w + l + \alpha\right)\right]\bar{M}_1.$$

It follows from this formula that, even with initial free trade, an inverse relation between government expenditure and private demand for importables, and a government marginal propensity to consume importables less than that of the private sector, an increase in the tariff rate can turn the terms of trade against the country. This requires the final term of the foregoing expression to be negative, which in turn requires $\left(\lambda+\frac{l+\alpha}{e_w}\frac{\bar{M}_1}{\bar{L}}\right)$ to be negative. This is possible in the following cases:

(i) Negative elasticity of supply of labour ($\lambda < 0$), requiring strong complementarity of the capital-intensive good (which may be either commodity) with leisure in consumption; the necessary condition for the term to be negative in this case is $-\lambda > \frac{l+\alpha}{\bar{L}e_w}\bar{M}_1$.

(ii) Positive elasticity of supply of labour ($\lambda > 0$) and negative elasticity of the wage-rate with respect to the price of importables ($e_w < 0$), which requires the exportable-goods industry to be relatively labour-intensive, together with $(l+\alpha)$ positive, which, since l is necessarily positive, is consistent with the quantity of labour supplied either increasing or decreasing as government expenditure increases; the necessary condition for the term to be negative in this case is $\frac{l+\alpha}{\lambda}\frac{\bar{M}_1}{\bar{L}} > -e_w$.

(iii) Positive elasticity of supply of labour ($\lambda > 0$) and positive elasticity of the wage-rate with respect to the price of importables ($e_w > 0$), which requires the importable-goods industry to be labour-intensive, together with $(l+\alpha)$ negative, which, since l is necessarily positive, requires that an increase in government expenditure reduce the quantity of labour supplied; the necessary condition for the term to be negative in this case is $-\alpha > \frac{\bar{L}\lambda e_w}{\bar{M}_1}+l$.

To obtain the formulae for the effect of the tariff increase on world excess demand for importables in the *disaggregated cases* it is necessary to introduce appropriately weighted averages of the expressions for the income and substitution effects of the increase in the domestic price of importables due to the tariff increase on the quantity of labour supplied, and of the effects on labour supplied of the change in the tariff revenue due to the tariff increase, for the two individuals. The resulting formulae will not be reproduced here; the general nature of the effects of allowing for differences between members of the private sector can be inferred from the argument of this and the preceding section.

V. The Effect of an Increase in the Tariff on the Domestic Price Ratio

The previous sections of this article have been concerned with generalizing the theory of the effect of a tariff increase on the terms of trade of the tariff-raising country. In this final section we consider the conditions under which a tariff increase may improve the terms of trade so much that the internal price of importable goods actually falls, a question which is of particular interest in connexion with the effect of the tariff in redistributing income between the owners of factors of production. The traditional analysis concludes (as mentioned in the introduction) that such an improvement requires that the marginal propensity to spend on domestic goods of the government or the private sector, whichever spends the tariff proceeds, must exceed the foreign elasticity of demand for the country's exports (so that, barring inferiority of importables in private or government consumption, that elasticity must be less than unity).

Like the terms of trade problem, this problem can be simplified by considering the effect of the tariff increase on world excess demand for importables at a given price for them; in this case we consider the effect on excess demand at the initial domestic price of importables. World excess demand for importables is symbolized below by $M' \equiv M - M_s$, where M is the quantity of imports demanded by the tariff-imposing country and M_s the quantity of imports supplied by the rest of the world; initially $M' = 0$. The tariff increase will raise or lower the internal price of importables according as it gives rise to an excess demand for or excess supply of importables in the world market at the initial domestic price of importables. We begin with our three aggregated cases, assuming that the private sector can be treated as homogeneous and that factor supplies are constant. The effect of the tariff increase on the world excess demand for importables is then the net resultant of three effects of the tariff increase:

(1) The tariff increase reduces the price offered to foreign suppliers for imports, and so alters the quantity supplied at the initial domestic price ratio. The change in the quantity supplied is

$$\frac{dM_s}{dt} = \frac{dM_s}{dp}\frac{dp}{dt} = \frac{dM_s}{dp}\frac{d}{dt}\left(\frac{\pi}{1+t}\right) = -\frac{\epsilon_f}{\pi}\overline{M}_s = \frac{1-\eta_f}{\pi}\overline{M}, \qquad (26)$$

where ϵ_f is the foreign elasticity of supply of imports and η_f is the elasticity of foreign demand for the country's exports. For the quantity of imports supplied to increase when the price offered for them falls, it is necessary for the foreign import demand elasticity to be less than unity. We shall not investigate the determinants of the foreign import demand elasticity; but the analysis of the preceding sections shows that, in addition to the usual possibility of a low demand elasticity due to a low elasticity of substitution between exportables and importables in foreign consumption, the foreign elasticity of demand for imports may be less than unity, and even negative, if the factor used intensively in foreign production of exportables has the higher marginal propensity to consume exportables, or if the supply curve of that factor is backward-rising.

(2) Where the government spends the tariff proceeds, and allocates expenditure between exportables and importables on the basis of world market prices, the reduction in the world market price increases the quantity of imports it demands from a given tariff revenue. The change in the quantity of imports demanded on this account is

$$\frac{\delta M_2}{\delta p}\frac{dp}{dt} = -\eta_g \bar{M}_2 \frac{d}{dt}\left(\frac{\pi}{1+t}\right) = \frac{\eta_g}{\pi}\bar{M}_2, \tag{27}$$

where η_g is the elasticity of government demand for imports.

(3) The increase in the tariff rate increases the tariff proceeds derived from the initial volume of imports and so increases the quantity of imports demanded to an extent which is differently determined in the different cases. The increase in the tariff revenue derived from the initial volume of imports is

$$\frac{\partial R}{\partial t} = \frac{\partial}{\partial t}\left(\frac{t}{1+t}\pi\bar{M}_1\right) = \frac{\bar{M}_1}{\pi}.$$

(*a*) Where the government spends the tariff revenue and private-sector demand is independent of the level of government activity (case (1)), the increase in the quantity of imports demanded due to the increase in the tariff revenue is:

$$\frac{\partial M_2}{\partial R}\frac{\delta R}{\delta t} = g\frac{\partial R}{\partial t} = \frac{g}{\pi}\bar{M}_1.$$

(*b*) Where the tariff revenue is redistributed to the private sector (case (2)), the increase in the quantity of imports demanded is

$$\frac{dM_1}{dt} = \frac{\partial M_1}{\partial R}\frac{dR}{dt} = \frac{c}{\pi}\left(\frac{\partial R}{\partial t}+t\frac{dM_1}{dt}\right) = \frac{c}{1+(1-c)t}\frac{\bar{M}_1}{\pi}.$$

(*c*) In case (3), where the government spends the tariff revenue and private demand for importables is dependent on the amount of governmental services provided, the tariff increase has a fourth effect, which is most conveniently considered in conjunction with the third. For, in addition to increasing the level of government consumption through increasing the amount of tariff revenue, the increase in the tariff rate, by reducing the price offered to foreign suppliers, both increases the real level and alters the composition of government consumption from the initial amount of tariff revenue. These changes, as well as the increase in tariff revenue, will have a dependence effect on the private demand for importables, which effect will differ according to the precise nature of the dependence of private demand on governmental activity. The latter must accordingly be specified, whereas it could legitimately be ignored in analysing the effect of the tariff increase on the terms of trade. Three cases can be distinguished: (3 *a*) dependence on total real governmental consumption, (3 *b*) dependence on the quantity of importables consumed by the government, and (3*c*) dependence on the quantity of exportables consumed by the government.

A *general formula for case* (*3*) which can be adapted to fit these alternative assumptions about the nature of dependence can be derived as follows: define B as the increase in quantity of importables privately demanded when government revenue (expenditure) increases by one unit, and A as the increase in government revenue that would produce the same effect on private demand for importables as the change in whatever aspect of government expenditure influences that demand that results from the tariff increase, tariff revenue being held constant. Then the increase in the quantity of importables privately demanded due to the effect of the tariff increase on governmental consumption is

$$\frac{dM_1}{dt} = \frac{\partial M_1}{\partial R}\left(\frac{dR}{dt}+A\right) = B\left(\frac{\delta R}{\delta t}+t\frac{dM_1}{dt}+A\right) = \frac{B(\bar{M}_1/\pi+A)}{1-Bt};$$

the increase in the quantity of imports demanded by the government due to the increase in tariff revenue is

$$\frac{dM_2}{dt} = \frac{\delta M_2}{\delta R}\frac{dR}{dt} = g\left(\frac{\delta R}{\delta t}+t\frac{dM_1}{dt}\right) = \frac{g(\bar{M}_1/\pi+ABt)}{1-Bt};$$

and the total change[1] in the quantity of importables demanded resulting from the effect of the increase in the tariff rate on governmental expenditure and the associated dependence effect on private demand for importables is

$$\frac{dM}{dt} = \frac{(g+B)(\bar{M}_1/\pi)+AB(1+gt)}{1-Bt} = \frac{g\bar{M}_1}{\pi}+\frac{(1+gt)B(\bar{M}_1/\pi+A)}{1-Bt}. \quad (28)$$

The reduction in the price of imports due to the increase in the tariff (tariff proceeds remaining constant) increases governmental real income by $-\bar{M}_2\, dp/dt = \bar{M}_2/\pi$, increases governmental consumption of importables by $(\delta M_2/\delta p)(dp/dt) = \eta_g(\bar{M}_2/\pi)$, and alters governmental consumption of exportables by $-\delta(p\bar{M}_2)/\delta t = (1-\eta_g)(\bar{M}_2/\pi)$. Hence the parameter A in the general formula is equal to $\bar{M}_2/\pi$ in case (3*a*), $(\eta_g/g)(\bar{M}_2/\pi)$ in case (3*b*), and $\{(1-\eta_g)/(1-g)\}(\bar{M}_2/\pi)$ in case (3*c*). The parameter B in the formula is equal to b_r/π in case (3*a*), $b_m g/\pi$ in case (3*b*), and $b_x(1-g)/\pi$ in case (3*c*), where the b's are coefficients relating the increase in private expenditure on importables to the increase in real government consumption, government consumption of importables, and government consumption of exportables, which induce it in the three cases. The total changes in the quantity of imports demanded resulting from the effects of the tariff increase under analysis in the three sub-cases are obtained by inserting these values in

[1] This change excludes the direct effect of the lower price of imports in increasing government consumption of them from the initial tariff revenue, discussed under (2) above.

the general formula; since the results are rather cumbrous, and are contained in the formulae for the effect of the tariff increase on the excess demand for importables presented below, they are not reproduced here.

In *case (1)* the total effect of the tariff increase on world excess demand for importables at the initial domestic price of importables is

$$\frac{dM'}{dt} = \frac{dM}{dt} - \frac{dM_s}{dt} = \left(g + \eta_g' \frac{\overline{M}_2}{\overline{M}} - 1 + \eta_f\right)\frac{\overline{M}}{\pi}, \tag{29) X}$$

where η_g' is the compensated elasticity of government demand for imports. For this to be negative, representing an excess supply of importables and necessitating a reduction in the world and domestic price of importables to restore equilibrium, requires[1]

$$(1-g) - \frac{\overline{M}_2}{\overline{M}}\eta_g' > \eta_f.$$

Whether free trade ($\overline{M}_2 = 0$) or a tariff ($\overline{M}_2 > 0$) is initially in force, the internal price of imports can fall only if the government's marginal propensity to spend on exportables $(1-g)$ exceeds the foreign elasticity of demand for imports (η_f), which in turn requires an inelastic foreign demand for imports unless importables are inferior in government consumption at the pre-existing level of tariff proceeds. Where a tariff is initially in force, an excess of $(1-g)$ over η_f is a necessary but not a sufficient condition for the internal price of importables to fall.

In *case (2)* the total effect of the tariff increase on the world excess demand for importables is[2]

$$\frac{dM'}{dt} = \left(\frac{c}{1+(1-c)t} - 1 + \eta_f\right)\frac{\overline{M}_1}{\pi}. \tag{30) XI}$$

A decrease in the world and domestic price of importables in this case requires

$$(1-c) > \frac{\eta_f}{\pi - \eta_f t}.$$

This requires the private sector's marginal propensity to spend on export-

[1] This result differs from that derived by Metzler in the supplementary paper referred to in n. 1, p. 226 (op. cit., especially equation (7), p. 439). The reason is that Metzler, in dealing with the case, writes governmental demand as a function of the tariff proceeds measured in importable goods. whereas we write it as a function of tariff proceeds measured in exportable goods. On his assumption, $\delta R/\delta t = \delta(tM_1)/\delta t = \overline{M}_1$, as contrasted with our $\delta R/\delta t = \overline{M}_1/1+t$. In dealing with our case (2), Metzler writes private demand as a function of tariff proceeds measured in exportable goods, and obtains a result identical with ours. Metzler's technique for the former case is inferior to ours, since it means that all the income effect of an import price change on government demand falls on the exportable good.

[2] Our earlier analysis of this case, presented in J. Bhagwati, 'Protection, Real Wages and Real Incomes', *Economic Journal*, vol. lxix, no. 276 (Dec. 1959), pp. 733–48, p. 746, and explained in note 3 to that page, is erroneous; in the derivation of the excess demand for importables, the changes in quantities of importables demanded and supplied are confused. The formula presented in that paper should be replaced by that presented here.

ables $(1-c)$ to exceed the foreign elasticity of demand for imports when free trade initially prevails, but not when there is a pre-existing tariff; it is always necessary, however, for the foreign demand for imports to be inelastic (barring inferiority of importables).

In *case (3)* the total effect of the tariff increase on world excess demand for importables is

$$\frac{dM'}{dt} = \left(\frac{b_r(1+gt)}{1+(1-b_r)t}+g+\eta_g'\frac{\bar{M}_2}{\bar{M}}-1+\eta_f\right)\frac{\bar{M}}{\pi} \quad \text{(31 a) XII}$$

when private demand is influenced by real government consumption;

$$\frac{dM'}{dt} = \left\{\frac{\pi+b_m}{1+(1-b_m g)t}\left(g\frac{\bar{M}_1}{\bar{M}}+\eta_g\frac{\bar{M}_2}{\bar{M}}\right)-1+\eta_f\right\}\frac{\bar{M}}{\pi} \quad \text{(31 b) XIII}$$

when private demand is influenced by governmental consumption of importables; and

$$\frac{dM'}{dt} = \left(\frac{b_x(1-g)+g\pi}{1+(1-b_x+b_x g)t}\frac{\bar{M}_1}{\bar{M}}+\frac{b_x(1+gt)+\pi(1-b_x)\eta_g}{1+(1-b_x+b_x g)t}\frac{\bar{M}_2}{\bar{M}}-1+\eta_f\right)\frac{\bar{M}}{\pi} \quad \text{(31 c) XIV}$$

when private demand is influenced by governmental consumption of exportables.

For simplicity we consider only the case in which private demand is influenced by the level of government consumption [case $(3a)$, equation (31 a)]. In this case the tariff increase will lower the domestic price of importables if

$$(1-g)-\frac{b_r(1+gt)}{1+(1-b_r)t}-\eta_g'\frac{\bar{M}_2}{\bar{M}} > \eta_f. \quad (32)$$

If an increase in government expenditure has the indirect effect of increasing private demand for importables $(b_r > 0)$ the tariff can reduce the domestic price of importables only if the government's marginal propensity to spend on exportables is greater than the foreign elasticity of demand for imports, which (barring inferior goods) must be less than unity.[1] But if an increase in government expenditure has the indirect effect of reducing private demand for importables $(b_r < 0)$, the tariff can reduce the domestic price of importables even though the government's marginal propensity to spend on exportables is less than the foreign elasticity of demand for imports and even though the latter is greater than unity.

Since the analysis of the effect of a tariff increase on the equilibrium domestic price of importables obtains its results from the effect of the tariff increase on world excess demand at the initial domestic price of importables, *relaxation of the assumption that the private sector can be treated*

[1] An exception is possible if $b_r > 1+t/t$.

as an aggregate makes no essential difference to the results: since domestic earned income and its distribution are unchanged if the domestic price of importables is unchanged, disaggregation requires merely the replacement of the aggregate marginal propensity to consume importables by an average of the marginal propensities of the two individuals, weighted by their shares in redistributed tariff proceeds, in case (2), and the replacement of the aggregate dependence coefficient by the sum of the coefficients for the two individuals, in case (3). For the same reason, *variability of the quantity of labour supplied* in response to changes in factor prices will make no difference to the various formulae, since the real wage-rate and real rent remain constant by the assumption of a constant internal price of importables. But variability in response to changes in the amount of tariff revenue redistributed will make a difference in case (2) and variability in response to changes in the amount and composition of real government consumption will make a difference in case (3).

In both cases, allowance for variability of the quantity of labour supplied involves introducing another effect of the tariff increase on the world excess demand for importables, the effect of the change in tariff revenue or real government consumption on the quantity of labour supplied and so on the quantity of importables domestically produced and the income available for private expenditure. These effects have already been discussed in connexion with the analysis of the effect of the tariff increase on the terms of trade.

Allowing for variability of the labour supply in response to changes in the amount of tariff revenue redistributed, the total effect of the tariff increase on world excess demand for importables in case (2) is

$$\frac{dM'}{dt} = \left(\frac{c+(\pi\rho-cw)l}{1+\{1-c-(\pi\rho-cw)l\}t}-1+\eta_f\right)\frac{\bar{M}_1}{\pi}. \qquad (33)\ \text{XV}$$

The corresponding condition for the tariff increase to lower the domestic price of importables is

$$(1-c)-(\pi\rho-cw)l > \frac{\eta_f}{\pi-\eta_f t}.$$

It follows from this inequality that, even in the case of initial free trade [where the inequality reduces to $(1-c)-(\rho-cw)l > \eta_f$] it is not necessary for the private marginal propensity to spend on exportables to exceed the foreign elasticity of demand for imports for the tariff to lower the domestic price of importables; since $\pi\rho$ is necessarily greater in absolute value than cw, a reduction of the domestic price of importables with $\eta_f > 1-c$ requires a negative ρ, which in turn means that labour is used intensively in the exportable-goods industry. If labour is used intensively in the exportable-goods industry, the domestic price of importables can fall even if the foreign demand for imports is elastic.

Allowing for variability of the labour supply in response to changes in the amount of real government consumption—the only variant of *case* (*3*) we shall consider[1]—the total effect of the tariff increase on world excess demand for importables is

$$\frac{dM'}{dt}=\left(\frac{\{b_r-(\pi\rho-cw)\alpha_r\}(1+gt)}{1+\{1-b_r+(\pi\rho-cw)\alpha_r\}t}+g+\eta_g'\frac{\bar{M}_2}{\bar{M}}-1+\eta_f\right)\frac{\bar{M}}{\pi}, \tag{34) XVI}$$

where α_r is the change in the quantity of labour supplied due to a unit increase in real government consumption. The corresponding condition for the tariff increase to lower the domestic price of importables is

$$(1-g)-\frac{b_r-(\pi\rho-cw)\alpha_r}{1+\{1-b_r+(\pi\rho-cw)\alpha_r\}t}(1+gt)-\eta_g'\frac{\bar{M}_2}{\bar{M}}>\eta_f.$$

In the initial free-trade case, this reduces to

$$(1-g)-b_r+(\rho-cw)\alpha_r>\eta_f;$$

and it follows from this formula that even if the dependence effect of a change in government revenue is positive, the internal price of importables may fall even though the government's marginal propensity to spend on exportables is less than the foreign elasticity of demand for imports and the latter is greater than unity. This can occur if *either* ρ is positive, implying that labour is used relatively intensively in the importable-goods industry, *and* α_r is positive, implying that the quantity of labour supplied increases when real government consumption increases, *or* ρ is negative, implying that labour is used relatively intensively in the exportable-goods industry, *and* α_r is negative, implying that the quantity of labour supplied decreases as real government consumption increases. Similar modifications apply to the general case in which a tariff is in force in the initial situation.

To allow for variability of the quantity of labour supplied in the disaggregated cases (2) and (3) it is necessary merely to replace c, b, $(\rho\pi-cw)l$ and $(\rho\pi-cw)\alpha_r$ by appropriately weighted sums of the corresponding expressions for the two separate individuals. The nature of the resulting modifications in the analysis of the effects of an increase in the tariff rate on the domestic price of importables is evident from the preceding analysis, and will not be developed further here.

Jagdish Bhagwati, Nuffield College, Oxford.
Harry G. Johnson, University of Chicago.

[1] Since allowing for variability of labour supply requires merely the addition of $(cw-\rho\pi)$, multiplied by the α relating labour supply to whatever aspect of governmental consumption it depends on, to the corresponding b term in the parameter B in the general formula developed above, the interested reader can easily work out the results for the other two variants for himself.

On the Equivalence of Tariffs and Quotas[1]

This paper examines the proposition that tariffs and quotas are equivalent in the sense that an explicit tariff rate will produce an import level which, if set *alternatively* as a quota, will produce an implicit tariff equal to the explicit tariff (and, pairwise, that a quota will produce an implicit tariff which, if set *alternatively* as an explicit tariff, will generate the same level of imports).

Such a notion of the equivalence between tariffs and quotas is widespread in the literature on trade theory – particularly in discussions relating to the protective effect of quantitative restrictions.[2] On the other hand, equivalence in the sense defined obtains as a logically true proposition only in a limited class of situations.

Indeed, it is easy to construct several possible situations where the equivalence breaks down. This paper demonstrates many such possibilities and then proceeds, in the light of this analysis, to correct some of the current misconceptions about tariffs and quotas which have their origin in the equivalence proposition.

1. Alternative Possibilities

The traditional equivalence proposition is deduced in the context of a model which assumes (a) competitive foreign supply, (b) perfect

[1] This revised version has profited as a result of a stimulating comment of Hirofumi Shibata [6]. The original version owed some improvements to Harry Johnson.

[2] C. P. Kindleberger [4], however, does explicitly analyse a case of non-equivalence. Kindleberger [4, pp. 621–3] concentrates on showing how a quota can create a monopoly domestically, and hence does not generalize the argument concerning non-equivalence in the way attempted here. Earlier, J. E. Meade [5, especially pp. 282–5] analysed various possibilities of monopoly arising from the administration of quota systems. The problem, as posed and analysed here, is mentioned in an earlier paper of mine [1].

competition in domestic production, and (c) a quota which is allocated so as to ensure perfect competition among the quota-holders, one consequence of which is that all quotas are used. This *universal* assumption of competitiveness ensures the equivalence which, as we shall soon see, generally breaks down with the introduction of monopoly elements in any one or more of the three listed areas.

We will begin the analysis with the case of universal perfect competition and then examine the following alternative cases: (a) perfect competition in (domestic) production replaced by pure monopoly in production; (b) perfect competition among quota-holders replaced by monopolist holding of quota; (c) simultaneous presence of monopoly in quota-holding and in domestic production; and (d) monopolistic supply of imports.

Throughout the analysis, we use the following notation:

P_F = foreign price
P_D = domestic price
t = tariff rate
S_D = domestic supply (production) of the commodity
S_F = foreign supply (production) of the commodity
D = total domestic demand for (consumption of) the commodity
D_D = net domestic demand for the commodity, available to the domestic suppliers
C = total cost of domestic production of the commodity

Case 1 Competitive supply from abroad, perfect competition in domestic production, and perfect competition among quota-holders.

We first set out the model for the case when a tariff, rather than a quota, is imposed.

$$S_D = S_D(P_D) \tag{1}$$
$$S_F = S_F(P_F) \tag{2}$$
$$P_F(1 + t) = P_D \tag{3}$$
$$S_P + S_F = D \tag{4}$$
$$D = D(P_D). \tag{5}$$

Equation (1) states that the domestic supply is a function of domestic price; equation (2) that the foreign supply is a function of foreign price; equation (3) that the domestic price exceeds the foreign price by the amount of the tariff; equation (4) that aggregate supply must equal domestic demand; and equation (5) that domestic demand is a function of domestic price.

We thus have five equations and six unknowns: S_D, S_F, D, P_D, P_F, and t. Thus, if t is given, the remaining unknowns are determined. Corresponding to every tariff rate t, therefore, there will be some import level S_F.

In the case where an import quota is set, the system is identical to that for the tariff case. Corresponding to every import level S_F chosen as the quota, therefore, there will be some (implicit) tariff rate, *i.e.*, discrepancy between P_D and P_F. Moreover, the systems being identical, a tariff will generate an import level which, set alternatively as a quota, will generate the *same* tariff rate.

Figure 9.1 shows graphically the equilibrium in this system. The tariff rate AV/VO shifts the S_F schedule upwards. The resulting total supply schedule S_T (aggregating S_F and S_D) cuts the D schedule to give the import level BC ($= EH$), foreign price OH, and domestic price OF. Conversely, with a quota of BC, the domestic price will turn out to be OF, the foreign price to be OH, and the (implicit) tariff rate therefore to be ($FH/OH =$) AV/VO. Equivalence thus obtains in this case.

Case 2 Competitive supply from abroad, monopoly in domestic production, and perfect competition among quota-holders.

Starting again with the case of tariffs, we find that the economic system is the following:

$$S_F = S_F(P_F) \tag{1}$$
$$D = D(P_D) \tag{2}$$
$$D_D = D(P_D) - S_F(P_F) \tag{3}$$
$$D_D = S_D \tag{4}$$
$$C = C(S_D) \tag{5}$$
$$\frac{d(P_D S_D)}{dS_D} = \frac{dC}{dS_D} \tag{6}$$
$$P_F(1+t) = P_D \tag{7}$$

Equation (1) states that the foreign supply is a function of foreign price; equation (2) that total domestic demand is a function of domestic price; equation (3) that the net demand available to the domestic monopolist is the difference between total demand and foreign supply; equation (4) that net domestic demand equals domestic supply; equation (5) that total cost of domestic production (supply) is a function of the level of production; equation (6) that marginal revenue in domestic production is equated by the monopolist with his marginal cost; and equation (7) that the domestic price is higher than the foreign price by the amount of the tariff.

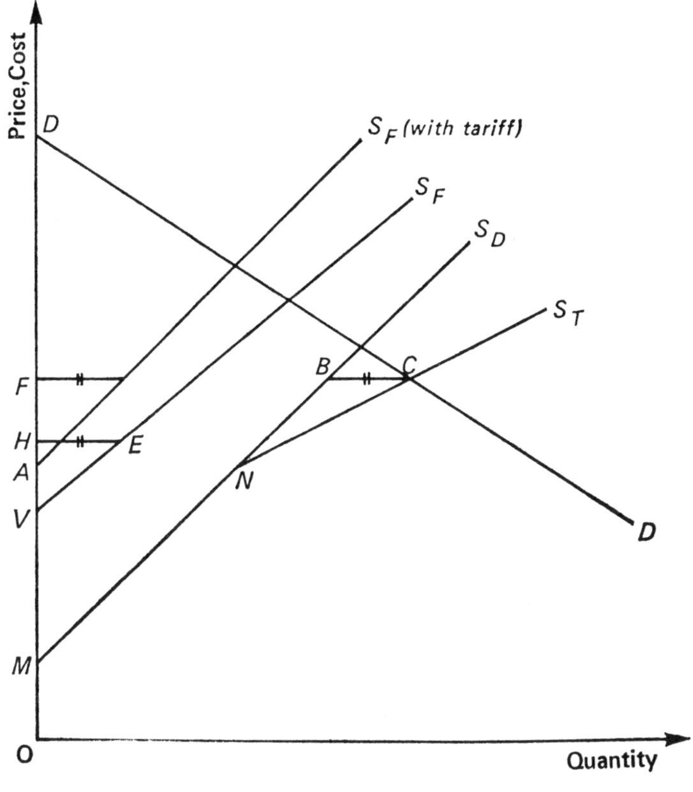

FIGURE 9.1

We have here seven equations and eight unknowns: D, D_D, S_F, S_D, P_D, P_F, C, and t. By choosing the tariff rate, t, therefore, we can determine the remaining values. Consequently, corresponding to every t there will be some level of imports, S_F.

But in contrast to Case 1, the present system shows non-equivalence. For a quota, the system is the following:

$$D = D(P_D) \tag{1}$$

$$S_F = S_F(P_F) \tag{2}$$

$$D_D = D(P_D) - S_F(P_F) \tag{3}$$

$$D_D = S_D \tag{4}$$

$$C = C(S_D) \tag{5}$$

$$\frac{d(P_D S_D)}{dS_D} = \frac{dC}{dS_D} \tag{6}$$

$$\frac{P_D}{P_F} = 1 + t \tag{7}$$

The system looks identical with that for a tariff.[1] However, the two systems are *not* identical, because the left-hand sides of equation (6), representing marginal revenue, are actually different. Under a tariff,

$$\frac{d(P_D S_D)}{dS_D} = P_D\frac{dD}{dS_D} + D\frac{dP_D}{dS_D} - P_D\frac{dS_F}{dS_D} - S_F\frac{dP_D}{dS_D};$$

whereas under a quota,

$$\frac{d(P_D S_D)}{dS_D} = P_D\frac{dD}{dS_D} + D\frac{dP_D}{dS_D} - S_F\frac{dP_D}{dS_D}$$

The difference of $-P_D(dS_F/dS_D)$ crucially divides the two systems, accounting for the non-equivalence of tariffs and quotas in this case. For, with this difference, a tariff rate will correspond to an import level which, if alternatively set as a quota, will not generate an identical (implicit) tariff rate. Indeed, the implicit tariff rate must be higher than the explicit one.

The difference is due to the fact that, with a tariff, the reduction in domestic price due to an increase in domestic output reduces the quantity of imports supplied, so that increased sales are effected partly by reducing imports, whereas with a quota imports are not reduced and the whole increase in sales must come from an increase in quantity demanded. Marginal revenue at any given output is therefore higher with the tariff than with a quota [$-P_D(dS_F/dS_D)$ is positive because (dS_F/dS_D) is negative]. Hence output will be higher, and domestic price, lower, under a tariff than it would be under a quota, for the same level of imports. This non-equivalence is easily illustrated graphically: Figures 9.2 and 9.3 show respectively the tariff and quota systems, two figures being employed instead of one to avoid confusion. In Figure 9.2, we set a tariff rate which generates an import level; in Figure 9.3, we set the *same* import level as a quota and show that a *different* (and higher) implicit tariff rate is generated.

In Figure 9.2, the tariff rate ($=AW/WO$) shifts the supply schedule S_F upwards. The net demand schedule for the domestic monopolist then is VUD, while VR is the marginal revenue schedule for the monopolist. Equilibrium exists where the latter cuts the marginal cost schedule for the monopolist, so that the monopolist's production (S_D)

[1] Of course, equations (2) and (7) are now to be understood differently. In the present, quota case, equation (2) gives the foreign price corresponding to the import quota set; whereas in equation (7) t is the *implicit* tariff rate, obtained merely as $(P_D/P_F - 1)$. Neither of these differences, however, affects the equivalence proposition.

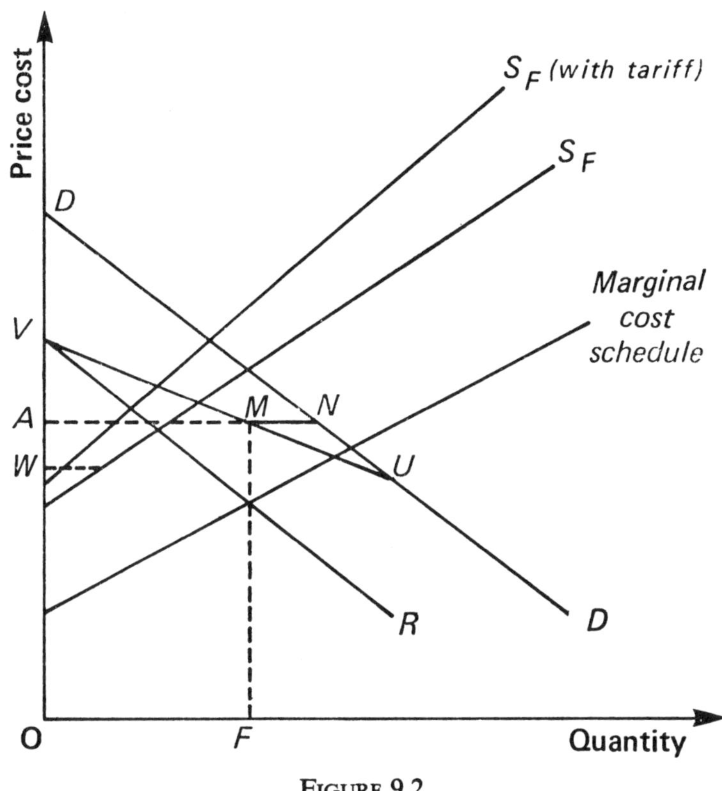

FIGURE 9.2

is at OF, the domestic price at OA, the foreign price at OW, and the import level (S_F) at MN.

We then use the *same* import level MN as the quota in Figure 9.3. The *net* demand schedule for the domestic monopolist is now D_D; it is steeper than the net demand schedule segment VU in the previous diagram. The corresponding marginal revenue schedule must lie farther below M (in Figure 9.2) than the previous marginal revenue schedule VR; it therefore cuts the monopolist's marginal cost schedule at a lower output than under the tariff, to yield OA as the domestic price and OB as the foreign price, the implicit tariff rate being AB/OB. Since OB in Figure 9.3 is equal to OW in Figure 9.2 (imports being the same in both cases), and OA in Figure 9.3 must be greater than OA in Figure 9.2, the implicit tariff rate under the quota must exceed the explicit tariff rate that would produce the same volume of imports. This demonstrates the non-equivalence between tariffs and quotas when there is monopoly in domestic production.

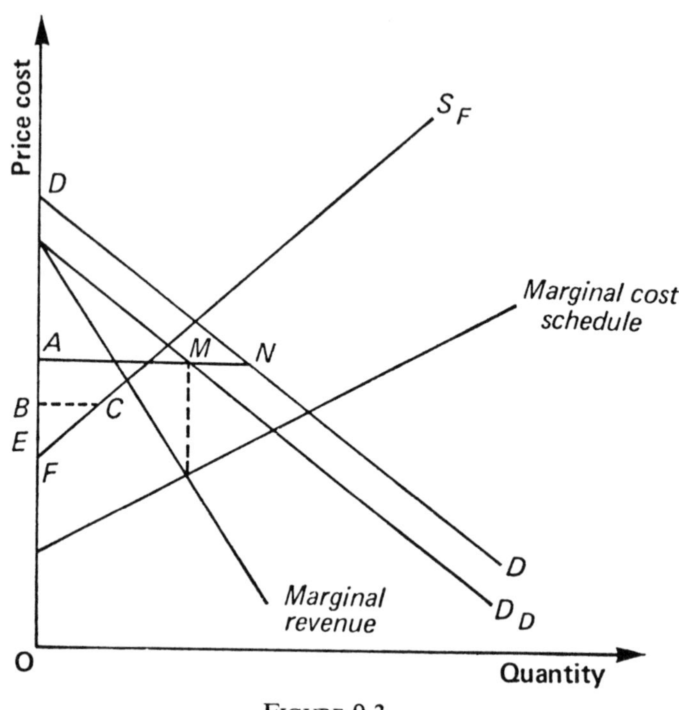

FIGURE 9.3

Case 3 Competitive supply from abroad, perfect competition in domestic production, and monopolist-holding of quotas.

Case A Assume that the imports are competitively demanded under the tariff situation. The analysis of a tariff in this case is identical with that in Case 1. With a quota, however, the system is now different. Since the quota-holder may be assumed to maximize his profits, he will vary his imports (within the quota set) so as to achieve this goal. The system then becomes the following:

$$D = D(P_D) \tag{1}$$

$$S_F = D(P_D) - S_D(P_D) \tag{2}$$

$$S_D = S_D(P_D) \tag{3}$$

$$S_F = S_F(P_F) \tag{4}$$

$$\frac{P_D}{P_F} = (1 + t) \tag{5}$$

$$\frac{d(P_D - P_F)S_F}{dS_F} \geqq 0. \tag{6}$$

The first five equations are already familiar. The last merely states the first-order, maximizing (equilibrium) condition for the monopolist quota-holder; the equality sign holds if the monopolist uses less than his full quota, the inequality if he uses all of his quota. There are thus six equations and six unknowns: P_F, P_D, S_F, S_D, D, and t. The import level which will maximize the quota-holder's profits is thus determinate;[1] and it is obvious that if this import volume is less than would occur under the tariff, the implicit tariff rate must exceed the explicit tariff rate. Since the tariff system and the quota system are different in this case, the equivalence proposition breaks down. It will hold only in the special case when the shapes of the various schedules make it most profitable for the monopolist to use his full quota.

Equilibrium in the quota system is easily illustrated in the three-quadrant Figure 9.4. The right-hand quadrant contains the usual S_D, S_F, and D schedules. The upper left-hand quadrant contains two schedules, one depicting the domestic price and the other the foreign price, corresponding to different levels of utilization of the quota $MN(=OR)$ by the quota-holder. The lower left-hand quadrant shows the level of profits corresponding to every level of utilization of the quota. $AB(=OE)$ then represents the level of quota utilization at which the profits of the quota-holder are at a maximum; and the corresponding (implicit) tariff rate is CD/DE.[2] This is necessarily greater than, or at least equal to, the tariff rate that would produce the level of imports OR.

Case B Assume, however, that imports are effected by a monopoly, such as a state trading corporation, under the tariff situation. In this variation of Case 3, monopolistic importation extends to *both* the quota and the tariff situation.[3]

[1] This import level will, however, be subject to an *upper bound* set by the quota.

[2] The equilibrium value of S_F can easily be shown to be:

$$\frac{P_D - P_F}{P'_F - (1/D' - S'_D)}$$

where

$$P'_F = \frac{dP_F}{dS_F}, \quad D' = \frac{dD}{dP_D},$$

and

$$S'_D = \frac{dS_D}{dP_D}.$$

[3] Case B was suggested by G. Yadav [7].

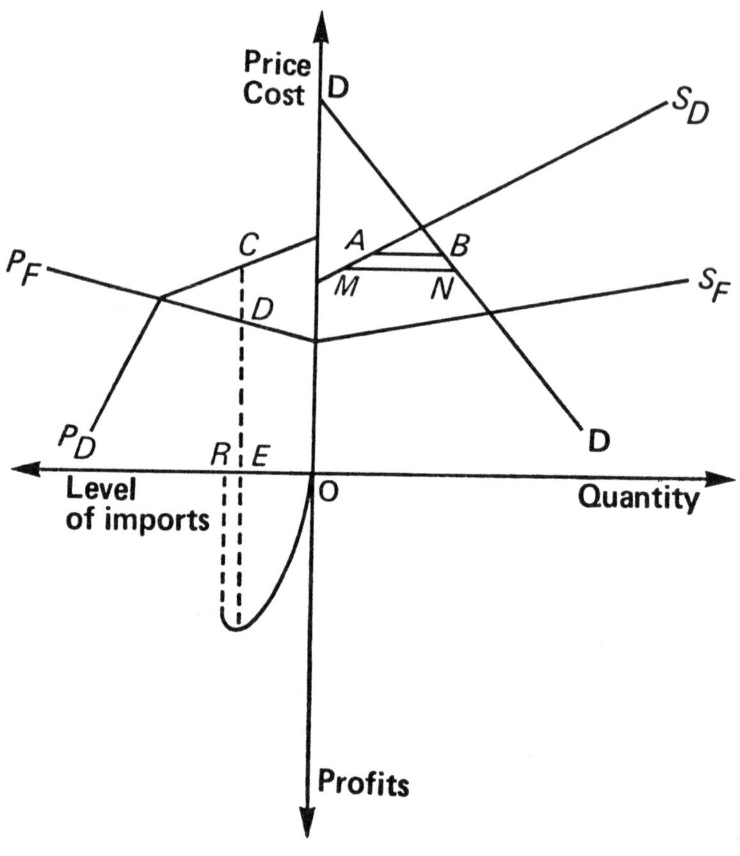

FIGURE 9.4

This case is readily analysed in Figure 9.5. Here, imports are made by a single importer, under *both* tariff and quota régimes, but competition holds everywhere else. Under tariff rate t, S_t is the foreign supply curve of imports; without the tariff, it is S. AR is the *net* demand curve for imports, the marginal revenue curve to it being MR. The intersection of the marginal cost curve MC_t, which is marginal to S_t, at F with MR, determines the maximum profit position for the monopolist importer under the tariff. The domestic price is EG, the foreign c.i.f. price is HG, the landed price is JG and hence the implicit tariff rate EH/HG exceeds the actual tariff rate JH/HG. When the quota is alternatively set at OG and the explicit tariff removed, equilibrium is again at domestic price EG, so that the implicit tariff rate is again EH/HG but this differs from, and exceeds, the explicit

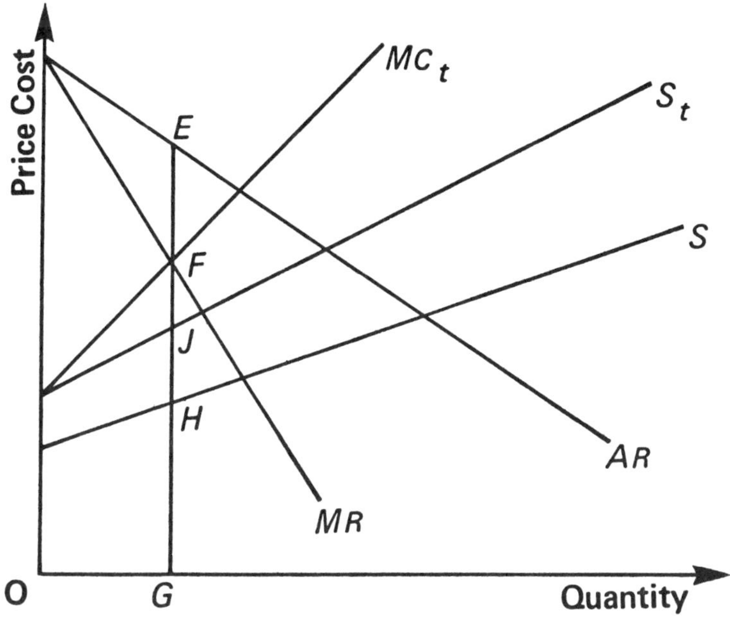

FIGURE 9.5

tariff rate JH/HG. Thus equivalence breaks down in this case as well.[1]

Case 4. Competitive supply from abroad, monopoly in domestic production, and monopolist holding of quotas.

The tariff system in this case is identical to that in Case 2 (and Figure 9.2). The quota system, however, will now differ – unless, of course, it is assumed that the quota-holder acts as a perfect competitor and fails to maximize his profits. Since the quota-holder may also be expected to maximize his profits, the problem becomes that of duopoly, and, as with that general class of problems, there are as many solutions as the behavioural assumptions one cares to make. We take only two simple cases here; they are sufficient for underlining the non-equivalence possibility.

Case A Assume that the producer maximizes his profits at every level of imports chosen by the quota-holder, and that the quota-

[1] If one takes the *pair-wise definition* of equivalence, that *a quota will give rise to an implicit tariff rate which, if alternatively set as a tariff, will generate the same level of imports as the quota*, it is again clear that equivalence breaks down when there is monopoly import under *both* tariff and quota: for, in this case, the quota *OG* will lead to an implicit tariff rate *EH/HG* which, then set alternatively as the tariff, will not lead to the same import level *OG*.

holder then chooses that level of imports which, given this assumption about the producer's behaviour, yields him the maximum profit.

In this case, the system is the following:

$$D = D(P_D) \tag{1}$$

$$S_F = S_F(P_F) \tag{2}$$

$$S_F + S_D = D \tag{3}$$

$$C = C(S_D) \tag{4}$$

$$\frac{P_D}{P_F} = (1 + t) \tag{5}$$

$$\frac{d(P_D - P_F)\,S_F}{dS_F} \gtreqless 0 \tag{6}$$

$$\frac{d(S_D P_D)}{dS_D} = \frac{dC}{dS_D} \tag{7}$$

The first five equations are familiar. Equation (6) is the profit-maximizing, equilibrium condition for the monopolist quota-holder, and equation (7) the corresponding condition for the monopolist producer. There are thus seven equations and seven unknowns: D, D_F, S_D, P_F, P_D, t, and C. The (implicit) tariff rate and the (actual) import level are thus determined simultaneously. Note further that the tariff and quota systems are again different so that non-equivalence will obtain,[1] except where conditions lead the monopolist quota-holder to use all his quota. Where the quota is not entirely utilized, the implicit tariff rate must be higher than the explicit tariff rate.

Case B Assume instead that the quota is allotted to the producer-monopolist himself.[2]

In this case, the producer becomes a pure monopolist, with two sources of supply – domestic and foreign. He will then use them in such a way as to maximize his profits. The system of equations is then the following:

$$D = D(P_D) \tag{1}$$

$$S_F + S_D = D \tag{2}$$

[1] This case could also be illustrated by adapting the three-quadrant diagram in Figure 9.4 so as to introduce monopoly instead of competition in domestic production.

[2] This is not as fanciful an assumption as it appears. In countries such as India, considerable concentration of ownership and control obtains in economic activity, owing to a variety of reasons such as strictly controlled entry and economies of scale combined with limited markets. It is thus not merely possible, but also probable, for the case described in the text to obtain in practice.

$$S_F = S_F(P_F) \tag{3}$$
$$C = C(S_D) \tag{4}$$
$$\frac{P_D}{P_F} = 1 + t \tag{5}$$
$$\frac{d(P_F S_F)}{dS_F} \leqq \frac{dC}{dS_D} = \frac{d(P_D D)}{dD}. \qquad \text{(6) and (7)}$$

We thus have seven equations (all familiar by now) and seven unknowns: D, S_F, S_D, C, P_F, P_D and t. Thus, both the (implicit) tariff rate and the rate of quota utilization are determined. Note again the differences in the tariff and quota systems in this case, implying non-equivalence.

This case is easily illustrated in Figure 9.6, where MC is the marginal cost schedule for imports, and the aggregate marginal cost schedule, for both sources of supply, is SRA_{mc}. The latter's intersection with the marginal revenue schedule at R yields the domestic price as EO,

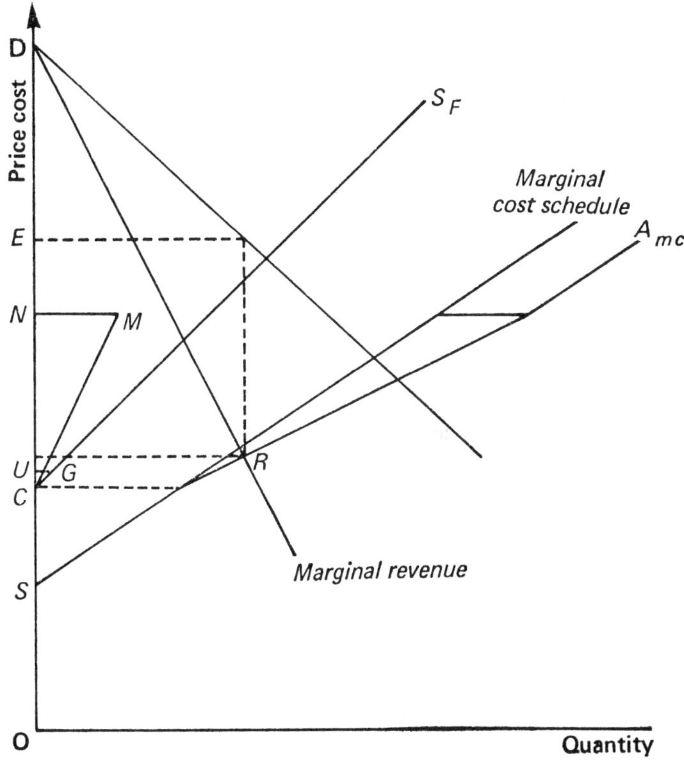

FIGURE 9.6

the foreign price as UO, the (implicit) tariff rate as EU/UO, and the level of imports as GU.[1]

Case 5 Monopolistic supply of imports from abroad, and competition elsewhere.

Consider finally the case where the foreign supply of imports is monopolistic under *both* tariff and quota.[2] In Figure 9.7, the mono-

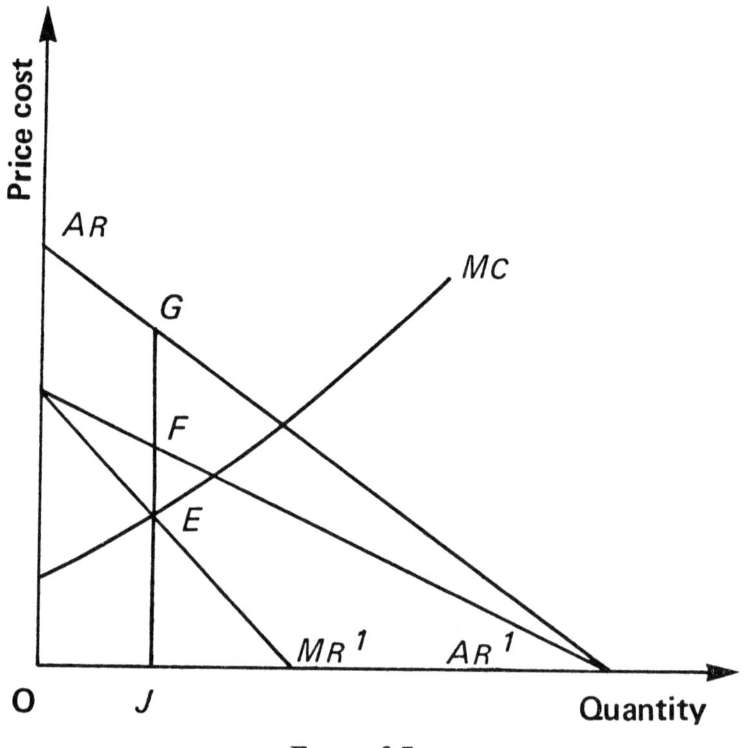

FIGURE 9.7

polist supplier of imports is faced with the net import demand schedule AR which, in case of a tariff at rate GF/FJ, will shift to AR' The marginal revenue curve to AR' is MR'. The intersection of the monopolist's marginal cost curve MC with MR' at E determines his maximum-profit point, giving OJ as the volume of imports, JG as the domestic price and hence FJ as the c.i.f. price. The shift to the

[1] The reader who wishes to illustrate non-equivalence in a simple fashion can use the (derived) tariff rate EU/UO and the same S_F, D, and marginal cost schedules to show how, if this tariff rate is actually imposed, the resulting import level can be different from GU.

[2] This is the case analysed by Shibata [6].

alternative situation where the tariff *GF*/*FJ* is removed and replaced by a quota of *OJ*, leads on the other hand to the same domestic price *GJ*, but the ci.f. price now shifts also to *GJ*, so that the implicit tariff rate is *zero*, and hence is *below* the explicit tariff.

The equivalence proposition thus breaks down unequivocally: an explicit tariff will not lead to an import level which, if set alternatively as a quota, will generate the same implicit tariff. (Nor will a quota lead to an implicit tariff which, if set alternatively as a tariff, will generate the same level of imports.) Hence, this case also is no exception to the presumption that equivalence will generally break down with the introduction of monopoly elements.

2. Implications of Non-Equivalence

The demonstration that the equivalence of tariffs and quotas can break down, once we move away from the universally competitive model, is not merely interesting in itself but also has important implications in several areas of analysis.

1 We can now answer directly the question whether under a quota régime the observed implicit tariff rates can be treated as equivalent to identical tariff rates (levied instead of the quota) in the sense of generating the same level of imports and domestic production. This is a question that comes up frequently and the general practice is *indeed* to treat the observed, implicit tariff rate under a *QR* régime as the 'effective tariff rate'. Examination of the equivalence proposition, in terms of the definition used here, throws up the limitations of these deductions when monopoly elements are present.

Thus, for example, in the case when foreign supply is monopolistic, the implicit tariff rate is zero under the quota – refer back to Figure 9.7 – but setting the actual tariff rate at zero and removing the quota restriction will *not* yield the same level of imports and domestic production; the truly equivalent tariff rate is *higher*. Similarly, in the case where there is domestic, import-monopoly instead, the truly equivalent tariff is *lower* than the implicit tariff rate in the quota alternative – refer back to Figure 9.5. Similar conclusions apply to the other cases analysed here: (i) where there is monopolistic-holding of quotas, but competition elsewhere, again the implicit tariff rate will *exceed* the explicit tariff rate, thus *overstating* the truly equivalent tariff rate, when the quota is under-utilized; (ii) where there is monopoly in domestic production as well as in the holding of quotas, again the under-utlization of the quota would imply an implicit tariff rate that exceeds the explicit tariff rate and hence *overstates* the truly equivalent, effective tariff; and (iii) where there is monopoly in domestic production but competition everywhere else, the implicit tariff will exceed the explicit tariff, thus *overstating* again the truly equivalent, effective tariff that the quota represents.

2 Yet another inference from the equivalence proposition has been that when both tariffs and quotas are applied to an industry, and the discrepancy between the foreign and domestic prices exceeds the tariff rate, the tariff is redundant (except insofar as it cuts into the profits of the quota-holders and yields corresponding revenue to the state). This inference is not necessarily valid, of course, when non-equivalence obtains, and it is important to note this in view of the widespread, simultaneous use of tariffs and quotas in many developing countries.[1]

The imposition of a tariff, even when the equilibrium solution with this tariff plus a specific quota shows a greater difference between P_f and P_D than the tariff would have produced, may still have a net supplementary protective effect, in the sense of increasing domestic production above what it would otherwise be. This can readily be illustrated in the framework of Case 4, assumption B, in which the domestic monopolist also has a monopoly of the quota. A tariff on imports (at less than the implicit tariff rate) would raise their marginal cost to the monopolist, inducing him to shift toward more domestic production while at the same time curtailing total sales. Similar interactions of quotas and tariffs could be demonstrated in other frameworks as well.

3 Note further that equivalence as defined in the present paper is *not* identical with equivalence defined as follows: that, corresponding to any tariff, there will exist *some* quota which will result in the same

[1] Firms frequently ask for tariff protection for their industries, even when the tariff may in fact be 'redundant' (in the sense of the text) by virtue of import control, because import control is subject to frequent revision – semiannually in India – and hence its protective effect is 'uncertain', whereas tariffs are revised in practice only after several years and hence can be 'relied upon'. Frequently also, there are built-in leakages, even in import control, which introduce uncertainty. Thus, for example, many countries now experiment with export-incentive schemes involving 'import-replacement' licences. Under these schemes, imports of a commodity earning a higher premium could well increase, thereby reducing the 'protective' effect of import control for the domestic producers of this commodity. A tariff could then be very useful indeed in reducing such a leakage!

level of imports and importable production. And it is equivalence in the *latter* sense that is implied in the literature on balance of payments theory, as in Johnson [3], Meade [5] and Fleming [2], for example, where it is customarily argued that the use of quantitative restrictions is identical with the use of *some* equivalent tariff, that the use of (further) tariffs is justified only insofar as the country is below the optimum tariff level, and that the use of quantitative restrictions to reduce an external deficit is therefore justified, from the welfare viewpoint, only when the country does not already have optimal restrictions. Equivalence in this latter sense *also* breaks down, generally speaking, with the introduction of monopoly elements, *along with* equivalence in the former sense used in this paper; but not always. For example, in Case 3 B and Case 5, equivalence breaks down in the sense of this paper but *not* in the sense relevant to payments theory. As a general proposition, however, it remains correct to argue that the introduction of monopoly elements will invalidate, generally speaking, the equivalence of tariffs and quotas in *either* sense; and hence balance of payments literature which relies on equivalence must be generally qualified.

4 It is often stated that quotas are preferred to tariffs because their import-restricting effect, although in principle equivalent to that of tariffs, is certain, whereas that of tariffs is not. The reason cited is the difficulty of estimating the supply and demand schedules, both domestic and foreign. In point of fact, the possible differences in market structure (at the level of foreign supply and domestic production) under the two systems have also to be assessed accurately – and these, as well as their effects, can be far more difficult to judge.

Moreover, the impression that quotas necessarily produce certain predictions about the level of actual imports is incorrect. They frequently set only an upper bound to the level of imports – not merely because foreign or domestic supply and/or demand schedules have changed or because of administrative delays in allocations of exchange, but also because the market structure may depart from the universally competitive model (as in Case 4, for example).[1]

Before concluding, we may spell out briefly two other propositions,

[1] Non-utilization due to administrative delays and changed supply or demand conditions is, of course, quite important. The time profile of utilization within the time horizon specified also can be interesting to analyse and would involve an inter-temporal, profit-maximizing solution.

relating to quotas *per se* rather than to the equivalence proposition, which seem to be of some interest.

1 It is frequently thought that import-quota auctions would be equivalent to ordinary quotas, while the profits made by quota-holders would accrue to the state as auction premiums. On the other hand, it is clear from the preceding analysis that the issue depends on *how* the auctions are conducted. For example, if quotas are allocated to a 'large' number of holders under the ordinary system, whereas the auction permits one buyer to bid highest, the latter will bid *until* the *monopolist*-profit is exhausted by way of premium, so that the resulting situation will become one of monopoly quota-holding instead of the original competition among quota-holders.[1] In this case, therefore, the auction would convert the situation from one system to another – from Case 1 to Case 3 (if we assume competition in domestic production). The equivalence of auctions and ordinary quotas would thus break down.

2 Another interesting policy proposition relates to the widely observed association of quantitative import restrictions with monopoly (or oligopoly) in domestic production and its consequently deleterious effects on *both* the level of output and the level of efficiency (with respect to minimizing the cost of producing a specified output).[2]

The restrictive effect on the level of output is implicit in the analysis of Case 2. The effect on efficiency, however, is perhaps far more significant – and has been the concern of planners, using import control régimes, in many developing countries.

It is pertinent, therefore, to consider seriously whether the import control régime should not be modified so as to build into the system a threat of 'liberalization' of imports when there is evidence of quality deterioration, inefficiency, or restrictive output policies. (This is, of course, similar to the traditional prescription with respect to removal of tariff protection.)

This prescription, however, runs counter to the present

[1] This argument, of course, presumes that the monopolistic buying-up occurs under auctions but that no monopoly is obtained by purchasing from the quota-holders under the non-auction system of allocation. These assumptions, however, may be realistic.

[2] The absence of foreign competition, combined with a planning set-up which rules out new entry and the driving out of inefficient producers, has resulted in considerable inefficiency in countries such as India. It is enough to be a consumer (or a producer using domestic intermediates) in India to see the force of this observation!

indiscriminate resort to quantitative restrictions and the tendency to ignore the economic costs of import control analysed here. But there is little doubt that it is imperative to experiment with this idea in practice if a way out of the current widespread 'featherbedding' and inefficiency in sheltered markets is to be reduced to less gigantic proportions.[1]

REFERENCES

1 Bhagwati, J., 'Quantitative Restrictions and Quotas in International Trade', *International Encyclopedia of the Social Sciences*, forthcoming.

2 Fleming, J. M., 'On Making the Best of Balance of Payments Restrictions on Imports', *Economic Journal*, March 1951.

3 Johnson, H. G., *International Trade and Economic Growth*, London, Allen and Unwin, 1958.

4 Kindleberger, C. P., *International Economics*, Homewood, Illinois, Richard D. Irwin, Inc., 1958.

5 Meade, J. E., *The Theory of International Economic Policy*, Volume I, *The Balance of Payments*, London, Oxford University Press, 1951.

6 Shibata, H., 'A Note on the Equivalence of Tariffs and Quotas', *American Economic Review*, March 1968.

7 Yadav, G., 'A Note on the Equivalence of Tariffs and Quotas', *Canadian Journal of Economics and Political Science*, February, 1968.

[1] Under balance-of-payments pressures, more countries may be expected to slide into such economic régimes. During a consulting assignment in Turkey in the summer of 1964, I found Turkey gradually moving into such a set-up. There, as soon as a domestic industry is established, the imports of that commodity are practically automatically 'deliberalized'. Aside from the adverse effects on quality and costs which may confidently be expected from this policy, its operation has led to interesting destabilization in the short term. Thus, as soon as the industry comes into operation, there is an excessive import of the commodity in the expectation that it will be deliberalized: this happened with rubber tyres, for example.

Editor's Note

The equivalence question has been further treated in J. N. Bhagwati, *The Anatomy and Consequences of Exchange Control Regimes*, Cambridge, MA: Ballinger, 1978, chapter 2.

Journal of International Economics 3 (1973) 259–282. © North-Holland Publishing Company

THE GENERAL EQUILIBRIUM THEORY OF EFFECTIVE PROTECTION AND RESOURCE ALLOCATION[1]

Jagdish N. BHAGWATI
Massachusetts Institute of Technology

and

T.N. SRINIVASAN
Indian Statistical Institute and M.I.T.

1. Introduction

The theory of effective rate of protection (ERP) has been developed in recent years in an attempt to seek a concept of protection which, in the presence of traded inputs, would be able to perform analytically the role that nominal tariffs played in the "older", traditional theory which was premised on a model which excluded traded inputs.

Thus, in the traditional model, with two traded goods produced with standard restrictions on the production functions[2] by two primary factors in given endowment, and the small-country assumption, a tariff on a good would lead to: (i) a rise in the (gross) output of the protected good; (ii) a rise in the nominal value of its output; (iii) a rise in the use of each primary factor therein; (iv) a rise in the real value-added therein (which coincides with output, when real value-added is defined as deflated by the price of "own output"); and (v) a rise in the nominal value-added therein (which coincides of course with the nominal value

[1] Thanks are due to the National Science Foundation for supporting the research reported in this paper. We have had the benefit of correspondence and/or mutual discussions over the last year with Chulsoon Khang and, in particular, Michael Bruno, whose paper (1973) in this Symposium complements ours admirably. The careful comments of John Chipman have also led to many improvements. Above all, we are greatly indebted to Yasuo Uekawa whose extremely careful reading has resulted in the removal of errors from earlier drafts.

[2] These should be linear homogeneous, concave, and factor-intensities should differ in equilibrium.

of output).[3] For two traded goods and n ($n > 2$) primary factors, a tariff on one good will continue to imply increase in its output and nominal value of output, though not necessarily in each of the primary factors used therein. For n ($n > 2$) traded goods and m ($m \geqslant n$) primary factors, a tariff on one good will still increase its output and nominal value of output, but, when more than one tariff is imposed (implying more than one price change), even this cannot be asserted for the good with the highest tariff.

The objective of ERP theory may then be taken as one of devising a concept of protection which, in the presence of tariff structures involving the imports of intermediates, constitutes in effect an index which will perform the same tasks as nominal tariffs do in the nominal tariff theory: i.e. predicting accurately the changes in these variables – gross output, nominal value of output, primary factor allocation, real value-added and nominal value-added. This, in fact, is the task which several analysts in the field of ERP theory have addressed themselves to, although a clear distinction has not always been made among these alternative ways of defining the objective of ERP theory. Thus, for example, Corden (1966) primarily addresses himself to prediction of gross outputs; Jones (1971), in the main text of his paper, also deals with gross outputs while an Appendix II is devoted to exploring value-added effects; Ramaswami and Srinivasan (1971) address their Impossibility theorem to the prediction of gross outputs and primary factor movements; Bhagwati and Srinivasan (1971a and 1971b) analyse the efficacy of ERP indices in predicting gross outputs and primary factor allocations; Khang (1973) is concerned exclusively with real value-added (i.e. nominal value added deflated by own-output-price) changes; and Bruno (1973) primarily investigates real value-added (similarly defined), gross outputs and primary resource shifts.[4]

When the problem of ERP theory is so defined, the analysis basically amounts to specifying an ERP index which will unambiguously predict the tariff-structure-induced changes in the variables specified. We note

[3] Proposition (i) follows from the concavity of the transformation function; Proposition (ii) follows from the identity of value-added with gross output; and Proposition (iii) follows from the Stolper-Samuelson theorem.

[4] We should emphasise that the references listed here are not meant to be exhaustive. The reader should not infer from them that this is all that each of the listed authors has written on the subject of ERP theory or that other economists have not written on the subject. Moreover, we have highlighted only those aspects which are of interest to us from the viewpoint of the problem as defined by us in this paper.

here merely that two *basic* definitions of such an ERP index have been developed in the literature: (i) the *Corden–Anderson–Naya* definition which defines it as the proportionate increment in value-added per unit output over the free-trade value-added per unit output,[5] and (ii) the *Corden–Leith* definition which defines it, meaningfully for only separable production functions, as the proportionate change in the "price of value-added".[6] It is well known then that the predictive power of these ERP indices is substantively limited relative to that of nominal tariff theory, especially in regard to predicting gross output changes (e.g. Jones, 1971; Ramaswami–Srinivasan, 1971; Bhagwati–Srinivasan, 1971a, to take just a few examples).

But it is also clear that this approach of making ERP theory attempt to do everything that nominal-tariff theory does, in regard to the prediction of the variables considered earlier, is to proceed by analytical analogy which is more apparent than real. For, clearly it is extremely improbable for example that an ERP index should be able to predict gross output changes despite the presence of intermediates. Hence, we need to pause and ask whether we can ask a somewhat different question, founded on an analytically more meaningful analogy, of ERP theory so as to compare it more sensibly with nominal-tariff theory. We think that this can indeed be done and proceed to do it as follows.

Thus note that, in the traditional analysis of nominal tariffs, the tariff leads to a change in the *price* of output and hence to change in output *quantity*: the change in value-added follows because value-added coincides with (gross) output and, in the two-primary-factors case, the uni-directional change in *each* primary factor used also follows because of the Stolper–Samuelson theorem. The basic proposition, however,

[5] This definition appears to have been suggested by analogy to nominal tariff theory, though no explicit statement to that effect has been found by us. Thus, if the domestic value-added per unit output is defined as $(1 + t)$ times the foreign-price value-added, t being then called the effective tariff, this would make it analogous to the nominal tariff where the domestic price is also one-plus-the-tariff times the foreign price. Cf. Bhagwati and Srinivasan (1971a).

[6] Cf. Corden (1966), Anderson–Naya (1969), and Leith (1968). When intermediate coefficients will change as a result of substitution, the Corden–Anderson–Naya definition (using symbols introduced later in this paper) becomes: $\hat{V}_i/V_i = \hat{P}_i - \Sigma a_j \hat{P}_{mj} - \Sigma \hat{a}_j P_{mj} \,/\, P_i - \Sigma a_j P_{mj}$. If then, as recommended by Corden (1966) and accepted by Jones (1971), Khang (1973) and Ray (1973), the changes in a_j are ignored, the definition reduces to: $\hat{V}/V_i = \hat{P}_i/P_i - \Sigma\theta_j \hat{P}_{mj}/P_{mj} \,/\, 1 - \Sigma\theta_j$ where θ_j is the share of j in i. And, where the production function is separable, it can be shown that this is, in fact, nothing but the Corden–Leith definition in terms of the proportionate increment in the "price of value added".

consists in relating the change in the *quantity of output* to the change in the *price of output*, thanks to the nominal tariff structure. Indeed, this may be taken as the primary proposition of the traditional theory concerning the effect of a tariff structure on *resource allocation*.

The task of the theory of effective protection may then be conceived essentially as one of examining, in a model allowing imported inputs, the question whether it is possible to devise a "price" of value-added, which can be used as an index to rank different activities such that, in exact analogy with the nominal tariff theory, the change in the "quantity" of value-added can be correctly predicted. If such an index can be devised, then we would be able to treat it as the total analog of the nominal tariff in the traditional model.

But one more dimension of the problem, which does not exist with nominal tariff theory, would be: can such an index be measured from observed or observable data without having to solve the general equilibrium (production) system for the two situations between which the resource-allocational shift is being predicted? For, if it cannot be, the index would not be of practical value because, to compute it, one would have to solve the full system and would thus *already know* the shift in value-added brought about by the tariff structure.[7]

In this paper, we use a general equilibrium, value-theoretic model with any number of primary factors, traded intermediates and goods, and discuss in terms thereof the question of the existence of a "price" of value-added that can serve as the "effective protection" index, predicting the shift in the "quantity" of value-added among the different activities. It is shown that, without loss of generality, one can express the proportionate change in nominal value added (consequent to a change in tariff structure) in an activity as the sum of two terms, the first of which is a suitably weighted average of the proportionate changes in the prices of inputs and outputs involved in that activity and the second of which is again a suitably weighted average of the proportionate changes in the quantities of primary factor inputs. It is further shown that, under two alternative sets of sufficient conditions, the first term can indeed be treated as a workable ERP index (with the second term serving as the measure of the change in quantity of value added that the ERP index is to predict).

[7] In the analysis that follows, we will therefore find that the range of possibilities over which the ERP index works analytically is larger than the range over which it can be measured "usefully" in the sense defined in the text.

The first set of conditions consists in restricting the class of production functions to separable production functions. In this case, a physical measure of value added can be defined so that the first term (i.e. ERP index) represents the proportionate change in the "price" of a physical unit of value added and the second-term represents the proportionate change in the quantity (in physical units) of value added.

The other set of conditions consists in restricting (a) the tariff changes to a range and (b) the number of final commodities to two, so that the first term, i.e. ERP index (in the absence of separable production functions, no longer representing the proportionate change in "price" of value added), nevertheless helps in predicting the sign of the second term (which again, in the absence of separable production functions, no longer represents the proportionate change in value added in physical units).

2. Sufficiency conditions for ERP theory

2.1. The model

Consider an economy producing n tradable goods for final use, using d $(d \geqslant n)$ domestic primary inputs and m imported inputs. Let the production function for the ith good be $F^i(D^i,M^i)$ where $D^i = (D_1^i,...D_d^i)'$ is the column vector of domestic inputs and $M^i = (M_1^i,...,M_m^i)'$ is the column vector of imported inputs used in its production. We shall assume, for simplicity, that all inputs enter into the production of each commodity and that each production function exhibits constant returns to scale and is concave. Let each domestic input be supplied inelastically to the extent of its availability.

Production is assumed to take place under perfect competition, given the domestic price vectors, $P^0 = (P_1^0,...,P_n^0)'$ and $P^M = (P_1^M,...,P_m^M)'$, respectively of the outputs and imported inputs. For any given P^0 and P^M, the equilibrium outputs and inputs are assumed to be unique. For simplicity, we shall be concerned only with equilibria in which every commodity is produced.

We need some further notations. Let:

$$F_D^i = \left(\frac{\partial F^i}{\partial D_1^i},...,\frac{\partial F^i}{\partial D_d^i}\right)', \qquad i = 1,2,...n. \tag{1}$$

$$F_M^i = \left(\frac{\partial F^i}{\partial M_1^i},\dots,\frac{\partial F^i}{\partial M_m^i}\right)', \qquad i = 1,2,\dots n\,. \tag{2}$$

$$F_{DD}^i = \left(\left(\frac{\partial^2 F^i}{\partial D_j^i \partial D_k^i}\right)\right) \qquad i = 1,2,\dots n;\, j,\, k = 1,2,\dots d. \tag{3}$$

$$F_{DM}^i = \left(\left(\frac{\partial^2 F^i}{\partial D_j^i \partial M_k^i}\right)\right) \qquad i = 1,2,\dots n;\, j = 1,2,\dots d;\ k = 1,2,\dots m. \tag{4}$$

$$F_{MD}^i = (F_{DM}^i)' \tag{5}$$

$$F_{MM}^i = \left(\left(\frac{\partial^2 F^i}{\partial M_j^i \partial M_k^i}\right)\right) \qquad i = 1,2,\dots n;\, j,\, k = 1,2,\dots m. \tag{6}$$

$$V^i = P_i^0 F^i - (P^M)' M^i = \text{domestic (nominal) value added in industry } i. \tag{7}$$

The competitive equilibrium conditions are:

$$P_i^0 F_D^i = P_n^0 F_D^n \qquad i = 1,2,\dots n-1. \tag{8}$$

$$P_i^0 F_M^i = P^M \qquad i = 1,2,\dots n. \tag{9}$$

$$\sum_{i=1}^{n} D_j^i = \bar{D}_j \qquad j = 1,2,\dots d. \tag{10}$$

Eqs. (8) state that the marginal value product of each domestic input in each of the first $(n-1)$ industries equals the marginal value product of the same input in the nth industry. Eqs. (9) state that the marginal value product of each imported input in any industry equals its price. Eqs. (10) state that the total amount used in all the n industries together of each domestic input equals the exogenously specified availability.

There are here $n(d+m)$ endogenous variables, namely, D_j^i, M_k^i where $i = 1,2,\dots n$; $j = 1,2,\dots d$; and $k = 1,2,\dots m$. There are $(n+d+m-1)$ exogenous variables, namely, P_i^0, $\bar{D}_j$, P_k^M where $i = 1,2,\dots n-1$; $j = 1,2,\dots d$;

$k = 1,2,...m$.[8] There are in all $n(d+m)$ equations, consisting of $d(n-1)$ in system (8), mn in system (9) and d in system (10). Thus the number of equations equals the number of endogenous variables. We have assumed throughout the analysis that the solution is unique and D^i_j, M^i_k are positive for all i, j, k.

2.2. The analysis

We can look upon a change in tariff structure as a change in the domestic price vectors P^0 and P^M. Let $\hat{P}^0$ and $\hat{P}^M$ denote a small change in P^0 and P^M brought about by a small change in tariff structure. Let us denote by $\hat{V}^i$, $\hat{D}^i$, $\hat{M}^i$, the changes in V^i, D^i and M^i respectively. Differentiating (7) totally we get:

$$\begin{aligned}\hat{V}^i &= \hat{P}^0_i F^i - (\hat{P}^M)' M^i + P^0_i \{(F^i_D)' \hat{D}^i + (F^i_M)' \hat{M}^i\} - (P^M)' \hat{M}^i \\ &= \hat{P}^0_i F^i - (\hat{P}^M)' M^i + P^0_i (F^i_D)' \hat{D}^i \text{ using (9).}\end{aligned}$$

$$\begin{aligned}\frac{\hat{V}^i}{V^i} &= \frac{\hat{P}^0_i F^i - (\hat{P}^M)' M^i}{P^0_i F^i - (P^M)' M^i} + \frac{P^0_i (F^i_D)' \hat{D}^i}{P^0_i - (P^M)' M^i} \\ &= \frac{(\hat{P}^0_i/P^0_i) - \sum_{k=1}^{k=m} \theta^M_{ik} (\hat{P}^M_k/P^M_k)}{1 - \sum_{k=1}^{k=m} \theta^M_{ik}} + \frac{\sum_{j=1}^{j=d} \theta^D_{ij} (\hat{D}^i_j/D^i_j)}{\sum_{j=1}^{j=d} \theta^D_{ij}},\end{aligned} \tag{11}$$

where $\theta^M_{ik} = \dfrac{P^M_k M^i_k}{P^0_i F^i} = \dfrac{M^i_k \dfrac{\partial F^i}{\partial M^i_k}}{F^i}$ = the competitive share of kth imported input in ith output. (12)

[8] We could have used the nth commodity as numeraire and set $P^0_n = 1$. However, there is no reason why a tariff cannot be imposed on this commodity. As such we have not set $P^0_n = 1$ by definition. Of course if a tariff structure changes all prices in the same proportion, i.e. $\hat{P}^0_i/P^0_i = \hat{P}^M_k/P^M_k$ $(i = 1,2,...n; k = 1,2,...m)$, the equilibrium outputs and inputs will be unchanged.

$$\theta_{ij}^D = \frac{D_j^i \dfrac{\partial F^i}{\partial D_j^i}}{F^i} = \text{the competitive share of } j\text{th domestic primary input in output.} \tag{13}$$

It is seen from (11) that the proportionate change in nominal value added in the ith industry, $\hat{V}^i/V^i$, is the sum of two terms. The first term is the weighted average of the proportionate change in the exogenously given prices relevant to the ith industry, the proportionate change in price of each input having a negative weight equal to its competitive share in output. This term can therefore be interpreted as a proportionate change in the "net" price (as it were) of industry i or, under conditions to be specified later in this paper, as a proportionate change in the "price" (P_v^i) of value added.

The second term, on the other hand, is a weighted average of the proportionate changes in domestic primary inputs used in industry i, each input having a weight equal to its competitive share in output. Thus, the second term can be interpreted as a proportionate change in "quantity" (as it were) of value added by industry i, or under conditions to be specified later in this paper, of the quantity Q_v^i in physical units of value added.

Using these symbols, we can thus write purely symbolically:[9]

$$\frac{\hat{V}^i}{V^i} = \frac{\hat{P}_v^i}{P_v^i} + \frac{\hat{Q}_v^i}{Q_v^i} \tag{14}$$

where
$$\frac{\hat{P}_v^i}{P_v^i} = \frac{(\hat{P}_i^0/P_i^0) - \Sigma_{k=1}^{k=m}\, \theta_{ik}^M\, (\hat{P}_k^M/P_k^M)}{1 - \Sigma_{k=1}^{k=m}\, \theta_{ik}^M} \tag{15}$$

and
$$\frac{\hat{Q}_v^i}{Q_v^i} = \frac{\Sigma_{j=1}^{j=d}\, \theta_{ij}^D\, (\hat{D}_j^i/D_j^i)}{\Sigma_{j=1}^{j=d}\, \theta_{ij}^D}. \tag{16}$$

[9] Note that $\hat{P}_v^i/P_v^i$ in (15) is not (in general) the "proportionate change in value-added per unit of output", which represents the original ERP definition of Corden (1966), Johnson (1965) and others. Rather, it is the ERP definition which is recommended by Corden (1969) for the case of substitution between imported inputs and domestic factors, and which is used by Jones (1971), Ray (1973) and others.

It should be emphasized that our notation $\hat{P}_v^i/P_v^i$ and $\hat{Q}_v^i/Q_v^i$ should not be taken to mean that we are implicitly defining a commodity whose output in physical units is Q_v^i and the unit price of which is P_v^i. Indeed, this is in general impossible. Of course, if one postulates that all tariffs are functions of a single policy parameter and changes in tariff structure are brought about by continuous changes in this parameter, one could interpret (15)–(16) as defining proportionate changes in P_v^i and Q_v^i as this parameter changes. As such, one could integrate (15) and (16) (assuming the right hand sides of (15) and (16) to be integrable as functions of this parameter) starting from arbitrary initial values to obtain P_v^i and Q_v^i. If we set the initial values so as to satisfy $V_{(0)}^i = P_v^i(0)Q_v^i(0)$, the same equality will hold true at all values of the policy parameter. But, in general (i.e. except for separable production functions), P_v^i so obtained will not represent in any meaningful sense a unit price of a quantity represented by Q_v^i.

Whether we are able to define a meaningful P_v^i and Q_v^i or not, however, it is nonetheless meaningful to ask whether an *index* of price change as represented by the right hand side of (15) is useful in inferring something about the *index* of quantity change as represented by the right hand side of (16).

More precisely, suppose that a tariff structure results in $\hat{P}_v^1/P_v^1 >$ $(<)$ $\hat{P}_v^2/P_v^2 = \ldots = \hat{P}_v^n/P_v^n$. When can we then infer whether the sign of $\hat{Q}_v^1/Q_v^1$ is the same as that of $\{\hat{P}_v^1/P_v^1 - \hat{P}_v^n/P_v^n\}$? For, if we could, then we would have the proposition analogous to that in nominal tariff theory: i.e. a change in the "price" (as it were) of value-added would predict the change in the "quantity" of value-added.[10] (From (15), note further that $\hat{P}_v^i/P_v^i$ depends upon $\hat{P}_i^0/P_i^0$, the changes in imported input prices $(\hat{P}_k^M/P_k^M)$ as well as the θ_{ik}^M. From (16), we see also that $\hat{Q}_v^i/Q_v^i$ depends on θ_{ij}^D and $\hat{D}_j^i/D_j^i$.)

One possible approach to establishing our sufficiency conditions then is to look for restrictions on the production function strong enough to ensure that $\{\hat{P}_v^1/P_v^1 - \hat{P}_v^n/P_v^n\}$ and Q_v^1/Q_v^1 have the same sign regardless of (1) the alternative patterns of $\hat{P}_i^0/P_i^0$ and $\hat{P}_k^M/P_k^M$ that can result in a given sign for $\{\hat{P}_v^1/P_v^1 - \hat{P}_v^n/P_v^n\}$ and $\hat{P}_v^i/P_v^i = \hat{P}_v^n/P_v^n$ for $i = 1,2,\ldots n-1$ and (2) the values of θ_{ij}^D and θ_{ik}^M.

[10] Several ERP-theory enthusiasts have implied a stronger proposition: i.e. that the ranking of two (or more) industries by their ERP index would rank them also by the changes in their resource use, in one sense or another: a result that would not hold in nominal tariff theory either!

The second approach is to look for restrictions on $\hat{P}_i^0/P_i^0$ and $\hat{P}_k^M/P_k^M$ such that $\{\hat{P}_v^1/P_v^1 - \hat{P}_v^n/P_v^n\}$ and $\hat{Q}_v^1/Q_v^1$ have the same sign regardless of θ_{1j}^D and θ_{1k}^M. Since we are not placing any special restrictions on the production functions in the latter approach, we have to look instead for restrictions on the price changes such that $\hat{D}_j^1/D_j^1$ has the same sign as $\{\hat{P}_v^1/P_v^1 - \hat{P}_v^n/P_v^n\}$ for all j, thus ensuring that $\hat{Q}_v^1/Q_v^1$ is also of that sign.

2.3. Sufficient restrictions on production functions

It turns out that the first approach leads to the following restriction on the production functions F^i: that there exist functions $\phi^i(D^i)$ which depend only on D^i such that F^i could be written as:

$$F^i \equiv G^i[\phi^i, M^i]. \tag{17}$$

Given linear homogeneity of F^i and its concavity, we can assume without loss of generality that ϕ^i is homogeneous of degree one and concave (see Arrow, 1972). In other words, each production function is "separable" in the sense that the domestic primary inputs used in each industry can be aggregated into an index ϕ^i.

Now, given (17), we can write:

$$F_D^i = G_D^i \phi_D^i \quad \text{where} \quad \phi_D^i = \left(\frac{\partial \phi^i}{\partial D_1^i}, \ldots, \frac{\partial \phi^i}{\partial D_d^i}\right)', \tag{18}$$

$$F_M^i = G_M^i, \tag{19}$$

where $$G_D^i = \frac{\partial G^i}{\partial \phi^i}, \tag{20}$$

$$G_M^i = \left(\frac{\partial G^i}{\partial M_1^i}, \ldots \frac{\partial G^i}{\partial M_m^i}\right)'. \tag{21}$$

Suppose now we define $\pi_v^i = P_i^0 G_D^i$. (22)

Then we can rewrite (8), (9) and (10) as:

$$\pi_v^i \phi_D^i = \pi_v^n \phi_D^n \qquad i = 1,2,\ldots n-1. \tag{8'}$$

$$P_i^0 G_M^i = P^M \qquad i = 1,2,\ldots n. \tag{9'}$$

$$\sum_{i=1}^{n} D_j^i = \bar{D}_j \qquad j = 1,2,\ldots d. \tag{10'}$$

It can be readily seen from (8′) and (10′) that the domestic input allocations D_j^i depend only on π_v^i $(i = 1,\ldots n)$ and the total availability of each input. Given the linear homogeneity and concavity of ϕ^i we are back to the traditional model, if we interpret ϕ^i as the net output of industry i with π_v^i as its net unit price.

Hence, if the π_v^i rises relative to π_v^n while all other π_v^i's remain the same relative to π_v^n, then the net output of i, i.e. ϕ^i, will go up. (Further, in the special case of a two-industry, two-primary factor world, this rise in net output (= value added) will come about by industry i attracting *each* domestic input from the other industry.) The gross output price P_0^i and imported input price vector P^M will influence domestic factor allocation only through their influence on π_v^i.

It is now easy to show that π_v^i, as defined by (22), satisfies (15) and that ϕ^i satisfies (16), thus linking up our results directly with the problem of ERP theory which we had formulated. For,

$$\begin{aligned} V^i &= P_i^0 F^i - (P_M)'M^i \\ &= P_i^0 G^i - (P_i^0 G_M^0)'M^i \\ &= P_i^0 [G^i - (G_M^0)'M^i] \\ &= P_i^0 G_D^i \phi^i \qquad \text{since } G^i \text{ is linear homogeneous} \\ &= \pi_v^i \phi^i \qquad \text{using (22).} \end{aligned}$$

Hence
$$\frac{\hat{V}^i}{V^i} = \frac{\hat{\pi}_v^i}{\pi_v^i} + \frac{\hat{\phi}^i}{\phi^i}, \tag{23}$$

but $\hat{\phi}^i = \Sigma \phi_j^i \hat{D}_j^i$ where $\phi_j^i = \partial \phi^i / \partial D_j^i$, and $\phi^i = \Sigma \phi_j^i D_j^i$ since ϕ^i is homogeneous of degree one.

Thus $$\frac{\hat{\phi}^i}{\phi^i} = \frac{\Sigma\phi^i_j\hat{D}^i_j}{\Sigma\phi^i_jD^i_j} = \frac{\Sigma\phi^i_jD^i_j(\hat{D}^i_j/D^i_j)}{\Sigma\phi^i_jD^i_j},$$

but $$\frac{\phi^i_jD^i_j}{\Sigma\phi^i_jD^i_j} = \frac{G^i_D\,\phi^i_jD^i_j}{\Sigma G^i_D\,\phi^i_jD^i_j} = \frac{(\partial F^i/\partial D^i_j)D^i_j}{\Sigma(\partial F^i/\partial D^i_j)D^i_j}\ \{\text{using (19)}\}$$

$$= \frac{\theta^D_{ij}}{\Sigma\theta^D_{ij}}\ \{\text{using (13)}\}.$$

Hence $$\frac{\hat{\phi}^i}{\phi^i} = \frac{\Sigma\theta^D_{ij}(\hat{D}^i_j/D^i_j)}{\Sigma\theta^D_{ij}} = \frac{\hat{Q}^i_v}{Q^i_v}. \tag{24}$$

Given (11), this implies that π^i_v, as defined by (22) satisfies (15). Since we have already established that, if π^1_v rises relative to π^n_v while all other π^i_v's remain the same relative to π^n_v, then ϕ^1 will go up as well, it then follows that the change in the sign of $\hat{Q}^1_v/Q^1_v$ *is* the same as that of $\{\hat{P}^1_v/P^1_v - \hat{P}^n_v/P^n_v\}$, so that the problem of ERP theory, as posed by us earlier, is indeed solved in this case.

It is further important to note that, in the case of separable production functions, we can also meaningfully talk of π^i_v as price per unit of value added and ϕ^i as quantity (in physical units) of value added in each industry. The reason is the following. Suppose we are given the prices $w_1,...w_d$, of the domestic primary inputs. The minimal cost of producing one unit of the value added product of industry i is obtained by minimizing $c^i = \Sigma^d_1 w_jD^i_j$ subject to $\phi^i(D^i) = 1$. The minimal value of c^i is $\tilde{\lambda}(w)$ where $(\tilde{D}^i,\tilde{\lambda})$ are solutions of $\tilde{\lambda}\phi^i_D(\tilde{D}^i) = w$ and $\phi^i(\tilde{D}^i) = 1$. Now this minimal unit cost $\tilde{\lambda}(w)$ is exactly equal to the price π^i_v of value added as defined by (22) if w is set equal to the value of $P^0_iF^i_0$ when D^i, M^i satisfy the equilibrium conditions (9)–(10). This is easily seen by appropriate substitutions and utilising the separability of F^i and linear homogeneity of ϕ^i.

2.4. Sufficient restrictions on tariff change

Let us now turn to the second approach, assuming that F^i are not separable.[11] Let us differentiate the system (8)–(10) totally. We get:

$$P_i^0[F_{DD}^i \hat{D}^i + F_{DM}^i \hat{M}^i] - P_n^0[F_{DD}^n \hat{D}^n + F_{DM}^n \hat{M}^n] = - \hat{P}_i^0 F_D^i + \hat{P}_n^0 F_D^n \tag{25}$$

$$P_i^0[F_{MD}^i \hat{D}^i + F_{MM}^i \hat{M}^i] = \hat{P}^M - \hat{P}_i^0 F_M^i \tag{26}$$

$$\sum_{i=1}^{n} \hat{D}^i = 0. \tag{27}$$

Eliminating $\hat{D}^n$ and $\hat{M}^i$ $(i = 1,2,...n)$, we get:

$$(P_i^0 A^i + P_n^0 A^n)\hat{D}^i + P_n^0 A^n \sum_{\substack{j=1 \\ j \neq i}}^{n-1} \hat{D}^j = s^i + t^i, \tag{28}$$

where $A^i = F_{DD}^i - F_{DM}^i (F_{MM}^i)^{-1} F_{MD}^i$ (barring pathologies, F_{MM}^i will have an inverse in the non-separable case)

$$s^i = (- \hat{P}_i^0 F_D^i + \hat{P}_n^0 F_D^n)$$

$$t^i = - F_{DM}^i (F_{MM}^i)^{-1} (\hat{P}^M - \hat{P}_i^0 F_M^i) + F_{DM}^n (F_{MM}^n)^{-1} (\hat{P}^M - \hat{P}_n^0 F_M^n).$$

Let Δ be the square matrix (in partitioned notation) of order $(n-1)$ whose (ij) element is the square matrix Δ_{ij} of order d given by:

$$\left.\begin{aligned} \Delta_{ij} &= P_i^0 A^i + P_n^0 A^n \qquad &\text{if } i = j \\ &= P_n^0 A^n \qquad &\text{if } i \neq j \end{aligned}\right\} \quad i = 1,2,...n-1. \tag{29}$$

[11] This automatically rules out the case of imported inputs being used in fixed proportions to output, of course.

Then: $$\Delta(\hat{D}_1',\ldots\hat{D}_{n-1}')' = \{(s^1+t^1)',\ldots,(s^{n-1}+t^{n-1})'\}'$$

$$= s + t. \tag{30}$$

2.4.1. Change in gross outputs

Let us evaluate the sign of the change in gross output of an industry, say the first industry, as well as the change in value added by it.

$$\begin{aligned}\hat{F}^1 &= (F_D^1)'\hat{D}^1 + (F_M^1)'\hat{M}^1 \\ &= (F_D^1)'\hat{D}^1 + (F_M^1)'(F_{MM}^1)^{-1}\left\{\frac{\hat{P}^M}{P_1^0} - \frac{\hat{P}_1^0}{P_1^0}F_M^1 - F_{MD}^1\hat{D}_1\right\} \\ &= \{(F_D^1)' - (F_M^1)'(F_{MM}^1)^{-1}F_{MD}^1\}\hat{D}^1 \\ &\quad + (F_M^1)'(F_{MM}^1)^{-1}\left\{\frac{\hat{P}^M}{P_1^0} - \frac{\hat{P}_1^0}{P_1^0}F_M^1\right\}\end{aligned} \tag{31}$$

$$\begin{aligned}\hat{V}^1 &= P_1^0\hat{F}^1 - (P^M)'\hat{M}^1 + \hat{P}_1^0F^1 - (\hat{P}^M)'M^1 \\ &= P_1^0(F_D^1)'\hat{D}^1 + \hat{P}_1^0F^1 - (\hat{P}^M)'M^1\end{aligned} \tag{32}$$

Suppose (as before) that protection is now conferred only on (against) industry 1 by the following change in the tariff structure:

$$\frac{\hat{P}_1^0}{P_1^0} > (<)\frac{\hat{P}_i^0}{P_i^0} = \frac{\hat{P}_k^M}{P_k^M}, \quad i = 2,\ldots n;\ k = 1,2,\ldots m$$

i.e. the relative prices (in terms of good 1) of goods 2,...n and all imported inputs fall in the same proportion. It can be seen from (15) that this structure results in $(\hat{P}_v^1/P_v^1) > (\hat{P}_v^i/P_v^i)$, $i = 2.3,\ldots n$. This would mean that:

$$s^1 + t^1 = P_1^0\left(\frac{\hat{P}_n^0}{P_n^0} - \frac{\hat{P}_1^0}{P_1^0}\right)\{(F_D^1) - F_{DM}^1(F_{MM}^1)^{-1}F_M^1\} \tag{33}$$

$$s^i + t^i = 0 \qquad i = 2,\ldots n-1. \tag{34}$$

Solving for $\hat{D}^1$ from (30) and substituting in (31) we get:

$$\hat{F}^1 = P_1^0 \left(\frac{\hat{P}_n^0}{P_n^0} - \frac{\hat{P}_1^0}{P_1^0}\right) \left[\frac{1}{P_1^0}(F_M^1)'(F_{MM}^1)^{-1}F_M^1 + \frac{1}{|\Delta|} \begin{vmatrix} 0_1 & (F_D^1)' - (F_M^1)'(F_{MM}^1)^{-1}F_{MD}^1 \quad 0_2 \\ -\left(F_D^1 - F_{DM}^1(F_{MM}^1)^{-1}F_M^1\right) & \\ & \Delta \\ 0_3 & \end{vmatrix}\right] \tag{35}$$

where: $|\Delta|$ = determinant of Δ, and 0_1, 0_2, 0_3 are null matrices of order 1×1, $1\times(n-2)d$ and $(n-2)d\times 1$ respectively.

It is clear that the first term in the square bracket in (35) is negative since $(F_{MM})^{-1}$ is a negative definite matrix. The second term is non-positive since $|\Delta|$ is of the same sign as $(-1)^{(n-1)d}$ (Δ is a negative definite matrix[12] of order $(n-1)d$) and

$$\begin{vmatrix} 0_1 & (F_D^1)' - (F_M^1)'(F_{MM}^1)^{-1}F_{MD}^1 \quad 0_2 \\ -\left(F_D^1 - F_{DM}^1(F_{MM}^1)^{-1}F_M^1\right) & \\ & \Delta \\ 0_3 & \end{vmatrix}$$

is of the sign of $(-1)^{(n-1)d+1}$

Thus $\hat{F}^1$ is of sign opposite to that of $\{\hat{P}_n^0/P_n^0 - \hat{P}_1^0/P_1^0\}$. Hence, if the first industry is conferred positive protection, i.e. $\{\hat{P}_1^0/P_1^0 > \hat{P}_n^0/P_n^0\}$,

[12] In general, Δ is negative semi-definite. To ensure that it is negative definite, we need to assume that the vector of equilibrium primary factor-ratios in the nth industry is not a scalar multiple of the appropriately weighted average of the vectors corresponding to the first $(n-1)$ industries, an assumption that reduces in the two-industry, two-factor case to the assumption that factor-intensities differ in equilibrium.

its *gross output* F^1 goes up and if protection is given against industry 1, i.e. $\{\hat{P}_1^0/P_1^0 < \hat{P}_n^0/P_n^0\}$ then its *gross output* goes down.

2.4.2. Change in (nominal) value added and in Q_v^i

This result on gross outputs paradoxically does not extend to (nominal) value added or to predicting the sign of $\hat{Q}_v^i/Q_v^i$ (which, of course, is our main objective). This is because, unfortunately, $(F_D^1)'\hat{D}^1$ is not of definite sign and hence it is not possible to assert, even with the earlier-imposed restrictions on tariff changes, that $\hat{Q}_v^1/Q_v^1$ is positive (negative) according as protection is given to (against) the first industry. In the general case of non-separable production functions, therefore, ERP theory breaks down (its objective being as defined by us in this paper).

2.4.3. The two-industry case

However, in a two-industry economy, with the added assumption that the marginal product of any input does not decrease as the quantity of any other input is increased, we can obtain the results we are after. This is seen as follows.

Given $n = 2$, Δ reduces to $P_1^0 A^1 + P_2^0 A^2$. Given our assumption on marginal products, the off-diagonal elements of F_{DD}^i, F_{MM}^i and all elements of F_{DM}^i $(= (F_{MD}^i)')$ are non-negative. This, together with the concavity of F^i, ensures that (a) $(F_{MM}^i)^{-1}$ consists of nonpositive elements and (b) the off-diagonal elements of A^i are non-negative. Since $\Delta = P_1^0 A^1 + P_2^0 A^2$ is thus a negative definite matrix with non-negative off-diagonal elements, Δ^{-1} consists of nonpositive elements. Now $\hat{D}_1 = \Delta^{-1}\{s^1 + t^1\} = P_1^0\{\hat{P}_2^0/P_2^0 - \hat{P}_1^0/P_1^0\}\Delta^{-1}\{F_D^1 - F_{DM}^1(F_{MM}^1)^{-1}F_M^1\}$ when the tariff change is restricted to $\{\hat{P}_2^0/P_2^0 = \hat{P}_k^M/P_k^M\}$, $k = 1,2,...m$. Since $\{F_D^1 - F_{DM}^1(F_{MM}^1)^{-1}F_M^1\} > 0$, it follows that $\hat{D}_1$ is of sign opposite to that of $\{\hat{P}_2^0/P_2^0 - \hat{P}_1^0/P_1^0\}$.

Hence, if the tariff structure results in protection being conferred on industry 1 (i.e. $\hat{P}_1^0/P_1^0 > \hat{P}_2^0/P_2^0 = \hat{P}_k^M/P_k^M$, $k = 1,2,...m$), this industry attracts all domestic resources and its gross output, nominal value added and Q_v^1 go up. If $\hat{P}_2^0/P_2^0 = \hat{P}_k^M/P_k^M > \hat{P}_1^0/P_1^0$, then it is industry 2 which gets protection and it will attract each domestic resource resulting in its gross output, nominal value added and Q_v^2 going up. ERP theory will work, in the sense defined by us; and we also have "nice" results on gross output and nominal value added changes consequent on change in the tariff structure.

2.5. The Ramaswami–Srinivasan and Jones–Khang analyses

Our analysis of the two-industry model has immediate implications for the existing analyses in the literature, especially those by Ramaswami–Srinivasan (1971) and by Jones (1971) and Khang (1973). In particular, the apparent divergence in the results obtained by Ramaswami–Srinivasan and by Jones, on the possibility of "perverse" changes in gross outputs, can now be easily explained by us and the results therefore reconciled.[13]

All these authors discuss effective protection in the context of a two-industry model with two domestic inputs and one imported input. However, while the R–S model allows the use of the imported input by both industries, the J–K model restricts its use only to the first industry. The change in tariff structure considered by R–S involves subsidisation of the imported input, leaving the output prices unchanged (thus placing it outside the range discussed earlier) while J–K change one output price (that of industry 1) and the price of its imported input, thus allowing for changes in tariff structure in as well as out of the range.

To relate their results with ours, let us tabulate Δ, $\hat{P}_i^0$, $\hat{P}_k^M$, and $(s^1 + t^1)$ for the R–S, J–K models and evaluate $\hat{D}_1 = \Delta^{-1}[s^1 + t^1]$. (See table 1.) Note further that, while the production functions assumed by R–S have the property that the marginal product of any input does not fall if the quantity used of some other input is increased, such a property is not postulated by the J–K model. In order to pinpoint the importance of resource endowment in the R–S counter example, let us therefore modify the J–K model by postulating the above assumption on marginal products.

With this assumption, in both models the off-diagonal elements of Δ are non-negative and hence the elements of Δ^{-1} and $(F_{MM}^i)^{-1}$ (in

[13] Khang (1973) uses the Jones model but deals with the predictability of (clearly-defined) real value added changes consequent on changes in the tariff structure whereas Jones' focus is on gross output changes. Jones' Appendix II considers changes in value added but it is not clear to us whether he intends to consider nominal or real value added shifts and, if the latter, what his definition is. His Appendix I, which attempts at reconciling the R–S analysis with Jones' own results on gross output changes, is on the other hand clear but (as is evident from our analysis in the text above) unfortunately not really to the point in ignoring wholly the really critical difference which exists between the two models in respect of the assumption with regard to the use of the intermediate input by the two industries and which makes the primary-factor resource endowment of the economy critical to the R–S conclusions and irrelevant to the J–K analyses.

Table 1
Critical values in the R–S and J–K models

Model	Δ	$\hat{P}_1^0$	$\hat{P}_2^0$	$\hat{P}_1^M$	(s^1+t^1)
R–S	$P_1^0\{F_{DD}^1 - F_{DM}^1(F_{MM}^1)^{-1}F_{MD}^1\}$	0	0	$=0$	$\{F_{DM}^2(F_{MM}^2)^{-1}$
	$+P_0^2\{F_{DD}^2 - F_{DM}^2(F_{MM}^2)^{-1}F_{MD}^2\}$				$-F_{DM}^1(F_{MM}^1)^{-1}\}\hat{P}_1^M$
J–K	$P_1^0\{F_{DD}^1 - F_{DM}^1(F_{MM}^1)^{-1}F_{MD}^1\}$	$\gtreqless 0$	0	$\gtrless 0$	$-\hat{P}_1^0F_D^1 - F_{DM}^1(F_{MM}^1)^{-1}$
	$+P_0^2F_{DD}^2$				$\times(\hat{P}_1^M - \hat{P}_1^0F_M^1)$

the J–K model, only F_{MM}^1 is defined) are nonpositive. Since $\hat{D}_1$, the change of domestic factors used in industry 1, is by definition $\Delta^{-1}(s^1+t^1)$, it follows that, if the elements of s^1+t^1 are of the same sign, then the elements of $\hat{D}_1$ are of the same sign. If, however, the elements of (s^1+t^1) are of opposite signs, then the sign of the elements of $\hat{D}_1$ cannot be determined without knowledge of the magnitudes of the elements of Δ^{-1} and of s^1+t^1.

For the tariff change considered by R–S, the signs of the elements of s^1+t^1 are a priori indeterminate while their magnitudes depend on the prices (P_1^0, P_2^0, P_3^0) as well as the factor allocations since the F_{DM}^i, F_{MM}^i depend on these. Hence the same change in the pattern of prices, (and hence the same pattern of protection), could (and in their numerical example, does) result in positive *or* negative signs for the elements of $\hat{D}_1$ depending on the aggregate factor endowment (which helps determine the factor allocations).

By contrast, in the J–K model, (modified, as noted earlier, for the restriction on the sign of marginal products), the elements of s^1+t^1 are necessarily of one sign, thus determining unambiguously the sign of $\hat{D}_1$ regardless of the factor endowments, as long as the tariff changes are confined to those noted immediately below. Thus:

$$\hat{D}_1 \geqq (\leqq)\ 0 \quad \text{if either:} \quad \text{(a) } \hat{P}_1^0 = 0 \text{ and } \hat{P}_1^M \leqq (\geqq)\ 0;\text{ or}$$

$$\text{(b) } \hat{P}_1^M/P_1^M = \hat{P}_1^0/P_1^0 \text{ and } \hat{P}_1^0 \geqq (\leqq)\ 0;\text{ or}$$

$$\text{(c) } \hat{P}_1^M/P_1^M < (>)\ \hat{P}_1^0/P_1^0 \text{ and } P_1^0 \geqq (\leqq) 0.$$

In all these three cases of tariff change, the industry gaining protection (i.e. increasing its $\hat{P}_v^i/P_v^i$ relative to that in the other industry) will gain domestic resources, increase its nominal value added (*and* have its $\hat{Q}_v^i/Q_v^i > 0$ – the last validating ERP theory in the sense defined by us). However, outside of the range of tariff changes described in (a)–(c), one could observe domestic factor movements and changes in nominal value added as also in Q_v^i in a direction opposite to that indicated by the pattern of protection.[14]

The breakdown of ERP theory in the (modified) J–K model is thus easily seen to arise in a substantively different manner from its breakdown in the R–S model. This is yet clearer when we note that the tariff change ($\hat{P}_1^0 = 0, \hat{P}_1^M < 0$) can yield opposite results for the sign of D_1, depending on the aggregate factor endowment in the R–S model, while in the modified J–K model it leads unambiguously to $\hat{D}_1 > 0$: this asymmetry in the two models is attributable entirely to the fact of the imported input entering only the first industry in the J–K model but both industries in the R–S model.

3. "Useful" measurability of ERP index

To sum up, one can define a measure of effective protection which performs, in the non-traditional model with imported inputs, a role completely analogous to that of nominal tariffs in the traditional model without imported inputs, only in the case of separable production functions. In the case of non-separable production functions, the analogy between effective protection and nominal protection breaks down except in cases where effective protection is conferred on an industry through particular forms of tariff change, and the number of final commodities is only two.

We now address ourselves to the question whether, even in the cases where sufficiency conditions obtain, for the ERP index to predict quantity-index shifts correctly, the ERP index can be measured "use-

[14] Note that, in the cases where there are only two primary factors, the "workability" of the ERP index (P_v^i), in both the cases of sufficiency conditions distinguished in this paper, is associated with the increment in value-added following ERP-protection being accompanied by the increase in employment in this industry of both the primary factors. The Stolper–Samuelson theorem's validity in each instance is thus critical to this outcome, as noted by Bhagwati–Srinivasan (1971a). Note also that the R–S counter-example is characterised by the primary-factor-ratios in the two activities going in contrary directions, thus invalidating the Stolper–Samuelson argument: also read Khang (1973) from this point of view.

fully", i.e. without having access to the kind of information which would enable us to solve directly for the resource allocational effects of the tariff structure. It turns out that this range of possibilities is even narrower.

Remember that our analysis has been in terms of "differentials." To be of any policy use at all, one should be able to assess the impact of non-infinitesimal changes in the tariff structure. Indeed, in the traditional model, we have the comparative static result that any increase in the tariff on imports of one commodity, ceteris paribus, will result in an increased production of that commodity in the new equilibrium. Formally of course, in the non-traditional model also, given that production functions are separable, we can say that any change in tariff structure which results in an increase in "price" of value added in one industry, ceteris paribus, will result in an increase in the "quantity" of value added of that industry in the new equilibrium.

However, one cannot in general compute the pattern of "prices" of value added from the knowledge of the *tariff structure alone* – one needs information on the production functions. This is in contrast to the traditional model where one can predict that, ceteris paribus, the equilibrium output of a commodity will go up consequent on an increase in the tariff on this commodity without drawing upon any knowledge of its production function.

This fact is evident from our definition of ERP in (15). In order to obtain the "price" of value added after a non-infinitesimal change in tariff structure, essentially we have to integrate (15). In the absence of imported inputs, (15) reduces to $\hat{P}_i^0/P_i^0$ and hence the integral is the proportionate change in output price alone and can be computed directly from the tariff change. However, once imported inputs are admitted, θ_{ik}^M or the share of each imported input in output enters the expression and in general θ_{ik}^M depends on the prices, a functional dependence that can be derived from the production function. Without a knowledge of this dependence, one cannot, in general, carry out the required integration. For instance, if this dependence takes the simple form that θ_{ik}^M are constant – a situation that arises in the case where the production function is Cobb–Douglas in the imported inputs and the index of domestic factors, such that $F^i = [\phi^i(D^i)]^{\alpha_0^i} (M_1^i)^{\alpha_1^i} \ldots (M_m)^{\alpha_m^i}$ with $\Sigma_{j=0}^{j=m} \alpha_j^i = 1$ and $\phi^i(D^i)$ is homogeneous of degree one in domestic inputs and concave – we can perform the integration with the information on θ_{ik}^M obtained from the initial equilibrium and with the knowledge of the proposed changes in tariff structure. Another instance is the case where each imported input is used in fixed proportions with output in each production function: in this case, also, the relevant information is contained in the initial equilibrium input/output ratios and the proposed changes in tariff structure.

In other cases, such as the general CES production function (which is, of course, separable) one can try to get by with "approximations" by assuming that the change in tariff structure is sufficiently small that either imported input coefficients or their shares in output remain approximately equal to their initial equilibrium values: but one really cannot get "correct" ERP indices measured usefully for the kinds of "real-life", "large" tariff structures which ERP-enthusiasts have been discussing in most recent contributions.

4. Conclusions

Our analysis thus leads us to conclude, somewhat nihilistically, that:

(i) A measure of ERP which will work *unfailingly* in analogy with nominal tariff theory does not always exist;

(ii) The range of sufficient conditions over which an ERP index will so work is significantly narrower than that over which the nominal tariff theory will so work in the traditional trade-theoretic model without imported inputs; and

(iii) The range of sufficient conditions over which such a working ERP index can be measured "usefully" – i.e. without solving the general equilibrium production system for both the situations over which the resource shift is sought to be predicted – is yet narrower.

These nihilistic conclusions are reinforced by four further observations:

(i) As we would expect, even when an ERP index works analogously to nominal tariffs, it does not necessarily work in predicting output shifts: and the latter are of greater interest in trade negotiations where ERP's may be thought of as replacing nominal tariffs in the future.

(ii) Recent studies, by Cohen (1969) and Guisinger and Schydlowsky (1970), of the relationship between the (calculated) nominal tariffs and ERP's in a number of empirical studies have shown that a remarkably high correlation exists between them: thus raising the question whether it is useful to spend vast resources on calculating ERP's when nominal tariffs seem to be adequate proxies for them anyway.

(iii) In a multi-commodity world where tariffs are levied on more than one commodity or input, we could not even tell, when the different processes were ranked by their ERP's in a chain, that the highest-ERP process would have gained resources and the lowest-ERP process would have lost them, in relation to the pre-trade situation. As with nominal tariffs, the scope of purely "qualitative economics" is negligible in this real-world case, so that once again the vast empirical effort required in making up the ERP numbers seems grossly disproportionate to what can be done to predict actual resource-allocational impacts of the tariff structure without resort to the full general-equilibrium solution.

(iv) It may finally be noted that attempts at arguing that the constancy of the (imported-factor) a_{ij}'s is a reasonable restriction because raw materials do not substitute with domestic factors and are in a fairly fixed proportion to output are based on a false equation of the imported factors with intermediates and raw materials. Most economies *import* capital goods and these do substitute with (domestic) labour quite generally. And, indeed, it is not at all uncommon for there to be substitution between intermediates and primary factors, though admittedly this is less important in practice than the substitution among the primary factors, capital and labour.

References

Anderson, J. and S. Naya, 1969, Substitution and two concepts of effective rate of protection, American Economic Review LIX, 607–611.

Arrow, K.J., 1972, The measurement of real value added, Technical Report No. 60, The Economics Series, Stanford University.

Bhagwati, J.N. and T.N. Srinivasan, 1971a, The theory of effective protection and resource allocation, M.I.T. Working Paper No. 67.

Bhagwati, J.N. and T.N. Srinivasan, 1971b, The theory of effective protection and resource allocation further examined, M.I.T. Working Paper No. 68.

Bruno, M., 1973, Protection and tariff change in general equilibrium, Journal of International Economics, this issue.

Corden, W.M., 1966, The structure of a tariff system and the effective protective rate, Journal of Political Economy LXXIV, No. 3; reprinted in: Bhagwati (ed.), 1969, International Trade (Penguin).

Corden, W.M., 1969, Effective protective rates in the general equilibrium model: A geometric approach, Oxford Economic Papers, 21.

Johnson, H.G., 1965, The theory of tariff structure with special reference to world trade and development, in: H.G. Johnson and P.B. Kenen, Trade and Development (Geneva).

Jones, R.W., 1971, Effective protection and substitution, Journal of International Economics 1, 1, 59–82.

Khang, C., 1973, Factor substitution in the theory of effective protection: A general equilibrium analysis, Journal of International Economics, this issue.

Leith, J.C., 1968, Substitution and supply elasticities in calculating the effective protective rate, Quarterly Journal of Economics LXXXII, 588–601.

Ramaswami, V.K. and T.N. Srinivasan, 1971, Tariff structure and resource allocation in the presence of substitution, in: Bhagwati et al. (eds.), Trade, Balance of Payments and Growth (North-Holland, Amsterdam).

Ray, A., 1973, Non-traded inputs and effective protection: A general equilibrium analysis, Journal of International Economics, this issue.

Errata

Page 264, lines 1 and 2 from bottom: "P_n^0" is also exogenous, giving $(n + d + m)$ exogenous variables.

Page 268, line 3: "θ_{1j}^D" should read "θ_{ij}^D", and "θ_{1k}^M" should read "θ_{ik}^M."

DOMESTIC DISTORTIONS, TARIFFS AND THE THEORY OF OPTIMUM SUBSIDY[1]

JAGDISH BHAGWATI AND V. K. RAMASWAMI
Indian Statistical Institute, New Delhi

There is confusion of varying degrees in the current literature on trade theory concerning the desirable form of intervention in foreign trade when the economy is characterized by domestic distortions (divergences of the commodity price ratios from the corresponding marginal rates of substitution). For instance, the age-old debate over whether tariffs or subsidies should be used to protect an infant industry is still carried on in terms of the respective political and psychological merits of the two forms of protection while their relative economic advantages are assumed not to point in the direction of a definite choice.[2]

Three questions about the use of tariffs when domestic distortions exist need to be distinguished here. (1) Is a tariff necessarily superior to free trade (that is, can a tariff rate always be found that yields a welfare position not inferior to that produced by free trade)? (2) Is a tariff policy necessarily superior to any other form of *trade* policy? (3) If the choice can be made from the entire range of policy instruments, which is the optimal economic policy?

In Section I we state the general theory that provides the answers to these three questions. In the light of this theory, we examine the propositions advanced in the two central contributions to trade theory in this field: Haberler's justly celebrated 1950 *Economic Journal* paper[3] and Hagen's recent analysis of wage differentials.[4] Sections II and III examine these two analyses. Section IV concludes with some observations concerning the relative advantages of tariffs and subsidies from the practical viewpoint.

I. GENERAL THEORY

The three questions posed here can be effectively answered by analyzing the characteristics of an optimum solution. Thus, for instance, the optimum tariff argument can be stated elegantly in terms of these characteristics. The achievement of an optimum solution is characterized by the equality of the foreign rate of transformation (FRT), the domestic rate of transformation in production (DRT), and the domestic rate of substitution in consumption (DRS). If the country has monopoly power in trade, a competitive free trade solution will be characterized by $DRS = DRT \neq FRT$. By introducing a suitable tariff, a country can achieve $DRS = DRT = FRT$. A subsidy (tax)

[1] An early draft of this paper was read to seminars at Massachusetts Institute of Technology, the University of Chicago, and Stanford University by one of the authors. C. P. Kindleberger and H. G. Johnson have made useful suggestions.

[2] For instance, C. P. Kindleberger in his *International Economics* (Homewood, Ill.: Richard D. Irwin, Inc., 1958), as does also G. Haberler in his *Theory of International Trade* (Glasgow: William Hodge & Co., 1936), states the economic argument in favor of subsidies and tariffs without stating definitely that one is invariably superior to the other from the economic viewpoint.

[3] G. Haberler, "Some Problems in the Pure Theory of International Trade," *Economic Journal*, LX (June, 1950), 223–40.

[4] E. Hagen, "An Economic Justification of Protectionism," *Quarterly Journal of Economics*, LXXII (November, 1958), 496–514.

on the domestic production of importables (exportables) could equalize *DRT* and *FRT* but would destroy the quality of *DRS* with *DRT*. Hence it is clear that a tax-cum-subsidy on domestic production is necessarily inferior to an optimum tariff. Moreover it may be impossible in any given empirical situation to devise a tax-cum-subsidy that would yield a solution superior to that arrived at under free trade.

By analogy we can argue that, in the case of domestic distortions, $DRS = FRT \neq DRT$ under free trade. A suitable tariff can equalize *FRT* and *DRT* but would destroy the equality between *DRS* and *FRT*. Hence it is clear that no tariff may exist that would yield a solution superior to that under free trade. A suitable tax-cum-subsidy on domestic production, however, would enable the policy-maker to secure $DRS = FRT = DRT$ and hence is necessarily the optimum solution. Hence a tariff policy is also necessarily inferior to an optimum tax-cum-subsidy policy. And the same argument must hold true of trade subsidies as well since they also, like tariffs, are directed at *foreign* trade whereas the problem to be tackled is one of *domestic* distortion.

Three propositions, therefore, follow in the case of domestic distortions. (*a*) A tariff is not necessarily superior to free trade. (*b*) A tariff is not necessarily superior to an export (or import) subsidy. (*c*) A policy permitting the attainment of maximum welfare involves a tax-cum-subsidy on domestic production. Just as there exists an optimum tariff policy for a divergence between foreign prices and *FRT*, so there exists an *optimum subsidy* (or an equivalent tax-cum-subsidy) policy for a divergence between domestic prices and *DRT*.

II. HABERLER ON EXTERNAL ECONOMIES

A divergence between the domestic commodity price ratios and the marginal rates of transformation between commodities may arise from what are usually described as "external economies." These may take various forms.[5] It is most fashionable at the moment to discuss the external economies arising from the interdependence of investment decisions.[6]

Haberler analyzes this problem in terms of the standard two-good, two-factor model of trade theory, using geometrical methods. Haberler is aware that a tariff is not necessarily superior to free trade. However, he is in error concerning the relative advantages of tariffs and trade subsidies. Further, he does not discuss the optimum economic policy under the circumstances.

Haberler distinguishes between two situations according to whether the domestic production of importables rises or falls (what he calls the direction of "specialization"). We shall analyze each case separately.

Case I.—In the former case, illustrated here in Figure 1*a*, *AB* is the production possibility curve. The discrepancy between the domestic price ratio and the domestic rate of transformation (*DRT*)

[5] According to Haberler, "there may be a deviation between social and private cost due to external economies or diseconomies, i.e. due to certain cost-raising or cost-reduction factors which would come into play if one industry expanded and the other contracted—factors which for some reason or other are not, or not sufficiently, allowed for in private cost calculations" ("Some Problems . . . ," *op. cit.*, p. 236).

[6] This has been analyzed in the context of international trade by J. Bhagwati, "The Theory of Comparative Advantage in the Context of Under-development and Growth," *Pakistan Development Review*, II, No. 3 (Autumn, 1962), 339–53. See also H. Chenery, "The Interdependence of Investment Decisions," in Moses Abramovitz *et al.*, *The Allocation of Economic Resources* (Stanford, Calif.: Stanford University Press, 1959).

leads to self-sufficiency equilibrium at S. Free trade, at the *given* international price PF, leads to production at P, consumption at F, export of agricultural goods, and a deterioration in welfare.[7]

The following comments are warranted. First, although Haberler does not state this explicitly, it can be shown that prohibitive protection may make the country worse off (Fig. 1*b*). Second, it follows from Section I that *no* tariff may be superior to free trade (this is implicit, we think, in Haberler's statements elsewhere in his paper). Finally, the optimum result could be achieved by a

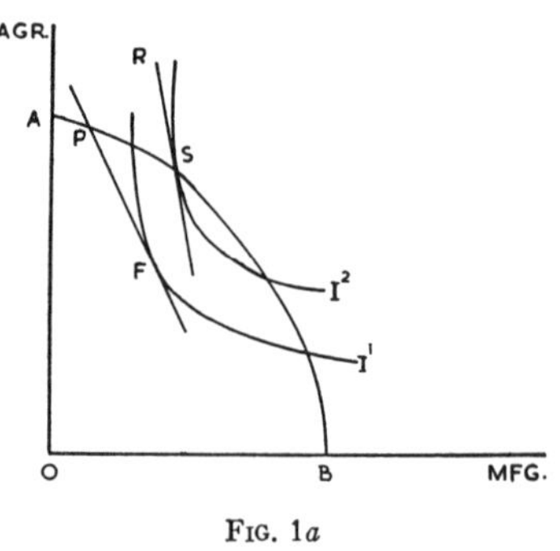

FIG. 1*a*

policy of tax-cum-subsidy on domestic production. Such a policy is illustrated in Figure 1*c* where the tax-cum-subsidy eliminates the divergence between commodity prices and DRT and brings production to P' and consumption to F'.

Case II.—Haberler distinguishes the other case by arguing that the self-sufficiency price ratio RS may be less steep than the *given* foreign price ratio PF. Here the production point is shifted to the right by free trade.[8] In this case, Haberler argues that "the country would specialize in the 'right' direction but not sufficiently. *It would after trade be better off than before, but it would not reach the optimum point. . . . In that case an export or import subsidy (rather than a tariff) would be indicated.*"[9]

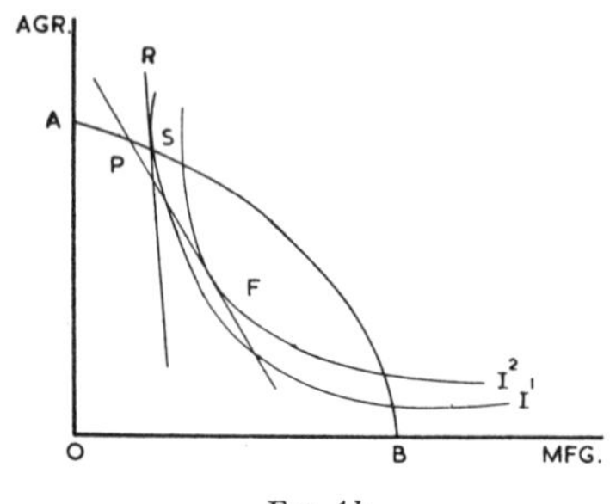

FIG. 1*b*

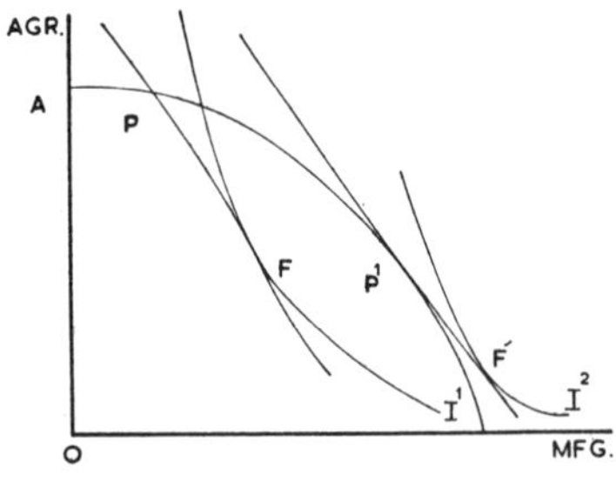

FIG. 1*c*

While Haberler is right in arguing that a movement to the right of S, when free trade is introduced, will necessarily be beneficial, his conclusion that an export

[7] Haberler wrongly seems to imply that the country must export agricultural goods in this case. There is no reason, *once there is a domestic distortion*, why a country should necessarily export the commodity that is cheaper than abroad in the absence of trade.

[8] This, of course, is erroneous, as noted in n. 7. Haberler implies that under free trade manufactures will now become the exported good. Haberler also describes this case as characterized by specialization in the "right" direction. He is right if, by this, he means that the movement of the production point to the right of S, caused by free trade, will necessarily improve welfare. He is wrong, however, if he means that the commodity exported will be that which would have been exported if the divergence did not exist.

[9] Haberler, "Some Problems . . . ," *op. cit.*, p. 237. Our italics.

(or import) subsidy is indicated and would be preferable to a tariff is erroneous in every rigorous sense in which it may be understood. First, it cannot be argued that the optimal solution when the policy used is an export (or import) subsidy will be necessarily superior to that when the policy used is a tariff. As argued in Section I, both policies are handicapped as they seek to affect *foreign* trade whereas the distortion is *domestic;* there is no reason why one should necessarily be better than the other. Second, nor can one maintain that an export (or import) subsidy will necessarily exist that will be superior to free trade, just as one cannot maintain that a tariff necessarily will be available that is superior to free trade. Third, the optimum solution again is to impose a tax-cum-subsidy on domestic production.

Case III.—Hagen on wage differentials. —A divergence between *DRT* and the domestic price ratio, arising from factor-market imperfections in the form of intersectoral wage differentials, has been discussed in relation to trade policy by Hagen. Before we proceed to Hagen's analysis, certain observations concerning the circumstances in which differential remuneration causes a distortion are in order.

The observed wage differentials between the urban and rural sector may *not* represent a genuine distortion. For instance, they may reflect (1) a utility preference between occupations on the part of the wage-earners, or (2) a rent (on scarce skills), or (3) a return on investment in human capital (by training), or (4) a return on investment in the cost of movement (from the rural to the urban sector). There *would* be a distortion, however, where the differential is attributable to (5) trade-union intervention, or (6) prestige-cum-humanitarian grounds ("I must pay my man a decent wage") that fix wages at varying levels in different sectors. Two other types of explanations may also be discussed: (7) Hagen argues that the differential occurs in manufacture because this is the advancing sector and growing activities inevitably have to pay higher wages to draw labor away from other industries. While this "dynamic" argument appears to provide support for the distortionary character of the differential, there are difficulties with it. For instance, the fact that a differential has to be maintained to draw labor away may very well be due to the cost of movement.[10] (8) A more substantive argument is that the rural sector affords employment to non-adult members of the family whereas, in the urban sectory, the adult alone gets employment (owing to institutional reasons such as factory acts). Hence, to migrate, an adult would need to be compensated for the loss of employment by the non-adult members of his family.[11] If this is the case, there is certainly a market imperfection (assuming that individual preferences rather than collective preferences, expressed in legislation, are relevant) and hence distortion.[12]

[10] Other difficulties also arise when the argument is used in conjunction with a static analysis. These will be discussed later.

[11] This hypothesis was suggested to us by D. Mazumdar.

[12] This "distortion," unlike the others, involves a contraction of the labor force as labor moves from one sector to another. Hence, the following analysis does not apply and a fresh solution, incorporating a changing labor supply, is called for. Note here also that the wage differential variety of distortion is quite distinct from the distortion caused when, although the wage is identical between sectors, it differs from the "shadow" optimal wage. This distinction has been blurred by recent analysts, especially W. A. Lewis, "Economic Development with Unlimited Supplies of Labor," *Manchester School,* XXII (May, 1959), and H. Myint, "Infant Industry Arguments for Assistance to Industries in

In the following analysis, we shall assume that the wage differential represents a genuine distortion while remaining skeptical about the degree to which such distortions obtain in the actual world.[13] We will also adopt Hagen's analytical framework of a two-commodity, two-factor model and a *constant* wage differential. The assumption of constancy of the wage differential raises some difficulties, probably with reasons (3) and (6) but certainly with reason (7), on which Hagen mainly relies. As will be seen presently, Hagen's analysis involves the *contraction* of manufactures after the introduction of trade; if the wage differential is due to the fact that manufactures are expanding and drawing labor away, it should surely reverse itself during the transition from autarky to free trade. The difficulty is that Hagen, in relying upon reason (7) while using traditional trade analysis, is illegitimately superimposing a dynamic argument upon a comparative statics framework. To analyze the distortion arising from reason (8) one needs an explicitly dynamic analysis. Hence, the following analysis applies, strictly speaking, only to distortions produced by reasons (5) and (6).

Hagen concludes that a tariff is superior to free trade when the *importable manufacturing* activity has to pay the higher wage.

> As a result of the wage disparity, manufacturing industry will be undersold by imports when the foreign exchanges are in equilibrium. Protection which permits such industry to exist will increase real income in the economy. However, a subsidy per unit of labour equal to the wage differential will increase real income further, and if combined with free trade will permit attaining an *optimum optimorum*.[14]

Hagen works successively with two models that differ only in the assumption concerning the number of factors of production. Since the first model has only one factor and is only a special case of the second, two-factor model, we shall concentrate here on the latter. It is assumed that all the standard Paretian conditions obtain except for the wage differential. We begin with Hagen's analysis and then comment on it.

In Figure 2*a*, *AQB* is the production possibility curve on the assumption of a wage uniform between the two sectors. *APB* is the production possibility curve, assuming the given wage differential.[15] The wage differential against manufac-

the Setting of Dynamic Trade Theory" (paper presented to a conference on "Trade in a Developing World," International Economic Association, September, 1961). Also see Bhagwati, *op. cit.*

[13] A. Kafka, "A New Argument for Protectionism," *Quarterly Journal of Economics*, LXXVI (February, 1962), 163–66.

[14] *Op. cit.*, p. 498. Hagen himself does not state explicitly that he is confining the analysis to the case where the differential operates against the importable activity. If the differential were to work in the contrary direction, the results would naturally have to be modified radically.

[15] The reader can satisfy himself as to the "shrinking in" of the production possibility curve by manipulating the Edgeworth box diagram. The careful reader of Hagen's paper will note that Hagen draws the "shrunk-in" production possibility curve so that it is convex (in the mathematical sense). This, however, is a property that does not necessarily follow from the assumptions made, and it is possible to produce counter-examples of concavity, although we have not been able to produce a general mathematical proof. (When this paper was read at Stanford, Paul David drew attention to A. Fishlow and P. David's "Optimal Resource Allocation in an Imperfect Market Setting," *Journal of Political Economy*, LXIX [December, 1961], 529–46, for a proof of this proposition. These writers have also anticipated our criticism concerning Hagen's confusion of statics and dynamics.) We shall use the convex curve, however, as it enables us to state our propositions in terms of equalities and without bothering about second-order conditions; the substance of the propositions *that interest us here* is unaffected by this complication. The divergence between the commodity price ratio and the domestic rate of transformation, which also results from the wage differential, needs a rigorous proof, which can be found by the reader in Hagen, *op. cit.*, pp. 507–8.

tures, aside from reducing the production feasibilities, will make the commodity price ratio, at any production point on *APB*, steeper than the rate of transformation along *APB* so that the price ratio understates the profitability of transforming agriculture into manufactures. *PT* being the foreign price ratio, the economy produces at *P* and consumes at *F* under free trade. Under self-sufficiency, however, the relative price of manufactures being higher, the economy would produce and consume at *S* and be better

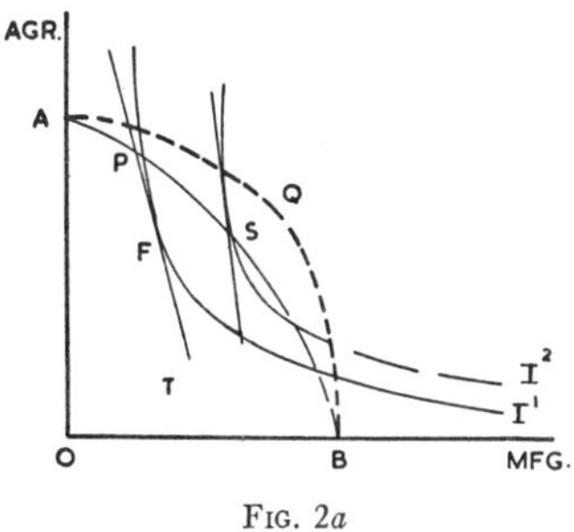

FIG. 2*a*

off. From this, Hagen concludes: "Protection of manufacturing from foreign trade will increase real income."[16]

However, the conclusion must be rectified. First, as illustrated in Figure 2*b*, where the contrary possibility is shown, prohibitive protection is not necessarily superior to free trade. Second, it may further be impossible, as argued in Section I, to find any level of tariff (or trade subsidy) that is superior to free trade. Third, a tax-cum-subsidy on the domestic production of the commodities, which eliminates the divergence between the price ratio and *DRT* (along *APB*) would necessarily yield a better solution than protection. In Figure 2*c*, *F'* represents the consumption and *P'* the production reached by the pursuit of such a tax-cum-subsidy policy.[17] Finally, a policy of tax-cum-subsidy on labor use would achieve equilibrium production at *P''* and consumption at *F''* in Figure 2*c* and produce the "first-best" result, as recognized by Hagen.

[16] Hagen, *op. cit.*, p. 510.

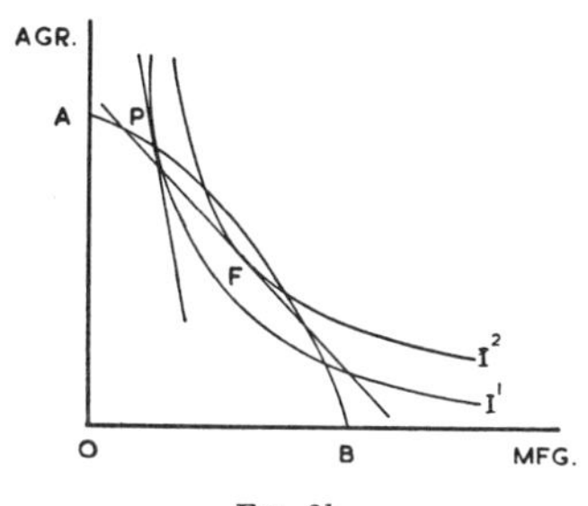

FIG. 2*b*

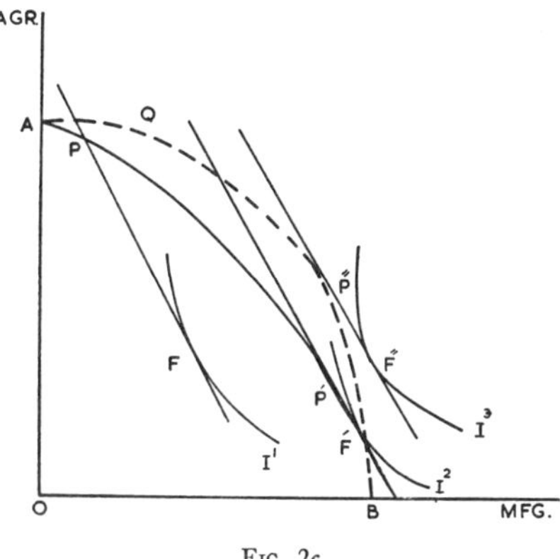

FIG. 2*c*

Note that, in contrast to the case of external economies, the optimum tax-cum-subsidy on domestic production, while superior to protection or trade subsidy,

[17] In relation to this point, it is also worth noting that the standard procedure adopted by several tariff commissions, of choosing a tariff rate that just offsets the differential between the average domestic cost at some *arbitrary*, given production of the existing units and the landed (c.i.f.) cost, is not necessarily correct. There is no reason why the tariff rate which just offsets this differential is necessarily the tariff rate which is optimum from the viewpoint of economic policy.

does not yield the ***optimum optimorum*** in the wage-differential case. The reason is straightforward. The wage differential causes *not merely* a domestic distortion but *also* a restriction of the production possibility curve. A tax-cum-subsidy on domestic production measure will, therefore, merely eliminate the domestic distortion but not restore the economy to the Paretian production possibility curve (AQB). It will thus achieve the equality of FRT and DRS with DRT along *the restricted production possibility curve* (APB) and hence constitute the optimal solution when the wage differential cannot be directly eliminated. Where, however, a direct attack on the wage differential is permitted, the fully optimal, "first-best" solution can be achieved by a policy of tax-cum-subsidy on factor use.

III. CONCLUSION

We have argued here that an optimum subsidy (or a tax-cum-subsidy equivalent) is necessarily superior to any tariff when the distortion is domestic. It may be questioned, however, whether this advantage would obtain in practice. This question, of course, cannot be settled purely at the economic level. A fully satisfactory treatment of this issue would necessarily involve disciplines ranging from politics to psychology. However, by way of conclusion, we think it would be useful to consider a few arguments that are relevant to the final, realistic choice of policy.

1. The contention that the payment of subsidies would involve the collection of taxes which in practice cannot be levied in a non-distortionary fashion is fallacious. A tax-cum-subsidy scheme could always be devised that would *both* eliminate the estimated divergence and collect taxes sufficient to pay the subsidies.

2. The estimation problem is also easier with subsidies than with tariffs. The former involves estimating merely the divergence between the commodity price ratio and DRT (at the relevant production point). The latter must extend the exercises necessarily to the estimation of the relevant DRS (which involves locating both the right level of income *and* the relevant consumption point).

3. The political argument has usually been claimed by free traders to favor the payment of subsidies under external economy arguments like infant industries. It is thought that it would be difficult to pay a subsidy longer than strictly necessary whereas a tariff may be more difficult to abolish. It must be pointed out, however, that this argument also pulls the other way because, precisely for the reasons which make a subsidy difficult to continue, a subsidy is difficult to choose in preference to a tariff.

Domestic Distortions, Tariffs, and the Theory of Optimum Subsidy: Some Further Results

Jagdish Bhagwati

Massachusetts Institute of Technology

V. K. Ramaswami

Indian Ministry of Finance

T. N. Srinivasan

Indian Statistical Institute

Bhagwati and Ramaswami (1963) showed that if there is a distortion, the Paretian first-best policy is to intervene with a tax (subsidy) at the point at which the distortion occurs. Hence a domestic tax-cum-subsidy with respect to production would be first-best optimal when there was a *domestic* distortion (defined as the divergence between domestic prices and the marginal rate of transformation in domestic production) just as a tariff policy would be first-best optimal under monopoly power in trade (which involves a *foreign* distortion). An important corollary, for the case of a distortionary wage differential, is that while a tax-cum-subsidy policy with respect to factor use would be first-best optimal, the second-best optimal policy would be a *domestic* production tax-cum-subsidy rather than a tariff policy.

While these central results are valid, Kemp and Negishi (1969) have correctly argued that two subsidiary propositions of Bhagwati and Ramaswami (1963) are false. These are (1) that no tariff (export subsidy) may exist which is superior to free trade in the presence of a domestic distortion, and (2) that no production tax-cum-subsidy may yield greater welfare than nonintervention when the nation has monopoly power.

We can demonstrate, however, that the Kemp-Negishi results are, in fact, special cases of the first of the following two theorems in the theory of second-best, which we shall prove:

Theorem 1.—If under laissez faire two of the variables *DRS*, *DRT*, and *FRT* are equal while the third has a different value, and the policy measure that will secure equal values of the three variables cannot be applied, some

H. G. Johnson has provided useful comments on an earlier draft of this note.

policy measure exists that will raise welfare above the laissez faire level, though it will destroy the equality of the first two variables.[1]

Theorem 2.—If under laissez faire all three variables *DRS*, *DRT*, and *FRT* have different values, and both of the policy measures that will secure equal values of the three variables cannot be applied, no feasible form of intervention may exist that will raise welfare.

We use the following notation:

- C_i, X_i denote the consumption and domestic output, respectively of commodity i, $i = 1, 2$.
- p_c denotes the ratio of the price of the first to that of the second commodity confronting consumers (*DRS*).
- p_t denotes $DRT = -dX_2/dX_1$.
- p_f denotes the ratio of the world price of the first commodity to that of the second commodity, that is, the *average* terms of trade. The marginal terms of trade $FRT = p_f$ only in the special case in which national monopoly power does not exist.

The welfare function $U(C_1, C_2)$ and the production functions are assumed to be differentiable as required. The U_i denotes the marginal utility of commodity i $(i = 1, 2)$. It is assumed throughout the analysis that under laissez faire there is nonspecialization in consumption and production, and that some trade takes place.

Our procedure is as follows. We derive the expression for the change in welfare when there is a slight movement away from an initial equilibrium in which there is no intervention. If the levy of some tax (subsidy) at a *small* rate will secure a positive value for this expression, we can conclude that welfare can be raised above the laissez faire level by applying this tax (subsidy). Note that in such a case some *finite* (and not merely infinitesimal) tax (subsidy) rate will exist which yields greater welfare than laissez faire. If the derivative of welfare with respect to the rate of some tax (subsidy) is nonzero at the laissez faire point, then by continuity it is nonzero for some finite interval of values of the tax (subsidy) rate around the laissez faire point. If, on the other hand, the levy of some tax (subsidy) at a small rate does not change welfare, then there may not exist any rate of this tax (subsidy) which secures more welfare than under nonintervention.[2]

[1] *DRS*, *DRT*, and *FRT* denote, respectively, the marginal domestic rate of substitution in consumption, the marginal domestic rate of transformation in production, and the marginal rate of transformation through trade.

[2] If the function relating the level of welfare and the rate of a specified tax (subsidy) is concave and has a local maximum at the laissez faire point, then this local maximum is a global maximum, and a finite tax (subsidy) *must* reduce welfare below the laissez faire level. If this function is not concave, however, the local maximum need not be a global maximum and therefore some finite tax (subsidy) *may* exist which raises welfare above the laissez faire level.

The change in welfare due to a small deviation from an initial laissez faire equilibrium is

$$dU = U_1 dC_1 + U_2 dC_2 = U_2\left(\frac{U_1}{U_2} dC_1 + dC_2\right).$$

The marginal condition for utility maximization is that $U_1/U_2 = p_c$. So,

$$\begin{aligned} dU &= U_2(p_c dC_1 + dC_2) = U_2[p_f dC_1 + dC_2 + (p_c - p_f)dC_1] \\ &= U_2[d(p_f C_1 + C_2) - C_1 dp_f + (p_c - p_f)dC_1]. \end{aligned}$$

Assuming balanced trade, $p_f C_1 + C_2 = p_f X_1 + X_2$. So,

$$\begin{aligned} dU &= U_2[d(p_f X_1 + X_2) - C_1 dp_f + (p_c - p_f)dC_1] \\ &= U_2[p_f dX_1 + dX_2 + (X_1 - C_1)dp_f + (p_c - p_f)dC_1] \\ &= U_2\left[dX_1\left(p_f + \frac{dX_2}{dX_1}\right) + (X_1 - C_1)dp_f + (p_c - p_f)dC_1\right] \\ &= U_2[dX_1(p_f - p_t) + (X_1 - C_1)dp_f + (p_c - p_f)dC_1]. \end{aligned} \tag{1}$$

Theorem 1

There are three ways in which, under laissez faire, two of the variables *DRS*, *DRT*, and *FRT* have equal values, while the third has a different value: $DRS = FRT \neq DRT$, $DRS = DRT \neq FRT$, and $DRS \neq DRT = FRT$. We consider these three cases in turn.

Case 1

Assume that national monopoly power does not exist. We then discuss two alternative cases in turn: (1) production externality,[3] and (2) wage differential in one activity.[4] In either case, $DRS = FRT \neq DRT$, and we have $p_c = p_f$, $dp_f = 0$ and $p_f \neq p_t$. so equation (1) reduces to:

$$dU = U_2[dX_1(p_f - p_t)]. \tag{2}$$

It is clear that any policy measure that slightly increases (reduces) the output of the first commodity will raise welfare, if p_f is greater (less) than p_t.

So if, in the externality case, it is not feasible to secure first-best through the levy of a production tax-cum-subsidy, greater welfare than under

[3] A production externality that would produce a domestic distortion, in the sense of a divergence between the domestic prices and *DRT*, is where the production functions are the following: $X = X(Lx, Kx)$; $Y = Y(Ly, Ky, X)$, where the output of commodity y is a function of not merely the inputs of labor (Ly) and capital (Ky) but also the output level of commodity x, but the market does not remunerate the x-producers for this productivity.

[4] We will be assuming that the wage differential is distortionary, as in Bhagwati and Ramaswami (1963).

laissez faire can be obtained if (1) a tariff (trade subsidy) or (2) a factor tax-cum-subsidy is imposed. Note further than a tariff is *not* necessarily superior to a factor tax-cum-subsidy policy. Which of these measures is preferable in a given situation will depend on the form of the welfare and production functions. Thus, in any specific situation, a factor tax-cum-subsidy policy may be the second-best optimal policy, and the tariff (trade subsidy) the *third-best* optimal policy.[5]

In the case of a distortionary wage differential, the first-best policy is a factor tax-cum-subsidy, the second-best policy is a production tax-cum-subsidy, and the third-best policy is the tariff.[6]

Case 2

Now assume that there is no domestic distortion but national monopoly power exists, so that $DRS = DRT \neq FRT$ under laissez faire. Then $p_c = p_t = p_f$ and $dp_f \neq 0$; so equation (1) reduces to

$$dU = U_2(X_1 - C_1)dp_f. \tag{3}$$

Thus production, consumption, and factor-use tax-cum-subsidies will exist that will raise welfare above the laissez faire level by changing the marginal rate of transformation through trade. It would appear, however, that we cannot determine a priori what the second-best, optimal policy will be; and the ranking of the three policies—production, consumption, and factor-use tax-cum-subsidies—which are available when the first-best tariff policy is ruled out, will depend on the specific situation being considered.

Case 3

Suppose now that there is no national monopoly power, or distortion, or externality in production but that the sellers of one commodity charge consumers a uniform premium over the cost of both domestic and imported supplies. Then, under laissez faire, $DRS \neq DRT = FRT$. We have $dp_f = 0$, $p_f = p_t$, $p_c \neq p_f$; so equation (1) reduces to

$$dU = U_2[(p_c - p_f)dC_1]. \tag{4}$$

Thus, clearly the levy of a consumption tax-cum-subsidy will secure Paretian first-best. Furthermore, levy of tariff is necessarily superior to laissez faire. Moreover, the imposition of production or factor-use taxes

[5] Thus Kemp and Negishi (1969), who do not consider the entire range of policies that may be available when the first-best policy is ruled out, imply incorrectly that the "second-best, optimal" policy in a situation with domestic distortions will be a tariff (trade subsidy) policy.

[6] Note that a finite consumption tax-cum-subsidy policy can only hurt the economy by adding a consumption loss to the loss already being suffered by the economy, thanks to the distortion.

(subsidies) *may* also be superior to laissez faire (unless inferior goods in social consumption were ruled out).[7]

This completes our proof and discussion of theorem 1. An intuitive explanation is perhaps in order. A *small* deviation as the result of the levy of a tax (subsidy) from an initial situation of *equality* of the values of two of the variables *DRS*, *DRT*, and *FRT* does not entail welfare loss. So if the tax (subsidy) brings the value of the third variable closer to those of the two variables which were initially equal, the welfare gain on this account will constitute a net improvement in welfare. More than one form of tax (subsidy) may secure this result; and the levy of any one of these will be superior to laissez faire.

But it should be noted that when only the policy that secures first-best can make *DRS*, *DRT*, and *FRT* equal and adoption of this policy is ruled out, as when national monopoly power exists but a tariff cannot be levied, alternative policies cannot be ranked except with reference to the facts of a given situation. The corollary of this proposition is that when a second-best policy alone can secure equality of *DRS*, *DRT*, and *FRT*, as when a distortionary wage differential cannot be directly attacked, the third-best policy cannot be determined a priori.

Theorem 2

Assume now that national monopoly power exists, and that there is a production externality or that factor taxes (subsidies) cannot be used to eliminate a distortionary wage differential. Then $DRT \neq DRS \neq FRT$. We rule out the case in which, by chance, $DRT = FRT$. So $p_f \neq p_t$, $dp_f \neq 0$ and $p_c = p_f$; and equation (1) reduces to

$$dU = U_2[dX_1(p_f - p_t) + (X_1 - C_1)dp_f]. \tag{5}$$

The simultaneous levy of both a tariff and a production tax (subsidy) would secure first-best in the case of a production externality and second-best in the case of a distortionary wage differential. But if only a tariff or a production tax (subsidy) is applied, there may be exactly offsetting changes in $dX_1(p_f - p_t)$ and $(X_1 - C_1)dp_f$, and welfare may not increase. So if both

[7] Note that in the present case, dealing with a domestic consumption distortion, a production or factor-use tax-cum-subsidy policy may improve welfare, whereas case 1, dealing with a domestic production, did not admit to a consumption tax-cum-subsidy raising welfare above the laissez faire level. The reason for this asymmetry is as follows. In the latter case, a consumption tax-cum-subsidy, whether small or large, cannot shift production and hence cannot improve welfare. In the former case, however, a production or factor-use tax-cum-subsidy can affect consumption through its income effect. The level of such a tax-cum-subsidy at an infinitesimal rate cannot, of course, change welfare because the income effect is zero to a first order of approximation; but when the rate is large, welfare may improve if the function relating welfare and the rate of tax (subsidy) is not concave (a possibility introduced by the presence of goods inferior in social consumption).

the policy measures needed to secure equality of *DRS*, *DRT*, and *FRT* cannot be applied, no feasible intervention may exist that will raise welfare above the laissez faire level.

References

Bhagwati, Jagdish, and Ramaswami, V. K. "Domestic Distortions, Tariffs, and the Theory of Optimum Subsidy," *J.P.E.* 71, no. 1 (February 1963): 44–50.

Kemp, M. C., and Negishi, T. "Domestic Distortions, Tariffs, and the Theory of Optimum Subsidy." *J.P.E.* 77, no. 6 (November/December 1969): 1011–13.

RANKING OF TARIFFS UNDER MONOPOLY POWER IN TRADE

JAGDISH BHAGWATI AND MURRAY C. KEMP

Kemp has argued that, for a country with no monopoly power in trade, a lower tariff is preferable to a higher tariff, in the sense that any distribution of individual utilities attainable with a higher tariff is attainable with a lower tariff, usually with something to spare.[1] Subsequently, Vanek[2] and Bhagwati[3] showed that if exportables are inferior (a) competitive equilibrium may not be unique, (b) one of the low-tariff equilibria may be inferior to one of the high-tariff equilibria and, therefore, (c) a reduction in the tariff might leave a country worse off. As a result,[4] Kemp's proposition has now been elaborated to read: "the (best) utility possibility curve under a lower tariff will indeed lie outside that under a higher tariff, regardless of the inferiority of the exportable good in social consumption; but a competitive price system could well result in equilibria involving a higher welfare level under a higher tariff, unless inferiority of the exportable good in social consumption were ruled out."[5]

Can anything be said about the ranking of tariffs when a country has monopoly power in trade? Or must one be content to know that an optimal tariff exists? This note shows that, under very modest restrictions on preferences and in spite of the necessity of ranking suboptimal policies, it is possible to establish the following propositions. Let the optimum tariff be t_w, the zero tariff t_o, and the (just) prohibitive tariff t_p.

Proposition (1): Successive increases in the tariff from the level t_o will raise welfare until the level t_w is reached; successive increases in the tariff thereafter will reduce welfare until the level t_p is reached; higher tariffs merely involve continuing autarky and hence are partially ordered.

Proposition (2): For a country with monopoly power in trade,

1. M. C. Kemp, "The Gains from International Trade," *Economic Journal*, LXXII (Dec. 1962).
2. J. Vanek, *General Equilibrium of International Discrimination: The Case of Customs Unions* (Cambridge, Mass.: Harvard University Press, 1965).
3. J. Bhagwati, "The Gains from Trade Once Again," *Oxford Economic Papers*, XX (July 1968).
4. Bhagwati, *op. cit.*, Vanek, *op. cit.*, and M. C. Kemp, "Some Issues in the Analysis of Trade Gains," *Oxford Economic Papers*, XX (July 1968).
5. Bhagwati, *op. cit.*

therefore, the choice of a social welfare function will *merely* determine the magnitudes of t_w and t_p; hence one could regard tariffs as continuously laid in a chain from zero to infinity, with the social welfare function (for a specific country) serving, as it were, as a spike which lifts this chain up to the level of the optimal tariff and drops it to the floor at the level of the (appropriate) prohibitive tariff — as illustrated by Figure I for five hypothetical welfare functions.

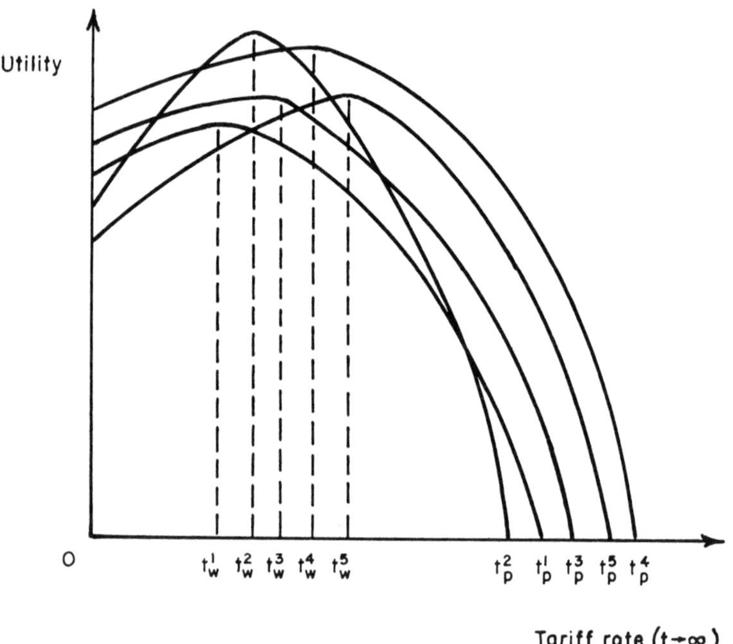

FIGURE I

Tariff-ranking for a given country, with monopoly power in trade, under five alternative social welfare functions. Note that no cardinal significance is to be attached to the utility axis. The figure merely ranks, in terms of utility, tariffs ranging from zero to infinity for each social welfare function. It also shows the optimum tariffs, for each of the five functions, at t^5_w, t^4_w, t^3_w, t^2_w, t^1_w and the corresponding prohibitive tariff levels at t^5_p, t^4_p, t^3_p, t^2_p, and t^1_p. The diagram could be readily extended to the second and third quadrants, to show the effects and ranking of export subsidies.

These propositions are not *generally* valid. To establish the conditions under which they *are* valid, consider Figure II, which shows the trade-indifference curves U^I_w, U^I_o and U^I_p reached by Country I successively under an optimum tariff, a zero tariff, and a prohibitive tariff. It is clear that Proposition (1), and hence Proposition

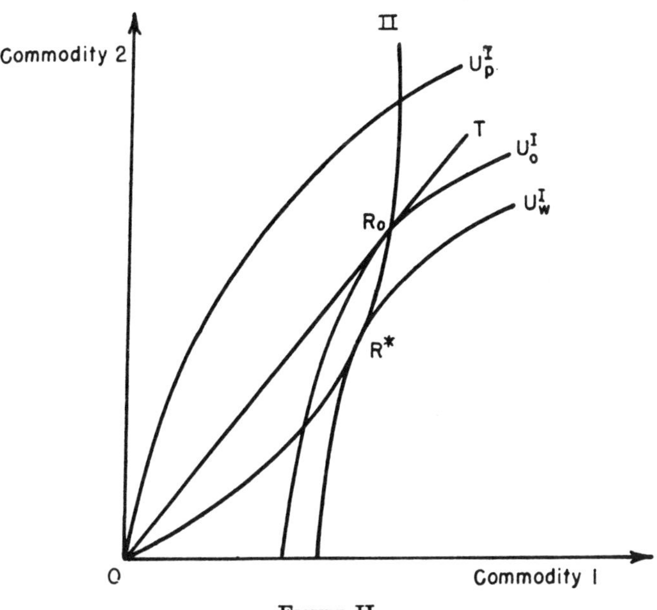

FIGURE II

This figure shows the optimum-tariff welfare level $U^I{}_w$, the zero-tariff welfare level $U^I{}_o$, and the self-sufficiency welfare level $U^I{}_p$ for Country I, the free-trade terms of trade OT and Country II's offer curve OII.

(2), will hold *if and only if* an increase in Country I's tariff will necessarily reduce the demand for imports. For, in such a case, an increase in the tariff, starting from a zero tariff at R_o, will take the economy through higher and higher trade indifference curves until it reaches R^* and then through successively lower trade-indifference curves to 0 and $U^I{}_p$.

Therefore, exceptions to Proposition (1), and hence Proposition (2), must constitute exceptions to the rule that an increase in the tariff will reduce the demand for imports. It can then be shown that this rule admits of exceptions only when the exportable commodity is inferior.[6]

Hold the terms of trade constant at unity. Suppose that Commodity 1 is imported and that Commodity 2 is the *numéraire*. The internal price ratio is, therefore, $(1+t)$ where t is the rate of duty. The demand for imports is $E_1(1+t, I_2)$ where

$$I_2 = (1+t)X_1 + X_2 + tE_1$$

6. Note, therefore, that the argument sometimes made in balance-of-payments theory, that tariffs must be preferred to devaluation *until* the optimum tariff is reached, is valid only insofar as inferiority of the exportable good is ruled out.

is income in terms of the *numéraire* commodity, X_i is the output of good i and tE_1 is the tariff revenue. We have

$$\frac{dE_1}{dt}=\frac{\partial E_1}{\partial t}+\frac{\partial E_1}{\partial I_2}\frac{dI_2}{dt}$$

$$\frac{dI_2}{dt}=X_1+E_1+t\frac{dE_1}{dt}\,.$$

Hence

$$\frac{dE_1}{dt}=\frac{\partial E_1}{\partial t}+\frac{m_1}{1+t}\left(X_1+E_1+t\frac{dE_1}{dt}\right)$$

$$=\frac{\dfrac{\partial E_1}{\partial t}+\dfrac{m_1}{1+t}D_1}{1-\dfrac{t}{1+t}m_1}$$

where m_1 is the marginal propensity to consume the first or imported commodity and D_1 is consumption of the first commodity. Introducing the Slutzky decomposition,

$$\frac{\partial E_1}{\partial t}=\left.\frac{\partial E_1}{\partial t}\right|-\frac{m_1}{1+t}D_1,\text{ where }\left.\frac{\partial E_1}{\partial t}\right|$$

is the pure substitution slope, we obtain, finally,

$$\frac{dE_1}{dt}=\frac{\left.\dfrac{\partial E_1}{\partial t}\right|}{1-\dfrac{t}{1+t}m_1}$$

OI is the low-tariff offer curve of Country I.
OI′ is the high-tariff offer curve of Country I.
OII is the offer curve of Country II.

which is negative unless the export is very inferior.

Figure III illustrates the possibility, ruled out by our restrictions on consumption inferiority, that an increase in the rate of duty may give rise both to an increase in import demand and to a deterioration in the terms of trade of the tariff-imposing country. With the lower tariff, production takes place at P, consumption at C, and the terms of trade are indicated by the slope of PC. With the higher rate of duty, production takes place at P', consumption at C'; and the (worsened) terms of trade are indicated by the slope of $P'C'$.

We have already stated that the possibility illustrated by Figure III can be ruled out if very modest restrictions are imposed on the

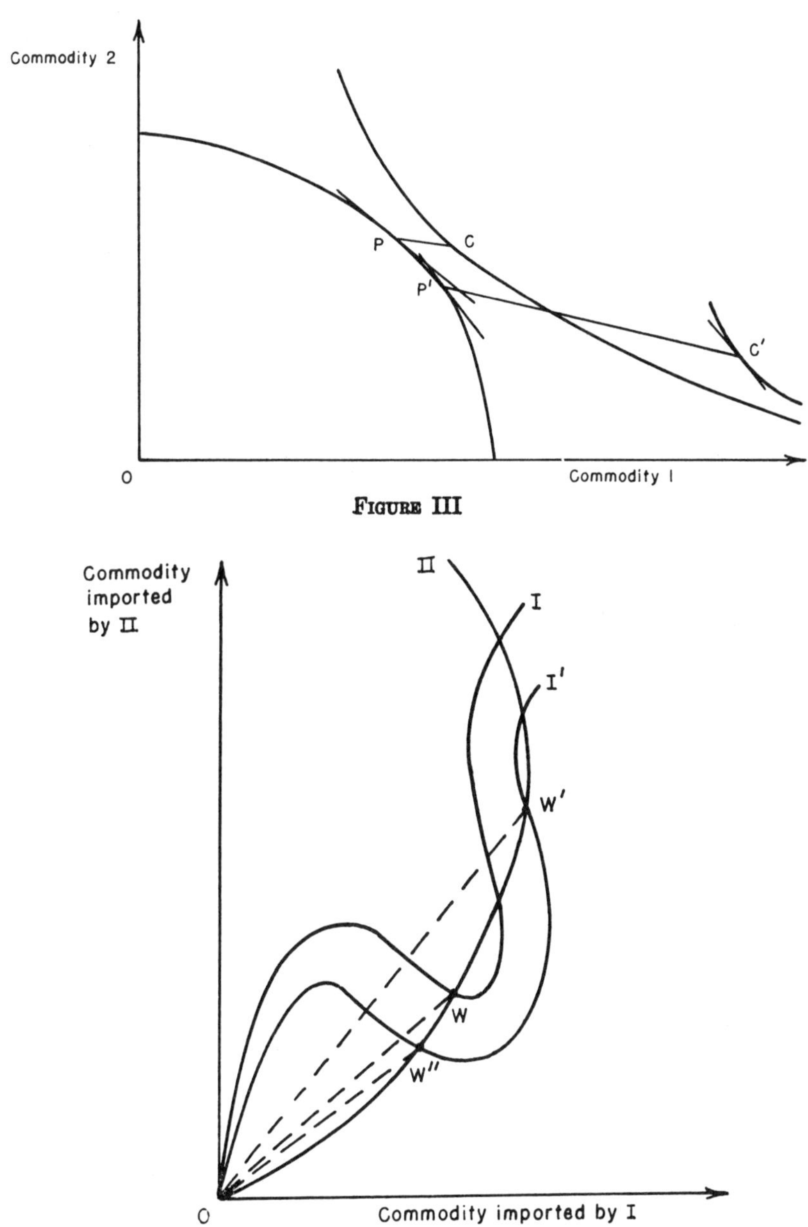

FIGURE III

FIGURE IV

community's preferences. We now offer two observations designed to emphasize just how modest those restrictions are.[7] First, we

7. The first observation emerged from a long correspondence with Harry G. Johnson.

recall that ". . . the reciprocal demand curve traced out by a higher tariff rate will always lie inside the curve traced out by a lower tariff rate. . . ."[8] It follows that the possibility illustrated by Figure III requires offer curves which yield multiple equilibria at given terms of trade, as in Figure IV. (Points W and W' of Figure IV correspond respectively to points C and C' of Figure III). Second, it follows from our mathematical analysis that dE_1/dt is positive if and only if $1-[tm_1/(1+t)]$ is negative, that is, if and only if

$$1+t(1-m_1)<0.$$

As Kemp has shown, however, this is precisely the condition for market instability when the terms of trade are given.[9]

Finally, we note that, even when an increase in the rate of duty is associated with a reduction in the demand for imports and a deterioration of the terms of trade, nevertheless there exists an alternative high-tariff equilibrium characterized by reduced import demand and improved terms of trade (shown by point W'' in Figure IV). It follows that by choosing carefully from alternative equilibria one can ensure that, as the rate of duty is raised, welfare rises steadily, reaches a maximum, then declines until the duty is prohibitive.

MASSACHUSETTS INSTITUTE OF TECHNOLOGY

UNIVERSITY OF NEW SOUTH WALES

8. H.G. Johnson, *International Trade and Economic Growth* (London: Allen and Unwin, 1958), p. 34, fn. 7.
9. Kemp, "Some Issues in the Analysis of Trade Gains," *op. cit.*

Erratum

Page 333, lines 11 and 13: "$\partial E_1/\partial t|$" should read "$\partial E_1/\partial t|U$" in all three occurrences.

IV
DIRECTLY UNPRODUCTIVE PROFIT-SEEKING (DUP) ACTIVITIES: ILLEGAL TRADE AND LOBBYING

Directly Unproductive, Profit-seeking (DUP) Activities

Jagdish N. Bhagwati

Columbia University

This paper proposes directly unproductive, profit-seeking (DUP) activities as a general concept that embraces a wide range of recently analyzed economic activities, including the subset of rent-seeking activities considered by Krueger. It then proceeds to provide a synthesis and generalization of the welfare-theoretic analysis of such activities by developing a fourfold categorization of cases depending on the levels of distortions before and after the DUP activity. Thus a unification and overview of the subject are achieved.

In recent years, economists have increasingly turned to a theoretical analysis of phenomena such as lobbying for protection, competing for a share of industrial or import licenses, inducing legislatures to enact monopolistic barriers to domestic entry, utilizing resources to evade "price" or "command" governmental regulations, etc.

In the area of international trade–theoretic analysis in particular, it would hardly be an exaggeration to say that this has been among the few leading topics of research focus recently. Thus, the theoretical analysis of *tariff evasion,* starting with Bhagwati and Hansen (1973),

Thanks are due to the National Science Foundation for grant no. 5-24718 and to the Guggenheim Foundation for partial financial support of the research underlying this paper. Correspondence with Richard Brecher, Max Corden, and Gordon Tullock has been valuable, and reactions and suggestions from participants at seminars at MIT, Yale, and Princeton, especially Carlos Diaz-Alejandro, T. N. Srinivasan, Susan Rose-Ackerman, Gene Grossman, Richard Brecher, Robert Feenstra, Jonathan Eaton, Avinash Dixit, and two anonymous referees of this *Journal* were extremely useful in revising the paper.

[*Journal of Political Economy*, 1982, vol. 90, no. 5]

has witnessed further contributions by Johnson (1972), Bhagwati and Srinivasan (1973), Sheikh (1974), Kemp (1976), Falvey (1978), Ray (1978), and Pitt (1981). The theoretical analysis of activity whereby claimants compete for premium-fetching import licenses, and what may therefore be christened *premium seeking,* was begun in a seminal paper by Krueger (1974) and extended by Bhagwati and Srinivasan (1980). The theoretical analysis of *revenue seeking,* where economic agents try to get a slice of the tariff revenue resulting from the adoption of a protectionist tariff, has been initiated by Bhagwati and Srinivasan (1980). The theoretical analysis of *tariff seeking,* on the other hand, where lobbies seek protectionist trade tariffs, has been pioneered by Brock and Magee (1978) and has been recently developed by Bhagwati (1980), Feenstra and Bhagwati (1982), and Findlay and Wellisz (1982). At the same time, in non-trade-theoretic literature as well, there has been growing concern with lobbying and related phenomena, as in the well-known papers of many distinguished writers, such as Tullock (1967, 1980) and Posner (1975).

In this paper, I begin in Section I by briefly discussing the common, unifying essence of the phenomena so analyzed and then arguing why they are best described as directly unproductive, profit-seeking (DUP) activities. Next, I proceed in Section II to differentiate analytically among different types of such activities, with a view to classifying them into categories which are analytically meaningful from the viewpoint of their welfare impact. Existing analyses of specific problems, such as tariff seeking and revenue seeking, are then readily identified in Section III as belonging to one such category or another, and the welfare consequences demonstrated in these analyses are then shown to be only specific illustrations of a wider class of DUP activities with identical welfare consequences.

I. Directly Unproductive, Profit-seeking (DUP) Activities: The Concept

The essential characteristic of the phenomena whose analysis has recently been undertaken, and many of which have been referenced above, is that they represent ways of making a profit (i.e., income) by undertaking activities which are directly unproductive; that is, they yield pecuniary returns but do not produce goods or services that enter a utility function directly or indirectly via increased production or availability to the economy of goods that enter a utility function. Insofar as such activities use real resources, they result in a contraction of the availability set open to the economy. Thus, for example, tariff-seeking lobbying, tariff evasion, and premium seeking for given import licenses are all privately profitable activities. However, their direct output is simply zero in terms of the flow of goods and services entering a conventional utility function: for example, tariff seeking yields pecuniary income by changing the tariff and hence factor rewards; evasion of a tariff yields pecuniary income by exploiting the differential price between legal (tariff-bearing) imports and illegal (tariff-evading) imports; and premium seeking yields pecuniary income from the premia on import licenses. Thus, these are aptly christened DUP activities. As an acronym, this can be pronounced "dupe" activities, coming close to the spirit in which economists must view these activities![1]

This distinction between directly unproductive and productive activities is somewhat reminiscent of the Physiocrats and the early Marxists but, in contrast, has, in strictly economic terms, a perfect claim to legitimacy. For example, lobbying to install a distortionary tariff is undoubtedly directly unproductive from an economic viewpoint, though it may possess a political legitimacy and value as constituting an element of a vigorous, pluralistic democracy!

Krueger's (1974) analysis of what she christened "rent-seeking" activities relates to a subset of the broad class of what are defined here as DUP activities. She is concerned with the lobbying activities which are triggered by different licensing practices of governments. Thus, she lists large numbers of licensing practices leading to lobbying to profit from the securing of such licenses. Also, her formal theoretical analysis is concerned with a welfare comparison between import licenses/quotas with attendant premium-seeking lobbying activity to earn the premia on these licenses vis-à-vis equivalent tariffs which were explicitly assumed not to attract any seeking activity. Thus, her focus is exclusively on licensing/quantity restrictions and the rents thereon,[2] and her rent-seeking activities exclude from their scope other DUP activities, for example, *price*-distortion-triggered DUP activities, or distortion-*triggering* DUP activities.[3]

[1] The other acronymic alternative, christening them ZOP (zero-output, profit-seeking) activities, is slightly less appealing on that account.

[2] Historians of concepts and phrase making may note that, parallel to Krueger's inspired phrase "rent seeking" to describe license-seeking activities, there is also the phrase "*rentier* society," used, e.g., in Bhagwati (1973) to describe much the same kind of phenomenon. In addition, there is also the Leninist (Lenin 1939) use of the phrase "*rentnerstaat*," by which was meant a "rentier state" or "usurer state" (1939, pp. 100–101), i.e., a rent-*receiving* society. Marxists, who consider Schumpeterian capitalism to be characterized by Joan Robinson's "animal spirits," also consider the *rentnerstaat* to be the antithesis of the creative impulses underlying robust capitalism.

[3] Krueger (1974, pp. 301–2) did mention minimum wage legislation, regulation of taxi fares, and capital gains tax treatment in her concluding remarks as also examples of rent seeking. However, her arguments concerning these are ambiguous, to say the least. Thus, consider the following: "Capital gains tax treatment results in overbuilding of apartments and uneconomic oil exploration" (p. 302). But this seems to be simply

II. DUP Activities: A Taxonomy

With the general concept of DUP activities spelled out, the analysis can now be addressed directly to the issue of the welfare consequences of DUP activities.

From the viewpoint of the analysis of the welfare consequences of DUP activities, evidently the most fruitful theory-informed taxonomy must build on the distinction between distorted (or suboptimal) and nondistorted (or optimal) situations. Thus, a DUP activity which uses up resources in the context of a distortion may be paradoxically welfare improving, whereas a similar DUP activity which destroys a distortion and achieves a first-best, optimal outcome may be paradoxically welfare worsening.

Noting that when distortions exist almost anything can happen, I hasten to add that the theory and the resulting taxonomy which is built into table 1, and which will be presently explained, presuppose that the world is indeed distortion free except for the distortions with which the DUP activity in question is related in an essential way. Thus, if one considers premium seeking in Krueger's (1974) analysis, the premium sought by the lobbyists is on distortionary quotas already in place in the model. In her model, therefore, there is an unchanging distortion in place when the directly unproductive premium seeking is introduced, but there are no other distortions.

Next, I should clarify that the DUP activities which are considered in the analysis that follows are wholly related to governmental policies: For example, they involve changing these policies or evading them. However, they can in principle be government free or exclusively private. Thus, effort and resources may be (legally) expended in getting a share of the "going" transfer by an economic agent, what may be described as "altruism seeking." Or they may be expended on (illegal) theft, as Tullock (1967) has considered. What I argue in this paper can be simply extended to private activities, therefore, even though virtually all examples chosen below concern governmental policy–related DUP activities exclusively.

Furthermore, I make no distinction between activities that utilize real resources directly and those that do not. For, while pure transfers/bribes are often supposed to be resource free, they are not.

---

stating the traditional resource-(mis)allocational effects of a tax. At the same time, another concluding paragraph does reiterate the view that her concept and theory of rent seeking are intended to be wholly license or restriction created: "Finally, all market economies have some rent-generating restrictions" (p. 302). The precise manner in which Krueger's generic class of quota intervention–triggered "rent-seeking" activities is a subset of the far more general class of DUP activities is set out fully in Bhagwati and Srinivasan (1981). Also, see the extended discussion in Bhagwati (1982).

TABLE 1

EXAMPLES AND CONSEQUENCES OF DUP ACTIVITIES

	TYPES OF DIRECTLY UNPRODUCTIVE ACTIVITY			
	1. Initially Distorted and Finally Distorted Situations		2. Initially Distorted but Finally Distortion-free Situations	
	Legal (1)	Illegal (2)	Legal (3)	Illegal (4)
1. Examples of such activity	1. Premium seeking: Krueger (1974); Bhagwati and Srinivasan (1980) 2. Revenue seeking: Bhagwati and Srinivasan (1980)	Tariff evasion or smuggling: Johnson (1972); Bhagwati and Hansen (1973); Bhagwati and Srinivasan (1973); Sheikh (1974); Kemp (1976); Ray (1978); Pitt (1981)	Tariff-destroying lobbying: Findlay and Wellisz (1982)	Tariff-destroying lobbying with aid of bribes to politicians
2. Consequences of such activity	Second-best analysis applies; therefore, paradox of beneficial outcome possible (except for pure quantity distortions: Bhagwati and Srinivasan [1981] and Anam [1982])		Second-best analysis applies; therefore, paradox of beneficial outcome possible (except for pure quantity distortions: Bhagwati and Srinivasan [1981] and Anam [1982])	
	3. Initially Distortion-free but Finally Distorted Situations		4. Initially Distortion-free and Finally Distortion-free Situations	
	Legal (5)	Illegal (6)	Legal (7)	Illegal (8)
1. Examples of such activity	1. Monopoly seeking: Posner (1975) 2. Tariff seeking: Brock and Magee (1978); Bhagwati (1980); Feenstra and Bhagwati (1982); Findlay and Wellisz (1982)	Tariff evasion from an optimal tariff situation	Zero-tariff-outcome lobbying: Tullock (1967); Findlay and Wellisz (1982)	Theft: Tullock (1967)
2. Consequences of such activity	Total outcome necessarily immiserizing. However, subsidiary paradox obtains: distortion imposed without DUP activity may produce lower welfare than when imposed with it.		Total outcome necessarily immiserizing. No paradoxes obtain.	

The direct demand on real resources that a successfully transacted bribe makes may be small, but it is not likely to be negligible.[4]

Finally, I distinguish between legal and illegal activities for two reasons. First, the latter introduce the added element that they constitute an independent element of the social loss insofar as illegality must be considered to be socially disapproved. Besides, it is interesting to note that, except on this dimension, the legal and illegal DUP activities can be shown to belong to analytically equivalent categories of our taxonomy, so that distinguishing between them is only with a view to underlining their analytical similarity in the present context.

With these clarifying remarks, let me then turn to the taxonomy underlying table 1. The taxonomy there, with an eye on welfare analysis, is critically built on the fact that all such DUP activities will involve either a distorted or a distortion-free situation, before and after the undertaking of such activity. Thus, four critical classes of DUP activities are distinguished as follows:

> Category 1. Here, the initial and final situations are both distorted.
>
> Category 2. Here, the initial situation is distorted, but the final situation (thanks to the DUP activity) is distortion free.
>
> Category 3. Here, the initial situation is distortion free, but the final situation is distorted.
>
> Category 4. Here, the initial situation is distortion free again, and so is the final situation (despite the DUP activity).

The fundamental distinction, however, remains that between categories 1 and 2 (which relate to initially distorted situations), on the one hand, and categories 3 and 4 (which relate to initially distortion-free situations).

I proceed then to demonstrate that, for DUP activities falling into categories 1 and 2, a beneficial rather than immiserizing outcome is paradoxically feasible, whereas for those falling into categories 3 and 4 it is not.[5] The critical difference is that the former set have initial

[4] Krueger (1974, p. 302) makes the interesting point that bribes can get reflected in the expected returns from qualifying to be a civil servant and thus divert resources via that route. However, the question is one of incidence here. If the government keeps civil service salaries low, expecting that the bribes will make up the required difference to attract a given volume of civil servants, the resource-impact analysis of bribes/transfers gets more complex. One would then have to compare the bribe-induced resource diversion with the resource diversion required to collect taxes to pay adequate salaries when lump-sum taxes are unavailable: a unique rank ordering again would not be generally possible.

[5] While the focus here is on whether the beneficial DUP activity paradox can arise, it is important to note that, with the second-best nature ignored, the problem in categories 1 and 2 (i.e., where there are initially distorted situations) will lead to other errors,

situations that are distorted, whereas the latter set start with distortion-free initial situations. The existing analyses of DUP activities, detailed above, are then assigned to these four categories, distinguishing further among legal and illegal activities.

III. Welfare Consequences of DUP Activities

The critical analytical point at issue is very simple. The diversion of resources from directly productive to directly unproductive activities, when undertaken in the context of initially distorted situations, is fundamentally different from such diversion occurring in the context of initially distortion-free situations. For, in the latter case, the loss of resources is occurring from a first-best situation and hence must represent a social loss as well, whereas in the former case it is occurring in a second-best situation and hence need not represent a social loss but may well be beneficial. Analytically the paradox constituted by the welfare improvement following from the undertaking of the directly unproductive activity in a second-best situation is the same as the paradox of immiserizing growth noted by Bhagwati (1958) and Johnson (1967) and generalized in Bhagwati (1968). For, in the former case, withdrawal of resources for unproductive activity and hence "negative growth" is beneficial, and in the latter case (positive) growth is immiserizing. And, of course, the "dual" of this is the phenomenon of negative shadow prices of factors noted and analyzed in Bhagwati, Srinivasan, and Wan (1978) and in Srinivasan and Bhagwati (1978).

Category 1

In this class of cases, the DUP activities are addressed to initially distortion-ridden situations in an essential fashion. Two legal activities so discussed in the literature are the Krueger (1974) phenomenon of premium seeking and the Bhagwati and Srinivasan (1980) phenomenon of revenue seeking.

Krueger's analysis of premium seeking postulates that, as a result presumably of protectionist demands, import quotas have materialized and characterize the initial situation. The premium-fetching import licenses then generate resource-using competition among po-

as noted for the case of revenue seeking and premium seeking by Bhagwati and Srinivasan (1980). The taxonomic distinctions drawn here, therefore, are critical even if the analyst is inclined to assert (fallaciously, in my judgment) that the beneficial DUP activity paradox is unimportant in practice. On the question whether such second-best paradoxes are likely to arise in practice, see the discussion in Bhagwati (1980) in the specific context of tariff seeking.

tential beneficiaries of the license allocation, and the analysis presupposes that the initial quota level remains unchanged. Therefore, the Kruegèr analysis of premium seeking is essentially of a legal process of DUP activity undertaken in the context of a distorted situation where the distortion triggering off the DUP activity remains unchanged through the analysis.

The same features characterize the Bhagwati and Srinivasan (1980) analysis of revenue seeking: legal directly unproductive competition for securing a share in the disbursement/transfer of tariff revenue resulting incidentally in the imposition of a tariff thanks to protectionist lobbying, the tariff thus being an exogenously specified, unchanging distortion that triggers off the revenue seeking which is being analyzed.

It is easy to demonstrate, as in fact Bhagwati and Srinivasan (1980) have done already, that the lobbying activity being modeled can be paradoxically beneficial despite being directly unproductive, the reason for this paradox being that outlined above already. This possibility can arise also in the premium-seeking case (unless the quota is defined purely in quantity terms, in which case the second-best possibility of welfare improvement through DUP activity–induced changes in outputs will be prevented by the pure trade constraint from spilling over into the paradoxical outcome).[6]

Next, the existing analyses of illegal trade in the presence of tariffs (and quotas) also fit immediately into the present category 1 of DUP activities. For they assume that there is an initially distorting tariff, and the tariff-evading activity is undertaken with this tariff remaining in place through the analysis. In view of the theoretical analysis developed above, it follows immediately that these analyses ought to yield the conclusion that such tariff evasion may be welfare improving (even allowing for the fact that the illegality carries an extra, negative dimension), as they in fact do. Bhagwati and Hansen (1973), for example, show this in a model where the extra real costs of illegality in trade are incurred in the form of the traded goods themselves, this being the "melting ice" assumption used by Samuelson (1954) to model transportation costs within the confines of the two-by-two model. Smuggling will be beneficial rather than immiserizing in this model, even though it uses up real resources (in the form of produced, tradable goods), since it confers production and consumption gains when the effective tariff is cut by the smuggling. The negative weight attached to the illegality may be considered to be outweighed by the gain noted above, which leaves the net evaluation still a benefi-

[6] General propositions concerning the contrast between DUP activities triggered by price and quantity distortions have been developed in Bhagwati and Srinivasan (1981) and in Anam (1982).

cial one. The paradox has repeated itself in the context of illegal trade.

The foregoing examples of category 1–type DUP activities—premium seeking, revenue seeking, and tariff or *QR* evasion—assume that the specified distortion which triggers off such activity remains exogenous to the activity. However, it is easy to imagine phenomena where the distortion may be endogenous to such activity. Thus, revenue seeking may affect adversely the protection implied by the tariff which triggered off the revenue seeking. Bhagwati and Srinivasan (1980) in fact demonstrate in the context of their general equilibrium analysis of revenue seeking that the revenue seeking may lead to a Metzler production paradox: The protectionist tariff plus revenue seeking may lead to a lower output of the importable than under free trade! If so, the protectionist lobby may well seek greater protection, thus influencing in principle the original tariff distortion itself, making therefore the eventual tariff level endogenous to revenue seeking. But even this complexity would leave the phenomenon of revenue seeking within the class of DUP activities squarely within category 1, with its attendant paradox of possible welfare improvement from such activities.

Category 2

In this class of DUP activities, the initial situation that triggers such activities is still distorted, but the outcome turns out to be distortion free.

This category is easily analyzed in light of the foregoing analysis of category 1. Thus, the overall welfare impact of a DUP activity starting from an initially distorted situation but ending in a distortion-free situation is the sum of two effects:

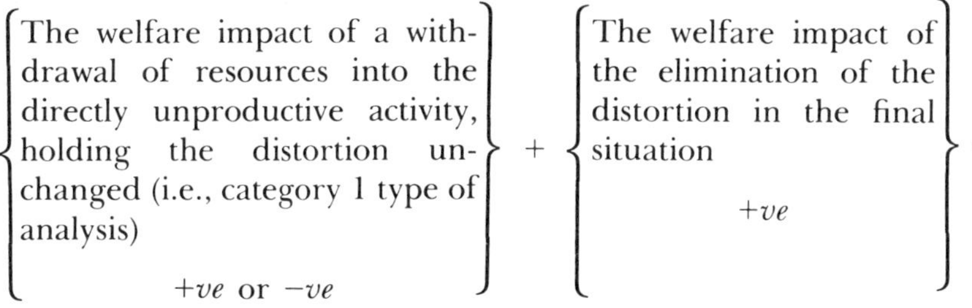

The former effect, as I have argued already, is either positive or negative; the latter, of course, is necessarily positive. The net outcome may therefore be positive or negative. The welfare-improving paradox obtains again, and so does the opposite quasi-paradox that a distortion-destroying lobbying activity may lead to immiserization and hence be only a Pyrrhic victory.[7]

An instance of this, as implied by Findlay and Wellisz (1982) in the context of the analysis of tariff seeking, would be when the resources used up in restoring free trade that is to the lobby's economic advantage are socially more valuable than the social gains from free trade. An instance of illegal DUP activity of a similar nature would be when the lobbying in the foregoing example was replaced by bribes to congressmen to change their vote to free trade.

Category 3

The paradox of beneficial DUP activities disappears, however, as soon as these activities are undertaken in the context of initially distortion-free situations. Category 3 relates to these when the final situation is the successful creation of a distorted situation.

Two classic examples of such category 3, legal DUP activities are successful lobbying efforts at creating government-sanctioned monopoly and lobbying to get tariff protection: monopoly seeking and tariff seeking. In each such case, the total social loss imposed by the DUP activity in question can be decomposed as the sum of two effects:

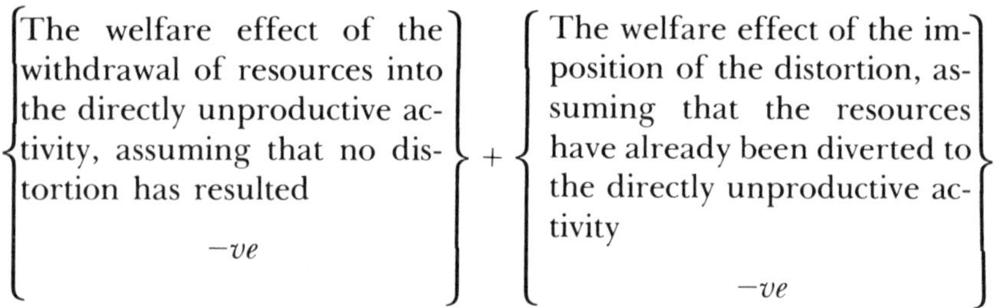

Evidently, there is no source of gain here and hence no room for the paradox of welfare improvement as with categories 1 and 2 above.

Thus, consider monopoly seeking in figure 1. In this small, closed economy which produces at P^* initially, with welfare at U^*, the lobby to secure a monopoly in good 1 production succeeds. The resources expended in securing the monopoly shift the production possibility curve down to $A'B'$, whereas the monopoly itself leads to nontangency of the goods-price ratio with $A'B'$ in equilibrium. Equilibrium production and consumption therefore shift to $P_{\ell m}$, $C_{\ell m}$ and welfare declines to $U_{\ell m}$ from U^*. The total decline in welfare then can be decomposed into (1) the shift from U^* to U_ℓ reflecting only the diver-

[7] Remember again the caveat concerning pure quantity distortions discussed in Bhagwati and Srinivasan (1981) and Anam (1982).

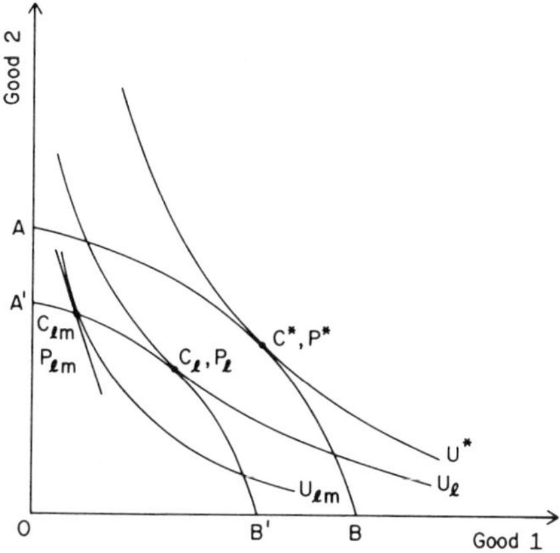

FIG. 1.—Monopoly seeking

sion of resources from directly productive use to the lobbying activity and the resulting move of production and consumption to P_ℓ, C_ℓ, if it is assumed hypothetically that monopoly has not resulted; and (2) the further shift from U_ℓ to $U_{\ell m}$ coming from the admission of the monopoly into the economy and the resulting move of production and consumption to $P_{\ell m}$, $C_{\ell m}$, respectively.[8]

Figure 2 illustrates the tariff-seeking case. The protectionist lobby, starting from free trade at P^*, manages in this small economy to spend resources to get a tariff enacted. If we take only the diversion of resources to lobbying into account, at free-trade prices production would shift from P^* to $\hat{P}^*_\ell$ on the shrunk-in production possibility curve $A'B'$, which represents therefore a loss of RS measured in terms of good 1. Moreover, the tariff resulting from the successful lobbying

[8] A referee has commented that the use of Samuelsonian social indifference curves to evaluate welfare may not be appropriate in figs. 1 and 2 on the following ground: "This construction is valid only if lump-sum transfers are being deployed to optimize income distribution. In response to any change in this distribution that the 'seeking' activities achieve, the government must recalculate the lump-sum transfers to optimize the Bergsonian welfare function again. This calls the whole process into question. Either the seek activities will be abandoned, or they will extend into persuading the government to abandon lump-sum transfer." However, the introduction of DUP activities is simply adding new activities to traditionally defined productive activities on the income-generating side in the model, with all of the given factors of production earning competitively determined incomes. In principle, therefore, it is not necessarily implausible to continue the use of Samuelsonian indifference curves as in the traditional analyses without DUP activities. If this were not so, one would have to agree with the referee that the analysis would then have to "do without social indifference curves, relying on the usual vague aggregate CV or EV measures" *or* shift to invoking Chipman-Moore type assumptions of identical, homothetic indifference curves for individuals combined with statements that are valid then for potential rather than actual welfare.

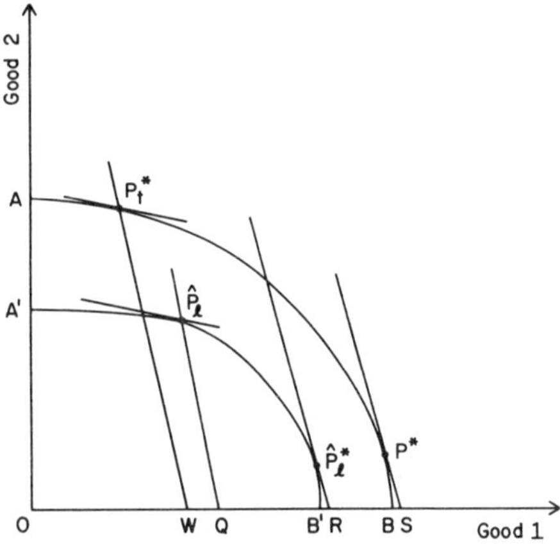

FIG. 2.—Tariff seeking

shifts the production point further to $\hat{P}_\ell$, which is the final observed equilibrium under tariff seeking; this is tantamount to a further loss of *QR* in terms of good 1. These measures are conventional Hicksian equivalent-variational measures, as before, at world prices. Thus the overall loss (*QS*), as already explained, is decomposed into two constituent elements, each of which is unambiguously negative.

A minor paradox does lurk here, however, which needs to be noted, and it reflects much prevailing confusion. Though I have recently dispelled it elsewhere (Bhagwati 1980), it merits a brief mention in the present context. In figure 2, suppose that the total social cost of tariff seeking, *QS*, were to be decomposed along an alternative route: (1) the shift from P^* to P_t^* along *AB*, which represents the social cost of the tariff, if one assumes hypothetically that lobbying resources are not yet expended so that it is as if the tariff has come about exogenously; and then (2) the shift from P_t^* to $\hat{P}_\ell$, from *AB* to *A'B'*, which represents the further shift as a result of the diversion of resources to lobbying, if one assumes the tariff distortion is in place. In this case, the first element of the decomposition will always yield a social loss (*WS*); however, as illustrated in figure 2 and reflecting the second-best considerations outlined in the analysis of categories 1 and 2 above, the second element may well yield a gain (*WQ*). While therefore the overall impact of category 3 activities must be necessarily negative (*QS*), it would be incorrect to assert or imply that the social cost of a distortion imposed without the aid of directly unproductive activity must be necessarily less than that of the same distortion imposed thanks to such activity; that is, in figure 2, the shift from P_t^* to $\hat{P}_\ell$ need not always be a social cost and is, in fact, shown to be a social gain worth *WQ*.

Finally, these conclusions can be readily extended to examples of illegal activities in category 3. An instance of this kind would be provided by tariff evasion or smuggling from an optimal, rather than a distortionary, tariff.

Category 4

The final category of DUP activities is provided by those which, starting with an initially distortion-free situation, wind up also with a distortion-free situation despite the resources expended in such activities. A simple but effective example of such an activity is provided by Findlay and Wellisz (1982) and suggested by Tullock (1967) as well, where tariff seeking by one lobby is offset by tariff-averting lobbying by another group, and the result is that resources are used up in mutually deterring lobbying that does not affect free-trade policy for the small country in the end. Figure 2 would illustrate this case, with a slight reinterpretation. Now, there is evidently a shrinking-in of the production possibility set for goods 1 and 2 from *AB* to *A'B'* as resources are diverted to the lobbying activities and therewith a social loss of *RS* in terms of good 1 since $\hat{P}^*_\ell$ is now the actual postlobbying equilibrium, characterized by continuing free trade. The diversion of resources from productive use when the first-best policy (of free trade in this small competitive economy) is in place throughout must obviously be immiserizing.[9] There is no room for paradoxes of any kind here.

Category 4 then is the clearest case of DUP activities where the simple claims of the early analysts of such activities about their negative impact can be sustained without the slightest qualification. But this is also clearly a very narrow subset of the entire range of activities that have been considered in the present paper.

IV. Concluding Remark

This paper has then provided a complete theory and taxonomy of the welfare consequences of DUP activities. The existing literature is in consequence synthesized within a general welfare-theoretic framework. The results are summarized in table 1.

[9] An inference of illegal profit-seeking DUP activity in category 4 would be that of theft which utilizes real resources in attempts at both undertaking and evading it but without creating any distortion (cf. Tullock 1967).

References

Anam, Mahmudul. "Distortion-triggered Lobbying and Welfare: A Contribution to the Theory of Directly-unproductive Profit-seeking Activities." *J. Internat. Econ.*, vol. 12 (August 1982).

Bhagwati, Jagdish N. "Immiserizing Growth: A Geometrical Note." *Rev. Econ. Studies* 25 (June 1958): 201–5.

———. "Distortions and Immiserizing Growth: A Generalization." *Rev. Econ. Studies* 35 (October 1968): 481–85.

———. *India in the International Economy: A Policy Framework for a Progressive Society*. Lal Bahadur Shastri Memorial Lectures. Hyderabad, India: Osmania Univ. Press, 1973.

———. "Lobbying and Welfare." *J. Public Econ.* 14 (December 1980): 355–63.

———. "Lobbying and Welfare: A Response to Tullock." *J. Public Econ.* (1982), in press.

Bhagwati, Jagdish N., and Hansen, Bent. "A Theoretical Analysis of Smuggling." *Q.J.E.* 87 (May 1973): 172–87.

Bhagwati, Jagdish N., and Srinivasan, T. N. "Smuggling and Trade Policy." *J. Public Econ.* 2 (November 1973): 377–89.

———. "Revenue Seeking: A Generalization of the Theory of Tariffs." *J.P.E.* 88, no. 6 (December 1980): 1069–87.

———. "The Welfare Consequences of Directly-unproductive, Profit-seeking (DUP) Activities: Price *versus* Quantity Distortions." Mimeographed. New Haven, Conn.: Yale Econ. Growth Center, March 1981.

Bhagwati, Jagdish N.; Srinivasan, T. N.; and Wan, Henry, Jr. "Value Subtracted, Negative Shadow Prices of Factors in Project Evaluation, and Immiserizing Growth: Three Paradoxes in the Presence of Trade Distortions." *Econ. J.* 88 (March 1978): 121–25.

Brock, William A., and Magee, Stephen P. "The Economics of Special Interest Politics: The Case of the Tariff." *A.E.R. Papers and Proc.* 68 (May 1978): 246–50.

Falvey, Rodney E. "A Note on Preferential and Illegal Trade under Quantitative Restrictions." *Q.J.E.* 92 (February 1978): 175–78.

Feenstra, Robert, and Bhagwati, Jagdish N. "Tariff-Seeking and the Efficient Tariff." In *Import Competition and Response,* edited by Jagdish N. Bhagwati. Chicago: Univ. Chicago Press (for Nat. Bur. Econ. Res.), 1982.

Findlay, Ronald, and Wellisz, Stanislaw. "Endogenous Tariffs: The Political Economy of Trade Restrictions and Welfare." In *Import Competition and Response*, edited by Jagdish N. Bhagwati. Chicago: Univ. Chicago Press (for Nat. Bur. Econ. Res.), 1982.

Johnson, Harry G. "The Possibility of Income Losses from Increased Efficiency or Factor Accumulation in the Presence of Tariffs." *Econ. J.* 77 (March 1967): 151–54.

———. "Notes on the Economic Theory of Smuggling." *Malayan Econ. Rev.* 17 (April 1972): 1–7. Reprinted in *Illegal Transactions in International Trade: Theory and Measurement,* edited by Jagdish N. Bhagwati. Amsterdam: North-Holland, 1974.

Kemp, Murray C. "Smuggling and Optimal Commercial Policy." *J. Public Econ.* 5 (April/May 1976): 381–84.

Krueger, Anne Osborne. "The Political Economy of the Rent-seeking Society." *A.E.R.* 64 (June 1974): 291–303.

Lenin, Vladimir I. *Imperialism: The Highest Stage of Capitalism.* New York: International Publishers, 1939.

Pitt, Mark. "Smuggling and Price Disparity." *J. Internat. Econ.* 11 (November 1981): 447–58.

Posner, Richard A. "The Social Costs of Monopoly and Regulation." *J.P.E.* 83, no. 4 (August 1975): 807–28.

Ray, Alok. "Smuggling, Import Objectives, and Optimum Tax Structure." *Q.J.E.* 92 (August 1978): 509–14.

Samuelson, Paul A. "The Transfer Problem and Transport Costs. II. Analysis of Effects of Trade Impediments." *Econ. J.* 64 (June 1954): 264–89.

Sheikh, Munir A. "Smuggling, Production and Welfare." *J. Internat. Econ.* 4 (November 1974): 355–64.

Srinivasan, T. N., and Bhagwati, Jagdish N. "Shadow Prices for Project Selection in the Presence of Distortions: Effective Rates of Protection and Domestic Resource Costs." *J.P.E.* 86, no. 1 (February 1978): 97–116.

Tullock, Gordon. "The Welfare Costs of Tariffs, Monopolies, and Theft." *Western Econ. J.* 5 (June 1967): 224–32.

———. "Efficient Rent-Seeking." In *Toward a Theory of the Rent-seeking Society,* edited by James M. Buchanan, Robert D. Tollison, and Gordon Tullock. College Station: Texas A&M Univ. Press, 1980.

Editor's Note

An empirical analysis of the opportunity cost to consumers of utilizing rationing entitlements in wheat, where the opportunity cost is the time spent in queues, is contained in J. N. Bhagwati and B. S. Sihag, "Dual Markets, Rationing, and Queues," *Quarterly Journal of Economics* (December 1980): 775–779.

Journal of International Economics 13 (1982) 33–44. North-Holland Publishing Company

THE WELFARE CONSEQUENCES OF DIRECTLY-UNPRODUCTIVE PROFIT-SEEKING (DUP) LOBBYING ACTIVITIES

Price versus quantity distortions*

Jagdish N. BHAGWATI

Columbia University, New York, NY 10027, USA

T.N. SRINIVASAN

Yale University, New Haven, CT 06520, USA

Received April 1982, revised version received June 1982

This paper is a contribution to the growing literature on the theory of what Bhagwati (1982) has christened the theory of DUP activities. These are activities that use up real resources in making profits (i.e. income) without producing directly or indirectly a 'good'. They result therefore in the contraction of the availability set defined on goods. For one generic subset of such DUP activities, namely distortion-triggered lobbying activities, the paper establishes asymmetrical propositions on the possibility of such DUP lobbying resulting in a paradoxical improvement of welfare.

1. Introduction: Concepts and questions

In the last decade a number of economists have turned to analyzing esoteric activities such as illegal transactions (e.g. smuggling or tariff evasion), lobbying for licenses, lobbying for tariffs or monopoly, etc. none of which is part of the economist's standard tool kit.

It has recently been argued [Bhagwati (1982)] that the key characteristic of these activities is that they represent, unlike the 'normal' or 'traditional' activities of economic models, ways of making profits that do not involve *directly* the production of *any output*. In short, they are directly-unproductive, profit-seeking (hereafter DUP) activities, and their effect is to contract the available set of consumption possibilities in the economy by diverting resources from directly-productive activities.[1]

*Thanks are due to the Guggenheim Foundation and the National Science Foundation for financial support of the first author's research. The comments of Richard Brecher, Alasdair Smith and Michael Roemer are gratefully acknowledged.

[1]Pronounced as 'dupe' activities, the phrase DUP activities also comes close to the spirit in which economists are likely to view such activities! The alternative of calling them ZOP (i.e. zero-output profit-seeking) activities is, on that ground, less appealing. Strictly speaking, these activities provide *income* to factors employed in them. As such, 'income-seeking' rather than 'profit-seeking' is a more appropriate way of characterizing them. However, given the aptness of the word 'dupe' in describing them, we have chosen to retain the phrase 'profit-seeking'.

When these DUP activities are policy-intervention-related in the economy — and they need not be, as in the case of theft, noted by Tullock (1967) — they can be classified to analytical advantage, as shown in fig. 1. There, the DUP activities are classified into two basic categories: I, those that seek policy intervention (including change therein) as in the case of protectionist lobbying to create tariffs or quotas; and II, those that are triggered by (exogenous) policy intervention. The intervention-triggered DUP activities are, in turn, classifiable into *lobbying* activities to secure a share in the resulting rents or revenues, and the intervention-*evading* DUP activities such as smuggling in the presence of tariffs or QRs. Each of the resulting three major classes of DUP activities, in turn, can relate to quantitative or price interventions.

This paper addresses the DUP activities of the lobbying class, and essentially contrasts the quantity and price distortion-triggered DUP lobbying on the dimension of their welfare impact. One precise point, considered in section 2, is the following. When the policy intervention that triggers such lobbying is distortionary (e.g. the quotas that are lobbied for happen to result in a suboptimal restriction of trade rather than constituting optimal restriction), we know from earlier analyses [e.g. Bhagwati and Srinivasan (1980)] that the diversion of resources into DUP lobbying has to be considered in a *second-best* context. As such, it is possible to argue that distortion-triggered lobbying may be paradoxically welfare-improving: reflecting the phenomenon of immiserizing growth [e.g. Bhagwati (1958) and Johnson (1967)] or, its dual, the phenomenon of negative shadow factor prices that can arise in a distortionary situation [Srinivasan and Bhagwati (1978)]. Section 2 considers whether such a paradox can arise symmetrically in the case of *both* quantity and price distortions, i.e. equally in the two cases, 3 and 4, distinguished in fig. 1. Section 2 derives two central propositions in this regard, which establish a basic asymmetry in regard to the paradoxical welfare-impact possibilities in the presence of quantity-intervention-triggered and price-intervention-triggered DUP lobbying activities. Section 3 extends the contrast between these two types of DUP lobbying activities to yet other questions which have important theoretical and policy implications.

2. Price versus quantity distortion-triggered DUP lobbying and welfare improvement

We show that:[2]

Proposition 1. Whenever the distortion that triggers DUP lobbying activity is the only distortion in the economy, and is a (pure) quantity constraint and

[2]These propositions are based upon there being just one distortion in the economy and need not hold when there is more than one distortion. For instance, if there are several foreign distortions, proposition 1 need not hold unless each distortion happens to be a quota. Alasdair Smith emphasized that we draw attention to these possibilities.

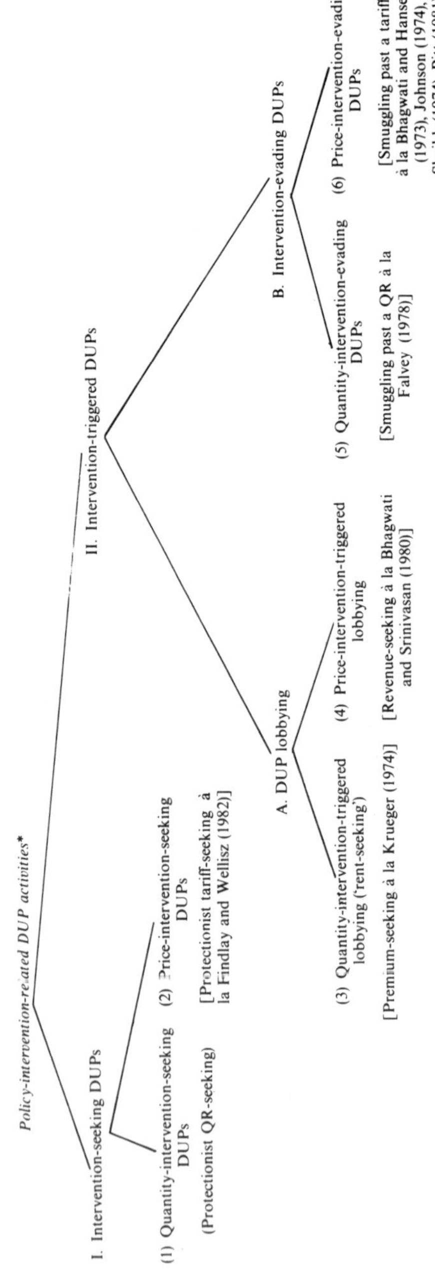

Fig. 1.

*The brackets give specific examples of the DUP category in question.

remains a binding constraint in the presence of the DUP lobbying activity, there can be no welfare improvement.

Proposition 2. When the only distortion is instead an ad valorem price distortion, DUP lobbying can raise welfare (except when the distortion does not affect productive efficiency).

The essential argument underlying proposition 1 is that, while the DUP lobbying activity takes place in a second-best distortionary situation, it fails to improve welfare because the quantity constraint 'bottles up' the source of positive gain that might outweigh the loss implied by the diversion of real resources to the DUP activity. This, on the other hand, does not happen when the distortion is instead of a price variety.

To see this in the traditional 2×2, small, open economy model, consider then the four classic distortionary cases,[3] in their quantity and price versions: (1) trade quota/constraint and trade tariff; (2) production quota/constraint and production tax; (3) factor use quota/constraint and factor tax; and (4) consumption quota/constraint and consumption tax.

2.1. Trade quota and trade tariff

A quota carries a premium which leads to 'premium-seeking' by lobbyists hoping to get hold of the trade quota. The price counterpart of this, of course, is the revenue that the tariff yields; and the corresponding DUP lobbying is then 'revenue-seeking'. Geometrically, it is easy to show how revenue-seeking may lead to paradoxical welfare-improvement, whereas premium-seeking cannot.

2.1.1. Trade tariff

Thus, imagine a tariff-seeking lobby has succeeded and a protective tariff has been put in place. Imagine next that the revenue that results from this (nonprohibitive) tariff attracts a revenue-seeking lobby. This revenue-seeking lobby therefore operates from an initially-distorted, tariff-ridden equilibrium (see fig. 2). There a small country with given terms of trade $P_t C_t$ and a production possibility curve AB is depicted. Then a tariff is imposed, making the importable good 2 more expensive domestically and leading to production at P_t at the point of tangency of the tariff-inclusive price-ratio $P_t S$ with AB, and consumption at C_t. Now, a DUP revenue-seeking activity which this tariff generates would lead to production of goods shifting from P_t

[3]These four cases have been distinguished and analyzed, from the viewpoint of the theory of policy intervention in the presence of noneconomic objectives, in Bhagwati and Srinivasan (1969).

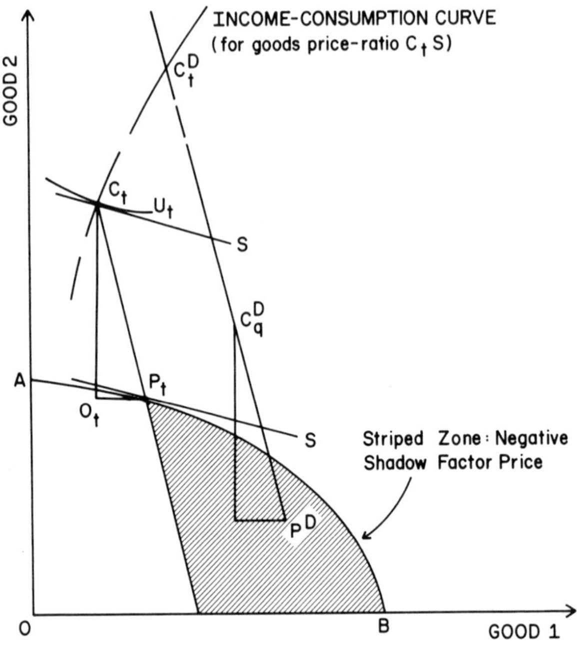

Fig. 2.

to somewhere inside *AB* and, if this shift occurred to a point such as P^D in the striped zone, the revenue-seeking activity would paradoxically *improve* welfare: as at C_t^D.

2.1.2. Trade quota

Now, does this paradoxical possibility not arise equally if the tariff is replaced instead by an import quota? It would seem at first blush that it would. But this is not so.[4] For, in the case of a quota on exports *or* imports, when defined purely in quantity (rather than value) terms, the trade triangle is fixed for the binding quota as $C_t O_t P_t$ and, no matter where P_t shifts to within *AB* as a result of premium-seeking, the attendant constrained-trade equilibrium must imply that the resulting consumption point C_q^D *cannot* rise above $C_t S$ and hence above U_t as well. As long as imports are fixed quantitatively, therefore, premium-seeking has to be immiserizing.

[4]Bhagwati and Srinivasan (1980) were in error on this issue and Mehmood-ul Anam of Carleton University spotted this.

2.2. Production quota and production tax

Next, consider fig. 3 for the case of production distortions. Assume that the initial equilibrium production is distorted to P_{ps} but consumption takes place at international prices at C_{ps}.

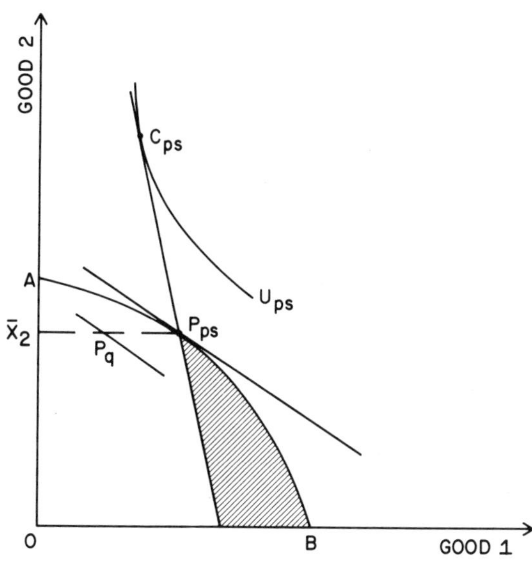

Fig. 3.

2.2.1. Production quota

Now, if the distortion is a quantitative one, i.e. $X_2 = \bar{X}_2$, the DUP activity generated to get the lucrative premia on production licenses (for producing good 2) will necessarily immiserize the economy. The reason is clearly that the loss of resources to the DUP activity will only shift the social budget line inwards and, given $\bar{X}_2$, this must reduce X_1 and hence social utility. In fig. 3, the shift of production is shown, under the quota, to P_q from the initial P_{ps}.

2.2.2. Production tax

However, if the distortion is of a price variety, i.e. a production tax, brings production initially to P_{ps}, DUP activity will raise welfare if it shifts the production point to within the striped area.

2.3. Factor employment quota and factor tax

Here again, a factor employment quantity constraint will eliminate the possibility of a negative shadow factor price, whereas a factor tax distortion will not.

2.3.1. Factor employment quota

With an employment quota of say $\bar{L}_1$, in the absence of DUP activity the transformation curve of the economy will be inside the curve without the quota (except at one point). The initial equilibrium will be characterized by the tangency of the international price line with this restricted transformation curve. As such the introduction of DUP activities will only shift the availability line inwards, as in the production quota case, thus resulting in a loss of welfare.

2.3.2. Factor tax

Suppose the employment level is implemented instead through a tax on employment in the production of good 2. With no DUP lobbying, but with the tax kept constant at this rate, the restricted transformation curve is AB in fig. 4 (though AB need not be concave as drawn, of course). At the initial position P^*, C^*, tangency of the price line with the transformation curve no longer obtains. Hence, introducing DUP can improve welfare if it shifts the production point from P^* to somewhere in the shaded area.

2.4. Consumption quota and consumption tax

Finally, we consider the consumption quota and tax cases and demonstrate that, in both cases, the paradox of negative shadow prices will not arise, despite the second-best nature of the problem at hand.

2.4.1. Consumption constraint

Let the initial situation be at P^*, C_{ct} and U_{ct} in fig. 5. Interpreting this as a consumption *quantity* constraint, such that $C_2 \leqq \bar{C}_2$, we can see that seeking will necessarily shift the social budget line to the left (i.e. from P^*C_{ct} to $C_q C_p$) and hence immiserize the economy (shifting it from U_{ct} to U_q).

2.4.2. Consumption tax

In this instance, however, even if the initial situation is treated as a consumption tax distortion, there will be a shift in welfare from U_{ct} to U_p as consumption shifts from C_{ct} to C_p down the income–consumption curve at

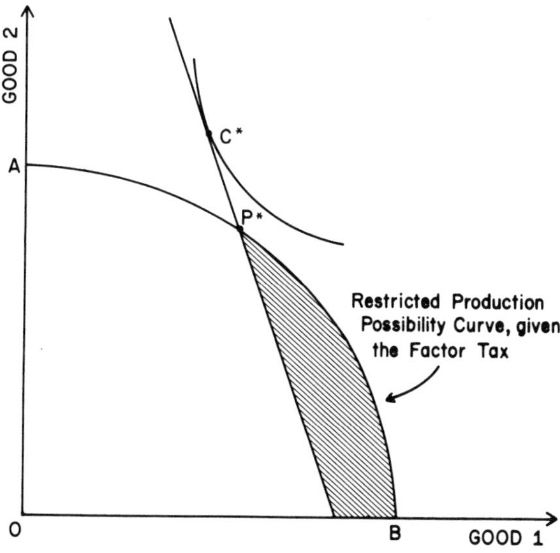
GOOD 2
A
C*
P*
Restricted Production
Possibility Curve, given
the Factor Tax
O
B
GOOD 1

Fig. 4.

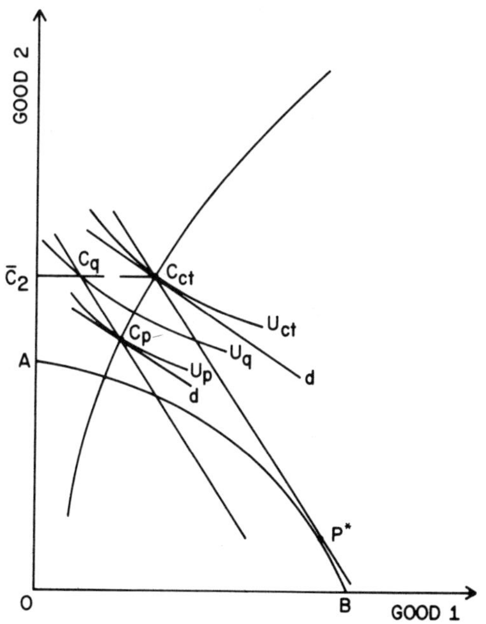
GOOD 2
$\bar{C}_2$
Cq
Cct
Cp
Uct
Uq
Up
d
d
A
P*
O
B
GOOD 1

Fig. 5.

constant (consumer) goods price-ratio d. Thus, in the case of a consumption distortion, there can be no welfare improvement even with a *price* distortion!

The reason why, in both the price and quantity cases, we now have immiserization is easily understood. Since the initial situation represents full production efficiency (at P^*), *any* lobbying must necessarily shift the social budget line inwards. For the fixed *price* distortion in consumption, by writing the indirect utility function in terms of the domestic goods price ratio p and the world-price-valued social income y, we see immediately that the former p is fixed and the latter y declines with DUP lobbying. Hence, a decline in social utility is inevitable. For the *quantity* distortion, again the decline in social income y implies that, given $\bar{C}_2$, the attainable C_1 must fall, and hence again a decline in social utility follows.

2.5. General principles

In all these cases the quantity distortion does not permit welfare improvement. Why? The answer is clear as soon as one understands that for welfare improvement through DUP lobbying to occur, the shadow price of a factor has to be negative. However, the marginal variation in factor supply is in *each* such quantity-constrained case undertaken from what can be regarded as a second-best optimal position; and, as Bhagwati's (1968) generalization of the theory of immiserizing growth shows, immiserizing growth and hence its mirror image phenomenon of a negative shadow factor price [see Bhagwati, Srinivasan and Wan (1978)] can arise only if suboptimality is present. The reason why the quantity-constrained cases can be regarded as involving marginal variation of factor supply from an optimal position is that, as we know from the theory of optimal policy intervention in the case of noneconomic objectives [Bhagwati and Srinivasan (1969)], the optimal way to achieve quantity constraints or objectives relating to production, consumption, trade and factor employment is to utilize implicit or explicit tax-cum-subsidies on production, consumption, trade and factor use, respectively. In fact, utilizing this very insight, Bhagwati (1970, pp. 82–84) had argued that the phenomenon of immiserizing growth could not arise when noneconomic objectives were being pursued with the aid of first-best policies,[5] but that it would resurrect itself if second-best or third-best policies were adopted to implement them in the first place. Proposition 1 above therefore follows immediately.

[5]Our unpublished algebraic derivation of shadow factor prices in the quota-constrained cases (concerning trade, production, factor use and consumption) shows correspondingly that the shadow factor prices in these cases are the *market* prices. This precise proposition is referred to in subsection 3.2 below. It is, of course, to be expected that the shadow prices would be the market prices when, as argued in the text, the quantity-constrained cases can be construed as involving a second-best *optimal* situation.

At the same time, it is equally clear that if the initial situation is regarded as one of *price* distortion, it cannot now be interpreted as one characterized by second-best optimality. Therefore, the possibility of a welfare improvement cannot be ruled out (except for the case of a consumption distortion since productive efficiency obtains in this case even under the distortion in consumption). Hence proposition 2 follows.

3. Other theoretical implications

3.1. Rank-ordering DUP lobbying activities triggered by quantity and price distortions

It is important to note that, while DUP lobbying is necessarily wasteful when triggered by price distortions but not generally when triggered by quantity distortions (as just demonstrated in section 2), this does not imply that one can uniquely rank-order these distortions in the presence of DUP activity. This point was raised by Krueger (1974) in her analysis of premium-seeking, and the attendant analysis of tariffs versus quotas. Hence, we may take up that comparison, but allowing for full revenue-seeking and premium-seeking to arise in the tariff and quota cases, respectively.

Thus, take fig. 2 again and consider two possibilities. First, let the equilibrium at P_t, without the DUP activity, be a tariff equilibrium and let it trigger a revenue-seeking DUP activity which is, for simplicity, *fully* competitive and results in *all* revenues being sought. Next, consider P_t to be a quota equilibrium and again allow it to trigger a premium-seeking DUP activity which is fully competitive and results in all premia on the import licenses being sought. Comparing now the two outcomes, we must conclude that it is not possible to rank-order the two outcomes, even if the technology of the revenue-seeking and premium-seeking DUP activities is assumed to be identical. This, and more, can be shown as follows.

At the full seeking equilibrium, consumer expenditure equals factor incomes that correspond to the production point on the production possibility curve at which the marginal rate of transformation equals the domestic price ratio. Hence, denoting by p this domestic price ratio and by $Y(p)$ the total factor income given p, we can write welfare in terms of the indirect utility function $V(p, Y(p))$. From the fact that p equals the marginal rate of transformation, we get $\mathrm{d}Y/\mathrm{d}p = X_2 \equiv$ output of good 2. Hence, $\mathrm{d}V/\mathrm{d}p = \partial V/\partial p + (\partial V/\partial Y)\cdot X_2$. Now, from Roy's identity, we know that $(\partial V/\partial Y)C_2 = -\partial V/\partial p$, where C_2 is the consumption of good 2. Thus, $\mathrm{d}V/\mathrm{d}p = -(\partial V/\partial Y)(C_2 - X_2) < 0$, given that $\partial V/\partial Y > 0$ and good 2 is the importable. Hence, if the domestic price-ratio corresponding to the equilibrium with a quota and full premium-seeking is greater (smaller) than the tariff-inclusive price, welfare in that equilibrium will be lower (higher) than that under a tariff with full revenue-seeking. In other words, the comparison of welfare levels will reflect a comparison of the implicit tariff under the quota (and full premium-seeking) with the explicit tariff!

3.2. Shadow factor prices in the presence of DUP lobbying

Yet another interesting issue is what the presence of DUP lobbying does to the estimation of shadow factor prices in cost–benefit analysis: a question raised recently by Foster (1981). Now, we know already from subsection 2.5 (and the unpublished algebraic analysis referred to in footnote 5, which corroborates the analysis of subsection 2.5), that the shadow price of each factor at the initial equilibrium, when such equilibrium is characterized by the *absence* of DUP lobbying, is its *market* price when this distortion is a *quantity* distortion (but *not* when it is a price distortion). However, we can show, following on from Foster's (1981) interesting analysis, that the shadow factor price will generally be the market price if the initial situation is itself defined to be DUP-lobbying-*inclusive*, when the distortion is a *price* distortion rather than a quantity distortion! In short, the equivalence of shadow and market factor prices occurs in exactly opposite cases, in regard to quantity and price distortions, depending on whether the initial situation is DUP-lobbying-exclusive or DUP-lobbying-inclusive. Why?

To see this, consider again the revenue-seeking and premium-seeking comparison. In the former case, with the entire revenue sought away, the consumer expenditure on *goods* equals income at market prices for factors. And these factor prices and goods prices do not change (as long as incomplete specialization continues) as we vary factor endowments, thanks to the tariff. As such, the value of change in the labour (capital) endowment by a unit is its market reward: hence, the shadow factor prices are the market prices. Asymmetrically, this proposition does not extend generally to shadow prices of factors at the premium-seeking equilibrium in the case of a quota. For, generally, the implicit tariff and hence factor prices will vary with marginal variation in the factor supply, in this instance.

References

Bhagwati, Jagdish N., 1958, Immiserizing growth: A geometrical note, Review of Economic Studies 25, June, 201–205.

Bhagwati, Jagdish N., 1968, Distortions and immiserizing growth: A generalization, Review of Economic Studies 35, October, 481–485.

Bhagwati, Jagdish N., 1970, The generalized theory of distortions and welfare, in: J. Bhagwati, R.W. Jones, R. Mundell and J. Vanek, eds., Trade balance of payments and growth: Essays in honor of Charles P. Kindleberger (North-Holland, Amsterdam).

Bhagwati, Jagdish N., 1982, Directly-unproductive, profit-seeking activities: A welfare-theoretic synthesis and generalization, Journal of Political Economy 90, October.

Bhagwati, Jagdish, N. and Bent Hansen, 1973, A theoretical analysis of smuggling, Quarterly Journal of Economics 87, May.

Bhagwati, Jagdish, N. and T.N. Srinivasan, 1969, Optimal intervention to achieve non-economic objectives, Review of Economic Studies, January.

Bhagwati, Jagdish, N. and T.N. Srinivasan, 1980, Revenue-seeking: A generalization of the theory of tariffs, Journal of Political Economy 88, December.

Bhagwati, Jagdish N., T.N. Srinivasan and Henry Wan Jr., 1978, Value subtracted, negative shadow prices of factors in project evaluation, and immiserizing growth: Three paradoxes in the presence of trade distortions, Economic Journal 88, March, 121–125.

Falvey, Rodney, 1978, A note on preferential and illegal trade under quantitative restrictions, Quarterly Journal of Economics 92.

Findlay, Ronald and Stanislaw Wellisz, 1982, Endogenous tariffs, the political economy of trade restrictions and welfare, in: J. Bhagwati, ed., Import competition and response, N.B.E.R. (University of Chicago Press).

Foster, Edward, 1981, The treatment of rents in cost-benefit analysis, American Economic Review 71, March, 171–178.

Johnson, Harry G., 1967, The possibility of income losses from increased efficiency or factor accumulation in the presence of tariffs, Economic Journal, March.

Johnson, Harry G., 1974, Notes on the economic theory of smuggling.' Malayan Economic Review, May 1972; reprinted in: J. Bhagwati, ed., Illegal transactions in international trade, Series in International Economics (North-Holland, Amsterdam).

Krueger, Anne Osborne, 1974, The political economy of the rent-seeking society, American Economic Review 64, June.

Pitt, Mark, 1981, Smuggling and price disparity, Journal of International Economics, November.

Sheikh, Munir, 1974, Smuggling, production and welfare, Journal of International Economics 4, November.

Srinivasan, T.N. and Jagdish N. Bhagwati, 1978, Shadow factor prices for project selection in the presence of distortions: Effective rates of protection and domestic resource costs, Journal of Political Economy 86(1).

Tullock, Gordon, 1967, The welfare cost of tariffs, monopolies and theft, Western Economic Journal 5.

A THEORETICAL ANALYSIS OF SMUGGLING *

JAGDISH BHAGWATI
AND
BENT HANSEN

In some underdeveloped countries smuggling takes on large proportions and is a major economic problem. In Afghanistan as much as one quarter to one fifth of total foreign trade is believed to be smuggling trade.[1] Other countries in the East, certainly Indonesia, and a number of African countries also have this problem. There is a need, therefore, to look at smuggling not only as a moral and legal problem but also as a purely economic phenomenon.

It is commonly argued that smuggling must improve economic welfare since it constitutes (partial or total) evasion of the tariffs (or quantitative restrictions), which, for a small country, would signify a suboptimal policy. We propose to demonstrate in Section I of this paper the falsity of this view, while also investigating the restrictive conditions under which smuggling may improve welfare.

Since, however, the tariff may be, and often is, levied to achieve specific objectives, such as protecting import-competing production or collecting revenue, we should also want to compare the welfare levels reached under tariffs with and without smuggling, *subject to such exogenously specified objectives.* In Section II we do this for the case of protecting production and show that the achievement of a given degree of protection to domestic importable production, in the presence of smuggling, produces lower welfare than if smuggling were absent. In Section III, we extend our analysis to the phenomenon of faked invoices.[2]

* Helpful comments were received on an earlier draft of this paper from Abba Lerner, Earl Rolph, Murray Kemp, and Ernest Nadel. Bhagwati's research has been supported by the National Science Foundation.

1. B. Hansen, *Economic Development in Afghanistan: An Appraisal* (submitted to Secretariat of United Nations ECAFE, Bangkok, 1971); H. H. Smith *et al., Area Handbook for Afghanistan* (Washington, D.C.: U.S. Government Printing Office, 1969).

2. Alan Manne has called our attention to an early attempt to analyze smuggling by the famous Italian eighteenth-century (1738–1794) criminologist and economist Cesare Bonesana, Marchese di Beccaria (Cesare Beccaria, "Tentativo Analitico Sui Contrabbandi," Estratto dal foglio periodico intitolato: *il Caffé* (Vol. I, Brescia, 1764–65); reprinted in *Scrittori Classici Italiani di*

I. Smuggling and Welfare

In the following analysis, we apply the Hicks-Samuelson value theoretic framework, which is customarily used in the traditional theory of international trade. We further assume that primary factors, in perfect competition, produce (two) traded goods and that the country is small — i.e., the terms of trade are fixed. We shall assume a given, well-behaved community indifference map. This assumption could be given up without altering any conclusions: it is retained only for convenience of exposition.

Since smuggling merely represents, from a welfare point of view, yet another way in which exportables are transformed into importables, we must represent it as a smuggling transformation (or offer) curve. However, it is clear that this transformation curve must be less favorable than the terms of trade.[3]

We next have the option of assuming that smuggling is either competitive or monopolistic and that the smuggling offer curve is

Economia Politica, parte moderna, tomo XII, Milano 1804, pp. 235–41). Beccaria's problem seems to be to find a method for rational determination of tariff rates and for that purpose he sets up a condition for smuggling to break even. Beccario does not explain his symbols very precisely, but there can be no doubt that the following interpretation is correct.

Assume that a merchant's investment in merchandise is u and that the tariff duty to be paid thereon is t. The rate of tariff is thus $\tau = t/u$. With smuggling the value of the merchandise successfully brought through the controls without payment of tariffs is x. Thus $(u-x)$ has been confiscated. Since the successfully smuggled commodities may be sold at domestic market price, the condition for smuggling to break even is clearly $x(1+\tau)=u$, or, as Beccario presents it, $x+tx/u=u$. He then develops this expression into something that perhaps can be described as isoprofit curves, but does not get anywhere with his analysis, and finally expresses the hope that it may prove useful as a starting point for further analysis.

It is, indeed, easy to develop Beccario's analysis. Let p denote the smuggler's total profit. We then have $p=x(1+\tau)-u$. Let $p/u=r$ be the rate of profit and $x/u=z$ be the probability for success in smuggling. We have then immediately $1+r=z(1+\tau)$. Assume now that the "normal" rate of profit is r^*. For smuggling to be unprofitable the tariff rate has to be set so that $\tau < \frac{1+r^*}{z} - 1$. If, on the other hand, the sovereign can work on the probability of successful smuggling through increased supervision — the more supervision, the lower is z — our relation shows the trade-off between increased supervision and increased tariff rates (revenues). To judge from his text it was precisely this trade-off that Beccario was looking for — natural for a criminologist.

From a national point of view commodities are not lost because they are confiscated, of course. Nonetheless, Beccario's analysis introduces a private cost factor, the risk of being caught, that certainly is important for determining the volume of smuggling and that our analysis does not deal with. (Pierluigi Molajoni translated Beccario's article and has helped us with the interpretation.)

3. As James Kearl has remarked to us, however, there may be relatively minor instances of smuggling at *more* favorable terms of trade — as when LDC-resident Americans with *subsidized* PX sources of foreign goods may be willing to resell these goods in their host-LDC's at prices that fall below legal channel prices.

characterized by either a constant rate of transformation or an increasing rate of transformation. We consider all these options in the following analysis.[4] For the sake of simplicity we shall assume that the individual smuggler has a constant marginal rate of transformation. When we assume increasing marginal rates of transformation for the smuggling industry as a whole, we retain the assumption of individual constant rates of transformation. The industry's increasing rate of transformation is thus exclusively due to intra-industrial, interfirm diseconomies of scale. This assumption permits us in a simple way to deal with both perfect competition and monopoly without loss of generality.

With perfect competition in smuggling, both the foreign price (the terms of trade) and the domestic price are given to the individual smuggler. With monopoly in smuggling, however, several possibilities are open. We shall use a minimum assumption to the effect that, whereas the monopolistic smuggler knows and takes into account the form of the (smuggling) industry's transformation curve, he does not consider the effect on domestic prices of a change in the volume of smuggling.[5] We have in fact also studied the case in which the monopolistic smuggler does consider domestic price effects. But our conclusions remain valid in this case as well. Hence, for reasons of space, we do not present this analysis here. Moreover, we cannot possibly take up here all possible cases of imperfect competition.

We also assume that, in the monopolistic smuggling case, the smuggler is a "nonresident" whose profits therefore do *not* constitute welfare for the country that experiences smuggling.[6] The question of the residence of the smuggler clearly does not arise, however, in the case of competitive smuggling; for, under our assumptions, the smuggling profits under competition would be zero.[7]

4. We disregard the petty smuggling of tourists that is done at zero marginal costs (economically). Our concern is large-scale smuggling on a commercial basis.

5. At constant costs our monopolistic smuggler clearly behaves in exactly the same way as a competitive smuggling industry would do. And at increasing costs he behaves as a competitive smuggling industry does at increasing costs for the individual smuggler without intra-industry diseconomies.

6. We could assume that the smuggler is a resident of the country or, which is very realistic in some primitive countries where smuggling is a large industry, that the smugglers really belong to no country. In Afghanistan nomadic tribes move across the borders to and from Pakistan and Iran, and some of them make a living from smuggling (Smith, *op. cit.*, pp. 328 ff.). They are "countries without fixed territory." Either country, or both, may include the nomads in their population and national income estimates, but such statistical conventions do not integrate the nomads with either country!

7. We should clarify, however, that the results for the monopolistic

Perfect Competition in Smuggling at Constant Costs

In Figure I, AB is the production possibility curve and the slope of P_fC_f (= the slope of P_tC_t) is the fixed, international terms of trade. The domestic price, inclusive of the tariff but in the absence of smuggling, is tangent to AB at P_t. If free trade prevailed, welfare would be at U_f, whereas with the tariff, but without smuggling, it would be at U_t.

With smuggling, however, the smuggling transformation curve is P_sC_s (steeper than P_fC_f, but less steep than the tangent at P_t); the domestic price faced by producers and consumers is P_sC_s, and the welfare is U_s.

Since $U_s < U_t$, we have here a case where smuggling has reduced welfare below what it would be in the absence of smuggling. Smuggling becomes a welfare-reducing phenomenon, contrary to common belief.

On the other hand, Figure II depicts a case where $U_s > U_t$: smuggling has improved welfare. We can therefore conclude:

> *For nonprohibitive tariffs, and constant costs smaller than the tariff-included price and perfect competition in smuggling, smuggling cannot be uniquely welfare-ranked vis-à-vis nonsmuggling.*

The rationale underlying this conclusion is readily seen by analogy with the analysis of the welfare effects of a trade-diverting customs union. Smuggling is analogous to admitting a "partner country" as an importer at higher cost than the "outside country"; smuggling therefore imposes a terms of trade loss, but the production and consumption gain may outweigh this loss, as they do in Figure II, but not in Figure I. Thus, we cannot tell in general whether smuggling is welfare-improving or not — compared to legal trade with the tariff.[8]

---

smuggling case, showing that smuggling may be harmful, do *not* critically depend on the assumption that the smuggler is a nonresident. While it may be thought that the country must be worse off from the exercise of monopoly power from abroad, it must be remembered at the same time that the monopolist smuggler maximizes along an "inferior" transformation curve and *not* along the "legal" offer curve.

8. We might add, however, that, if we were to draw the tangent to the production possibility curve AB and the no-smuggling tariff situation utility curve U_t in Figures I and II, and define the point of tangency with AB as P_z, we can distinguish two zones (in analogy with the trade-diverting customs union theory): Zone I, defined as the range of smuggling offers that would yield smuggling situation equilibrium production between P_f (excluded) and P_z (excluded), where the smuggling must necessarily improve welfare over the nonsmuggling situation; and Zone II, defined similarly over the range from P_z (excluded) to P_t (included), where the smuggling must necessarily worsen welfare.

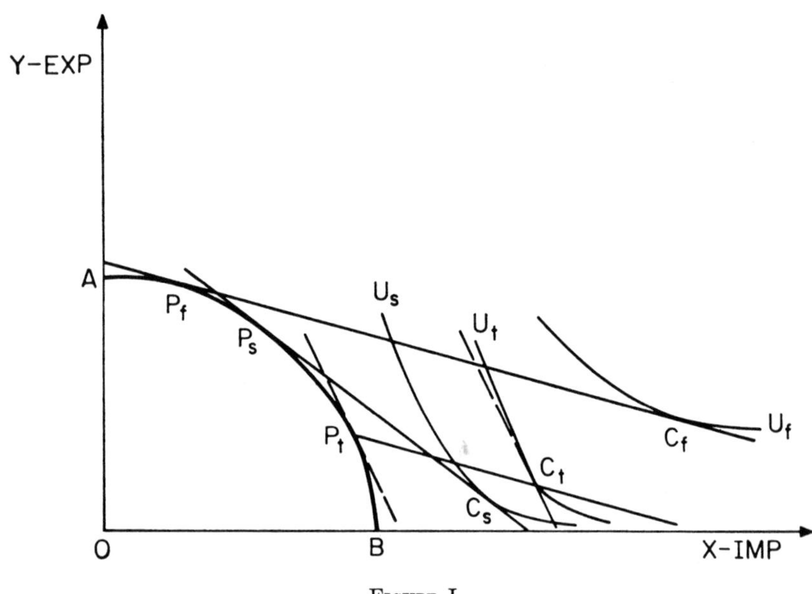

FIGURE I

Perfect Competition in Smuggling at Constant Costs

With free trade, production possibility curve AB, and given international price line P_fC_f, the welfare (maximum) is at U_f. With tariff, the production, consumption, and welfare are at P_t, C_t and U_t, respectively, provided that no smuggling takes place. With smuggling, at constant price line (transformation line) P_sC_s, less steep than the tangent to AB at P_t, *legal trade ceases* and welfare ends up at $U_s<U_t$. Hence, smuggling *reduces* welfare.

In both Figures I and II legal trade is eliminated, given the assumption that the smugglers' transformation line is less steep than the tangent to the country's production frontier at P_t; when the competitive smugglers' costs are constant and lower than the tariff-included price, legal trade cannot survive.[9] Were the smugglers' transformation line steeper than the tangent at P_t, smuggling would, on the other hand, cease completely, and legal trade prevail. But there is here a borderline case in which smuggling and legal trade may coexist. When the smugglers' transformation line coincides with the tangent at P_t, smugglers' constant costs are equal to the tariff-included price and smuggling may or may not prevail. Unfortunately our assumptions leave, strictly speaking, the division

9. John Pettengill has remarked to us, however, that governmental agencies may be compelled to buy through legal channels, in which case legal imports at higher cost *could* coexist with illegal imports by the nongovernmental sector at lower cost. We exclude this possibility in the analysis in the text.

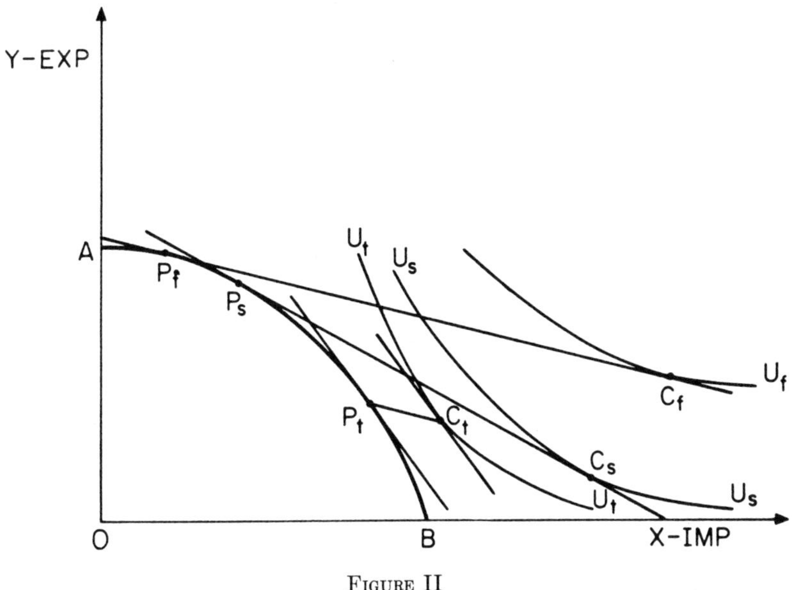

FIGURE II

Perfect Competition in Smuggling at Constant Costs (cont.)

This figure is identical with Figure I, except that now smuggling *improves* welfare: $U_s > U_t$. With the smugglers' transformation line less steep than the tangent at P_t, legal trade is again eliminated.

of trade between smuggling and legal trade indeterminate. Nevertheless, we can state unequivocally that in this case smuggling must be a welfare-reducing activity. Figure III shows that no matter how much or how little smugglers trade, trade exclusively on a legal basis would be better. If the smugglers have all trade, as at point C_s at welfare level U_s, C_t at the welfare level U_t must clearly be better: $U_t > U_s$. And with smuggling at Q and legal trade at $C_{s,\,t}$, we have $U_t > U_{s,\,t}$. We have thus the following result:

For nonprohibitive tariffs, and constant costs equal to the tariff-included price and perfect competition in smuggling, legal trade and smuggling may coexist. In this case, no smuggling is better than any amount of smuggling; and the less smuggling, the better.

Perfect Competition in Smuggling at Increasing Costs

We now consider the case where there are increasing costs in smuggling, while it continues to be competitive. It is clear that, in this case, we can have smuggling coexisting with legal trade, whereas in the preceding case, with constant costs in both smuggling and

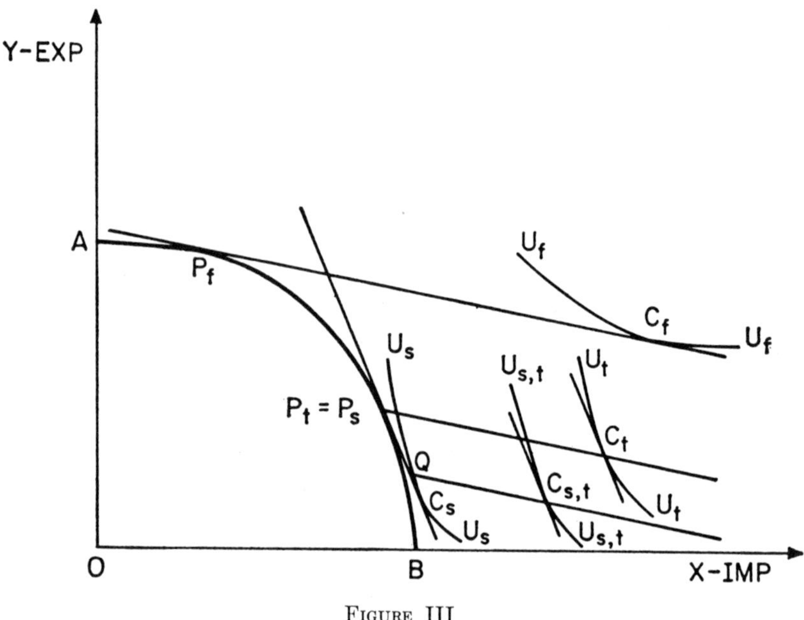

FIGURE III

Perfect Competition in Smuggling at Constant Costs (cont.)

In this figure, the smugglers' transformation line, P_s C_s, coincides with the tangent to AB at P_t $(=P_s)$. If the smugglers have all trade, the welfare level will be U_s with the consumption point C_s. C_s is clearly inferior to C_t; therefore $U_s<U_t$. With smuggling at Q, legal trade will lead to the consumption point $C_{s,\,t}$ at welfare level $U_{s,\,t}$. We have always $U_s<U_{s,\,t}<U_t$. The first inequality is obvious; it means that some legal trade is better than no legal trade. The second inequality follows from the circumstance that, if $U_t<U_{s,\,t}$, which is easily seen to be possible, there would exist at least one more equilibrium point on the trade line, P_tC_t, at a higher welfare level than $U_{s,\,t}$ (J. Bhagwati, "The Gains from Trade Once Again," *Oxford Economic Papers*, XX (1968), 137–48).

legal trade, smuggling, if profitable at all, eliminated legal trade apart from a special borderline case. This possibility of legal trade coexisting with smuggling is not merely a theoretical curiosum: in real life it is probably the most common case, and, as we show below, it turns out to be critical to the welfare effects of smuggling (indeed, as we have already seen in the borderline case above).

Let us initially discuss the cases where smuggling eliminates trade, despite increasing costs. Figure IV illustrates this possibility. The smuggling transformation curve, P_sC_s, now exhibits diminishing returns, and the equilibrium under smuggling shows the domestic price ratio, at which production and consumption take place, to be

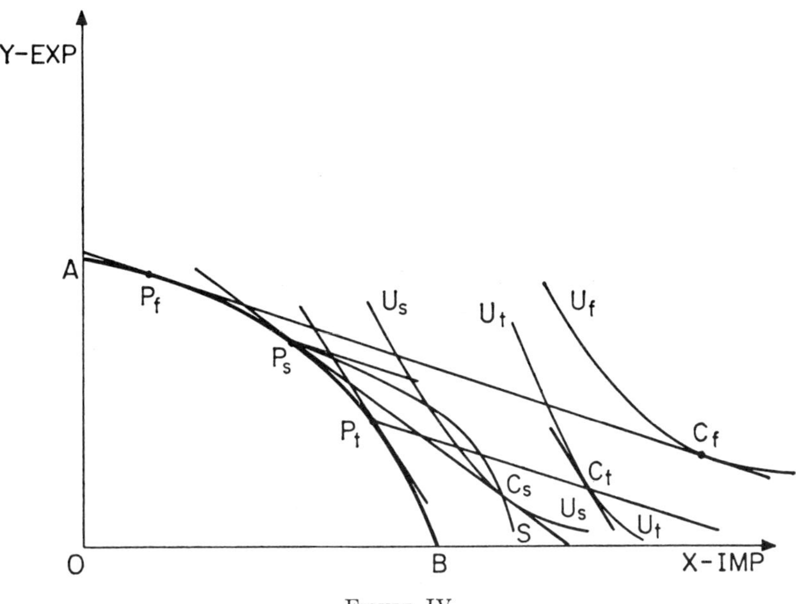

FIGURE IV

Perfect Competition in Smuggling at Increasing Costs

This figure is identical with Figure I, but we now have increasing costs in smuggling. The transformation curve for smuggling is P_sC_sS, and the equilibrium for the smuggling situation is characterized by production at P_s, where the *average* (recall the assumption of individual constant rate of transformation) transformation rate in smuggling (the straight line, P_sC_s) is tangential to AB and by consumption at C_s, where the same rate is tangential also to U_s. Again, legal imports are eliminated, and $U_s < U_t$.

the line P_sC_s. Since P_sC_s is steeper than the legal trade price line, P_fC_f, legal trade has been eliminated. Smuggling is shown to lower welfare vis-à-vis the nonsmuggling situation: $U_s < U_t$.

On the other hand, Figure V shows just the opposite: $U_t < U_s$, and smuggling has improved welfare. Thus, we have the following result:

For nonprohibitive tariffs, and increasing costs and perfect competition in smuggling, smuggling cannot be uniquely welfare-ranked vis-à-vis nonsmuggling when legal trade is eliminated by smuggling.

Consider, however, the case where legal trade is *not* eliminated in the smuggling situation. Figure VI, which is variant on Figures IV and V, illustrates this case. In the smuggling situation, the domestic price will now be the tariff-inclusive price: so both production (at P_s) and consumption (at C_s) must be at tariff-inclusive

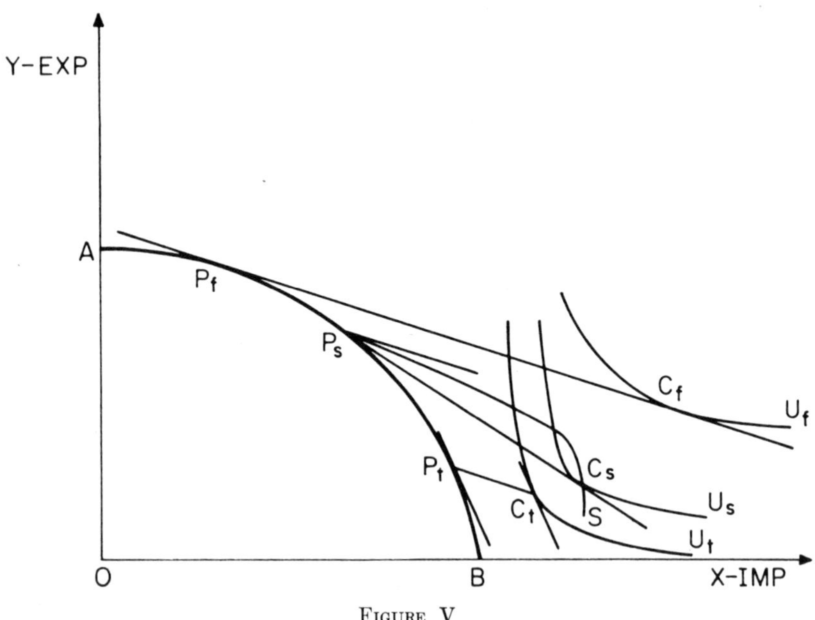

FIGURE V

Perfect Competition in Smuggling at Increasing Costs (cont.)

This figure is identical with Figure IV, except that we now show smuggling to result in greater welfare than legal trade: $U_s > U_t$. Again, in the smuggling situation, legal imports are eliminated.

prices. The point of trade on the *smuggling* transformation curve, P_sQS, must be (at Q) where the *average* terms of trade (we have individual constant returns) are again the same as the *domestic* price ratio. However, *legal* trade must occur at the *international* price ratio, the slope of QC_s. It is clear, then, that smuggling worsens welfare, and we thus have the result:

For nonprohibitive tariffs, and increasing costs and perfect competition in smuggling, when legal trade is not eliminated, smuggling necessarily reduces welfare vis-à-vis the nonsmuggling situation.

The rationale for this result is again readily seen. The smuggling situation, vis-à-vis the nonsmuggling situation, now imposes *identical* production and consumption distortions on the economy, while *also* imposing a terms of trade loss; smuggling must therefore necessarily be a welfare-reducing phenomenon in this instance.

Monopoly in Smuggling at Constant Costs

When smuggling is monopolistic, the *marginal* rate of trans-

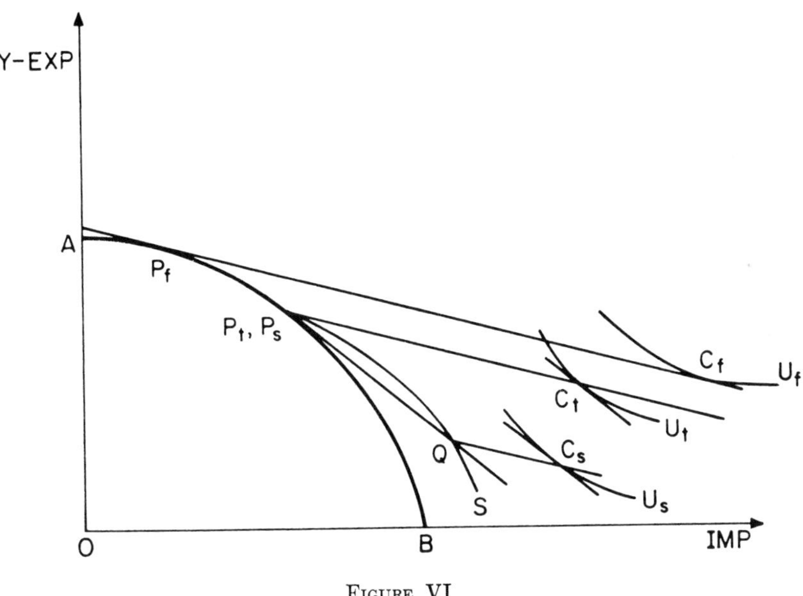

FIGURE VI

Perfect Competition in Smuggling at Increasing Costs (cont.)

This diagram shows a situation where smuggling and legal trade *coexist* in equilibrium. The production points, P_t and P_s, therefore coincide; smuggling takes the availability point to Q and legal trade takes it then, at international prices, to C_s and welfare $U_s < U_t$ (the welfare that would be achieved under legal trade alone); see caption for Figure III concerning the possibility of $U_s > U_t$, in case of multiple equilibria.

formation in smuggling will be equated with the domestic price ratio. However, for constant costs in smuggling, the marginal and average rates of transformation are identical, and hence the results are identical with the case where smuggling is competitive. Hence we can conclude:

For nonprohibitive tariffs, and constant costs and monopoly in smuggling, smuggling cannot be uniquely welfare-ranked vis-à-vis nonsmuggling.

Monopoly in Smuggling at Increasing Costs

However, when there are increasing costs in smuggling, we have to distinguish between marginal and average terms of trade in smuggling. As with the competitive case, we find that the ranking of smuggling vis-à-vis nonsmuggling is critically dependent on whether smuggling eliminates legal trade.

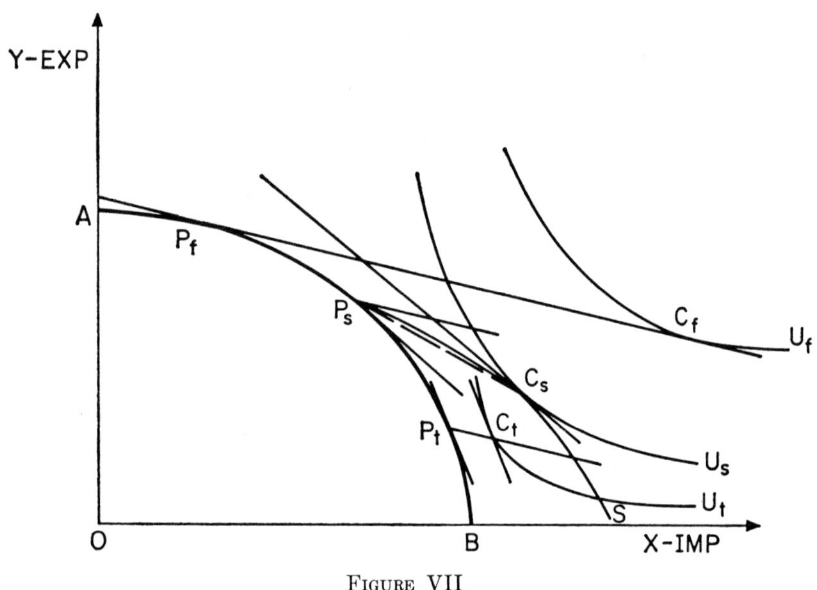

FIGURE VII

Monopoly in Smuggling at Increasing Costs

This figure is similar to Figure V: legal trade is eliminated and $U_s > U_t$. However, instead of depicting smuggling on the perfectly competitive assumption, we now equate the *marginal* rate of transformation in smuggling (at C_s) with the marginal rate of transformation in domestic production and domestic prices (at P_s). Smuggling improves welfare over the legal trade situation.

In Figure VII, we illustrate a case where smuggling does eliminate legal trade. The difference from Figure V, where the case of competitive smuggling under increasing costs was discussed, is that the smuggling equilibrium is characterized by equality of domestic prices and the *marginal* rate of transformation in smuggling — the tangents to the production possibility curve AB at P_s, to the transformation curve P_sS at C_s, and to the social indifference curve U_s at C_s are parallel. We here depict a case where $U_s > U_t$: smuggling is welfare-improving. We could, however, equally readily have redrawn the diagram to show $U_s < U_t$ — i.e., that smuggling had reduced welfare.

We thus have the following proposition:

For nonprohibitive tariffs, and increasing costs and monopoly in smuggling, smuggling cannot be welfare-ranked vis-à-vis nonsmuggling when legal trade is eliminated by smuggling.

We note, therefore, that the conclusions are identical regardless of whether smuggling is competitive or monopolistic.

Consider now, however, the case where smuggling fails to eliminate legal trade. Figure VIII illustrates this case. As with the com-

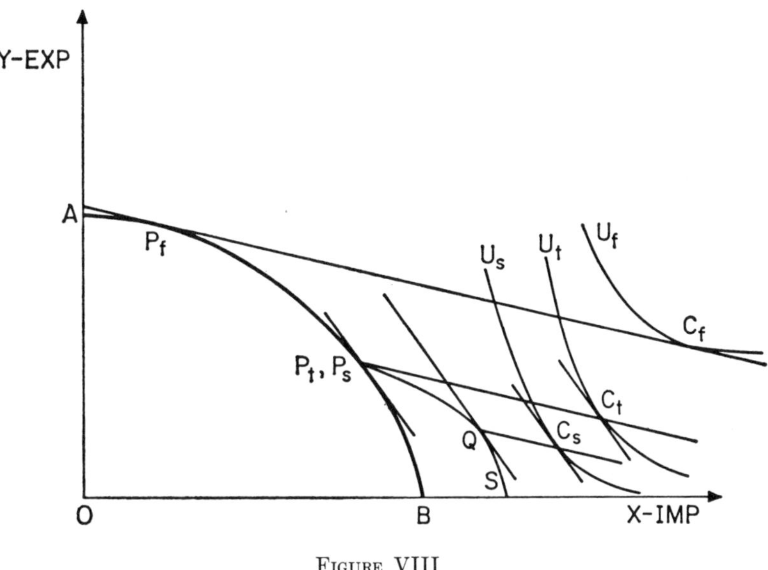

FIGURE VIII

Monopoly in Smuggling at Increasing Costs (cont.)

This diagram shows the *simultaneous* presence of smuggling and legal trade in equilibrium. It is easy to see that, *in this case of continued legal trade in the presence of smuggling,* smuggling is necessarily inferior to nonsmuggling: $U_t > U_s$. Concerning the possibility that $U_t < U_s$, in case of multiple equilibria, see caption to Figure III.

petitive smuggling case, we find that $U_s < U_t$ and that smuggling necessarily reduces welfare. Again, it is easy to see why: with legal trade continuing, the distortion in domestic production and consumption must be *identical* between the smuggling and nonsmuggling situations, whereas the presence of smuggling imposes an (additional) terms of trade loss. Thus we can conclude:

> *For nonprohibitive tariffs, and increasing costs and monopoly in smuggling, smuggling is necessarily inferior to nonsmuggling when smuggling does not eliminate legal trade.*

Prohibitive Tariffs

Note, however, that we have explicitly qualified all our propositions by stating them as valid for *nonprohibitive tariffs* alone. The reason for this is clear enough. When we consider a prohibitive tariff, the nonsmuggling situation is autarkic. Smuggling then makes trade feasible; the appropriate analogy now is with a *trade-creating* customs union, as distinct from a trade-diverting customs union, and clearly gains must necessarily accrue from smuggling. We can thus conclude:

For prohibitive tariffs, smuggling is necessarily superior to nonsmuggling, whether smuggling is competitive or monopolistic, and whether subject to constant or increasing costs.

Perfect Competition vs. Monopoly in Smuggling

A comparison between Figures VI and VIII leads directly to the conclusion:

When legal trade and smuggling coexist at nonprohibitive tariffs and increasing costs in smuggling, monopoly in smuggling is better than perfect competition.

In other words, the more smugglers we put in jail, the better! This sounds quite reasonable and proper: economics and morality coincide in their prescriptions! (When legal trade is eliminated, however, monopoly and competition cannot be ranked thus. And at constant costs the two are identical (on our assumptions).) Our result is analogous to the familiar proposition in optimum tariff theory that the exercise of monopoly power by a country improves its welfare. In this instance, the smuggler's exercise of his monopoly power is tantamount (on our assumptions) to the country's adopting an optimum tariff policy along the smuggling transformation curve; hence it clearly yields a superior welfare level than if smuggling were competitive.

II. Exogenously Specified Objectives: Target Increase in Importable Production

The preceding analysis is essentially of interest where the economist thinks either that the tariff policy is misconceived or that it is a historical accident. In either case, the economist is likely to argue — and indeed such arguments are frequently asserted in practice — that smuggling *must* be welfare-improving, a notion that we have just demonstrated to be unsustainable as a general proposition.

But suppose now that the tariff has been imposed to achieve some definite end. Assume that the government wishes to achieve a prespecified degree of protection for the import-competing industry. We then have the following proposition.

To attain a feasible target increase in domestic production of the importable good, a tariff with no smuggling is superior to a tariff with smuggling.

This proposition is illustrated in Figure IX. With the production point fixed by the target specification at $P_s(P_t)$, it follows that $U_s < U_t$. Again, the rationale of this result can be readily grasped by noting that the *fixing* of the production point makes the production distortion *identical* between the smuggling and the nonsmuggling situations, whereas the terms of trade under smuggling are inferior to those under legal trade. Consumption is again at identically distorted prices (at C_t and C_s under the nonsmuggling and the smuggling situations, respectively). Hence smuggling must necessarily worsen welfare.

This result is of interest not merely because it reinforces our critique of the customarily complacent view of smuggling, but also because it would seem to us to provide yet another argument in support of the view that, for a *production* noneconomic objective, a

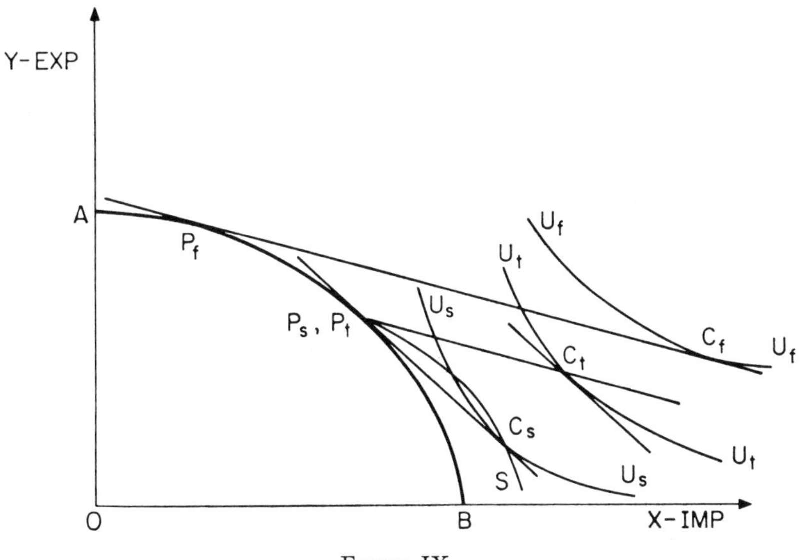

FIGURE IX

Smuggling at Predetermined Production Point

Note that the production of X, the importable good, cannot fall below $P_s = P_t$. A suitable tariff, in the absence of smuggling, will take welfare to U_t. A *higher* tariff, in the presence of smuggling (at transformation curve P_sC_sS), would (necessarily) produce lower welfare at U_s. The same result could be illustrated for the case where smuggling does *not* eliminate legal trade, as also for monopolistic smuggling.

production tax cum subsidy policy is superior to a tariff policy.[1] In the presence of smuggling, the tariff rate needed to encourage domestic import-competing production is clearly *greater* than if smuggling is not present, and this conclusion is clearly of considerable significance to countries such as Afghanistan and Indonesia, where smuggling assumes significant dimensions.

III. Overinvoicing and Underinvoicing of Transactions

Our analysis of smuggling can also be readily extended to quasi-smuggling phenomena, such as the overinvoicing and underinvoicing of transactions on *legal* trade.[2] We demonstrate how this can be done for the case where the presence of a tariff duty leads to underinvoicing of imports.

We should distinguish between two possibilities: (1) where the underinvoicing of imports amounts merely to a de facto reduction in the tariff, so that the smuggling situation is equivalent to a lowering of the tariff; and (2) where the resulting gain to the importer has to be shared, in some degree, with the exporter who collaborates in the faking of the invoices, in which case the effective c.i.f. price of importation to the importing country rises, entailing a terms of trade loss.

Clearly, the latter case is equivalent to our analysis of smuggling, and therefore no modification in our conclusions is necessary. However, in the former case, our conclusions get critically affected. For, with underinvoicing amounting only to a lower tariff, it follows that it must necessarily be superior to a non-underinvoicing situation, and for the case where a target-specified degree of domestic production of the importable must be achieved, it clearly makes no difference now whether there is faking of invoices or not; with faking, the tariff will just have to be set higher, and the faking-inclusive real situation will then be identical with that which would have obtained without faking but with a lower tariff.[3]

1. See W. M. Corden, "Tariffs, Subsidies, and the Terms of Trade," *Economica*, XXIV (1957), 235–42, and J. Bhagwati and T. N. Srinivasan, "Optimal Intervention to Achieve Non-Economic Objectives," *Review of Economic Studies*, XXXVI (1969), 27–38.

2. For earlier analyses of such phenomena, seeking different answers, see Bhagwati, "Fiscal Policies, the Faking of Foreign Trade Declarations and the Balance of Payments," *Trade, Tariffs, and Growth* (Cambridge: M.I.T. Press, 1969), pp. 266–94; Bhagwati and Padma Desai, *India: Planning for Industrialization* (London: Oxford University Press, 1970); and G. Winston, "Overinvoicing, Underutilization and Distorted Industrial Growth," *Pakistan Development Review*, X (1970), 405–21.

3. As with smuggling, however, the degree of protection sought may be unattainable in the presence of faking of invoices.

IV. Conclusions

We have thus managed to incorporate successfully the phenomena of smuggling and faked invoicing into the welfare analysis of tariffs. Our analysis is clearly generalizable, and in a sequel to this paper we propose to extend our analysis into two major areas: (1) the welfare analysis of domestic taxation, and (2) other propositions in the theory of trade and welfare.[4]

Massachusetts Institute of Technology
University of California, Berkeley

4. In particular, our analysis must be extended to a multiple-good model, while the present analysis has explored only the two-good model throughout. Further, we have dealt in the present paper only with the smuggling of goods rather than of "bads" (such as heroin) or of assets (such as gold), whose analysis must be conducted in the framework of differently constructed models. Finally, we may note explicitly that we (correctly, in our view) conceive of smuggling as necessarily taking place in the presence of governmental attempts at enforcing the tariff. (Norman Mintz has pointed out to us that if we were to postulate instead that the government does not do so, the smuggling equilibrium would be identical with the free-trade equilibrium: the real cost of smuggling trade would be no different from that of legal trade in this case because the smugglers would be merely walking past the customs officers, choosing not to pay the tariff and not being penalized for doing so! This situation would be both nonsensical and unrealistic; we have therefore assumed that smuggling necessarily takes place in the context of enforcement.) As with traditional analysis, however, where the cost of operating the tariff is not explicitly taken into account by, say, a shrunk-in production possibility curve, we have simply ignored this aspect of the tariff-enforcement costs.

Editor's Note

See also J. N. Bhagwati and T. N. Srinivasan, "An Alternative Proof of the Bhagwati-Hansen Results on Smuggling and Trade Policy," in J. N. Bhagwati, ed., *Illegal Transactions in International Trade*, Amsterdam: North-Holland, 1974, chapter 2, pp. 23–26.

Journal of Public Economics 2 (1973) 377–389. © North-Holland Publishing Company

SMUGGLING AND TRADE POLICY *

Jagdish BHAGWATI and T.N. SRINIVASAN
MIT and Indian Statistical Institute, U.S.A. and India

First version received January 1973, revised version received April 1973

Bhagwati and Hansen (1973) have shown that the phenomenon of smuggling in an open economy can be incorporated readily into standard trade–theoretic analysis by treating smuggling as essentially involving a less favourable transformation curve insofar as smuggling involves a real cost. [1]

In this paper, we utilise the same analytical device and extend the Bhagwati–Hansen analysis to a number of other issues traditionally considered in the theory of international trade policy. We use the same analytical simplifications:

(i) Smuggled goods and legal imports are cleared at the same final price: consumers do not discriminate in their purchases between the two sources of supply.

(ii) Changes in social welfare are analysed by reference to a standard Crusoe-type social utility function defined on the *current* availability of goods and services.

(iii) Goods constituting consumption and directly entering the utility function are smuggled, and not bads (e.g. heroin) or assets (e.g. gold): the model used for our analysis is the traditional trade–theoretic model where non-traded primary factors produce traded final goods entering the utility function.

(iv) Expenditure on enforcement of the tariff is held implicitly constant in comparing the tariff-with-smuggling and tariff-without-smuggling situations and is not explicitly considered, in keeping with

* The research for this paper was supported by the National Science Foundation. The paper was written while T.N. Srinivasan was Visiting Professor of Economics at MIT. Thanks are due to Yasuo Uekawa and the referees for very helpful comments.

[1] This real cost arises insofar as the avoidance of normal trade channels leads to increased costs – e.g. more expensive transport and higher f.o.b. price for imports.

the tradition of trade theory, in comparing either with the free-trade situation; one important effect is to rule out analysis of the possible trade-offs between increased enforcement expenditure and reduced smuggling.

(v) Finally, the bulk of our formal analysis is based on the two-traded-goods model.

Sec. 1 considers a country with monopoly power in (legal) trade (the small-country analytical results then being derivable as a special case) and derives the first-order conditions for an optimal solution when smuggling is possible and examines the set of policies that would yield this optimum. Noting that this set of policies is not operationally feasible in general, we proceed to examine therefore in sec. 2 the following issues in the 'second-best' domain where a tariff is the only policy instrument available. The following questions are considered:

(i) How does the optimal tariff without smuggling – which is clearly the first-best policy instrument – rank with the optimal tariff with smuggling – which is clearly, in light of sec. 2, not a first-best policy instrument?

(ii) How does the maximal-revenue tariff in the presence of smuggling compare with the optimal tariff in the presence of smuggling? [2]

(iii) How does the maximal-revenue tariff in the presence of smuggling compare with the maximal-revenue tariff in its absence?

(iv) Is the maximal revenue that can be collected with smuggling lower than the maximal revenue in the absence of smuggling?

(v) For any *given* revenue, is the tariff rate with smuggling greater than the tariff rate without smuggling?

In sec. 3, we summarise our results in tabular form.

1. Consider a country producing two goods at levels X_1, $G(X_1)$ when G is the transformation function ($G > 0$, $G' < 0$, $G'' < 0$ for $0 \leqq X_1 \leqq \bar{X}_1$). Let foreign trade take place through two channels: legal and smuggler's. Let the first commodity be imported. Let the second commodity (exportables) be the numeraire.

Let p_d be the domestic price ratio and p_ℓ, p_s the foreign price ratios for legal trade and smuggler's trade. Let C_i be the consumption of commodity i. Let x_ℓ, x_s be the imports of commodity 1 through the

[2] Harry Johnson (1950–51) has shown that, without smuggling, the maximal-revenue tariff is greater than the optimal tariff.

legal and smuggler's channels respectively. Let $U(C_1, C_2)$ be the concave social utility function.

Let $p_\ell = g(x_\ell)/x_\ell$ where $g(x_\ell)$ represents the exports of commodity 2 needed for getting imports of x_ℓ units of commodity 1 through legal trade. We shall assume that $g(0) = 0$, $g' > 0$, $g'' \geqq 0$ (where primes denote derivatives of appropriate order) implying that p_ℓ is a non-decreasing function of x_ℓ and $p_\ell < g'$. Clearly the case where $g'' \equiv 0$ will correspond to a situation where there is no monopoly power in trade. Analogously, let us assume $p_s = h(x_s)/x_s$ where $h(0) = 0$, $h' > 0$, $h'' \geqq 0$ will correspond to the case where there are constant costs in smuggling.

$$C_1 \leqq X_1 + x_\ell + x_s \tag{1}$$

$$C_2 \leqq G(X_1) - g(x_\ell) - h(x_s) \tag{2}$$

$$C_1, C_2, X_1, x_\ell, x_s \geqq 0\,.$$

Maximising the Lagrangean $\Phi = U - \lambda_1[C_1 - X_1 - x_\ell - x_s] - \lambda_2[C_2 - G + g + h]$, we get (for our interior solution):

$$U_1 = \lambda_1 \tag{3}$$

$$U_2 = \lambda_2 \tag{4}$$

$$\lambda_1 + \lambda_2 G' = 0 \tag{5}$$

$$\lambda_1 - \lambda_2 g' = 0 \tag{6}$$

$$\lambda_1 - \lambda_2 h' = 0 \quad \text{or} \tag{7}$$

$$\frac{U_1}{U_2} = -G' = g' = h'\,. \tag{8}$$

In other words the marginal rate of substitution in consumption is equated to the marginal rate of transformation in production, in legal trade and in smuggling.

If we do not wish to rule out corner solutions we can rewrite (3)–(7) as follows:

$$U_1 - \lambda_1 \leqq 0 \text{ with equality if } C_1 > 0$$

$$U_2 - \lambda_2 \leqq 0 \text{ with equality if } C_2 > 0$$

$$\lambda_1 + \lambda_2 G' \leqq 0 \text{ with equality if } X_1 > 0$$

$$\lambda_1 - \lambda_2 g' \leqq 0 \text{ with equality if } x_\ell > 0$$

$$\lambda_1 - \lambda_2 h' \leqq 0 \text{ with equality if } x_s > 0 .$$

One particular corner solution is of some interest. Suppose there is no monopoly power in legal trade, i.e., $g = p^f x$ where p^f is the fixed world terms of trade. Ruling out specialisation in consumption and production, the optimal solution will be characterised by free trade and no smuggling if:

$$U_1 = \lambda_1, \quad U_2 = \lambda_2, \quad \lambda_1 + \lambda_2 G' = 0, \quad \lambda_1 = \lambda_2 g' = \lambda_2 p^f$$

$$\text{and} \quad h'(0) \geqq \lambda_1 / \lambda_2 = p^f .$$

In other words, free trade will be the optimal policy in the absence of monopoly power in trade if, as we have assumed, the marginal terms of trade of the smuggler at zero level of smuggling are not superior to the legal world terms of trade, i.e., there is no incentive for smuggling when free trade prices prevail in domestic markets.

Returning, however, to an interior solution and the case of monopoly power in trade, and assuming competitive smuggling, production and consumption, we can sustain the optimal solution obtained above by:

(i) consumption tax at an ad valorem rate c so that $\dfrac{h(x_s)}{x_s}(1 + c) = h'$

(ii) tariffs (subsidies) on legal imports at an ad valorem rate t so that $\dfrac{g(x_\ell)}{x_\ell}(1+t) = \dfrac{h(x_s)}{x_s}$

(iii) production subsidies at the rate s so that $\dfrac{h(x_s)}{x_s}(1+s) = -G'$.

In this framework, if we introduce a non-economic objective of raising the production of importables X_1 to some preassigned level X_1^* in the form of a constraint $-X_1 \leqq -X_1^*$, we add the expression

$-\lambda_3(-X_1 + X_1^*)$ to the Lagrangean and maximise. The first order conditions (3), (4), (6) and (7) continue to hold. Eq. (5) gets modified to

$$\lambda_1 + \lambda_2 G' + \lambda_3 = 0 . \tag{9}$$

Of course, the solutions for C_1, C_2, X_1, X_2, x_ℓ, x_s, λ_1, λ_2 will be different with the non-economic objective present. The form of policy interventions, however, are the same: [3] Consumption tax, tariff (subsidy) on legal imports and a production subsidy. In the presence of the non-economic objective, the production subsidy at rate s that equates $[h(x_s)/x_s](1+s)$ to $-G'$ will be higher than the consumption tax c that equates $[h(x)_s/x_s](1+c)$ to h' since $-G' = \lambda_1/\lambda_2 + \lambda_3/\lambda_2 = h' + \lambda_3/\lambda_2 > h'$, whereas in the absence of the non-economic objective the two rates will be equal.

2. While the analysis of the optimal policy mix in the presence of smuggling and monopoly power in (legal) trade that we have just set out is technically correct, it does assume the oddity that the smuggled goods be subject to consumption taxes in the same way as legally-traded goods. If we rule this out, and assume instead that smuggled goods fetch to the smuggler the tariff-inclusive price plus or minus the tax or subsidy on consumption of the legal imports and production, then the achievement of the optimal solution is impossible. We then have a second-best problem which we propose to tackle in a subsequent paper.

Instead we proceed to examine the question of the optimum level at which the tariff can be set, in the presence of smuggling, when the tariff is the only policy instrument available. [4] We also extend the analysis, using only the tariff as a policy variable, to questions posed by revenue as an objective.

Let us then set out the conditions of equilibrium, given a tariff rate t, in the absence of (A) and in the presence of (P) smuggling:

[3] Other non-economic objectives analysed by Bhagwati–Srinivasan (1969) can be introduced in the presence of smuggling with exactly the same type of policy consequences as for the case of production analysed in the text.

[4] This is a problem of policy relevance as a number of LDCs are not equipped to utilise other instruments (such as production and consumption taxes) with quite the same efficacy.

A		P	
$C_{1A} = X_{1A} + x_{\ell A}$	(10A)	$C_{1P} = X_{1P} + x_{\ell P} + x_{sP}$	(10P)
$C_{2A} = G(X_{1A}) - g(x_{\ell A})$	(11A)	$C_{2P} = G(X_{1P}) - g(x_{\ell P}) - h(x_{sP})$	(11P)
$\dfrac{U_{1A}}{U_{2A}} = p_{dA}(t)$	(12A)	$\dfrac{U_{1P}}{U_{2P}} = p_{dP}(t)$	(12P)
$-G'(X_{1A}) = p_{dA}(t)$	(13A)	$-G'(X_{1P}) = p_{dP}(t)$	(13P)
$\dfrac{g(x_{\ell A})(1+t)}{x_{\ell A}} = p_{dA}(t)$	(14A)	$\dfrac{g(x_{\ell P})(1+t)}{x_{\ell P}} = p_{dP}(t)$	(14P)
		$\dfrac{h(x_{sP})}{x_{sP}} = p_{dP}(t).$	(15P)

As a preliminary to deriving the tariff rates that maximise revenue or welfare, let us derive the rates of change of the equilibrium values of some of the variables (denoted by a dot over the variable) with respect to changes in tariff. It can be shown that:

$$\dot{X}_{1A} = \frac{G'(1-\theta_A)}{G''(1+t)} > 0 \qquad \dot{X}_{1P} = \frac{G'(1-\theta_P)}{G''(1+t)} > 0$$

$$\dot{x}_{\ell A} = \frac{-\theta_A}{(1+t)\left(\dfrac{g'}{g} - \dfrac{1}{x_{\ell A}}\right)} < 0 \qquad \dot{x}_{\ell P} = \frac{-\theta_P}{(1+t)\left(\dfrac{g'}{g} - \dfrac{1}{x_{\ell P}}\right)} < 0$$

$$\dot{p}_{dA} = \frac{p_{dA}(1-\theta_A)}{(1+t)} > 0 \qquad \dot{p}_{dP} = \frac{p_{dP}(1-\theta_P)}{(1+t)} > 0$$

$$\dot{x}_{sP} = \frac{(1-\theta_P)}{(1+t)\left(\dfrac{h'}{h} - \dfrac{1}{x_{sP}}\right)} > 0$$

where

$$\theta_A = \frac{P_A/G'' + U_2}{P_A/G'' + U_2 - Q_A/p_{dA}} \qquad \theta_P = \frac{P_P/G'' + U_2 - R_P/p_{dP}}{P_P/G'' + U_2 - (Q_P + R_P)/p_{dP}}$$

$$P_A = (U_{11} - p_{dA} U_{21}) - p_{dA}(U_{12} - p_{dA} U_{22}) < 0 \qquad P_P = (U_{11} - p_{dP} U_{21}) - p_{dP}(U_{12} - p_{dP} U_{22}) < 0$$

$$Q_A = \{(U_{11} - p_{dA} U_{21}) - g'(U_{12} - p_{dA} U_{22})\} \times (g'/g - 1/x_{\ell A})^{-1} < 0 \qquad Q_P = \{(U_{11} - p_{dP} U_{21}) - g'(U_{12} - p_{dP} U_{22})\} \times (g'/g - 1/x_{\ell P})^{-1} < 0$$

$$R_P = \{(U_{11} - p_{dP} U_{21}) - h'(U_{12} - p_{dP} U_{22})\} \times (h'/h - 1/x_{sP})^{-1} < 0 .$$

Since $U_2 > 0$, $G'' > 0$ it is clear that $0 < \theta_A, \theta_P < 1$. Neither good is assumed inferior in consumption to ensure P_A, P_P, Q_A, Q_P, R_P are negative.

(1) Maximal-revenue tariffs: Let us first consider the maximization of revenue: T_A, T_P. Now:

$$T_A = g(x_{\ell A})t \qquad T_P = g(x_{\ell P})t$$

$$\dot{T}_A - g + tg'\dot{x}_{\ell A} \qquad \dot{T}_P = g + tg'\dot{x}_{\ell P} .$$

Let us assume that T_A and T_P attain a unique maximum at the solution of $\dot{T}_A = 0$ and $\dot{T}_P = 0$ respectively. Let us denote the solutions by t^*_{AT} and t^*_{PT}. By definition,[5] $\dot{T}_A \gtreqless 0$ according as $t \lesseqgtr t^*_{AT}$ and $\dot{T}_P \gtreqless 0$ ac-

[5] This is true, in general, only for values of t in a neighbourhood of t^*_{AT} and t^*_{PT} respectively.

cording as $t \lesseqgtr t^*_{PT}$. By substituting for $\dot{x}_{\ell A}$, $\dot{x}_{\ell P}$, in the expressions for $\dot{T}_A$ and $\dot{T}_P$ respectively, we can then show that:

$$\frac{1+t}{t} \gtreqless \frac{\theta_A(g'/g)}{g'/g - 1/x_{\ell A}} \qquad \text{according as } t \lesseqgtr t^*_{AT} \,;$$

$$\frac{1+t}{t} \gtreqless \frac{\theta_P(g'/g)}{g'/g - 1/x_{\ell P}} \qquad \text{according as } t \lesseqgtr t^*_{PT} \,.$$

(2) Optimal tariffs: Denoting the welfare levels achieved in the absence and in the presence of smuggling by U_A and U_P, we can next show that:

$$\dot{U}_A = U_2\{p_{dA} - g'\}\dot{x}_{\ell A} \,;$$

$$\dot{U}_P = U_2[(p_{dP} - g')\dot{x}_{\ell P} + (p_{dP} - h')\dot{x}_{sP}] \,.$$

Let us assume that U_A and U_P attain their unique maximum at the solution t^*_{AU} and t^*_{PU} respectively of $\dot{U}_A = 0$ and $\dot{U}_P = 0$. Then, by definition, $\dot{U}_A \gtreqless 0$ according as $t \lesseqgtr t^*_{AU}$ and $\dot{U}_P \gtreqless 0$ according as $t \lesseqgtr t^*_{PU}$. By substituting for $\dot{x}_{\ell A}$, $\dot{x}_{\ell P}$, $\dot{x}_{sP}$ in the expression for $\dot{U}_A$ and $\dot{U}_P$ respectively, we can thus show that:

$$\frac{1+t}{t} \gtreqless \frac{g'/g}{g'/g - 1/x_{\ell A}} \qquad \text{according as } t \lesseqgtr t^*_{AU} \,;$$

$$\frac{1+t}{t} \gtreqless \frac{\theta_P(g'/g) - (1-\theta_P)\{g'/g - 1/x_{\ell P}\}(h/g)}{(g'/g - 1/x_{\ell P})\{\theta_P - (1-\theta_P)(h/g)\}}$$

$$\text{according as } t \lesseqgtr t^*_{PU} \,.$$

These inequalities hold in a neighborhood of t^*_{AU} and t^*_{PU} respectively.

We can now proceed to answer the questions which we posed in the introduction:

2.1. Comparison of maximal-revenue and optimal tariffs in the absence of smuggling

This implies ranking t^*_{AT} and t^*_{AU}; and, as is already known from Johnson's (1950–51) classic analysis, $t^*_{AT} > t^*_{AU}$. This follows because $(1+t)/t$ is a decreasing function of t; t^*_{AT} and t^*_{AU} are the solutions of

$$\frac{1+t}{t} = \frac{\theta_A(g'/g)}{g'/g - 1/x_{\ell A}} \quad \text{and} \quad \frac{1+t}{t} = \frac{g'/g}{g'/g - 1/x_{\ell A}};$$

and θ_A lies between 0 and 1, and $(g'/g)/(g'/g - 1/x_{\ell A})$ crosses $(1+t)/t$ from below at $t = t^*_{AU}$.

2.2. Comparison of optimal tariffs in the presence and in the absence of smuggling

We can see that, for constant-elasticity offers such that $\eta_g = xg'(x)/g(x)$ is constant for all $x \geqq 0$, $t^*_{PU} < t^*_{AU}$: i.e. the optimal tariff in the presence of smuggling is less than in the absence of smuggling. This follows from the facts that $t^*_{AU} = (\eta_g - 1)$ and $t^*_{PU} = (\eta_g - 1)[1 - (1/\theta_P - 1)(h/g)] < \eta_g - 1$. However, η_g is in general a function of the particular x at which it is evaluated; hence, in general, we cannot rank t^*_{AU} and t^*_{PU}.

2.3. Comparison of the maximal-revenue and optimal tariffs in the presence of smuggling

We can show that, with smuggling $t^*_{PT} > t^*_{PU}$; i.e. the maximal-revenue tariff is higher than the optimal tariff, just as in the (traditional) case without smuggling. Note that t^*_{PT} and t^*_{PU} are respectively solutions of

$$\frac{1+t}{t} = \frac{\left(\frac{g'}{g}\right)\theta_P}{\frac{g'}{g} - \frac{1}{x_{\ell P}}} \quad \text{and} \quad \frac{1+t}{t} = \frac{(\theta_P)\frac{g'}{g} - (1-\theta_P)\frac{h}{g}\left(\frac{g'}{g} - \frac{1}{x_{\ell P}}\right)}{\left(\frac{g'}{g} - \frac{1}{x_{\ell P}}\right)\left\{(\theta_P) - (1-\theta_P)\frac{h}{g}\right\}}.$$

Further, $(1+t)/t$ is a decreasing function t. It can be shown that, when $t = t^*_{PU}$, $(1+t^*_{PU})/t^*_{PU} > \theta_P(g'/g)/(g'/g - 1/x_{\ell P})$. Since $\theta_P(g'/g)/(g'/g - 1/x_{\ell P})$ crosses $(1+t)/t$ from below at $t = t^*_{PT}$, we can conclude that $t^*_{PT} > t^*_{PU}$. Fig. 1 illustrates the situation.

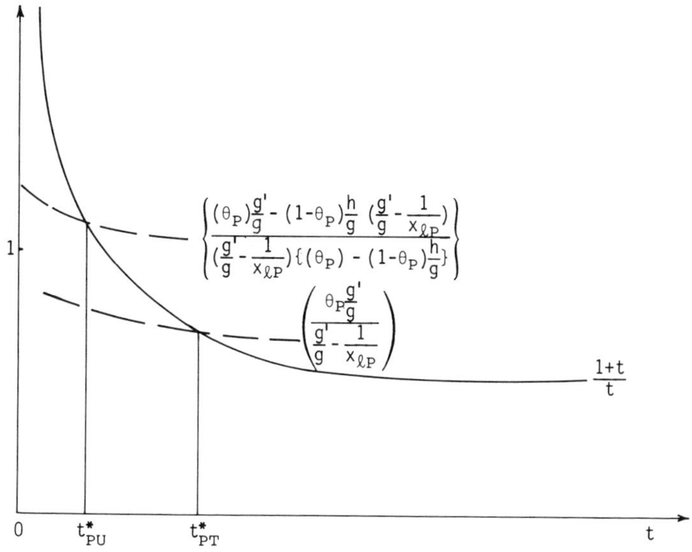

Fig. 1

2.4. *Comparison of maximal-revenue tariffs in the presence and in the absence of smuggling*

As we noted earlier,

$$\frac{1+t^*_{AT}}{t^*_{AT}} = \frac{\theta_A \frac{g'}{g}}{\frac{g'}{g} - \frac{1}{x_{\ell A}}} = \frac{\theta_A \eta_g}{\eta_g - 1} \quad \text{and} \quad \frac{1+t^*_{PT}}{t^*_{PT}} = \frac{\theta_P \frac{g'}{g}}{\frac{g'}{g} - \frac{1}{x_{\ell P}}} = \frac{\theta_P \eta_g}{\eta_g - 1}\,.$$

Now θ_A and θ_P involve second derivatives of the welfare and transformation functions and in general we cannot assert anything about the ratio of θ_A to θ_P. Thus even if we were to assume that η_g is a constant, we cannot rank t^*_{AT} and t^*_{PT} and this conclusion holds a fortiori if η_g was not a constant.

2.5. *Comparison of revenue collected, given the tariff rate, in the presence and in the absence of smuggling*

We may now investigate whether the revenue collected, given the tariff rate, will reduce in the presence of smuggling. This is readily shown as follows.

First, we can show that $x_{\ell A}$ reduces as the tariff increases. Let $\bar{t}$ be the tariff that reduces $x_{\ell A}$ to zero. Clearly $\bar{t}$ is determined by $(1+\bar{t})g'(0) = -G'(X_1^*)$ where X_1^* is the output of X_1 under autarky.[6] Let us confine ourselves to tariffs in the range $(0, \bar{t})$. Given our assumptions about G, U and g already made and assuming further that neither good is inferior, corresponding to any tariff t there exists a unique equilibrium in the absence of smuggling.

Consider now a tariff t under which an equilibrium exists in the absence as well as in the presence of a smuggling. It is clear that $p_{dP}(t) < p_{dA}(t)$. For if $p_{dP}(t) \geqq p_{dA}$, then:

(i) (13A) and (13P) will imply $X_{1A} \leqq X_{1P}$ since $G'' < 0$;

(ii) (14A) and (14P) will imply $x_{\ell A} \leqq x_{\ell P}$ since $g(x)/x$ is an increasing function of x;

(iii) by assumption, $x_{sP} > 0$; and

(iv) (10A), (10P), (11A) and (11P) will imply $C_{1A} < C_{1P}$ and $C_{2A} > C_{2P}$.

However, given the concavity of U and non-inferiority of either good, $C_{1A} < C_{1P}$, $C_{2A} > C_{2P}$ will imply $U_{1A}/U_{2A} = p_{dA} > U_{1P}/U_{2P} = p_{dP}$, contradicting the assumption that $p_{dP} \geqq p_{dA}$.

Thus, for the same tariff, $p_{dP} < p_{dA}$ and consequently $x_{\ell P} < x_{\ell A}$. Since at $t = \bar{t}$, $x_{\ell A} = 0$ it follows that (the maximal tariff $\bar{\bar{t}}$) for co-existence of smuggling and legal trade will be less than t. Let us now confine our attention to tariffs in the interval $(0, \bar{\bar{t}})$. Clearly at $t = \bar{\bar{t}}$, $x_{\ell P} = 0$ and $x_{\ell A} > 0$.

From the above, it immediately follows that given a tariff, the revenue that can be collected in the presence of smuggling is less than the revenue in the absence of smuggling. For the same tariff, the equilibrium domestic price ratio and legal imports are higher in the absence of smuggling; hence the tariff revenue will be higher. This also means that the maximum tariff revenue that can be collected is greater in the absence of smuggling. However, as we have already argued, we cannot in general rank the tariff rates that generate maximum revenue in the two cases.

2.6. *Comparison of tariff rates generating given revenue, in the presence and in the absence of smuggling*

We may now investigate yet another problem: In generating a given,

[6] Implicitly we are assuming $g'(0) < -G'(X_1^*)$. This simply means that there is an incentive to import commodity 1 at the autarky point, if there is no tariff.

feasible revenue, can we argue that smuggling will require necessarily a higher or a lower tariff than if smuggling were not possible?

To analyse this question, consider any tariff revenue $\bar{T}$ that can be collected in the presence and absence of smuggling. If we now assume the revenue $\{T_A(t), T_P(t)\}$ collected by a tariff to increase, reach a maximum and then decrease as t increases,[7] there will be pairs of tariffs $(\hat{t}_A, \hat{\hat{t}}_A)$ and $(\hat{t}_P, \hat{\hat{t}}_P)$ that yield $\bar{T}$. Since $T_A(t) > T_P(t)$ for all relevant t, it is clear that $\hat{t}_A \leqq t_{AT} \leqq \hat{\hat{t}}_A$, $t_P \leqq t_{PT} \leqq \hat{\hat{t}}_P$ and $\hat{t}_A < \hat{t}_P \leqq \hat{\hat{t}}_P < \hat{\hat{t}}_A$. Thus, of the two tariffs that collect a given revenue in the absence of smuggling, the lower one is less than the lower tariff that collects the same revenue in the presence of smuggling and the higher one is larger than the higher one.

3. The results reached in sec. 2 may now be summarised in table 1, as follows:[8]

Table 1
Summary of results obtained in section 2.

Variables \ State of the economy	Absence of smuggling	Presence of smuggling	Ranking
1. Optimal tariff rate	t^*_{AU}	t^*_{PU}	no ranking [a]
2. Revenue maximizing tariff rate	t^*_{AT}	t^*_{PT}	no ranking [a]
3. Revenue collected given a tariff	T_A	T_P	$T_A > T_P$
4. A given revenue R is collected by: [b]	$[\hat{t}_A, \hat{\hat{t}}_A]$	$[\hat{t}_P, \hat{\hat{t}}_P]$	$\hat{t}_A < \hat{t}_P$ $\hat{\hat{t}}_A > \hat{\hat{t}}_P$
Ranking	$t^*_{AU} < t^*_{AT}$	$t^*_{PU} < t^*_{PT}$	

[a] For constant elasticity offers it is shown that $t^*_{PU} < t^*_{AU}$.
[b] The revenue collected by a tariff is assumed to increase, reach a maximum and then decrease as the tariff rate increases. $[\hat{t}_i, \hat{\hat{t}}_i]$ refer to the lower and higher rate that collects the given revenue; see illustrative diagram on the following page.

[7] This is an additional restriction to those we have specified earlier; in general, there is no reason to assume that the revenue collected is not identical at more than two values.

[8] We are thankful to an anonymous referee for having suggested this tabular presentation.

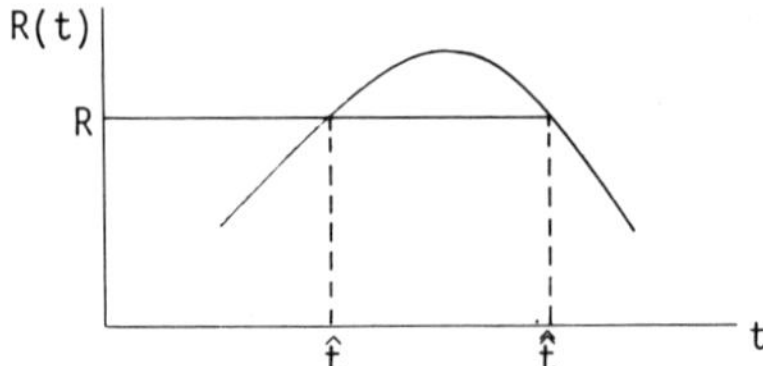

References

Bhagwati, J. and T.N. Srinivasan, 1969, Optimal intervention to achieve non-economic objectives, Review of Economic Studies XXXVI.

Bhagwati, J. and Bent Hansen, 1973, A theoretical analysis of smuggling, Quarterly Journal of Economics 87.

Johnson, H.G., 1950–1951, Optimum welfare and maximum revenue tariffs, Review of Economic Studies XIX.

Erratum

Page 388, table 1: In the second row and third column, superscript a should be omitted.

ON THE UNDERINVOICING OF IMPORTS*

Jagdish N. BHAGWATI

1. Introduction

In many developing countries, it is customary to rely on severe import and exchange control regimes. Typically these regimes give rise to 'black' markets for various prohibited or restricted uses of foreign exchange. It is well known, for instance, that in countries limiting allocations of exchange for foreign travel, black exchange leaks into this area; and so on.

The supply of illegal exchange comes from several sources. Underinvoicing of exports and overinvoicing of imports are the most obvious sources. For countries, such as Turkey, where the earnings of workers abroad constitute a major source of invisible receipts through remittances, this represents at least as important a source of foreign exchange in the black market[1].

The demand for illegal exchange, on the other hand, comes largely from tourists (as noted above) and from the flight of capital abroad[2]. It also comes from the underinvoicing of imports, which requires the purchase of black-market exchange to make the full payment to the foreign exporter.

* This paper was written during my assignment as an Organization for Economic Development and Co-operation (OECD) Consultant in Turkey during April–July 1964. Its originality consists neither in discovering that underinvoicing of imports can occur nor in finding out that c.i.f. import statistics can be less than the corresponding f.o.b. export statistics, a fact well known to statisticians of international trade. It consists in (i) inferring the former from the latter; (ii) linking it to the phenomenon of tariffs and import control; and (iii) using the exercise to make informed inferences about the areas into which 'black' exchange is leaking and hence to assess better the 'losses' imposed by such a leakage. In my statistical work on the Turkish trade data, I have profited greatly from conversation with R. Gross, who had already noticed discrepancies between Turkish c.i.f. and partner-countries' f.o.b. values for a single year. My thanks are also due to Professors Bent Hansen and Besim Ustunel for useful discussions in the preparation of this paper.

[1] In fact, it was while trying to assess where the remittances were leaking – the official remittances being well below the expected level – that I undertook the present exercise in Turkey.

[2] It is known, for example, that accounts in Swiss banks are operated by the nationals of many developing countries such as Turkey and India.

The present paper deals with this phenomenon of underinvoiced imports. Sect. 2 states the general analysis that explains such underinvoicing. Sect. 3 concerns the application of this analysis to recent Turkish experience.

2. Reasons for underinvoicing of imports

Underinvoicing of imports – a discrepancy between the stated value of imports and their actual value (payable to the exporter abroad), such that the latter exceeds the former – may arise characteristically in two cases: when the imported commodity carries a tariff duty; and when the imports of the commodity are strictly controlled, resulting in a premium on it in the domestic market.

Take the case of a tariff duty, to begin with. It will pay the importer to understate the value of his imports when the resulting saving in tariff duties outweighs the extra price that he must pay to purchase the foreign exchange in the black market. For the individual domestic importer, who may be assumed to have access to illegal foreign exchange at a given premium, and whose imports face an *ad valorem* duty, the understatement of import values will become profitable as soon as the tariff rate exceeds the premium.

There is, however, a risk attached both to the understatement of value and to engaging in illegal foreign exchange transactions. Hence the understatement will not occur unless the discrepancy between the tariff rate and the black-market premium exceeds the evaluated risk factor. The extent of understatement will also be constrained by the increasing risk attached to greater understatement and, failing that, by the degree of understatement it is reasonably possible to claim successfully under existing regulations.

Similar arguments apply to the case where quantitative import restrictions are in use. If the understatement of import unit values enables the importer to import a larger quantity under his licence (stating the permissible total import value) and if the premium on the imported commodity in the domestic market is higher than the premium to be paid for black-market exchange, underinvoicing becomes profitable.

3. An empirical investigation

An analysis of the Turkish situation is attempted here, with a view to investigating the presence of underinvoicing of imports and its possible causes and effects.

The analysis rests crucially on a comparison of the f.o.b. export values recorded by Turkey's principal trading partners with the c.i.f. import values recorded by

Turkey. One would expect the latter to exceed the former (by the amount of the insurance and freight). If the c.i.f. values turn out to be less than the f.o.b. statistics, and if we cannot produce any other reason to explain this, we may reasonably infer that underinvoicing of imports appears to have occurred. This conclusion would be strengthened if these commodities could also be shown to be carrying high tariff duties which exceed the black-market premium for foreign exchange[3], and if they were such as to make underinvoicing feasible and easy – manufactures, especially capital goods (usually made to order), qualify readily.

In this sequence of inferences, the requirement that other reasons explaining the perverse discrepancy between c.i.f. and f.o.b. statistics must be ruled out (before we can reasonably infer underinvoicing) is naturally the most difficult to fulfil. There are, in fact, several reasons which may explain such discrepancies:

(1) There are frequently errors of commodity classification: an item belonging to code no. 319 may be wrongly put under code no. 316, making for an understatement in 319 if the error is committed only by the importing country. This type of error, however, is usually easy to trace by checking the data carefully for it.

(2) There may be exports from (say) Italy which have not reached (say) Turkey or have not yet passed through customs and been recorded. The goods may then be recorded as exported to Turkey but not as imported by it, causing the discrepancy in the 'wrong' direction, i.e. making c.i.f. imports smaller than f.o.b. exports. This argument, however, will not be persuasive if the level of imports does not change over time: in this case, the imports of this year, which are not recorded currently but carry over into the next year's c.i.f. statistics, will be more or less offset by the imports of last year carried over into this year's statistics. If, however, imports are rising, there will be a tendency towards understatement though it is unlikely to be large enough to produce a perverse discrepancy[4].

(3) There may be a misallocation of imports by country: imports from (say) Italy are wrongly attributed to Germany, and so on. This happens frequently. It is to be traced usually to confusion over the origin and ownership of imported goods. For example, Malayan exports of rubber to Turkey may be wrongly attributed to the United Kingdom because an English exporter is handling the transaction; and so on. Though this sort of error can usually be detected, omissions cannot be ruled out.

[3] Alternatively, these commodities may be shown to be subject to stringent import control, carrying higher domestic premiums than the premium in the black market for foreign exchange.

[4] Thus, even if we assume that the carry-over applies to six months in every year, and equally generously that trade grows by 10% per annum, the understatement in import value will only be 4.5% of the actual import value and is unlikely to exceed the insurance and freight charges in international commerce (especially for machinery and other manufactures where we find the perverse discrepancies in Turkish statistics).

(4) We must not rule out the possibility of overinvoicing of exports at the other end.

Clearly all these complicating factors must be carefully considered. Bearing them in mind, I have found in the Turkish case that, for 1960 and 1961, there is strong evidence of understatement of import values of manufactures, especially in the field of transport equipment and machinery. Let me now state the analysis

Table 1.
1960 trade between France and Turkey (thousands of dollars).

SITC code no.	Commodities	France's exports	Turkey's imports	Dis-crepancy
313	Petroleum products	9 059	617	– 8 442
6	Main manufactured goods	3 212	3 196	– 16
66	Non-metallic mineral manufactures	343	266	– 77
68	Non-ferrous metals	4 412	3 464	– 948
69	Metal manufactures	3 915	544	– 3 371
7	Machinery and transport equipment	5 270	3 820	– 1 450
8	Miscellaneous manufactured goods	1 246	595	– 651
	Others	4 197	3 834	– 363
	Total	31 654	16 336	–15 318

Table 2.
1960 trade between Italy and Turkey (thousands of dollars).

SITC code no.	Commodities	Italy's exports	Turkey's imports	Dis-crepancy
313	Petroleum products	13 093	713	–12 380
6	Main manufactured goods	3 576	3 559	– 17
65	Files, textiles, etc.	2 737	1 590	– 1 147
66	Non-metallic minerals manufactures	265	173	– 92
68	Non-ferrous metals	4 700	1 317	– 3 383
69	Metal manufactures	3 151	2 258	– 893
7	Machinery and transport equipment	18 913	15 213	– 3 700
8	Miscellaneous manufactured goods	1 591	1 035	– 556
	Others	4 391	4 176	– 215
	Total	52 417	30 034	–22 383

Table 3.
1960 trade between Germany and Turkey (thousands of dollars).

SITC code no.	Commodities	Germany's exports	Turkey's imports	Discrepancy
6	Main manufactured goods	4 094	4 023	− 71
66	Non-metallic minerals manufactures	3 111	1 259	− 1 852
68	Non-ferrous metals	20 623	21 357	+ 734
69	Metal manufactures	7 620	5 260	− 2 360
7	Machinery and transport equipment	62 884	51 097	−11 787
8	Miscellaneous manufactured goods	6 916	4 043	− 2 873
	Others	9 984	10 987	+ 1 003
	Total	115 232	98 026	−17 206

Table 4.
1960 trade between U.S.A. and Turkey (thousands of dollars).

SITC code no.	Commodities	U.S.A.'s exports	Turkey's imports	Discrepancy
313	Petroleum products	7 130	24 660	+17 530
412	Vegetable oils	5 673	14 828	+ 9 155
5	Chemical products	4 424	3 894	− 530
6	Main manufactured goods	5 258	4 529	− 729
66	Non-metallic minerals manufactures	350	563	+ 213
68	Non-ferrous metals	4 599	4 108	− 491
69	Metal manufactures	1 084	922	− 162
7	Machinery and transport equipment	62 032	53 942	− 8 090
8	Miscellaneous manufactured goods	2 422	1 711	− 711
	Others	31 808	11 310	−20 498
	Total	124 780	120 467	− 4 313

Table 5.
1960 trade between Netherlands and Turkey (thousands of dollars).

SITC code no.	Commodities	Netherlands' exports	Turkey's imports	Discrepancy
6	Main manufactured goods	4 298	4 062	− 236
7	Machinery and transport equipment	5 400	3 561	− 1 839
8	Miscellaneous manufactured goods	498	382	− 116
	Others	3 402	4 094	+ 692
	Total	13 598	12 099	− 1 499

Table 6.
1961 trade between Germany and Turkey (thousands of dollars).

SITC code no.	Commodities	Germany's exports	Turkey's imports	Dis-crepancy
6	Main manufactured goods	3 726	3 710	− 16
66+ 67	Non-metallic mineral manufactures + Iron and steel	14 700	16 620	+ 1 920
68	Non-ferrous metals	949	1 211	+ 262
69	Metal manufactures	4 795	2 848	− 1 947
7	Machinery and transport equipment	52 629	46 158	− 6 471
8	Miscellaneous manufactured goods	4 410	3 377	− 1 033
	Others	12 079	11 152	− 927
	Total	93 288	85 076	− 8 212

Table 7.
1961 trade between Italy and Turkey (thousands of dollars).

SITC code no.	Commodities	Italy's exports	Turkey's imports	Dis-crepancy
352	Petroleum products	15 526	592	−14 934
6	Main manufactured goods	4 368	4 503	+ 135
65	Files, textiles, etc.	1 749	1 461	− 288
66	Non-metallic mineral manufactures	373	363	− 10
67	Iron and steel	2 579	2 169	− 410
69	Metal manufactures	1 450	1 188	− 262
7	Machinery and transport equipment	21 801	24 465	+ 2 664
8	Miscellaneous manufactured goods	1 719	1 660	− 59
	Others	6 468	6 473	+ 5
	Total	56 033	42 874	−13 159

Table 8.
1961 trade between U.S.A. and Turkey (thousands of dollars).

SITC code no.	Commodities	U.S.A.'s exports	Turkey's imports	Dis-crepancy
352	Petroleum products	7 167	21 722	+14 555
5	Chemical products	7 637	6 526	− 1 111
6	Main manufactured goods	12 850	12 161	− 689
7	Machinery and transport equipment	39 380	30 513	− 8 867
8	Miscellaneous manufactured goods	2 721	1 548	− 1 173
	Others	71 893	67 609	− 4 374
	Total	141 738	140 079	− 1 659

Table 9.
1961 trade between France and Turkey (thousands of dollars).

SITC code no.	Commodities	France's exports	Turkey's imports	Dis-crepancy
332	Petroleum products	8 601	127	− 8 474
6	Main manufactured goods	6 355	6 050	− 305
7	Machinery and transport equipment	9 063	6 874	− 2 189
	Others	5 409	4 648	− 761
	Total	29 428	17 699	−11 729

Table 10.
Turkey's imports of petroleum products, 1960 (thousands of dollars).

Exporting country	Exporting country's statistics	Turkey's statistics	Dis-crepancy
France	9 059	617	− 8 442
Italy	13 093	713	−12 380
United Kingdom	2 166	8 819	+ 6 653
United States	7 130	24 660	+17 530
Total	31 448	34 809	+ 3 361

Table 11.
Turkey's imports of petroleum products, 1961 (thousands of dollars) (SITC 332).

Exporting country	Exporting country's statistics	Turkey's statistics	Dis-crepancy
France	8 601	127	− 8 474
Italy	15 526	592	−14 934
United Kingdom	1 339	10 030	+ 8 691
United States	7 167	21 722	+14 555
Total	32 633	32 471	− 162

fully. The data for Turkey–Italy, Turkey–Germany, Turkey–United States, Turkey–France and Turkey–Netherlands (tables 1–9), relating to Turkey's principal trading partners, testify to substantial excesses of f.o.b. over c.i.f. values in petroleum products and in the categories of main manufactured goods (code no. 6), machinery and transport equipment (code no. 7) and miscellaneous manufactures (code no. 8).

Not all of these testify to underinvoicing of imports. The discrepancies in petroleum products, for instance, are offsetting between France, Italy, United States and United Kingdom (tables 10, 11). They arise from the misallocation of imports among sources, resulting from confusion over the ownership of refineries and petroleum[5]. But I have not been able to think of similar explanations for the other discrepancies[6].

It is not valid to argue that the time lag between exports and imports will explain the discrepancies observed[7]. Significant overinvoicing by exporters to Turkey is unlikely, given the existence of convertibility during this period for the relevant currencies and countries[8].

We are therefore left with some significant discrepancies for which the only explanation appears to be underinvoicing. How does this explanation stand up in relation to Turkey's organization of its international trade? Quite well, as it turns out.

Turkey, during the early 1960s, was operating a substantially 'liberalized' trade system. It relied on tariffs – other price-instruments such as devaluation, licence fees, stamp duty also being used occasionally – to regulate imports. I expected, therefore, that the underinvoicing would in this case turn out to be related to tariffs, rather than to import control. This turned out to be the case.

In the statement on Turkey's tariffs in 1961 (which also adequately serves our purpose for 1960), see sect. 4, the reader will find that the categories of goods which show perverse discrepancies (in tables 1–9) also generally had tariff rates ranging up to 30% and rarely below 10%[9].

As the black-market premium for foreign exchange has rarely exceeded 15% according to official observations, and has been usually below this level, it seems reasonable to conclude that the discrepancies represent underinvoicing of imports,

5 I am indebted to R. Gross, who spotted the offsetting nature of the petroleum discrepancies.

6 In ships and boats I found that the discrepancy was to be explained by foreign registration: but this, in turn, might be linked to high tariffs on import of ships.

7 This is for much the same reason as set out in footnote 4.

8 It is true that the relief from the cascading turn-over taxes in some Western European countries was related, during this period, to the *value* of exports. Hence there could have been some overinvoicing of exports to secure greater relief. But I doubt whether much can be made of this point.

9 Some puzzling tariffs seem to be those on non-ferrous metals – at 5%. I have not been able to think of a suitable explanation in these cases.

by and large. This conclusion is further reinforced by the fact that understatement of value in the field of manufactures – especially machinery, which is frequently made to order and rarely carries standard prices that the customs can readily check – is readily possible. And it is precisely in these areas that the perverse discrepancies occur in the Turkish case.

Let me emphasize again that the preceding analysis provides, not a conclusive proof, but only a strong indication of the presence of underinvoicing of imports in the Turkish case. Indeed, for many the case may appear totally convincing. What are we to conclude from this analysis? Some of the more interesting implications seem to me to be the following.

First of all, if black market foreign exchange is being used to buy manufactures, and in particular machinery and equipment, this is certainly less disastrous from the Turkish viewpoint than if it were leaking entirely into Turkish tourists' expenditure abroad and/or illegal export of capital. After all, even if the exchange had come into official channels, it would probably have been allocated for much the same uses as it gets into through illegal channels[10].

Secondly, certain fiscal measures may be of fortuitous assistance in reducing such underinvoicing. Take, for example, the accelerated depreciation allowance, introduced in Turkey in 1963. This type of measure is, in general, an 'inefficient' way of increasing investment in a country with an excess supply of labour (as Turkey is generally considered to be). Because it links the subsidy on investment to the value of (fixed) capital, it creates a bias in favour of capital-intensive techniques. In view of the understating of import values on equipment and machinery that appears to obtain in Turkey, however, it is possible to claim that the accelerated depreciation allowance has, in the Turkish case, the offsetting virtue of making undervaluation of capital goods imports less attractive: an undervaluation would mean a corresponding loss of the benefit from the accelerated depreciation allowance.

4. Turkish tariffs during 1961

There was a stamp duty, i.e. a *de facto* tariff, of 5% on all visible imports. Moreover, the tariff rates on the items covered in our analysis ranged up to 30–40%,

[10] Of course, this is not to argue that there is, therefore, *no* cost attached to illegal inflow of exchange. Aside from the usual costs, I may mention that nothing would seem to make the nations giving aid to Turkey happier, and more willing to support the Turkish developmental effort through large-scale aid, than the evidence of increasing exchange earnings which indicate the possibility of Turkish viability, without external aid, in the long run. One of the costs of exchange receipts going through illegal channels, therefore, could well be a reduction (even a sizeable reduction) in foreign aid.

in some cases going even higher. The only exceptions among the items which appear to have been understated in value were nickel, aluminium and zinc, which carried a duty of only 5%, and copper for which the duty was 10%.

Among transport equipment and different kinds of machinery, the following may be taken as illustrative: 20% on locomotives, trains, buses and wagons, 25% on tractors, 40% on automobiles, buses and pick-ups, 50% on ships and other craft, 20–25% on generators, motors and transformers, 20–30% on other machinery (including agricultural).

Some 'protective' duties were quite high and obviously related to categories of imports for which underinvoicing of imports seemed to be important. Examples are: 60% on knives, 70% on spoons and forks, 100% on lamps, 50% on bells, 50% on mirrors, 100% on metal necklaces, etc., 100% on decorative sculpture (figurines, etc.).

There is a minor complication in interpreting these duties. It was possible, in several cases, to get exemption from these duties and pay *lower* duties under certain circumstances. I have found it difficult to judge how important this exemption was, but my impression is that its effect was not significant from the viewpoint of the present analysis.

Editor's Note

Further analysis of the effects of faked invoicing on the balance of payments is in J. N. Bhagwati, "Fiscal Policies, The Faking of Foreign Trade Declarations, and The Balance of Payments," *Bulletin of the Oxford University Institute of Statistics* (February 1967). See also chapter 10, with the same title, in J. N. Bhagwati, *Trade, Tariffs and Growth*, Cambridge, MA: MIT Press, 1969.

Alternative Theories of Illegal Trade: Economic Consequences and Statistical Detection

By

Jagdish N. Bhagwati

Contents: I. Different Types of Illegal Trade. — II. Some Key Concepts. — III. Alternate Models: A. Illegal Trade through Legal Entry Points; B. Illegal Trade through Illegal Entry Points. — IV. Concluding Remarks.

Recently, the theoretical analysis of illegal trade has received fresh impetus from the imaginative work of Mark Pitt [1981]. The earlier analysis (initiated by the Bhagwati and Hansen [1973] paper and extended in subsequent contributions by Johnson [1974], Sheikh [1974] and others) had assumed that legally and illegally traded goods, as long as they were homogeneous, would be cleared in the domestic market at identical prices, and that this identical price would have to be equal to the tariff-inclusive price on legal trade since any domestic price below that would make legal trade unprofitable.

Observing that legal trade in Indonesia co-exists with illegal trade and that despite this the domestic price is *below* the tariff-inclusive price (so that legal trade is presumably unprofitable), Pitt constructs a model that permits such "price disparity" to exist in the model. Basically, he argues that some legal trade is required if the trader is to handle illegal trade without unnecessary risk of detection; hence the loss on legal trade is to be seen as a way of permitting the profits on illegal trade to be earned.

Pitt's ingenious work opens up therefore the question as to how illegal trade is optimally analyzed, and how it may then be best detected in empirical analysis. In the following analysis, I take the view that reality is complex and that there are different ways in which illegal trade will

Remark: Thanks are due to the Guggenheim Foundation and the National Science Foundation for research support. In synthesizing and extending the theoretical work on modelling illegal trade, I have drawn on much earlier research where I collaborated with Bent Hansen and T. N. Srinivasan. To these distinguished economists, as also to Mark Pitt [1981] whose paper provided the immediate impetus to write the present paper, I wish to express my thanks. I have also profited from conversations with Richard Brecher and Padma Desai and from the stimulating reactions of participants in seminars arranged by the Ford Foundation at the University of Philippines, the Bank of Indonesia and Thammasat University in Thailand. The comments of Mark Pitt have been most helpful, especially in correcting an important error.

arise; that therefore there are different ways in which they need to be modelled and their positive and normative consequences analyzed; and there are correspondingly different ways in which they might be empirically detected. I therefore take successive models of illegal trade below and consider them from the viewpoint of both their economic consequences and attendant implications for their detection.

I. Different Types of Illegal Trade

There are two basic types of illegal trade that need to be distinguished in the following, all triggered by either quantitative restrictions, which may be set in pure quantity or (as is more frequently the case) in value terms, or by tariffs. (i) The illegal trade may simply consist in bringing the goods through *legal checkpoints* but bypassing the control of the customs by simply bribing the customs officer or by concealing the importation in one form or another. (ii) On the other hand, the illegal trade may be conducted through *illegal checkpoints,* as in the popular conception of *dhows* pulling in from Bahrain et al. onto inadequately patrolled coastlines and offloading their illegal cargos.

The distinction between illegal trade through legal and illegal places of entry is of importance insofar as it has a bearing on the kinds of illegal trade that can arise in the two cases. Thus, if illegal trade takes place through illegal entry points, such trade is surely likely to be that associated with "ships in the night" type of operation, which will in turn imply that definite real costs will be incurred in undertaking it. On the other hand, the illegal trade that arises in the shape of faked invoicing, where trade values are faked in order to reduce assessed payments or to increase assessed subsidies, evidently requires that such illegal trade occur through legal checkpoints where customs officers will confront the faked invoices in determining the tax payments or subsidy benefits on the alleged trade. Such faked invoicing is unlikely to involve the kinds of real costs that are associated with smuggling through illegal entry points and will therefore have differential implications, in consequence. In the analysis that follows in this paper, therefore, I will initially begin with those types of illegal trade that are typically associated with legal entry points, and then turn to the illegal trade that comes in through illegal entry points.

II. Some Key Concepts

In addition, the analysis below will focus on certain key concepts of "price disparities," distinguishing several types of relevant price discrepancies other than that noted by Mark Pitt, as also other disparities.

These will be of importance in yielding statistical methods of detecting the alternative types of illegal trade in the real world. I will also confine the analysis to import tariffs throughout.

Thus, define the following symbols (assuming in each case that they relate to a specific imported good):

p_f the f.o.b. price of the commodity, as recorded in partner-country's export data, plus estimated insurance and freight where excluded;

p_c the landed price of the commodity, as declared in valuation to customs when trade is through legal entry points;

p_c^t the landed price of the commodity, as it "truly" is as distinct from its declared value which may be faked, *excluding* the cost of misinvoicing, α, below;

p_d domestic price of the commodity (assuming no further distinction between wholesale, retail, internal transportation charges between different locations etc.);

q_f the foreign, recorded export quantity of the commodity;

q_c the recorded import quantity of the commodity;

t the legal tariff rate;

t_e the "effective" (i.e. actual) tariff rate;

α the unit cost charged by exporter to fake importer's invoice and make underinvoiced importation possible;

β the unit bribe paid to customs officers to overlook misinvoicing.

The distinction between legal and illegal trade, when relevant, is to be denoted by an added suffix, *l* for legal and i for illegal trade. With this notation, the following concepts may now be defined:

(1) *Landed Value versus Domestic Price (LVDP) Price Disparity*

This price disparity implies that $p_c(1 + t) \neq p_d$, i.e. that the domestic price of the commodity is different from — in fact, is below — the tariff-inclusive, landed, *declared* value of the commodity, implying losses on the imports of the commodity.

(2) *"True" Landed Value versus Domestic Price (TLVDP) Price Disparity*

Where the declared and the "true" values differ, the LVDP measure must be distinguished from the TLVDP measure such that $p_c^t(1 + t) \neq p_d$. This is presumably Pitt's price disparity.

(3) *Partner-Country-Comparison (PCC) Price Disparity*

In this case, there is a discrepancy between the declared unit value (price) of a commodity in the records of the exporting and importing

28*

countries, when these are duly adjusted for differences in freight and insurance. This implies that $p_f \neq p_c$.

(4) *PCC Quantity Disparity*

Again, there may be disparity in recorded quantities in partner-country trade data, i.e. $q_f \neq q_c$.

(5) *PCC Value Disparity*

Similarly, there may be *total* value disparity in partner-country data, i.e. $p_f q_f \neq p_c q_c$, reflecting $p_f \neq p_c$ and/or $q_f \neq q_c$.

(6) *Legal versus Illegal Trade (LI) Price Disparities*

Finally, one may have discrepancies between the prices in legal and illegal trade, implying for instance that *either* $p_{dl} \neq p_{di}$, i.e. the domestic price of a commodity is different depending on whether it is legally or illegally imported; *or* $p^t_{cl} \neq p^t_{ci}$, i.e., the true cost of importation in legal and illegal trade is different.

III. Alternate Models

In the following analysis, I consider altogether 6 different models, of which 4 are based on the assumption that illegal trade is conducted through legal entry points whereas the remaining 2 are formulated on the premise that it is conducted through illegal points of entry[1]. The analysis, it should be reemphasized, is confined to tariffs and to imports: but it can be readily extended, *mutatis mutandis,* to quantity restrictions and to exports. Moreover, none of the models considered here allows for the illegally imported, homogeneous goods to be transacted in the domestic market at prices different from legally imported goods, thus imposing on them identical prices at identical locations regardless of how they are imported. This assumption may not make sense in reality as transacting in illegally-imported goods may impose a discount on them. Moreover, when it comes to durables, the extended service and maintenance components of the goods may simply not be available on illegally-imported goods; also the assurance of quality may not be identical when a consumer buys around the dark corner as when he buys from a well-heeled shopkeeper handling legally-imported goods. While this possible element of reality is assumed away in the six models considered below, many other complexities are

[1] These models represent polar types and reality reflects, at times, combinations thereof. Thus, faked invoicing may involve *both* unit-value and quantity faking; and it may involve *both* bribing of customs and sharing gains from faking with the exporter, whereas the four possibilities are modelled below as exclusive of one another.

allowed for and the models offer important abstractions of the kinds of illegal-trade phenomena to be encountered in practice.

A. Illegal Trade through Legal Entry Points

Where illegal trade occurs through legal entry points, i.e., where it is actually declared and passed through customs, the manner in which it occurs must involve some form of faked invoicing. A few observations are in order before the analysis is undertaken.

Note first that faked invoicing may be undertaken *without* the bribe-induced cooperation of customs officers. Alternatively, it may be undertaken with such cooperation. The implications of the two methods of faking invoices to secure illegal importation are different since the former is likely to involve a (direct) real cost to the country insofar as the faking will require the collaboration of the exporter at greater risk and hence compensation whereas the latter requires a bribe which is, in economic terms, only a transfer payment between nationals of the importing country[1].

Moreover, an implication of both basic model types here is that they blur the meaningfulness of the popular distinction between legally and illegally imported goods. For, in either case, the goods come in through legal channels but with illegal assessments of charges.

Furthermore, the analysis below builds on the distinction between faking that concerns quantity declarations and that which works through false price (or unit value) declarations: the implications are again different. Finally, it should be noted that the analysis deployed here assumes throughout that an import tariff creates an economic incentive to underinvoice so as to avoid the full tariff. However, as was noted in the articles by Bhagwati [1964; 1967] which initiated the analysis of faked invoicing by using partner-country trade data comparisons, this does not always follow. For example, in countries with exchange control regimes and black market premia on foreign exchange, the faking incentive will be to overinvoice imports when the tariff rate is below the black market premium on foreign exchange; and it will be to underinvoice, as assumed throughout here, when the tariff rate exceeds the black market premium (as would automatically be the case under full convertibility).

[1] It is conceivable, of course, that the illegal trade is transacted by foreign nationals, as noted by Bhagwati and Hansen [1973] in their early analysis of smuggling. In that event, the argument in the text would need to be suitably modified.

Model I: *Faked Invoicing of Unit Values or Prices, without Bribing of Customs*

In this case, the faking of the invoice, so as to underinvoice imports, occurs through understatement of the unit value at which the quantities (which are correctly invoiced) are imported.

Such underinvoicing may occur costlessly to the importer, and hence to the country (assuming that the importer is a national), in the sense that the exporter is prepared to give the importer the faked invoice at negligible cost. Alternatively, it may occur at a non-negligible real cost, as when the importer has to share some fraction of his resulting gains with the exporter to induce him to supply the necessary faked invoice. The latter may be a possibility if the trade in the commodity is by reputable firms and is subject to a non-negligible prospect of detection: in which case the risk of potential damage to the exporter from detection is non-negligible and hence may require inducement in the form of a share in the gains from underinvoicing. The welfare implications as also some of the "positive" implications will be different in each of the two cases.

Case (1): Consider first the case where the real cost to the importer of faking the invoice is negligible. What are then the consequences for the different "disparities" distinguished above? Now, the effective tariff rate will be: $t_e = tp_c/p_c^t$ since $p_d = p_c^t + tp_c$. Therefore, the following consequences can be noted.

(i) With $p_c < p_c^t$ due to underinvoicing of imports, $p_d > p_c(1+t)$ and therefore *LVDP price disparity*, which relates to the declared unit value, will exist. However, it will exist with a reversed sign from Pitt's: importation will appear as if it was yielding "abnormal" profits.

(ii) Next, *TLVDP price disparity* will also exist, with Pitt's sign, with $p_c^t(1+t) > p_d$ (as $p_c < p_c^t$ and $p_d = p_c^t + tp_c$).

(iii) At the same time, *PCC price disparity* will arise since the recorded, true export price (or unit value) will exceed the declared, understated import price, i.e., $p_f > p_c$.

(iv) *PCC quantity disparity* will not arise, of course: $q_f = q_c$.

(v) But *PCC value disparity* will, since $p_f q_f > p_c q_c$.

(vi) Finally, there are no *LI price disparities*: legal and illegal trade are not meaningfully distinguishable in the fully competitive case, since all trade will be costlessly underinvoiced.

The implications for statistical detections of this kind of illegal trade are evident. Price disparities of the LVDP, TLVDP and PCC variety have to be looked for. The TLVDP price disparity would require extracting the "true" landed value. This and the PCC price and value disparities may be spotted through a careful use of the partner-country trade comparison technique which has been developed in Bhagwati [1964] who analyzed the faked invoicing of Turkish imports and in many other papers[1].

The welfare implications of such illegal trade are easily seen if a conventional social-utility-function approach is taken. In the Bhagwati-Hansen [1973] 2 x 2 model, the effect as illustrated in Figure 1 (adapted from Bhagwati and Hansen) is seen readily as that of a simple reduction

Figure 1

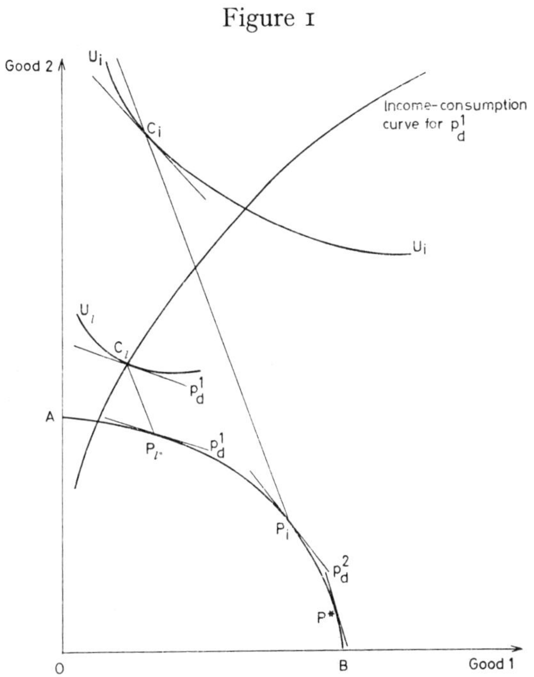

in the "effective" tariff level. Thus, in the legal case without faked invoicing, the tariff-inclusive domestic goods price-ratio is p_d^1 and consumption, production and welfare are at C_l, P_l and U_l, respectively. With reduction in effective tariff, the goods price-ratio shifts to p_d^2 and consumption, production and welfare to C_i, P_i and U_i, respectively. $U_i \geqslant U_l$ necessarily obtains since, ruling out inferior goods and associated multiple equilibria, a lower tariff will not be inferior to a higher tariff.

[1] Essentially, the analyst has to be able to correct for the many statistical reasons for discrepancies in PCC trade data, to be able to sift through to the faking that is sought to be pinned down. For a fuller discussion, see Bhagwati [1964; 1967] and Bhagwati *et al.* [1974].

Of course, this conclusion is strictly limited to conventional welfare analysis. If import substitution, for instance, were valued as a "non-economic" objective or if revenues were important, the analysis would have to be suitably amended — as already done by several theorists of illegal trade for Model V below. Again, the sheer fact of illegality may constitute a negative element in the evaluation of the overall welfare impact. This factor is ignored in this paper but can be suitably allowed for in a fuller analysis. Equally, non-economic and revenue objectives can be allowed for: these are ignored here so as to focus rather on the major distinctions among the different models of illegal trade[1].

Case 2: Consider now the other case where the faked invoicing requires non-negligible real cost *via* sharing a fraction of the importer's gains from faking with the foreign exporter. This will modify critically the disparity and welfare outcomes. Note now that, with α representing the unit cost charged by the exporter to fake invoices for the importer, we have $p_d = p_c^t + tp_c + \alpha$. Therefore, the effective tariff is $t_e = (tp_c + \alpha)/p_c^t$. The following consequences then arise for disparities.

(i) With $p_c < p_c^t$ due to underinvoicing of imports, we again have $p_d > p_c\,(1+t)$. Therefore, *LVDP price disparity* again exists, with the reversed sign from Pitt's.

(ii) At the same time, *TLVDP price disparity* will also arise, with Pitt's sign, since $\{p_c^t\,(1+t) - p_d\} = t\,(p_c - p_c^t) + \alpha < 0$ as $\alpha > 0$ but cannot exceed in absolute magnitude the total gain from underinvoicing measured by $t\,(p_c^t - p_c)$.

(iii) *PCC price disparity* will exist whether p_f, the recorded export value adjusted for insurance and freight, includes the share in the gain from faking or not. In the former case, the disparity will be smaller.

(iv) *PCC quantity disparity* does not exist, of course.

(v) *PCC value disparity* will exist, reflecting the price disparity.

(vi) *LT price disparity* cannot arise.

The major difference in disparities when the faking of unit values occurs with real cost therefore is that the real cost now implies that the reduction in the domestic goods price-ratio, p_d, that follows is no longer an unmixed gain. For, it is accompanied by a terms-of-trade loss as a result of the "true" landed price rising by the amount of the gain from faking that is shared with the foreign exporter. Therefore, as Bhagwati

[1] The contrasting implications of different models for issues such as the rank-ordering of the maximal revenue tariff with and without illegal trade are treated, for Models V and VI below, in Pitt [1981] for instance.

and Hansen [1973] demonstrated, the net welfare impact may be a gain *or* a loss. The reader can readily illustrate this by modifying Figure 1 to compare a (legal) higher-tariff situation with a (faked, illegal) lower-tariff situation, but with the latter now characterized by inferior terms of trade.

Model II: *Faked Invoicing of Quantity, without Bribing of Customs*

In this case, the faked invoicing occurs *via* misstatement of the quantity being imported. Typically, the containers may contain a larger quantity than invoiced. This rather common form of illegality may be safely assumed to require non-negligible real resource cost since quantity faking is more detectable than unit value faking and therefore more risky to the exporter's goodwill and future business, requiring therefore some compensation. It is also likely to involve special packing, which may be more expensive. In this case, the following consequences arise.

(i) *LVDP price disparity* will exist because the effective tariff will have been lowered and therefore $p_c\ (1+t) > p_d$, with $t > t_e$.

(ii) Similarly, *TLVDP price disparity* will also exist, with $p_c^t\ (1+t) > p_d$ since $p_c^t = p_c$.

(iii) If the recorded export data include the exporter's share in the gain from faking, $p_f > p_c$ and the *PCC price disparity* will exist.

(iv) At the same time, since quantities are being faked, *PCC quantity disparity* must evidently exist: $q_f > q_c$.

(v) This will imply that *PCC value disparity* will exist: $p_f q_f > p_c q_c$.

(vi) *LI price disparities* will not arise under competitive import trade (unless differences are introduced in the ability of different importers/economic agents to manage illegal faking).

The significant difference between unit-value and quantity faking, i.e. between Models I (2) and II, is then clearly that the latter generates the *LVDP price disparity* with the Pitt inequality sign whereas the former does with the sign reversed, thus providing the analyst with a method of discriminating between these two types of faking that may sometimes work. So also the PCC comparisons, properly conducted, may be able to distinguish between cases where the value discrepancies arise from unit price as distinct from quantity differences.

The nature of the welfare consequences, of course, is identical between the two models: since the (direct) real cost of faking is positive, both models leave open the possibility of a loss from the faking, even though the domestic price of the importable is reduced.

Model III: *Faked Invoicing of Unit Values, with Bribes*

Consider now the case where Model I is modified so as to permit bribing of customs officers. This will change the picture insofar as the faking of invoices poses much-diminished risk of detection at the border now. Thus, one may consider the possibility of non-negligible resource costs (as against "transfer payments") being involved here as relatively remote and hence unnecessary to analyze. In the case where these real costs are negligible, therefore, the following disparity results follow:

(i) For *LVDP price disparity*, the results are naturally identical to those of Model I (2): the price disparity does arise. The identity arises because, whereas in Model I (2) the domestic price p_d reflects element α (the real cost to the importer of the sharing of the gain from faking with the exporter) in the present model it reflects instead element β (the financial cost to the importer of the bribe paid to the customs officer). Elements β and α play, therefore, identical roles in regard to LVDP price disparity but, as noted below, are different in their welfare implications.

(ii) Again, *TLVDP price disparity* will arise, as with Model I (2). For, $\{p_c^t(1+t) - p_d\} = t(p_c - p_c^t) + \beta < 0$ as $\beta > 0$ but cannot exceed in absolute magnitude the total gain from underinvoicing measured by $t(p_c^t - p_c)$.

(iii) *PCC price disparity* evidently exists, $p_f > p_c$, since the declared value in the importing country is faked at a lower value.

(iv) Quantities are not faked, so $q_f = q_c$, i.e., *PCC quantity disparity* does not arise.

(v) *PCC value disparity* will exist because $p_f q_f > p_c q_c$.

(vi) *LI price disparities* will not exist under competitive import trade by uniform economic agents.

As for conventional welfare implications, Model III implies a straightforward cut in the effective tariff charged. Therefore, as with Model I (1) where also the real costs of faking are negligible, the effect is to increase welfare unambiguously.

Model IV: *Faked Invoicing of Quantity, with Bribes*

In this case, the customs officer clears an understated quantity of imports, charging the legal duty on a fraction of the actual imports. The rationale for this practice is obvious. The customs officer, to protect himself, must show *some* legal imports of the item and faces a seriously enhanced prospect of detection if no legal imports are registered at all. There is, therefore, some fraction of overall imports that will be declared for legal-duty-rate assessment. However, the effective tariff rate will be reduced since the actual imports will exceed the imports on which duty is assessed. Therefore, the practice embodied in Model IV amounts to simply cutting the actual, effective tariff rate. And it is done at negligible real cost since the bribing of the customs officer (constituting a transfer payment, and hence a financial rather than real cost) makes it unnecessary to share the gains from faking with exporters or to incur extra costs of packaging to avoid detection etc[1]. The results are therefore fairly straightforward.

(i) Since the effective tariff is lowered, while the declared unit value or price is not faked, the domestic price will be lower than the landed price inclusive of the ineffective, legal tariff: $p_c\,(1+t) > p_d$.[2] *LVDP price disparity* will therefore obtain.

(ii) Similarly, since $p_c = p_c^t$, *TLVDP price disparity* also follows.

(iii) *PCC price disparity* does not obtain, since it is quantities that are faked.

(iv) The quantity faking implies that $q_f > q_c$, so that *PCC quantity disparity* obtains.

(v) *PCC value disparity* follows: $p_f\,q_f > p_c\,q_c$.

(vi) *LI price disparities* do not obtain under competitive imports with uniform agents.

The welfare implications are also straightforward. The absence of real costs in faking, combined with the fact that the model implies a cut in the effective tariff, mean that unambiguous welfare improvement results.

B. Illegal Trade through Illegal Entry Points

The other, major class of illegal trade is what occurs through illegal entry points. This trade fits better the popular conception of illegality, of course. In this case it is conceivable, but highly improbable, that there

[1] As noted later, therefore, this model, while it is built on the notion of some legal trade permitting some illegal trade, à la Pitt [1981], departs radically from it in terms of its economic implications. In fact, Model IV makes it somewhat meaningless to distinguish between legal and illegal trade since all trade is illegal here: some fraction of it is recorded and some not. Pitt's model, Model VI below, instead makes more sense when the legal trade is through legal channels and the illegal trade is through illegal channels, the trader handles both sources of imports, and the legal imports make it possible for the trader to escape detection on his handling of the illegal imports.

[2] The domestic price, p_d, will reflect of course the bribe to the customs officer. It is only if the bribe fully absorbs the gain from faking that there will be equality of $p_c\,(1+t)$ and p_d, eliminating the LVDP price disparity. But that is only a limiting, and improbable, case.

are no significant real costs involved in the illegal trade. Typically, costs will result from damage in transit owing to the highly unorthodox methods of transportation involved and owing to the risks of detection[1]. Besides, unlike in the case of illegal trade through faking at legal entry points, the distinction between legal and illegal trade is now clearly meaningful.

There are two major classes of models that exist now in the literature that seek to embody such illegal trade into general equilibrium analysis. These are discussed below, and their consequences for disparities and welfare spelled out.

Model V: *Smuggling of Untaxed Commodities by Firms Engaging in Illegal Trade*

In this model, the illegal and legal trade are assumed to be carried out by separate firms, with illegally imported commodities clearing in the market alongside with homogeneous, legally imported commodities at identical prices (whenever legal and illegal trades co-exist). This is the model in the early analysis of Bhagwati and Hansen [1973], and in the papers subsequently written by many authors such as Johnson [1974], Bhagwati and Srinivasan [1974], Falvey [1978], Ray [1978] and others. It also is the model underlying the analysis of Sheikh [1974]. In contrast however to Bhagwati and Hansen's assumption that the real costs of illegal trade (are higher than those of legal trade and) are incurred in the form of the traded commodities themselves (much like Samuelson's famous "melting ice" assumption for dealing with transport costs), Sheikh assumes instead that these added costs are incurred in the form of an intermediate good that uses primary factors directly.

The contrast between the Bhagwati-Hansen and Sheikh methods of modelling the added real costs of illegal trade has implications for welfare under certain conditions; but these are of no immediate concern in the present context[2]. Hence, the precise analysis below will assume that the Bhagwati-Hansen model is relevant: so that the added costs of illegal trade can be portrayed as simply amounting to the importing country facing a less favourable foreign offer curve on illegal trade.

Now, this model reduces in principle to Models I (2) and II (assuming that bribery is negligible in this type of illegal importation). However, aside from the fact that the price-disparity implications will be different

[1] Bhagwati and Hansen [1973] mention the gruesome example of slaves being thrown overboard in the infamous slave trade after abolition when detection was imminent, so that more slaves were "lost" in illegal transit than if the trade were legal.

[2] Thus, if legal and illegal trade co-exist, the Bhagwati-Hansen model implies necessary welfare loss from illegal trade. Not so, under the Sheikh model.

in the present instance, an important difference is that the effective tariff on illegally imported goods now will be zero whereas in Models I (2) and II it will not be. Therefore, in depicting the economic analysis of Model V, Figure 1 must be modified to show the illegal trade as occurring at zero tariff rather than at just a reduced tariff.

Thus, in Figure 2, which illustrates for simplicity the case of constant costs in illegal and legal transformation and also a case where illegal trade dominates and drives out legal trade, the legal trade equilibrium in absence of smuggling is portrayed with consumption, production and welfare

Figure 2

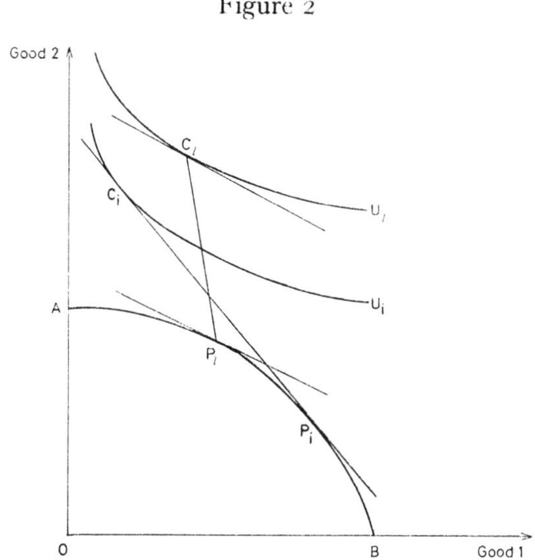

at C_l, P_l, and U_l, respectively, and with illegal trade at C_i, P_i, and U_i, respectively. Here $U_i < U_l$, though one could well have shown that $U_i > U_l$.[1] The welfare implications of Model V, given the terms-of-trade deterioration implied by the added costs of illegal trade, are therefore not unambiguous. The disparity implications are as follows:

(i) On legal (recorded) trade, where it exists, *LVDP price disparity* does not arise: $p_{cl}(1+t) = p_d$.

(ii) Similarly, since $p_{cl} = p^t_{cl}$, *TLVDP price disparity* also does not exist.

[1] Cases where illegal and legal trade co-exist have been illustrated and discussed in Bhagwati and Hansen [1973].

(iii) For PCC disparities, the answer depends on whether the illegal importation is recorded or not in the exporting country's statistics[1]. The *PCC price disparity* will, however, be non-existent regardless.

(iv) *PCC quantity disparity* will arise, $q_f > q_{cl}$, if the exporting country records the illegal trade — which is perfectly possible since the illegality is in importation; it will not arise, $q_f = q_{cl}$, if it does not.

(v) *PCC value disparity* will arise or not, depending on whether PCC quantity disparity does.

(vi) *LI price disparity* can now meaningfully exist as illegal and legal trades can always be differentiated. Since there is an added real cost to illegal trade, this will imply that $p^t_{cl} < p^t_{ci}$.

Model VI: *Smuggling of Untaxed Commodities by Firms Engaging Simultaneously in Legal and Illegal Trade*

Pitt [1981] departs from the above model and essentially argues that the legal trade is undertaken so as to make illegal trade possible (at reduced risk)[2]. In this case, illegal trade cannot be undertaken by itself — as it, of course, is in practice in cases where there are outright prohibitions on legal importation. Once this link is established, legal trade can arise even at a loss as long as the loss is offset by the gain on the illegal trade that the legal trade makes possible[3].

Since the illegal trade occurs through illegal entry points in the present case, the present model assumes that the illegal trade occurs at an augmented real cost. The following implications then follow.

[1] For detecting unrecorded trade see also Nayak [1977].

[2] Pitt [1981] himself seems to imply that this model would work for illegal trade through legal entry points. Thus, he argues: "A large share of smuggling occurs not via 'ships in the night' but rather in broad daylight off the wharves of customs administered ports. Traded goods are misweighed, misgraded, misinvoiced or not invoiced at all with or without the cooperation of customs authorities. Some legal trade is necessary for this type of activity. The greater the legal trade [by a trading firm], the easier it is to hide smuggling activity from enforcement agencies and therefore the less costly will be smuggling. Thus, legal trade can be viewed as an input into the smuggling activity." However, illegal trade that occurs through legal entry points, such as customs administered wharves, involves surely some form of misinvoicing that must imply one of the four Models I—IV distinguished above, depending on whether the customs officers are bribed or not and on whether the misinvoicing implies unit value or quantity faking. Pitt's argument that legal trade is required to support illegal trade, as developed by him, is surely more appropriate when the illegal trade is through illegal entry points, whether the offloading of the illegal trade is by day or by night!

[3] The loss on legal trade does not necessarily arise in all variants of this model. One cannot rule out, in general, the possibility that both legal and illegal trade co-exist and yield "normal" profits. But this possibility is ignored in the text which follows Pitt's formulation in this regard.

(i) In this case, the model yields the *LVDP price disparity* with the correct inequality à la Pitt, as it should since it was specifically devised to explain such a disparity: $p_{cl}(1+t) > p_d$.

(ii) Since $p^t_{cl} = p_{cl}$, *TLVDP price disparity* also follows in this model[1].

(iii) *PCC price disparity* will not arise: $p_f = p_{cl}$.

(iv) However, as in Model V, *PCC quantity disparity* will exist, i.e. $q_f > q_{cl}$, or not exist depending on whether the illegal imports are recorded in the exporting country's statistics or not.

(v) This is equally true of *PCC value disparity*.

(vi) Again, *LI price disparity* will exist since illegal trade will incur non-negligible real costs, so that $p^t_{cl} < p^t_{ci}$.

As for welfare impact, this will again be ambiguous since the terms-of-trade loss on illegal trade will imply a loss to be set against the gain implied by the effective lowering of the importable good's domestic price, p_d.[2]

IV. Concluding Remarks

In the foregoing analysis, several different forms of illegal trade are modelled, reflecting different ways in which illegal trade actually arises in the real world. The models are analyzed for their implications for conventionally-defined welfare impact as also for their implications regarding observable price, quantity or value data on trade so that the empirical analyst of illegal trade can detect the different types of illegal trade and possibly discriminate among them from the statistical evidence. The full set of results has been tabulated in the following table.

[1] Note of course that these LVDP and TLVDP price disparities were shown to arise in other models also in this paper.

[2] Pitt also considers the case where the real costs on illegal trade are negligible. In that case, the welfare impact owing to reduced domestic price of the imported good is unambiguously favourable, of course.

Disparity and Welfare Implications of Alternative Models of Illegal Trade [a]

Model	Direct real cost of illegal trade	Disparity implications						Welfare implication (on assumption that the tariff is the only distortion)
		LVDP price	TLVDP price	PCC price	PCC quantity	PCC value	LI price	
A. Illegal Trade through Legal Entry Points								
I. Faked invoicing of unit values, without bribes Cf. Bhagwati [1964; 1967] (1)	negligible (faked invoices available costlessly from foreign exporters)	YES $P_c\,(1+t) < P_d$ (reversed inequality sign)	YES $P_c^t\,(1+t) > P_d$	YES $P_f > P_c$	NO $q_f = q_c$	YES $P_f\,q_f > P_c\,q_c$	NONE	welfare improvement (same as a simple cut in the tariff)
(2)	non-negligible (foreign exporter shares in gain from faked invoicing)	YES $P_c\,(1+t) < P_d$ (reversed inequality sign)	YES $P_c^t\,(1+t) > P_d$	YES $P_f > P_c$	NO $q_f = q_c$	YES $P_f\,q_f > P_c\,q_c$	NONE	welfare loss now possible (because of terms-of-trade deterioration) Cf. Bhagwati and Hansen [1973]; Johnson [1974]; Bhagwati and Srinivasan [1974]
II. Faked invoicing of quantity, without bribes Cf. Bhagwati [1964; 1967]	non-negligible (only probable case since detection more likely)	YES $P_c\,(1+t) > P_d$	YES $P_c^t\,(1+t) > P_d$ since $P_c = P_c^t$	YES *If* P_f includes exporter's share in gain from faked invoicing, then: $P_f > P_c$ NO otherwise	YES $q_f > q_c$	YES $P_f\,q_f > P_c\,q_c$	NONE	again, non-negligible real cost implies that welfare loss is possible
III. Faked invoicing of unit values, with bribes Cf. Bhagwati [1964; 1967]	negligible (in view of customs collaboration)	YES $P_c\,(1+t) < P_d$ (reversed inequality sign)	YES $P_c^t\,(1+t) > P_d$	YES $P_f > P_c$	NO $q_f = q_c$	YES $P_f\,q_f > P_c\,q_c$	NONE	welfare improvement (since tariff is effectively cut at no cost)

IV. Faked invoicing of quantity, with bribes Cf. Bhagwati [1964; 1967]	negligible (in view of customs collaboration)	YES $p_c(1+t) > p_d$	YES $p_c^t(1+t) > p_d$ since $p_c = p_c^t$	NO $p_f = p_c$	YES $q_f > q_c$	YES $p_f q_f > p_c q_c$	NONE	welfare improvement (since tariff is effectively cut at no cost)
B. Illegal Trade through Illegal Entry Points								
V. Smuggling of untaxed commodities by firms engaging in illegal trade Cf. Bhagwati and Hansen [1973]; Sheikh [1974]	non-negligible	NO $p_{cl}(1+t) = p_d$ if legal trade exists	NO $p_{cl} = p_{cl}^t = p_d$ therefore $p_{cl}^t(1+t) = p_d$ if legal trade exists	1. Assuming that illegal trade is recorded in exporting country's data: NO $p_f = p_{cl}$	YES $q_f > q_{cl}$	YES $p_f q_f > p_{cl} q_{cl}$	YES $p_{cl}^t < p_{ci}^t$	either welfare improvement or welfare loss possible Cf. Bhagwati and Hansen [1973]; and Sheikh [1974]; both papers model the real cost of illegal trade differently
				2. Assuming that illegal trade is not recorded in exporting country's data: NO $p_f = p_{cl}$	NO $q_f = q_{cl}$	NO $p_f q_f = p_{cl} q_{cl}$		
VI. Smuggling of untaxed commodities by firms engaging simultaneously in legal and illegal trade to reduce risk on illegal trade Cf. Pitt [1981]	non-negligible	YES $p_{cl}(1+t) < p_d$	YES $p_{cl}^t = p_{cl}$ therefore $p_{cl}^t(1+t) < p_d$	1. Assuming that illegal trade is recorded in exporting country's data: NO $p_f = p_{cl}$	YES $q_f > q_{cl}$	YES $p_f q_f > p_{cl} q_{cl}$	YES $p_{cl}^t < p_{ci}^t$	either welfare improvement or welfare loss possible Cf. Pitt [1981]
				2. Assuming that illegal trade is not recorded in exporting country's data: NO $p_f = p_{cl}$	NO $q_f = q_{cl}$	NO $p_f q_f = p_{cl} q_{cl}$		

[a] The results tabulated here were derived in the text.

References

Bhagwati, Jagdish N., "On the Underinvoicing of Imports". *Bulletin of the Oxford University Institute of Economics and Statistics,* Vol. 26, Oxford, 1964, pp. 389—397.

—, "Fiscal Policies, the Faking of Foreign Trade Declarations, and the Balance of Payments". *Ibid.,* Vol. 29, 1967, pp. 61—77.

—, and **Bent Hansen,** "A Theoretical Analysis of Smuggling". *The Quarterly Journal of Economics,* Vol. 87, Cambridge, Mass., 1973, pp. 172—187.

—, and **T. N. Srinivasan,** "Smuggling and Trade Policy". In: Jagdish N. Bhagwati (Ed.), *Illegal Transactions in International Trade. Theory and Measurement.* Studies in International Economics, 1, Amsterdam, 1974, pp. 27—38.

—, **Anne Krueger** and **Chaiyawat Wibulswasdi,** "Capital Flight from LDCs: A Statistical Analysis". In: *Ibid.,* pp. 148—154.

Falvey, Rodney E., "A Note on Preferential and Illegal Trade under Quantitative Restrictions". *The Quarterly Journal of Economics,* Vol. 92, New York, 1978, pp. 175—178.

Johnson, Harry G., "Notes on the Economic Theory of Smuggling". In: Jagdish N. Bhagwati (Ed.), *Illegal Transactions in International Trade. Theory and Measurement.* Studies in International Economics, 1, Amsterdam, 1974, pp. 39—46.

Nayak, Satyendra S., "Illegal Transactions in External Trade and Payments in India: An Empirical Study". *Economic and Political Weekly,* Vol. 12, Bombay, 1977, pp. 2051—2062.

Pitt, Mark M., "Smuggling and Price Disparity". *Journal of International Economics,* Vol. 11, Amsterdam, 1981 forthcoming.

Ray, Alok, "Smuggling, Import Objectives, and Optimum Tax Structure". *The Quarterly Journal of Economics,* Vol. 92, New York, 1978, pp. 509—514.

Sheikh, Munir A., "Smuggling, Production and Welfare". *Journal of International Economics,* Vol. 4, Amsterdam, 1974, pp. 355—364.

Revenue Seeking: A Generalization of the Theory of Tariffs

Jagdish N. Bhagwati

Columbia University

T. N. Srinivasan

Yale University and World Bank

The theory of commercial policy has recently addressed three phenomena: (i) tariff (quota) seeking or lobbying by potential beneficiaries for the imposition of a tariff (quota), (ii) tariff (quota) evasion, and (iii) rent seeking or lobbying for getting an allocation of the import quota to earn the rents generated. Revenue seeking or lobbying to secure a share in the disposition of the tariff revenues is analyzed here. It is shown that revenue seeking may, even for a small country, result in a reduction in importable output. Furthermore, revenue seeking may be welfare improving. Rent seeking may be welfare improving as well.

I. The Problem

The formal theory of commercial policy, as constituted by the theory of trade and welfare, has traditionally failed to incorporate three types of phenomena that attend the imposition of tariffs:

Thanks are due to the National Science Foundation grant no. SOC79-07541 for financial support of Bhagwati. The comments of Clark Leith, Peter Kenen, Ed Tower, Alan Deardorff, Anne Krueger, Peter Diamond, Peter Neary, Max Corden, Michael Michaely, Alasdair Smith, and Gordon Tullock on an earlier draft (Bhagwati 1979), which this substantially augmented and revised version replaces, have been very helpful. The comments of two anonymous referees and of the editor, Jacob Frenkel, have been helpful as well. Views expressed are not necessarily those of the institutions with which we are affiliated.

[*Journal of Political Economy*, 1980, vol. 88, no. 6]

1. Tariff seeking (or tariff making): Where tariffs are imposed, for example, for protective (or other income-distributional) reasons, the potential beneficiaries of these protective tariffs will often lobby for their imposition.

2. Tariff evasion (or smuggling): Where tariffs exist, there is an incentive to evade them via smuggling, whether overt or in the form of overinvoicing and underinvoicing.

3. Revenue seeking: Where tariffs are imposed for, say, protective reasons, they will simultaneously happen to generate revenue. This, in turn, will generate a lobbying process to secure a share in the disposition of the revenues.

For each of the tariff (or "price") phenomena, there are corresponding *QR* (or "command") phenomena. Thus we have (1) *QR* seeking for protective reasons, (2) *QR* evasion, and (3) rent seeking, where there is (perfect or imperfect) competition and lobbying to get the licenses and hence earn the premia/rents that are associated with them, the licenses themselves having emerged from the (conceptually distinct) *QR*-seeking lobby's success at having the *QR*s established.

The first area of neglect has been addressed in much recent work, especially that of Brock and Magee (1978), and is attracting attention from analysts whose main objective is to explain why tariffs are what they are and, as in Cheh (1974), why they change in the way they do.[1]

Recent analytical developments have also addressed the second area of neglect, beginning with the analysis of smuggling in the presence of tariffs by Bhagwati and Hansen (1973), utilizing the 2 × 2 HOS (Heckscher-Ohlin-Samuelson) model of trade theory. Numerous extensions of their work have followed, especially by Johnson (1972), Bhagwati and Srinivasan (1973), Bhagwati (1974), Sheikh (1974), and Ray (1978). Falvey (1978) has extended the analysis to smuggling in the presence of *QR*s, noting the nonequivalence of tariffs and *QR*s that follows in this case.[2]

However, the third area of neglect curiously continues to remain so. The familiar Meade (1952) assumption of lump-sum redistribution of tariff revenues has been widely used, preventing the analysis of revenue seeking, that is, the expenditure of real resources in the activity of getting a share of the revenues resulting from tariff imposition. That lobbies exist, and utilize real resources for pursuit of a share in the revenues that are disbursed by the state, is so obvious from the most

[1] There has been practically no integration of this work into general-equilibrium analysis or into the theory of trade and welfare. An important beginning has, however, been made by Findlay and Wellisz (1979).

[2] The phenomena of overinvoicing and underinvoicing, whose detection and economic causation have been analyzed in Bhagwati (1964, 1967), can also be analyzed identically as smuggling.

casual observation as to require no extended justification. However, whether the share of such revenues that gets to be sought through such lobbying is unity or less, on the average or for marginal increment in revenues, is a matter for empirical evaluation, and the setting up of "rules" subject to which revenues are disbursed is evidently a factor that tends to reduce this ratio below unity in many empirical contexts. The analysis of revenue seeking below, therefore, allows for the share of tariff revenues that is sought to vary below unity.

Our analysis of revenue seeking is developed in Sections II–V and is conducted within the general-equilibrium framework of the HOS model, thus permitting us to relate our findings readily to the main corpus of the general equilibrium theory of trade. Thus we are able, for example, to demonstrate how revenue seeking may, even for a small country, result in a reduction, rather than an increase, in the output of the importable industry.

By also focusing on the fact that, given the tariff, the introduction of resource-diverting revenue-seeking activity implies the withdrawal of factors from gainful employment into a zero-output activity in a tariff-distorted economy, we demonstrate the not-insignificant possibility (Sec. III) that revenue seeking may be welfare improving, and we establish the conditions for it to arise (Sec. IV), indicating therewith that this is a paradox but not a "theoretical curiosum."

As already noted, the "command" or *QR* counterpart of our revenue-seeking phenomenon is what Krueger (1974) has called "rent seeking." Her invaluable analysis of this phenomenon, conducted with the framework of a rather special, simplified model of complete specialization on one good but complicated via the introduction of a "distribution" sector, reached, however, the conclusion that rent seeking is always welfare worsening. This central conclusion is unfortunately not sustainable, as our analysis of revenue seeking, extended readily to rent seeking under a *QR* instead (in Sec. V), readily shows.

This reversal of her central conclusion, as also her exclusion of the possibility of revenue seeking, vitiates, furthermore, her "nonequivalence" proposition, that *QR*s are always inferior to tariffs because they attract rent seeking, embodied in the conclusion that "the major proposition of this paper is that competitive rent-seeking for import licenses entails a welfare cost *in addition to* the welfare cost that would be incurred if the same level of imports were achieved through tariffs" (1974, p. 295; emphasis added). Quite aside from the fact that rent seeking may be welfare improving and hence a *QR* with rent seeking may dominate a tariff without revenue seeking, Krueger's conclusion presupposes inappropriately that whereas the success of a protectionist lobby in getting a *QR* imposed will result in a rent-seeking scramble for all the resulting premia/rents on the import licenses, an equivalent success of the protectionist lobby in getting a tariff enacted[3] will be characterized by a total absence of a revenue-seeking scramble for a share of the resulting tariff revenues![4] Since even *QR*s are often allocated by reference to "rules," or assigned to public-sector trading agencies or public-sector user corporations, a substantial fraction of the *QR*-generated rents is not "sought" in practice, whereas doubtless some fraction of revenues is sought, so that the extreme and opposed assumptions concerning tariffs and *QR*s underlying Krueger's comparison thereof are unpersuasive.

A proper welfare comparison of tariffs and quotas, with both revenue seeking and rent seeking, is therefore undertaken by us in Section VI and is shown nonetheless to imply nonequivalence between the two under alternative, precise definitions of nonequivalence. Quite remarkably, different assumptions concerning the extent of revenue seeking and rent seeking are not necessary for this outcome.

Finally, in Section VII, we briefly reexamine the question of measuring the cost of protection, once revenue seeking is introduced.

II. Tariff Equilibrium with Revenue Seeking: The Geometry

Consider the standard 2 × 2 HOS model, with factors K and L, goods 1 and 2, a set of social indifference curves,[5] and the "small-" country assumption so that the world goods price ratio is given.

The standard representation of a tariff equilibrium in this case is as in figure 1, with world price ratio (equal to minus the slope of the line)

[3] The protectionist lobby will be indifferent whether it gets its protection through a tariff or a *QR*—in a world with certainty and full flexibility of *QR*s and tariffs in response to changing conditions. Evidently, this is not realistic, as noted in Bhagwati (1965).

[4] The problem with Krueger's argument stems evidently from the focus of the trade-and-developmental economists during the early 1970s on *QR*-generated rents. Thus, in analyzing the Indian economy's reliance on industrial and import licensing, one of us had argued (Bhagwati 1973) that the system was creating a rentier society rather than encouraging the emergence of Schumpeterian entrepreneurs. The growth of a rentier class, and the rent-seeking activities, in a society with reliance on *QR*s was thus foremost in our thoughts. What one forgot then was that such rent seeking would be paralleled by revenue seeking if the same objectives were to be sought by "price" rather than "command" instruments, and therefore that a proper comparison between, say, a tariff and a quota to achieve a target increase in importable production, for example, would have to include revenue seeking for the tariff case if rent seeking was included in the quota case. This problem with the Krueger analysis was noted and discussed in Bhagwati (1978), but the need for a corrected analysis was merely indicated there and is being responded to in this paper.

[5] For those who may find it offensive to assume social indifference curves (with attendant lump-sum transfers) in an analysis of revenue seeking, we may note that our conclusions are equally robust if we use the increment in the availability locus at world prices as a welfare improvement criterion in itself.

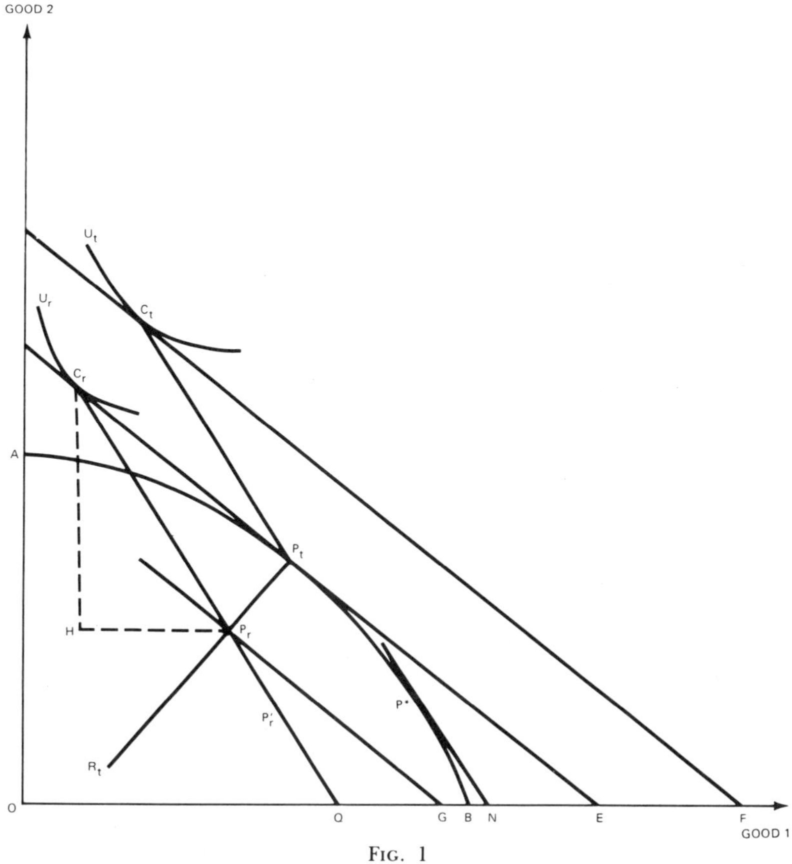

FIG. 1

P_tC_t, free-trade production at P^*, tariff-policy production and consumption at P_t and C_t, and the associated tariff revenue as EF in terms of good 1. Lump-sum transfer of revenues to consumers is assumed.

Now introduce revenue seeking into this HOS model. Envisage a production function in revenue seeking, with K_r and L_r being the factors used in rent seeking. It is evident that, given competition in this activity, the K_r/L_r ratio will be chosen to minimize costs, given the market values of the rental (r) and the wage (w).

In the 2 × 2 model, as long as we confine ourselves to incomplete specialization in production (as we do throughout Secs. II and III, but not in Sec. IV), the tariff-inclusive domestic goods price ratio ($C_tF = P_tE$ in fig. 1) will determine the factor price ratio, that is, the w and r faced by revenue seekers, and forthwith the K_r/L_r ratio.

Given this choice of K_r/L_r ratio, the total factors withdrawn from use in goods production at P_t will equal the amount of tariff revenue that we assume to be subject to seeking. This follows from the fact that throughout we assume competitive revenue seeking. Our analysis will divide the total tariff revenue into two parts: the revenue that is sought and the Meade-type lump-sum transfer that escapes the seeking process. However, we will focus presently on the (empirically improbable) case where all revenue is sought and, only in Secs. III and IV, consider the case where some Meade-type transfer is permitted.[6]

Finally, the withdrawal of K_r and L_r for rent seeking will correspondingly reduce the total amount of factors available for production of goods 1 and 2. On the other hand, given the fixity of goods and factor prices, it is equally evident that the domestic consumption of goods will lie on the domestic expenditure line which is identical to the national-income-at-factor-cost line P_tE in figure 1. For domestic expenditure must equal domestic income in the revenue-seeking equilibrium, and the latter is nothing but the value of factors used in goods production plus the value of factors diverted to revenue seeking, which adds up to the value of all factors at w and r associated with P_t and hence to national income at factor cost at P_t.

The resulting revenue-seeking equilibrium is readily illustrated in figure 1. The domestic expenditure (or national income at factor cost) line is P_tE. Consumption must therefore occur at C_r. Moreover, the world price line must pass through C_r, so C_rQ is the world price line through C_r. At the same time, the new production point must lie on C_rQ, while it also lies on the generalized Rybczynski line P_tR_t—which is the locus of successive production points, at constant domestic goods price ratio P_tE, as factors are successively withdrawn for revenue seeking in proposition K_r/L_r. The production point that satisfies both the requirements is therefore clearly P_r. Then the difference between C_r and P_r defines C_rH as the import level, with tariff revenue now at GE: the value of factor income in goods production being OG, in revenue seeking being GE, and in aggregate being OE.

Note immediately that welfare falls, with the introduction of competitive revenue seeking, from U_t to U_r. This appears to be a thoroughly intuitive conclusion since resources are being diverted by revenue seeking to a "wasteful" activity with zero output (in terms of social valuation).[7] However, as we note in Section III, this intuition

[6] We will not, however, consider imperfectly competitive revenue seeking. As Tullock (1978) has noted in an interesting contribution, imperfectly competitive rent seeking may result in resource diversion that is less than the rents sought, and this is true, of course, of revenue seeking as well.

[7] We are not assuming, with Tullock (1967), that tariff revenues are applied to wasteful projects such as building "tunnels that lead nowhere." However, revenue seeking leads to an outcome, in our analysis, that implies an identical zero-output diversion of resources.

needs correction: The welfare-worsening outcome is not the only possibility.[8]

III. Possible Paradoxes in the Presence of Revenue Seeking

Among the less compelling "paradoxical" outcomes, the following are evident from figure 1 on a little reflection.

i) The new, revenue-seeking equilibrium level of imports may exceed or be less than the original (prior to revenue seeking) equilibrium, that is, in view of similar triangles, as $C_rP_r \gtreqless C_tP_t$. This has implications for the equivalence of tariffs and quotas, as argued in Section VI.

ii) The tariff revenue in the revenue-seeking equilibrium may exceed, equal, or be less than the original tariff revenue ($GE \gtreqless EF$).

iii) Quite remarkably, the cost of revenue seeking shown in figure 1 is independent of any change in the production function of the revenue-seeking activity as long as the resulting shift in the Rybczynski line P_tR_t continues to keep it intersecting C_rQ at a point P_r representing incomplete specialization in the production of goods 1 and 2.[9]

However, the most remarkable paradoxes are the following in the positive and welfare analyses of tariffs.

iv) If the objective in imposing a tariff was to protect and thus increase the output of the importable good 2, the small-country assumption does ensure the absence of the Metzler production paradox (P_t, relative to P^*, implies an increase in the output of the protected good 2), when revenue seeking is absent. However, once revenue seeking is introduced, the Metzler paradox may arise despite the small-country assumption as when P_r is shifted to P_r' with C_rQ and a modified P_tR_t intersecting at P_r' to the southwest of P^*.

v) Again, the change in the production of the importable good following on revenue seeking opens up the interesting possibility that, in the presence of welfare-worsening revenue seeking, a target increase in the production of the importable good above the free-trade level may involve a lower (or a higher) tariff than in the absence of the revenue-seeking activity and, correspondingly, a lower (or a higher) welfare loss than that arising from a tariff without revenue seeking.

vi) More remarkably, we can show that revenue seeking may be welfare improving. To do this simply, we now consider the possibility

[8] The full range of outcomes, and the conditions determining them, are the subject of the analysis in Sec. IV.

[9] This proposition, however, does not hold for less than full competitive revenue seeking or where only a fraction of the revenue earned is sought and where complete specialization in production results.

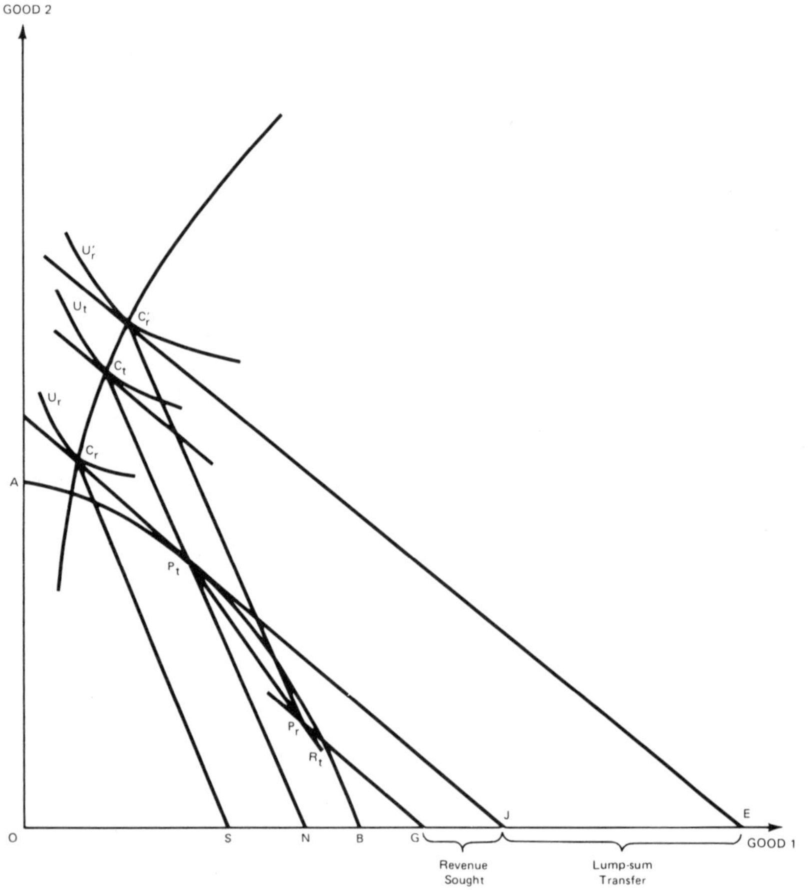

Fig. 2

that part of the revenue is handled as a Meade-type lump-sum transfer and only the remainder is competitively sought, so that the value of factors diverted to revenue seeking is less than the total revenue. Thus, consider figure 2, which uses much the same lettering as figure 1, and the income-consumption line at the tariff-inclusive domestic price ratio has been drawn. The difference is that the Rybczynski line P_tR_t is now drawn flatter than the international price line P_tN. A possible revenue-seeking equilibrium is then shown at P_r, C_r' with total revenue collected at GE, the revenue offered and sought at GJ, and the lump-sum Meade-type transfer being JE. Thus welfare improves with revenue seeking to U_r' ($> U_t$), and the proportion of tariff revenue disbursed to revenue seekers is less than unity, the proportion being GJ/GE.

This paradox is immediately resolved as soon as we recognize that the welfare-improving diversion of resources to the zero-output revenue-seeking activity in the tariff-distorted situation is formally identical to, and indeed the mirror image of, the phenomenon of immiserizing growth where the augmentation of resources in a tariff-distorted economy can immiserize the economy (as shown by Johnson [1967] and generalized in Bhagwati [1968]). Alternatively, the paradox can be understood by recognizing that the analytical problem of revenue seeking is equivalent formally to the problem of project evaluation in trade-distorted, small economies. In the latter case, given the trade distortion, resources are withdrawn for project use and can have a *negative* shadow price, as demonstrated and discussed in Bhagwati, Srinivasan, and Wan (1978) and Srinivasan and Bhagwati (1978), such that even a zero-output "project" (such as a "Keynesian" project to dig ditches and fill them up, under full employment) may be socially desirable. Analogously, in the former case, the zero-output, "wasteful" diversion of resources into revenue seeking from the trade-distorted equilibrium can be welfare improving: The shadow price of (one of the two) factors being withdrawn into revenue seeking may be negative.[10]

Once we have formulated the problem in mathematical terms, in the next section, it will be possible for us to go beyond a mere demonstration of this paradox and to delineate "zones" into which the Rybczynski line (R-line) may lie and thereby establish the conditions under which the outcome of revenue seeking may be welfare worsening or welfare improving. We therefore turn immediately to this analysis.

IV. Tariff Equilibrium with Revenue Seeking: The Mathematics

A. Formally, our model is simply stated as follows. We have:[11] $\hat{k}_i$ = the (distorted-equilibrium) capital-output ratio, $\hat{\ell}_i$ = the (distorted-equilibrium) labor-output ratio, and X_i = output (activity) level, where $i = 1, 2, r$; $\Sigma X_i k_i = \bar{K}$, the fixed factor endowment of capital; $\Sigma X_i \ell_i = \bar{L}$, the fixed factor endowment of labor; and there are two goods, 1 and 2, and the revenue-seeking activity denoted by suffix r. As long as incomplete specialization in the production of goods 1 and 2 holds, as we assume initially, the coefficients $\hat{k}_i$ and $\hat{\ell}_i$ are as at the nonseeking tariff-distorted equilibrium (i.e., as at P_t in figs. 1, 2). As considered

[10] As Bhagwati et al. (1978) argue, the negative shadow price of a factor is a necessary, but not a sufficient, condition for a zero-output project to be welfare improving.

[11] The "hats" on the variables $\hat{k}_i$ and $\hat{\ell}_i$ refer to their values reflecting the tariff-distorted equilibrium. For incomplete specialization, $\hat{k}_i$ and $\hat{\ell}_i$ are obviously fixed parameters.

later, these coefficients will generally change after specialization in production is reached on good 1 or 2 with sufficient primary factor withdrawal to revenue seeking, and our analysis must be changed correspondingly.

The question at hand is, What is the welfare impact of factor withdrawal for revenue seeking? To consider this question, assume a standard social utility function, $U = U(C_1, C_2)$. We can then show that dU/dX_r has the same sign as dC_1/dX_r, and therefore the sign of the latter is sufficient to determine the welfare impact of revenue seeking. Thus, note that $C_1 = X_1 - E_1$ and $C_2 = X_2 + E_1/p^*$, where C_1, C_2 are the consumption levels of goods 1 and 2, E_1 is the export of good 1, and p^* is the relative international price of good 1.

It follows that, given the tariff rate t, we have:

$$\frac{U_2}{U_1} = p^*(1+t) \Rightarrow \frac{dC_2}{dX_r} = -\left(\frac{U_{21}U_1 - U_{11}U_2}{U_{22}U_1 - U_{12}U_2}\right)\frac{dC_1}{dX_r}$$

$$\equiv \theta \frac{dC_1}{dX_r},$$

where $\theta > 0$ under normality in consumption of both goods. Now,

$$\frac{dU}{dX_r} = U_1 \frac{dC_1}{dX_r} + U_2 \frac{dC_2}{dX_r} = U_1[1 + \theta p^*(1+t)] \cdot \frac{dC_1}{dX_r}, \quad (1)$$

so that Sgn (dU/dX_r) = Sgn (dC_1/dX_r). Next, note that $C_1 + p^*C_2 = X_1 + p^*X_2$, from the balance of payments being assumed zero. Hence

$$\frac{dC_1}{dX_r} + p^* \frac{dC_2}{dX_r} = \frac{dX_1}{dX_r} + p^* \frac{dX_2}{dX_r},$$

and therefore[12]

$$(1 + \theta p^*)\frac{dC_1}{dX_r} = \frac{(\hat{k}_2\hat{\ell}_r - \hat{\ell}_2\hat{k}_r) + (\hat{\ell}_1\hat{k}_r - \hat{k}_1\hat{\ell}_r)p^*}{(\hat{k}_1\hat{\ell}_2 - \hat{k}_2\hat{\ell}_1)}. \quad (2)$$

But we can now introduce the concept of second-best shadow prices of primary factors at the tariff-distorted equilibrium, $\hat{w}^*$ and $\hat{r}^*$, these being calculated à la Srinivasan and Bhagwati (1978) as the solution to the two equations,[13] $1 = \hat{\ell}_1\hat{w}^* + \hat{k}_1\hat{r}^*$, and $p^* = \hat{\ell}_2\hat{w}^* + \hat{k}_2\hat{r}^*$, which yields

$$\hat{w}^* = \frac{p^*\hat{k}_1 - \hat{k}_2}{\hat{k}_1\hat{\ell}_2 - \hat{k}_2\hat{\ell}_1}, \quad (3)$$

[12] This is derived by substituting for dX_i/dX_r $(i = 1, 2)$ from $\hat{k}_1(dX_1/dX_r) + \hat{k}_2(dX_2/dX_r) = -\hat{k}_r$ (full utilization of capital) and $\hat{\ell}_1(dX_1/dX_r) + \hat{\ell}_2(dX_2/dX_r) = -\hat{\ell}_r$ (full employment of labor).

[13] The hats on $\hat{w}^*$ and $\hat{r}^*$ refer to the fact that these shadow prices reflect the tariff-distorted equilibrium coefficients, $\hat{k}_i$ and $\hat{\ell}_i$, while the asterisks refer to the optimi-

and

$$\hat{r}^* = \frac{\hat{\ell}_2 - p^*\hat{\ell}_1}{\hat{k}_1\hat{\ell}_2 - \hat{k}_2\hat{\ell}_1}. \tag{4}$$

Substituting (3) and (4) into (2), we then get

$$(1 + \theta p^*)\frac{dC_1}{dX_r} = -(\hat{\ell}_r\hat{w}^* + \hat{k}_r\hat{r}^*). \tag{5}$$

Therefore, given (1) and (5), we deduce that

$$\text{Sgn}\,\frac{dU}{dX_r} = \text{Sgn}\,-(\hat{\ell}_r\hat{w}^* + \hat{k}_r\hat{r}^*). \tag{6}$$

This result is easily understood, for revenue seeking withdraws primary factors from the tariff-distorted resource allocation. The "output" from this revenue-seeking activity has a zero social valuation. Therefore, the welfare impact of the revenue seeking will be negative or positive exclusively as the social cost of the factors withdrawn; that is, $(\hat{\ell}_r\hat{w}^* + \hat{k}_r\hat{r}^*)$ is positive or negative.[14] Note, moreover, that the social cost of the factors withdrawn is equal to, and in fact derived from, the social cost defined in terms of the revenue-seeking-caused change in output of goods 1 and 2, valued at the international prices; that is, it equals $(\Delta X_1 + p^*\Delta X_2)$.

B. Next we can delineate three zones, around the initial tariff-determined production equilibrium P_t in figures 1 and 2, wherein the R-line may lie, with corresponding welfare-impact implications.[15]

In figure 3, we show P_t and the relevant segment of the production possibility curve. The three zones, I, II, and III, are then evidently designated by drawing the vertical and horizontal lines through P_t. Since the entry of the R-line into the three zones implies differential behavior of X_1 and X_2 vis-à-vis P_t, since this behavior can, in turn, be tied into the social cost of the factors diverted to revenue seeking (as noted at the end of the preceding subsection A) and therefore directly into the welfare impact of revenue seeking, we first derive the formulae governing ΔX_1 and ΔX_2 in response to revenue seeking.

Thus, assuming X_1^0 and X_2^0 to be the initial output levels at P_t, and the production levels with revenue-seeking activity at level $X_r > 0$ (but with incomplete specialization in production) to be X_1 and X_2, and

zation; they are therefore second-best shadow factor prices. Also see the important paper of Findlay and Wellisz (1976) on second-best shadow prices.

14 Seen thus, the criterion for the sign of the welfare impact of revenue seeking in (6) is a special case of the criterion for evaluating the desirability of a project, the special case consisting in the "project" having zero output.

15 For an analogous delineation of welfare-improving and welfare-worsening cones in the context of making resource-allocational inferences from domestic resource calculations in trade-distorted economies, see Bhagwati and Srinivasan (1979).

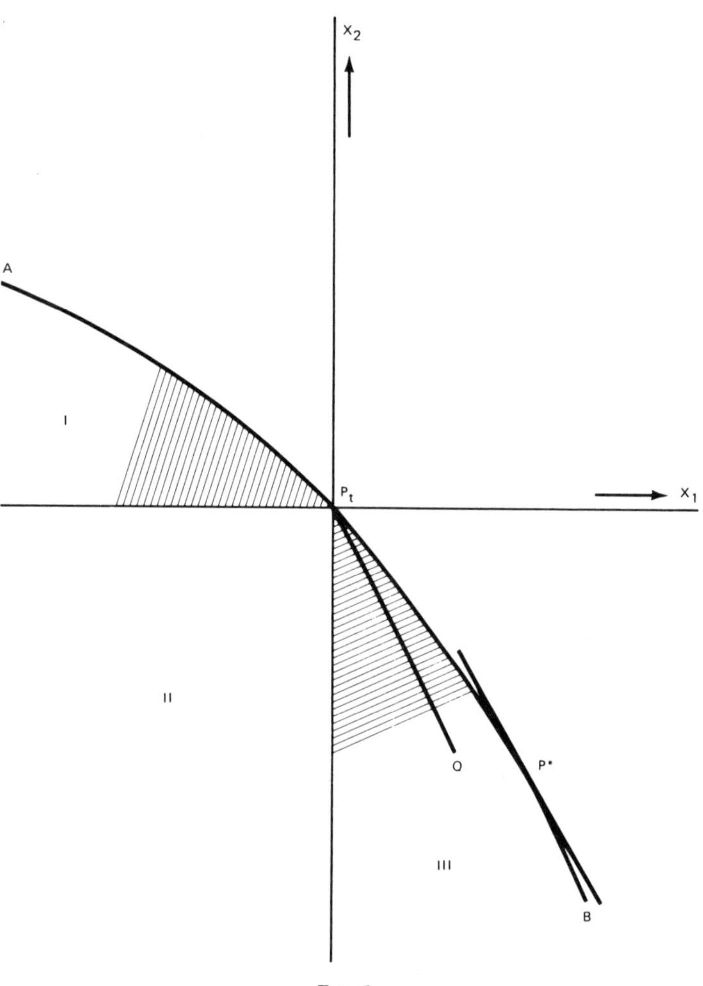

FIG. 3

defining $\Delta X_1 = X_1 - X_1^0$ and $\Delta X_2 = X_2 - X_2^0$, we have the following: $X_1\hat{k}_1 + X_2\hat{k}_2 + X_r\hat{k}_r = \bar{K} = X_1^0\hat{k}_1 + X_2^0\hat{k}_2$, and $X_1\hat{\ell}_1 + X_2\hat{\ell}_2 + X_r\hat{\ell}_r = \bar{L} = X_1^0\hat{\ell}_1 + X_2^0\hat{\ell}_2$. Then $\hat{k}_1\Delta X_1 + \hat{k}_2\Delta X_2 = -X_r\hat{k}_r$, and $\hat{\ell}_1\Delta X_1 + \hat{\ell}_2\Delta X_2 = -X_r\hat{\ell}_r$. Hence

$$\Delta X_1 = -\left(\frac{\hat{k}_r\hat{\ell}_2 - \hat{\ell}_r\hat{k}_2}{\hat{k}_1\hat{\ell}_2 - \hat{k}_2\hat{\ell}_1}\right)X_r, \tag{7}$$

and

$$\Delta X_2 = -\left(\frac{\hat{k}_1\hat{\ell}_r - \hat{\ell}_1\hat{k}_r}{\hat{k}_1\hat{\ell}_2 - \hat{k}_2\hat{\ell}_1}\right)X_r. \tag{8}$$

Now, without loss of generality, assume that good 1 is the exportable and, moreover, capital intensive, that is, $\hat{k}_1/\hat{\ell}_1 > \hat{k}_2/\hat{\ell}_2$, and, further, that $X_r > 0$. Then we can conclude:

Zone I: $\Delta X_1 < 0$ and $\Delta X_2 > 0$. This zone will necessarily be entered by the R-line if $\hat{k}_r/\hat{\ell}_r > \hat{k}_1/\hat{\ell}_1 > \hat{k}_2/\hat{\ell}_2$, as evident from (7) and (8). Recall that the social cost of revenue seeking is $(\Delta X_1 + p^*\Delta X_2)$, which is, of course, the same as $X_r(\hat{\ell}_r\hat{w}^* + \hat{k}_r\hat{r}^*)$. Therefore, we can see from figure 3 that, given the fact that the free-trade production point P^* is to the right of P_t (because good 1 is assumed to be the exportable), welfare improvement cannot occur in zone I since the output of the exportable (importable) decreases (increases) compared with P_t. Revenue seeking will therefore be necessarily welfare worsening.

Zone II: $\Delta X_1 \leqslant 0$ and $\Delta X_2 \leqslant 0$. This zone will necessarily be entered by the R-line if $\hat{k}_1/\hat{\ell}_1 \geqslant \hat{k}_r/\hat{\ell}_r \geqslant \hat{k}_2/\hat{\ell}_2$, as evident from (7) and (8). Again, it follows that revenue seeking cannot be welfare improving, as seen immediately from the social-cost formula, $(\Delta X_1 + p^*\Delta X_2)$.

Zone III: $\Delta X_1 > 0$ and $\Delta X_2 < 0$. This zone will necessarily be entered by the R-line if $\hat{k}_1/\hat{\ell}_1 > \hat{k}_2/\hat{\ell}_2 > \hat{k}_r/\hat{\ell}_r$. In this zone (and this zone alone), therefore, it is evident from figure 3, as also from the social-cost formula, that welfare-improving revenue seeking can occur. It will occur, furthermore, if and only if $(\hat{\ell}_r\hat{w}^* + \hat{k}_r\hat{r}^*) < 0$.

Moreover, we may subdivide zone III with the dashed international price line P_tQ. The R-lines in the subzone to the left of P_tQ evidently must result in necessary welfare worsening, whereas the R-lines in the subzone to the right of P_tQ must result in welfare improvement.[16]

V. Quota Equilibrium with Rent Seeking

Consider now the replacement of a tariff with a quota that is equivalent to it if there is neither revenue seeking nor rent seeking. Furthermore, let there be fully competitive rent seeking.

Note first that, in the final rent-seeking equilibrium, the rents on imports must equal the value of factors devoted to rent seeking, exactly as the tariff revenues equaled the value of the factors devoted to revenue seeking. Next, the generalized R-line P_tR for rent seeking (at the initial implicit tariff) need not be identical to that for revenue seeking since the K/L ratio in the two seeking activities may differ.

Thus consider figure 4, where the initial quota equilibrium, in the absence of rent seeking, is at P_t, C_t and the quota is for import-level $\overline{M}$. Assuming that P_tR_r is the generalized R-line (at the initial implicit

[16] Note, however, that an R-line in the welfare-improving subzone of zone III, on reaching complete specialization, will wind back toward the origin and so will eventually enter the welfare-worsening zones. Finally, we may note that (as we have shown at some length in a subsection which is not being published for reasons of economy of space but which is available from us on request) the paradoxical possibility of welfare-improving revenue seeking is compatible with the share of revenue seeking in total revenue being unity, although, that would imply, in our model, that the economy would have reached complete specialization. Where the economy is incompletely specialized, the share of revenue seeking is less than unity.

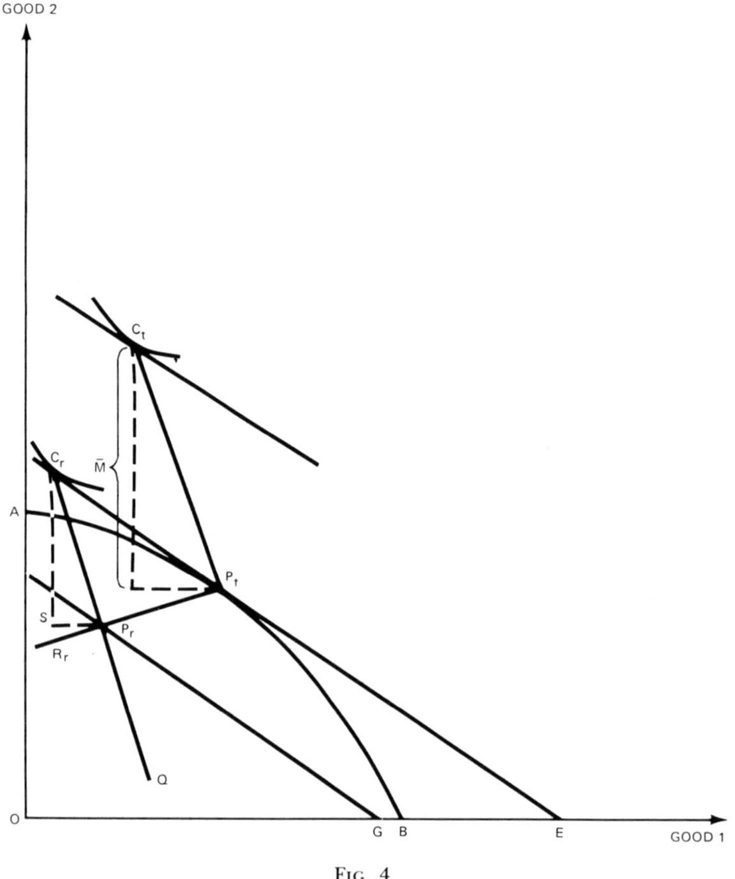

FIG. 4

tariff) for diversion of factors to rent seeking and that the implicit tariff will remain unchanged in the rent-seeking equilibrium, production will shift P_r with consumption at C_r. Evidently, in that event, the import level would be C_rS and the resources diverted to rent seeking would be worth GE, the value of the rents in terms of X_1.

However, the critical difference now from the tariff analysis is that $C_rS < \overline{M}$ so that the quota is not binding, thus contradicting the premise underlying the analysis! The rent-seeking equilibrium will therefore involve a different implicit tariff, with its associated R-line (which will be different from the original R-line because it will start from a different point on AB *and* the K/L ratio in rent seeking will have changed with the implicit tariff). If normality of each good in consumption is assumed and we assume that the R-lines do not cross despite the changing K/L ratios in rent seeking, the situation depicted in figure 4 will involve equilibrium at a lower implicit tariff.

Among the important conclusions that follow from the rent-seeking analysis is that the Metzler production paradox can evidently arise now as much as with the tariff plus revenue-seeking equilibrium: A *QR* may wind up deprotecting the importable industry!

The other paradoxes established for the revenue-seeking case in Section III will hold, *mutatis mutandis*, in the rent-seeking case. In particular, we should note that rent seeking can be welfare improving as much as revenue seeking was shown to be. And the condition for this paradox to arise can be put into the same shadow-wage format as in (6) for revenue seeking. This can be done by noting that, with the *QR* resulting in changes in factor-use coefficients and prices facing consumers even for "small" changes in rent-seeking activity, we cannot work with changes in value of output foregone at international prices as our welfare-impact index. The shadow prices of factors must therefore be expressed directly in terms of the effect on the utility function and can be derived to be

$$\hat{w}^* = U_1\left(\frac{dX_1}{d\bar{L}} + \frac{f_1^1}{f_1^2}\cdot\frac{dX_2}{d\bar{L}}\right)(X_r \text{ fixed}), \tag{9}$$

and

$$\hat{r}^* = U_1\left(\frac{dX_1}{d\bar{K}} + \frac{f_1^1}{f_1^2}\cdot\frac{dX_2}{d\bar{K}}\right)(X_r \text{ fixed}), \tag{10}$$

where $f^i(\hat{k}_i, \hat{\ell}_i) = 1, i = 1, 2, r$, are the "intensive" production functions in the three activities. We can then get the welfare impact of rent seeking quite simply into the now-familiar format as

$$\frac{dU}{dX_r} = -(\ell_r\hat{w}^* + k_r\hat{r}^*), \tag{11}$$

and the welfare-improving paradox will evidently reappear when the bracketed social cost is negative and leads to $dU/dX_r > 0$.

VI. The Nonequivalence of Tariffs and Quotas

The preceding analysis has immediate implications for the question of whether tariffs and quotas are equivalent once seeking activities are introduced. Specifically, if the import level in the revenue-seeking equilibrium were turned into a quota (with attendant rent seeking), and all revenues and rents were fully and competitively sought, would this quota lead to an identical implicit tariff as the explicit tariff that was being replaced—this being the equivalence definition of Bhagwati (1965)? That is, if the import level in the tariff-with-revenue-seeking equilibrium (i.e., C_rH in fig. 1) were turned into a quota and rent seeking were then present, would not this quota lead to an identical real equilibrium, with the implicit tariff equal to the earlier explicit tariff and therefore with production at P_r and consumption at C_r? It should be evident now that this can happen only if the generalized Rybczynski locus P_tR_t for revenue seeking and the locus P_tR_r for rent seeking were the same. Otherwise, the quota C_rH will exceed or fall short of the imports in the rent-seeking equilibrium (at the implicit tariff defined by domestic price line P_tE), and the final rent-seeking equilibrium with import level C_rH will involve a reduced or increased implicit tariff.

In this important sense just defined, therefore, tariffs and quotas cease, generally speaking, to be equivalent when revenue seeking and rent seeking accompany them, respectively, and the nonequivalence arises essentially from the differences in capital intensity that can exist between the revenue-seeking and rent-seeking activities. This nonequivalence is at a much deeper level and is based on a more appropriate formulation of the problem than the Krueger (1974) proposition of nonequivalence which rests on permitting rent seeking for the quota and omitting altogether revenue seeking for the tariff.

An implication of the immediately preceding argument is that, if revenue seeking is admitted on the tariff side just as rent seeking is admitted on the quota side, this renders invalid Krueger's (1974, p. 295) central conclusion that, subject to an identical import level, the quota equilibrium will necessarily involve lower welfare vis-à-vis the tariff equilibrium. Thus, fixing the import level at the amount reached in the revenue-seeking equilibrium, it is easily seen that the rent-seeking equilibrium will imply lower or higher welfare than the revenue-seeking equilibrium according as the implicit tariff is higher or lower in the rent-seeking equilibrium. The outcome therefore may imply, in particular cases, that a quota is worse than a tariff, but it may imply the opposite as well.

VII. Measuring the Cost of Protection with Seeking

Finally, what happens to the familiar Hicksian measures of the cost of protection, as in Johnson's (1960) classic paper on the cost of protection? Lack of space forbids us to illustrate our argument fully. But it is evident that, in the presence of revenue seeking, the cost of protection can be decomposed in two alternative ways: either (1) take the "true" shift in production (e.g., from P^* in free trade to P_r in tariff-with-revenue-seeking equilibrium in fig. 1) in measuring the production cost (which would then be QN in terms of good 1 in fig. 1) and add to it the usual consumption cost; or (2) decompose the "true" production cost (QN) into two elements: (i) the production cost corresponding to the production shift as it would occur in the absence of revenue seeking under the tariff (i.e., from P^* to P_t in fig. 1) and (ii) the further cost (or gain) corresponding to the added shift in production thanks to revenue seeking (i.e., from P_t to P_r in fig. 1).

Correspondingly, if the analyst is considering the cost of a quota with rent seeking that has led to an identical equilibrium shift in production (P^* to P_r in fig. 1), the two alternative ways of approaching the cost of protection are equally applicable (with GE representing, not tariff revenue, but the rents on the quota).

What does one make of Krueger's proposition that the cost of quota protection is now the cost of its "tariff equivalent" (without revenue seeking) "plus the value of the rents" (1974, p. 302), that is, that the total cost in figure 1 is (i) the production cost corresponding to the shift from P^* to P_t plus (ii) the consumption cost plus (iii) the value of the rents (GE)?

This is evidently inappropriate for two reasons: First, the value of the rents is always positive, whereas, under conditions established in Section IV above, the production cost of the seeking activity may be negative and hence a gain (as in the shift from P_t to P_r in fig. 2 rather than fig. 1), and second, even when the added production shift imposed by rent seeking imposes a production cost, this will be less than the value of the rents except under complete specialization in production of the exportable good.[17] Moreover, an empirical analyst must also note that it is extremely unlikely that all rents will be sought competitively.

For all these reasons, it is certain that the valid procedure to estimate the cost of protection in the presence of seeking activities is to measure this cost conventionally, taking the production cost as that defined by the shift in production to the seeking equilibrium from the free-trade equilibrium. This does mean that the analyst must estimate, in general equilibrium with suitable specification of the seeking activities as in this paper, the shift in production from the observed seeking equilibrium (P_r) to the hypothetical free-trade equilibrium (P^*). But this has to be done in any case, even if seeking activity is at zero level as in the conventional analysis.

VIII. Concluding Observations

We hope to have opened up an entirely new, and important, aspect of the theory of tariffs and welfare by analyzing revenue seeking. The

[17] Both of these possibilities were excluded by the restrictive model of Krueger (1974), which assumed complete specialization on the exportable good and that all rents were sought competitively.

analysis is further applicable, it should be evident, quite without qualification to the welfare effect of tariffs (in the absence of revenue seeking) when their collection involves a direct cost. For, in this case, we would be considering a situation that is formally equivalent to revenue seeking: The use of primary factors in revenue seeking associated with tariffs is, to that extent, identical with the use of these factors instead for revenue collection.

It should be emphasized that one of our central conclusions, that is, that revenue seeking may be welfare improving, follows from the fact that resource diversion to seeking activities occurs in a second-best situation since the economy is characterized by a tariff distortion. Therefore, conclusions based on first-best intuitions, that is, that resource diversion to "unproductive" activities must be wasteful, will not carry over into the analysis of seeking activities. It is this inadvertent confusion between first-best and second-best analyses which really accounts for the erroneous conclusion by the analysts of rent-seeking activities in the QR case that they necessarily increase the losses imposed by the QR directly.

Finally, many extensions suggest themselves. For example, it would be fruitful to establish the conditions under which the Metzler production paradox, demonstrated only as a possibility in this paper, would arise. Similarly, the conditions under which a tariff would have to be increased (decreased) in order to maintain a certain target level of importable production could also be established. The interaction of tariff evasion with revenue seeking also provides yet another example of the kind of policy-relevant welfare-theoretic analysis that could be undertaken.

References

Bhagwati, Jagdish N. "On the Underinvoicing of Imports." *Bull. Oxford Univ. Inst. Statis.* 26 (November 1964): 389–97.

———. "On the Equivalence of Tariffs and Quotas." In *Trade, Growth and the Balance of Payments*, edited by Richard E. Caves, Peter B. Kenen, and Harry G. Johnson. Chicago: Rand McNally, 1965.

———. "Fiscal Policies, the Faking of Foreign Trade Declarations, and the Balance of Payments." *Bull. Oxford Univ. Inst. Statis.* 29 (February 1967): 61–77.

———. "Distortions and Immiserizing Growth: A Generalization." *Rev. Econ. Studies* 35 (October 1968): 481–85.

———. *India in the International Economy: A Policy Framework for a Progressive Society.* Lal Bahadur Shastri Memorial Lectures. Hyderabad, India: Osmania Univ. Press, 1973.

———, ed. *Illegal Transactions in International Trade: Theory and Measurement.* Amsterdam: North-Holland, 1974.

———. *The Anatomy and Consequences of Exchange Control Regimes.* Cambridge, Mass.: Ballinger (for Nat. Bur. Econ. Res.), 1978.

———. "Revenue-Seeking and Rent-Seeking: The Theory of Commercial Policy." Mimeographed. Cambridge, Mass.: Massachusetts Inst. Tech., May 1979.

Bhagwati, Jagdish N., and Hansen, Bent. "A Theoretical Analysis of Smuggling." *Q.J.E.* 87 (May 1973): 172–87.

Bhagwati, Jagdish N., and Srinivasan, T. N. "Smuggling and Trade Policy." *J. Public Econ.* 2 (November 1973): 377–89.

———. "On Inferring Resource Allocational Implications from DRC Calculations in Trade-distorted, Small Open Economies." *Indian Econ. Rev.*, n.s. 14 (April 1979): 1–16.

Bhagwati, Jagdish N.; Srinivasan, T. N.; and Wan, Henry, Jr. "Value Subtracted, Negative Shadow Prices of Factors in Project Evaluation and Immiserizing Growth: Three Paradoxes in the Presence of Trade Distortions." *Econ. J.* 88 (March 1978): 121–25.

Brock, William A., and Magee, Stephen P. "The Economics of Special Interest Politics: The Case of the Tariff." *A.E.R. Papers and Proc.* 68 (May 1978): 246–50.

Cheh, John H. "United States Concessions in the Kennedy Round and Short-Run Labor Adjustments Costs." *J. Internat. Econ.* 4 (November 1974): 323–40.

Falvey, Rodney E. "A Note on Preferential and Illegal Trade under Quantitative Restrictions." *Q.J.E.* 92 (February 1978): 175–78.

Findlay, Ronald, and Wellisz, Stanislaw. "Project Evaluation, Shadow Prices, and Trade Policy." *J.P.E.* 84, no. 3 (June 1976): 543–52.

———. "Rent-Seeking, Welfare, and the Political Economy of Trade Restrictions." Mimeographed. New York: Columbia Univ., 1979.

Johnson, Harry G. "The Cost of Protection and the Scientific Tariff." *J.P.E.* 68, no. 4 (August 1960): 327–45.

———. "The Possibility of Income Losses from Increased Efficiency or Factor Accumulation in the Presence of Tariffs." *Econ. J.* 77 (March 1967): 151–54.

———. "Notes on the Economic Theory of Smuggling." *Malayan Econ. Rev.* 17 (April 1972): 1–7. Reprinted in *Illegal Transactions in International Trade: Theory and Measurement*, edited by Jagdish N. Bhagwati. Amsterdam: North-Holland, 1974.

Krueger, Anne O. "The Political Economy of the Rent-seeking Society." *A.E.R.* 64 (June 1974): 291–303.

Meade, James E. *A Geometry of International Trade.* London: Allen & Unwin, 1952.

Ray, Alok. "Smuggling, Import Objectives, and Optimum Tax Structure." *Q.J.E.* 92 (August 1978): 509–14.

Sheikh, Munir A. "Smuggling, Production and Welfare." *J. Internat. Econ.* 4 (November 1974): 355–64.

Srinivasan, T. N., and Bhagwati, Jagdish N. "Shadow Prices for Project Selection in the Presence of Distortions: Effective Rates of Protection and Domestic Resource Costs." *J.P.E.* 86, no. 1 (February 1978): 97–116.

Tullock, Gordon. "The Welfare Cost of Tariffs, Monopolies, and Theft." *Western Econ. J.* 5 (June 1967): 224–32.

———. "Efficient Rent-Seeking." Mimeographed. Blacksburg: Center Study Public Choice, Virginia Polytechnic Inst. and State Univ., 1978.

Revenue Seeking: A Generalization of the Theory of Tariffs—a Correction

Jagdish N. Bhagwati

Columbia University

T. N. Srinivasan

Yale University

In our paper on "Revenue Seeking: A Generalization of the Theory of Tariffs" (1980), we extended the theory of tariffs to include revenue seeking. We also compared tariffs with quotas, under seeking activities associated with the revenues from the former and with the rents (i.e., license premia) from the latter. We argued, among other propositions, that: (1) Revenue seeking was a zero-output activity undertaken in the presence of, and triggered by, a distortion. (2) Therefore the questions about whether and what losses it imposed were second-best (rather than first-best) questions, and thus such a seeking activity could be beneficial rather than immiserizing (i.e., the shadow price of a primary factor of production could be [sufficiently] negative). (3) Correspondingly, premium seeking[1]—the "command" counterpart of the revenue-seeking phenomenon—was also a second-best phenomenon. (4) Therefore, premium seeking may also be beneficial rather than immiserizing, contrary to Krueger's (1974) argument reflecting first-best intuition. (5) The welfare cost of a quota could not, in view of the second-best nature of the problem, be measured generally (as Krueger [1974] had proposed) as the cost of an equivalent tariff (in the absence of any seeking) plus the value of the rents even if all rents were competitively sought. (6) A proper comparison of tariffs and quotas would have to compare a tariff with revenue seeking vis-à-vis a quota with premium seeking, in preference to Krueger's (1974) comparison of a quota with full premium

Thanks are due to Richard Brecher for drawing to our attention the work of Mahmudul Anam at Carleton University, who spotted the error noted in this *erratum*. Partial financial support by the National Science Foundation is acknowledged.

[1] Krueger (1974) and we, after her, called this "rent seeking," but "premium seeking" is a more appropriate term (see Bhagwati 1981; Bhagwati and Srinivasan 1981).

[*Journal of Political Economy*, 1982, vol. 90, no. 1]

seeking vis-à-vis a tariff with no revenue seeking at all. (7) In that event, tariffs and quotas could not be uniquely rank ordered in welfare terms.

All these propositions are valid except for 4. It is impossible (except in ways which are spelled out later in this note) for premium seeking to be beneficial. The reason is that, when a quota is binding, it prevents the second-best nature of the problem from resulting in welfare improvement since the quantity constraint "bottles up" the source of positive gain that may outweigh the loss implied by the diversion of real resources to the zero-output-seeking activity.

The economic argument underlying this result is straightforward. Recall, from the theory of policy intervention to achieve a non-economic objective that requires imports to be constrained (Johnson 1967; Bhagwati and Srinivasan 1969), that the optimal policy for this is a tariff policy. It follows that, for the level of binding imports associated with the preseeking equilibrium, the implicit tariff at that equilibrium is indeed the least-cost tariff. *Any* move away from that equilibrium, therefore, will be suboptimal, that is, immiserizing if imports remain fixed at the same level. Therefore premium seeking, since it does shift production and therefore the preseeking equilibrium, will always be welfare worsening. As long as imports are fixed quantitatively, therefore, premium seeking has to be immiserizing.

Note further that the result holds equally for export and import quotas when the country is small. Again, for a small country, the result will hold if the quotas are defined in foreign values rather than in pure quantity. However, even for a small country, the critical constraint on import quantity may be relaxed, opening up the possibility of beneficial premium seeking if an import quota is defined in domestic values: For, as the implicit tariff falls, the same domestic value constraint can accommodate an increasing quantity of imports.

For a large country, however, the possibility of admitting the paradox of beneficial premium seeking is enhanced. Thus, while an import quota will eliminate this possibility, an export quota does not (unless one imposes the restriction that the foreign offer curve be elastic). Thus the same export level may be compatible with more than one import quantity, and the critical import quantity constraint may not operate to exclude the paradox of beneficial premium seeking. Again, even if the import quota is fixed in foreign values, the variable terms of trade implied by the large-country assumption can relax the import constraint and open up the paradoxical possibility.[2]

[2] The important issue of comparing seeking activities triggered generally by price versus quantity distortions has been treated elsewhere by us in depth (Bhagwati and Srinivasan 1981).

References

Bhagwati, Jagdish N. "Directly-Unproductive Profit-Seeking (DUP) Activities: A Theoretical Generalization." Working Paper no. 80, Columbia Univ., Dept. Econ., April 1981.

Bhagwati, Jagdish N., and Srinivasan, T. N. "Optimal Intervention to Achieve Non-economic Objectives." *Rev. Econ. Studies* 36 (January 1969): 27–38.

———. "Revenue Seeking: A Generalization of the Theory of Tariffs." *J.P.E.* 88, no. 6 (December 1980): 1069–87.

———. "The Welfare Consequences of Directly-Unproductive Profit-Seeking (DUP) Activities: Price versus Quantity Distortions." Mimeographed. Discussion Paper no. 375, Yale Univ., Econ. Growth Center, March 1981.

Johnson, Harry G. "The Possibility of Income Losses from Increased Efficiency or Factor Accumulation in the Presence of Tariffs." *Econ. J.* 77 (March 1967): 151–54.

Krueger, Anne O. "The Political Economy of the Rent-Seeking Society." *A.E.R.* 64 (June 1974): 291–303.

Journal of Public Economics 14 (1980) 355–363. © North-Holland Publishing Company

LOBBYING AND WELFARE*

Jagdish N. BHAGWATI**

Columbia University, New York, NY 10027, USA

Received May 1980, revised version received June 1980

The paper shows that the cost of any distortion, arising without the aid of resource-using lobbying addressed to having the distortion implemented, is not necessarily less than the cost of the same distortion arising with the aid of such lobbying. This refutation of the prevalent assertions to the contrary reflects the second-best nature of the problem at hand.

1. Introduction

A great deal of interest has arisen recently in the analysis of lobbying activities and their welfare impact. Much of this interest has been a result of the general feeling that economists have traditionally underestimated the overall cost to society that arises from protection, monopoly, etc. once the entire lobbying process that accompanies the rise of such protection, monopoly, etc. is also taken into account. Consider therefore the following quotes from three prominent economists. For example, in the context of the cost of tariff protection, Tullock (1967, p. 228) has argued as follows:

> Generally governments do not impose protective tariffs on their own. They have to be lobbied or pressured into doing so by the expenditure of resources in political activity. One would anticipate that the domestic producers would invest resources in lobbying for the tariff until the marginal return on the last dollar so spent was equal to its likely return producing the transfer. There might also be other interests trying to prevent the transfer and putting resources into influencing the government in the other direction. *These expenditures*, which may simply offset each

*This paper was written while the author was Ford International Professor of Economics at MIT.

**Thanks are due to the NSF Grant no. SOC79-07541 for financial support of the research underlying this paper. My thoughts on this subject have developed in the course of work on cost–benefit analysis and on revenue-seeking, undertaken with T.N. Srinivasan, where the second-best nature of the required analysis and the possibility of negative shadow prices for factors in distorted economies first rose to our attention and Srinivasan should therefore share in the credit for such merits as this paper might have. Cf. Srinivasan and Bhagwati (1978) for the cost–benefit analysis and Bhagwati and Srinivasan (1980) for the analysis of revenue-seeking.

> other to some extent, *are purely wasteful from the standpoint of society as a whole;* they are spent not in increasing wealth, but in attempts to transfer or resist transfer of wealth. I can suggest no way of measuring these expenditures, but the potential returns are large, and it would be quite surprising if the investment was not also sizable. (Emphasis added.)

Again, in her analysis of lobbying to secure a share of the rents that characterize import quotas, Krueger (1974) concludes that the cost of protection is understated in the case of quotas by the usual 'triangles' calculation because the rents fetched by the import quotas lead to lobbying for a share of these licenses: a phenomenon she christens as 'rent-seeking'. Citing other such rents and associated lobbying activities that they generate, she concludes (1974, p. 302):

> Each of these and other interventions lead people to compete for the rents although the competitors often do not perceive themselves as such. In each case, *there is a deadweight loss associated with that competition over and above the traditional triangle.* (Emphasis added.)

And Rachel McCulloch (1979, p. 83), in reviewing the current literature on the cost of protection, accepts the general position that lobbying is necessarily welfare-worsening and that therefore the 'traditional' measures of the cost of protection are understatements of the true social costs:

> Economists have never been fully satisfied with measured costs of protection as calculated by the standard Marshallian approach — the 'tiny triangles' of lost consumers' and producers' surplus . . . tariff or quota protection, subsidies, and special tax treatment can be beneficial to any industry or special interest group, irrespective of whether these measures contribute to the efficiency of the economy as a whole. Thus, a government receptive to arguments for intervention in the name of increased efficiency will receive petitions from all sectors of the economy, based on claims by each firm and industry group that it also falls into one or another of these categories. The net effect is to turn economic activity away from the production of goods and services available to the final consumer and toward attempts to influence the legislative and administrative process . . . *The loss thus incurred is probably far greater than any of the present estimates of the cost of protection;* . . . (Emphasis added.)

Now, there are two quite *distinct*, but evidently undistinguished, propositions that seem to be implied by these quotes: first, that the cost of (say) protection when this protection is levied without resource-using lobbying (addressed to having it levied) will be necessarily *below* the cost of identical protection which results instead as a consequence of such lobbying;[1] and second, that the conventional estimates of the cost of distortions such as protection are *underestimates* insofar as they ignore the lobbying that gives rise to such distortions.

As it happens, the first contention is false, as argued in section 2 below. However, as will be discussed in section 3, the second assertion may well be justified.

2. The cost of protection with and without tariff-seeking lobbying: First-best versus second-best

The assertion that the cost of a distortion levied with the aid of resource-using lobbying must necessarily exceed its cost if levied without such lobbying is based on the *first-best* intuition that resources devoted to lobbying have a positive social cost. However, the distortion implies that the resources devoted to lobbying are being withdrawn from productive use in a *second-best* situation, and thus their social cost *may* by negative! That lobbying may therefore be welfare-improving rather than immiserizing (in the sense that the distortion imposed without such lobbying may be more costly than when imposed with such lobbying), since the situation is a second-best rather than a first-best one, is a conclusion of the same order of importance analytically as Viner's (1950) pathbreaking conclusion that a move *towards* a free trade area was not the same as a move to free trade, that a customs union therefore may be (trade-diverting and hence) immiserizing even though a nonpreferential move to full free trade was necessarily welfare-improving.

While the conclusion that lobbying may be welfare-improving applies evidently to all classes of lobbying, it is useful to consider here the original Tullock problem of lobbying for a tariff, what Bhagwati and Srinivisan (1980) christen as 'tariff-seeking'. It is readily shown then that the lobbying may be welfare-improving *vis-à-vis* a situation where the resulting tariff happens to be exogenously imposed without the lobbying.

Thus, consider the traditional 2×2 Heckscher–Ohlin–Samuelson model in fig. 1. AB is the production possibility curve, P^* the free trade production for this small economy at the *given* world price-ratio p^*, and P_t the production at the tariff-inclusive domestic price-ratio p_t when this tariff is considered as arbitrarily imposed without lobbying. However, lobbying does occur and absorbs real resources, withdrawing primary factors from the production of goods X_1 and X_2. Therefore, the equilibrium production lies at P_t^l, under lobbying-inclusive protection on the shrunk-in production possibility curve A_tB_t, which is based on primary factor endowment *net* of the factors used in the lobbying process that yields the tariff depicted.

[1]In fact, Krueger (1974) explicitly compares a quota (or equivalent tariff) without rent-seeking with the same quota attended by rent-seeking.

Now, the way P_t^l is drawn relative to P_t, it is evident that the valuation of national income at world prices, p^*, has *increased*, rather than fallen, as a result of the lobbying: by QS in terms of good X_1. With a well-behaved social utility function, therefore, lobbying has improved welfare![2]

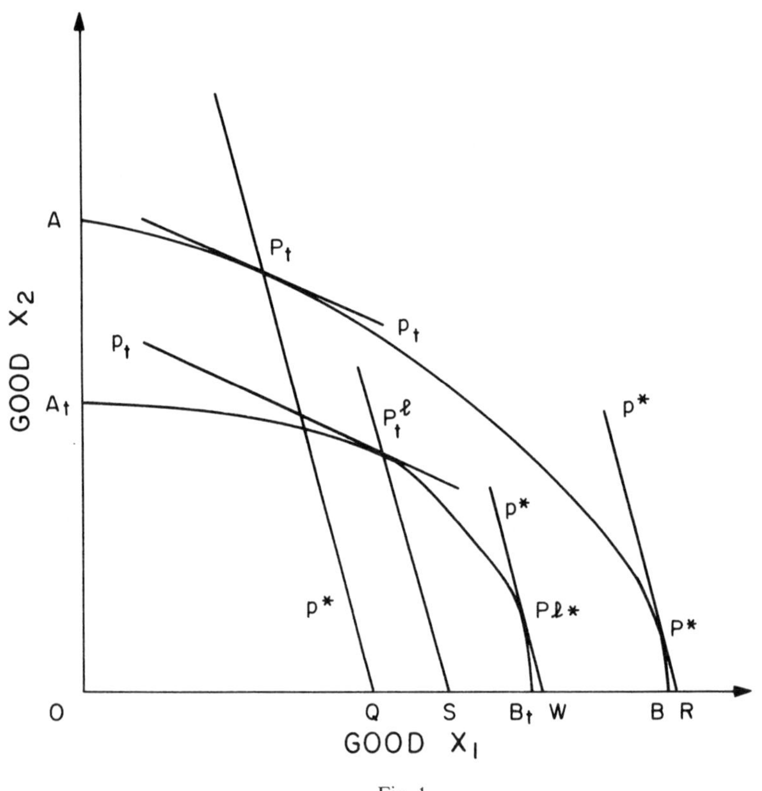

Fig. 1.

Fig. 2 delineates two zones into which lobbying may take the production point P_t^l from P_t: zone I where lobbying will be immiserizing and zone II where it will be beneficial. These zones are divided by the world price-ratio p^* and evidently therefore, since P_t and P_t^l must lie on a Rybczynski (1955) line (defined at the tariff-inclusive domestic price-ratio p_t), the relative slopes

[2]Inferior goods, leading to multiple equilibrium, may imply that an improvement in national income at world prices still leads to welfare worsening. However, a welfare-improving equilibrium will necessarily exist, so that *potential* improvement in welfare can always be inferred.

of the world price-ratio and the Rybczynski-line will determine whether the lobbying will be immiserizing or beneficial.[3]

Of course, zone II with beneficial welfare-impact from tariff-seeking lobbying is where the shadow price of the primary factors withdrawn from productive use into the lobbying activity (with its zero-productive-output) is negative [cf. Srinivasan and Bhagwati (1978) and Bhagwati, Srinivasan and Wan (1979)]. And it is equally the reverse of the case analyzed by Johnson (1967) where the *augmentation* of factor supply in productive use is *immiserizing.*

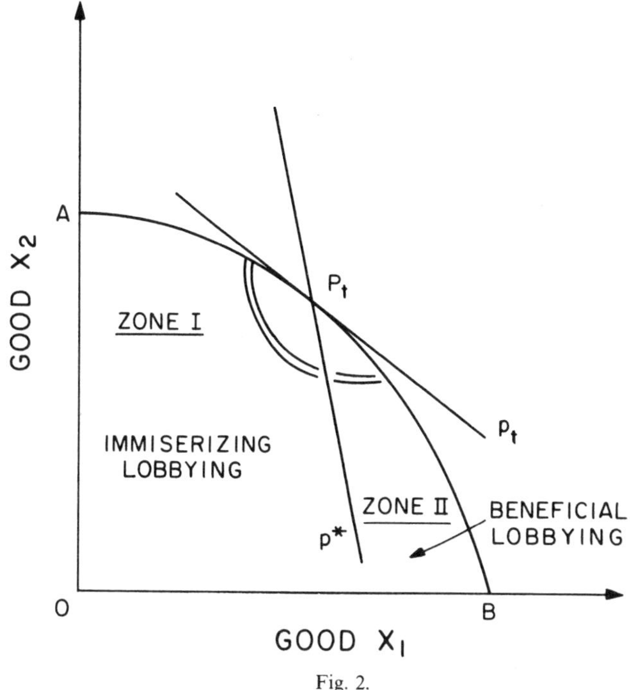

Fig. 2.

The cost of protection therefore may be reduced, rather than increased, by the presence of lobbying that diverts resources from (directly) productive use. The total cost of any level of protection, if imposed with resource-using lobbying, is thus *not* necessarily greater than the cost of an identical level of

[3]The slope of the Rybczynski line, in turn, will reflect the relative factor intensities of the goods X_1 and X_2, and of the lobbying activity [cf. Bhagwati and Srinivasan (1980)]. For readers unfamiliar with Rybczynski (1955), it may be noted that the Rybczynski line is derived, for varying factor endowments (the variation being done identically at each successive stage), at a *constant* goods price-ratio.

protection imposed without the aid of such lobbying, contrary to what is implied by the distinguished economists cited at the outset.

A few remarks are in order concerning what has just been proven, precisely because it runs counter to the widespread presumptions in the literature. First, it should be emphasized that there is a fundamental difference between asserting that the world is characterized by distortions and therefore we cannot say anything definite in the resulting second-best environment, and arguing that the world is first-best but that the problem at hand *itself* introduces an inherently second-best situation. The latter is what characterizes the present problem: the lobbying itself introduces a second-best situation insofar as it brings about the distortion the total cost of which is being considered.[4] Second, the fact that one cannot sign the welfare effect of resource-using lobbying in general, with the customary restrictions, does diminish the scope of 'qualitative economics'. But in opening up the need for parametric estimates in making the correct inference in specific situations, it increases rather than diminishes the need for economic analysis. Third, one may well ask whether this welfare-improving possibility is a 'likely' one (ignoring the fact that the second-best nature of the problem, once demonstrated, implies that the sensible thing to do in general is to evaluate each specific case separately). This question may be approached in two different ways.

(1) Can we think of reasonable conditions under which, in models normally used in our analysis, lobbying may shift the economy into the welfare-improving zone II of fig. 2? Note that zone II can be entered only if the output of the (nonlobbying) sector producing good X_1 goes up. We now take two models, in turn. First, take the Jones (1971)–Neary (1978) sector-specific model where one factor (say labor) is mobile and goods X_1 and X_2 each have a specific factor. Assume that lobbying for protection of good X_2 uses intensively the factor specific to X_2.[5] In that case the marginal product of the mobile factor will fall in X_2 and hence the output of X_1 will rise as a result of this lobbying (although it may not rise sufficiently to enter zone II). Second, in the standard 2×2 model with all factors mobile, it is easily shown that if lobbying is capital-intensive (labor-intensive) relative to X_2 when X_2 is capital-intensive (labor-intensive) relative to X_1, that will again increase the output of X_1 and thus satisfy the necessary condition for welfare-improving lobbying. 'Strange' conditions are therefore not necessary, in

[4] It is probably worth noting that lobbying that does not succeed in its intended target will leave the first-best situation undisturbed and hence will indeed represent welfare-worsening lobbying.

[5] As this paper is being written the MIT corridor walls are plastered with posters advertising lectures by Ford and United Automobile Workers Union executives on the plight of the US auto industry and its need for protection!

familiar models, to generate the lobbying-caused output changes that are necessary for beneficial lobbying.[6]

(2) Moreover, if we consider empirical observation as a guide to making *a priori* judgements on the subject, it is pertinent to note that many empirical studies of trade-distorted economies have turned up observations of value subtraction at world prices in certain sectors. Evidently, withdrawal of resources from such sectors would be welfare-improving even if these resources were then not put to productive use. It is not unreasonable, when one thinks more deeply about it, that distortions occasionally can get out of hand resulting in what appears at first blush to be improbable outcomes.

3. Are conventional estimates of the cost of protection underestimates?

The preceding analysis does not map wholly into the question which looks superficially identical to that just analyzed: whether the conventional estimates of the cost of protection (and other distortions for that matter) are *underestimates* because they do not bring into the analysis the lobbying process leading to the protection. For the answer to this question will vary depending on how one interprets the conventional estimates. Indeed, for one of three different interpretations it is possible to sustain the assertion that the conventional estimates are underestimates, whereas for others they are not.

To see this, first note that the overall production cost of protection in fig. 1, in the lobbying-inclusive equilibrium, is SR, measured in units of good X_1. Next, there are two alternative ways of decomposing this cost into two constitutent elements: the cost of the protection itself and the cost of the resources lost in the lobbying process.

Method I. Here, following the procedure implicit in the argument of section 2, the cost of the protection is measured as QR, reflecting the distortion of production along AB from P^* to P_t; and the lobbying cost (or gain, as it happens, in fig. 1) as QS, reflecting the further shift in production from P_t to P_t^l. Thus, the total production cost of protection is decomposed as follows:

$$\underset{\substack{\text{(total}\\\text{production}\\\text{cost)}}}{SR} = \underset{\substack{\text{(cost of}\\\text{protection,}\\\textit{per se}\text{)}}}{QR} + \underset{\substack{\text{(cost, or}\\\text{gain, of}\\\text{lobbying)}}}{(-QS)}$$

Method II. Here, we decompose SR along an alternative route. Thus, put the world price-line tangent to the 'restricted' production possibility curve A_tB_t at P^{l*} (this restricted curve A_tB_t being defined of course on the primary factors *net* of those used up in the lobbying). Then, the decomposition of SR

[6]Cf. Bhagwati and Srinivasan (1980). On the other hand, if lobbying uses X_1 and/or X_2 directly or, in the Jones–Neary model, the lobbying is intensive in the use of the mobile factor, zone II is necessarily excluded as an outcome.

can be as follows: WR, reflecting the cost of resource-loss in lobbying with production moving from P^* to P^{l*} and SW, reflecting the cost of the protection and the attendant move of production from p^{l*} to P^l_t. Thus, the total production cost of protection is now decomposed as follows:

SR	$=$	SW	$+$	WR
(total production cost)		(cost of protection, *per se*)		(cost of lobbying)

Note, in particular, that the cost of lobbying is now necessarily positive because it is being measured at first-best policies between the two situations, with and without the use of resources in lobbying.

Now, there are three alternative views which may be taken of the conventional estimates of the production cost of protection in the literature.

(1) The conventional estimates may be taken as measuring SR correctly simply because the econometrician must start with the *observed* P^l_t and must estimate the *hypothetical* shift of resources to their optimal situation without the distortion. If the econometrician does this hypothetical estimate for the entire set of factor endowments, using the production functions on the two productive activities (X_1 and X_2) and the given world price vector, evidently he would be estimating P^* and therefore the resulting estimate of the production cost of protection would indeed be the correct one. It would then be incorrect to infer that the estimate was an understatement.

(2) Alternatively, it may be assumed, however, that the econometrician will calculate the cost of protection as QR, reflecting the difference between P_t and P^*. Then evidently he will be missing out QS, the shift between P_t and P^l_t. In this case the estimate may be, as we have already seen, either an underestimate or (as in fig. 1) an overestimate. However, it is highly implausible that this is in fact what the conventional estimate does, for it presupposes that the econometrician estimates two hypothetical production vectors (P^* and P_t) to make the erroneous calculation.

(3) The third and final assumption may be that the econometrician will estimate, starting from the observed P^l_t, a shift under free trade to P^{l*} rather than a shift to the fully optimal P^*, thereby estimating the production cost of protection as SW. If this is the case, then the conventional estimate will indeed be an underestimate, for it will then leave out WR, the cost attributable to lobbying. It is arguable that the conventional 'triangles', based as they are on partial-equilibrium elasticities of supply (and demand), come closer to estimating the shift from the observed production equilibrium as being to P^{l*} rather than to P^*.[7] In that case there is indeed reason to think

[7]In fact, even if the econometrician undertakes a *general-equilibrium* exercise but reallocates efficiently *only* the factors that are employed in the productive activities, this will move the econometrician from p^l_t to p^{l*}, and not to P^*. Such an exercise is, for example, carried out in the brilliant paper by Desai and Martin (1979) where a new measure of inefficiency in resource-allocation among different branches of Soviet industry is evolved and calculated.

that the existing *econometric* estimates of the cost of protection are underestimates.

And this conclusion is quite consistent, as should be obvious by now, with the conclusion of section 2 that it is theoretically inappropriate to assert that protection imposed without lobbying must necessarily be less costly than equal protection imposed with the aid of (resource-using) lobbying.

References

Bhagwati, Jagdish and T.N. Srinivasan, 1980, Revenue-seeking: A generalization of the theory of tariffs, Journal of Political Economy.

Bhagwati, Jagdish, T.N. Srinivasan and Henry Wan, Jr., 1978, Value subtracted, negative shadow prices of factors in project evaluation and immiserizing growth: Three paradoxes in the presences of trade distortions, Economic Journal 88, 121–125.

Desai, Padma and Ricardo Martin, 1979, On measuring resource-allocational efficiency in Soviet industry, Harvard Russian Research Center, August, mimeo.

Johnson, H.G., 1967, The possibility of income losses from increased effieicncy or factor accumulation in the presence of tariffs, Economic Journal 77, 151–154.

Jones, Ronald W., 1971, A three factor model in thepry, trade, and history, in: J.N. Bhagwati et al., eds., Trade, balance of payments, and growth: Essays in honor of Charles P. Kindleberger (North-Holland, Amsterdam), 3–21.

Krueger, A.O., 1974, The political economy of the rent-seeking society, American Economic Review 64 (3), 291–303.

McCulloch, Rachel, 1979, Trade and direct investment: Recent policy trends, in: R. Dornbusch and J. Frenkel, eds., International Economic Policy: Theory and Evidence (Johns Hopkins Press, Maryland), 76–105.

Neary, J. Peter, 1978, Short-run capital specificity and the pure theory of international trade, Economic Journal 88, 488–410.

Rybczynski, T.N., 1955, Factor endowment and relative commodity prices., Economica 22, 336–341; Reprinted in R.E. Caves and H.G. Johnson, eds., 1968, Readings in international economics (Richard D. Irwin, Homewood, Illinois), 58–71.

Srinivasan, T.N. and Jagdish Bhagwati, 1978, Shadow prices for project evaluation in the presence of distortions: Effective rates of protection and domestic resource costs, Journal of Political Economy 86 (1), 97–116.

Tullock, G., 1967, The welfare costs of tariffs, monopolies and theft, Western Economic Journal 5, 224–232.

Viner, Jacob, 1950, The Customs Union Issue (Carnegie Endowment for International Peace, New York).

Journal of Public Economics 19 (1982) 395–401. North-Holland Publishing Company

LOBBYING, DUP ACTIVITIES AND WELFARE

A response to Tullock*

Jagdish N. BHAGWATI

Columbia University, New York, NY 10027, USA

Received February 1982, revised version received June 1982

Professor Tullock (1981), in trying to understand the results in my (1981) paper on lobbying and welfare, has raised issues that require further clarification and analysis. For brevity's sake, I shall concentrate here on the essentials, leaving minor remarks of Tullock's aside.

(1) The specific case of lobbying which I addressed originally was tariff-seeking by protectionist lobbies: so that the tariff would be endogenous. I then showed that one could not argue, in this instance, that an exogenously-specified tariff at $x\%$ was *necessarily* welfare-superior to an endogenous tariff at $x\%$.[1] All other forms of lobbying were excluded, of course.

(2) Tullock argues that this result obtains because he and Krueger (1974) think, whereas I do not, that tariff revenues can be wasted. As it happens, Krueger (1974) made no such assumption. She explicitly compared, in her analysis of the specific case of premium-seeking for import quotas already in place, quotas (with such premium-seeking) with tariffs that had *no* corresponding revenue-seeking or, for that matter, any waste resulting from the government directly expending the tariff revenue. Bhagwati and Srinivasan (1980) were the first to introduce the revenue-seeking concept and to argue that it was wholly inappropriate for Krueger to compare tariffs and quotas on the assumption that the latter gave rise to *full* premium-seeking whereas the former gave rise to *zero* revenue-seeking!

*Thanks are due to the National Science Foundation Grant No. NSF SCS-8-25401 for support of the research underlying this note. Conversations with John Wilson and Richard Brecher, and correspondence with Gordon Tullock, have led to improvements over the first draft of this note.

[1]Incidentally, since this suggested counter-intuitively that lobbying for a tariff was welfare-improving, I also proceeded to show that one *could* decompose the overall loss from the endogenous tariff, vis-a-vis free trade, in an alternative manner which would always sign the 'normal' cost of protection and the lobbying cost agreeably. Tullock seems to have missed this section; it was not present in some of the earlier drafts of my paper which he saw in personal correspondence.

(3) Since Tullock raises the question of wastage resulting from revenues in connection with the impact of tariff seeking, let me first clarify that it is extremely important here to distinguish among three different ways in which revenues can be (wholly or fractionally) wasted. (i) In revenue-seeking, the waste is caused because lobbies seek a share in the revenue disposal and, in competition, the value of the factor services expended in revenue-seeking will equal the revenues lobbied for. (ii) Alternatively, the government may directly spend revenues on purchasing factor services (e.g. in hiring bureaucrats), but the resulting governmental 'output' or consumption is held to be worth less than the revenues. (iii) Finally, the government may directly spend revenues on purchasing goods, in which case one may again regard some or all governmental consumption as wasteful and having zero social value. The first two cases are qualitatively equivalent. But the third is not, since the relationship between the tariff-inclusive goods prices and factor prices ceases to be unique in the first two cases, even with the standard restrictions, when complete specialization can ensue as in the negative-shadow-factor-prices case at issue in my (1980) analysis. Let me distinguish therefore between *case 1* where the revenues cause waste because of revenue-seeking and *case 2* where the waste arises because government spends revenues on goods and this is deemed to have zero value.

Case 1: Revenue-seeking[2]

Before I turn to what I consider to be Tullock's way of looking at the problem of tariff-seeking, let me stress that I would myself insist that the two different kinds of lobbying — tariff-seeking to impose, say, a protectionist tariff, and revenue-seeking to seek the resulting tariff revenues — be kept distinct. It can, in fact, be shown that *each* of these two lobbying activities can yield the paradoxical conclusion that lobbying may be welfare-improving.

To see this best, consider fig. 1 which shows both tariff-seeking and revenue-seeking. Free trade would be at P^*, with AB the production possibility curve. $\hat{P}$ is where an exogenous tariff would take the economy. An endogenous tariff at the same rate, resulting from lobbying, would take the economy to $\hat{\hat{P}}$ where the tariff-inclusive price line is tangent to A^tB^t which is the production possibility curve *net* of resources used up in tariff-seeking. Since $\hat{\hat{P}}$ is to the right of $\hat{P}$, and the world price ratio in this small economy is WP, it is clear that the economy is better off. The paradox Tullock is unhappy with is seen.

[2]Or, equivalently, the case where the government spends tariff revenues directly on factor services and these are assumed to amount to socially worthless output or consumption.

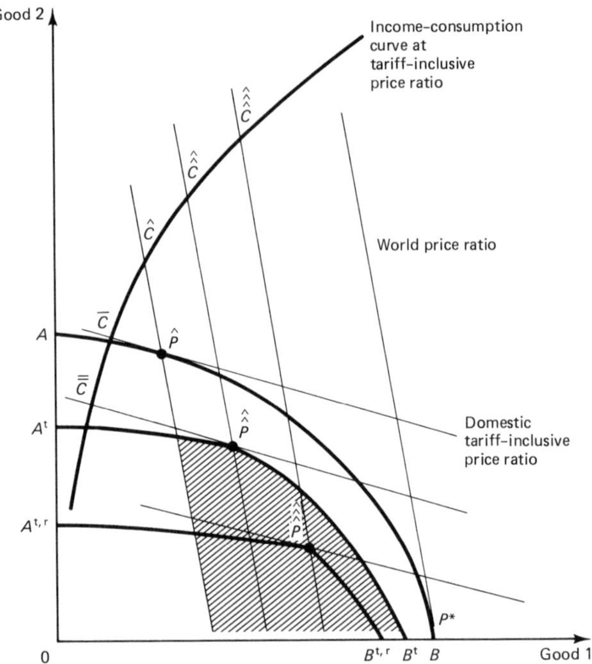

Fig. 1. (*AB*: production possibility curve without any lobbying; A^tB^t: production possibility curve with tariff-seeking; $A^{t,r}, B^{t,r}$: production possibility curve with both tariff-seeking and revenue-seeking.)

Now, introduce revenue-seeking (For simplicity, I assume that the level of tariff-seeking is exogenous to the introduction of revenue-seeking.) The tariff at $\hat{\hat{P}}$ yields revenues which trigger lobbying for some of these revenues. Following Bhagwati and Srinivasan (1980), one can solve for the resulting equilibrium. Let this be at $\hat{\hat{\hat{P}}}$ where the tariff-inclusive price line is tangent now to production possibility curve $A^{t,r}B^{t,r}$ which reflects factor endowments net of those used up in *both* the tariff-seeking and revenue-seeking lobbies. As drawn, $\hat{\hat{\hat{P}}}$ yields a yet further gain, vis-a-vis $\hat{\hat{P}}$. As Bhagwati and Srinivasan (1980) note, in the Komiya–Salter model they use, equilibrium at a point of incomplete specialization such as $\hat{\hat{\hat{P}}}$ implies that *all* revenues are not lobbied for.[3]

On the other hand, as I now read Tullock, he would like to ask a different question: what is the rank-ordering between tariff-seeking (i.e. an *endogenous*

[3]In their fig. 2 (1980, p. 1076), the fraction of the total revenue that is lobbied for and which then equals the market-valued waste of resources is clearly shown for an arbitrary revenue-seeking equilibrium such as $\hat{\hat{\hat{P}}}$ above. This fraction will vary along the Rybczynski line drawn through $\hat{\hat{P}}$ and $\hat{\hat{\hat{P}}}$ in fig. 1 above.

tariff) with 100% revenue-seeking and an *exogenous* tariff with 100% revenue-seeking? Must my (1980) conclusion that an endogenous tariff may be welfare-superior to an exogenous tariff at an identical rate, both being considered without any revenue-seeking or other assumption of direct government waste, be reversed if 100% revenue-seeking is admitted as part of this comparison? In fig. 1, therefore, he ought to be comparing (i) an exogenous tariff at $\hat{P}$ with full revenue-seeking (or equivalently, with the government directly wasting resources through buying factor services towards no socially valuable purpose) *vis-a-vis* (ii) an endogenous tariff at $\hat{\hat{P}}$ with full revenue-seeking. If one does that, then Tullock seems to assume that the 'private' economy will operate on the budget line $\hat{P}\bar{C}$ in case (i) and on the budget line $\hat{\hat{P}}\bar{\bar{C}}$ in case (ii): the latter is then dominated by the former. But, unfortunately, even this cannot be maintained. For, if indeed the Rybczynski line lies in the stripped zone of negative shadow factor prices, full revenue-seeking will simply mean that the economy will specialize completely on good 1. It is then still possible for full revenue-seeking to yield higher welfare than at $\hat{C}$ in case (i) and at $\hat{\hat{C}}$ in case (ii), and, regardless, for the welfare level in case (ii) to exceed that in case (i), thus sustaining my (1980) paradox that an endogenous tariff may be superior to an exogenous tariff at the same rate.[4]

Case 2: Direct waste on goods

Where instead the government directly spends all revenue, on goods, and the entire resulting governmental consumption is regarded as socially worthless, the endogenous tariff (combined with this assumption) will indeed lead 'private' consumption to $\bar{\bar{C}}$ and the exogenous tariff (combined with this assumption) to $\bar{C}$. The paradox of the latter being inferior to the former will not arise.

Tullock's contention therefore would be necessarily correct if he made all of the following three assumptions: that the government directly wastes revenues, that all revenues are wasted, and that the waste is occurring wholly through government expenditure on goods rather than factor services.[5] Needless to say, therefore, the possibility of my (1980) paradox is by no means ruled out if 'wastage of revenues' is simply admitted into the analysis. In particular, I should reemphasise that I find it highly improbable that all revenues of the government lead directly or *via* revenue-seeking to fully matching waste of resources any more than I would consider it agreeable to assume that no revenues are so wasted. (Also, I should stress, as I did in

[4]See Bhagwati and Srinivasan (1980, p. 1081, footnote 16).

[5]Tullock has pointed out in private correspondence that his view is that in reality all governmental revenue is not wasted. If so, the conditions for ruling out the paradox at issue are *not* satisfied.

relation to case (1), that it is important to keep tariff-seeking and revenue waste analytically separate. If one does that in case (2), one goes in fig. 1 from $\hat{C}$ to $\hat{\hat{C}}$ with tariff-seeking *alone* and with no wastage of revenues assumed. Then one goes from $\hat{\hat{C}}$ to $\bar{\bar{C}}$ when wastage of all revenues through governmental purchase of goods is introduced.)

(4) Much of the confusion in this literature on lobbying can be cleared up if we focus on the true nature of the activities being analyzed. In my view, the essential nature of the activities such as lobbying, evasion, etc. is that they are ways of making a profit (or rather, an income) by undertaking activities which are directly unproductive, i.e. they yield pecuniary returns but do not produce goods or services that enter a utility function directly or indirectly via increased production or availability to the economy of goods that enter a utility function.[6] Insofar as such activities use real resources, they result in a contraction of the availability set open to the economy. Thus, for example, tariff-seeking lobbying, tariff evasion, and premium-seeking for given import licenses are all privately profitable activities. However, their direct 'output' is simply zero in terms of the flow of goods and services entering a conventional utility function.

Functionally, the DUP activities can be classified as in fig. 2, which is constructed on the assumption that the DUP activities are generated by policy-intervention-imposed distortions — though, they can equally be generated by optimal policy interventions (as when smuggling is around an optimal tariff) or without policy intervention at all (as in Tullock's case of theft). The functional classification in fig. 2 divides the DUP activities into 3 classes: (a) distortion-seeking DUPs, such as tariff-seeking analyzed in my 1980 paper and Tullock's comment thereon; (b) distortion-triggered DUP lobbying, and (c) distortion-evading DUPs. The latter two, of course, immediately imply that the economy *begins* with a distortion that triggers the DUP activity: hence they represent an intrinsically *second-best* problem, with possible paradoxes of the type that Tullock is addressing with puzzlement.

In this schema, Krueger's (1974) generic class of 'rent-seeking' activities comes readily under the category of QR-triggered lobbying, for she is concerned *generically* with lobbying activities that are prompted by the existence of QRs and licenses, whereas her *specific* analysis relates to import quotas. As such, the phrase 'rent-seeking' should apply to simply one, and possibly small, subset of DUP activities in the real world.[7]

[6]The word 'directly' is necessary since, in the inherently second-best cases noted below, DUP activities may be (indirectly) beneficial. See the extended conceptual discussion in Bhagwati (1982).

[7]It is not clear to me that the Marshallian notion of 'rent' is readily extendable to all classes of DUP activities, even if one were willing to overlook the fact that Krueger used the phrase to categorise only the subset of QR-triggered lobbying activities. Furthermore, I have the rather different problem with the focus on rents in thinking about DUP activities, that rents arise also in models where DUP activities are not present at all. Thus, in the traditional models with fixed

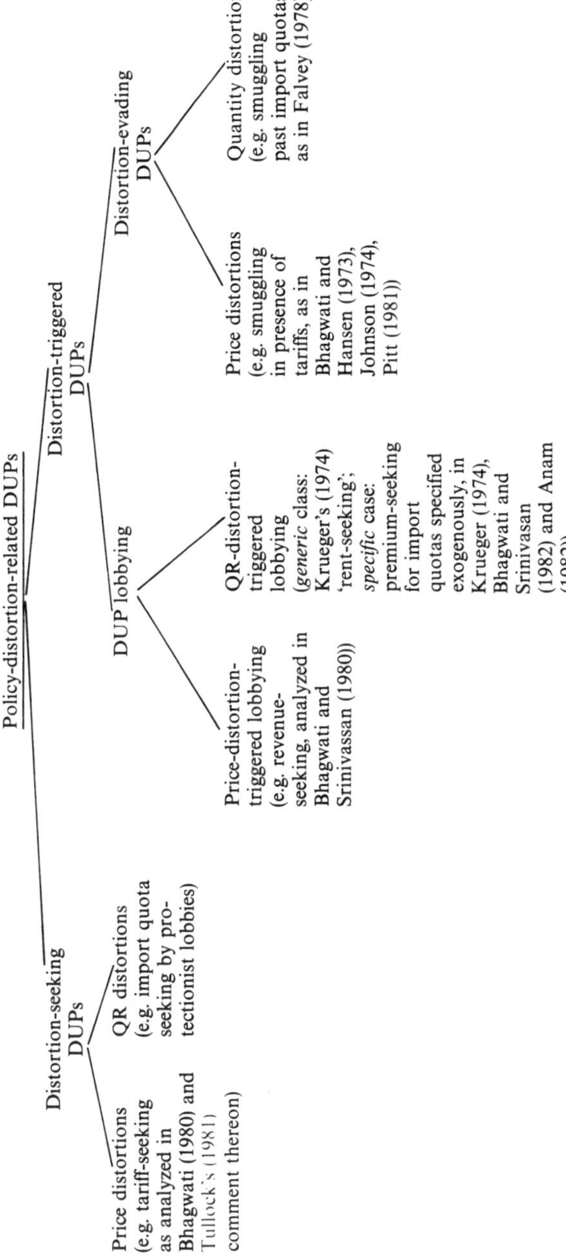
Policy-distortion-related DUPs
Distortion-seeking DUPs
Distortion-triggered DUPs
Price distortions (e.g. tariff-seeking as analyzed in Bhagwati (1980) and Tullock's (1981) comment thereon)
QR distortions (e.g. import quota seeking by pro-tectionist lobbies)
DUP lobbying
Distortion-evading DUPs
Price-distortion-triggered lobbying (e.g. revenue-seeking, analyzed in Bhagwati and Srinivassan (1980))
QR-distortion-triggered lobbying (generic class: Krueger's (1974) 'rent-seeking'; specific case: premium-seeking for import quotas specified exogenously, in Krueger (1974), Bhagwati and Srinivasan (1982) and Anam (1982))
Price distortions (e.g. smuggling in presence of tariffs, as in Bhagwati and Hansen (1973), Johnson (1974), Pitt (1981))
Quantity distortions (e.g. smuggling past import quotas as in Falvey (1978))

factor supplies in full employment, each factor earns only rents since the minimum supply price of the factors is zero. Thus, focussing on rents does not help to distinguish between DUP and traditional non-DUP activities, which I presume is what one wants to do. Hence, the phrase 'DUP activities' seems the logical candidate, in focussing directly on the relevant essence of such activities.

I also note with pleasure that Tullock does approve of the phrase DUP (pronounced as 'dupe'). As for his fear that it may be too late to have it adopted, I think that this may be too pessimistic. It has already begun to gain currency in the trade-theoretic literature, as in Anam (1982).

References

Anam, Mahmudul, 1982, Distortion-triggered lobbying and welfare: A contribution to the theory of directly-unproductive profit-seeking activities, Journal of International Economics 13, August, 15–32.

Bhagwati, Jagdish N. (ed.), 1974, Illegal transactions in international trade: Theory and policy (North-Holland, Amsterdam).

Bhagwati, Jagdish N., 1980, Lobbying and welfare, Journal of Public Economics 14, December, 355–363.

Bhagwati, Jagdish N., 1982, Directly-unproductive, profit-seeking (DUP) activities, Journal of Political Economy 90, October, 988–1002.

Bhagwati, Jagdish N. and Bent Hansen, 1973, A theoretical analysis of smuggling, Quarterly Journal of Economics, May, 172–187.

Bhagwati, Jagdish N., and T.N. Srinivasan, 1980, Revenue seeking: A generalization of the theory of tariffs, Journal of Political Economy, December, 1069–1087.

Bhagwati, Jagdish N. and T.N. Srinivasan, 1982, The welfare consequences of directly-unproductive, profit-seeking (DUP) activities: Price versus quantity distortions, Journal of International Economics 13, August, 33–44.

Buchanan, James, Gordon Tullock and R. Tollison, (eds.), 1980, Towards a general theory of the rent-seeking society (Texas A&M University Press, College Station).

Falvey, Rodney, 1978, A note on preferential and illegal trade under quantitative restrictions, Quarterly Journal of Economics, February, 175–178.

Johnson, Harry C., 1974, Notes on the economic theory of smuggling, in: Bhagwati (1974).

Krueger, Anne Osborne, 1974, The political economy of the rent-seeking society, American Economic Review, June, 291–303.

Pitt, Mark, 1981, Smuggling and price disparity, Journal of International Economics, November, 447–458.

Tullock, Gordon, 1981, Lobbying and welfare: A comment, Journal of Public Economics 16, 391–394.

Tariff Seeking and the Efficient Tariff

Robert C. Feenstra and
Jagdish N. Bhagwati

9.1 Introduction

A common reaction to increased import competition is tariff lobbying by interest groups adversely affected by the competition, a phenomenon christened "tariff seeking" in Bhagwati and Srinivasan (1980). Empirical analyses by Cheh (1974), Pincus (1975), Caves (1976), and several others have pointed to the importance of interest group pressures in determining the level of tariffs and, in particular, the importance of tariff lobbying within labor-intensive industries.

In this paper we shall model the lobbying activities of labor, used intensively in the import-competing industry, as a game between labor and the government, where the actions of the government are determined jointly by its willingness to grant (or perhaps its inability to resist the granting of) tariffs in the face of political pressure and by its desire to maximize social welfare.

We shall suppose that a decrease in the relative price of imports due to increased foreign competition triggers lobbying activity by labor and that this political pressure leads the government to grant tariff protection. The tariff improves the real wages of labor, but under the assumption that we are dealing with a small country, is welfare-inferior to a position of no

Jagdish N. Bhagwati is the Arthur Lehman Professor of Economics at Columbia University. He has written on trade theory, developmental theory and policy, internal and international migration, and education models. He is editor of the *Journal of International Economics* and author (with T. N. Srinivasan) of *Lectures on the Theory of International Trade*, to be published by MIT Press. Robert C. Feenstra is assistant professor of economics at Columbia University and was a Post-Doctoral Fellow in International Economics at the University of Chicago. He has published in the *Journal of International Economics* and has written on international trade theory and econometrics.

Financial support for the research underlying this paper was provided by NSF Grant SOC 79-07541.

tariff and no lobbying. It should be expected, then, that the government will search for policies to reduce the lobbying activity and resulting tariff. If lump-sum taxation were feasible, then the government could simply bribe labor to stop its lobbying activity by offering sufficiently high compensation, thereby restoring the economy to its first-best position with no tariff.

However, in the more realistic case where the government faces a budget constraint, its ability to bribe labor is limited, and in this case it may turn to the revenue created by the tariff itself as a source of funds. By using this revenue to increase labor's real income (defined as the sum of its real wages and this subsidy, as in Bhagwati 1959), the government can change the amount of lobbying activity and tariff, and improve welfare. It cannot, however, eliminate the lobbying activity completely since in that case the tariff is zero and there is no revenue with which to compensate labor. So in general the equilibrium after *optimal* government intervention will have a nonzero tariff, and we shall refer to this as the *efficient* tariff.[1]

Note that the efficient tariff is a second-best concept in that lump-sum taxation to raise funds to compensate labor is assumed infeasible. The idea makes a good deal of sense insofar as the revenue raised for redistribution is being generated as a side effect of the protection itself and is *not* being raised *ab initio* for the redistribution.[2] Our underlying assumption that one part of the government responds to the protectionist pressures while another tries to maximize welfare subject to this response suggests, as some conference participants wittily remarked, a "left-brain, right-brain" or an "ego versus id" type of approach to the political economy at hand. It does reflect, however, the classic division and confrontation between the (protrade) executive and the (lobbying-dominated) legislature in countries such as the United States.

In section 9.2 we determine the equilibrium tariff level based on optimal lobbying activity by labor. In section 9.3 we introduce the possibility of government intervention in the form of conditional subsidies to labor and derive the efficient tariff. While one might expect that it is optimal for the government to *reduce* the amount of lobbying and the resulting tariff, it is also possible for the optimal policy to involve an *increase* in the level of lobbying and tariff. This paradox can arise if, given the existing distortion caused by the tariff, the shadow price of the lobbying activity is *negative*, so that an increase in the lobbying activity may be socially desirable (for analyses of negative project shadow prices see Srinivasan and Bhagwati 1978; Bhagwati, Srinivasan, and Wan 1978; Bhagwati and Srinivasan 1980). In section 9.4 we derive a necessary and sufficient condition for this possibility to arise. Further discussion and conclusions are given in sections 9.5 and 9.6.

9.2 Optimal Lobbying

We shall adopt the usual 2 × 2 HOS (Heckscher-Ohlin-Samuelson) model, with industry 1 labor-intensive and import-competing. Choosing commodity 2 as the numeraire, let p^* and $p = p^*(1 + t)$ denote the foreign and domestic relative price of commodity 1, respectively, where t is the *ad valorem* tariff rate and, under the assumption of a small country, p^* is given as a parameter by world trade. The consumption and production of good i are denoted by X_i and Y_i, $i = 1,2$, and the factor prices and given endowments of labor and capital are denoted by w, r, $\bar{L}$, and $\bar{K}$, respectively.

Suppose that the foreign relative price of good 1 falls from p_0^* to p^* due to increased import competition and that this triggers tariff lobbying by labor, whose real wages have fallen. Following Findlay and Wellisz (chapter 8 of this volume), we shall assume that this lobbying activity takes the form of hiring labor L_t and capital K_t to determine a tariff level $t = f(L_t, K_t)$, where f is increasing and concave. This lobbying function should be interpreted as derived from given political behavior and institutions, such as the desire of politicians to maximize their probability of reelection.[3] We shall denote minimum costs at which the tariff rate t can be obtained as $C(t,w,r)$. A reasonable form for the lobbying cost function is

$$C(t,w,r) = \left\{\frac{t\phi(w,r)}{\max\{0,(p_0^* - p^*(1+t)\}}\right\}, \tag{1}$$

where $\phi(w,r)$ is increasing and quasi-concave. For this cost function, as the tariff increases and $p^*(1 + t)$ approaches p_0^* so that labor's real wages approach the level obtained *before* the increased import competition, costs become arbitrarily large. Also, if import competition were to *decline* ($p^* > p_0^*$) and labor's real wages improve, then the costs of lobbying for any positive tariff would be arbitrarily large. This cost function is meant to embody the notion that *before* the change in the terms of trade the historically determined distribution of income between labor and capital was "acceptable" in the sense that lobbying would have been ineffective (lobbying costs would have been arbitrarily large), and it is only *after* the shift in the terms of trade that lobbying becomes feasible for the factor whose real wages have deteriorated. Adopting an analogous lobbying cost function for capital, and for the case we are considering where $p_0^* > p^*$, capitalists will *not* lobby after the change in the terms of trade because their real rental has improved.[4]

We shall assume that all laborers have an identical linearly homogeneous utility function, and denote the maximum utility obtainable with the relative price p and income I by $V(p,I)$. After the fall in the foreign relative price of commodity 1 from p_0^* to p^*, labor's lobbying problem is

$$\max_{t\geq 0} V\{p^*(1+t), w\bar{L} - C(t,w,r)\}, \tag{2}$$

where $(w\bar{L} - C(t,w,r))$ is labor's income net of lobbying costs. Using Roy's identity,[5] the first-order conditions for this problem can be written as

$$p^*(\bar{L}\frac{dw}{dp} - X_1^L) = \frac{dC}{dt}, \tag{3a}$$

where

$$\frac{dC}{dt} = \left(w\frac{\partial L_t}{\partial t} + r\frac{\partial K_t}{\partial t}\right) + p^*\left(L_t\frac{dw}{dp} + K_t\frac{dr}{dp}\right). \tag{3b}$$

The left-hand side of (3a) is the change in labor's real income due to a change in the tariff, $dw/dp > 0$ and $(\bar{L}\,(dw/dp) - X_1^L) > 0$, where X_1^L is labor's consumption of good 1;[6] the right-hand side is the marginal cost of the tariff, including both the direct effect on costs of hiring more inputs and the indirect effect of changing factor prices.

The solution t^* to labor's lobbying problem is illustrated in figure 9.1, where $C(t)$ are costs as a function of t including general equilibrium changes in factor prices, and the "benefits" curve $B(t)$ has slope p^* $(\bar{L}$ (dw/dp) $-$ $X_1^L)$. For the lobbying cost function given in (1), costs approach infinity as t approaches $\tilde{t} = (p_0^*/p^*) - 1$, and this implies that $t^* < \tilde{t}$; so the domestic price ratio $p = p^*(1 + t^*)$ after tariff lobbying lies between the foreign price ratios p_0^* and p^* obtaining before and after the increase in import competition, respectively. Note that multiple solutions to (3) are possible.[7] Assuming that lobbying costs are shared equally by all laborers, the net wage after lobbying is $(w - C(t^*,w,r)/\bar{L})$.

9.3 Government Intervention

The equilibrium with optimal lobbying by labor is welfare-inferior to a position of no lobbying and no tariff. Thus, as argued in section 9.1, the government may turn to the revenues created by the tariff itself as a source of funds to compensate labor and improve welfare. In order to be effective, this compensation will take the form of subsidy payments which are *conditional* on the tariff rate: for the case in which the government wishes to reduce the level of lobbying and tariff to $\hat{t} < t^*$ it would offer the subsidy $\hat{S}(t)$ defined by

$$\hat{S}(t = \begin{cases} S(\hat{t}) \text{ for } t \leq \hat{t} \\ 0 \text{ for } t > \hat{t}, \end{cases} \tag{4}$$

where $S(\hat{t})$ is chosen such that labor will *accept* the conditional subsidy. This bribe is illustrated in figure 9.1, from which it is clear that the minimum level of $S(\hat{t})$ that labor will accept is

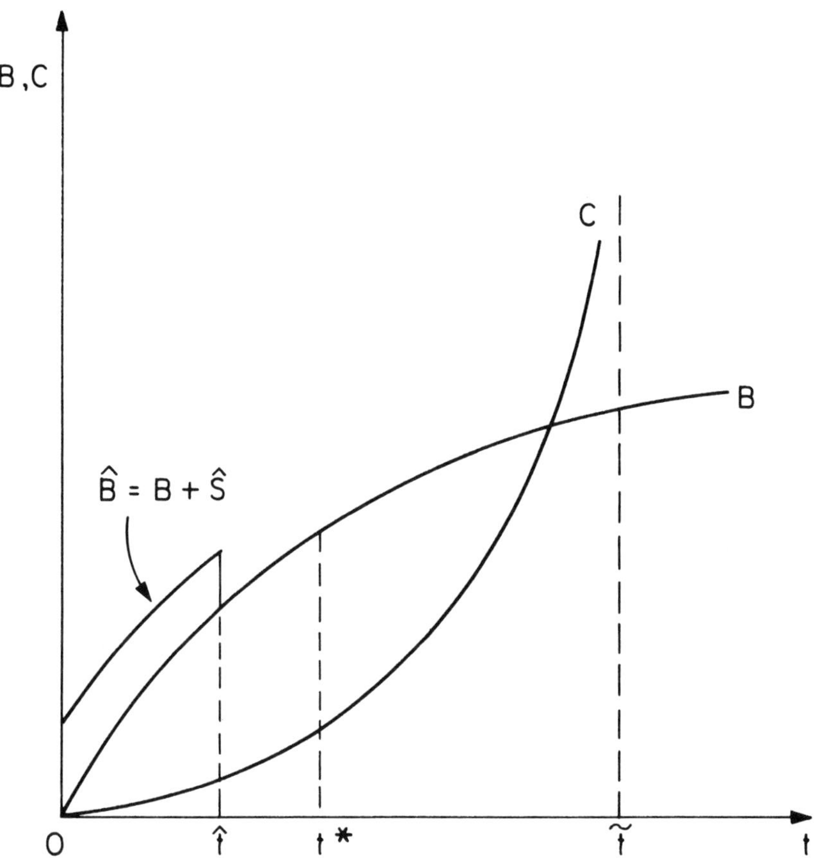

Fig. 9.1

(5) $$S(\hat{t}) = \left[B(t^*) - C(t^*)\right] - \left[B(\hat{t}) - C(\hat{t})\right],$$

in which case labor is indifferent between $\hat{t}$ and t^*. The schedule of minimum subsidy payments $S(t)$ is implicitly defined by (5) or, equivalently,

(5′) $$V(p^*(1+t), w\bar{L} - C(t,w,r) + S(t)) = V_L^*,$$

where V_L^* is the utility of labor in the optimal lobbying equilibrium. The subsidy payments are illustrated in figure 9.2. Note that for the case in which the government wishes to increase the level of lobbying and tariff to $\hat{t} > t^*$, it would offer the conditional subsidy $\hat{S}(t)$ defined by

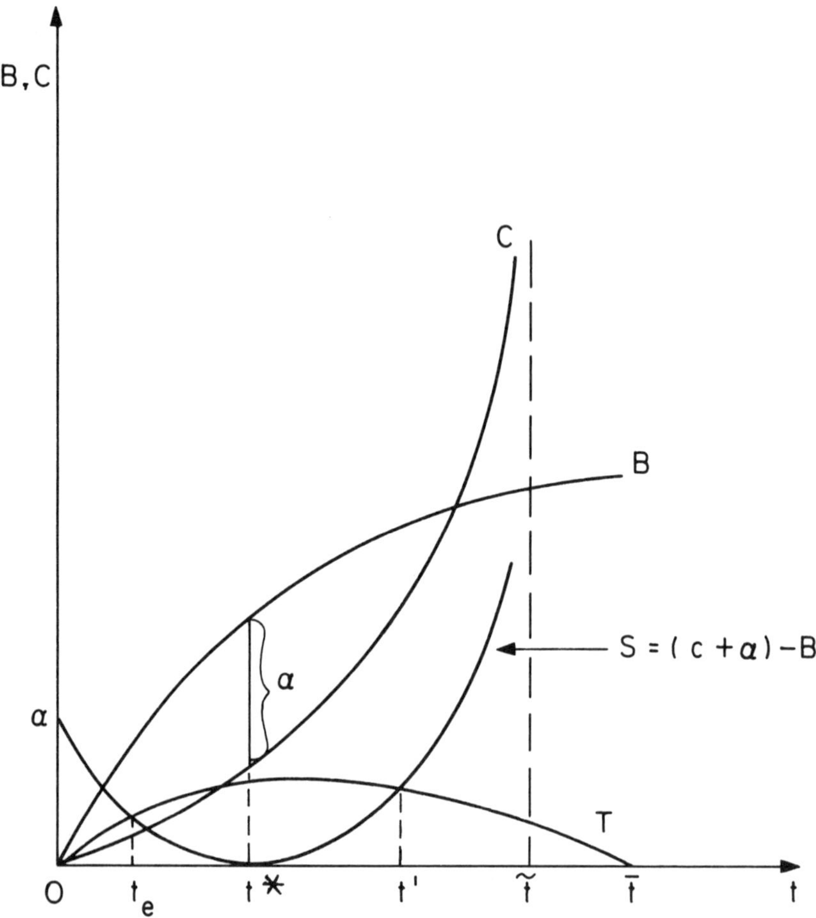

Fig. 9.2

$$\hat{S}(t) = \begin{cases} 0 \text{ for } t < \hat{t}, \\ S(\hat{t}) \text{ for } t \geq \hat{t} \end{cases}$$

where with $S(t)$ chosen according to (5) or (5′) labor would be willing to accept this compensation.

Using the subsidy payments $S(t)$, the government can shift the equilibrium of the economy to any desired position with $0 \leq t < \tilde{t}$, and we assume that it wishes to choose the position which maximizes social welfare.[8] Assuming that the government places equal weight on all individuals when evaluating social welfare and that capitalists have the same linearly homogeneous utility function as laborers, social welfare is given by

$$\begin{aligned} U &= V(p^*(1+t), w\bar{L} + r\bar{K} + T - C(t,w,r)) \\ &= V(p^*(1+t), w\bar{L} - C(t,w,r,) + S(t)) \\ &\quad + V(p^*(1+t), r\bar{K} + T - S(t)) \\ &= V_L^* + V(p^*(1+t), r\bar{K} + T - S(t)), \end{aligned}$$

where T denotes redistributed tariff revenues. Since V_L^* is a constant, maximizing social welfare is equivalent to maximizing $V_k \equiv V(p^*(1 + t), r\bar{K} + T - S(t))$, which is the utility of capitalists when they receive their rental income and redistributed tariff revenues less subsidy payments. We explicitly rule out the possibility of lump-sum taxation of capital, and so the net income distributed to capital must be *nonnegative*. Thus, the government's problem can be stated as

(6) $$\max_{t \geq 0} V_K \text{ subject to } T - S(t) \geq 0.$$

The tariff rate t_e given by the solution to (6) is the *efficient* tariff. The game-theoretic equilibrium at which the efficient tariff obtains is a *Stackelberg* equilibrium with the government as the Stackelberg leader: in choosing its optimal policy, labor takes any conditional subsidy offer $\hat{S}(t)$ as given, whereas the government includes the reaction of labor to different subsidy offers in its decision framework.

The efficient tariff may be below or exceed the optimal labor-lobbying tariff t^*, where the latter possibility can arise if the shadow price of the lobbying activity is negative. Consider first the "normal" case, where it is optimal for the government to bribe labor to *reduce* the lobbying activity and resulting tariff. Then the *minimum* feasible tariff rate and maximum social welfare is clearly attained where $T = S(t)$, so that all of the tariff revenue is used to compensate labor and none is distributed to capital. This corner solution is shown as $t_e < t^*$ in figure 9.2, where $\bar{t}$ is the prohibitive tariff, and $\bar{t} > \tilde{t}$ since it is assumed that industry 1 was import-competing before the initial shift in the terms of trade.[9] For the latter case where it is optimal for the government to *increase* the level of lobbying and tariff from t^*, social welfare is maximized at a tariff rate *between* t^* and t'. The point t' is defined by $t' > t^*$ and $T = S(t')$, and the efficient tariff is necessarily less than t'. This result can be demonstrated as follows. Using the subsidy payments $S(t)$, labor obtains the same utility at t^* and t', but since at t' *all* tariff revenues are used to compensate labor and the rental on capital is less than at t^* (by the Stolper-Samuelson theorem), capital is necessarily worse off at t' as compared with t^*. Therefore, social welfare is lower at t' than at t^*, and so for the case we are considering where a marginal rise in the tariff rate from t^* increases social welfare, the maximum is clearly obtained between t^* and t'.[10]

When can the latter paradoxical case arise? As we shall demonstrate in the following section, starting at any tariff rate t, $0 \leq t < \tilde{t}$, an *increase* in the amount of lobbying activity and resulting tariff due to government intervention is welfare-improving if and only if

$$(7)\qquad -\frac{d}{dt}\left(p^*Y_1 + Y_2\right) < t(p^*)^2\left(\frac{\partial X_1}{\partial p}\bigg|_u - \frac{\partial Y_1}{\partial p}\right),$$

whereas the optimal intervention is to decrease the amount of lobbying and tariff if the inequality in (7) is reversed.[11] The left-hand side of (7) is the change in national income evaluated at *international* prices due to a change in the level of lobbying activity and tariff, which is the *shadow price* of the lobbying activity. The right-hand side of (7) reflects the change in tariff revenue due to substitution effects in consumption and production, and is negative since

$$\frac{\partial X_1}{\partial p}\bigg|_u < 0 \text{ and } \frac{\partial Y_1}{\partial p} > 0.$$

Thus, an increase in the lobbying activity and tariff is optimal if and only if the shadow price of the lobbying activity is negative and sufficiently large in absolute value.

9.4 Derivation of Optimal Government Intervention

The change in the subsidy given to labor needed to keep labor's utility at its optimal lobbying level can be calculated from (5′) as

$$(8)\qquad \frac{dS}{dt} = -\{p^*(\bar{L}\frac{dw}{dp} - X_1^L) - \frac{dC}{dt}\}.$$

When the tariff revenues less subsidy payments are redistributed to capitalists, their utility is $V_K = V(p^*(1+t), r\bar{K} + T - S(t))$, and

$$\frac{dV_k}{dt} = \frac{\partial V}{\partial I}\{p^*(\bar{K}\frac{dr}{dp} - X_1^K) + \frac{dT}{dt} - \frac{dS}{dt}\},$$

where X_1^K is the consumption of good 1 by capitalists and $dr/dp < 0$. Then $dV_K/dt > 0$, in which case it is optimal for the government to bribe labor to *increase* the amount of lobbying and resulting tariff, if and only if

$$(9)\qquad \left(\frac{dT}{dt} - \frac{dS}{dt}\right) > -p^*\left(\bar{K}\frac{dr}{dp} - X_1^K\right).$$

The right-hand side of (9) is the real income loss of capitalists due to a higher tariff, and so the higher tariff is preferred if and only if the net gain in tariff revenue exceeds this loss.

Equation (9) clarifies the nature of the optimal intervention for the case where it is optimal for the government to increase the level of lobbying and tariff from t^* (i.e., [9] holds at t^*). The right-hand side of (9) is positive (by the Stolper-Samuelson theorem), and in a neighborhood of t' it can be seen that $dT/dt < dS/dt$, so that (9) cannot hold. The efficient tariff in this case is obtained when (9) holds with equality, which will occur at a point between t^* and t'. We can also see that the efficient tariff satisfies $dT/dt > 0$, which implies that the efficient tariff is necessarily less than the *maximum revenue* tariff for which $dT/dt = 0$.

Tariff revenues are given by

$$T = tp^*(X_1(p^*(1+t), w\bar{L} + r\bar{K} + T - C) - Y_1),$$

where $X_1 = X_1^L + X_1^K$, from which we can calculate that

$$\begin{aligned} \frac{dT}{dt} &= \beta\{p^*(X_1 - Y_1) + t(p^*)^2(\left.\frac{\partial X_1}{\partial p}\right|_u - \frac{\partial Y_1}{\partial p})\} \\ &+ \beta tp^*(\frac{\partial Y_1}{\partial \bar{L}}\frac{dL_t}{dt} + \frac{\partial Y_1}{\partial \bar{K}}\frac{dK_t}{dt}) \\ &+ (\beta - 1)(p^*\bar{L}\frac{dw}{dp} + p^*\bar{K}\frac{dr}{dp} - p^*X_1 - \frac{dC}{dt}), \end{aligned} \tag{10}$$

where $\beta = (1 - tp^*(\partial X_1/\partial I)^{-1} > 0$ so long as good 2 is not inferior.[12] We also have

$$\begin{aligned} \frac{dS}{dt} &- p^*(\bar{K}\frac{dr}{dp} - X_1^K) \\ &= -(p^*\bar{L}\frac{dw}{dp} + p^*\bar{K}\frac{dr}{dp} - p^*X_1 - \frac{dC}{dt}) \end{aligned}$$

using (8);

$$\begin{aligned} &= -(p^*(\bar{L} - L_t)\frac{\partial Y_1}{\partial \bar{L}} \\ &+ p^*(\bar{K} - K_t)\frac{\partial Y_1}{\partial \bar{K}} - p^*X_1 - C_t) \end{aligned}$$

using (3b), using the reciprocity relations $dw/dp = \partial Y_1/\partial \bar{L}$ and $dr/dp = \partial Y_1/\partial \bar{K}$, and since $C_t = w(\partial L_t/\partial t) + r(\partial K_t/\partial t)$;

$$= p^*(X_1 - Y_1) + C_t \tag{11}$$

since $$Y_1 = (\bar{L} - L_t)\frac{\partial Y_1}{\partial \bar{L}} + (\bar{K} - K_t)\frac{\partial Y_1}{\partial \bar{K}}.$$

Using (10) and (11), condition (9) becomes

(9′)
$$t(p^*)^2\left(\frac{\partial X_1}{\partial p}\bigg|_u - \frac{\partial Y_1}{\partial p}\right) + tp^*\left(\frac{\partial Y_1}{\partial \bar{L}}\frac{dL_t}{dt} + \frac{\partial Y_1}{\partial \bar{K}}\frac{dK_t}{dt}\right) - C_t > 0.$$

To further simplify (9′) we must introduce the concept of *shadow prices* of primary factors at the tariff-distorted equilibrium. Letting a_{ij} denote the cost-minimizing unit-output requirement of factor i in industry j, evaluated at the tariff-distorted domestic price ratio $p = p^*(1 + t)$, the factor prices w and r satisfy

(12a)
$$p^*(1+t) = a_{L1}w + a_{K1}r,$$
$$1 = a_{L2}w + a_{K2}r,$$

whereas the *shadow* factor prices w^* and r^* are defined by

(12b)
$$p^* = a_{L1}w^* + a_{K1}r^*,$$
$$1 = a_{L2}w^* + a_{K2}r^*.$$

Using (12a) and (12b), it can be shown that

(13)
$$tp^*\frac{dw}{dp} = w - w^*,$$
$$tp^*\frac{dr}{dp} = r - r^*.$$

Using (13) and the reciprocity relations, we then have

(14)
$$tp^*\left(\frac{\partial Y_1}{\partial \bar{L}}\frac{dL_t}{dt} + \frac{\partial Y_1}{\partial \bar{K}}\frac{dK_t}{dt}\right) = C_t - \left(w^*\frac{\partial L_t}{\partial t} + r^*\frac{\partial K_t}{\partial t}\right) + \theta,$$

where

$$\theta = t(p^*)^2\left\{\frac{\partial L_t}{\partial w}\left(\frac{dw}{dp}\right)^2 + 2\frac{\partial L_t}{\partial r}\left(\frac{dw}{dp}\right)\left(\frac{dr}{dp}\right) + \frac{\partial K_t}{\partial r}\left(\frac{dr}{dp}\right)^2\right\}$$
$$= t^{-1}(w^*, r^*)\begin{bmatrix} C_{ww} & C_{wr} \\ C_{rw} & C_{rr} \end{bmatrix}\begin{pmatrix} w^* \\ r^* \end{pmatrix} \leq 0,$$

since $C(t,w,r)$ is concave in (w,r).

Substituting (14) into (9′), the necessary and sufficient condition for an increase in the level of lobbying and tariff to be welfare-improving is

$$(w^* \frac{\partial L_t}{\partial t} + r^* \frac{\partial K_t}{\partial t}) - \theta < t(p^*)^2 (\frac{\partial X_1}{\partial p}\bigg|_u - \frac{\partial Y_1}{\partial p}). \tag{9''}$$

Finally, note that national income evaluated at international prices is given by

$$p^* Y_1 + Y_2 = w^*(\bar{L} - L_t) + r^*(\bar{K} - K_t),$$

from which it can be shown that

$$-\frac{d}{dt}(p^* Y_1 + Y_2) = (w^* \frac{\partial L_t}{\partial t} + r^* \frac{\partial K_t}{\partial t}) - \theta. \tag{15}$$

Substituting (15) into (9″), we obtain condition (7), as desired.

9.5 A Sufficient Condition for Welfare Improvement in the Lobbying Equilibrium

In the absence of any tariff lobbying the fall in the relative price of imports due to foreign competition, while harmful to the real wages of labor, is welfare-improving. The lobbying activity reduces welfare from that point by establishing a tariff and using resources, and so it is possible for social welfare to be *lower* after the improvement in the terms of trade and resulting lobbying and tariff than before. However, as shown in figure 9.3, a *sufficient* condition for welfare to be *higher* after the improvement in the terms of trade and lobbying is easily derived. (Note that the efficient tariff equilibrium is no worse than the lobbying equilibrium, so that our sufficiency condition extends to it as well.)

In figure 9.3 the equilibrium production points before and after the fall in the relative price of imports (and with no lobbying) are P_0 and P_1, respectively, and $0I$ is the income-consumption path corresponding to the domestic price ratio in the tariff-distorted equilibrium. For the lobbying cost function given in (1), the domestic price ratio with optimal labor lobbying lies between the international price ratios obtaining before and after the change in the terms of trade (so that $\tilde{P}$ is spanned by P_0 and P_1). Production is shifted from $\tilde{P}$ to P_t by the lobbying activity, and consumption is at C_t. For the given tariff, an increase in lobbying costs would shift consumption down along $0I$, but so long as the consumption point does not fall below $\tilde{C}$, welfare U_t must be higher than U_0. (Note that this condition is sufficient but *not* necessary and that $\tilde{C}$ is a hypothetical

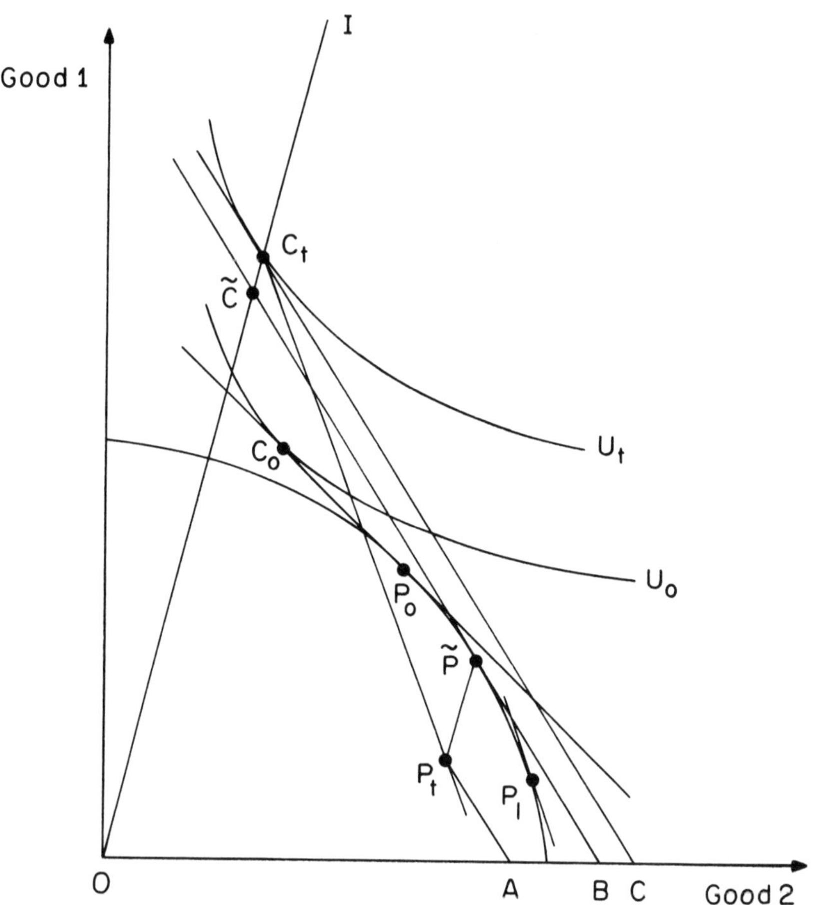

Fig. 9.3

consumption point which does *not* correspond to any trade equilibrium.) The condition for C_t to exceed $\tilde{C}$ is that tariff revenues AC exceed lobbying costs AB, and so this is a sufficient condition for welfare to *improve* due to the initial fall in the relative price of imports.

9.6 Conclusions

We have derived the efficient tariff obtaining in the Stackelberg equilibrium of a game between the government and labor, where labor lobbies for a tariff and the government responds by granting some tariff protection but also by using tariff revenues to compensate labor directly, thereby changing the amount of lobbying. For the lobbying cost function given in (1), the real rental on capital improves as a result of the improvement in the terms of trade despite the lobbying (i.e., in moving from P_0 to P_t in figure 9.3), labor's real income is damaged by the increased foreign competition but is higher than in the absence of lobbying, and so long as tariff revenues exceed lobbying costs in the final equilibrium the improved terms of trade improve social welfare.

Notes

1. Johnson's (1960) concept of the "scientific tariff" related to that tariff structure which would minimize the cost of certain "noneconomic" objectives such as "diversification, industrialization, or agriculturization" and "national self-sufficiency and independence." As such, it was a constrained, second-best concept, the second-best nature of the tariff structure relating to the fact that the first-best solution is additionally being constrained by the noneconomic objectives. As noted in the text, however, our concept of the "efficient tariff" is also a second-best one insofar as the lobbying activity cannot be eliminated by bribing labor with lump-sum transfers in a first-best solution. The efficient tariff, however, minimizes the welfare loss from the successful lobbying for a tariff by utilizing an added policy instrument which is perfectly appropriate to the problem (and which was earlier disregarded by trade theorists following the Meade assumption that all tariff revenues are given away as lump-sum transfers), namely, the tariff revenues which can be used to bribe labor into accepting a lower tariff.

2. Gene Grossman has pointed out to us that something very similar in spirit to the efficient tariff notion is implied by the Carter administration's proposal to use the revenue raised from the oil tariff and the windfall profits tax to compensate the losers from higher-priced oil. In chapter 12 Richardson also notes that a provision of the Trade Act of 1974 earmarked funds out of tariff revenues for the retraining of trade-displaced workers.

3. Brock and Magee (1978) model politicians as maximizing their probability of reelection in a very general game-theoretic framework.

4. Aside from the direct costs of hiring factors to lobby, the lobbying cost function can also be interpreted as including costs of labor *union* activity which induces tariff lobbying by *entrepreneurs*. For example, if workers strike in response to lowered real wages, this could lead to greater tariff lobbying by entrepreneurs in an attempt to meet union wage demands without reducing the return on capital. Labor would have to bear the costs of not receiving wage income during the strike (though these costs may be mitigated by government compensation), as well as some portion of the opportunity costs of capital unemployed during the strike. Within the context of our model we are assuming that the costs to labor $C(t,w,r)$ include the *full* opportunity cost of unemployed capital as well as the lobbying costs of entrepreneurs in industry 1; we also do not consider the role of government unemployment compensation.

5. Roy's identity states that $X_1 = (-\partial V/\partial p)/(\partial V/\partial I)$.

6. We have $(\bar{L}\,(dw/dp) - X_1^L) > 0$ since, by the Stolper-Samuelson theorem, labor's real wages improve in terms of *either* good and so the rise in real income exceeds the increased cost of consumption.

7. Of course, if $C(t)$ is convex and $B(t)$ concave, then the solution is unique. The convexity of $w(p)$, which is a component of $B(t)$, is investigated in Kemp and Khang (1975).

8. Note that the government's desire to maximize social welfare is consistent with its willingness to grant tariff protection, in that the latter can represent its reaction to distributive equity whereas the former corresponds to allocative efficiency.

9. Note that the tariff revenue T need *not* be "single-peaked" as shown in figure 9.2. If $T = S(t)$ at numerous values of t, then the optimal value of t when the government wishes to reduce the lobbying activity and resulting tariff is the *minimum* t for which $T = S(t)$.

10. If $T = S(t')$ and $t' > t^*$ at numerous values of t', then the efficient tariff when the government wishes to increase the level of lobbying and tariff from t^* must lie between t^* and the *maximum* value of t'.

11. An interior maximum of social welfare is obtained when (7) is satisfied with equality (and the second-order conditions for maximization are satisfied).

12. Since marginal propensities to consume must add up to unity, we have $(1 - tp^* (\partial X_1/\partial 1)) = (p^* (\partial X_1/\partial I) + (\partial X_2/\partial I))$, and this expression is positive so long as good 2 is not inferior.

References

Bhagwati, J. N., 1959, Protection, real wages, and real incomes. *Economic Journal* 69: 733–44.

Bhagwati, J., and T. N. Srinivasan. 1979. On inferring resource allocational implications from DRC calculations in trade-distorted, small open economics. *Indian Economic Review* 14, no. 1 (April): 1–16.

———. 1980. Revenue-seeking: A generalization of the theory of tariffs. *Journal of Political Economy* 88, no. 6 (December): 1069–87.

Bhagwati, J., T. N. Srinivasan, and H. Wan, Jr. 1978. Value subtracted, negative shadow prices of factors in project evaluation and immiserizing growth: Three paradoxes in the presence of trade distortions. *Economic Journal* 88 (March): 121–25.

Brock, W. A., and S. P. Magee. 1978. The economics of special interest politics: The case of the tariff. *American Economic Review Papers and Proceedings* 68, no. 2 (May): 246–50.

Caves, R. E. 1976. Economic models of political choice: Canada's tariff structure. *Canadian Journal of Economics* 9, no. 2 (May): 278–300.

Cheh, J. 1974. United States concessions in the Kennedy Round and short-run labour adjustment costs. *Journal of International Economics* 4, no. 4 (November): 323–40.

Johnson, H. C. 1960. The cost of protection and the scientific tariff. *Journal of Political Economy* 68, no. 4 (August): 327–45.

Kemp, M. C., and C. Khang, C. 1975. A convexity property of the two-by-two model of production. *Journal of International Economics* 5: 255–61.

Pincus, J. J. 1975. Pressure groups and the pattern of tariffs. *Journal of Political Economy* 83, no. 4 (August): 757–78.

Srinivasan, T. N., and J. Bhagwati. 1978. Shadow prices for project evaluation in the presence of distortions: Effective rates of protection and domestic resource costs. *Journal of Political Economy* 86, no. 1: 96–116.

Errata

Page 248, equation (4): "$\hat{S}(t$" should read "$\hat{S}(t)$".

Page 251, line 6: "V_k" should read "V_K".

Page 252, equation following equation (8): "V_k" should read "V_K".

Page 258, footnote 12, line 2: "$\partial X_1/\partial 1$" should read "$\partial X_1/\partial \Gamma$".

V
NONECONOMIC OBJECTIVES AND GATT REFORM

Reprinted from THE REVIEW OF ECONOMIC STUDIES, Vol. XXXVI (1), January, 1969, J. N. BHAGWATI AND T. N. SRINIVASAN, pp. 27-38.

Optimal Intervention to Achieve Non-Economic Objectives[1]

International trade theorists have been almost alone in considering seriously the question of devising the optimal economic policy when social utility, defined as a function of the currently available flow of goods and services, cannot take the maximum value that is attainable within the framework of technological, resource and trading opportunities, owing to constraints provided by " non-economic " objectives.[2]

Four major varieties of non-economic objectives can be distinguished: (1) the *output* level in specific activities may be considered to be of strategic importance and hence may not be allowed to fall below specified magnitudes; (2) *self-sufficiency*, that is, the value of imports (or exports, under balanced trade), may be considered to be sufficiently strategic to entail that its level not exceed a specified magnitude; (3) *factor employment* in certain activities, for example labour in agricultural activities, may be considered vital for defence or " national character " and hence may not be allowed to fall below specified levels; and finally (4) *domestic availability* of certain commodities may be considered to be relevant to " social policy ", requiring that it not exceed certain specified levels, as for example with " luxury " consumption.

In each of these cases, the question of maximizing social utility becomes a problem in the theory of the second-best, for each such non-economic objective constitutes an additional constraint subject to which the social utility function would be maximized. And corresponding to each such constrained solution, there is an optimal form of policy intervention that will enable a competitive system to maximize social utility.

This paper is addressed to an analysis of the optimal policies, when the economist is faced with these non-economic objectives (each taken in turn, during the ensuing analysis). Throughout, the model assumed involves two primary factors, two final outputs, production functions embodying constant returns to scale and diminishing returns along isoquants, a well-behaved concave social utility function, and fixed supplies of factors of production. In Section I, it is also assumed that there is no monopoly power in trade, so that the external terms of trade are fixed throughout the analysis. This assumption is relaxed in Section II.

The analysis involves the derivation of necessary (and under our assumptions, sufficient) conditions for a solution to the constrained maximum problem implicit in each case. However, all cases in Section I are illustrated diagrammatically as well, so as to bring out the essence of the analysis more clearly. It can be shown that an optimum solution exists in all cases, and the analysis will be devoted to a characterization of the optimum solution.

[1] This paper was written when Bhagwati was a Visiting Professor of Economics at Columbia University and Srinivasan was a Visiting Professor of Economics at Stanford University. Srinivasan's research was supported by the Ford Foundation under a faculty research fellowship grant to Stanford University. Thanks are due to Professor Harry Johnson for valuable comments on an earlier draft.

[2] See Bhagwati [1] for a survey of this literature as of early 1964. A discussion of the optimal policies in the presence of non-economic objectives using different production models can be found in Johnson [4] and Ramaswami, V. K. and Srinivasan, T. N. [5].

I. ABSENCE OF MONOPOLY POWER IN TRADE

The basic model, and the optimality of free trade when additional constraints in the form of some non-economic objective are not present, are first outlined here. The problem is to:

maximize:

$$U = U(X_d, Y_d); \qquad \text{...(0)}$$

subject to:

$$X_d \leqq X(L_x, K_x) - X_e, \qquad \text{...(1)}$$

$$Y_d \leqq Y(L_y, K_y) + X_e, \qquad \text{...(2)}$$

$$L_x + L_y \leqq \bar{L}, \qquad \text{...(3)}$$

$$K_x + K_y \leqq \bar{K}, \qquad \text{...(4)}$$

$$L_x,\ L_y,\ K_x,\ K_y,\ X_d,\ Y_d \text{ non-negative,} \qquad \text{...(5)}$$

where U stands for social welfare; X_d, Y_d stand for domestic availability of goods x and y respectively; $X(.,.)$, $Y(.,.)$ represent domestic production of x and y respectively using factor combination of (L_x, K_x) and (L_y, K_y) of labour and capital. $\bar{L}$ and $\bar{K}$ denote total availability of labour and capital in this economy. X_e denotes the net *exports* of x. From the assumption that trade is balanced and the foreign prices are unity for both commodites, X_e also denotes the net *imports* of y. Under the assumption of concavity of production functions the constraint set is convex. The solution to this well-known problem is as follows: First, we form the Lagrangean:

$$\Phi = \theta U - \lambda[X_d - X(L_x, K_x) + X_e] - \mu[Y_d - Y(L_y, K_y) - X_e]$$
$$-\omega[L_x + L_y - \bar{L}] - \rho[K_x + K_y - \bar{K}], \qquad \text{...(6)}$$

where θ, λ, μ, ω, ρ are Lagrangean multipliers associated with U and constraints (1)-(4) respectively. Unconstrained maximization of the Lagrangean yields the necessary conditions for an optimum. These are: (subscript i of a function denotes the derivative of the function with respect to its ith argument)

$$\frac{\partial \Phi}{\partial X_d} = \theta U_1 - \lambda \leqq 0 \text{ with equality if } X_d > 0, \qquad \text{...(7)}$$

$$\frac{\partial \Phi}{\partial Y_d} = \theta U_2 - \mu \leqq 0 \text{ with equality if } Y_d > 0, \qquad \text{...(8)}$$

$$\frac{\partial \Phi}{\partial X_e} = -\lambda + \mu = 0, \qquad \text{...(9)}$$

$$\frac{\partial \Phi}{\partial L_x} = \lambda X_1 - \omega \leqq 0 \text{ with equality if } L_x > 0, \qquad \text{...(10)}$$

$$\frac{\partial \Phi}{\partial K_x} = \lambda X_2 - \rho \leqq 0 \text{ with equality if } K_x > 0, \qquad \text{...(11)}$$

$$\frac{\partial \Phi}{\partial L_y} = \mu Y_1 - \omega \leqq 0 \text{ with equality if } L_y > 0, \qquad \text{...(12)}$$

$$\frac{\partial \Phi}{\partial K_y} = \mu Y_2 - \rho \leqq 0 \text{ with equality if } K_y > 0. \qquad \text{...(13)}$$

Given the concavity of the functions U, X, and Y and the fact that the constraint qualification is satisfied, the necessary conditions (with the multipliers positive) are also sufficient for an optimum. From the fact that X_e, net exports of x, has no sign restriction it follows $\partial\Phi/\partial X_e$ will be zero at an optimum. This is nothing but a restatement of the optimality condition that the marginal rate of substitution between x and y in social consumption must equal their foreign price ratio. It is also clear that $\lambda>0$, i.e., shadow price of a unit of exports of x will be positive, for if $\lambda = 0$, then from (7) it will follow that $\theta U_1 \leqq 0$. This implies $\theta U_1 = 0$ since U_1 and θ are both non-negative. Hence either $\theta = 0$ or $U_1 = 0$. This can happen only if there is either satiation in consumption overall, or in consumption of x. Ruling these out we can assert $\theta>0$ and $\lambda>0$. This enables one to choose λ conveniently as the foreign price of x, namely unity. Then μ will also equal 1; ω and ρ will become wage and rental rates in terms of foreign prices. θ can be interpreted as foreign exchange cost of a unit of welfare.

It is clear that free trade, defined as the absence of impediments to the equalization of foreign with domestic prices, combined with perfect competition, will lead to optimality by satisfying the conditions resulting from the preceding solution. Thus, given the prices unity for x and y and the wage and rental rates ω and ρ respectively, (9)-(13) represent necessary and sufficient conditions for profit maximization in the production of x and y. Similarly (7) and (8) represent necessary and sufficient conditions for welfare maximization.

We can now consider the four non-economic objectives successively.

Case I: Production Level

The case where production of the importable commodity is not allowed to fall below a specified level has been examined previously by Corden [2] and Johnson [3]. Corden shows that, for the case where there is no monopoly power in trade, a production subsidy policy will be superior to a tariff policy in achieving the stated non-economic objective at least cost in terms of utility derived from the flow of currently available goods and services. It can, however, be shown that the policy of tax-cum-subsidy to domestic production of importables is the *optimal* policy under the circumstances, so that it is superior also to the policy of reaching the stated non-economic objective by use of a factor-subsidy policy, for example. More generally, a domestic production tax-cum-subsidy policy will be the optimal policy whenever there is a constraint on the level of production (of exportables *or* importables) that turns out to be binding.

Formally, the problem amounts to introducing an additional constraint in the model:

$$-X \leqq -X^*.$$

In this case, the first order conditions (10) and (11) are altered to the following:

$$(\lambda+\delta)X_1 - w \leqq 0 \quad \text{with equality if } L_x>0, \qquad \text{...(10')}$$

$$(\lambda+\delta)X_2 - \rho \leqq 0 \quad \text{with equality if } K_x>0, \qquad \text{...(11')}$$

where δ is the shadow price associated with the additional constraint. The additional constraint will be binding because otherwise the objective $X \geqq X^*$ is attained under free trade. This means that $\delta>0$. As earlier we can choose $\lambda = \mu = 1$.

It is clear from the above solution that the optimal policy (under pure competition) will entail a tax-cum-subsidy policy with respect to domestic production, designed to bring domestic production of the importable good to the required level when free trade will result in too low a level of its production (i.e. the additional constraint is binding). For (7), (8) and (9) imply that the marginal rate of substitution in consumption will continue to be the foreign price ratio unity, if both commodities are consumed. Also from (10′), (11′), (12) and (13) we can deduce that the marginal rate of substitution of L and K is the same in the production of x and y, provided both commodities are produced and both factors are used in the production of each. Thus, there is no factor subsidy (except possibly in the trivial sense of equiproportionate subsidy on L_x and K_x) involved in the production of x in the optimal solution. However (10′) and (11′) imply that a subsidy of δ per unit over foreign price in the production of x is the optimal policy for bringing the level of production to X^* from its free-trade level.[1]

The superiority of a suitable tax-cum-subsidy policy with respect to domestic production over a tariff policy or a factor subsidy policy can be illustrated as follows. In Fig. 1, the case where the production of importables cannot be allowed to fall below level P^* is illustrated. AB is the efficient production possibility curve and the terms of trade are fixed at $P^*C_t = P_{fs}C_{fs}$. Under a production tax-cum-subsidy policy, the production mix can be shifted to P^* while consumption can occur at international prices at C_{ps} whereas, under a tariff policy, consumption too will occur at distorted prices, at C_t, leading to a loss of welfare even below the level under a production tax-cum-subsidy policy. A policy of subsidizing one of the factors, within the importable industry, can also take production of importables to the desired level; but it will lead to a production point " below " the efficient production possibility curve. The reason is that subsidizing a factor used in one

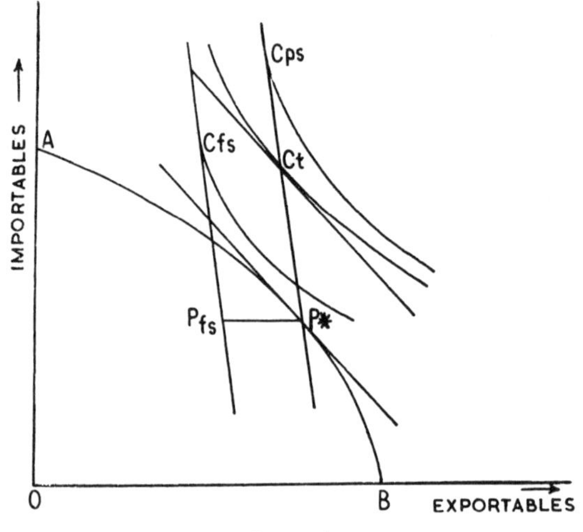

FIGURE 1

industry implies that the marginal rate of substitution of one factor for another differs between industries whereas at any point on the efficient production possibility curve this rate is the same in the two industries. The resulting equilibrium can be illustrated with production at P_{fs} and consumption at C_{fs}, with welfare level below that under the production tax-cum-subsidy policy. This ranking of the two policies is inevitable as the "availability line" $P_{fs}C_{fs}$ must necessarily lie behind the "availability line" P^*C_{ps}. Note that the diagram could be readily adapted to show that, where the production of exportables must exceed the level reached by an optimal free-trade policy, a domestic tax-cum-subsidy policy with respect to production will be superior to a policy of subsidizing the use of one of the factors *and* to a policy of export subsidization, each policy suitably used to achieve the required non-economic objective.

1 A tax on the production of y is an alternative but equivalent policy. This can be seen easily if we choose the normalization $\lambda+\delta = 1$, rather than $\lambda = 1$. Then $\lambda = \mu = 1-\delta$. Thus the domestic producer receives $1-\delta$ per unit of y rather than its foreign price unity. This sort of equivalence between an optimal tax on one commodity (or factors used in one industry) and a subsidy on the other commodity (or factors used in the other industry) arises also in other cases of non-economic objectives. Also a tax (subsidy) on the production of y is equivalent to equiproportionate taxes (subsidies) on the factors used in the production of y. To save space, we will not touch on these sets of equivalence in each case.

Case II: Reduction of Trade or " Self-Sufficiency "

The case where the non-economic objective is to reduce the value of trade and move towards self-sufficiency has been analyzed by Johnson [3] who has noted that, in contrast to the case where the objective is defined in terms of *production* levels, the use of a tariff policy turns out to be superior in this instance to the use of a tax-cum-subsidy policy with respect to domestic production. However, it is possible again to generalize the results, to argue that a tariff policy will be the *optimal* method of reaching the stated non-economic objective, and that it will be superior not merely to a domestic tax-cum-subsidy policy designed to encourage the production of importables but also to a consumption tax-cum-subsidy policy designed to discourage the consumption of importables and to a factor-use tax-cum-subsidy policy designed to encourage the production of importables.

Remembering that, with constant terms of trade, the present non-economic objective can be defined merely as requiring that the import *level*, say of y, does not exceed a certain magnitude, the formal problem amounts to introducing the following additional constraint into the model:

$$X_e \leqq X_e^*$$

Note the constraint says that net exports of x should not exceed X_e^*. Under balanced trade, this is equivalent to requiring that the net imports of y do not exceed X_e^*. In this case, the first order condition (9) is altered to:

$$-\lambda+\mu-\eta = 0 \qquad \ldots(9')$$

where η is the Lagrangean multiplier associated with the additional constraint. As before choose $\lambda = 1$, then μ will become $1+\eta$. Obviously $\eta>0$ since the additional constraint will have to be binding for it to qualify as a non-economic objective.

It is clear from the solution that the optimal policy under pure competition will entail a tariff policy, designed to bring the level of imports to the required level when free trade will result in too high a level of imports. For, from (7)-(8), (10)-(13), we know that the marginal rate of substitution of x for y in consumption as well as production is the same value λ/μ. But λ/μ is now different from the foreign price ratio unity and equals $1/(1+\eta)$. Thus a tariff at the rate η per unit on imports of Y is the optimal policy. Incidentally, (10)-(13) also imply that the marginal rate of substitution of L and K is the same in the production of x and y, indicating that factor subsidization is not optimal.

The result can be illustrated by elaborating further the diagram used by Johnson [3] to show the superiority of a tariff policy over a domestic production tax-cum-subsidy policy. In Fig. 2, AP_tB is the efficient production possibility curve and P_tC_t is the fixed terms of trade. The tariff brings production to P_t, consumption to C_t and the import level to the difference between the production and consumption levels. Now, it can be shown readily that, subject to the constraint that each policy lead to the same utility level (U), the level of imports under the tariff policy will be the *least* as compared with the (illustrated) policies of production tax-cum-subsidy, consumption tax-cum-subsidy and factor tax-cum-subsidy. The consumption tax-cum-subsidy leads to production at P_{cs} at international prices and to consumption at C_{cs} and it is clear that the import level exceeds that under the tariff. The production tax-cum-subsidy leads to production at P_{ps} and to consumption at C_{ps}, again necessarily involving a level of imports in excess of that under the tariff. A suitable tax-cum-subsidy on factor use (excluding of course equiproportionate tax or subsidy on both factors, which would be equivalent to a production tax or subsidy) will lead to production at P_{fs} and consumption at C_{fs}, again leading to excess of imports over that level reached under the tariff. Note further that the factor tax-cum-subsidy policy will, in turn, be inferior to a production tax-cum-subsidy policy, although no unique ranking between the consumption and production tax-cum-subsidy policies is possible but will rather depend upon the relative elasticities of substitution in consumption and domestic production.

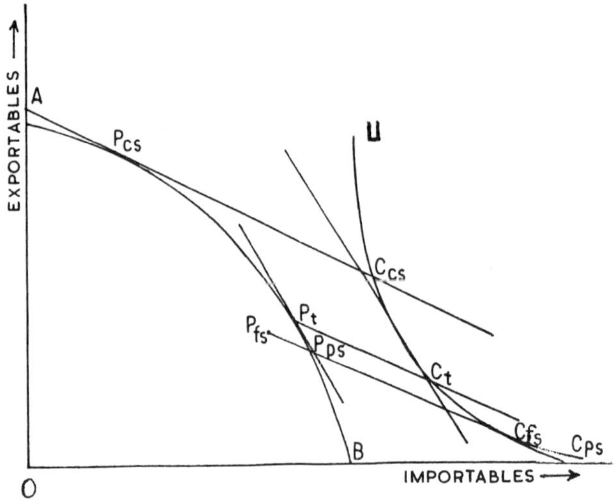

FIGURE 2

Case III: Factor Employment

The case where the non-economic objective is to prevent the employment of a factor in an occupation from falling below a specified level may now be examined. It will be shown that in this case, the optimal policy will consist of a subsidy for the use of the factor in the sector, when the level of use of the factor in the sector under free trade falls below the required magnitude.

From a formal point of view, the problem amounts to introducing the following additional constraint in the model: $-L_x \leqq -L_x^*$. This says that employment in the production of x, namely L_x, must not fall below L_x^*. In this case, condition (10) is altered to the following:

$$X_1 - \omega + \omega^* = 0, \qquad \text{...(10')}$$

where ω^* is the shadow price associated with the additional constraint. As before we can safely assume that the new constraint will be binding and hence $\omega^* > 0$. We can normalize the shadow prices as before so that $\lambda = 1$.

It is clear from the solution that the optimal policy will involve a subsidy policy with respect to the use of the factor in the activity. i.e., production of x where its employment is not to be allowed to fall below the specified level L_x^*. The optimal rate of subsidy is ω^* per unit of employment. From (7)-(9) we can conclude that the marginal rate of substitution in consumption is the foreign price ratio, namely unity. With $\lambda = \mu = 1$, one can conclude from (10')-(13) that no production subsidy on output is optimal.

This conclusion can be illustrated readily. Remember that the shift to the required level of employment can be achieved in either of two ways: (i) by shifting the level of production in favour of the activity whose employment of the factor in question is sought to be increased above the level under free trade, by use of either trade policy or domestic production tax-cum-subsidy policy; or (ii) by directly subsidizing the use of the factor in that activity. Thus, we need to compare essentially three policies with one another: (i) domestic production tax-cum subsidy policy; (ii) trade tax (or subsidy) policy; and (iii) factor-use subsidy policy. The comparison between the first two policies is easily illustrated: the domestic production tax-cum-subsidy policy is clearly superior as it will shift production, and hence factor employment, to the required level without inflicting the consumption loss that would be entailed by the use of a trade tariff (or subsidy) policy. But the comparison between the production tax-cum-subsidy policy and the factor-use subsidy policy requires the deployment of the box diagram.

Thus take Fig. 3 where *ASB* represents the efficient production possibility curve. Each point on *ASB* corresponds to a point on the contract curve *OSO′* in the Edgeworth box diagram of Fig. 4 where the size of the box is determined by total factor availability and the curves represent production isoquants. The constraint $L_x \geqq L_x^*$ means that the

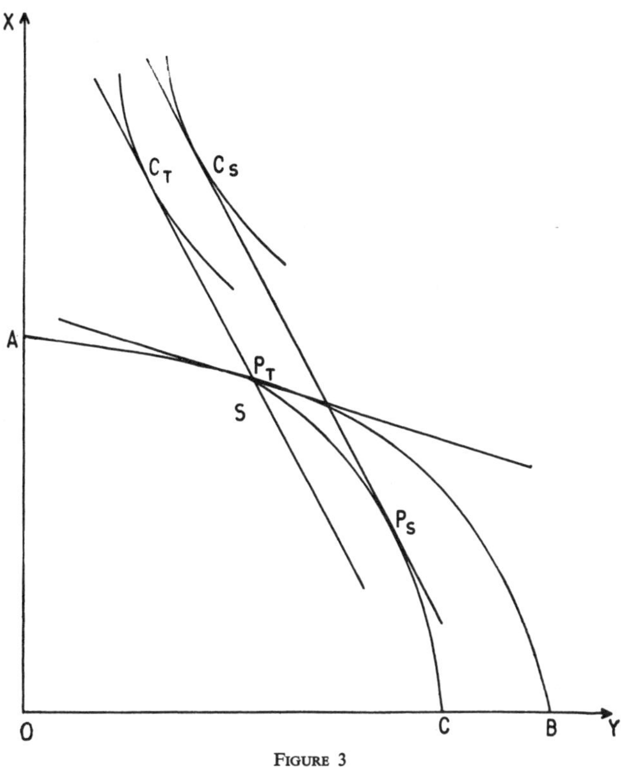

FIGURE 3

chosen production point (i.e., factor allocation point) must lie in the smaller box *PQRO′*. Thus, the efficient production possibility curve, given the constraint $L_x \geqq L_x^*$ is no longer the entire contract curve *O′SO*, but consists of two parts. The first part is obtained by following the contract curve from *O′* to the point *S* where $L_x = L_x^*$. The second part is obtained by following the factor allocations corresponding to points on the vertical line *SQ*. Thus, the new production possibility curve is *ASC* rather than *ASB* as in Fig. 3, the points on *SC* being dominated by points on *SB*. It will also be clear that a point on *ASC* on the segment *SC* can be reached under pure competition only by a factor subsidy policy, the reason being that at such a point the marginal rate of substitution of one factor for another differs as between industries. Having obtained the constrained production possibility curve *ASC*, the standard argument that free trade in outputs is the optimal policy follows. The fact that the employment constraint is binding implies that, if the

C

constraint were removed, the free trade production point would fall on the *SB* portion of *ASB* in Fig. 3. This means, given diminishing marginal rate of substitution of x for y along *ASB*, that once the employment constraint is introduced and the relevant production possibility curve becomes *ASC*, free trade in outputs will result in production at some point on *SC*. Such a point can be reached by a subsidy on labour used in the production of x. Suppose on the other hand we use a production tax-cum-subsidy policy to bring production to point S and achieve our non-economic objective. Then, as Fig. 3 clearly indicates, such a policy will result in consumption point C_T lying on a lower indifference curve as compared to the consumption point C_S associated with the policy of factor subsidy and free trade. It may be observed that Fig. 4 implies that some capital is needed for producing x. This is not essential to the argument.

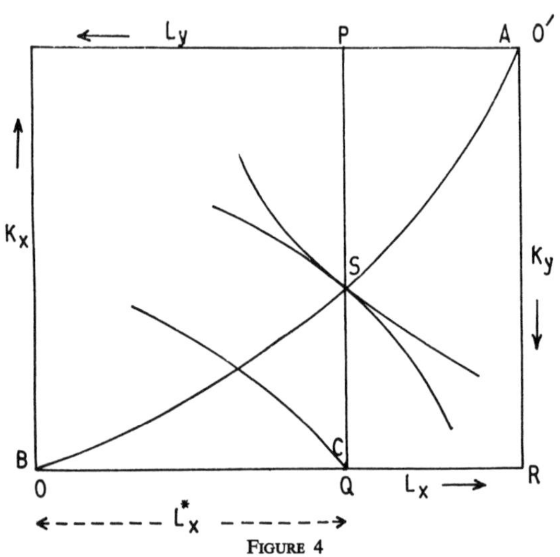

FIGURE 4

Case IV: Domestic Availability

The case where domestic *availability*, rather than domestic production, is sought to be restrained for social or political reasons, requires optimal intervention in the form of a *consumption* tax-cum-subsidy policy when the constraint is binding.

From a formal point of view, the problem amounts to including the following constraint in the model:

$$X_d \leqq X_d^*.$$

In this case, condition (7) is altered to the following:

$$\theta U_1 - (\lambda + \lambda^*) \leqq 0, \qquad \text{...(7')}$$

with equality if $X_d > 0$ where λ^* is the shadow price associated with the additional constraint. The additional constraint can be assumed to be binding, in which case $\lambda^* > 0$. As earlier we can choose $\lambda = 1$, which implies $\mu = 1$. Then (7′) and (8) imply that the marginal rate of substitution of x and y in consumption is $(\lambda + \lambda^*)/\mu = 1 + \lambda^*$, while (10)-(13) imply that the marginal rate of substitution in production is $\lambda/\mu = 1$ = foreign price ratio of x and y. The marginal rates of substitution of the two factors are the same in the production of x and y. Thus no production or factor-use subsidy is involved in an optimal solution.

It is clear from the solution that the optimal intervention will involve taxing the consumption of the commodity whose availability under free trade exceeds the level specified as an additional constraint. This follows from the difference between the foreign price ratio and the marginal rate of substitution in consumption.

This conclusion can be readily illustrated. In Fig. 5, AP_fB is the efficient production possibility curve, P_f is the production under free trade and C_f the consumption under free trade. Thus, under free trade, the domestic availability of Y will be at OQ and will exceed OR^*, the maximum amount specified as possible. A consumption tax-cum-subsidy policy will then take consumption to C_{ct}, maintaining production at P_f and reducing the consumption of Y to OR^*. It is clear then that any other policy will enable the consumption of Y to occur at OR^* (or below) *only* by shifting the consumption point along

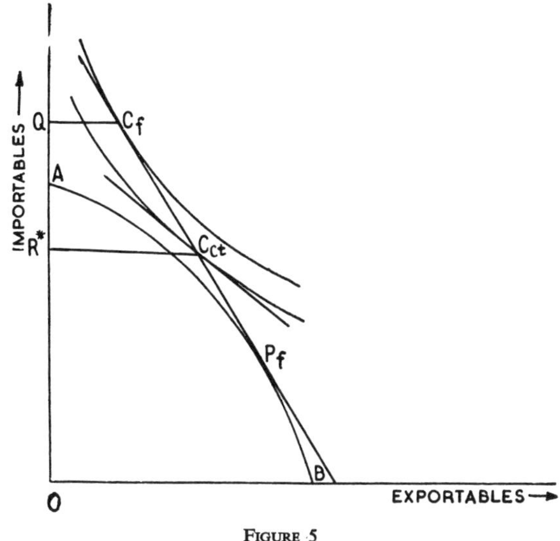

FIGURE 5

$C_{ct}R^*$ to the left (or to the southwest of C_{ct}) and hence will necessarily result in a *lower* level of welfare than at C_{ct} which is reached by an appropriate consumption tax-cum-subsidy policy.

II. MONOPOLY POWER IN TRADE

The analysis of Section I was based on the assumption that the foreign price ratio was fixed (by choice of units of x and y this ratio was assumed to be unity) and was independent of the quantities traded. In this section we relax this assumption and allow terms of trade to vary with the volume of trade. The paper by Corden [2] mentioned earlier considers this case when the non-economic objective is to ensure that the domestic production of the importable commodity does not fall below a specified level. It is shown that the optimal policy for achieving this objective is to use a production subsidy together with an optimum tariff. We shall consider the other non-economic objectives as well and show that the optimal policy is to use the same instrument (though not necessarily at the same level) as in the corresponding fixed terms of trade case in conjunction with an optimum tariff. The mathematical analysis will be provided only for the cases of (*a*) absence of non-economic objectives in which case an optimum tariff policy will emerge and (*b*) the non-economic objective of ensuring that the level of employment in a specified activity (say production of x) does not fall below a specified level L_x^* in which case a wage subsidy in the production of x along with an optimum tariff will emerge as optimal.

With the presence of monopoly power in trade the number of units of x that can be obtained (or have to be given up) by giving up (or to obtain) a unit of y through trade will depend on the number of units of x imported (or exported). Let X_e denote the net exports of x as before. Then the net imports of Y_e under balanced trade will now be $p(X_e)X_e$ where $p(X_e)$ represents the price of y per unit of x when X_e units of x are traded. We shall assume that $F(X_e) = p(X_e)X_e$ is such that $F'(X_e)>0$, $F''(X_e)<0$ for all X_e. This means that the marginal revenue derived from exports is positive but declines as the volume of exports increases. This can be seen as follows. Suppose x is the export commodity, i.e., $X_e>0$; then $F(X_e)$ represents the total export earnings measured in units of y. Thus $F'(X_e)$ is the marginal revenue and by assumption it is positive. The assumption $F''(X_e)<0$ means that marginal revenue declines as X_e increases. Suppose, on the other hand, x is the import commodity, then X_e is negative, and $Y_e = -F(X_e)$ is the volume of exports of y. The value of exports of y in terms of x, that is, the quantity of x that can be imported from exporting a given quantity Y_e of y, will then be $-X_e = -F^{-1}(-Y_e)$ where F^{-1} is the inverse of the function F. Let $G(F_e) = -F^{-1}(-Y_e)$. The assumption $F'>0$, $F''<0$ will imply $G'>0$, $G''<0$, i.e., the marginal revenue in terms of x of exporting Y_e units of y is positive and declines as Y_e increases.

With this notation, constraint (2) will now read

$$Y_d \leqq Y[L_y, K_y]+p[X_e]X_e = Y[L_y, K_y]+F(X_e). \qquad \text{...(2')}$$

All other constraints remain unchanged. Given our assumption about F, the constraint set continues to be convex and satisfies the constraint qualification. When there are no non-economic objectives, the only first order condition that gets altered is (9) which will now read:

$$-\lambda+\mu F'(X_e) = 0. \qquad \text{...(9')}$$

From the fact that the other conditions do not get altered, it follows that (in the case of non-specialization of production and consumption) the marginal rate of substitution in production of x for y is λ/μ, and that the marginal rate of substitution of labour for capital is the same in the production of each good. However, λ/μ does not equal the average terms of trade, i.e., the foreign price ratio $p(X_e)$, but equals the marginal terms of trade $F'(X_e) = p(X_e)+X_e p'(X_e)$. If this optimal solution is to be achieved through competitive markets at home, domestic price ratio will have to be λ/μ while foreign price ratio is $p(X_e)$. Thus an optimum tariff corresponding to this difference emerges.

If we introduce now the additional constraint $-L_x \leqq -L_x^*$ into the model, (10) becomes changed to

$$\lambda X_1-\omega+\omega^* = 0. \qquad \text{...(10')}$$

Condition (9') continues to hold. Thus the optimal policy will now take the form of a tariff plus a wage subsidy of ω^* per unit of labour in the production of x.

It can be easily seen from a similar analysis that the optimal policy instrument in addition to a tariff designed to exploit the assumed monopoly power in trade, will be (i) a production subsidy if the non-economic objective is to ensure that the production of importables does not fall below a specified level; (ii) a consumption tax, if domestic availability of a commodity is not to exceed a specified level; and (iii) a tariff if the imports are not to exceed a specified level.

If will be realized that the shadow prices associated with the constraints relating to non-economic objectives (in Section I and II) represent the " marginal cost " of such a constraint, in the following sense. Take for instance the case where the non-economic objective is to ensure that the production of importables does not fall below the level X^*. The shadow price δ associated with this constraint means that if the specified level

X^* is increased by a sufficiently small positive amount ε, the welfare level attained will go down by $(\delta/\theta)\varepsilon$ where θ is the shadow price of utility. If we choose the normalization $\theta = 1$, instead of $\lambda = 1$, the value of δ indicates the "marginal cost" in utility terms of increasing X^*. A similar interpretation holds for other shadow prices.

III. ALTERNATIVE FORMULATION OF THE PROBLEM

An alternative approach to the problem of non-economic objectives is to incorporate these directly into the utility function. Such an approach, however, raises the question whether it is meaningful at all to distinguish between economic and non-economic objectives when both sets of objectives enter the utility function as arguments. We illustrate this approach for the case of the non-economic objective $X \geqq X^*$, in order to highlight the similarities and differences between it and our approach. Let us define a new concave utility function $V(X_d, Y_d, X)$ as follows:

$$V(X_d, Y_d, X) = U(X_d, Y_d) \quad \text{for all } X \geqq X^* \text{ and } (X_d, Y_d),$$

$$V(X_d, Y_d, X) < U(X_d, Y_d) \quad \text{for all } X < X^* \text{ and all } (X_d, Y_d),$$

$$\lim_{X \to X^*_-} V(X_d, Y_d, X) = U(X_d, Y_d) \quad \text{for all } (X_d, Y_d),$$

$$\frac{\partial V(X_d, Y_d, X)}{\partial X} > 0 \quad \text{for } X < X^* \text{ and all } (X_d, Y_d),$$

$$\lim_{X \to X^*_-} \frac{\partial V(X_d, Y_d, X)}{\partial X} = 0 \quad \text{for all } (X_d, Y_d).$$

This formulation means that the level of output of x is relevant for welfare only when $X < X^*$. The marginal utility of x falls to zero as X approaches X^* from below. Also the utility of a given (X_d, Y_d) when the non-economic objective is present is *less*, when the output of x is less than X^*, than the utility of the same (X_d, Y_d) when such an objective is absent. More importantly, this formulation accommodates a trade-off between economic and non-economic objectives in the sense that an optimal solution could conceivably result in $X < X^*$ whereas in our earlier approach $X \geqq X^*$ appears as a constraint and as such cannot be violated in any feasible, let alone optimal, solution.

Now maximization with V as welfare function rather than U yields the following:

$$\theta V_1 - \lambda \leqq 0 \quad \text{with equality if } X_d > 0, \qquad \ldots(7'')$$

$$\theta V_2 - \mu \leqq 0 \quad \text{with equality if } Y_d > 0, \qquad \ldots(8'')$$

$$(\theta V_3 + \lambda) X_1 - \omega \leqq 0 \quad \text{with equality if } L_x > 0, \qquad \ldots(10'')$$

$$(\theta V_3 + \lambda) X_2 - \rho \leqq 0 \quad \text{with equality if } K_x > 0. \qquad \ldots(11'')$$

Inequalities (9), (12) and (13) are the same as before.

From a comparison with (7), (8), (10′) and (11′), it will be seen that (7″) and (8″) have the same form as (7) and (8), since V_1 and V_2 represent the same things as U_1 and U_2 respectively, namely marginal utilities of the domestic availabilities of x and y. The inequalities (10″) and (11″) differ from (10′) and (11′) only in that θV_3 occurs in (10″) and (11″) in place of δ that occurred in (10′) and (11′). But, a moment's reflection will suggest that θV_3 and δ represent the same thing. For V_3 is the marginal utility of domestic output of x and, by definition of V, this is different from zero only when the output of x is less than X^*. Thus, given a sufficiently small $\varepsilon > 0$, εV_3 is nothing but the utility loss of a reduction in output of x by ε, i.e., utility cost of an ε deviation away from or the utility gain in an ε deviation towards X^*. As before, θ is the shadow price of utility; then $\varepsilon\theta V_3$

is the shadow cost or benefit of a deviation of ε from or towards X^*. We saw earlier $\varepsilon\delta$ represents the shadow price of an ε increase or decrease in X^*, when the constraint is set as $X \geqq X^*$. Thus both approaches yield an estimate of the marginal cost of the non-economic constraint. However, there is the important difference mentioned earlier, namely, that the above approach permits X to fall below X^*, if it will increase welfare, where a constraint of the form $X \geqq X^*$ will not permit this. In other words, the two approaches are not equivalent unless we define V in such a way that even though it is feasible to have an output of x less than X^* in the sense that a solution to all variables with $X < X^*$ exists satisfying all the other constraints, it is not optimal to do so.

Massachusetts Institute of Technology J. N. BHAGWATI
Indian Statistical Institute T. N. SRINIVASAN

First version received 12.2.68; *final version received* 18.9.68

REFERENCES

[1] Bhagwati, J. " The Pure Theory of International Trade: A Survey ", *Economic Journal* (March 1964).

[2] Corden, W. M. " Tariffs, Subsidies, and the Terms of Trade ", *Economica* (August 1957).

[3] Johnson, H. G. " Optimal Trade Intervention in the Presence of Domestic Distortions " in Baldwin *et al.*, *Trade, Growth and Balance of Payments* (North-Holland Publishing Company, Amsterdam, 1965).

[4] Johnson, H. G. " The Cost of Protection and the Scientific Tariff ", *Journal of Political Economy* (October 1960).

[5] Ramaswami, V. K., and Srinivasan, T. N. " Optimal Subsidies and Tariffs when Some Factors are Traded ", *Journal of Political Economy* (December 1968).

Erratum

Page 29, equation (10′): "w" should read "ω".

Trade Liberalization among LDCs, Trade Theory, and Gatt Rules

Jagdish Bhagwati

Political attitudes change rapidly and astonishingly in the field of international commercial policy. To those accustomed to the protectionist policies of the LDCs in the decade and a half since the war, it is remarkable that the LDCs today are actively discussing the issue of trade liberalization among themselves.

Not merely are they discussing it, but several of them have actively engaged in mutual negotiations to get action started. The most striking developments have undoubtedly been those in South America, where the Treaty of Montevideo represented the formal inauguration of LAFTA (The Latin American Free Trade Area),[1] of which Ecuador, Colombia, Peru, Chile, Argentina, Uruguay, Paraguay, Brazil and Mexico are already members, and the Treaty of Managua on *Central American Economic Integration* which has already accelerated significantly the integration process among the member countries Salvador, Guatemala, Costa Rica, Honduras, and Nicaragua (Bell, 1966, chapter 4).

Elsewhere, the current picture is not as much in character, but the outlook points the same way. The *East African Federation*, comprising Tanganyika, Uganda and Kenya, and the UDEAC (Union Douanière et Economique de l'Afrique Centrale), with Congo (Brazzaville), Gabon, the Central African Republic, Chad and the Federal Republic of Cameroon in French Equatorial Africa as its members, are two of the conspicuous examples in the African continent. But they trace their ancestry to colonial periods and their 'integrated markets' have recently been witness to disruption by measures such as *inter-member* QRS, tariffs and surcharges.[2] However, the measures taken by the members to review these developments and *retain* the framework of a generally reduced and low level of trade barriers between member countries, rather than follow post-independence policies of industrialization behind universal trade barriers, themselves signify an *implicit* decision to liberalize trade among themselves.

There have also recently been developments such as the *Regional Cooperation for Development* between Pakistan, Iran and Turkey, which aims explicitly to create 'regional' division of labour with attendant liberalization of mutual trade barriers, and the still-undefined moves towards a *Middle Eastern Common Market*. Asia, however, has witnessed little concrete efforts or ideas in this direction, despite ECAFE's efforts to initiate regional liberalization of trade.[3]

Reasons for Trade Liberalization

The reasons for these efforts at trade liberalization among LDCs are several. First, there is a growing appreciation of the simple fact of inefficiency of specialization which industrialization behind indiscriminate, high trade barriers involves. Many LDCs, especially in the ECAFE region, feel that, starting from the present position of QRs, it is possible to relax restrictions on a mutual basis with other LDCs and reduce 'overlapping' import substitution or industrialization (provided that balance of payments difficulties resulting, if any, are not excessive and payments arrangements are forthcoming to assist in the short-run). The emphasis here is on *economic inefficiency arising from producing things which could well be imported more cheaply from others who are better placed, by natural resources or otherwise, to produce them.*

This argument, however, is eclipsed by the more recent emphasis on *the inefficiency which arises from the inability to exploit economies of scale in industrial activities if one has to industrialize within essentially national markets.* This argument has come up in both African and Latin American contexts and there are three ways in which it can be encountered.

(1) It is often presented, in the African and Central American contexts, in the strongest conceivable terms as a *sine qua non* of industrialization. Individual countries are absolutely *non-viable* because it is impossible to conceive of any industrial activity which can be set up even remotely within sight of its optimum scale in view of the extremely small effective demand. Thus, industrialization cannot be conceived of at all *unless* the markets are widened through trade. Hence the case for international trade liberalization.

(2) The preceding argument overstates the case. The real point is that,

if scale economies cannot be exploited, the real return to investment in industrial activity will fall, raising thereby the resources necessary to achieve the same level of industrialization. The scale of the effective demand in many African countries, for example, is perhaps so small in relation to achievable economies that the increase in costs may be significant; but it is not meaningful to describe the resulting situation as one of 'non-viability'. In the reformulated version, therefore, the argument merely amounts to stating that industrialization, with access to extra-national markets, would be achievable by an LDC at lower cost *via* the resulting exploitation of economies of scale.

(3) Indeed, the 'non-viability' argument comes up, in a different version, in Latin America, among the industrialized countries of Brazil, Argentina and Mexico. They discuss their problems of industrialization in a Fraserian, evolutionary framework and argue that they have 'completed the first stage of industrialization, involving the production of consumer goods', reasonably adequately within national markets. But the 'next stage', involving the establishment of heavy industry, is impossible to contemplate, in view of the scale economies involved, within national frontiers and is conditional upon access to international markets.[4]

Finally, there is the traditional argument that foreign trade can be an instrument for increasing competitiveness and hence the efficiency of industrial activity.[5] The experience of the LDCs has underlined the inefficiencies which arise from domestic monopolies sheltering behind trade barriers. This has been a powerful argument, in Latin America especially, for initiating reductions from very high tariff levels so as to reintroduce some 'measured degree' of competition. Note, however, that this argument presupposes that investment *is* forthcoming; since in most LDCs this itself is frequently a result of fenced-off national markets, the concern with efficiency of investment is something which comes at a *later* stage in the process of industrialization; after all, the LDCs cannot be expected to worry about efficiency unless there is something to be efficient about!

These arguments for trade liberalization are quite sensible, of course, and familiar to economists. Not that they are always used to advantage or with a correct appreciation of their limitations. For example, the fact that economies of scale operate in industrial activities should not make the LDCs, operating a customs union and an industrial allocation policy in harness (as in East Africa, Equatorial Africa and Central America) forget that (i) the spatial distribution of demand, (ii) transportation costs, (iii) the inter-temporal growth of demand at different points of consumption and (iv) the external economies obtaining *via* the geographical clustering of certain industries are *also* factors to be considered and that the optimal solutions, even when trade barriers are absent, may still demand that 'uneconomic scale' plants be constructed in different member countries in the same activity.[6]

Distinguishing Features of LDC *Trade Liberalization*

However, the most interesting aspect of the LDC efforts at trade liberalization is that they are characterized by certain patterns which are both readily discernible and difficult to reconcile with what traditional trade theory would predict as the behaviour of governments 'rationally' pursuing economic welfare. The most notable of these features may be listed here at the outset.

(1) The trade expansion efforts are sought to be on a *preferential* basis, among a few or all LDCs but *excluding the developed countries*. Where the preferential groupings fall within the purview of Gatt's Article XXIV (exempting 100 per cent preferential arrangements from the contractual commitment to extending MFN treatment to all other Gatt members), there is no institutional change involved in this demand. But the LDCs clearly would like to extend the operation of such an exemption to less-than-100 per cent preferential arrangements among LDCs. They are thus demanding really the suspension of automatic MFN rights by the developed Gatt members with respect to the LDC members.

(2) Furthermore, the experience in Latin America in particular shows that the LDC efforts at tariff cuts and trade liberalization are oriented very clearly towards *trade diversion*. Looked at from the viewpoint of traditional trade theory, therefore, the LDC efforts seem to be directed at the wrong kind of tariff cuts altogether! The acceptance of the increment in intra-regional trade in LAFTA as an index of its success, without any attempt at separating out trade diversion from this figure, as also the impatience exhibited in Latin American circles with the requirement of Gatt's Article XXIV[7] that the average external tariff must not be greater after a customs union or free trade area (which would, among other things, make trade diversion *via* the raising of external tariffs impossible), are pointed

reminders of this divergence between LDC demands and behaviour on the one hand and traditional predictions and prescriptions on the other.

(3) The LDC negotiations and literature are unanimous in insisting upon 'reciprocity' of benefits. This is familiar from the history of tariff negotiations anywhere. The reciprocity takes the form, quite acutely in most LDC cases, of balancing of *incremental* trade flows rather than demands of identical tariffs cuts or any other method. Both the strict insistence on reciprocity and the specific form taken by it are not readily reconciled with what traditional trade theory, as analyzed below, would indicate as the likely pattern of LDC behaviour.

(4) As a corollary to this concern with this form of reciprocity, there is also discernible among many LDCs a preference for negotiations and action on trade liberalization among smaller rather than larger groups. As a consequence, there is already discernible a growing conflict of opinion on whether any *sub*-set of LDCs should be allowed to discriminate against the other LDCs when a less-than-100 per cent programme of tariff cuts, outside the purview of Gatt's Article XXIV, is involved. The dominant trend, however, seems to be in favour of the more 'liberal' version which would permit discriminatory tariff cuts applicable even within a sub-set of LDCs.

There are broadly two sets of issues that arise from these patterns of LDC behaviour and demands. First, is it possible to 'explain' them in terms of the traditional theory of preferential trade liberalization (associated mainly with Viner, Meade and Lipsey[8]) if one makes the additional assumption that the LDC governments act 'rationally' in pursuit of economic welfare? Or do we have to modify the theory itself so that it leads to predictions of behaviour which are consistent with those observed? It is argued, later in this paper, that we indeed require a modified, new theory which fits the observable facts very much better and that such a theory can be obtained by modifying the LDC governments' assumed 'utility function'.

Secondly, in the light of such an 'explanation' of LDC behaviour and demands, the question immediately arises as to what attitude economists *ought* to take concerning the amendments proposed by LDCs in the Gatt rules. The following analysis formulates a conceptual framework which provides a possible case for accepting such amendments, while also examining its limiting assumptions.

Explanation of Distinguishing Features of LDC *Trade Liberalization*

It is possible, of course, to say that the LDCs are 'muddled' and 'irrational'; such views are not as uncommon as one would imagine. They are in fact held especially by those who have not reconciled themselves to the exercise of governmental action and hence cannot admit of its possible rationality.

On the other hand, purely *political* explanations are both possible and undoubtedly relevant. Thus, for example, the desire to liberalize trade *within* the LDC group, to the exclusion of the developed countries, could be explained, partly at least, by reference to a desire to attain 'solidarity' within the LDC group. There are most certainly overtones of such notions as 'solidarity', 'bargaining power', 'political cohesion and strength' and the like in some of the regional LDC groups such as LAFTA and in Central America; they are to be traced to the political dominance of the United States in the area as also the example of the European Common Market which too was enveloped in a political cloak of similar cloth.

There also seems to have been considerable interest shown by some of the developed countries themselves in getting the LDCs to liberalize trade *among* themselves as an 'act of self-help'. This too is to be explained, at least partially, in political terms as an attempt to (i) divert LDC attention away from pressing on with their claims at UNCTAD for concessions from the developed countries, (ii) create predictable dissensions among the LDCs (on issues such as that of discrimination among themselves) and thus break the LDC-block (such as it is) at UNCTAD, and (iii) promote, in particular, *regional* groupings of LDCs which would then be easier to attract into preferential groupings with the developed countries in the region, thus reinforcing the traditional economic and political ties[9] (as with United States and Latin America or EEC and French Africa).[10]

Similarly, the interest in trade-diverting trade expansion may be explained in terms of a *political* inability to lower tariffs on protected, domestic industries. Since producers typically tend to turn into articulate and powerful pressure groups, it is plausible to argue that the politics of democratic systems will reflect producer interests more readily than any others, so that trade-diverting trade expansion is certainly likely to be preferred to trade-creating trade expansion.

While such explanations are certainly relevant, it is also of equal interest to note that practically the entire range of LDC behaviour can be 'explained' by recasting traditional trade theory into a somewhat different mould. This is, in fact, readily done.

Traditional Analysis

The traditional analysis classifies preferential tariff reduction into two ideal categories: (i) trade diverting and (ii) trade creating. Each of these well-known types may be considered, in turn, from the viewpoint of predictions of behaviour that they would generate on the assumption of 'rational' behaviour in the sense discussed earlier.

I. *Trade diverting tariff reduction.* Looked at from the viewpoint of a tariff-cutting country (M), and the partner-country (P) in whose favour the tariff is cut, a trade diverting tariff cut leads to the following situation according to the traditional theory:[11]

(*a*) country M will lose from the trade diversion shifting the source of imports to the higher cost supplier, country P;

(*b*) on the other hand, the cheapening of the commodity, on which the tariff is cut preferentially, may lead to a net consumption gain (Lipsey, 1957);

(*c*) country M can therefore be left as before, or may gain or lose from a trade-diverting tariff cut;

(*d*) as for country P, it will *either* gain from opening trade with country M or by improving its terms of trade with it *or* have its welfare position unchanged if it is a 'large' country (in the Samuelson sense).

The matrix of welfare possibilities from a preferential tariff cut by country M in favour of country P, according to traditional theory, is shown on page 28. Note that, in two cases at least, (1) and (2), there seems to be a clear reason why reciprocity by country P does not represent a *sine qua non* for a tariff cut by country M; whereas, only in three cases (3–5) would it seem that country M could not be induced to cut its tariff on country P without demanding some measure of reciprocity from it. Note also that whereas reciprocity would not be necessary in the cases where trade diversion leads to welfare gains, the insistence on reciprocity would arise most compellingly only in cases where the trade diversion leads to a loss (as will happen in cases 3 and 4) where again all that reciprocity may lead to is a loss to *both* countries instead of one. Thus we *either* fail to provide rationale for reciprocity at all or provide it in cases where the possibility of there being preferential tariff cuts at all is dismal.

So far, therefore, the theory fails to explain why the LDCs seem to prefer trade diverting tariff cuts and simultaneously to insist on reciprocity (of incremental trade flows). We can, however, go somewhat further than we have. Within the framework of this analysis itself, there are two ways in which the reciprocity demands may be justified even in cases where country M gains from a unilateral, preferential tariff cut causing trade diversion. On the one hand, we could introduce a game-theoretic formulation into the analysis. For example, in the two cases, (1) and (2), where country M stands to benefit unambiguously from a preferential tariff cut, its insistence on a reciprocal tariff cut *could* lead perhaps to a mutual, simultaneous tariff cut which may make country M even *better off than under a unilateral, discriminatory tariff cut.*[12]

MATRIX (1). Welfare possibilities under a trade diverting tariff cut by one country (M) – on traditional theory

possibility	COUNTRY M	COUNTRY P
(1)	gains	gains
(2)	gains	unchanged
(3)	loses	gains
(4)	loses	unchanged
(5)	unchanged	gains
(6)	unchanged	unchanged

At the same time, we could well argue that the alternative to a unilateral preferential tariff cut by country M is not merely the status quo but could well be a unilateral *non-discriminatory* tariff cut. Thus it could be argued that the willingness to cut a tariff preferentially in favour of country P involves a *potential* loss (or reduction in gain) as compared with a situation where country M would have cut its tariff non-preferentially, and therefore the reciprocity demand follows from the consequential (implicit) loss to country M.[13]

We can somewhat strengthen, therefore, the case for expecting 'rational' governments to press for reciprocity. Note, however, that while reciprocity may be explained along these lines, we cannot so explain the desire for balancing the incremental trade flows – that is, the *specific form* that reciprocity demands take. Moreover, the analysis does not really explain why the sub-set of countries M and P are interested in negotiations for trade liberalization with each other and not with others. To make this implicit but important assumption plausible, we would have to bring in some extraneous, political argument; as argued earlier, a sub-set of countries may well decide to undertake liberalization among only themselves consequent upon a political decision to 'integrate their political and economic systems'. Indeed, some such political assumption would be necessary even to explain why it is that, since *both* countries M and P can lose from such trade diverting trade liberalization despite reciprocity, and such possibilities do not seem to be excluded by any means by recent LDC experience, the LDCs in fact seem to opt nonetheless for such trade liberalization. Unless, therefore, one relies on such political arguments at a crucial stage of the analysis, the traditional theory will not be able to come to grips with even the most obvious features of LDC attempt at trade liberalization.

II. *Trade creating tariff reduction*: When we analyse the case of trade creating tariff cuts, the inability of traditional theory to come to grips with LDC behaviour seems even more evident. Assuming that country M is preferentially cutting its tariff again, if it is a trade creating tariff cut it will lead to the following situation according to traditional theory:

(*a*) country M will lose its inefficient industry, partially or wholly, to country P;

(*b*) country M will consider itself as having improved its allocation or resources and will also derive a consumption gain, leaving it a net gainer; and

(*c*) country P will not or will have gained depending on whether it is or is not 'large'.

The matrix of welfare possibilities under the traditional theory is then as indicated on page 30.

By contrast with the case of trade diverting tariff cuts, we now have one case of harmony of interests and another where the tariff-cutting country gains anyway. In neither case, therefore, would reciprocity appear to be a prime requisite before country M would cut its tariff.[14]

Traditional analysis would then also imply that trade creating tariff cuts will be profitable whereas trade diverting tariff cuts would not be so except where the consumption gain is decisive. Hence we would infer from traditional analysis that trade creating tariff cuts are more likely to occur in practice than trade diverting tariff cuts. This is yet another conclusion which seems to contradict LDC experience.

MATRIX (2). Welfare possibilities under a trade creating tariff cut by one country (M)–on traditional theory

possibility	COUNTRY M	COUNTRY P
(1)	gains	unchanged
(2)	gains	gains

Modified 'Utility Function'

Consider, however, the following modification to each LDC's objective or utility function:

(1) let each LDC attach intrinsic significance to the level of import-competing industrial output that trade diversion attracts to each country and trade creation attracts to one country 'at expense of' the other; and

(2) let each country ignore the significance of any possible consumption gain from the cheapening of products in domestic markets subsequent on tariff cuts.[15]

Note further that the addition of these new arguments in the LDC objective function seems quite plausible because, in particular:

(1) the LDCs typically wish to industrialize and hence use tariffs (and/or quantitative restrictions) for this purpose, so that the attraction of import-competing industrial production would be considered a desirable result *in itself*; and

(2) in most cases, the trade pattern of the LDCs involves imports of components, materials and machines, to which the notion of a *consumption* gain is only indirectly applicable.[16]

If these modifications are made, consider what happens in the case of trade diversion examined earlier on traditional lines. The matrix of welfare possibilities will change radically. Country M will now feel that it has 'lost' through having to import the commodities from country P at a higher cost whereas, in its opinion, country P has registered a definite 'gain' because it has now started or expanded production of these commodities. Given therefore this change in the objective function, the matrix reduces to a simple, conflict situation where the tariff cutting country M feels it has lost and the other country P has gained. Reciprocity thus becomes extremely important and no trade diverting tariff cuts or free trade areas/customs unions may therefore be expected to make progress unless reciprocity is built into the arrangements from the beginning.

At the same time, it becomes easy to see that reciprocity would ensure that, by satisfactory distribution of trade-diverted industrialization, both countries could emerge feeling that they have gained from the reciprocal discriminatory tariff cuts.[17] Again, it is easy to see now that the LDCs would prefer to liberalize trade with one another rather than with the advanced countries. Since industrial production has value in itself, the LDCs would consider it disadvantageous to negotiate tariff cuts (on industrial products) with advanced countries (whose competitive strength in manufactures is assumed to be greater) *unless* they are one-way, in their favour, thus ruling out reciprocal tariff cuts (including customs unions and free trade areas) except among the LDCs (who are presumed to be at a more comparable or 'similar' stages of development vis-a-vis one another) and also explaining their well-known insistence on 'non-reciprocity' by LDCs for tariff cuts made by the advanced countries.[18]

For similar reasons, trade creating tariff cuts would, under the modified theory, equally exhibit demands for reciprocity *and* would appear less attractive than under traditional theory, thus corresponding again more closely to observable facts about LDCs. Thus, for example, the matrix of welfare possibilities from such a unilateral tariff cut (Matrix 2) will now be changed. Country M will reduce its estimate of gain (by the amount of the consumption gain, if any) and, more significantly, has a new 'loss' factor because the contraction or elimination of its import-competing manufactures will be considered undesirable *per se*. At the same time, country P will be thought to have *definitely* gained because it has attracted to itself or expanded the manufacturing activity which has declined in country M. The matrix of welfare possibilities thus reduces again to a simple conflict situation where country P is supposed to have gained and country M to have lost. A unilateral tariff cut by country M is thus ruled out and reciprocal tariff cuts by country P become a *sine qua non* of country M's tariff cuts even in trade creating situations. Moreover, since value is attached to industrial production *per se*, the LDCs fail to see any rationale in contracting the output of existing manufactures, so that trade creating tariff cuts seem to them to be 'unnecessary' or 'unfruitful' and hence inferior to trade diverting tariff cuts, which bring more industrial activity to the member LDCs.

If therefore the new theory is accepted, it is possible to explain practically all the puzzling features of LDC negotiations, from reciprocity to preference for trade diverting tariff cuts. The most interesting of these implications may now be brought together and further spelled out:

(1) trade liberalization will *inevitably* be accompanied by considerable interest in 'reciprocity' arrangements, even though traditional theory does not so imply;

(2) trade diverting tariff cuts, provided reciprocity is worked out, are far more likely to be acceptable than traditional theory would imply (the creation or expansion of import-competing, industrial production being a desirable objective in itself);

(3) trade creating tariff cuts will be far less likely to be acceptable, even when reciprocity is worked out, than traditional theory would imply (the decline of import-competing, industrial production being an undesirable objective in itself);

(4) trade diverting tariff cuts, in consequence, are more likely to occur in practice than trade creating tariff cuts, again contrary to what traditional theory would imply;

(5) the 'reciprocity' requirement is further likely to take the form of attention to whether the resulting *incremental trade flows* between the participating countries are balanced: this, in turn, would be an indication of the degree of the production 'advantage' which the new theory stresses as a significant source of gain;[19]

(6) the new theory would also reinforce political explanations in predict-

ing that LDCs would turn to one another for tariff-cutting exercises: trade diversion is more readily practised against the developed countries which still continue overwhelmingly to be the major exporters of industrial manufactures to the LDCs;

(7) the new theory would simultaneously explain the demand to have Gatt's Article XXIV amended so as to allow the *raising* of the average external tariff in a preferential tariff cut (in a 100 per cent programme); if tariffs were to be preferentially cut only from existing levels, and if these tariffs may be expected to be higher on items where trade creation rather than trade diversion is likely,[20] the effort at preferential tariff cuts could be jeopardized by having to concentrate on trade creating rather than trade diverting cuts;

(8) further, in view of the insistence on reciprocity, the preference is likely to be for tariff cuts among smaller groups of LDCs rather than larger groups; reciprocity is easier to work out within smaller groups especially when it takes the specific forms outlined earlier *and* is so important to the participants, whereas smaller groups also make it easier to supplement an 'unpredictable' trade mechanism by a 'more direct' and simultaneous policy of 'industrial allocations' among members;[21] and

(9) the preference for trade diversion is likely to accentuate still further the tendency to prefer smaller groups, for the simple reason that there are more outsiders to divert trade from when the group is smaller.

Indeed, these are all very distinctly the special features of LDC attempts at trade liberalization and of their consequential demands for Gatt revision.

Should Gatt Rules be Changed?

The logical question then is whether it makes economic sense to amend the Gatt rules so as to accommodate the LDC patterns of behaviour and demands. There are three main types of position which can be taken on this general issue.

(1) Either one can be cynical and argue that, after all, countries act exactly as they want to *despite* Gatt membership, so that there is little point in amending these rules. While there is force in the contention that actual practice manages frequently to bypass international obligations–as, for example, with the Gatt rules on export subsidies, which are widely flouted in devious ways–their nuisance value is very evident and they

3

frequently involve resort to indirect and inefficient ways of achieving legal consistency between international obligations and national action. The very fact that LDCs want Gatt rules changed implies that they must, at least sometimes, be constrictive. So this cynical dismissal of the question must be rejected.

(2) Alternatively, one may argue the opposite case: that, if a sufficient number of countries want a change in the Gatt rules, it will go through and there is no point in arguing the matter any further. Such a cynic may well point to the insertion of Article XXIV, undoubtedly to accommodate an impending European Economic community, which enjoyed equally the support of the United States, while the LDCs were apathetic or reconciled to impotence in influencing events; after all, even traditional theory cannot show that a 100 per cent tariff cut, on a preferential basis, is invariably superior to a partial cut or no cut at all and yet that is exactly what Article XXIV implicitly asserts! If LDCs manage to muster enough bargaining strength, eventually they may well succeed in changing Gatt rules around to suit their demands. But again, unless the developed countries can be persuaded to acquiesce in these amendments, the progress towards them would be inevitably slow and halting. So this form of cynical dismissal of the question must also be rejected.

(3) Indeed, even from an intellectual standpoint, it is necessary to argue through the question whether the LDC demands *ought* to be supported.

In answering this question, one has to be clear about what exactly is the alternative to *not* amending the Gatt rules in accordance with LDC demands. This, in turn, amounts to asking what is really the alternative to LDCs not being allowed to liberalize trade *among* themselves and whether, from an economic point of view, that alternative is superior.

Emphasis is being placed here quite deliberately on defining the most realistic alternative, in comparison with which the possibility of amending Gatt rules in the LDC-suggested direction must be judged. Much too often economic issues are mis-judged because the alternatives considered are really irrelevant. Thus, for example, devaluation was widely considered to be inflationary in its impact because the alternative implicitly considered was that of utilization of reserves to ease the deficit. It was later realized that the correct comparison, from a policy viewpoint, was with alternative adjustment policies, *all* being evaluated subject to non-availability of reserves, and that once this was done it was by no means obvious that devaluation would be inflationary by comparison with, for example, QRS.[22]

The starting point in finding the right alternative to answer our present question seems to be the fact that *industrialization* is among the primary, immediate objectives of the LDCs. One may debate whether this is a desirable, legitimate 'economic' objective or whether it is to be classified as a 'non-economic' objective. Regardless of the precise reasons for considering industrialization as an LDC objective, that the LDCs so consider it is the essential fact to be noted.

If then industrialization is to proceed in an LDC, the immediate consequence of such a decision for most LDCs would be for the imports, of the items in which the import-substitution occurs, to shrink below their level otherwise.[23] *Trade diversion*, in this sense, *is already implicit in the decision to industrialize.* Nothing in current Gatt rules can effectively block an LDC member from undertaking such trade diversion in pursuit of its policy of industrialization.

1. *Case for Gatt Revisions.* From this way of looking at things, the most favourable case for accepting the LDC behaviour and demands emerges as follows.[25]

If the LDCs could be allowed to reduce tariff barriers *among* themselves, this could permit the given trade diversion (implicit in *each* LDC's decision to industrialize) to be carried out at *lower cost* because the trade diversion, while continuing against the non-members, would be eliminated or reduced as among the (member) LDCs. To put it yet differently, and more illuminatingly, the tariff cuts (among the LDCs) would in fact be permitting trade creation among the LDCs in relation to the situation where they would have industrialized behind national tariff walls. The contention then is that, regarded in this light, the apparently trade diverting attempts by LDCs at mutual tariff preferences turn out really to be effectively trade creating.

On this line of argument, several arguments for modifying Gatt rules seem to become persuasive. For example, the automatic extension of MFN treatment by LDCs to the developed members could be removed on the ground that the trade diversion away from the developed countries will take place anyway, thanks to *individual* LDC action, so why hold up the (implicit) trade creation among the LDCs that such an amendment would facilitate?

Similarly, why not modify Article XXIV of Gatt so as to permit the raising of the external average tariff when entering a 100 per cent preferential agreement? If the alternative again is the raising of *national* LDC tariff barriers which Gatt cannot effectively prevent (except when the duties are 'bound'), why not consider the suggested modification of Article XXIV as permitting a less undesirable, alternative procedure which would reduce the LDC-cost of industrialization?

Again, if LDCs will not readily wish to dismantle *existing* lines of industrialization and would rather concentrate instead on ensuring that the *future* doses of industrialization are efficiently made by having wider markets among the LDCs–thus concentrating on the gains from *implicit* trade creation, as defined here–it would appear that the alternative to not letting them discriminate between tariffs on existing and on new industries to come, as Article XXIV would require, is likely to make the LDCs continue the present policies of industrialization in small, domestic markets and thus forgo even the advantages that could accrue from implicit or potential trade creation. By this argument, therefore, there would again be a good case for letting LDCs, even in Article XXIV situations where the LDCs would commit themselves to eventual full integration, discriminate in their progressive tariff cuts between existing and newer industries (much as there is now accepted an asymmetry between manufactures and agriculture).[25]

II. *Arguments against Gatt Revisions.* The above case is, in fact, the most favourable one that can be built up for making some of the Gatt revisions that the LDCs have been demanding. But it rests on two crucial assumptions which need to be spelled out very clearly, for it is around them that economists are likely to divide in their judgment of what changes in Gatt are desirable.

The first crucial assumption (already stated explicitly) is that the LDCs would, in fact, if Gatt rules are not changed, use non-discriminatory tariffs (or quotas) in pursuit of industrialization. While this assumption is plausible, in the light of LDC experience, it *could* be challenged on the dubious argument that the increased cost of the resulting attempt at industrialization behind national tariff walls would itself reduce the degree of trade diversion (and hence economic inefficiency) which LDCs are willing to undertake in pursuit of industrialization.[26]

The second crucial assumption is more serious. The preceding case for

Gatt revisions really presupposes that the LDCs will undertake tariff negotiations in a way which, while discriminatory, does in fact reduce (if not minimize) the mutual cost of any given degree of industrialization among the member countries. There is an important difference between arguing that discriminatory arrangements among LDCs could reduce the mutual cost of member-LDC industrialization and asserting that it would necessarily do so.[27]

Indeed, from the analytical point of view, this way of posing the problem leads to at least three questions of importance and relevance to the present discussion:

(1) If an *arbitrarily-defined* sub-group of LDCs desires to achieve a *given* level of industrialization, within *each* country, what is the *optimal* level and structure of the external tariff which will permit this to be done at *least cost* within the framework of an integrated market? (No such solution need exist, of course, if the level of industrialization within any member cannot be sustained without protection from the other members, thereby violating the presence of an integrated market within the sub-group.)

(2) Within the same, arbitrarily-defined sub-group of LDCs, what is the optimal set of policy instruments for achieving the required level of industrialization within each LDC? Here, the range of policy instruments being considered extends beyond tariff policy.

(3) Given a set of LDCs, each with its own target of industrialization, what is the *optimum sub*-set of LDCs from any *one* LDC's point of view which will permit it to achieve its objective at least cost, assuming for example that the subset will act so as to minimize cost for the group as in (*a*) or (*b*) preceding?[28] It is not clear that LDCs would, in fact, examine their possibilities of preferential arrangements in the careful way that is necessary, so that it is inevitable that economists would be divided on the set of rules that they would like to see at Gatt on the question of preferential tariff arrangements.

The questions concerning Gatt revisions are thus not easily answerable; they involve resort to judgments of a fairly crucial type about what is likely to happen in response to the changes. Even the framework devised in this paper, to strengthen the case for these revisions, cannot make the case for them definitive.

Ultimately, the issue is likely to be judged also in the light of the views which economists have concerning whether the possibility of preferentially reducing trade barriers among LDCs is likely to constitute the only feasible route by which the world will move closer towards freer trade or whether it will only lead to a sustained and more marked fragmentation of the world economy.

ACKNOWLEDGMENTS

This paper has grown out of my having been a member of two United Nations 'Expert Groups', in November 1964 at ECAFE and in February 1966 at UNCTAD, on this general subject. It is really an academic economist's attempt at discovering the rationale, if any, behind the attempts of the developing countries to liberalize trade in certain specific ways which do not 'square with' what economic analysis would predict as 'rational'. Throughout the paper, LDCs mean less developed countries, an identifiable bloc of countries at the UNCTAD now, and Gatt stands for the General Agreement on Tariffs and Trade. I should like to record my general indebtedness to the numerous colleagues on the two United Nations Groups as also to members of a Seminar at I.B.R.D. for their comments. My thanks are also due to Harry Johnson for incisive comments on the penultimate draft of this paper and for drawing my attention to his own work (1965a). The recent work of Linder, Cooper and Massell also relates to some of the questions touched upon in this paper. I am also happy to recall that Sir John Hicks has often shown considerable insight into questions of international trade policy (see *Essays in World Economics*).

NOTES AND REFERENCES

[1] As far as tariff reductions are concerned, Sidney Dell (1966) records that '. . . the LAFTA countries achieved a certain initial measure of success following the entry of the Treaty of Montevideo into force. The first round of negotiations was held in Montevideo from 24 July to 12 August 1961, the second in Mexico City from 27 August to 21 November 1962, the third in Montevideo again from 5 October to 31 December 1963, and the fourth in Bogotá from 20 October to 11 December 1964' (p. 70). For details and evaluation, see chapter 5.

[2] A useful account of the disruptionist trends, immediately after independence of the three East African Territories, is contained in a contribution of Arthur Hazlewood to a forthcoming publication, of the Royal Institute of International Affairs, on Integration in Africa, edited by Hazlewood himself.

[3] The ASA (between Malaya, Thailand and Philippines) and the MAPHILINDO (between Malaya, Philippines and Indonesia) have remained politically utopian in their concept altogether. Several ECAFE conferences have also resulted in Ministerial resolutions on trade liberalization with practically no concrete results. On the other hand, the recent establishment of the Asian Development Bank, with the contribution mainly of Japan and the United States, may lead to the beginning of a more active interest in region-oriented tariff cuts or quota liberalization.

[4] This 'two-stage' method of argument is absolutely 'classical', based on historical observation of industrialization, and has frequently been used to 'establish' the inadvisability of beginning *first* with heavy industry *à la* Soviet Union. It is now well recognized, of course, that no such 'laws' can be derived and the 'Soviet model', which reverses the stages, *can* make considerable sense.

[5] The inefficiency here relates to the lack of incentive, in a sheltered market, for reducing costs to the minimum at *whatever* level of output is chosen by the entrepreneur.

[6] Not merely are these qualifications infrequently appreciated but also there is danger that the industrial allocations among members of a union may, in practice, be the product of 'horse trading'.

[7] 'With respect to a free-trade area, or an interim agreement leading to the formation of a free-trade area, the duties and other regulations of commerce maintained in each of the constituent territories and applicable at the formation of such free-trade area or the adoption of such interim agreement to the trade of contracting parties not included in such area or not parties to such agreement shall not be higher or more restrictive than the corresponding duties and other regulations of commerce existing in the same constituent territories prior to the formation of the free-trade area, or interim agreement, as the case may be.'

[8] The main literature is: J. Viner (1950); J. Meade (1955) and R. Lipsey (1960). There is also the 'monetary' theory of trade discrimination, associated with the names of Frisch, Fleming and Meade, which is not touched upon in this paper, but which would be relevant in understanding payments problems and assessing current IMF rules.

[9] That Raul Prebisch, Secretary General of UNCTAD, has been worried by this aspect of the problem is clear from his address to United Nations Trade and Development Board, stating: 'Unfortunately, there are some symptoms that the spirit of Geneva is not being applied, and that on the contrary there is an aggravation of the tendency towards a system of discriminatory preferences in certain parts of the world. I cannot hide from the Board my great concern at signs in

certain Latin American circles, which are manifesting themselves with increasing force in requests to the United States for a preferential system to be exclusive to Latin American countries' (Dell, 1966, p. 34). Indeed, the fact that LAFTA exists now is likely to make both the demand for, and granting of, such discriminatory preferences by the United States a significant possibility.

[10] Economists are particularly prone to scoffing at such 'fears'. They would be well advised to read, in case they are sceptical, E. M. Carr's (1946) brilliant account of the inevitable interaction of economic philosophy and national political interest.

[11] Note that, in analysis that follows, only the *simpler* analytical models of Viner (1950) and Lipsey (1960), are used. Complications can arise, however, if this is not done. For example, as Lipsey has pointed out, even the consumption effect can be negative if one takes a *three-good* model. Also, as Mundell has shown recently, unless gross substitutability is assumed between the goods of each country in a *three-good*, three-country model, the terms of trade of the partner country (P) with the third country can worsen, thus presumably opening up the possibility of a loss to it.

[12] This aspect of tariff bargaining, which may rationalize certain reciprocity demands even within the *traditional* theoretical framework, has always been ignored by those who voice puzzlement as to the insistence of many countries on reciprocity of one kind or another in tariff negotiations. See, for example, Harry Johnson (1965a) whose elegant analysis neglects altogether this line of argument. Failure to see this line of argument can be traced to many liberal writers, such as Lionel Robbins (1954, pp. 137–8) who recognizes the problem explicitly and tries to account for reciprocity by arguing unconvincingly that the burden of adjustment with unilateral tariff cuts would be less.

[13] This point can be readily seen from Lipsey's well-known diagram. Assume that country M, specialized on producing OR of Y, has an initial, non-discriminatory tariff which leads to trade with country C at price-ratio OC, and consumption at Q with domestic, tariff-inclusive price ratio being P_t and welfare at U_i. If the tariff is eliminated altogether, welfare will increase to U_c. If the tariff is cut only for country P, trade will occur along price-line RP and welfare will be at U_p. Note that $U_p > U_i$ but $U_p < U_c$. See figure opposite.
Therefore, in terms of U_c, there *is* a loss from a preferential tariff removal, even though it is a case where trade diversion increases welfare ($U_p > U_i$).

[14] Again, as with the analysis of trade diversion, we could strengthen somewhat the case for reciprocity by using a game-theoretic formulation or by pointing out the *potential* loss from a discriminatory, as distinct from a possible non-discriminatory, tariff cut.

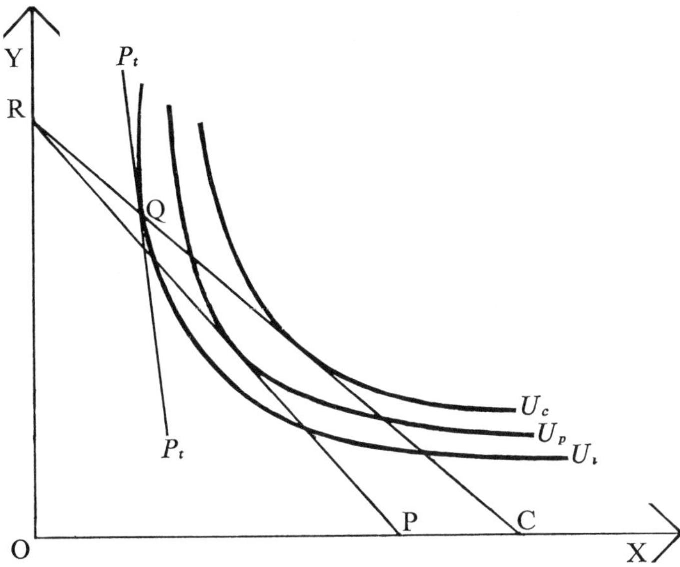

[15] For this reason, though more so by virtue of the difficulty of accepting the notion of 'given preferences' on which the whole theory rests, I have found it useful to develop the welfare theory of trade in my lectures in Delhi in terms of technological efficiency rather than utility rankings. For details on this, see my forthcoming paper (Bhagwati, to appear) on 'Gains from Trade Once Again'.

[16] There is also an associated 'revenue' problem. Where LDCs have levied tariffs for earning revenue, their removal or reduction, on other LDCs, could well result in a loss of revenue in case of trade diversion, if the increment in imports from the resulting cheapening of the item in domestic consumption is not large enough to offset the reduction in the tariff rate. Experience in East Africa and French Equatorial Africa, in particular, suggests that this possible loss of revenue is considered an important 'loss' factor by LDCs in continuing or entering upon integration schemes. This factor is ignored in the text.

[17] It is assumed, in the following analysis, that a decisive weight will usually be attached by LDCs to the question of whether industrial activity expands or contracts in the economy.

[18] This 'principle' of non-reciprocity has been brought up even *within* preferential groupings, as in the special treatment meted out to the less 'developed' members of both EEC and LAFTA, with respect to implementation of tariff cuts.

[19] Evidence of such behaviour by LDC members of common markets and free trade areas is to be found in the experience in LAFTA and in

East Africa. The Kampala Agreement of 1964 explicitly refers to *balanced trade flows* within the East African Federation, for example.

[20] This appears to have been the case in LAFTA countries (Dell, 1966, chapter 5).

[21] Indeed, one of the important features of all LDC attempts on trade expansion, to date, has been the unwillingness to initiate tariff cuts and trust them to result in efficient industrial division of labour in the classical, textbook manner. Even where the classical method was initially adopted, as in East Africa and with LAFTA, direct, industrial allocations of one kind or another among the member countries have now been envisaged and machinery actually set up to deal with the question. There are two major reasons for this: (i) the LDCs recognize, from experience, that wasteful duplication, or even multiplication, of industrial capacity, which the enlargement of markets *via* tariff cuts is intended to avoid, cannot frequently be eliminated in practice without governmental intervention, and (ii) the LDCs feel that market forces would tend to gravitate industrial activity towards the already industrialized areas within the group, so that interference with the market mechanism would be necessary to direct part of the industrialization towards the 'weaker' members. On the other hand, the offsetting disadvantages of such industrial allocations by political agencies, unless managed with reference to economic criteria, could also be significant.

[22] Credit for this insight goes to Egon Sohmen (1958) who, to my knowledge, was the first to reformulate the question of the impact of devaluation upon the price level in this manner.

[23] This argument presupposes, of course, that industrialization will lead to the imposition of tariff (or equivalent QR) protection and that the level of industrialization which free trade will permit falls short of the desired level. Both of these seem to be realistic assumptions, of course, about LDCs.

[24] At the I.B.R.D. seminar, where this paper was presented, Bela Balassa pointed out to me that my way of presenting the strongest case in favour of accepting LDC demands is implicit in the writings of Raul Prebisch, Cooper and Massell and Balassa, although the precise formulation of the argument is different.

[25] This could be done quite readily by permitting a different rate of progressive tariff cuts on these two classes of products and thus effectively lengthening considerably the time over which the existing industries would have to adjust. The fact of growing industrialization and incomes, as also the prospect of an eventually integrated market, would then both induce and permit an orderly decline in the relative and/or absolute level of the industry in the LDC where it is inefficient.

[26] This is, in fact, the type of argument which has long been used by the opponents of foreign aid, such as Milton Friedman, who claim that foreign aid featherbeds many inefficiencies which would become insupportable if the countries receiving aid had to make do with their own resources. This argument, of course, presupposes that the recipient countries agree with these commentators in regarding certain policies as 'inefficient', an assumption which is notoriously invalid – there is a well-known law of intransitivity which operates in these matters: X thinks his economics is better than Y's and Y thinks the other way around. The effect of withdrawal of aid is more likely to be the reinforcing of the very same policies that these opponents of foreign aid dislike.

[27] The experience in LAFTA, where the tariff cuts seem to have been *undiscriminatingly* trade diverting, can only make one sceptical with respect to the second assumption being discussed here.

[28] Cooper and Massell (1965) raise the somewhat more limited question of whether the LDCs could *reduce* their mutual cost of industrialization through preferential arrangements. They use a constant-cost model, which is somewhat limited for dealing with the questions of importance to LDCs (such as economies of scale); but it is nonetheless a useful device, exploited with great skill by the authors.

Editor's Note

The following is the list of references for this essay, drawn from the list of contributors' references at the end of the volume in which this essay appeared:

Bhagwati, J. N. (1969) "The Gains from Trade Once Again," in *Trade, Tariffs and Growth*, chapter 3, pp. 149–163. Cambridge, MA: MIT Press, 1969.

Carr, E. H. (1946) *The Twenty Years' Crisis, 1919–1939*, 2nd edition. London.

Cooper, C. A., and Massel, B. F. (1965) "Towards a General Theory of Customs Unions for Developing Countries," *Journal of Political Economy* 73: 461–476.

Dell, S. (1966) *A Latin American Common Market?* London.

Johnson, H. G. (1965a) "An Economic Theory of Protectionism, the Tariff Bargaining, and the Formation of Customs Unions," *Journal of Political Economy* 73: 256–283.

Lipsey, R. (1957) "The Theory of Customs Unions: Trade Diversion and Welfare," *Economica* (N.S.) 24:40–46.

Lipsey, R. (1960) "The Theory of Customs Unions: A General Survey," *Economic Journal* 70:496–513.

Meade, J. E. (1955) *The Theory of Customs Unions*. Amsterdam.

Robbins, L. (1954) *The Economist in the Twentieth Century*, pp. 137–138. London.

Sohmen. E. (1958) "The Effect of Devaluation on The Price Level," *Quarterly Journal of Economics* 72:273–282.

Viner, J. (1950) *The Customs Union Issue*. London.

Journal of International Economics 6 (1976) 317–336. © North-Holland Publishing Company

OPTIMAL TRADE POLICY AND COMPENSATION UNDER ENDOGENOUS UNCERTAINTY: THE PHENOMENON OF MARKET DISRUPTION

Jagdish N. BHAGWATI*

Massachusetts Institute of Technology, Cambridge, MA 02139, U.S.A.

T.N. SRINIVASAN

Indian Statistical Institute, New Delhi 110029, India

Received August 1975, revised version received May 1976

The paper examines the nature of optimal policy intervention required in the exporting country when there is the possibility of a market-disruption-induced trade restriction being invoked by the importing country. The analysis is conducted primarily with a two-period model, with and without adjustment costs, and the results are related to the well-known policy prescriptions of Bhagwati, Ramaswami, Srinivasan, Johnson et al. in the theory of trade and welfare. The last section extends the argument briefly to steady state analysis. The applicability of the analysis to the symmetric, embargo problem is also noted.

1. Introduction

The fact that 'market disruption' permits or prompts importing countries to invoke quantitative import restrictions (or, what is more fashionable in recent times, voluntary export restrictions by the exporting countries, at the urging of the importing countries) immediately implies that the exporting country faces a situation of endogenous uncertainty: its own export level can affect the probability of such quantitative restrictions (QR's) being imposed. It simultaneously raises the following analytical questions which have obvious policy implications:

(1) What is the optimal trade policy for an exporting country which is faced by such potential QR-intervention?

(2) Since the possibility of such QR-intervention must restrict the trade opportunity set relative to that which would obtain in the absence of the QR-

*The research underlying this paper was financed partly by UNCTAD, through its Manufactures Division; needless to say, the paper does not necessarily represent the views of the UNCTAD Secretariat. Our thanks are due to Peter Diamond, Murray Kemp, Paul Krugman, Clive Bell, Charles Blitzer, Graham Pyatt, and Wolfgang Mayer for helpful comments on an earlier draft.

possibility, can one meaningfully define the loss that such a QR-possibility imposes on the exporting country and therefore the compensation that could be required to be paid to the exporting country under, say, a modified set of GATT rules?

2. Optimal trade policy: Two-period model with zero adjustment costs

To analyze the problem of optimal trade policy for the exporting country in the presence of a market-disruption-induced possibility of QR-intervention, we will deploy the usual trade-theoretic model of general equilibrium, but will extend it to a two-period framework in sections 2–5. In section 4, we will also introduce adjustment costs, beginning with a simple formulation which has putty in period 1 and clay in period 2, and then extending the analysis in section 5 to lesser rigidity of redeployment of resources in period 2. In section 6, we will consider a steady state with an infinite time horizon rather than a two-period analysis, so that we can analyze the effects of continuous uncertainty (as against just period-1 uncertainty).

Thus, consider a two-commodity model of international trade. We then assume a two-period time horizon such that the level of exports E in the first period affects the probability $P(E)$ of a quota $\bar{E}$ being imposed at the beginning of the next period.[1]

Let $U[C_1, C_2]$ be the standard social utility function defined in terms of the consumption C_i of commodity i $(i = 1, 2)$. By assumption, it is known at the beginning of the next period whether the quota $\bar{E}$ has been imposed or not. Thus, the policy in the next period will be to maximize U subject to the transformation function $F[X_1, X_2] = 0$ and the terms of trade function π if no quota is imposed, and with an additional constraint $E \leqq \bar{E}$ if the quota is imposed.

Let now the maximal welfare with and without the quota be $\underline{U}$ and $\bar{U}$ respectively. Clearly then, we have $\bar{U} > \underline{U}$ when the quota is binding. The expected welfare in the second period is then clearly

$$\underline{U}P(E) + \bar{U}[1-P(E)].$$

The objective function for the first period is therefore:

$$\phi = U[X_1 - E, X_2 + \pi E] + \rho[\underline{U}P(E) + \bar{U}\{1-P(E)\}],$$

[1]This method of introducing market disruption presupposes that the QR-level is prespecified but that the probability of its being imposed will be a function of how deeply the market is penetrated in the importing country and therefore how effective the import-competing industry's pressure for protection will be vis-a-vis the importing country's government. The effect of modifying this simplifying assumption so as to allow for varying levels of a quota is noted later in this section.

where ρ is the discount factor. This is then to be maximized subject to the domestic transformation constraint, $F[X_1, X_2] = 0$. In doing this, assume that $P(E)$ is a convex function of E, i.e. the probability of a quota being imposed increases, at an increasing rate as E is increased, and that, in the case where π depends on E, πE is concave in E. Then, the first-order conditions for an interior maximum are:

$$\frac{\partial \phi}{\partial X_1} = U_1 - \lambda F_1 = 0, \tag{1}$$

$$\frac{\partial \phi}{\partial X_2} = U_2 - \lambda F_2 = 0, \tag{2}$$

$$\frac{\partial \phi}{\partial E} = -U_1 + U_2\{\pi + E\pi'\} - \rho(\bar{U} - \underline{U})P'(E) = 0. \tag{3}$$

Now, eqs. (1) and (2) yield the familiar result that the marginal rate of substitution in consumption equals the marginal rate of transformation. Eq. (3) moreover can be written as

$$\frac{U_1}{U_2} = (\pi + \pi' E) - \frac{\rho\{\bar{U} - \underline{U}\}}{U_2} P'(E). \tag{3'}$$

If (*i*) monopoly power is absent ($\pi' = 0$) and if (*ii*) the first period's exports do not affect the probability of a quota being imposed in the second period, then (3′) clearly reduces to the standard condition that the marginal rate of substitution in consuption equals the (average = marginal) terms of trade. If (*i*) does not hold but (*ii*) holds, then U_1/U_2 equals the marginal terms of trade $(\pi + \pi' E)$, leading to the familiar optimum tariff. If both (*i*) and (*ii*) are present, there is an *additional* tariff element: $(\rho[\bar{U} - \underline{U}]/U_2)P'(E)$. This term can be explained as follows: if an additional unit of exports takes place in period 1, the probability of a quota being imposed and hence a discounted loss in welfare of $\rho(\bar{U} - \underline{U})$ occurring, increases by $P'(E)$. Thus, at the margin, the expected loss in welfare is $\rho(\bar{U} - \underline{U})P'(E)$ since there is no loss in welfare if the quota is not imposed. Converted to numeraire terms, this equals $[\rho(\bar{U} - \underline{U})P'(E)]/U_2$, and must be subtracted from the marginal terms of trade $(\pi + \pi' E)$, the effect of an additional unit of exports on the quantum of imports.[2]

[2]Instead of assuming that the fixed quota of $\bar{E}$ will be imposed with probability $P(E)$, one could assume that a quota of $\bar{E}$ will be imposed with probability density $P(\bar{E}, E)$. In other words, the quota level $\bar{E}$ is variable and the probability of imposition depends both on the level $\bar{E}$ and on the quantum of exports E in the first period. Let $f(\bar{E})$ denote the maximum of $U(C_1, C_2)$ subject to $F(X_1, X_2) = 0$ and $E_1 \leqq \bar{E}$, where $C_1 = (X_1 - E_1)$ and $C_2 = (X_2 + \pi E_1)$.

It is then clear that the market-disruption-induced QR-possibility requires optimal intervention in the form of a tariff (in period 1). It is also clear that, compared to the optimal situation *without* such a QR-possibility, the resource allocation in the QR-possibility case will shift against exportable production, i.e. comparative advantage, in the welfare sense, shifts away, at the margin, from exportable production. Moreover, denoting the utility level under the optimal policy intervention with quota possibility as ϕ_{Q}^{OPT}, that under laissez faire with the quota possibility as ϕ_{Q}^{L}, and that under laissez faire without this quota possibility as ϕ_{NQ}^{L}, we can argue that

$$\phi_{Q}^{OPT} > \phi_{Q}^{L}, \qquad \phi_{NQ}^{L} > \phi_{Q}^{L}.$$

This result is set out, with the attendant periodwise utility levels achieved under each option, in table 1 (which is self-explanatory).[3]

For the case of a small country, with no monopoly power in trade (except for the quota possibility), the equilibria under alternative policies are illustrated in fig. 1.[4] Thus, U represents the utility level in the absence of a quota, $\underline{U}$ the utility level when the quota is imposed, and U^* the first-period utility level reached under the optimal policy intervention option. Note that equilibrium with U^* naturally requires that the export level is being restricted below the level that would be reached with nonintervention (at $\bar{U}$), while exceeding the level reached in equilibrium when the quota is invoked (at $\underline{U}$). Also, note that the optimal policy for restricting the first-period level of exports is a tariff: a conclusion that is, of course, familiar from the theory of optimal intervention under noneconomic objectives as considered in Johnson (1965) and Bhagwati and Srinivasan (1969).

Then the expected welfare in period 2, given the export level E in the first period, is $\int f(\bar{E}) P(\bar{E}, E)\,d\bar{E}$. Let us denote this by $h(E)$. Thus the maximand ϕ now becomes $U[X_1-E, X_2+\pi E] + \rho h(E)$ and condition (3′) becomes $U_1/U_2 = \pi+\pi'E+\rho h'(E)/U_2$. Now $h'(E)$ is the change in expected welfare in period 2 due to an additional unit of export in period 1 and this has to be added to the marginal terms of trade $\pi+\pi'E$. Nothing substantive therefore changes. Note however that if we allow for *many* exporting countries and if the *share* in the overall quota level granted in period 2 to *one* exporting country will increase with the export level achieved by that country in period 1, this would produce an incentive to *increase*, rather than decrease, the export level in period 1, *ceteris paribus*. Hence, our analysis based on one exporting country would need to be modified correspondingly.

[3]However, we cannot assert that $\phi^{L}_{NQ} > \phi_{Q}^{OPT}$ except in the case of a small country with no influence on the terms of trade; this follows from the fact that ϕ^{L}_{NQ} is no longer the first-best policy in the presence of monopoly power in trade, so that U^* may well exceed $\bar{U}$ in table 1.

[4]Needless to say, for a country with no monopoly power, it is not meaningful to think of market-disruption leading to QR's: if the country is indeed atomistic in foreign markets, its exports surely will not cause market disruption. Our analysis, of course, allows for monopoly power; only fig. 1 illustrates the simple case of a small country.

Table 1
Alternative outcomes under different policies.[a]

	Alternative outcomes		
	Optimal policy intervention with possible quota	Laissez faire with possible quota	Laissez faire with no quota possibility
Period 1	U^*	$\bar{U}$	$\bar{U}$
Period 2	$\rho[\underline{U}P^* + \bar{U}(1-P^*)]$	$\rho[\underline{U}\bar{P} + \bar{U}(1-\bar{P})]$	$\rho\bar{U}$
ϕ: social utility level	$\phi_Q{}^{OPT}$	$\phi^L{}_Q$	$\phi^L{}_{NQ}$
	$\phi_Q{}^{OPT} > \phi^L{}_Q, \quad \phi^L{}_{NQ} > \phi^L{}_Q$		

[a]*Notation*: (1) $\underline{U}$ is utility level if quota is imposed.
(2) $\bar{U}$ is utility level if quota is not imposed.
(3) U^* is utility level with optimal policy intervention when quota can be imposed in second period.
(4) $P(E)$ is the probability of second-period quota of $\bar{E}$ being imposed, as a function of the first-period exports E. With optimal policy intervention in the situation with possible quota, the exports of the first period result in a value of P^* for $P(E)$. With laissez faire, the exports in the first period will be different and the corresponding value for $P(E)$ is $\bar{P}$.
(5) ρ is the discount factor.
(6) $\phi^L{}_{NQ} > \phi_Q{}^{OPT}$ necessarily only for small countries with no influence on terms of trade.
(7) $\phi_{NQ}{}^{OPT}$, when the country is optimally exercising its monopoly power in trade and there is no QR possibility, is not listed above.

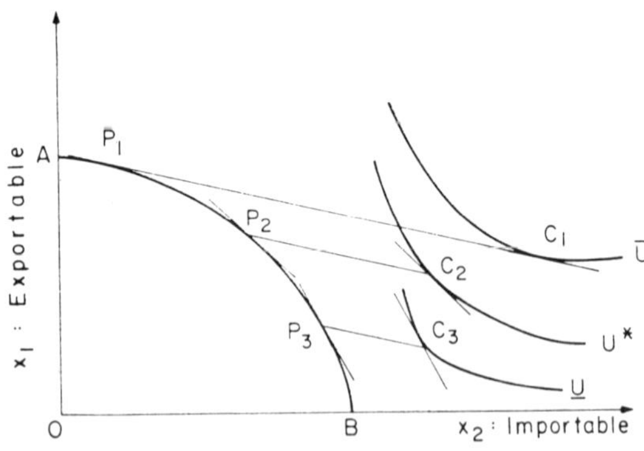

Fig. 1

3. Defining the loss from market-disruption-induced QR-possibility

Consider now the measure of the loss to the exporting country from this possibility of a market-disruption-induced QR. One can think of alternative ways in which this loss could be defined:

Measure I: Taking expected utilities, one can define the loss of welfare to the exporting country as the difference between $\phi^{\mathrm{L}}_{\mathrm{NQ}}$ and $\phi^{\mathrm{L}}_{\mathrm{Q}}$: i.e. the loss in expected welfare that follows, in the absence of optimal intervention by the exporting country, from the QR-possibility.

This measure clearly is $\rho\bar{P}\ \{\bar{U}-\underline{U}\}$ and is, of course, nothing but the expected loss in period 2 from the possible imposition of the quota, duly discounted.

Now, it is also clear that this measure will lie between the ex post period-2 loss if the quota *is* invoked (which loss, duly discounted, is $\rho(\bar{U}-\underline{U})$) and the ex post period-2 loss if the quota is not invoked (which loss is, of course, zero). Thus, one must regard the actual period-2 loss when the quota *is* invoked as an upper bound on the loss in this model.

It also follows that there is a welfare loss, measured as $\rho\bar{P}\{\bar{U}-\underline{U}\}$ *even if the quota is not actually invoked in period* 2 and, (in our two-period model), the actual equilibrium allocations in each period are identical between the QR-possibility and the no-QR-possibility situations. This follows clearly from the fact that, in period 1, consumers face the prospect of uncertain prices in period 2 as the QR may or may not be invoked.

Measure II: Alternatively one may measure the loss to the exporting country as the difference between $\phi^{\mathrm{OPT}}_{\mathrm{NQ}}$ and $\phi^{\mathrm{OPT}}_{\mathrm{Q}}$: the difference between expected welfare when there is no QR possibility, but the optimal tariff to exploit monopoly power *is* being exercised, and that when the government of the exporting country intervenes with optimal policy to maximize expected welfare when there *is* a QR-possibility. This alternative measure would be more meaningful for exporting countries with governmental trade agencies or exporters' associations with the ability to regulate their overall export levels, whereas Measure I would be more meaningful for exporting countries with (only) atomistic exporters.

4. Adjusting for adjustment costs: A putty–clay model

So far, our analysis was based on the assumption that the choice of optimal production in period 2 was not constrained by the choice of production in period 1. Thus, in fig. 1, the economy could move from P_1 or P_2 in period 1 to P_3 in period 2, along the (long-run) transformation curve AB. However, this procedure fails to take into consideration possible adjustment costs: i.e. we were essentially dealing with a putty model.

However, this procedure eliminates an important aspect of the problem raised by market disruption. So, in this section, we modify our model and analysis to allow for adjustment costs. However, to simplify the analysis, we take initially the extreme polar case of a putty–clay model, where the production choice made in period 1 cannot be modified *in any way* in period 2.

With this modification, the choice variables now are: X_i, the production of commodity i in periods 1 and 2 ($i = 1, 2$); E_1, the net exports of commodity 1 in period 1; and E_2, the net exports of commodity 1 in period 2 when *no* quota is imposed. As before, $\bar{E}$ is the net export of commodity 1 when the quota *is* imposed. Superscripts refer to periods 1 and 2.

Clearly then, the expected welfare ϕ is now as follows:

$$\phi = U^1[X_1-E_1, X_2+\pi E_1]+\rho P(E_1)\underline{U}^2[X_1-\bar{E}, X_2+\pi\bar{E}]$$

$$+\rho\{1-P(E_1)\}\bar{U}^2[X_1-E_2, X_2+\pi E_2].$$

This is then maximized subject to the implicit transformation function, $F(X_1, X_2) = 0$, as before. The first-order conditions for an interior maximum then are:

$$\frac{\partial\phi}{\partial X_1} = U_1^1+\rho P(E_1)\underline{U}_1^2+\rho\{1-P(E_1)\}\bar{U}_1^2-\lambda F_1 = 0, \tag{4}$$

$$\frac{\partial\phi}{\partial X_2} = U_2^1+\rho P(E_1)\underline{U}_2^2+\rho\{1-P(E_1)\}\bar{U}_2^2-\lambda F_2 = 0, \tag{5}$$

$$\frac{\partial\phi}{\partial E_1} = -U_1^1+\{\pi(E_1)+E_1\pi'(E_1)\}U_2^1-\rho P'(E_1)\{\bar{U}^2-\underline{U}^2\} = 0, \tag{6}$$

$$\frac{\partial\phi}{\partial E_2} = \rho[-\bar{U}_1^2+\{\pi(E_2)+E_2\pi'(E_2)\}\bar{U}_2^2]\{1-P(E_1)\} = 0, \tag{7}$$

where

$$U_j^1 = \frac{\partial U[X_1-E_1, X_2+\pi E_1]}{\partial X_j},$$

$$\bar{U}_j^2 = \frac{\partial U[X_1-E_2, X_2+\pi E_2]}{X_j},$$

$$\underline{U}_j^2 = \frac{\partial U[X_1-\bar{E}, X_2+\pi\bar{E}]}{\partial X_j},$$

and λ = the Lagrangean multiplier associated with the constraint, $F(X_1, X_2) = 0$.

The interpretation of these first-order conditions is straightforward. Condition (7) states that, *given the optimal production levels*, the level of exports in period 2 *when no quota is imposed* must be such as to equate the marginal rate of substitution in consumption to the marginal terms of trade. Condition (6) is identical in form to the one obtained earlier: the optimal experts in period 1 must *not* equate the marginal rate of substitution in consumption in *that* period to the marginal terms of trade, but must instead also allow for the marginal change in expected welfare arising out of the change in probability of a quota being imposed – the latter equals $P'(E_1)(\overline{U}^2-\underline{U}^2)$, where $\overline{U}^2 = U[X_1-E_2, X_2+\pi E_2]$ and $\underline{U}^2 = U[X_1-\bar{E}, X_2+\pi\bar{E}]$. Thus, condition (6) ensures the optimal choice of exports in period 1, *given the production levels*. Conditions (4) and (5) then relate to the optimal choice of production levels and, as we would expect, the introduction of adjustment costs does make a difference. Writing (4) and (5) in the familiar ratio form, we get

$$\frac{F_1}{F_2} = \frac{U_1^1+\rho P(E_1)\underline{U}_1^2+\rho\{1-P(E_1)\}\overline{U}_1^2}{U_2^1+\rho P(E_1)\underline{U}_2^2+\rho\{1-P(E_1)\}\overline{U}_2^2}. \qquad (8$$

Clearly therefore the marginal rate of transformation in production (in periods 1 and 2, identically, as production in period 1 will carry over into period 2 by assumption), i.e. F_1/F_2, must *not* equal the marginal rate of substitution in consumption in period 1, i.e. U_1^1/U_2^1 (unlike our earlier analysis without adjustment costs in sections 2 and 3). Rather, F_1/F_2 should equal a term which properly takes into account the fact that production choices once made in period 1 cannot be changed in period 2 to suit the state (i.e. the imposition or absence of a quota) obtaining in period 2. Eq. (8) can be readily interpreted as follows.

The LHS is, of course, the marginal rate of transformation in production. The RHS represents the marginal rate of substitution in consumption, if *reinterpreted* in the following sense. Suppose that the output of commodity 1, the exportable, is increased by one unit in period 1 (and hence in period 2 as well, by assumption). Given an optimal trade policy, then, the impact of this on welfare can be examined by adding it to consumption in each period. Thus social utility is increased in period 1 by U_1^1 while in period 2 it will increase by $\overline{U}_1^2$ if no quota is imposed and by $\underline{U}_1^2$ if the quota is imposed. Thus, the discounted increase in period-2 expected welfare is given as $\rho[\underline{U}_1^2P(E_1)+\overline{U}_1^2(1-P(E_1))]$. Thus, the total expected welfare impact of a unit increase in the production of commodity 1 is

$$U_1^1+\rho[\quad {}_1^2P(E_1)+\overline{U}_1^2(1-P(E_1))].$$

Similarly, a decrease in the production of commodity 2 by a unit in period 1 (and hence in period 2 as well) reduces expected welfare by

$$U_2^1+\rho[\underline{U}_2^2P(E_1)+\overline{U}_2^2(1-P(E_1))].$$

Hence, the ratio of these two expressions, just derived, represents the 'true' marginal rate of substitution, and this indeed is the RHS in eq. (8) to which the marginal rate of transformation in production $-F_1/F_2$, the LHS in eq. (8) – is to be equated for optimality.

The optimal policy interventions in this modified model with adjustment costs are immediately evident from eqs. (6)–(8) and the preceding analysis. Thus, in period 1, the ratio U_1^1/U_2^1 is clearly the relative price of commodity 1 (in terms of commodity 2) facing consumers, while $\pi(E_1)$ is the average terms of trade. Thus U_1^1/U_2^1 differs from $\pi(E_1)$ by $[\pi' E_1 - (\rho P'(E_1)\{\overline{U}^2 - \underline{U}^2\}/U_2^1)]$ and this difference constitutes a consumption tax on the importable, commodity 2. An identical difference between F_1/F_2, the relative price facing producers, and $\pi(E_1)$ would define a production tax on commodity 2 at the same rate, so that a tariff at this rate would constitute the appropriate intervention in the model with no adjustment costs. However, *with adjustment costs*, eq. (8) defines, for period 1, the appropriate production tax-cum-subsidy which, in general, will diverge from the appropriate consumption tax: so that the optimal mix of policies in the model with adjustment costs will involve a tariff (reflecting both the monopoly power in trade and the QR possibility) *plus* a production tax-cum-subsidy in period 1.[5] In period 2, in both the models (with and without adjustment costs), an appropriate intervention in the form of a tariff (to exploit monopoly power) would be called for; however, with production fixed at period 1 levels in the adjustment-cost model, a consumption tax-cum-subsidy would equally suffice. Specifically, note that in period 2, with adjustment costs, the price ratio facing consumers would be $\overline{U}_1^2/\overline{U}_2^2$ if no quota is imposed, with the average terms of trade at $\pi(E_2)$ and the producer's price ratio (as defined along the putty-transformation frontier) would be F_1/F_2; on the other hand, if the quota is imposed, these values change to $\underline{U}_1^2/\underline{U}_2^2$, $\pi(\overline{E})$ and F_1/F_2 respectively. The consumption tax-cum-subsidy and the equivalent tariff (with no impact on production decision already frozen at period-1 levels) are then defined by these divergences, depending on whether the quota obtains or not.

A tabular comparison of the characteristics of the optimal solution, with and without adjustment costs, is presented in table 2 and should assist the reader.

Note that the above results are quite consistent with the basic propositions of the theory of distortions, as developed in Bhagwati–Ramaswami (1963), Johnson (1965) and Bhagwati (1971): the first-best, optimal policy intervention for the case with adjustment costs requires a trade policy to adjust for the foreign distortion (represented by the effect of current exports on the period-2 probability of a quota being invoked)[6] and a production tax-cum-subsidy to adjust

[5]It should be pointed out that atomistic firms in period 1 are assumed to respond to that period's prices only. This assumption can be justified on the ground that they are likely to assume that these prices will carry over into the next period, since there is no other, obvious mechanism by which they can anticipate the 'true' period 2 prices.

[6]*In addition*, of course, to the usual optimal tariff if there is also monopoly power in trade.

for the existence of adjustment costs in production. It also follows, from the equivalence propositions, that the combination of the optimal tariff and the optimal production tax-cum-subsidy can be reproduced identically by a tariff set at the 'net' production tax-cum-subsidy required by the optimal solution plus a consumption tax-cum-subsidy. Similarly, while our analysis has been focussed on first-best policy intervention, the fundamental results of the theory of distortions and welfare on second-best policies also can be immediately applied to our problem. Thus, if there are zero adjustment costs so that there is only the foreign distortion in period 1, then clearly a production tax-cum-subsidy will *improve* (but not maximize) welfare. Similarly, if there are adjustment costs as well, then there will be *two* distortions, and then applicable here would be the Bhagwati–Ramaswami–Srinivasan (1969) proposition that no feasible, welfare-improving form of intervention may exist if both of the policy measures that will secure optimal intervention cannot be used simultaneously.

Table 2

Characteristics of optimal solutions in models with and without adjustment costs.[a]

	No adjustment costs	Adjustment costs
Period 1	$DRS_1 \neq FRT_1$ $DRS_1 = DRT_1$	$DRS_1 \neq FRT_1$ $DRS_1 \neq DRT_1$
Period 2	$DRS_2 = DRT_2$ $= FRT_2$	$DRS_2 = FRT_2$ (DRT_2 not relevant as production is frozen at period-1 levels)

[a] *DRS*, *DRT* and *FRT* represent the marginal rates of substitution in consumption, domestic transformation, and foreign transformation respectively. For an earlier use of these abbreviations see Bhagwati, Ramaswami and Srinivasan (1969). Since we are considering an interior maximum, the inequalities do *not* include corner equilibria, of course. The subscripts refer to the periods, 1 and 2.

5. Adjustment costs: A general formulation

So far, we have considered only the extreme version of an adjustment-costs model, where the period-1 production levels are frozen in period 2. We may now briefly consider however a more general formulation, (with basically the same results, of course, for optimal policy intervention), where the clay nature of period 1 allocation is partially relaxed: some reallocation is now permitted in period 2.

The simplest way to do this is to write out the period-2 implicit transformation function as $\underline{G}[\underline{X}_1^2, \underline{X}_2^2, X_1^1, X_2^1] = 0$ for the quota case and as $\bar{G}[\bar{X}_1^2, \bar{X}_2^2, X_1^1, X_2^1$ $= 0$ for the no-quota case, such that the feasible output levels in period 2 are explicitly made a function of the (allocation-cum-) output levels of period 1, X_1^1

and X_2^1. Our welfare problem then becomes one of maximizing,[7]

$$\phi = U[X_1^1 - E_1,\, X_2^1 + \pi E_1] + \rho P(E_1)\underline{U}[\underline{X}_1^2 - \underline{E}_2, \underline{X}_2^2 + \underline{E}_2\pi]$$
$$+ \rho\{1 - P(E_1)\}\overline{U}[\overline{X}_1^2 - \overline{E}_2, \overline{X}_2^2 + \overline{E}_2\pi],$$

subject to:

$$F(X_1^1, X_2^1) = 0, \tag{9}$$

for period 1;

$$\underline{G}[\underline{X}_1^2, \underline{X}_2^2, X_1^1, X_2^1] = 0, \tag{10}$$

for period 2, with quota imposed;

$$\overline{G}[\overline{X}_1^2, \overline{X}_2^2, X_1^1, X_2^1] = 0, \tag{11}$$

for period 2, with no quota imposed; and

$$\underline{E}_2 \leqq \overline{\overline{E}}, \tag{12}$$

where $\overline{\overline{E}}$ is the quota level.

The first-order conditions for an interior maximum then are

$$\frac{\partial \phi}{\partial X_1^1} = U_1^1 - \lambda_1 F_1 - \lambda_2 \underline{G}_3 - \lambda_3 \overline{G}_3 = 0, \tag{13}$$

$$\frac{\partial \phi}{\partial X_2^1} = U_2^1 - \lambda_1 F_2 - \lambda_2 \underline{G}_4 - \lambda_3 \overline{G}_4 = 0, \tag{14}$$

$$\frac{\partial \phi}{\partial \underline{X}_1^2} = \rho P(E_1)\underline{U}_1^2 - \lambda_2 \underline{G}_1 = 0, \tag{15}$$

$$\frac{\partial \phi}{\partial \underline{X}_2^2} = \rho P(E_1)\underline{U}_2^2 - \lambda_2 \underline{G}_2 = 0, \tag{16}$$

$$\frac{\partial \phi}{\partial \overline{X}_1^2} = \rho\{1 - P(E_1)\}\overline{U}_1^2 - \lambda_3 \overline{G}_1 = 0, \tag{17}$$

$$\frac{\partial \phi}{\partial \overline{X}_2^2} = \rho\{1 - P(E_1)\}\overline{U}_2^2 - \lambda_3 \overline{G}_3 = 0, \tag{18}$$

[7]The underbar and the overbar refer to the quota and no-quota values respectively.

$$\frac{\partial \phi}{\partial E_1} = -U_1^1+(\pi+\pi' E_1)U_2^1-\rho[\bar{U}^2-\underline{U}^2]P'(E_1) = 0, \tag{19}$$

$$\frac{\partial \phi}{\partial \underline{E}_2} = \rho P(E_1)[-\underline{U}_1^2+(\pi+\pi'\underline{E}_2)\underline{U}_2^2]-\gamma = 0, \tag{20}$$

$$\frac{\partial \phi}{\partial \bar{E}_2} = \rho\{1-P(E_1)\}[-\bar{U}_1^2+(\pi+\pi'\bar{E}_2)\bar{U}_2^2] = 0, \tag{21}$$

where λ_1, λ_2, λ_3 and γ are the Lagrangean multipliers associated with constraints (9)–(12) respectively, and G_i is the partial derivative with respect to the ith argument.

It is then easy to see that, while $\underline{DRS}_2 = \underline{DRT}_2$ (because eqs. (15) and (16) imply that $\underline{U}_1^2/\underline{U}_2^2 = \underline{G}_1/\underline{G}_2$) and $\overline{DRS}_2 = \overline{DRT}_2$ (because eqs. (17) and (18) imply that $\bar{U}_1^2/\bar{U}_2^2 = \bar{G}_1/\bar{G}_2$), as before, one can see the effect of adjustment costs more readily, from eqs. (13) and (14), i.e. $DRT_1 \neq DRS_1$, as follows:

$$\frac{F_1}{F_2} = \frac{U_1^1-\lambda_2\underline{G}_3-\lambda_3\bar{G}_3}{U_1^2-\lambda_2\underline{G}_4-\lambda_3\bar{G}_4}, \tag{22}$$

or, alternatively,

$$\frac{F_1}{F_2} = \frac{U_1^1-\rho P(E_1)\underline{U}_1^2\left(\dfrac{\underline{G}_3}{\underline{G}_1}\right)-\rho\{1-P(E_1)\}\bar{U}_1^2\left(\dfrac{\bar{G}_3}{\bar{G}_1}\right)}{U_1^2-\rho P(E_1)\underline{U}_2^2\left(\dfrac{\underline{G}_4}{\underline{G}_2}\right)-\rho\{1-P(E_1)\}\bar{U}_2^2\left(\dfrac{\bar{G}_4}{\bar{G}_2}\right)}. \tag{22'}$$

Now, it is easy to see that, if we have the polar case with no reallocation possible in period 2 (the putty–clay model of section 4), the transformation curve in period 2 reduces to the single point (X_1^1, X_2^1). As such, the partial derivatives $\underline{G}_i$, $\bar{G}_i$ ($i = 1, 2, 3, 4$) are not defined. However, one could define G in such a way that putty clay is a limiting case and, in the limit, $\bar{G}_3 = \underline{G}_3 = -G_1$ and $\bar{G}_4 = \underline{G}_4 = -G_2$. This is analogous to obtaining the Leontief fixed coefficient production function as a limiting case of the CES production function. Therefore, eq. (22′) reduces to eq. (8), as it should. If, however, we have no adjustment costs (as in section 2), then $\bar{G}_3 = \underline{G}_3 = \bar{G}_4 = \underline{G}_4 = 0$ and eq. (22′) will reduce to $U_1^1/U_2^1 = F_1/F_2$ (which is what eqs. (1) and (2) imply in section 2). For any situation with *some*, but not total, inflexibility of resource allocation in period 2, the ratios $-\underline{G}_3/\underline{G}_1$, $-\bar{G}_3/\bar{G}_1$, $-\underline{G}_4/\underline{G}_2$ and $-\bar{G}_4/\bar{G}_2$ will lie between 0 and 1.

The parametric values of these ratios will clearly reflect the 'pattern of inflexibility' that one contends with. Thus, if one assumes total factor price flexibility but no resource mobility, as in Haberler (1950), then the putty–clay model is relevant. On the other hand, one might assume just the opposite, where factor prices are inflexible but resources are fully mobile – this being the case systematically analyzed by Brecher (1974). Variations on these two polar possibilities include analyses such as that of Mayer (1974) which assumes an activity-specific factor with no mobility in the short run (interpret 'short run' as period 2 for our purposes) but with factor price flexibility.

Whatever the source of adjustment costs in period 2, what they do imply is that the transformation curve of period 1 is not feasible in period 2. Hence the illustration of optimal-policy equilibrium in period 2 would be as in fig. 2, where AB is the (putty) period-1 transformation curve, P^1 the production point on it in period 1 representing therefore (X_1^1, X_2^1), CP^1D the clay transformation curve for period 2 and QP^1R the (partial-clay) transformation curve when resources in period 2 are partially mobile. With equilibrium production at P^1

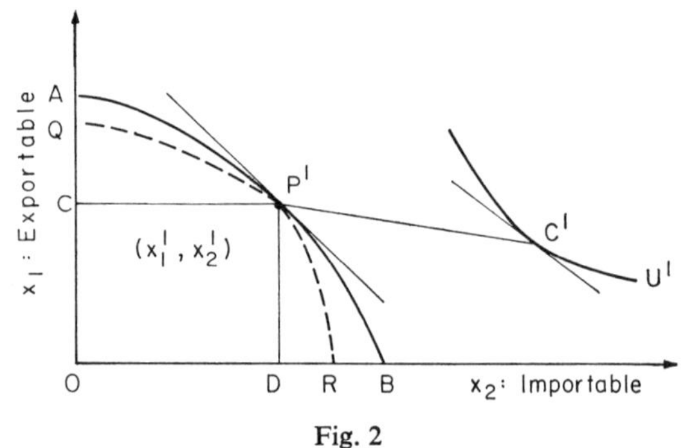

Fig. 2

(with tangency in period 1 to AB) and consumption at C^1, and assuming for simplicity that the international terms of trade are fixed at P^1C^1, we can then illustrate that $F_1/F_2 \neq U_1^1/U_2^1$ (i.e. that the tangents to AB and to the social utility curve U^1 are not equal), as required by eq. (22′) for the case of adjustment costs.

6. Steady state analysis: Infinite time horizon

So far, we have worked with a 2-period horizon, where the uncertainty essentially obtains in period 1 and is resolved in period 2. However, it would be useful to consider an infinite-time-horizon model where each period can face unresolved uncertainty. In this section, therefore, we consider now an infinite-time-horizon steady state analysis of our basic model.

However, to simplify the analysis, we will assume that the quota, once imposed, will not be lifted. The analysis therefore applies to the case where the prospect of a quota being levied is not certain but the prospect that, once levied, it will persist is certain: a situation that is fairly approximated by commodities/items falling within the scope of, say, the long-term agreement on textiles, and other similar commodities.

Thus, consider now that, aside from a quota persisting forever once invoked, the probability of a quota being invoked in any period depends only on the level of exports in the previous period, and that this relationship remains invariant over time. Further, assume that the chance of the event of a quota not being invoked in any period is independent of the same event in the previous periods. Then it is clear that, in the event that the quota is not imposed in any period, the optimal production and trade policies in that period will be the same regardless of the calendar time at which this event occurs.

Let us then start from an initial period at which the quota is not in force, and let $W[X_1, X_2, E]$ denote the discounted sum of expected welfare levels at all future points, given that the production and export levels are X_1, X_2 and E respectively. In other words, W is the welfare associated with the stationary policy (X_1, X_2, E) in any period in which no quota has been imposed till then.

It then follows (as will be demonstrated below) that

$$W = U[X_1-E,\ X_2+\pi E]+\rho\{1-P(E)\}W+\frac{\rho}{1-\rho}P(E)\underline{U}. \tag{23}$$

This is seen as follows. The policy (X_1, X_2, E) yields a utility of $U[X_1-E, X_2+\pi E]$ in the first period. In the second period, if the quota is not imposed (the probability of which event is $1-P(E)$), the policy is again (X_1, X_2, E) so that one can regard the welfare from that point on as $W[X_1, X_2, E]$ as in period 1. This W would however have to be discounted back to the first period, thus yielding the second term on the RHS of eq. (23): $\rho\{1-P(E)\}W$. However, if the quota *is* imposed in the second period, (the probability of which event is $P(E)$), the optimal policy from then on remains the same (as the quota persists forever by assumption) and yields welfare $\underline{U}$ in each period. The discounted sum of this series is clearly $\underline{U}\rho/(1-\rho)$, so that the result is to yield the third term on the RHS of eq. (23): $[\rho/(1-\rho)]P(E)\underline{U}$.

In the following analysis, note first that the maximizing procedure will, as before, be different for the cases with and without adjustment costs. In the case where adjustment costs are zero, $\underline{U}$ will be obtained by maximizing $U[\hat{X}_1-\bar{E}, \hat{X}_2+\pi\bar{E}]$ with respect to $\hat{X}_1$, $\hat{X}_2$ subject to $F(\hat{X}_1, \hat{X}_2) = 0$, and where $\bar{E}$ is the specified quota. In the case where there are adjustment costs, however, X_1 and X_2 cannot be altered (altogether, if we take the putty–clay model) once chosen; hence $\underline{U}$ must be defined as $U[X_1-\bar{E}, X_2+\pi\bar{E}]$, the optimal X_1 and X_2 now being chosen so as to maximize $W[X_1, X_2, E]$.

6.1. Zero adjustment costs

In this case, we must now maximize

$$W[X_1, X_2, E] = \frac{U[X_1 - E, X_2 + \pi E + \frac{\rho}{1-\rho}\underline{U}P(E)}{1-\rho(1-P(E))},$$

subject to

$$F(X_1, X_2) = 0.$$

Recalling that, in this case, $\underline{U}$ does not depend on X_1, X_2 and E, we can derive the first-order conditions for an interior maximum:

$$\frac{\partial W}{\partial X_1} = \frac{U_1}{1-\rho\{1-P(E)\}} - \lambda F_1 = 0, \tag{24}$$

$$\frac{\partial W}{\partial X_2} = \frac{U_2}{1-\rho\{1-P(E)\}} - \lambda F_2 = 0, \tag{25}$$

$$\frac{\partial W}{\partial E} = \frac{\{1-\rho(1-P(E))\}\left[-U_1 + (\pi+\pi' E)U_2 + \frac{\rho}{1-\rho}\underline{U}P'(E)\right] - \rho P'(E)\left[U + \frac{\rho}{1-\rho}\underline{U}P(E)\right]}{\{1-\rho(1-P(E))\}^2}$$

$$= 0. \tag{26}$$

As one would expect, eqs. (24) and (25) imply, (given that $1-\rho(1-P(E)) > 0$), that $U_1/U_2 = F_1/F_2$, so that $DRS_1 = DRT_1$. And, rewriting eq. (26) as

$$-U_1 + (\pi+\pi' E)U_2 - \frac{\rho P'(E)(U-\underline{U})}{1-\rho(1-P(E))} = 0, \tag{26'}$$

we can see that U_1/U_2 differs from the marginal terms of trade $(\pi+\pi' E)$ by the term $\rho P'(E)(U-\underline{U})/(1-\rho\{1-P(E)\})$ and hence the optimal policy intervention is a tariff that suitably corresponds to the difference between U_1/U_2 and π.

This result, of course, is identical to that derived in the two-period model, except that the infinite time horizon model leads to a different tariff rate. In particular, this difference arising from the fact that a quota may be imposed at any time in the future, with probability $P(E)$, reflects itself in the tariff term in two ways: (*i*) the utility in a period in which no quota is imposed is now U, whereas

$\bar{U}$ ($> U$) is the maximum feasible utility and enters the tariff for the two-period case in eq. (3′); and (*ii*) the term $\{1-\rho(1-P(E))\}$ now enters the denominator. This difference is commented on below.

6.2 Non-zero adjustment costs[8]

We now must maximize

$$W[X_1, X_2, E] = \frac{U[X_1-E,\ X_2+\pi E]+\dfrac{\rho}{1-\rho}\underline{U}[X_1-\bar{E},\ X_2+\bar{E}]P(E)}{1-\rho\{1-P(E)\}}$$

subject to $F(X_1, X_2) = 0$.

The first-order conditions for an interior maximum now are:

$$\frac{\partial W}{\partial X_1} = \frac{U_1+\dfrac{\rho}{1-\rho}\underline{U}_1P(E)}{1-\rho\{1-P(E)\}}-\lambda F_1 = 0, \tag{27}$$

$$\frac{\partial W}{\partial X_2} = \frac{U_2+\dfrac{\rho}{1-\rho}\underline{U}_2P(E)}{1-\rho\{1-P(E)\}}-\lambda F_2 = 0, \tag{28}$$

$$\frac{\partial W}{\partial E} = \frac{\left\{-U_1+U_2(\pi+\pi'E)+\dfrac{\rho}{1-\rho}\underline{U}P'(E)\right\}\{1-\rho(1-P(E))\} - \rho P'(E)\left\{U+\dfrac{\rho}{1-\rho}\underline{U}P(E)\right\}}{\{1-\rho(1-P(E))\}^2}$$

$$= 0. \tag{29}$$

Since $\{1-\rho(1-P(E))\} > 0$, we then get

$$\frac{F_1}{F_2} = \frac{U_1+\dfrac{\rho}{1-\rho}\underline{U}_1P(E)}{U_2+\dfrac{\rho}{1-\rho}\underline{U}_2P(E)} = \frac{(1-\rho)U_1+\rho\underline{U}_1P(E)}{(1-\rho)U_2+\rho\underline{U}_2P(E)}, \tag{30}$$

$$-U_1+U_2(\pi+\pi'E)-\frac{\rho P'(E)}{\{1-\rho(1-P(E))\}}(U-\underline{U}) = 0. \tag{31}$$

[8]We should note, of course, that the assumption of 'adjustment costs' in the infinite time horizon case makes little sense as all reallocations should presumably be possible in this case. This subsection is therefore retained only from the viewpoint of completeness of the theoretical argument.

Hence, it is evident from eq. (30) that, as in the two-period model of sections 4 and 5, the introduction of adjustment costs results in establishing a wedge between the marginal rate of transformation, F_1/F_2, in any period and the marginal rate of substitution in consumption (U_1/U_2 or $\underline{U}_1/\underline{U}_2$, depending on whether the quota has not, or has, been imposed). And, eq. (31) shows that the first-order condition relating to exports (E) continues to be of the same essential form as in the case without adjustment costs.[9]

6.3. Welfare comparisons

Confining ourselves to the simpler case of zero adjustment costs, we can now see that, in the infinite time horizon model, laissez faire will lead to a welfare level (given that a quota may be imposed at any time) of

$$W_{\mathrm{Q}}^{\mathrm{L}} = \frac{\bar{U} + \frac{\rho}{1-\rho}\underline{U}P(\hat{E})}{1-\rho(1-P(\hat{E}))} \tag{32}$$

where

$$\bar{U} = \max_{X_1, X_2, E} U[X_1 - E, X_2 + \pi E],$$

subject to $F(X_1, X_2) = 0$, and $\hat{E}$ is the corresponding optimal export level; and

$$\underline{U} = \max_{X_1, X_2, E} U[X_1 - E, X_2 + \pi E],$$

subject to $F(X_1, X_2) = 0$ and $E \leqq \bar{E}$.

The same laissez faire policy, when the probability of a quota being imposed is zero, will clearly lead to the welfare level:

$$W_{\mathrm{NQ}}^{\mathrm{L}} = \frac{\bar{U}}{1-\rho}. \tag{33}$$

Finally, the optimal-policy solution to the situation with the probability of a quota being imposed leads to the welfare level:

$$W_{\mathrm{Q}}^{\mathrm{OPT}} = \frac{U^* + \frac{\rho}{1-\rho}\underline{U}P(E^*)}{1-\rho\{1-P(E^*)\}}, \tag{34}$$

[9] The $\underline{U}$ values, in the two cases, will not of course be equal. Nor, of course, will the values of E be equal in the two cases.

where $U^* = U[X_1^* - E^*, X_2^* + \pi E^*]$ and X_1^*, X_2^*, E* maximize

$$\frac{U[X_1 - E, X_2 + \pi E] + \frac{\rho}{1-\rho} \underline{U}P(E)}{1-\rho(1-P(E))},$$

subject to $F(X_1, X_2) = 0$.

Clearly, then, we have the ranking:

$$W_{\mathrm{NQ}}^{\mathrm{L}} > W_{\mathrm{Q}}^{\mathrm{OPT}} > W_{\mathrm{Q}}^{\mathrm{L}}.$$

6.4. Interpreting the difference between infinite-time-horizon and two-period results

In concluding the analysis of section 6, it would be useful to comment on the difference in the optimal tariffs that obtains between the infinite time horizon and the two-period models, that was noted explicitly above for the simpler case of zero adjustment costs.

For this purpose, it is best to take the two-period model and to turn it into an infinite time horizon model by assuming that, in the second period, the uncertainty is resolved *fully* forever: i.e. that, whether the quota is imposed in period 2 or not, that will also be the case thereafter. In this event, welfare will continue to be $\underline{U}$ (or $\overline{U}$), depending on whether the quota is (or is not) imposed. And, discounted to the present, this yields a welfare of $\rho\underline{U}/(1-\rho)$ (or $\rho\overline{U}/(1-\rho)$). Thus the maximand becomes

$$U[X_1 - E, X_2 + \pi E] + \frac{\rho}{1-\rho}\{\underline{U}P(E) + \overline{U}(1-P(E))\},$$

and yields the following first-order conditions for an interior maximum:

$$U_1 - \lambda F_1 = 0, \tag{35}$$

$$U_2 - \lambda F_2 = 0, \tag{36}$$

$$-U_1 + U_2[\pi + \pi' E] - \frac{\rho}{1-\rho}[\overline{U} - \underline{U}]P'(E) = 0. \tag{37}$$

On the other hand, in the infinite time horizon model with continuing uncertainty as to whether a quota, still not imposed, will be imposed or not (as in this section), the equivalent conditions were derived as eqs. (24), (25), and (26′). To contrast this case with the preceding case of infinite time horizon with uncertainty resolved in period 2, we will use a tilde (~) to denote the present case of unresolved uncertainty.

This contrast, between eqs. (35)–(37) and eqs. (24)–(26′), shows that the *same* values of X_1, X_2, and E will solve *both* sets of equations [of course $\tilde{\lambda}[1-\tilde{\rho}\{1-P(\tilde{E})\}] = \lambda$] if

$$\frac{\tilde{\rho}(\tilde{U}-\underline{U})}{1-\tilde{\rho}\{1-P(\tilde{E})\}} = \frac{\rho(\overline{U}-\underline{U})}{1-\rho}. \tag{38}$$

But eq. (38), in turn, implies that

$$1-\frac{\rho}{\tilde{\rho}} = \frac{(1-\tilde{\rho})\left[1-\left(\dfrac{\tilde{U}-\underline{U}}{\overline{U}-\underline{U}}\right)\right]+\tilde{\rho}P(\tilde{E})}{\{1-\tilde{\rho}(1-P(\tilde{E})\}\left\{1+\tilde{\rho}\left(\dfrac{\tilde{U}-\underline{U}}{\overline{U}-\underline{U}}\right)\dfrac{1}{1-\tilde{\rho}(1-P(\tilde{E})}\right\}} > 0\,. \tag{38′}$$

since $\overline{U} > \tilde{U} > \underline{U}$ and $1-\tilde{\rho}(1-P(\tilde{E})) > 0$. Thus, we must have $\rho < \tilde{\rho}$, for the two infinite-time-horizon cases, without and with unresolved uncertainty, to yield identical results (i.e. values of X_1, X_2 and E). It is easy to see now that the residual-uncertainty model has a larger discount factor ($\tilde{\rho}$) than the resolved-uncertainty model (ρ): as one would expect, the risk involved in the unresolved-uncertainty case has to be compensated by lowering the discount rate (or by increasing the discount factor).

7. Concluding remarks

The preceding analysis of the phenomenon of market-disruption-induced QR-imposition can be shown both to have other applications and to be generalizable in many directions.

Thus, it is readily seen that the phenomenon of a trade *embargo* on a country's *imports* can be analyzed in the same way as the market-disruption phenomenon. The analysis, and results, would in fact be identical if we were to assume that the probability of the imposition of an export embargo (e.g. by OPEC) by the exporting country was an increasing function of the import level by the importing country (e.g. import of oil by the U.S.).[10] In this case, the optimal policy intervention by the importing country, faced by such an (import-level-related) embargo-prospect of reduced (or eliminated) feasible import level, would be a trade tariff if there were no adjustment costs, and a trade tariff plus production tax-cum-subsidy if there were adjustment costs as well. The analysis would however have to be slightly modified if the embargo problem were modeled

[10]The economic rationale for this assumption is that the probability of the exporter invoking an export embargo may be a function of the 'import dependence' of the importer.

rather as one where the probability of the exporting country allowing reduced, permissible exports were made a function instead of the ratio of imports to domestic production (as this may be a better index of import dependence). In this case, since the probability of the quota being invoked is now a function of a ratio involving *both* trade and production levels, one should expect that the optimum tariff would now be replaced by a *combination* of a tariff *and* a production tax-cum-subsidy, on this account (even in the absence of adjustment costs). Finally, if one models the probability of an embargo imposition as independent of a country's trade level or import-to-production ratio, so that the uncertainty is *exogenous*, then clearly the optimal policy for a small country (with no monopoly power in trade) is free trade with zero adjustment costs and, if there are adjustment costs, it will consist of a production tax-cum-subsidy related to these adjustment costs.

As for the generalizations of our analysis in other directions, we may indicate some. Thus, for example, an important extension would be to incorporate technical change as a source of export expansion and hence accentuated probability of a triggering of market-disruption-induced QR's: this would provide yet another instance of immiserizing growth, while also carrying implications for optimal imports of technology in developing countries, to mention only two possible analytically-interesting consequences. Again, our analysis has explicitly modeled only the exporting country as far as welfare implications of the market-disruption phenomenon are concerned. However, one could take a 'world-welfare' approach and model the importing country also more explicitly. If this was done, then one could no longer meaningfully take the importing country's QR-imposition policy as 'given,' and the basic model of this paper would have to be modified in an essential manner.

References

Bhagwati, J. and V.K. Ramaswami, 1963, Domestic distortions, tariffs and the theory of optimum subsidy, Journal of Political Economy 71, 44–50.

Bhagwati, J. and T.N. Srinivasan, 1969, Optimal intervention to achieve non-economic objectives, Review of Economic Studies 36, 27–38.

Bhagwati, J., V.K. Ramaswami and T.N. Srinivasan, 1969, Domestic distortions, tariffs, and the theory of optimum subsidy: Some further results, Journal of Political Economy 77, 1005–1010.

Bhagwati, J. 1971, The generalized theory of distortions and welfare, in: J. Bhagwati, et al., eds., Trade, balance of payments and growth (North-Holland, Amsterdam) 69–90.

Brecher, R., 1974, Optimal commercial policy for a minimum-wage economy, Journal of International Economics 4, 139–150.

Haberler, G., 1950, Some problems in the pure theory of international trade, Economic Journal 60, 223–240.

Johnson, H.G., 1965, Optimal trade intervention in the presence of domestic distortions, in: R.E. Caves et al., eds., Trade, growth and the balance of payments (North-Holland, Amsterdam) 3–34.

Mayer, W., 1974, Short-run and long-run equilibrium for a small open economy, Journal of Political Economy 82, 955–967.

Erratum

Page 324, line 4 from bottom: "U" should appear in the blank space in the equation.

Editor's Note

In section 6.3, p. 333, note that $\bar{U}$ is defined as the maximum utility when the optimal tariff is imposed [equation following (32)], and the ranking on page 334, line 5, then follows. If, however, $\bar{U}$ is defined as the utility level under laissez-faire when the quota is not imposed, then the ranking on page 334, line 5, would instead be analogous to that on page 320, line 10 and footnote 3.

Market Disruption, Export Market Disruption, Compensation, and GATT Reform

Jagdish N. Bhagwati

Introduction

This work addresses the issue of market disruption and suggests schemes for compensating the less developed countries (LDCs) who face what may aptly be described as export market disruption when the importing, developed countries (DCs) invoke protective devices, such as "voluntary" export restraints, to assist domestic industries seeking relief from foreign competition.

Section 1 deals with the problem of defining market disruption. Section 2 considers the GATT Article XIX on the subject and its relationship to national legislations. Section 3 goes on to outline the principal forms in which market-disruption-related restrictions have been invoked, focusing on "voluntary" export restraints (VERs) and the more sustained and formal multilateral arrangements (the LTA which restricts the exports of textiles). Section 4 discusses the welfare impact of the possibility of market-disruption-induced restrictions that LDCs face on their exports of manufactures. Section 5 assesses the need for compensation that the welfare losses to LDCs imply from this analysis, and develops specific proposals for such compensation. Section 6 suggests ways in which the GATT Article XIX could be modified to implement these suggestions. Appendix 1 contains a brief review of one precedent, where the "importing" country provided compensation to the "exporting" country for "export market disruption," so to speak. This is the case of the United States compensating Turkey for adjustment assistance to Turkish poppy farmers (the objective being to enable the farmers to shift to nonpoppy farming at no loss). Appendix 2, on the other hand, is a theoretical exercise, in a general-equilibrium framework, of the phenomenon of export market disruption and provides the necessary analytical support to the compensation schemes discussed in the text.

1. The Concept of Market Disruption

In a basic sense, market disruption is an old, protectionist concept: imports are considered disruptive of the domestic industry in the domestic market and hence must be curtailed and regulated. In this sense, virtually all imports are market disrupting, and indeed if one examines, in a "revealed preference" fashion, the demands for protection by many industries in almost all countries, this loose and all-embracing version is, in fact, what would most nearly reflect the intent of the spokesmen for these industries.

However, in an international economy, which, in the postwar, post-GATT world has been geared to increasing trade liberalization, the institutions governing the use of protective devices for manufactures have taken a narrower view of market disruption.

This is particularly true of the GATT, where Article XIX is designed to handle cases of "serious injury" to domestic industries and is set within the context of other rules designed to constrain the use of protection by member countries.[1]

It is correspondingly true also of national legislations enacted to correspond to Article XIX and related GATT provisions. Thus the United States had established corresponding "escape-clause" procedures by Executive Order 9832 from 1947 to 1951, by Section 7 of the 1951 Trade Agreements Extension Act between 1951 to 1962, and by Section 301 of the Trade Expansion Act from 1962.[2]

Under these legislations, for example, the successful invoking of protection required the public demonstration of injury, caused by tariff-concession-led imports, to the U.S. Tariff Commission which would, in turn, convey its finding to the president who, in turn, could act on it, consistently with the national legislation and the GATT rules.

On the other hand, the national executive has often been willing to sidetrack GATT restrictions and associated national processes for seeking relief under market disruption, and to invoke measures, outside of the GATT framework, to regulate the flow of such imports. The most potent such measure has been the VERs, which have tended to proliferate since the 1950s.

In consequence, it would be appropriate to say that, if we were to rank the different groups and institutions seeking to define market disruption and to seek relief from imports therewith, according to the degree of restrictiveness that they would apply to the concept, the ranking would be as follows:

$$\left\{\begin{array}{c}\text{Domestic}\\ \text{Industry}\\ \text{in}\\ \text{Importing}\\ \text{Country}\end{array}\right\} < \left\{\begin{array}{c}\text{National}\\ \text{Executive}\\ \text{in}\\ \text{Importing}\\ \text{Country}\end{array}\right\} \lesseqgtr \left\{\begin{array}{c}\text{National}\\ \text{Legislative}\\ \text{in}\\ \text{Importing}\\ \text{Country}\end{array}\right\} < \left\{\begin{array}{c}\text{GATT}\\ \text{(in}\\ \text{particular,}\\ \text{Article}\\ \text{XIX)}\end{array}\right\}$$

That is to say, the domestic industry, seeking relief from imports, would apply the least restrictive criteria to define market disruption; and the highest, in restrictiveness, would be the GATT, which seeks generally to minimize interferences with expanding trade. In between are the national executives and legislatures whose relative actions and attitudes on the issue of market disruption are likely to vary. Thus, in the United States the executive has been, via VERs, de facto less restrictive in the interpretation of market disruption, whereas the legislative statutes have been closer to GATT. On the other hand, this is quite consistent with the legislative representatives, interested in specific industries in their constituencies, being the effective moving force in getting a free-trade-oriented executive to enact the VERs. Hence one must distinguish between executive actions and legislation, on the one hand, and the executive and legislative bodies' attitudes toward the issue of market disruption, on the other hand.[3]

It is clear that the loosest, industry-based view of market disruption would extend to all competition with imports in the domestic market and indeed no evidence of any serious injury would need to be established. Thus, as Metzger has noted, the provisions of H.R. 18970, the so-called U.S. Trade Act of 1970, if it had become law, would have effectively elevated this view of market disruption to the status of the operating criterion for invoking protection (thus going beyond what GATT Article XIX envisaged).[4] The escape clause would have retained a Tariff Commission investigation but reduced the definition of injury to one where the domestic industry's relative share in the domestic market had fallen, while also removing presidential discretion in vetoing Tariff Commission recommendations for escape-clause action.[5]

By contrast, Article XIX of GATT restricts the "emergency action on imports of particular products" to situations which satisfy three conditions: (1) that the alleged disruption should have been the result of "the obligations incurred by a contracting party under this Agreement, including tariff concessions"; (2) that the product must be imported in "increased quantities"; and (3) that conditions must exist which "cause or threaten serious injury to domestic producers." While these conditions, and shifts in their interpretation over time, are discussed in the next section, it is pertinent to note immediately that the GATT envisions a much narrower interpretation of market disruption and hence a correspondingly smaller scope for invoking legitimate interferences with imports.

In keeping with this view of the matter, the associated national legislation has been relatively strict in interpreting market disruption as well. Thus, in the United States, the invoking of the escape clause has had to involve a public inquiry by the U.S. Tariff Commission which had to apply legislated criteria, similar to those of Article XIX, to the case at hand: the U.S. industries going the escape-clause route have had to argue that concession-induced imports were causing serious injury, and have often failed to win their case.

The invoking of protective devices by industries seeking curtailment of imports despite the GATT Article XIX and corresponding national legislations has therefore taken the route of executive action, typically in the form of VERs, outside of this framework; hence, the de facto definition of market disruption has turned out to be substantially closer to the importing industry's viewpoint than the GATT rules might suggest.

A review of the existing VERs, including the LTA governing the trade in textiles, reveals that the concept of market disruption that can successfully be invoked to get political, executive action in DCs tends to include the following "weakly restrictive" features:

1. There need not be a sharp rise in imports; it is enough for the relative *share* of foreign imports to increase sharply in the domestic market.

2. It is usually helpful to appeal to the notion that foreign competition is from "low-priced" imports. The Europeans have the term "abnormal competition" to refer to this phenomenon and claim market disruption when, according to J. De Bandt, the import price is below the domestic price by "the portion of value added which they are unwilling to forego."[6] This is a strange notion indeed for economists to contemplate: after all, trade will reflect comparative advantage and imports will be effected when they are cheaper than domestic output. But it is a notion that is widely held and presumably is occasionally successful in getting protection.

The reliance on criteria such as decline in domestic industry's share in the domestic market and the need to compete with "low-priced" imports have thus replaced the need to show that there is "serious injury" in any other sense (that unemployment is rapidly resulting in the industry) and that it is attributable to increasing imports.

Hence the matter has become of serious concern to LDCs whose ("low-priced," "low-cost") exports have now come fairly significantly to face the prospect of market-disruption-induced restrictions, and, indeed, are in some important cases (such as the LTA) already under such restraints.[7] Therefore prior to discussing the manner in which such prospects can be regulated and compensated for, it is necessary to examine in greater depth the history and present status of GATT rules on the subject, proceeding then to a fuller exploration of the growth of VERs and other restrictions outside of the GATT-and related framework.

2. GATT Rules and National Legislations

It is useful to put the current GATT rules on the phenomenon of "serious injury," as applicable to market disruption, in historical perspective as well as in relation to the rest of GATT articles.

It is fair to say that GATT has had built into its basic structure an asymmetry under which agriculture has managed to be relatively easy to protect but interferences with trade in manufactures have been made more difficult. Thus, for example, the GATT Article XI is explicit in ruling out quotas as follows:

1. No prohibitions or restrictions other than duties, taxes or other charges, whether made effective through quotas, import or export licenses or other measures, shall be instituted or maintained by any contracting party on the importation of any product of the territory of any other contracting party or on the exportation or sale for export of any product destined for the territory of any other contracting party.

2. The provisions of paragraph 1 of this Article shall not extend to the following:

(a) Export prohibitions or restrictions temporarily applied to prevent or relive critical shortages of foodstuffs or other products essential to the exporting contracting party;

(b) Import and export prohibitions or restrictions necessary to the application of standards or regulations for the classification, grading or marketing of commodities in international trade;

(c) Import restrictions on any agricultural or fisheries product, imported in any form . . . necessary to the enforcement of governmental measures which operate:

(i) to restrict the quantities of the like domestic product permitted to be marketed or produced, or, if there is no substantial domestic production of the like product, of a domestic product for which the imported product can be directly substituted; or

(ii) to remove a temporary surplus of the like domestic product, or, if there is no substantial domestic production of the like product, of a domestic product for which the imported product can be directly substituted, by making the surplus available to certain groups of domestic consumers free of charge or at prices below the current market level; or

(iii) to restrict the quantities permitted to be produced of any animal product the production of which is directly dependent, wholly or mainly, on the imported commodity, if the domestic production of that commodity is relatively negligible.

It is clear from the above that the essential exemptions contemplated under Article XI.2 relate to agricultural commodities (with domestic price support programs, and so forth) and do not help manufacturing industries desiring protection.

The basic *protective* outlet for manufactures (as distinct from articles such as XII relating to balance of payments and XXI concerning security exceptions) which seek protection from imports on alleged grounds of "market disruption" is provided under Article XIX whose full text states:

1. (a) If, as a result of unforeseen developments and of the effect of the obligations incurred by a contracting party under this Agreement, including tariff concessions, any product is being imported into the territory of that contracting party in such increased quantities and under such conditions as to cause or threaten serious injury to domestic producers in that territory of like or directly competitive products, the contracting party shall be free, in respect of such product, and to the extent and for such time as may be necessary to prevent or remedy such injury, to suspend the obligation in whole or in part or to withdraw or modify the concession.

(b) If any product, which is the subject of a concession with respect to a preference, is being imported into the territory of a contracting party in the circumstances set forth in subparagraph (a) of this paragraph, so as to cause or threaten serious injury to domestic producers of like or directly competitive products in the territory of a contracting party which receives or received such preference, the importing contracting party shall be free, if that other contracting party so requests, to suspend the relevant obligation in whole or in part or to withdraw or modify the concession in respect of the product, to the extent and for such time as may be necessary to prevent or remedy such injury.

2. Before any contracting party shall take action pursuant to the provisions of paragraph 1 of this Article, it shall give notice in writing to the CONTRACTING PARTIES as far in advance as may be practicable and shall afford the CONTRACTING PARTIES and those contracting parties having a substantial interest as exporters of the product concerned an opportunity to consult with it in respect of the proposed action. When such notice is given in relation to a concession with respect to a preference, the notice shall name the contracting party which has requested the action. In critical circumstances, where delay would cause damage which it would be difficult to repair, action under paragraph 1 of this Article may be taken provisionally without prior consultation, on the condition that consultation shall be effected immediately after taking such action.

3. (a) If agreement among the interested contracting parties with respect to the action is not reached, the contracting party which proposes to take or continue the action shall, nevertheless, be free to do so, and if such action is taken or continued, the affected contracting parties shall then be free, not later than ninety days after such action is taken, to suspend, upon the expiration of thirty days from the day on which written notice of such suspension is received by the CONTRACTING PARTIES, the application to the trade of the contracting party taking such action, or, in the case envisaged in paragraph 1 (b) of this Article, to the trade of the contracting party requesting such action, of such substantially equivalent concessions or other obligations under this Agreement the suspension of which the CONTRACTING PARTIES do not disapprove.

(b) Notwithstanding the provisions of subparagraph (a) of this paragraph, where action is taken under paragraph 2 of this Article without prior consultation and causes or threatens serious injury in the territory of a contracting party to the domestic producers of products affected by the action, that contracting party shall, where delay would cause damage difficult to repair, be free to suspend, upon the taking of such action and throughout the period of consultation, such concessions or other obligations as may be necessary to prevent or remedy the injury.

The GATT view of the invoking of "escape-clause" protection in the matter of market disruption, as implicit in Article XIX, was therefore traditionally a rather strict one. However, its interpretation has been somewhat less strict than the language would suggest.

Thus, the "unforeseen developments" in para. 1(a) have been interpreted as inclusive of situations deriving from the fulfillment by a member of its obligations (under Articles III or IX).[8] More important, the interpretation of the phrase "increased quantities" in para. 1 has been formally agreed to as including the case where imports may have increased only *relatively* to domestic production (as, in fact, was explicit in the corresponding Havana

Charter, Article 40 text).[9] Finally, the article clearly states that the relaxation of commitments under it will be "for such time as may be necessary": this, in turn, has been clarified to imply that while the expectation is one of short-term, temporary invoking of protection, the phrasing does allow for longer and continuous invoking of Article XIX.[10]

But, subject to these liberal interpretations, the scope of Article XIX is essentially narrow. Basically, it does require that concession-led increasing imports be a cause of serious injury. It also builds into the mechanism the *possibility* of compensation to the exporting member countries that thereby lose the tariff concessions to be suspended: reflecting, of course, the fact that Article XIX explicitly pertains to imports of articles on which a concession had earlier been granted and which is being suspended by the invoking of Article XIX.[11]

Of these two restrictive aspects of Article XIX, the former has caused the critical difficulty for industries seeking relief from imports, by claiming market disruption, under national legislations. Thus, in the United States (until the 1974 legislation), for example, the escape-clause actions (under the U.S. legislations, noted in Section 1) have been remarkably unsuccessful. Thus, of 134 investigations instituted by the commission until 1962, the process terminated in presidential invocation of the escape clause in only fifteen cases, with yet more dramatic failure rates for the post-1962 period!

The result has been a rather limited resort to GATT Article XIX for relief by industries alleging market disruption: national legislations and processes, reflecting the tougher criteria of Article XIX, have eliminated the bulk of the protectionist demands under the broad umbrella of "market disruption." The corresponding paucity of actions under Article XIX is therefore only natural.

It may also be noted that the invoking of Article XIX has generally taken the form of an increase in bound tariffs and, to a lesser degree (in about a third of the cases), of the imposition of QRs.[12] Furthermore, it has been estimated that the developing countries' exports were involved in more than half of the developed countries' invoking of Article XIX. The restrictions imposed in these cases were removed within a year in a third of the cases involving developing countries whereas in half the total number of cases the measures had been in force for over five years.

3. Growth and Existence of Principal Forms of Market-Disruption-Related Instruments of Protection

Basically, therefore, national governments in DCs responding to the protectionist pressures from their industries have responded in two principal ways: (1) by trying to weaken the restrictive nature of GATT rules on market disruption; and (2) by bypassing the GATT framework altogether.

Of these, the former has been the less important and has, in fact, not resulted in any major changes at the GATT to date. Apparently, the first public reference to "market disruption" specifically appears to have been made by the United States, via Mr. Douglas Dillon in Tokyo at the Fifteenth GATT Session in 1959.[13] This was to lead to the appointment of a GATT working party in June 1960 to examine the issue of market disruption. Their initial efforts amounted to defining market disruption to include four elements "in combination":[14]

(i) a sharp and substantial increase or potential increase of imports of particular products from particular sources;
(ii) these products are offered at prices which are substantially below those prevailing for similar goods of comparable quality in the market of the importing country;
(iii) there is serious damage to domestic producers or threat thereof;
(iv) the price differentials referred to in paragraph (ii) above do not arise from governmental intervention in the fixing or formation of prices or from dumping practices.

The working party advocated a multilateral and "constructive" approach toward this problem, one that would permit trade expansion. Its recommendation that there be a permanent Committee on Market Disruption was accepted and this committee, in collaboration with the International Labor Organization, was to consider the economic, social, and commercial aspects of market disruption and report on the matter.[15] As it happened, this report never materialized, and, in fact, the most important market-disruption-type restriction that soon materialized, the LTA (Long-Term Arrangement Regarding International Trade in Cotton Textiles), was to be negotiated in 1962 quite without regard to this committee! In the years that have lapsed since then, the GATT has not managed to regulate market disruption any more than the DCs have managed to alter the basic GATT framework to accommodate less restrictive criteria for invoking market-disruption-related protection.

The fact is that the alternative route, of bypassing the GATT altogether to seek successfully restraints on trade in cases of market disruption defined far more weakly than in GATT, is the one that has been chosen by DCs. And the most fashionable policy instrument chosen has been the VERs, ironically described as "voluntary" but, in fact, imposed on reluctant exporting countries threatened with more drastic treatment in the absence of the VERs. And the most serious of the VERs, those on cotton textiles, have been formally signed multilaterally into continuing quantitative restrictions under the LTA.

Before discussing the scope of these VERs, it is interesting to note that an analysis of the U.S. VERs, as in Table 6.1, shows how industries that failed to win protection by the escape-clause route then proceeded, through executive action, to secure VERs on imports (from Japan): the correlation is revealing. At the same time, note that several industries with VERs have not even bothered to go the escape-clause route first; this is true, for example, of cotton textiles in the United States, now under the LTA! In fact, the great

Table 6.1 The Relationship Between Japanese Voluntary Export Restraints and United States Escape-Clause Investigations

Items Subject to Japanese Voluntary Export Restraints	Items in Previous Escape-Clause Action	Finding in Previous Escape-Clause Action
1. Bicycle parts	Bicycle parts	Negative
2. Malleable cast-iron joints	Cast-iron soil-pipe fittings	Negative
3. Bicycles, assembled	Bicycles	First investigation: Negative Second investigation: Positive (president invoked escape clause) Third investigation: Negative
4. Thermometers	Clinical thermometers	Positive (president invoked escape clause)
5. Wood screws	Wood screws	First investigation: Negative Second investigation: Negative Third investigation: Evenly divided (president declined to invoke escape clause)
6. Gloves, woolen, knitted	Knit gloves and mittens, wool	Dismissed (at applicant's request)
7. Scarves, silk and rayon	Screen-printed silk scarves	Positive (president declined to invoke escape clause)
8. Silk fabrics	Silk woven fabrics	Dismissed (after preliminary inquiry)
9. Flatware, stainless steel	Stainless steel table flatware	Positive (president invoked escape clause)
10. Gloves and mittens, baseball use	Baseball and softball gloves	Positive (president declined to invoke escape clause)
11. Raincoats, vinyl	Plastic raincoats	Negative
12. Smoking accessories	Tobacco pipes and bowls	Positive (president declined to invoke escape clause)
13. Tableware, hard porcelain	Household china tableware	Negative
14. Umbrellas	Umbrellas	Dismissed (at applicant's request)
15. Umbrella frames	Umbrella frames	First investigation: Positive (president declined to invoke escape clause)

Table 6.1 (continued)

Items Subject to Japanese Voluntary Exports Restraints	Items in Previous Escape-Clause Action	Finding in Previous Escape-Clause Action
		Second investigation: Dismissed at applicant's request)
16. Glass- and crystal-ware	Handmade glassware	First investigation: Evenly divided (president declined to invoke escape clause) Second investigation: Negative
17. Rosaries	Rosaries	Negative
18. Tiles, mosaic, unglazed	Ceramic mosaic tiles	Positive (president declined to invoke escape clause)

Source: Constructued from Lynch (1968, p. 200) and Kelly (1963, pp. 169-173) by John Cheh (1974, Table VI-2).

advantage of VERs is that the industry does *not* have to satisfy the relatively stringent requirements such as the demonstration to an officially designated agency (say, the U.S. Tariff Commission) of serious injury from concession-led increase in imports: all that is truly necessary is sufficient political clout with one's government, and, in turn, the latter's clout with the government and/or traders of the exporting countries. As Metzger has put it pointedly in relation to the historical Potato Agreement of 1948 between the U.S. and Canada, an early example of a VER:

On the U.S. side, strong domestic interests desired to protect themselves against competitive imports. They either believed that they could not qualify for escape clause relief (i.e., Cotton Textiles, Man-made Textile Fibers, Shoes), or, if they might qualify for National Security Amendment relief (i.e., Steel), they were aware of the foreign relations problems involved in imposing unilateral quotas, which are often considered to be "unfriendly" acts by America's trading partners. Cognizant Congressional Committees, made aware of these problems by their own experience no less than by that communicated by the Chief Executive, have not desired to force the Administration's hand by passing mandatory legislative quotas; indeed, they have had grave doubts that in the last analysis they could muster the strength to repass such a bill over a determined Chief Executive. Yet, they, like the Administration, have been loathe to treat all domestic industries—those with and those without major political strength—alike. Those without sufficient domestic political strength have simply had to live with the foreign competition which cannot be stemmed under generally applicable domestic legal criteria. Those with such strengths have secured the extraordinary remedy of the United

States raising to the highest international negotiating levels the matter of securing curtailment of imports from friendly foreign countries, developing and developed alike, in the interest of those who can not show, or at any rate have not attempted to show, serious injury in consequence of increased importation.

Indeed, similar exertion of political muscle by industry and, in turn, by government against the exporting country were to mark the four early VERs between Japan and the United States in the 1930s.[16]

Information regarding VERs is, by the standards of international trade data, occasionally difficult to come by: this is in the nature of the case, given the extra-GATT-framework, political arm twisting that precedes their incidence. For the United States, we have Magee's estimates that are seen, in Table 6.2, to yield an estimated value of trade (affected by VERs) as exceeding $5 billion in 1971: a figure that, as one would expect, exceeds greatly the Canadian 1968 estimate of $57 million (Canadian). On the other hand, Canada and the United States are only two of many DCs practicing VERs.

By far the most important existing, as distinct from potential, VERs relate to textiles and currently are embodied in the Arrangement Regarding International Trade in Textiles, negotiated by some fifty governments in 1973 and entering into force on January 1, 1974. This arrangement goes back proximately, in essence, to the initial Short-Term Arrangement (STA) negotiated in 1961 at U.S. initiative and remaining in force between October 1961 and September 1962, and then succeeded by the LTA which was to be repeatedly renegotiated. The original agreements were restricted to cotton textiles whereas the latest agreement extends to "wool, man-made fibres, or blend thereof."[17]

The VERs, including the Arrangement on Textiles, suggest certain broad characteristics and conclusions.

Table 6.2 Major U.S. Imports Subject to Voluntary Export Restraints and Import Quotas, 1971 (in millions of dollars)

	VERs	QRs
Petroleum		3,278
Sugar		813
Dairy products		70
Total		4,161
Cotton textiles	590	
Synthetic and woolen textiles	1,840	
Steel	2,009[a]	
Meat	598	
Total	5,037	

Source: Stephen P. Magee (1972, p. 662); cited also in Fred Bergsten (1975).
[a]1969 figure, excluding several categories of steel products covered by the VERs. Thus the figure for total VER coverage should be somewhat higher. In 1973, the total coverage approximated $2.3 billion.

1. They can be invoked successfully at extremely low levels of imports, both absolutely and as a share of domestic absorption. Thus, the early VERs on textiles from Japan, imposed by the United States in the 1930s, were at a time when total imports of textiles into the United States were no more than 3 percent of domestic production and total imports from Japan were only about 1 percent.[18] From 1951 to 1962, straddling the renewal of such VERs in the mid-1950s, the shares were, if anything, even lower. Similarly, the steel VERs invoked by the United States have also been in the face of imports as low as 17 million tons against domestic production of 141 million tons in 1969.[19]

2. The industries profiting from VERs almost always allege fears of "low-price" imports offering undue competition and *threatening* injury, rather than actually causing it.[20]

3. The length of duration of the VERs, at a time, would seem to be around one year but can extend to five years. In several cases, they have been renewed beyond the period of first imposition.[21] Some have been allowed to lapse as well.

4. The VERs are an inefficient instrument, compared to domestic tariffs or quotas, in restricting imports. The principal cause is that VERs apply to specific exporters and they cannot effectively rule out new suppliers from entering the market. In consequence, the progress of most VERs on specific countries (with notable exceptions as in the case of U.S. VERs on steel) has been toward increasing coverage of other exporters and, in the case of textiles, to a fully multilateral arrangement of exporters and importers.[22] In other cases, for instance, Canada, there is "back-up" legislation in case VERs fail to hold back imports effectively.[23]

5. While the VERs build in permissible rates of growth of exports from specific countries, these are invariably controlled at low levels. Thus the latest Arrangement on Textiles builds in a ceiling of 6 percent (as against the earlier 5 percent), but, at the same time, allows for an escape route (seized under the earlier arrangement by Canada, for example, at 3 percent) under which a "lower positive growth rate may be applied."[24]

6. Furthermore, there is literally no sanction against the expansion of capacity in the domestic industry of the importing country while the VERs operate. This is the case even for the 1974 Arrangement on Textiles; and, in fact, while the earlier LTA operated, the exporting LDCs noted and complained about the growth of such capacity in member DCs to no avail. Therefore VERs are, in this respect, one-sided.

7. Finally, unlike the compensation *possibility* in the GATT Article XIX, there is practically no evidence that any of the existing and past VERs have incorporated explicit compensation to the countries whose export markets are being disrupted.[25]

4. Impact of "Export Market Disruption" on Welfare of Exporting LDCs

The *threat* of protectionist restrictions being invoked by the importing countries, on grounds of market disruption, can be shown to impose a welfare loss on the exporting countries, as is in fact done in the theoretical Appendix 2.

It is shown there that, taking expected utilities, economic welfare of the exporting country will be less in the absence of such a threat. It is also shown that if the exporting country, in turn, reacts with an optimal policy intervention in the nature of restricted exports so as to reduce the probability of VERs or other such market-disruption-related restrictions being invoked, then the reduction in welfare from the *threat* of such invocations will be less than if the exporting country took no such action: but the loss will still be there. And, furthermore, if investment allocations cannot be costlessly readjusted, once in place, then the presence of such "adjustment costs" will further increase the loss of welfare from the threat of such trade restraints. Finally, the *actual* invoking of the trade restraints would inflict a welfare loss on the exporting country that would exceed the expected loss from the *threat* of such an invocation at a future date.

From these general theoretical propositions, certain compensatory proposals would seem to follow.

First, there is a case for asking importing DCs to compensate the exporting LDCs faced with mere *threats* of market-disruption-related trade restraints. The DCs can reasonably be asked to "buy," with compensation payments, the right to invoke a market-disruption-related trade restraint on a product, and to forego the right to resort to such trade restraints on all products *not* so bought for. Thus a list of "restrainable" items can be prepared under multilateral auspices, such as GATT, and the compensation required for affected exporting countries, whose welfare is correspondingly reduced, would have to be paid to put a product on such a list.

Second, the actual invoking of such restraints, by imposing a greater loss, would equally call for further compensation to the affected exporters.

Compensation, for potential and actual export market disruption, to the exporting countries affected by trade restraints related to market disruption would thus be the natural consequence of our analysis. In Section 5, therefore, we consider the possible rules in this regard in greater depth, proceeding in Section 6 to consider the implications these rules would have for modifications in GATT Article XIX and related provisions.

5. Compensation for Export Market Disruption, Potential and Actual: Suggested Rules

The rules for compensation for market-disruption-related trade restraints can then be defined on a number of dimensions as follows.

1. *Penalty/compensation for potential restriction.* In accordance with the arguments of the preceding section, a list of "items potentially subject to

market-disruption-related trade restrictions" ought to be maintained. This list might be described as the *list of potentially restrainable items.*[26] For putting an item on such a list, the DCs would be required to pay a "penalty" which could be utilized to compensate the exporting countries subject to welfare loss from the threat of trade restraints on the item.

2. *Penalty compensation for actual invoking of trade restraints on potentially restrainable items.* Moreover, as and when the trade restraints are actually invoked, a further penalty should be used for compensating the exporting country whose export market is thus restrained.[27] The penalty so imposed, if it is to reflect the compensation to be paid to the exporting countries, must then be less than the actual cost of the trade restraint by the adjusted sum already paid for putting the item, in the first place, on the list of potentially restrainable items.

3. *Escape clause from list of potentially restrainable items.* While the preceding two rules should, in principle, divide all items into those that are restrainable and those that are not, this is politically inadequate. There will almost certainly be cases where unforeseen *and* politically unmanageable difficulties will arise on items not already put on the list of potentially restrainable items and the DC of importation will be unable to avoid responding to political pressures for trade restraint.

An escape-clause action for items not on this list would therefore be appropriate. At the same time, given the fact that this should not provide an incentive to escape from the option of putting such items on the restrainable list, it would be equally appropriate to make the invoking of this escape clause both more difficult and more costly. Thus, the escape clause should require that the importing DC be allowed nonetheless to invoke a trade restraint on items not on the list of potentially restrainable items, provided that (a) it makes a demonstrable case, under multilateral (GATT) auspices, of the existence of serious injury (as under the current GATT Article XIX) *and* (b) it then makes a considerably larger penalty payment for the compensation of the exporting countries. It may also be noted that one would, in practice, need a substantial time limit for an item to be on the restrainable list before permitting the invoking of trade restraints under it. Otherwise, when this period could be a few weeks or months, it would pay countries to go this route rather than the proposed escape-clause route where the proposed penalties are higher.

4. *Automaticity of compensation.* The penalty/compensation would be automatic under the preceding rules, rather than constituting a mere possibility as in the current GATT Article XIX. This would rule out the use of political muscle to get out of this obligation when invoking trade restraints.

5. *Financial form of compensation.* Moreover, the above rules require financial compensation. This is in contrast, for example, to the Article XIX variety of "compensation," which takes the form of either grant of a new tariff concession (on something else) or of withdrawal of a tariff concession

by the exporting country. This latter method reflects the tariff-bargaining framework in which GATT rules are enmeshed; it makes little sense since compensation to the exporter in the form of enabling the latter to raise a tariff in retaliation, for example, presupposes that the latter is advantageous while in fact, it is likely to cause yet more damage by further restraining trade; at the same time, it disrupts yet another market in seeking redress for the original market disruption. The financial form of penalty/compensation provided for in the rules suggested above is free from these obvious defects.

6. *Compensation to exporting country*. Furthermore, the financial compensation is designed here for payment to the exporting *country*, rather than to the exporting industry: as called for by the theoretical analysis of Appendix 2. In turn, the payment is to be made by the importing country. It may be noted that the latter, financial penalty to be paid from the budget would, in turn, serve to generate executive counterpressures against the industrial pressure groups for trade restraints, potential and actual.

7. *Compensation only for LDCs.* The preceding rules in regard to compensation may be applied only to exporting LDCs. They are, after all, the countries which have been seriously affected by the textiles restrictions and by VERs, as we have already seen.[28] Further, there is greater willingness, as part of the new international economic order, to grant LDCs reasonable accommodation via framing new rules regarding their trade. Moreover, the flows of funds to be so generated are far more likely to be significant, relative to their needs, for LDCs than for DCs. Finally, discriminatory adjustment of trade rules, in favor of LDCs, is well-embedded in GATT reform, as in the enactment of Article XXIII for them at GATT.

The foregoing set of rules, involving essentially compensation for exporting LDCs by importing DCs, are not entirely novel in their reference to the *potential* use of trade restraints since the well-established practice of the "binding" of tariffs does imply that the potential use of restrictions is given up. In regard to the notion of the compensation itself, however, there are no obvious precedents. At the same time, a precedent of sorts, which certainly suggests that what is being proposed here is fully feasible, relates to the payment by the United States of compensation to the Turkish government of a sizable sum in order to enforce the ban on poppy production: by using this money to compensate Turkish farmers, in turn, this would theoretically have made it possible for them to shift to other cultivation at no financial loss.[29] This "precedent" is spelled out in some detail in Appendix 1. There would therefore appear to be nothing insuperable, politically, in putting the suggested compensatory rules here onto the agenda for GATT reform.

At the same time, it would be useful to note that; in complementarity to the rules suggested above, two DC policies would be extremely valuable, only one of which is being gradually extended in scope.

Insofar as the response to foreign imports, or to domestic decline due to other reasons, is to provide domestic adjustment assistance to assist factors of production to retrain and relocate, this will correspondingly reduce the need to resort to trade restraints by making the pressures for such restraints from the industry both less intense and politically less difficult to resist. In this regard, the easing of the criteria for such adjustment assistance in the recent U.S. Trade Act of 1974 is welcome news for the exporting LDCs.[30]

Next, it is clear from elementary principles that trade restraint, to protect the production level of the domestic industry, is inferior to the use of a production subsidy: from the viewpoint of the importing DC itself.[31] Equally, it is obvious that the use of the production subsidy will increase the overall market in the DC for the imported item while a tariff, by increasing the price for consumers, will reduce it. Hence, given the fact that domestic production must be maintained at a desired level, the use of a production subsidy by the importing DC will be preferable, from the viewpoint of the exporting LDC, than the use of a trade policy.[32] Thus it would be useful if the overall reform in regard to the phenomenon of market-disruption-related trade restraints, as suggested in this section, were to include a multilateral agreement by DCs to use production subsidies rather than tariffs or trade quotas, whenever trade restraints are invoked under the rules specified above.[33] The only exceptions to this code could include emergency situations where an immediate trade quota may be necessary: in this case, the quota could be phased out and replaced gradually by a production subsidy on a multilaterally agreed schedule.

6. Proposed Modification in GATT Article XIX

If the rules suggested in Section 5 are to be implemented, the logical place for them is the GATT; and there, the logical candidate for replacement by these rules is Article XIX.

The GATT is already being reexamined—as, in fact, it has been continuously since its inception in regard to new phenomena such as the growth of customs unions—in regard to the manifestation and growth of new problems such as the use of export quotas,[34] for example, to hold back commodities for an objective such as anti-inflationary policy. The recent thrust toward a new international economic order also provides an ideal climate in which to reexamine long-standing issues, for instance, market disruption, which have been addressed but for which suitable solutions have not been provided.

The rules suggested in Section 5 therefore provide an agenda for replacing the basic content of Article XIX, in an international economic climate where such a concrete proposal is likely to be examined without immediate hostility on the part of DCs. At the same time, in being concrete and specific, the suggested changes provide the necessary content and shape to the long-standing demands by LDCs that something be done about the phenomenon of market-disruption-related trade restraints from DCs. They constitute therefore an essential and useful input into the basic agenda for reforming GATT as part of a new international economic order.

The formal adoption of such rules, replacing Article XIX, would also have to bring the *existing* VERs, including the 1974 Textiles Agreement, into line with them. This would be done most naturally by formally sanctioning them, but insisting on the payment of the penalty by the importing DCs to compensate the LDCs whose exports are being constrained by these restraints. Otherwise, there would be an advantage to invoking VERs prior to the reaching of agreement on the new rules.[35] Also, there would be an advantage in bringing *all* such trade restraints under one institutional umbrella, where they can be watched, monitored, and regulated according to the suggested, new rules.

The dynamics of reaching an agreement on these rules, finally, presumably would have to involve an initiative by the LDCs themselves, as they are the parties injured by the current and potential market-disruption-related trade restraints. The logical place for their initiative is therefore the UNCTAD, to be followed by action by the LDC members of the GATT at the GATT. The proposals advanced here certainly provide an alternative and consistent set of reform rules that needs to be considered seriously alongside the suggestions in regard to market disruption recently aired by the LDCs.[36]

Notes

This paper was originally commissioned by the UNCTAD, Geneva, Switzerland, but does not represent or reflect the UNCTAD Secretariat's views. Thanks are due to Michael Pelcovits and Paul Krugman for excellent research assistance and to T. N. Srinivasan for coauthoring Appendix 2, which is an abbreviated version of a full-length theoretical analysis, published in the *Journal of International Economics*, November 1976. Helpful comments on an earlier draft were received from Robert Baldwin, Fred Bergsten, Charles Blitzer, Peter Diamond, Murray Kemp, Hendrik Houthakker, R. Krishnamurti, C. P. Kindleberger, Gerry Helleiner, Jan Tumlir, Stanley Metzger, John Williamson, Bela Balassa, Wolfgang Mayer, and Koichi Hamada.

1 Article XIX is one of several, so-called "safeguard" provisions in GATT which enable the contracting parties to reenact trade barriers for a number of specific reasons. Article VI, for example, allows the enacting of countervailing and antidumping duties.

2 Cf. Stanley Metzger (1971, p. 168).

3 It is thus well known that the U.S. executive has been generally more liberal on trade barriers reduction than the U.S. Congress, and that the VERs were imposed often so as to prevent more serious protectionist legislation from becoming enacted in the Congress.

4 Metzger (1971, p. 173).

5 This notion of market disruption as occurring whenever the domestic industry loses its relative share in the domestic market is implicit or explicit in trade legislation introduced earlier in the U.S. House of Representatives. Thus H.R. 2511, introduced on January 8, 1969, begins typically as follows: "A Bill to provide for the orderly marketing of flat glass imported into the United States by affording foreign supplying nations a *fair share* of the growth or change in the United States flat glass market . . ." (91st Congress, 2nd

Session, Committee Print, Committee on Ways and Means, U.S. House of Representatives, June 1970, U.S. Government Printing Office, Washington, 1970, p. 172, italics inserted). Or take H.R. 993 which begins with: "A Bill to provide for *an equitable sharing* of the United States market by electronic articles of domestic and of foreign origin . . ." (ibid., p. 150, italics inserted).

6 See Caroline Pestieau and Jacque Henry (1972, pp. 139-140). The work referred to here is by Henry.

7 Thus, according to Pestieau and Henry (1972), Canada had official VERs in 1971 with twenty countries, of which only six were DCs.

8 Thus a Working Party at GATT had concluded that "developments occurring after the negotiation of the relevant tariff concession which it would not be reasonable to expect that the negotiations of the country making the concession could and should have foreseen at the time when the concession was negotiated." Cf. GATT (1970-1971, p. 107).

9 GATT (1970-1971, p. 107).

10 GATT (1970-1971, p. 107). In fact, in the case of Germany, in regard to hard coal, the 1958 invoking of Clause XIX was in force as late as 1975.

11 The article builds in provision for consultations with interested contracting parties, which is the usual forum for granting the compensation if indeed granted. (Where the action is taken prior to consultation, the interested contracting parties may retaliate. However, such retaliation has been quite rare, having occurred only in three cases to present date.) Furthermore, as corroborated by unpublished tabulations at GATT, compensation is only a possibility, as noted in the text, and is often *not* provided when Article XIX is invoked. In fact, dissatisfaction with the compensation aspect of Article XIX has prompted occasional suggestions to do away with it and instead modify Article XIX so as to insist on the following of certain stricter criteria by the country invoking the article.

12 In some cases, the action taken took the form of establishing minimum valuations for imports, thus effectively raising the tariff rate for items with actual values below these minimums.

13 GATT (1961b, p. 25). In fact, it was at the United States' initiative that Article XIX had been included in GATT originally.

14 Cf. GATT (1961a); also cited in Pestieau and Henry (1972, pp. 137-138), in Metzger (1971, pp. 175-176), and discussed in GATT (1961b, pp. 25-26).

15 Cf. Pestieau and Henry (1972, pp. 137-138).

16 Metzger (1971, pp. 170-171). "As Henry states, the 'entire story shows clearly that the U.S.-Japan voluntary export restraint agreements of the 1930's resulted mainly from American pressures and threats of unilateral, permanent, and possibly more restrictive action. Nothing indicates,' he asserts, 'that this pattern has changed since.' The Japanese, for their part, accepted the agreements as the most practicable means of preserving a portion of their textile exports to the United States, and in the interest of political harmony in this sphere of their relationships with the United States."

17 Cf. GATT (1974), Article 12, pp. 17-18.

18 Cf. Metzger (1971, p. 170).

19 Cf. Metzger (1971, p. 182).

quotas under uncertainty shows that if the uncertainty comes from foreign supply, the welfare superiority of tariffs over quotas as methods of restricting imports to a given level if the tariff rate is high: precisely 100 percent in the case of linear supply and demand schedules. Cf. the interesting work of Michael Pelcovits (1975).

21 Pestieau and Henry (1972) note that the duration of a formal agreement is not identical with its incidence: occasionally, as with GATT Article XIX as well, the restriction will go into force before formal papers are exchanged. They also note that most Canadian VERs have duration of one year.

22 Besides, export quotas have always been known to earn the monopoly rents (from restriction) for the exporters whereas domestic quotas will earn them for the importer under competition.

23 Pestieau and Henry (1972, p. 168): "Several Canadian laws include clauses that can be used to supplement or reinforce VERs, and the various amendments enacted in the context of the present government's textile policy lessen the previous dependence on exporters' voluntary collaboration. Prior to January, 1969, subsection (7c) of section 40A of the Customs Act was used to apply special values for duty in instances where imports were found to have injured the interest of Canadian producers. However, this subsection was repealed and replaced on January 1, 1969, by the new section 8 of the Customs Tariff Act. As stated in section 37 of the Anti-dumping Act (1969), the new section authorizes the imposition of a surtax on imports that cause or threaten to cause injury to Canadian producers of similar or directly competitive goods. The Export and Import Permits Act has also been amended to permit unilateral imposition of import-licensing quotas to deal with problems of disruptive imports whenever VER arrangements would not be feasible. Furthermore, section 5(c) of this Act enables the federal government to control imports and 'to implement an intergovernmental arrangement or commitment'—clearly opening up a method for making VER arrangements more effective.

"These are the powers on which the efficiency of the Canadian VER system rests."

Examples can be found in U.S. Legislation as well, as in the Public Law 87-488 (H.R. 10788) which amended Section 204 of the Agricultural Act of 1956 by the insertion of the following sentence:

In addition, if a multilateral agreement has been or shall be concluded under the authority of this section among countries accounting for a significant part of world trade in the articles with respect to which the agreement was concluded, the President may also issue, in order to carry out such an agreement, regulations governing the entry or withdrawal from warehouse of the same articles which are the products of countries not parties to the agreement.

This legislation was approved on June 19, 1962.

Note that both the United States and Canada have back-up legislation for VERs in cases of textiles and meat.

24 Cf. GATT (1974, Annex B, p. 22).

25 However, from a theoretical standpoint, it may be noted that VERs, as contrasted with import QRs, will transfer the monopoly rents from the trade restriction to the exporters, so that one may well consider this to constitute an implicit compensation under a VER arrangement. In fact, as Bergsten has pointed out, textile export quota tickets are actively sold throughout the Far East at a premium that reflects this rent. See Fred Bergsten (1975, pp. 239-271).

26 An analogue to this recommendation may be found in the practice of "binding" tariffs in advance.

27 The loss inflicted by actual invoking of restraints is, of course well understood in trade-theoretic literature. For measurement of the cost of sugar protectionism to exporting LDCs, for example, see the work of Snape and Johnson, reviewed in H. G. Johnson (1967).

28 VERs have also affected Japan seriously; and, in some cases, such as the steel VERs in the United States, the impact was felt by the developed country exporters and imports were initially diverted to developing countries which thereby benefited.

29 The compensation rules suggested for trade restraints in this paper, however, relate only to financial compensation to the exporting *country*, and *not* to the exporting industry. For other contrasts, refer to Appendix 1.

30 For an excellent account of the U.S. policies in regard to adjustment assistance, and evidence on the efforts to ease the criteria for it until 1973, see Robert Baldwin and John Mutti, "Policy Issues in Adjustment Assistance: The United States," in Helen Hughes, ed. (1973), especially Section IV. Adjustment assistance in the EEC is also discussed in Ch. 7 of this volume.

31 This is one of the important policy prescriptions from the theory of optimal policy intervention in the presence of "noneconomic" objectives and follows from the fact that the tariff imposes a consumption cost (by raising prices for consumers) which is avoided, while equally protecting domestic output, by a production subsidy. Cf. J. Bhagwati and T. N. Srinivasan (1969).

32 This conclusion would have to be modified, but is not altogether nullified, if the domestic industry wishes to maintain a certain *share* of sales in the domestic market. The optimal policy intervention in this case, from the DC viewpoint, would be the combination of an import tariff and a production subsidy.

33 A code of conduct, along these lines, is mentioned also by Henry (1972, p. 175), who states that this "has been suggested in various places" and cites one example from Bela Balassa.

34 See, in this regard, the excellent pamphlet by C. Fred Bergsten (1974). Bergsten does not consider VERs or market-disruption problems in this study.

35 For a long-standing restraint such as the Textiles Arrangement, it may be politically easier and also quite sensible to have the penalty enacted at the time of the next renewal, since there has been a short time limit on each such arrangement.

36 The latter have been neatly summarized in UNCTAD document TC/B/C.2/R.4.

References

Baldwin, R., and J. Mutti, 1973, "Policy Issues in Adjustment Assistance: The United States," in Helen Hughes (ed.), *Prospects for Partnership*, IBRD, Johns Hopkins University Press, Baltimore.

Bergsten, C. F., 1974, *Completing the GATT: Toward New International Rules to Govern Export Controls*, British-North American Committee, United States, October.

________, 1975, *On the Non-Equivalence of Import Quotas and "Voluntary" Export Restraints*, Technical Series Reprint T-009, Brookings Institution, Washington, D.C.

Bhagwati, J., and T. N. Srinivasan, 1969, "Optimal Intervention to Achieve Non-

Economic Objectives," *Review of Economic Studies*, January.

Cheh, J., 1974, *U.S. Trade Policy and Short-run Domestic Adjustment Costs*, Ph.D. dissertation, M.I.T.

Dominion Bureau of Statistics, several years, *Trade of Canada, Imports by Commodities*, Queen's Printer, Ottawa.

GATT, 1961a, *Basic Instruments and Selected Documents*, 9th Supplement, Sixteenth and Seventeenth Sessions, February, Geneva.

_______, 1961b, *The Activities of GATT, 1960/61*, April, Geneva.

_______, 1970-1971, *Analytical Index, Third Revision, March 1970, Notes on the Drafting, Interpretation and Affirmation of the Articles of the General Agreement*, Geneva.

_______, 1974, *Arrangement Regarding International Trade in Textiles*, Geneva.

Johnson, H. G., 1967, *Economic Policies Towards the Developing Countries*, Brookings Institution, Washington, D.C.

Kelly, W., 1963, *Studies in United States Commercial Policy*, University of North Carolina Press, Chapel Hill.

Lynch, J., 1968, *Toward an Orderly Market*, Sophia University; Voyager's Press, Tokyo.

Magee, S. P., 1972, "The Welfare Effects of Restrictions on U.S. Trade," *Brookings Papers on Economic Activity*, 3 (edited by A. Okun and G. Perry).

Metzger, S., 1971, "Injury and Market Disruption from Imports" in *United States International Economic Policy in an Interdependent World*, U.S. Commission on International Trade and Investment Policy, Vol. 1, Washington, D.C., July.

Pelcovits, M., 1975, "Tariffs *versus* Quotas," M.I.T. *mimeo.*, September; forthcoming in the *Journal of International Economics*, November 1976.

Pestieau, C., and J. Henry, 1972, *Non-Tariff Trade Barriers as a Problem in International Development*, Canadian Economic Policy Committee and the Private Planning Association of Canada, Canada, April.

UNCTAD, Document No. TD/B/C.2/R.4.

Appendix 1
On Compensating for Market Loss of a Bad: The Turkish Poppy and the United States

Outside of the GATT Article XIX framework (where compensation is nonautomatic and furthermore applies only if the market disruption being nullified is a result of "obligations incurred by a contracting party under this Agreement, including tariff concessions," and whose applicability in any event has been emasculated by actions such as the LTA and VERs undertaken outside of its domain), the only major example of an importing country paying compensation to the exporting country when trade is sought to be eliminated or reduced is that of the United States paying Turkey a significant compensation to enforce the ban on Turkish poppy cultivation.

This precedent is not perfect, although it illustrates what is feasible. Its major difference from the compensation proposed for export market disruption is that its objective is to *induce* adjustment by compensating the exporting activity so that the exports will *in consequence* effectively cease, whereas the proposed compensation here is when exports have *already* ceased (or been reduced) and the compensation is for the adjustment that *has to occur* with the decline in exports. This difference, of course, stems from the fact that the case deals with trade in a bad, rather than a good, and hence with illegal trade that was sought to be eliminated at source through banning the production activity itself. Its similarity, however, with the proposed compensation for export market disruption (for goods) consists in the fact that the importing country provided the compensation to the farmers in the exporting country for the adjustment necessary if the heroin trade was to be curtailed. Hence, a brief account and review of the salient features of the case of Turkish poppy and the U.S. adjustment assistance is relevant.

The United States had for a long time been putting pressure on Turkey to reduce poppy cultivation. In response to this pressure, the number of provinces in which cultivation was legal was reduced from forty-two (out of seventy) in 1960 to seven in 1970, and four in 1971.[1] On June 30, 1971, the United States and Turkey announced a total ban on poppy cultivation. On February 14, 1974, Turkey unilaterally lifted the ban.

The logistics of the poppy trade before the ban were as follows. By a simple process poppies can be turned to opium gum, which can in turn be manufactured into morphine base. Turkey produced around 120,000 kilograms of opium gum per year. Legally, all of this was supposed to be sold to a state marketing agency, at thirteen dollars a kilo. But about half of the crop went on the black market, selling at around thirty-five dollars a kilo. (Refined into morphine base—a cheap process—this became \$550 to \$600 a kilo in Marseilles.)[2]

The agreement to ban cultivation called for U.S. payments of \$15 million a year, plus \$20 million for agricultural development investments in the affected regions. This was to compensate the farmers, and also the Turkish government, for the \$3.5 million a year it earned from morphine export. The Turkish marketing organization was to pay farmers a compensation of forty dollars per kilo for poppies not grown.[3]

For more than a year after the ban, there was little impact on the flow of heroin, as dealers drew down their stockpiles.[4] But eventually the ban had a major effect, doubling heroin prices in the United States.[5]

The ban was unpopular with farmers, and politicians in a seven-province area agitated for an end.[6] In the October 1973 elections all political parties promised to review the ban.[7] When cultivation was resumed, the Turkish government said that it was because of hardships to the peasants, that it was unfair to ask Turkey to bear this burden.

It would appear that the Turkish farmers were compensated only at the legal prices presumably available on their poppy, so that the premium from illegal sales for heroin was lost by them under the ban, despite the compensation; hence the discontent. Furthermore, it is apparent that the ban was somewhat sudden and so little of the developmental aid was actually spent in the poppy-growing region by the time the discontent surfaced.[8] Finally, the ban having been forced initially on a reluctant Turkey by the United States, which was naturally frantic to stem the heroin traffic, questions of Turkish sovereignty appear eventually to have played some role also in termination of the ban.[9]

Notes

1 *New York Times* (February 21, 1974).

2 *New York Times* (August 9, 1973).

3 *New York Times* (August 9, 1973).

4 *New York Times* (October 10, 1972).

5 *New York Times* (February 21, 1974).

6 *New York Times* (August 9, 1973).

7 *New York Times* (February 21, 1974).

8 *New York Times* (February 21, 1974).

9 *Wall Street Journal* (June 23, 1974).

Editor's Note

Appendix 2 of this paper appears under the same title in expanded form as essay 30 in this volume.

VI
FACTOR MARKET IMPERFECTIONS AND POLICY INTERVENTION

Journal of International Economics 1 (1971) 19–35. © North-Holland Publishing Company

THE THEORY OF WAGE DIFFERENTIALS: PRODUCTION RESPONSE AND FACTOR PRICE EQUALISATION

Jagdish N.BHAGWATI
Department of Economics, Massachusetts Institute of Technology, Cambridge, Mass. 02139

T.N. SRINIVASAN
Indian Statistical Institute, Planning Unit

Previous analyses of the case where there is a distortionary wage differential between different activities, by writers such as Fishlow and David (1961), Hagen (1958), Bhagwati and Ramaswami (1963), and Johnson (1966) have led to the discovery of the following pathologies:

(i) the feasible production possibility curve will shrink inside the "best" production possibility curve (Hagen, 1958);

(ii) the commodity–price ratio will not be tangential (at points of incomplete specialisation in production) to the feasible production possibility curve (Hagen, 1958); and

(iii) the production possibility curve may become convex to the origin, instead of concave (Fishlow and David, 1961; Bhagwati and Ramaswami, 1963; and Johnson, 1966).

However, this is not the end of the story. It can be further shown that (i) the shift in the production of a commodity, as its relative price changes, may be either positive or negative; and that the shift is not necessarily predictable from the convexity or concavity of the feasible production possibility curve; and (ii) given the commodity–price ratio, we cannot necessarily have unique capital–labour ratios in the two activities or unique factor price ratios: an important and interesting implication of which result is that the factor price-equalisation theorem breaks down, despite all the Samuelson conditions being met, even if there is an identical wage differential in the same sector in both countries.

We would like to note that research in the field of wage differentials is independently being conducted by Steve Magee, P.J.Lloyd, Ronald Jones, and by Murray Kemp and Horst Herberg. Thanks are due to Harry Johnson and Ronald Jones for comments on an earlier draft of the paper. The research of the former author has been supported by a grant from the National Science Foundation.

1. The model

We consider the standard two-factor, two-commodity model of trade theory. The production function for each commodity will be assumed to be homogeneous of degree one, and strictly concave with non-negative marginal products for both factors. Each factor is limited in availability and supplied inelastically to the extent of availability. The price paid for the use of one of the factors in the production of one of the commodities is, however, assumed to be a given constant times the price paid for the use of the same factor in the production of the other commodity. Given the international commodity–price ratio, production is assumed to take place under purely competitive conditions.

Let R_i denote the factor intensity (ratio of the amount of the first factor to that of the second) in the production of commodity i. Let R be the aggregate factor endowment ratio. Without loss of generality, we shall assume that the total availability of the second factor is unity. Let L be the amount of the second factor employed in the production of the first commodity. Let $f^i(R_i)$ be the average physical product of the second factor in the production of commodity i when the factor-intensity is R_i. Let Q_i be the output of commodity i. Let γ be the ratio of the reward of the second factor in the production of the second commodity to that in the production of the first commodity. Let $f^i_1(R_i)$ be the derivative of $f^i(R_i)$ with respect to R_i. Clearly $f^i_1(R_i)$ is the marginal physical product of the first factor in the production of commodity i. Let p be the international price of the second commodity in terms of the first.

Given our assumptions we can now describe our model algebraically as follows:

$$Q_1 = Lf^1(R_1)\,, \tag{1}$$

$$Q_2 = (1-L)f^2(R_2)\,, \tag{2}$$

$$LR_1 + (1-L)R_2 = R\,, \tag{3}$$

$$f^1_1(R_1) = pf^2_1(R_2)\,, \tag{4}$$

$$\{f^1 - R_1 f^1_1(R_1)\}\gamma = p\{f^2 - R_2 f^2_1(R_2)\}\,. \tag{5}$$

Eqs. (1), (2), and (3) represent the production functions and factor allocations. Eq. (4) states that the reward of the first factor (i.e. its marginal value product) is the same in the production of either commodity. Eq. (5) states that the reward of the second factor in the production of the second commodity is γ times its reward in the production of the first.

2. The comparative statics of equilibrium outputs

In order now to investigate the response of output of either of the two commodities as the commodity–price ratio changes, it is convenient to work in terms of the variable w representing the ratio of the reward of the second factor to that of the first in the production of the first commodity. Then we can write:

$$\frac{f^1 - R_1 f_1^1}{f_1^1} = w \,, \tag{6}$$

$$\frac{f^2 - R_2 f_1^2}{f_1^2} = \gamma w \,. \tag{7}$$

Given our concavity assumptions we can solve (6) and (7) uniquely [1] to obtain R_1 and R_2 as functions $R_1(w)$ and $R_2(w)$ of w. It is easily seen that $R_i(w)$ is an increasing function of w. Given R, let $w_i(R)$ be the unique solution of $R_i(w) = R$. Then the relevant range of values for w is the interval $[\underline{w}, \overline{w}]$ where $\underline{w}(\overline{w})$ is the smaller (larger) of $w_1(R)$ and $w_2(R)$ (see fig. 1). The value of L corresponding to any given w in this interval is obtained from eq. (3). The equilibrium value (or values) of w corresponding to a given p is (are) obtained from eq. (4).

Let us examine this equation more closely. Let us first rewrite it as:

$$\frac{f_1^1(R_1)}{f_1^2(R_2)} = p \,. \tag{8}$$

[1] If we wish to ensure that a solution exists for all non-negative values of w, we have to assume the Inada conditions:

$$\lim_{R_i \to 0(\infty)} \frac{f^i - R_i f_1^i(R_i)}{f_1^i(R_i)} = 0(\infty) \,.$$

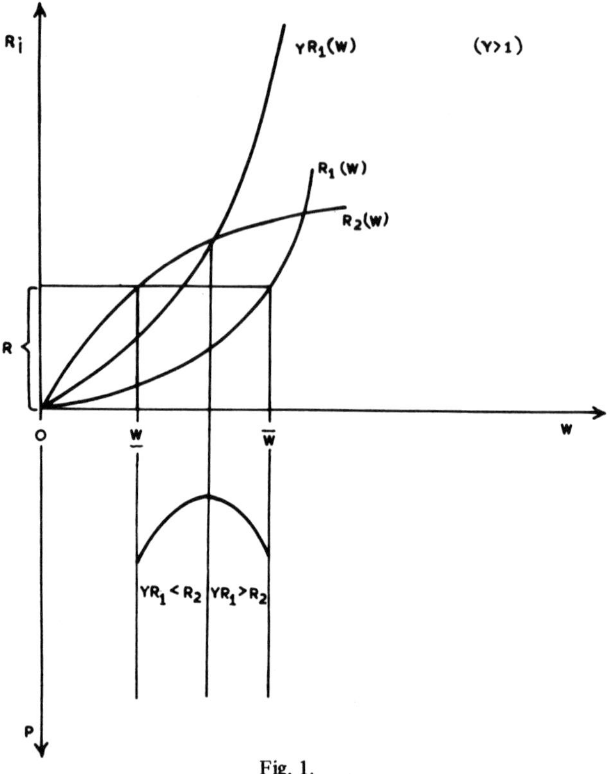

Fig. 1.

The left-hand side of eq. (8) is a function of w alone. Denoting this function by $p(w)$ we get:

$$\frac{p'(w)}{p(w)} = \frac{1}{p(w)} \frac{\mathrm{d}p(w)}{\mathrm{d}w} = \frac{f_{11}^1(R_1)}{f_1^1(R_1)} \frac{\mathrm{d}R_1(w)}{\mathrm{d}w} - \frac{f_{11}^2(R_2)}{f_1^2(R_2)} \cdot \frac{\mathrm{d}R_2(w)}{\mathrm{d}w}$$

where $f_{11}^i(R_i)$ is $[\mathrm{d}^2 f^i(R_i)]/\mathrm{d}R_i^2$.

From (6) and (7) we get:

$$-\frac{f_{11}^1(R_1) f^1(R_1)}{\{f_1^1(R_1)\}^2} \cdot \frac{\mathrm{d}R_1(w)}{\mathrm{d}w} = 1 \ , \tag{9}$$

$$-\frac{f_{11}^2(R_2) f^2(R_2)}{\{f_1^2(R_2)\}^2} \cdot \frac{\mathrm{d}R_2(w)}{\mathrm{d}w} = \gamma \ . \tag{10}$$

Hence

$$\frac{p'(w)}{p(w)} = -\frac{f_1^1(R_1)}{f^1(R_1)} + \frac{f_1^2(R_2)}{f^2(R_2)}$$

$$= -\frac{1}{w+R_1} + \frac{\gamma}{\gamma w + R_2} \qquad \text{[using (6) and (7)]}$$

$$= \frac{(\gamma R_1 - R_2)}{(w+R_1)(\gamma w + R_2)} \; . \tag{11}$$

Eq. (11) points at once to an interesting set of possibilities.

First, if in the relevant interval $[\underline{w}, \overline{w}]$ of values of w, $[\gamma R_1(w) - R_2(w)]$ changes sign, then $p'(w)$ also changes sign, since $w + R_1(w)$ and $\gamma w + R_2(w)$ are both non-negative. In other words, $p(w)$ is not a monotonic function of w. Thus eq. (8) can have more than one value of w in $[\underline{w}, \overline{w}]$ as a solution. This means that the same commodity–price ratio p can be consistent with more than one equilibrium combination of the outputs of the two commodities.

Second, consider two countries with identical production functions and the same type and degree of distortion (i.e. the second factor in the production of the second commodity receives γ times its reward in the production of the first commodity in both countries). Suppose they face the same commodity–price ratio p. If $\gamma R_1(w) - R_2(w)$ changes sign in both countries within the respective interval of values of w, then one country's equilibrium value w could be different from that of the other. In other words, factor price equalisation will fail to take place. It is important to note that this failure could take place, even though there is no factor-intensity reversal in the usual sense: even though $[R_1(w) - R_2(w)]$ has the same sign for all relevant values of w, for both countries, $[\gamma R_1(w) - R_2(w)]$ can still change its sign.[2]

The precise conditions under which such multiple equilibria will arise can be readily derived and related to the conditions defining the nature of output response to price change. To do this, we proceed now to

[2] It should of course be kept in mind that $R_2(w)$ is the factor intensity in the production of the second commodity when the factor price ratio faced by producers of this commodity is γw.

derive first the slope of the production possibility curve, given γ. Using (1), (2), and (3), we get:

$$\frac{\mathrm{d}Q_1}{\mathrm{d}w} = \frac{\mathrm{d}L}{\mathrm{d}w} f^1 + L f_1^1 \frac{\mathrm{d}R_1}{\mathrm{d}w},$$

$$\frac{\mathrm{d}Q_2}{\mathrm{d}w} = -\frac{\mathrm{d}L}{\mathrm{d}w} f^2 + (1-L) f_1^2 \frac{\mathrm{d}R_2}{\mathrm{d}w},$$

$$\frac{\mathrm{d}L}{\mathrm{d}w} = \frac{(R_2-R)(\mathrm{d}R_1/\mathrm{d}w) + (R-R_1)(\mathrm{d}R_1/\mathrm{d}w)}{(R_2-R_1)^2}$$

Hence

$$\frac{\mathrm{d}Q_1}{\mathrm{d}w} = \frac{f^2\left\{(R_2-R)\dfrac{\mathrm{d}R_1}{\mathrm{d}w} + (R-R_1)\dfrac{\mathrm{d}R_2}{\mathrm{d}w}\right\} + f_1^1(R_2-R)(R_2-R_1)\dfrac{\mathrm{d}R_1}{\mathrm{d}w}}{(R_2-R_1)^2}$$

$$= \frac{\{(f^1-R_1f_1^1) + R_2f_1^1\}(R_2-R)\dfrac{\mathrm{d}R_1}{\mathrm{d}w} + f^1(R-R_1)\dfrac{\mathrm{d}R_2}{\mathrm{d}w}}{(R_2-R_1)^2}$$

$$= \frac{f_1^1\left[\left\{\left(\dfrac{f^1-R_1f_1^1}{f_1^1}\right) + R_2\right\}(R_2-R)\dfrac{\mathrm{d}R_1}{\mathrm{d}w} + \dfrac{f^1}{f_1^1}(R-R_1)\dfrac{\mathrm{d}R_2}{\mathrm{d}w}\right]}{(R_2-R_1)^2}$$

$$= \frac{f_1^1\left\{(w+R_2)(R_2-R)\dfrac{\mathrm{d}R_1}{\mathrm{d}w} + (w+R_1)(R-R_1)\dfrac{\mathrm{d}R_2}{\mathrm{d}w}\right\}}{(R_2-R_1)^2} \quad \text{[using (6)]}$$

and

$$\frac{\mathrm{d}Q_2}{\mathrm{d}w} = \frac{f_1^2\left\{(\gamma w+R_2)(R_2-R)\dfrac{\mathrm{d}R_1}{\mathrm{d}w} + (\gamma w+R_1)(R-R_1)\dfrac{\mathrm{d}R_2}{\mathrm{d}w}\right\}}{(R_2-R_1)^2}$$

Now:

$$\frac{\mathrm{d}R_1}{\mathrm{d}w} = \frac{-(f_1^1)^2}{f_{11}^1 f^1} \quad \text{and} \quad \frac{\mathrm{d}R_2}{\mathrm{d}w} = \frac{-(f_1^2)^2\gamma}{f_{11}^2 f^2} \, .$$

Next, let $\sigma(R_i)$ denote the elasticity of substitution of the factors in the production of the ith commodity. It is well known that

$$\sigma(R_i) = -\,\frac{f_1^i(f^i - R_i f_1^i)}{R_1 f^i f_{11}^i} \, .$$

Using (6) and (7) therefore we can write:

$$\frac{\mathrm{d}Q_1}{\mathrm{d}w} = \frac{f_1^1\{(w+R_2)(R_2-R)\sigma_1 R_1 + (w+R_1)(R-R_1)\sigma_2 R_2\}}{w(R_2-R_1)^2} \tag{12}$$

$$\frac{\mathrm{d}Q_2}{\mathrm{d}w} = \frac{-f_1^2\{(\gamma w+R_2)(R_2-R)\sigma_1 R_1 + (\gamma w+R_1)(R-R_1)\sigma_2 R_2\}}{w(R_2-R_1)^2} \tag{13}$$

Hence

$$\frac{\mathrm{d}Q_1}{\mathrm{d}Q_2} = -\,\frac{f_1^1}{f_1^2}\left\{\frac{(w+R_2)(R_2-R)\sigma_1 R_1 + (w+R_1)(R-R_1)\sigma_2 R_2}{(\gamma w+R_2)(R_2-R)\sigma_1 R_1 + (\gamma w+R_1)(R-R_1)\sigma_2 R_2}\right\}$$

$$= -p\left\{\frac{(w+R_2)(R_2-R)\sigma_1 R_1 + (w+R_1)(R-R_1)\sigma_2 R_2}{(\gamma w+R_2)(R_2-R)\sigma_1 R_1 + (\gamma w+R_1)(R-R_1)\sigma_2 R_2}\right\} . \tag{14}$$

It is seen from (14) that if there is no distortion, i.e. if $\gamma = 1$, then $\mathrm{d}Q_1/\mathrm{d}Q_2 = -p$, showing that the domestic rate of transformation $(-\mathrm{d}Q_1/\mathrm{d}Q_2)$ equals the commodity–price ratio p. However, if $\gamma \neq 1$, we see from (14) that:

$$p - \left(-\frac{\mathrm{d}Q_1}{\mathrm{d}Q_2}\right)$$

$$= p(\gamma - 1)w\left\{\frac{(R_2 - R)\sigma_1 R_1 + (R-R_1)\sigma_2 R_2}{(\gamma w+R_2)(R_2-R)\sigma_1 R_1 + (\gamma w+R_1)(R-R_1)\sigma_2 R_2}\right\}. \tag{14a}$$

The expression in the square parentheses is always positive; hence $p \gtreqless -\mathrm{d}Q_1/\mathrm{d}Q_2$ according as $\gamma \gtreqless 1$. This means that the commodity–price ratio, p, will not equal and will indeed exceed (fall short of) the domestic rate of transformation $(-\mathrm{d}Q_1/\mathrm{d}Q_2)$ according as the degree of distortion in the factor price ratio faced by the producers of the second commodity as compared to those of the first, i.e. γ, exceeds (falls short of) unity.

Note further that, in general, the degree of divergence between the commodity–price ratio and the marginal rate of transformation can be expected to vary with the equilibrium point on the production possibility curve at which this divergence is being measured (although this is not inevitable).[3] It is also clear that this variation in the degree of divergence can obtain under CES production functions (where σ_1 and σ_2 are constant) and even under Cobb–Douglas production functions (where $\sigma_1 = \sigma_2 = 1$). Furthermore, the possibility of multiple equilibria which we have already noted, also implies that, corresponding to the *same* commodity–price ratio, there could be different divergences between the price ratio and the marginal rate of transformation at alternative equilibirum points on the production possibility curve.

We are now in a position to examine the response of the equilibirum output Q_2 of the second commodity to change in the international price ratio p. From (13), it is clear that $\mathrm{d}Q_2/\mathrm{d}w \gtreqless 0$ according as $R_2(w) \gtreqless R_1(w)$. By definition (except in the trivial case where $\underline{\mathbf{w}} = \overline{w}$, either $R_2(w) > R_1(w)$ or $R_2(w) < R_1(w)$ for all w in $[\underline{\mathbf{w}}, \overline{w}]$. Since the interval $[\underline{\mathbf{w}}, \overline{w}]$ is determined uniquely once the aggregate factor endowment is known, the sign of $\mathrm{d}Q_2/\mathrm{d}w$ is also uniquely determined. To get the response of Q_2 with respect to p we have to evaluate $\mathrm{d}Q_2/\mathrm{d}p = (\mathrm{d}Q_2/\mathrm{d}w) \cdot (\mathrm{d}w/\mathrm{d}p)$. Remember also that $\mathrm{d}w/\mathrm{d}p$ will have the same sign as $p'(w)$ in eq. (11); and that $p'(w) \gtreqless 0$ according as $[\gamma R_1 - R_2] \gtreqless 0$. Using these arguments, we can now proceed to analyse the following six cases (excluding the degenerate case of $\underline{\mathbf{w}} = \overline{w}$):

Case I: $R_1(w) > R_2(w)$ and $\gamma R_1(w) > R_2(w)$ for all w in $[\underline{\mathbf{w}}, \overline{w}]$. Given $R_1(w) > R_2(w)$, this case will arise when either $\gamma \geq 1$ or when γ is less than unity but not sufficiently less than unity to make $\gamma R_1(w)$

[3] This can be seen readily by dividing (14a) on both sides by 'p', which yields the formula for $-p/(\mathrm{d}Q_1/\mathrm{d}Q_2)$, the relative degree of divergence. Note also that, except for the multiple-equilibrium possibility discussed in the text, any movement along the production possibility curve in equilibrium will require a change in the commodity–price ratio.

less than $R_2(w)$ for some w in $[\underline{w}, \overline{w}]$. In this case, $dQ_2/dw > 0$ and assuming incomplete specialisation $dw/dp > 0$. Hence $dQ_2/dp > 0$. Thus, if we compare the equilibrium output Q_2 corresponding to two different international price ratios, the one associated with the higher price of the second commodity in terms of the first will be larger. Thus the (comparative static) response of equilibrium output to a price change is 'normal'.

Case II: $R_1(w) < R_2(w)$ *and* $\gamma R_1(w) < R_2(w)$ for all w in $[\underline{w}, \overline{w}]$. Given $R_1(w) < R_2(w)$, this case will arise when either $\gamma \leq 1$ or when γ is greater than unity but not sufficiently greater to make $\gamma R_1(w)$ exceed $R_2(w)$ for some w in $[\underline{w}, \overline{w}]$. In this case $dQ_2/dw < 0$ and again assuming incomplete specialisation $dw/dp < 0$. Hence $dQ_2/dp > 0$. Thus the output response is again 'normal'.

Case III: $R_1(w) > R_2(w)$ but $\gamma R_1(w) < R_2(w)$ for all w in $[\underline{w}, \overline{w}]$. Given $R_1(w) > R_2(w)$ this can happen only when γ is sufficiently less than unity. In this case $dQ_2/dw > 0$ and, assuming incomplete specialisation, $dw/dp < 0$. Hence $dQ_2/dp < 0$. Thus if we compare the equilibrium outputs corresponding to two different international prices for the second commodity in terms of the first, then the output corresponding to a *higher* price will be *smaller*. This is a case of 'perverse' comparative-static response.

Case IV: $R_1(w) < R_2(w)$ but $\gamma R_1(w) > R_2(w)$ for all w in $[\underline{w}, \overline{w}]$. Given $R_1(w) < R_2(w)$, this can arise only when γ is sufficiently greater than unity. In this case also the output response in a comparative-static sense is 'perverse'.

Case V: $R_1(w) > R_2(w)$ but $\gamma R_1(w) - R_2(w)$ changes sign at one or more w in $[\underline{w}, \overline{w}]$. We saw earlier than when $\gamma R_1(w) - R_2(w)$ changes sign in $[\underline{w}, \overline{w}]$, the same international price ratio p *may* correspond to more than one equilibrium value for w and hence for the outputs Q_1 and Q_2. Thus the derivative dw/dp will be different depending on the particular equilibrium value of w at which it is evaluated. Hence the sign of dQ_2/dp will depend on the particular equilibrium point at which it is evaluated. It is easy to see that if we order the equilibrium points in increasing order of the value of Q_2 then dQ_2/dp will alternate in sign as we move from one equilibrium point to the next. Thus if at one equilibrium point the comparative static response is 'normal', then at the next it will be 'perverse'.

Case VI: $R_1(w) < R_2(w)$ but $\gamma R_1(w) - R_2(w)$ changes sign at one or more w in $[\underline{\mathbf{w}}, \bar{w}]$. Here again the possibility of multiple equilibria arises and the conclusions in Case V apply to this case also.

We may finally note that these results can be readily translated into, and derived via, the familiar Lerner technique as revived by Findlay and Grubert (1959). Thus, for example, the central result of our analysis, which demonstrates the possibility of multiple w-values corresponding to a single p-value, can be illustrated in terms of the Lerner technique as follows.

In fig. 2, the commodity–price ratio involves an exchange of $\bar{1}$ for $\bar{2}$ units of the two commodities. Then, it is easy to see that, consistent with commodity 1 remaining intensive in the use of factor 2 in two alternative equilibria (i.e. OM^2 is steeper than OM^1, and so is ON^2 steeper than ON^1), two alternative values of the factor price ratio are possible when the commodity–price ratio is fixed at an exchange of $\bar{1}$ for $\bar{2}$ units of the two commodities. These two alternative factor price ratios are: [AC, AB] and [DF, DE] (such that the wage of factor 2 in commodity 2 is higher in each case by the same multiplicative factor than in commodity 1).

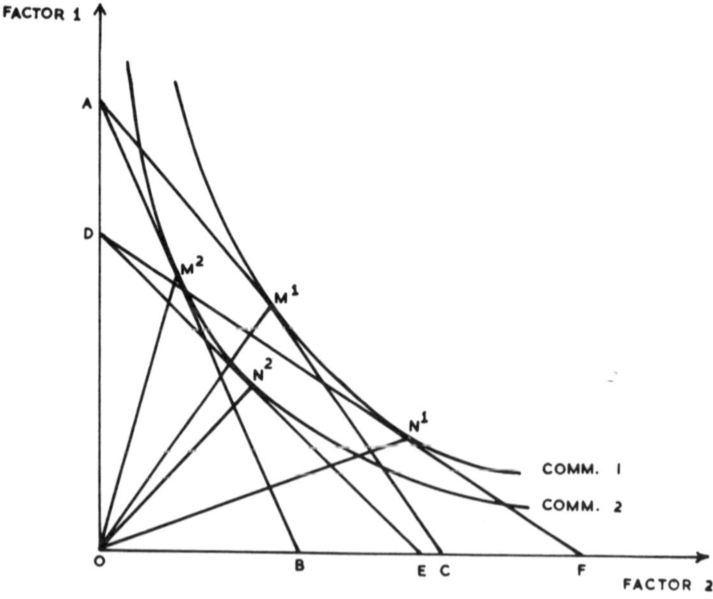

Fig. 2.

3. Relationship of output response to shape of the production possibility curve

The possibility of 'perverse' production response to change in the commodity–price ratio, in the presence of the wage differential, raises in turn the question as to whether the 'perverse' response will arise if and only if the production possibility curve is convex to the origin.

Such an inference is implicit in the earlier literature (Bhagwati and Ramaswami, 1963; Hagen, 1958), in the way the diagrams are drawn, for example, to show that the output of a commodity increases with its relative price when the production possibility curve is concave to the origin. However, such an inference is logically valid only when there is no wage differential. In the absence of such a differential the commodity–price ratio will be tangential to the production possibility curve and hence the output response to price change depends entirely on the curvature of this curve. But, once the differential is present, the commodity–price ratio no longer equals the domestic rate of transformation and hence there is no *a priori* reason to expect any necessary connection between output response and the curvature of the production possibility curve. Our numerical example in the Appendix does in fact show that there is no such connection. However, it is nevertheless of interest to derive analytically the curvature of the production possibility curve. To this we now turn. We showed (eq. (14)) that:

$$\frac{\mathrm{d}Q_1}{\mathrm{d}Q_2} = -\frac{f_1^1}{f_1^2}\left[\frac{(w+R_2)(R_2-R)\sigma_1 R_1+(w+R_1)(R-R_1)\sigma_2 R_2}{(\gamma w+R_2)(R_2-R)\sigma_1 R_1+(\gamma w+R_1)(R-R_1)\sigma_2 R_2}\right]$$

We can then derive $\mathrm{d}^2 Q_1/\mathrm{d}Q_2^2$ by using the relation $\mathrm{d}^2 Q_1/\mathrm{d}Q_2^2 = \mathrm{d}[\mathrm{d}Q_1/\mathrm{d}Q_2]/\mathrm{d}w.\ \mathrm{d}w/\mathrm{d}Q_2$ and $\mathrm{d}w/\mathrm{d}Q_2 = 1/(\mathrm{d}Q_2/\mathrm{d}w)$. We have already derived the expression for $\mathrm{d}Q_2/\mathrm{d}w$ in eq. (13). Let us denote the numerator of the detailed expression for $\mathrm{d}Q_1/\mathrm{d}Q_2$, with the negative sign, by $N(w)$ and the denominator by $D(w)$. Then

$$\frac{\mathrm{d}}{\mathrm{d}w}\frac{\mathrm{d}Q_1}{\mathrm{d}Q_2} = \frac{D(w)\dfrac{\mathrm{d}N}{\mathrm{d}w} - N(w)\dfrac{\mathrm{d}D}{\mathrm{d}w}}{D^2}\ .$$

Now, using the relations $\mathrm{d}R_i/\mathrm{d}w = \sigma_i R_i/w$, we can show that:

$$\frac{\mathrm{d}N}{\mathrm{d}w} = -\,[(w+R_2)(R_2-R)\,\sigma_1 R_1 + (w+R_1)(R-R_1)\sigma_2 R_2]$$

$$\times \frac{f_1^1}{w}\left[\frac{\sigma_1 R_1 f_{11}^1}{f_1^1} + (\sigma_1+\sigma_2)\right] - f_1^1\Big[(R_2-R)\sigma_1 R_1 + (R-R_1)\,\sigma_2 R_2$$

$$+ \frac{\sigma_1\sigma_2}{w}\,(R_2-R_1)(R_1R_2-wR)$$

$$+ R_1(w+R_2)(R_2-R)\,\frac{\mathrm{d}\sigma_1}{\mathrm{d}w} + R_2(w+R_1)(R-R_1)\,\frac{\mathrm{d}\sigma_2}{\mathrm{d}w}\Big]\,.$$

Next, we can deduce that:

$$\frac{\mathrm{d}D}{\mathrm{d}w} = [(\gamma w+R_2)(R_2-R)\sigma_1 R_1 + (\gamma w+R_1)(R-R_1)\,\sigma_2 R_2\,]$$

$$\times\,\frac{f_1^2}{w}\left[\frac{f_{11}^2\sigma_2 R_2}{f_1^2} + \sigma_1+\sigma_2\right] + f_1^2\Big[\gamma\{(R_2-R)\sigma_1 R_1 + (R-R_1)\,\sigma_2 R_2\}$$

$$+\frac{\sigma_1\sigma_2(R_2-R_1)}{w}\,(R_1R_2-wR) + R_1(\gamma w+R_2)(R_2-R)\,\frac{\mathrm{d}\sigma_1}{\mathrm{d}w}$$

$$+R_2(\gamma w+R_1)(R-R_1)\,\frac{\mathrm{d}\sigma_2}{\mathrm{d}w}\Big]\,.$$

Hence

$$D\,\frac{\mathrm{d}N}{\mathrm{d}w} - N\,\frac{\mathrm{d}D}{\mathrm{d}w} = \frac{DN}{w}\left[\frac{-w}{w+R_1} + \frac{\gamma w}{\gamma w+R_2}\right] + (\gamma-1)\,R_1R_2 f_1^1 f_1^2$$

$$\times\,\{\sigma_1(R_2-R) + \sigma_2(R-R_1)\}\{(R_2-R)\sigma_1 R_1 + (R-R_1)\,\sigma_2 R_2$$

$$-\,R\sigma_1\sigma_2(R_2-R_1)\} - (\gamma-1)\,f_1^1 f_1^2$$

$$\times \{(R_2-R)\sigma_1 R_1 + (R-R_1)\sigma_2 R_2\}\, \sigma_1 \sigma_2 R_1 R_2 (R_2-R_1)$$

$$-(\gamma-1)(R_2-R_1)\, w(R-R_1)(R_2-R)$$

$$\times R_1 R_2 f_1^2 f_1^1 \left\{\sigma_2 \frac{\mathrm{d}\sigma_1}{\mathrm{d}w} - \sigma_1 \frac{\mathrm{d}\sigma_2}{\mathrm{d}w}\right\} .$$

Hence [using $\dfrac{\mathrm{d}Q_2}{\mathrm{d}w} = \dfrac{-D}{w(R_2-R_1)^2}$] we get :

$$\frac{\mathrm{d}^2 Q_1}{\mathrm{d}Q_2^2} = \frac{-w(R_2-R_1)^2}{D^2} \Bigg[\frac{N(\gamma R_1 - R_2)}{(w+R_1)(\gamma w + R_2)} + \frac{(\gamma-1)R_1 R_2 f_1^1 f_1^2}{D}$$

$$\times \Big\{ \{(R_2-R)\sigma_1 R_1 + (R-R_1)\sigma_2 R_2 - R\sigma_1\sigma_2(R_2-R_1)\}$$

$$\times \{\sigma_1(R_2-R) + \sigma_2(R-R_1)\}$$

$$-\sigma_1\sigma_2(R_2-R_1)\{(R_2-R)\sigma_1 R_1 + (R-R_1)\sigma_2 R_2\}$$

$$-w(R_2-R_1)(R_2-R)(R-R_1)\left\{\sigma_2 \frac{\mathrm{d}\sigma_1}{\mathrm{d}w} - \sigma_1 \frac{\mathrm{d}\sigma_2}{\mathrm{d}w}\right\}\Big\}\Bigg] \qquad (15)$$

It should be obvious from (15) that it is difficult in general to determine the sign of $\mathrm{d}^2 Q_1/\mathrm{d}Q_2^2$. One has therefore to consider special cases.

(1) If there is no differential (i.e. $\gamma = 1$), then $\mathrm{d}^2 Q_1/\mathrm{d}Q_2^2 < 0$ since the lengthy right-hand-side term in the bracket in (15) cancels out and $(R_1 - R_2)N$ is always positive. Thus we get the standard result that the production possibility curve is concave to the origin.

(2) Where, however, $\gamma \neq 1$, we can show that the production possibility curve may have *both* convex and concave stretches. We can do this by evaluating $\mathrm{d}^2 Q_1/\mathrm{d}Q_2^2$ at two extreme points: complete speciali-

sation in Q_1 (so that $R_1 = R$) and in Q_2 (so that $R_2 = R$), and showing that the production possibility curve is concave at one end and convex at the other. Assuming that $\mathrm{d}\sigma_i/\mathrm{d}w$ is well-behaved for $i = 1, 2$, we can see from (15) that, quite generally:

$$\frac{\mathrm{d}^2 Q_1}{\mathrm{d}Q_2^2} \text{ (given } R_1 = R) = \frac{-w(R_2 - R)^2}{D^2}$$

$$\left[\frac{N(\gamma R - R_2)}{(w+R)(\gamma w + R_2)} + \frac{(\gamma-1)R_2 f_1^1 f_1^2 (R_2 - R)^2 \sigma_1^2 R^2 (1-2\sigma_2)}{D}\right]$$

$$\frac{\mathrm{d}^2 Q_1}{\mathrm{d}Q_2^2} \text{ (given } R_2 = R) = \frac{-w(R - R_1)^2}{D^2}$$

$$\left[\frac{N(\gamma R_1 - R)}{(w+R_1)(\gamma w + R_1)} + \frac{(\gamma-1)R_1 f_1^1 f_1^2 (R - R_1)^2 \sigma_2^2 R^2 (1-2\sigma_1)}{D}\right]$$

Suppose now that $R_1(w) > R_2(w)$ for all w in $[\underline{w}, \overline{w}]$. Then $R_1(\underline{w}) = R = R_2(\overline{w})$ and $R_1(w) > R > R_2(w)$ for all w in $(\underline{w}, \overline{w})$. In this case, it follows that $N > 0$ and $D < 0$. Assume further the specific values: $\gamma > 1$ and $\sigma_1(\overline{w}) \geq \frac{1}{2}$. Then clearly $\mathrm{d}^2 Q_1/\mathrm{d}Q_2^2 < 0$ when $R_2 = R$ (i.e. $w = \overline{w}$). If it so happens that when $R_1 = R$ (i.e. $w = \underline{w}$), $\gamma R < R_2(\overline{w})$ and $\sigma_2(\underline{w}) \leq \frac{1}{2}$, then $\mathrm{d}^2 Q_1/\mathrm{d}Q_2^2 > 0$. Thus the production possibility curve will be convex in the neighbourhood of one specialisation point and concave in the neighbourhood of the other.

(3) We may finally consider the case where $\sigma_1 = \sigma_2$ equals a constant, showing that this can lead to a production possibility curve which is smoothly convex (to the origin) throughout.[4] In this case of CES production functions, with identical elasticities for both industries, (15) reduces to:

$$\frac{\mathrm{d}^2 Q_1}{\mathrm{d}Q_2^2} = \frac{-w(R_2 - R_1)^2}{D^2}$$

$$\left[\frac{N(\gamma R_1 - R_2)}{(w+R_1)(\gamma w + R_2)} + \frac{\sigma^2(\gamma-1)R_1 R_2 R (R_2 - R_1)^2 f_1^1 f_1^2 (1-2\sigma)}{D}\right]$$

[4] Kemp and Herberg have independently arrived at this conclusion for CES production functions.

If we write $f^i = [\alpha_i R_i^{-\epsilon} + (1-\alpha_i)]^{-1/\epsilon}$ (where $\sigma = 1/(\epsilon+1)$) then we get $R_1(w) = (\alpha_1/(1-\alpha_1))^\sigma w^\sigma$ and $R_2(w) = (\gamma\alpha_2/(1-\alpha_2))^\sigma w^\sigma$. This means that $R_2 = \eta R_1$ where $\eta = (\beta\gamma)^\sigma$, and $\beta = (\alpha_2/(1-\alpha_2))/(\alpha_1/(1-\alpha_1))$. Since $\sigma > 0$, $\eta \gtreqless 1$ according as $\beta\gamma \gtreqless 1$. It can be shown that $N = -f_1^1(\eta-1)\,\sigma R_1(wR + \eta R_1^2)$ and $D = f_1^2(\eta-1)\,\sigma R_1(\gamma wR + \eta R_1^2)$. Substituting these into the expression for $\mathrm{d}^2Q_1/\mathrm{d}Q_2^2$ we get:

$$\frac{\mathrm{d}^2Q_1}{\mathrm{d}Q_2^2} = \frac{-wR_1^4(\eta-1)^3 f_1^1}{D^2} \tag{16}$$

$$\times\left[\frac{(\eta-\gamma)(wR+\eta R_1^2)}{(w+R_1)(\gamma w+\eta R_1)} + \frac{(\gamma-1)(1-2\sigma)\eta RR_1}{(\gamma wR+\eta R_1^2)}\right].$$

It is clear from (16) that if $\alpha_1 = \alpha_2$ and $\frac{1}{2} \leq \sigma \leq 1$ (i.e. when $\beta = 1$), $\mathrm{d}^2Q_1/\mathrm{d}Q_2^2 > 0$ for all $\gamma \neq 1$. The reason is that, in this case, either $1 > \eta > \gamma$ or $\gamma > \eta > 1$. Thus the production possibility curve is convex throughout.

APPENDIX: a numerical example

The following numerical example demonstrates the possibilities of (a) multiple equilibria corresponding to a given commodity–price ratio, (b) perverse comparative–static response to changes in this price ratio and (c) 'normal' response being associated with 'perverse' curvature of the production possibility curve.

Let $f^1 = [\frac{1}{2} R_1^{-1} + \frac{1}{2}]^{-1}$ and $f^2 = [\frac{1}{9} R_2^{\frac{1}{2}} + \frac{8}{9}]^2$. Let $\gamma = 8$ and $R = 4$. It is easy to deduce, using eqs. (6) and (7), that $R_1(w) = w^{\frac{1}{2}}$, $R_2(w) = w^2$, $\underline{\mathbf{w}} = 2$ and $\overline{w} = 16$. Hence $[\gamma R_1(w) - R_2(w)] = 8w^{\frac{1}{2}} - w^2$ and thus is positive in $\underline{\mathbf{w}} = 2 \leq w < 4$, zero when $w = 4$ and negative in $4 < w \leq 16 = \overline{w}$. Of course $R_2(w) > R_1(w)$ for all w in (2, 16). The resulting production possibility curve is presented in fig. 3. This curve is convex throughout, as can be verified also by algebraic analysis.

In fig. 4, the function $p(w)$ is plotted. As was proved earlier (recall eq. (11)) and as is evident from the figure, $p(w)$ increases with w when $\gamma R_1(w) > R_2(w)$, i.e. when w is in the interval (2, 4) and decreases as w increases when $\gamma R_1(w) < R_2(w)$, i.e. when w is in the interval

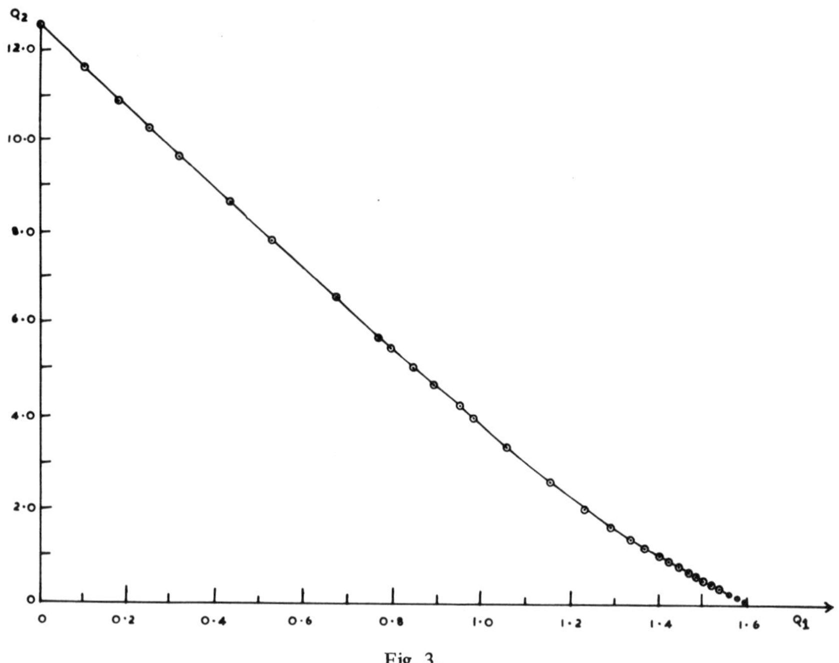
Q2
12·0
10·0
8·0
6·0
4·0
2·0
0
0
0·2
0·4
0·6
0·8
1·0
1·2
1·4
1·6
Q1

Fig. 3.

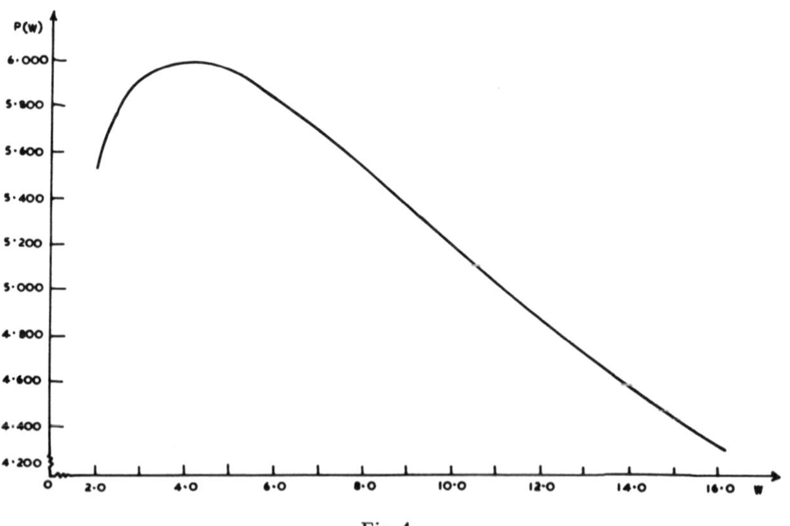
P(W)
6·000
5·800
5·600
5·400
5·200
5·000
4·800
4·600
4·400
4·200
0
2·0
4·0
6·0
8·0
10·0
12·0
14·0
16·0
W

Fig. 4.

(4, 16). Thus $p(w)$ starts from a value of about 5.56 when $w = 2$, reaches a maximum of 6 when $w = 4$, and declines steadily to a value of 4.32 when $w = 16$. Thus it follows that if the commodity–price ratio happens to be anywhere in the range $5.56 \leq p < 6$, there are *two* equilibrium values of w corresponding to *each* such p, one in the interval (2, 4) and the other in the interval (4, 7.81). If either $4.32 \leq p < 5.56$ or $p = 6$, there is one and only one equilibrium value of w.

Next, note that with $R_2(w) > R_1(w)$ for all w in (2, 16), $dQ_2/dw < 0$. Suppose we now increase p from $p = 4.32$ upto $p = 5.56$. Then the equilibrium value of w decreases steadily from $w = 16$ to $w = 7.81$ (approximately) and Q_2 increases steadily from $Q_2 = 0$ to $Q_2 = 0.66$ (approximately). Thus the response is 'normal', i.e. the equilibrium output of the second commodity is larger when its relative price is higher, even though the production possibility curve is convex to the origin.

References

Bhagwati, J. and V.K.Ramaswami, 1963, Domestic distortions, tariffs and the theory of optimum subsidy, J. Political Economy 71, 44–50.

Findlay, R. and H.Grubert, 1959, Factor intensities, technological progress and the terms of trade, Oxford Economic Papers 11, 111–121.

Fishlow, A. and P.David, 1961, Optimal resource allocation in an imperfect market setting, J. Political Economy 69, 529–546.

Hagen, E., 1958, An economic justification of protectionism, Quart. J. Economics 72, 496–514.

Johnson, H., 1966, Factor market distortions and the shape of the transformation curve, Econometrica 34, 686–708.

On Reanalyzing the Harris-Todaro Model: Policy Rankings in the Case of Sector-Specific Sticky Wages

By Jagdish N. Bhagwati and T. N. Srinivasan*

In a brilliant and pioneering paper, John Harris and Michael Todaro introduced a model with two sectors, manufacturing (urban) and agriculture (rural), a (sticky) minimum wage in manufacturing and consequent unemployment. They also introduced a labor allocation mechanism under which, instead of the usual equalization of *actual* wages, the actual rural wage was equated with the expected urban wage; the latter was defined as the (sticky) minimum wage weighted by the rate of employment, so that, unlike in the standard rigid-wage models of trade theory (for example, Gottfried Haberler, Bhagwati, Harry Johnson, Louis Lefeber, and Richard Brecher), the unemployment resulting from the minimum wage is to be construed as *specific* to the urban sector.

In the context of this model, Harris and Todaro analyze two policies: 1) a wage subsidy policy in the manufacturing sector (alone); and 2) a labor-mobility restriction policy. They argue that the former, as well as the latter, can be used to improve welfare, defined as a function of available goods in the usual way; but that, to attain the optimal first best solution, *both* policies are necessary. The authors express regret at the necessity of using migration restrictions in view of the "... ethical issues involved in such a restriction of individual choice and the complexity and arbitrariness of administration" and end their exercise with the sentiment that:

> All of the above suggests that altering the minimum wage may avoid the problems of taxation [to finance the wage subsidy in manufacturing], administration, and interference with individual mobility attendant to the policy package just discussed. Income and wage policies designed to narrow the rural-urban wage gap have been suggested by D. P. Ghai, and Tanzania has formally adopted such a policy along with migration restriction. In the final analysis, however, the basic issue at stake is really one of political feasibility and it is not at all clear that an incomes policy is any more feasible than the alternatives. [p. 138]

We argue in this paper that this dilemma is unnecessary *in principle*, the reasons being that:

1) a *uniform* wage subsidy, regardless of the sector of employment, will yield the optimal, first best solution;

2) equivalently, a wage subsidy in manufacturing *plus* a production subsidy to agriculture will yield the optimal, first best solution;

3) in either case, no resort to "ethical compromises" in the direction of sanctioning migration restrictions will be necessary;

4) proposition 2) implies that the authors' argument that the traditional prescription to use shadow pricing of labor (i.e., a wage subsidy in employment) is inapplicable to their model is not correct and their conclusion stems from equating this prescription with the prescription that the wage subsidy be given for employment in the manufacturing sector alone; and

5) proposition 2) also implies that the authors' contention that *two* policies are necessary to attain the first best optimum is not valid *unless* one construes a general wage subsidy to constitute *two* policies when there are *two* sectors employing labor.

* Professors of economics, Massachusetts Institute of Technology and the Indian Statistical Institute, respectively. The paper was written while Srinivasan was visiting professor of economics at M.I.T. and the research underlying it has been supported by the National Science Foundation. The paper has profited from seminars at Minnesota, Stanford, and Harvard. Thanks are due to David McClain for computational assistance, and to Peter Diamond, John Harris, John Chipman, Anne Krueger, and a referee for helpful comments.

In demonstrating these propositions, we should note that the Harris-Todaro formal model has a demand function which is not related to the utility function in their (later) welfare analysis, so that their analytical system is open to the possibility of being overdetermined. We therefore rewrite their model, with the utility function explicitly incorporated into the model, eliminating the "additional" demand equation of Harris and Todaro.

Since the basic problems with the Harris-Todaro analysis relate to their first best optimal-policy characterization, we begin with analysis of the first best, optimal policy in the model.[1] However, we also take the opportunity to extend the analysis in Section II to two second best policy measures: wage subsidy in manufacturing and production subsidy to agriculture; both policies can be shown to be equivalent, singly or in combination, to all other conceivable policy interventions in the model. However, rather than prove these results with rigor—we have done this elsewhere in a companion paper—we produce numerical examples in the Appendix to establish and illustrate the least intuitive among them.

I. The Model

We may now restate the Harris-Todaro model. First, there are two production functions:

$$X_A \leqq f_A(L_A) \tag{1}$$

$$X_M \leqq f_M(L_M) \tag{2}$$

where X_A and X_M are the output levels of agriculture (rural sector) and manufactures (urban sector), respectively, and L_A, L_M are the labor-input levels in the two sectors. The functions are strictly concave. The labor supply is fixed and assumed to be unity by choice of units:

$$L_A + L_M \leqq 1 \tag{3}$$

We then have a standard, social utility function:

$$U = U(X_A, X_M) \tag{4}$$

[1] An error of detail is picked up later in this paper.

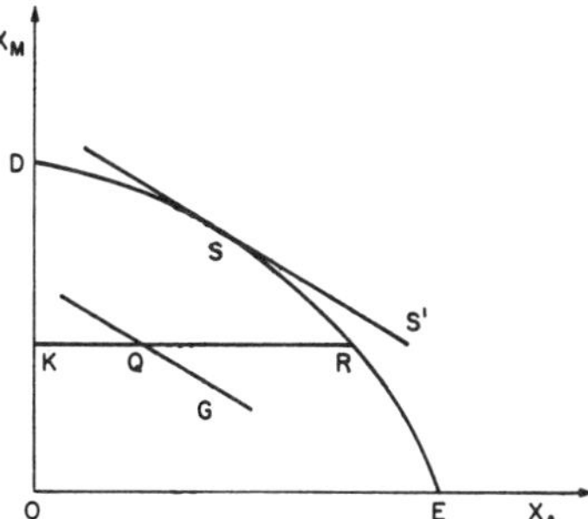

DE is the production possibility curve when wage rigidity is absent. With the wage rigidity constraint, equilibrium production under *laissez-faire* can lie only along *RK* instead of *RD*, because equilibrium on *RD* (excluding *R*), as at *S*, implies wage in manufacturing *below* the minimum wage. *Q* is the *laissez-faire* production point under price-ratio *QG* under the wage constraint. For simplicity, the diagram depicts the price-ratio at *S* and *Q* to be identical, implying *either* a linear utility function for a closed economy *or* a "small," open economy with unchanging terms of trade. The formal analysis in the text is not restricted to linear utility functions; but it does *not* apply, without amendment, to a "large" open economy with monopoly power in trade.

FIGURE 1

where U is concave with positive marginal utilities for finite $[X_A, X_M]$.

For a fully competitive economy, the resulting equilibrium can be shown in Figure 1 at S where the production possibility curve DE is tangent to SS' and

$$\frac{U_1}{U_2} = \frac{f'_M}{f'_A} \tag{5}$$

with U_1/U_2 equal to the negative of the slope of SS', and U_1 and U_2 representing the partial derivatives of U with respect to X_A and X_M, respectively.

But we now assume that the wage in manufacturing is fixed as a minimum, so that for this competitive economy, we must have:

$$f'_M(L_M) = \bar{w} \tag{6}$$

If we then assume that this constraint is

binding at S, the first best optimal solution is inadmissible and unemployment ensues.[2] The system could then have been characterized nonetheless by the equalization of *actual* wages in the two sectors. Harris and Todaro, however, chose to rewrite the wage-equalization equation in terms of the *expected* wage in manufacturing, defined as the actual wage there weighted by the rate of employment, so that the critical equilibrium conditions in their model, relevant for our analysis, are

$$f'_M = \bar{w} \tag{7}$$

$$\frac{U_1}{U_2} f'_A = \bar{w} \frac{L_M}{1 - L_A} \tag{8}$$

where the total labor force is assumed to be one by choice of units and where consumption and production price of the agricultural good is identical and equal to U_1/U_2.

With $\bar{w}$ specified, (7) and (8) can be solved for L_M and L_A, using the two production functions. The *laissez-faire* equilibrium, with unemployment ($L_M < 1 - L_A$), will then lie in Figure 1 along RK (where X_M and hence L_M are fixed at the value that makes $f_M = \bar{w}$) at Q. (It may be emphasized that the *laissez-faire* equilibrium would so lie along RK even if actual wages were equalized in the two sectors: nothing critical to our interests hangs on the *expected*-wage wrinkle in the Harris-Todaro analysis.)

As for the available policy instruments (that use the price mechanism as distinct from direct allocation mechanisms) in this model, we note now the following:

(i) *laissez-faire*;
(ii) wage subsidy in manufacturing;
(iii) production subsidy to agriculture.

The structure of the model also implies the following equivalences:

(iv) a wage subsidy in agriculture is equal to policy (iii);[3]
(v) a uniform wage subsidy in all employment is a combination of policies (ii) and (iii);
(vi) for a closed economy, a consumption tax-cum-subsidy is equivalent to policy (iii), i.e., a production tax-cum-subsidy;[4]
(vii) for an open economy, a tariff (trade subsidy) policy would, as usual, be equivalent to policy (iii), i.e., a production tax-cum-subsidy policy, *plus* a consumption tax-cum-subsidy policy.[5]

One final point may be noted. Our analysis does *not* explicitly distinguish between a

[2] Needless to say, unemployment is inevitable only if we assume that the unemployed labor will not prefer certain employment at a lower wage in the agricultural sector to uncertain employment in the manufacturing sector at a higher wage. One has to contemplate therefore *either* a randomized process by which everyone in the manufacturing labor force gets an equal crack at the manufacturing jobs, so that *each* on the average gets the expected wage *or* that the unemployed workers return to employment in the agricultural sector. In the latter case, we could wind up with the wage differential, full employment model which has already been extensively analyzed in trade-theoretic literature.

[3] We are assuming, in writing equation (7), that the producer and consumer prices of the manufacturing good (in terms of any arbitrary unit of account) are the same, i.e., in effect, the producers of the manufacturing good are paying the workers the wage $\bar{w}$ in kind. Hence, the effect of a production subsidy to manufacturing is essentially not to affect any real decisions, as those made *via* equations (7) and (8), but merely to increase each commodity price in terms of the (arbitrary) unit of account. However, if we were to assume instead that the producer and consumer prices of the manufacturing good could be made to differ by policy, then the worker in manufacturing would earn the value of his marginal product at the producer price and then, *qua* consumer, must have enough income (in terms of the unit of account) to buy $\bar{w}$ units of the manufacturing good. In that case, a wage subsidy policy to manufacturing would be equivalent to a production subsidy policy to manufacturing, as is the case in the agricultural sector. Thus note that, if we did shift to the latter, alternative assumption on wage payment in the manufacturing sector, then the analysis would not change but our policy equivalences would. In particular, the first best optimal policy mix would then include: a uniform production subsidy to both sectors; and a production subsidy in manufacturing and a wage subsidy in agriculture.

[4] Thus, let $\pi_p = \bar{w}L_M/(1-L_A)f_A'$ be the production price of the agricultural good and $\pi_c = U_1[X_A, X_M]/U_2[X_A, X_M]$ be the consumption price of the agricultural good. The production tax-cum-subsidy is then $(\pi_p - \pi_c)/\pi_c$; and the consumption tax-cum-subsidy is $(\pi_c - \pi_p)/\pi_p$.

[5] Thus, if π^* is the international price of the (importable) agricultural good, a tariff at *ad valorem* rate t would imply: $\pi^*(1+t) = \pi_p = \pi_c$.

closed and an open economy. Since it relates essentially to the *production* equilibrium in the economy, and since it allows the utility function to be linear or non-linear, it can be interpreted as applying *either* to a closed economy *or* to an open economy with given terms of trade.[6]

II. Optimal Policy Intervention

It is easy to see that the first best optimum can be reached in this model by the use of a uniform wage subsidy *or*, equivalently, by the use of a wage subsidy in manufacturing and a production subsidy to agriculture. Thus, let

$$s^* = \bar{w} - f_M'(L_M^*)$$

be the wage subsidy (financed by appropriate lump sum taxation) in manufacturing, with the asterisks denoting first best values. If this subsidy is also extended to employment in agriculture, we should write the equilibrium condition in production as:

$$f_M' = \bar{w} - s^* \tag{9}$$

$$\pi_c^* f_A' = \bar{w} - s^* \tag{10}$$

where $\pi_c^* = U_1(X_A^*, X_M^*)/U_2(X_A^*, X_M^*)$ is the consumption price (equal to the producer's price $\pi_p^* = f_M'/f_A'$) of the agricultural good. It is clear then that the constraints of the model are met (i.e., the wage rate in manufacturing is at $\bar{w}$ *and* the wage rates are equalized at the producer's prices in both sectors) and full employment optimal equilibrium is reached with wage subsidy at level s^* in both sectors. Thus, in Figure 2 (which illustrates for a closed economy case), the resulting full employment, optimal equilibrium is at S, with $\pi_c^* = \pi_p^*$, (and the domestic, marginal rates of transformation in production and in consumption are equal at S).

Alternatively, we could have used a wage subsidy in manufacturing (alone) at level s^*

[6] The analysis would have to be amended to bring in the foreign reciprocal demand function explicitly into the formal model if we were to consider the case of a country with monopoly power in trade. For a "small," open economy, the analysis in the text for a linear utility function would be applicable without modification.

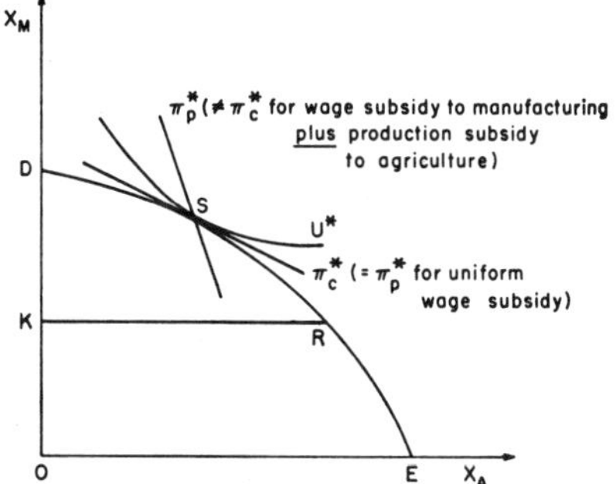

S is the first best, optimum for a closed economy, with the social utility curve U^* tangent to the production possibility curve DE. A suitable, uniform wage subsidy to both sectors, A and M, will equate the consumption and production prices with the domestic rates of transformation in production and substitution in consumption at S. A suitable wage subsidy to manufacturing *plus* production subsidy to agriculture will not equate the consumption and production prices but will equate the two rates of substitution in consumption and transformation in production at S with each other and with the consumption price alone.

FIGURE 2

and combined it with a production subsidy in agriculture. Thus, with

$$\pi_p^* = \frac{\bar{w}}{f_A'(L_A^*)}$$

as the producer's price of the agricultural good, and π_c^* as the consumer's price of the agricultural good, as before, we have:

$$t^* = \frac{\pi_p^* - \pi_c^*}{\pi_c^*}$$

as the optimal subsidy to agriculture. With the optimal values for s^* and π_p^*, we then have:

$$f_M' = \bar{w} - s^* \tag{11}$$

$$\pi_p^* f_A' = \bar{w} = \bar{w} \cdot \frac{L_M^*}{1 - L_A^*} \tag{12}$$

and, once again, we note that the constraints in the model are met, and full employment, optimal equilibrium is reached with wage

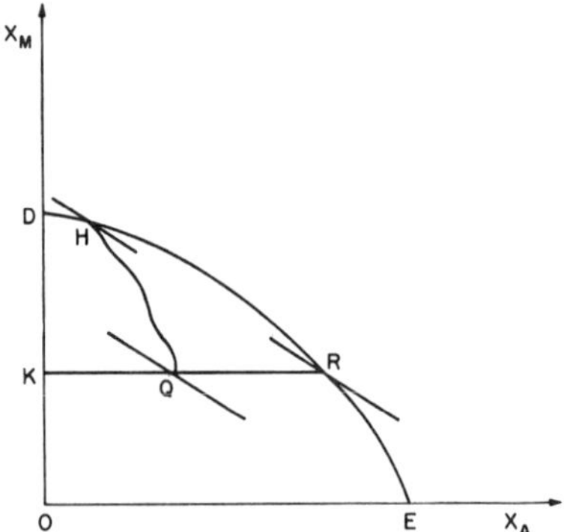

QH is the locus of production equilibria, traced out by increasing the wage subsidy in manufacturing from $s=0$ to s_{max} yielding full employment at H. QR is the locus of production equilibria, traced out by increasing the production subsidy to agriculture. While the diagram assumes the linear utility function case, as does Figure 1, for sake of simplicity, the formal analysis in the text is not so restricted. Note that, in the restricted case illustrated here, an increasing wage subsidy to manufacturing would necessarily reduce agricultural output; not so, in the general case which admits nonlinear utility functions.

FIGURE 3

subsidy in manufacturing at level s^* and production subsidy to agriculture at rate t^*.

However, while the equilibrium is again optimally at S, it is characterized now by $\pi_p^* \neq \pi_c^*$ (though of course the domestic, marginal rates of transformation in production and substitution in consumption remain equal to each other and identical to that under the uniform wage-subsidy policy at S).

Hence we have established the validity of criticisms 1)–5) leveled at the Harris-Todaro analysis at the outset of this paper.

III. Second Best Policy Intervention

The two second best policies which then can be considered are: a wage subsidy to manufacturing (considered by Harris-Todaro at some length); and a production subsidy to agriculture (not considered by Harris-Todaro, although their "migration-restriction" policy is the "quota-equivalent" thereof).

Wage Subsidy in Manufacturing: We only sketch here briefly the analysis of this policy as the Harris-Todaro results are totally correct.[7] With s as the wage subsidy in manufacturing, the equilibrium is now characterized by:

$$(13) \qquad f'_M = \bar{w} - s$$

$$(14) \qquad \frac{U_1}{U_2} f'_A = \bar{w} \cdot \frac{L_M}{1 - L_A}$$

Clearly, given $\bar{w}$ and s, (13) and (14) can be solved for L_M and L_A. We can then demonstrate (see our 1973 paper) that:

Starting from a *laissez-faire* equilibrium ($s=0$), on RK at Q in Figure 3, increasing s means shifting the production equilibrium Q steadily north;

the locus of successive production equilibria, mapped out by increasing s, must reach full employment (at an s_{max}) on the production possibility curve: such a locus being QH;[8]

the full employment equilibrium may be inferior welfarewise to *laissez-faire*—a proposition which we illustrate with a numerical example in the Appendix;

a wage subsidy will necessarily improve welfare (i.e., $dU/ds > 0$ at $s=0$); and

the second best wage subsidy need not be characterized by full employment, so that tradeoff possibilities between increased welfare (*via* a standard social utility function of the type deployed by Harris and Todaro, and in this paper) and reduced unemployment may be pertinent.

Production Subsidy to Agriculture: For the case where the policy instrument is a production subsidy to agriculture, the equilib-

[7] We have also developed the second best analysis at much greater length, and with formal rigor, in the companion paper cited earlier. Instead, we give numerical examples in the Appendix to illustrate the major propositions listed here.

[8] Harris and Todaro incorrectly argue, p. 134, that the full employment equilibrium with a wage subsidy in manufacturing can be inside DE, off the production possibility curve. They forget that labor is the only factor in the model, in effect; they seem to have erred by relying on analogy with the standard two-factor model.

rium conditions are clearly rewritten as:

$$f'_M = \bar{w} \tag{15}$$

$$\pi_p f'_A = \frac{\bar{w}L_M}{1 - L_A} \tag{16}$$

where, as before, π_p is the producer's price of the agricultural good and the implied production subsidy is $(\pi_p - U_1/U_2)/(U_1/U_2)$. Clearly, given π_p and $\bar{w}$, we can solve for L_M and L_A. It is also then easy to show that:

Starting from a *laissez-faire* equilibrium ($\pi_p = U_1/U_2$), on RK at Q in Figure 3, increasing π_p will steadily shift the production equilibrium to the right along QR until full employment is reached at $\bar{\pi}_p$ at R;

the equilibrium at R is also the second best optimal equilibrium, so that the full employment, second best equilibrium is reached when $\pi_p = \bar{\pi}_p$ and there is an implied production subsidy to agriculture; and

the second best wage subsidy in manufacturing cannot be ranked uniquely with the second best production subsidy to agriculture—as illustrated by a numerical example in the Appendix.

IV. Concluding Remarks

Where do the migration-restriction policies of Harris and Todaro fit in?

If one is willing to contemplate direct, physical allocations, one can clearly reach the first best, optimal solution, S in Figure 1, by assigning the corresponding labor to the two sectors (L_A^* and L_M^*) and enforcing the rule that all labor be employed regardless of private profitability (thus yielding X_A^* and X_M^*). The Harris-Todaro policy package for reaching S, consisting of a wage subsidy in manufacturing and migration restrictions is thus a "mixed" package: one policy being of the price-mechanism variety and the other of the direct physical-mechanism variety. One could equally turn this mixed package on its head and have manufacturers forced to employ all available labor and let a production subsidy to agriculture allocate the labor force at the optimal values (L_A^* and L_M^*).

Nothing can be said, in principle, about the relative suitability of all these equivalent alternatives without bringing in other considerations, including the ethical considerations mentioned by Harris and Todaro, to introduce asymmetries/nonequivalences among them.

Further, as for second best policies, we might be able to justify the Harris-Todaro concentration on the wage subsidy to manufacturing policy, as against a uniform wage subsidy policy, on feasibility grounds. It may well be that the government's capacity to intervene is confined to the (modern) urban sector and that a wage subsidy in agricultural employment is infeasible. This is, however, a question of empirical import, and it does not really justify the exclusion from the theoretical analysis of the first best price-mechanism variety intervention.

Finally, we may note explicitly that an attempted extension of our policy rankings to actual policy implementation would have to take into account the following, well-known problems:

The administration costs *and* feasibility of alternative policies must be taken into account.

Since taxes must be collected to disburse subsidies, the question arises whether those who ask for minimum real wages will not, even when such taxes are imposed on them in a lump sum fashion, seek to revise the minimum real wage that is demanded. We have assumed, of course, that the minimum real wage demanded is independent of the tax policy chosen.

Appendix

We produce numerical examples to show that:

A full employment yielding wage subsidy in manufacturing may be inferior to *laissez-faire*.

The second best wage subsidy in manufacturing may be inferior or superior to the second best production subsidy to agriculture; the two policies cannot be uniquely ranked.

Let us consider the following production and utility functions: $f_A(L_A) = L_A^{0.75}$, $f_M(L_M) = L_M^{1/2}$, $U = pX_A + X_M$. Let p take two al-

TABLE 1

		$p=1.5$	$p=0.5$
Minimum Wage $=(L_M^*)^{-1/2}$		2.363709	1.119195
First Best Optimum	L_A	0.821017	0.201660
	X_A	0.862510	0.300929
	L_M	0.178983	0.798340
	X_M	0.423064	0.893499
	U	1.716828	1.043963
Laissez-Faire Equilibrium	L_A	0.908222	0.499286
	X_A	0.930345	0.593967
	L_M	0.044746	0.199585
	X_M	0.211532	0.446749
	U	1.607048	0.743733
Second Best Wage Subsidy Equilibrium	L_A	0.904517	0.012604
	X_A	0.927497	0.037617
	L_M	0.046600	0.987396
	X_M	0.215869	0.993678
	U	1.607114	1.012486
Full Employment Wage Subsidy Equilibrium	L_A	0.051314	0.012604
	X_A	0.107814	0.037617
	L_M	0.948684	0.987396
	X_M	0.974004	0.993678
	U	1.135726	1.012486
Second Best Production Subsidy Equilibrium	L_A	0.955254	0.800415
	X_A	0.966249	0.846226
	L_M	0.044746	0.199585
	X_M	0.211532	0.446749
	U	1.660906	0.869862

ternative values 1.5 and 0.5. Let the specified minimum wage (in terms of manufactured good) in manufacturing be twice the equilibrium wage associated with the first best optimum. The following table gives the equilibrium factor allocations, output, and welfare associated with each of the following policies: first best optimum; *laissez-faire*; second best wage subsidy to manufacturing; full employment wage subsidy to manufacturing; and second best production subsidy to agriculture.

It is seen that when $p=0.5$, the second best optimum wage subsidy[9] to manufacturing happens to be the full employment wage subsidy, and it dominates the second best production subsidy (to agriculture) whereas, when $p=1.5$, the second best production subsidy dominates the second best wage subsidy. Further, the full employment wage subsidy is inferior to *laissez-faire*, when $p=1.5$.

[9] Note that the values for U in the table represent a global maximum because p is fixed.

REFERENCES

J. Bhagwati, "The Theory and Practice of Commercial Policy," in *Special Papers in International Economics*, no. 8, Princeton 1968, 1–69.

——— **and T. N. Srinivasan**, "The Ranking of Policy Interventions Under Factor Market Distortions: The Case of Sector-Specific Sticky Wages and Unemployment," *Sankhya* 1973, forthcoming.

R. Brecher, "Minimum Wage Rates and the Theory of International Trade" unpublished doctoral dissertation, Harvard Univ. 1971.

G. Haberler, "Some Problems in the Pure Theory of International Trade," *Econ. J.*, June 1950, *60*, 223–40.

J. Harris and M. Todaro, "Migration, Unemployment and Development: A Two-Sector Analysis," *Amer. Econ. Rev.*, Mar. 1970, *60*, 126–42.

H. G. Johnson, "Optimal Trade Intervention in the Presence of Domestic Distortions," in R. E. Caves et al., eds., *Trade, Growth, and the Balance of Payments*, Amsterdam 1965, 3–34.

L. Lefeber, "Trade and Minimum Wage Rates," in J. Bhagwati et al., eds., *Trade, Balance of Payments, and Growth*, Amsterdam 1971, 91–114.

Editor's Note

Also see J. N. Bhagwati and T. N. Srinivasan, "The Ranking of Policy Interventions under Factor Market Imperfections: The Case of Sector-Specific Sticky Wages and Unemployment," *Sankhya* 35 (Scrics B), Part 4 (1974):405–420, for fuller, formal analysis of the linear utility case. The more general case with monopoly power in trade is treated in essay 34 in this volume.

Reprinted from JOURNAL OF ECONOMIC THEORY Vol. 11, No. 3, December 1975

Printed in Belgium

Alternative Policy Rankings in a Large, Open Economy with Sector-Specific, Minimum Wages*

T. N. SRINIVASAN

Indian Statistical Institute

AND

JAGDISH BHAGWATI

Massachusetts Institute of Technology

Received July 10, 1975

The analysis by international trade theorists of factor market imperfections, and alternative policy rankings in the presence thereof, has distinguished between two major, polar types: (i) a distortionary wage differential between two sectors, while the wage is perfectly flexible in each sector; and (ii) a sticky (or minimum) wage which is equal, however, between the two sectors.

The analysis of the former class of distortions was pioneered by Hagen [7] and has subsequently been extensively explored by Bhagwati and Ramaswami [3], Kemp and Negishi [9], and Bhagwati, Ramaswami and Srinivasan [2].

The analysis of the second class of distortions was pioneered by Gottfried Haberler [6] and has subsequently been extended fully for the traditional two-sector model of trade theory by Brecher [5].

The purpose of this paper is to analyze policy rankings in the presence of a yet different type of factor market imperfection, introduced in a pioneering paper by Harris and Todaro [8] which *combines* specificity of wages (in one sector) with a (*resulting*) wage differential between the two sectors in an ingenious manner. In earlier papers [3, 4], we have analyzed the Harris–Todaro model, for this range of issues, in the context of a closed economy or a "small," open economy with given terms of trade. In this paper, we analyze alternative policy rankings in the context

* This paper was written while T. N. Srinivasan was Visiting Professor of Economics at M.I.T. during 1972–1973. It was M.I.T. Economics Working Paper No. 109 in its first version.

of the fully general assumption of a "large" country, which has monopoly power in trade.

Section 1 outlines the model. Section 2 briefly outlines the principal results of our analysis. Section 3 analyzes the policy instrument defined by a wage subsidy in the sector with minimum wages. Section 4 discusses the policy instrument defined by a production tax-cum-subsidy. Section 5 analyzes the policy instrument defined by a consumption tax-cum-subsidy. Section 6 discusses a tariff policy. Finally, Section 7 derives the combination of policies yielding the first-best optimum.

1. The Model

The basic Harris–Todaro model consists of a set of relations which can be stated as follows.

There are two commodities (A and M), produced in quantitites X_A and X_M, using L_A and L_M units of labor, with strictly concave production functions. (Thus, implicitly, there is a second factor (K_A, K_M) which yields the diminishing returns to labor input.)

$$X_A \leqslant f_A(L_A), \tag{1}$$

$$X_M \leqslant f_M(L_M). \tag{2}$$

Next, with the fixed, overall labor supply assumed by choice of units to equal unity, we have

$$L_A + L_M \leqslant 1, \tag{3}$$

$$L_A, L_M \geqslant 0. \tag{4}$$

We now introduce foreign trade. Let E denote net exports of the agricultural good, exchanging for $g(E)$ of net imports of manufacturing. (Since we do not wish to prejudge the question as to which commodity will be imported, E is allowed to take on negative values as well, in which case $g(E)$ will also be negative. In such a case, agricultural goods will be imported and manufactured goods will be exported.) We further assume that $g(0) = 0, g' > 0, g'' < 0$. This implies that the marginal (g') and average (g/E) terms of trade decline as E increases and the marginal is less than the average. The domestic consumption of the two commodities will then be

$$C_A = X_A - E, \tag{5}$$

$$C_M = X_M + g(E). \tag{6}$$

It is well known that if we now add a standard utility function

$$U = U[C_A, C_M], \tag{7}$$

where U is concave with positive marginal utilities for finite $[C_A, C_M]$, neoclassical free trade equilibrium will be characterized by

$$U_1/U_2 = f_M'/f_A', \tag{8}$$

$$U_1/U_2 = g(E)/E, \tag{9}$$

together with (1)–(6) being satisfied (where U_1 and U_2 represent the partial derivatives of U with respect to C_A and C_M, respectively, and f_i' is the derivation of f_i with respect to its argument, $i = A, M$). (We rule out corner solutions by assuming $f_A'(0) = f_M'(0) = \infty$.)

Figure 1 shows the production possibility curve BJ and the foreign offer curve PDC superimposed on it at P a la Baldwin. At the production

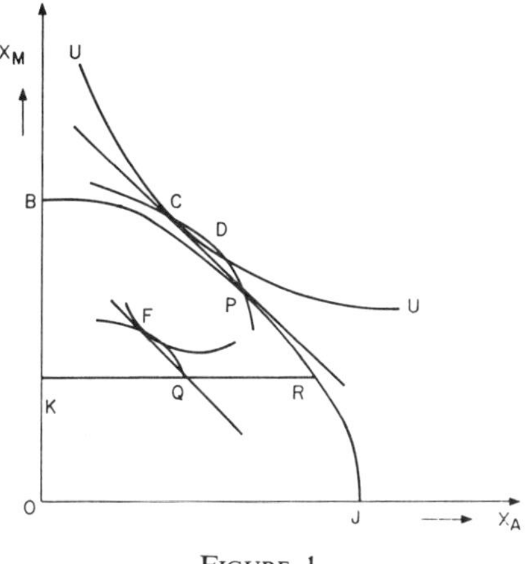

FIGURE 1

point P, the price ratio faced by producers (i.e., the negative of the slope of PC) is the same as the marginal rate of substitution in production as represented by the (negative of the) slope of the tangent to the production possibility curve at P. At the consumption point C, this price ratio equals the marginal rate of substitution in consumption as represented by the (negative of the) slope of the indifference curve at C. (The production and consumption points are so located that the price ratio equals the external terms of trade. The curve PDC corresponds to the graph of $g(E)$.)

The Harris–Todaro problem of sector-specific rigid wages and resulting unemployment can now be readily introduced. Let the free trade solution above (at P and C in Fig. 1) be $X_A^*, X_M^*, L_A^*, L_M^* (=1 - L_A^*)$, E^*, C_A^*, C_M^*. Assume now, however, that there is an exogenously specified, minimum wage constraint in manufacturing, such that

$$w \geqslant \bar{w}, \tag{10}$$

where w is the wage in manufacturing, in units of the manufacturing good (M). For a competitive economy, this implies that

$$f_M'(L_M) \geqslant \bar{w}. \tag{10'}$$

This constraint becomes binding, and P in Fig. 1 is inadmissible, when

$$f_M'(L_M^*) < \bar{w}.$$

The competitive economy, when characterized by this wage constraint, will then experience unemployment of labor. We then have two options to characterize the labor market equilibrium in this situation: *either* assume that the wage in agriculture (A) will be equalized with the wage in manufacturing (M) despite the unemployment; *or* that the wage in agriculture will be equalized with the *expected* wage in manufacturing, the expected and the actual wage in manufacturing being different as the former would be defined, as the latter weighted by the rate of employment, i.e.

$$\bar{w}L_M/(1 - L_A),$$

where $L_M < (1 - L_A)$ when there is unemployment.

The analysis of Harris–Todaro is based on the latter assumption, so that we can then write the equilibrium production conditions in competition and laissez-faire, as follows.

$$f_M' = \bar{w}, \tag{11}$$

$$(U_1/U_2) f_A' = \bar{w}L_M/(1 - L_A), \tag{12}$$

$$U_1/U_2 = g(E)/E. \tag{13}$$

We assume, in (12), that the production and consumption prices for the agricultural good are the same. (In writing Eq. (11), we assume that the producer and consumer prices of the manufacturing good are identical, with wage $\bar{w}$ paid in kind. Hence, the effect of a production subsidy to manufacturing is essentially not to affect any real decisions, as those made *via* equations (11) and (12), but merely to increase each commodity price in terms of the (arbitrary) unit of account. However, if we were to assume instead that the producer and consumer prices of the manufacturing good could be made to differ by policy, then the worker in manufacturing would earn the value of his marginal product at the producer price and then, *qua* consumer, must have enough income (in terms of the unit of account) to buy $\bar{w}$ units of the manufacturing good. In that case, a wage subsidy policy to manufacturing would be equivalent to a production subsidy policy to manufacturing, as is the case in the agricultural sector. Thus, note that, if we did shift to the latter, alternative assumption on wage payment in the manufacturing sector, then the analysis would not change but our policy equivalences would. In particular, the first best optimal policy mix would then include a uniform production subsidy to both sectors, and a production subsidy in manufacturing and a wage subsidy in agriculture.) Given $\bar{w}$, we can solve (11), (12) and (13) for L_M, L_A, and E after setting $X_A = f_A(L_A)$, $X_M = f_M(L_M)$, $C_A = f_A(L_A) - E$ and $C_M = f_M(L_M) + g(E)$. The equilibrium production point corresponding to this situation of nonintervention, with unemployment, will then lie, in Fig. 1, along RK (where X_M and hence, L_M are fixed at the value that makes $f_M' = \bar{w}$) at Q. (It is worth noting that the nonintervention equilibrium would lie along RK even if we assumed actual wages to be equalized between the two sectors.) The consumption point will be at F.

The policy question that emerges then, is: What alternative policies can be used in this model for intervention and what would be their impact on welfare and on unemployment?

2. The Basic Results

In this model, there are a number of policy options which can be explored; however, many can be shown to be equivalent to one another or to combinations of other policies.

Thus, we will discuss the following policies: (i) nonintervention or laissez-faire; (ii) wage subsidy in manufacturing (M); (iii) production subsidy to agriculture (A); and (iv) consumption subsidy to agriculture (A).

Note that, as a little reflection will show, the simple structure of the model implies that: (v) a wage subsidy in agriculture is equivalent to policy (iii); (vi) a uniform wage tax-cum-subsidy in all employment is a combination of policies (ii) and (iii); and (vii) a tariff policy is a combination of policies (iii) and (iv).

We will proceed to establish the following propositions.

Theorem 1. *There exists a unique equilibrium corresponding to each wage subsidy s to manufacturing in an interval* $[0, \bar{s}]$. *At $\bar{s}$, full employment is reached.*

THEOREM 2. *A wage subsidy (in manufacturing) will exist which will improve welfare over laissez-faire.*

Thus, laissez-faire (i.e., wage subsidy = 0) can be necessarily improved upon by some wage subsidy. In fact, any positive subsidy in some interval with zero as its left end point will be welfare-improving.

THEOREM 3. *The full-employment wage subsidy $\bar{s}$ may not be the "second-best" wage subsidy and may be inferior even to laissez-faire.*

THEOREM 4. *There exists a unique production subsidy which will enable full employment to be reached and which is also the second-best production subsidy.*

THEOREM 5. *The second-best wage subsidy (to manufacturing) and production subsidy (to agriculture) cannot be ranked uniquely.*

THEOREM 6. *There exists a unique consumption subsidy which will enable full employment to be reached and which is also the second-best consumption subsidy.*

THEOREM 7. *The second-best wage subsidy (to manufacturing) and the second-best consumption subsidy (to agriculture) cannot be ranked uniquely.*

THEOREM 8. *The second-best production and consumption subsidies cannot be ranked uniquely.*

THEOREM 9. *A tariff (or trade subsidy) policy may not improve welfare but can improve employment.*

THEOREM 10. *The first-best optimum can be reached if, in addition to the monopoly-power-in-trade tariff, a combination of a production tax-cum-subsidy and wage subsidy (to manufacturing) or any equivalent thereof (including a uniform wage subsidy on employment of labor in both sectors), is provided.*

The combination of a suitable production subsidy to agriculture plus an appropriate wage subsidy in manufacturing, or its equivalents, such as a uniform wage subsidy in all employment, will yield the first-best optimum, when also combined with an appropriate tariff to exploit the postulated monopoly power in trade (as discussed in Section 7).

3. Wage Subsidy in Manufacturing

Let us now consider the wage subsidy as the policy intervention in this economy. Denoting by s the subsidy per unit of labor employed in manufacturing, we find that the equilibrium is now characterized by

$$f_M' = \bar{w} - s, \tag{14}$$

$$(U_1/U_2) f_A' = \bar{w} L_M/(1 - L_A), \tag{15}$$

$$(U_1/U_2) = g(E)/E. \tag{16}$$

Equation (14) assumes that each worker in manufacturing receives remuneration $\bar{w}$, of which only $(\bar{w} - s)$ is paid by the employer and s by the state out of some form of nondistortionary taxation. With the consumer and producer price of the agricultural good assumed to be identical, and equal to U_1/U_2, we then have the actual wage in agriculture being equated to the employment-rate-weighted (i.e., expected) wage in manufacturing in Eq. (15).

Existence of equilibrium is established once we show that values of L_A, L_M, and E exist that satisfy (14)–(16) and the conditions that (i) L_A and L_M are nonnegative and their sum does not exceed the available labor force, namely, unity; and (ii) the value of E is such that whichever commodity is exported, the volume of exports does not exceed production. We now proceed to show that, in fact, unique values of L_A, L_M and E exist that satisfy all the above conditions. In doing so, we shall use, in addition to the assumptions already made, the assumption that both goods are normal in consumption.

Denoting the average terms of trade $g(E)/E$ by $\phi(E)$, we see that our assumptions on g imply that $\phi > 0$, $\phi' < 0$, and $g' < \phi$ for all E. Substituting (16) into (15) we get

$$\phi(E) f_A' = \bar{w} L_M/(1 - L_A). \tag{15'}$$

Given $\bar{w}$, s, concavity of f_M, and the assumption that $f_M' \to \infty$ as $L_M \to 0$, Eq. (14) uniquely determines L_M as a function $L_M(s)$ of s for all s in $0 \leqslant s \leqslant \bar{w}$. Given the value $L_M(s)$ for L_M, the range of feasible values of L_A is $[0, 1 - L_M(s)]$. For any value of L_A in this range, the feasible values of E are confined to the interval $[g^{-1}\{-f_M(L_M(s))\}, f(L_A)]$, the reason being that if A is exported the volume of exports E cannot exceed the production $f(L_A)$ and if A is imported, then $-E$ is the *value* of exports of M. The physical volume of exports of M is $-g(E)$ and this cannot exceed the production $f_M(L_M(s))$. Thus $-g(E) \leqslant f_M(L_M(s))$ or

$$E \geqslant g^{-1}\{-f_M(L_M(s))\},$$

where g^{-1} is the inverse function of g. We first show that given any feasible L_A there exists a unique, feasible E that satisfies (16). We then substitute this value of E (denoting it $E(L_A, s)$ to indicate its dependence on the specified values of L_A and s) into the left-hand side of (15′) and show that a unique feasible value of L_A satisfies (15′).

Now consider (16). The right-hand side is a decreasing function of E while the left-hand side is an increasing function of E for given values of L_A and $L_M(s)$, since

$$\frac{\partial}{\partial E}\left(\frac{U_1}{U_2}\right) = \frac{(-U_{11} + U_{12}g')\,U_2 - (-U_{21} + U_{22}g')\,U_1}{U_2^{\,2}} > 0$$

by virtue of the facts that $g' > 0$ and the normality assumptions ensure that $U_{11}U_2 - U_{21}U_1 > 0$ and $U_{22}U_1 - U_{12}U_2 < 0$. Further, as E approaches its lowest feasible value, the volume of exports of the manufactûred good approaches its production; the result is that its domestic consumption C_M approaches zero. Similarly, as E approaches its highest feasible value, the domestic consumption C_A of the agricultural good approaches zero. Now, if we assume that the marginal utility $U_1(U_2)$ of agricultural good (manufactured good) tends to ∞ as its consumption $C_A(C_M)$ tends to zero, the left-hand side of (16) increases from zero to $+\infty$ as E increases from its lower to upper limiting value and hence, given s, for any feasible L_A there exists a unique E denoted by $E(L_A, s)$ which satisfies (16).

It is easily seen that $\partial E(L_A, s)/\partial L_A > 0$. For, given s (and hence, X_M) and a feasible E (and hence, C_M), C_A increases as L_A increases resulting in a decrease in U_1/U_2 (given our assumption of normality for both goods). Thus, as L_A increases, the graph of the left-hand side of (16) shifts to the right while the graph of the right-hand side stays put, resulting in a larger value for the E at which the two graphs intersect. The reader can readily verify, using a similar argument, that $\partial E/\partial s < 0$.

Let us now substitute the function $E(L_A, s)$ for E in (15′). Then, for any given s, both sides of (15′) are functions of L_A only. The left-hand side of (15′) is then a decreasing function of L_A since

$$(\partial/\partial L_A)\{\phi f_A'\} = \phi'(\partial E/\partial L_A) + \phi f_A'' < 0$$

because $\phi > 0$, $\phi' < 0$, $\partial E/\partial L_A > 0$, and $f_A'' < 0$. The right-hand side is an increasing function of L_A. Further, as $L_A \to 0$, the left-hand side (i.e., $\phi f_A'$) also $\to \infty$, and hence, exceeds the right-hand side which takes the value $\bar{w}L_M(s)$. Hence, if we show that as $L_A \to$ its maximum feasible value $1 - L_M(s)$, the left-hand side is less than the right-hand side, we would have shown the existence of a unique feasible L_A satisfying (15′).

Consider $s = 0$. Then $L_M(0)$ satisfies $f_M' = \bar{w}$. By assumption, L_M^* (the laissez-faire value of L_M without the minimum wage constraint) results in $f_M' < \bar{w}$ and hence, $L_M^* > L_M(0)$. This means that $L_A^* = 1 - L_M^* < 1 - L_M(0)$. Thus if we set $L_A = 1 - L_M(0)$, its maximum feasible value given $s = 0$, the following hold true:

(i) $f_A'(1 - L_M(0)) < f_A'(L_A^*)$ (concavity of f_A) ;
(ii) $E\{1 - L_M(0), 0\} > E\{(1 - L_M^*), 0\}$ (since $\partial E/\partial L_A > 0$) ;
(iii) $\phi[E\{1 - L_M(0), 0\}] < \phi[E\{1 - L_M^*, 0\}]$ (since $\phi' < 0$).

Thus, $\phi f_A'$ (left-hand side of (15′)) evaluated at the largest feasible value of L_A (given $s = 0$), i.e., at $1 - L_M(0)$, is less than its value evaluated at $L_A = 1 - L_M^*$. But at $L_A = 1 - L_M^*$, $\phi f_A' = (U_1/U_2) f_A' = f_M' < \bar{w}$. Hence, a fortiori, the value of $\phi f_A'$ at $L_A = 1 - L_M(0)$ is less than $\bar{w}$. This in turn implies that, for $s = 0$, the graphs of the two sides of (15′) intersect at a unique L_A between zero and $1 - L_M(0)$, as shown in Fig. 2.

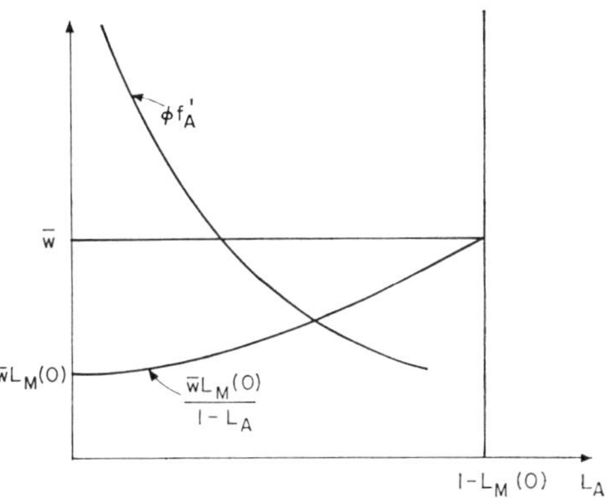

FIGURE 2

Thus we have established the existence of a unique laissez-faire equilibrium with unemployment under the minimum wage constraint.

Existence of Unique Equilibrium for Each Value of s in $[0, \bar{s})$

Now, as s is increased, for any given L_A the left-hand side of (15′) increases, since $(\partial/\partial s)(\phi f_A') = \phi' f_A'(\partial E/\partial s) > 0$, and hence, its graph shifts to the right. The right-hand side also increases since $L_M(s)$ increases with s. Thus, its graph shifts to the left, with its value at $L_A = 1 - L_M(s)$ always equal to $\bar{w}$. Hence, the two graphs continue to intersect at a unique L_A in the interval $\{0, 1 - L_M(s)\}$ as s increases up to a maximum value $\bar{s}$, when this value of L_A equals its upper bound $1 - L_M(\bar{s})$, and full employment is reached. This is shown in Fig. 3. For values of $s > \bar{s}$, no equilibrium exists. Thus, we have shown the existence of a unique equilibrium for each value of s in $[0, \bar{s}]$.

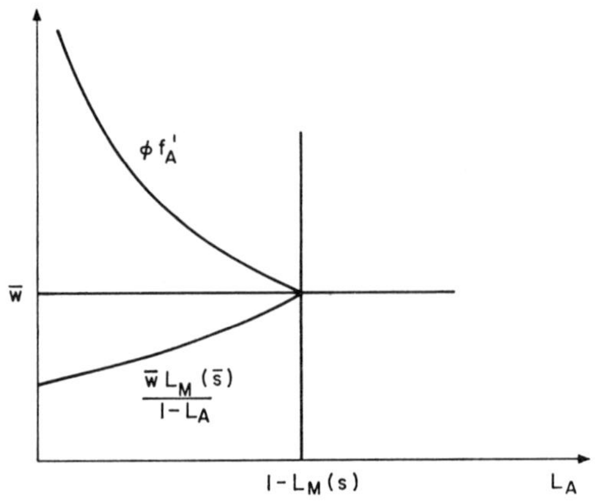

FIGURE 3

Impact on Welfare of Change in s

Let us now evaluate the change in welfare, i.e., dU/ds, as s increases. After some manipulation, the following can be derived,

$$\frac{dE}{ds} = -\left[\left\{\phi f_A'' - \frac{\bar{w}L_M}{(1-L_A)^2}\right\}\frac{\partial}{\partial L_M}\left(\frac{U_1}{U_2}\right) + \frac{\bar{w}}{1-L_A}\frac{\partial}{\partial L_A}\left(\frac{U_1}{U_2}\right)\right]\Big/ Df_M'' , \tag{17}$$

$$\frac{dL_A}{ds} = \left[\phi' f_A' \frac{\partial}{\partial L_M}\left(\frac{U_1}{U_2}\right) + \left\{\frac{\partial}{\partial E}\left(\frac{U_1}{U_2}\right) - \phi'\right\}\frac{\bar{w}}{(1-L_A)}\right]\Big/ Df_M'' , \tag{18}$$

$$\frac{dU}{ds} = -U_2 \frac{N}{Df_M''} , \tag{19}$$

where

$$D = \phi' f_A' \frac{\partial}{\partial L_A}\left(\frac{U_1}{U_2}\right) + \left\{\phi f_A'' - \frac{\bar{w}L_M}{(1-L_A)^2}\right\}\left\{\phi' - \frac{\partial}{\partial E}\left(\frac{U_1}{U_2}\right)\right\} , \tag{20}$$

$$\begin{aligned} N = {} & \left[-\phi\left\{\phi f_A'' - \frac{\bar{w}L_M}{(1-L_A)^2}\right\} - \phi\phi'(f_A')^2 - \frac{\bar{w}\phi f_A' g'}{(1-L_A) f_M'}\right] \\ & \times \frac{\partial}{\partial L_M}\left(\frac{U_1}{U_2}\right) \\ & + \left[\frac{g'\bar{w}}{(1-L_A)} + \frac{f_M'}{f_A'}\left\{\phi f_A'' - \frac{\bar{w}L_M}{(1-L_A)^2}\right\} + f_M' f_A' \phi'\right]\frac{\partial}{\partial L_A}\left(\frac{U_1}{U_2}\right) \\ & + \phi' f_M' \phi f_A'' + \frac{s\bar{w}L_M\phi'}{(1-L_A)^2} . \end{aligned} \tag{21}$$

Now, if we assume normality of both goods in consumption, then

$$\frac{\partial}{\partial L_M}\left(\frac{U_1}{U_2}\right) > 0, \qquad \frac{\partial}{\partial L_A}\left(\frac{U_1}{U_2}\right) < 0,$$

$$\frac{\partial}{\partial E}\left(\frac{U_1}{U_2}\right) = -\frac{1}{f_A'}\frac{\partial}{\partial L_A}\left(\frac{U_1}{U_2}\right) + \frac{g'}{f_M'}\frac{\partial}{\partial L_M}\left(\frac{U_1}{U_2}\right) > 0.$$

Further, $\phi > 0$, $\phi' < 0, f_A' > 0, f_A'' < 0, f_M' > 0$ and $U_2 > 0$. Hence, $D > 0$. It is seen that $dE/ds < 0$, i.e., the net export of the agricultural commodity decreases as the wage subsidy to manufacturing increases. However, the signs of dL_A/ds and dU/ds are in general indeterminate. But, using the fact that the marginal terms of trade g' is by assumption less than the average terms of trade ϕ, we can show that

$$N > \left[-\phi^2 f_A'' - \phi\phi'(f_A')^2 - \frac{s\phi\bar{w}L_M}{(1-L_A)^2 f_M'}\right]\frac{\partial}{\partial L_M}\left(\frac{U_1}{U_2}\right)$$
$$+ \left[f_M' f_A' \phi' + \frac{\phi f_M' f_A''}{f_A'} + \frac{s\bar{w}L_M}{(1-L_A)^2 f_A'}\right]\frac{\partial}{\partial L_A}\left(\frac{U_1}{U_2}\right)$$
$$+ \phi' f_M' \phi f_A'' + \frac{s\bar{w}L_M\phi'}{(1-L_A)^2}.$$

In the above inequality, all terms involving s explicitly are negative and the rest are positive. When $s = 0$, the terms involving s drop out making N and hence, $dU/ds > 0$ at $s = 0$. By continuity this means that welfare can be increased over its laissez-faire level by giving any positive wage subsidy in an interval. It is also clear that the full-employment wage subsidy need not be the second-best optimum subsidy.

4. Production Subsidy

We now consider the policy of subsidizing production in agriculture. To do this, we rewrite the critical equilibrium conditions as follows:

$$f_M' = \bar{w}, \tag{22}$$

$$\pi_p f_A' = \bar{w}L_M/(1 - L_A), \tag{23}$$

$$U_1/U_2 = \phi(E), \tag{24}$$

where π_p is the producer's price of the agricultural good, the production subsidy being $(\pi_p - \phi)/\phi$ per unit.

Now (22) determines L_M uniquely as $L_M(0)$ (its laissez-faire value). The feasible values of L_A then lie in the interval $[0, 1 - L_M(0)]$. Equation (24) is the same as (16) when $s = 0$ and hence, for any feasible L_A, there exists a unique $E(L_A, 0)$ which satisfies (24) and clearly $\partial E/\partial L_A > 0$. Now the left-hand side of (23) is a decreasing function of L_A (for any given π_p) and the right-hand side is an increasing function of L_A. We have already seen that when π_p is at its laissez-faire value, the graphs of the two sides intersect at a unique $L_A(0)$ such that $0 < L_A(0) < 1 - L_M(0)$. Now, as we increase π_p continuously above its laissez-faire value, thus increasing the rate of production subsidy, the graph of the left-hand side of (23) shifts to the right and continues to intersect the right-hand side (which does not shift) at a feasible value of L_A until π_p reaches a value $\bar{\pi}_p$ at which the intersection occurs at $L_A = 1 - L_M(0)$. At this point, full employment is attained; and for values of $\pi_p > \bar{\pi}_p$, no equilibrium exists.

It is also clear that as π_p increases, L_A increases and hence, X_A increases, i.e., $dL_A/d\pi_p > 0$ and $dX_A/d\pi_p = f_A'(dL_A/d\pi_p) > 0$. It can thus be shown that

$$\frac{dU}{d\pi_p} = U_2 \left[\frac{g'\left\{-\frac{\partial}{\partial L_A}\left(\frac{U_1}{U_2}\right) + \frac{\phi f_A'}{f_M'}\frac{\partial}{\partial L_M}\left(\frac{U_1}{U_2}\right)\right\} - \phi\phi' f_A'}{-\frac{1}{f_A'}\frac{\partial}{\partial L_A}\left(\frac{U_1}{U_2}\right) + \frac{g'}{f_M'}\frac{\partial}{\partial L_M}\left(\frac{U_1}{U_2}\right) - \phi'} \right] \frac{dL_A}{d\pi_p} > 0. \tag{25}$$

Hence, clearly the second-best optimum production subsidy is the full-employment subsidy (which is the maximum, feasible subsidy).

5. Consumption Subsidy

We now consider the policy of subsidizing the consumption of agricultural goods. To do this, we must rewrite the equilibrium conditions as follows,

$$f_M' = \bar{w}, \tag{26}$$

$$\phi(E) f_A' = \bar{w}\, L_M/(1 - L_A), \tag{27}$$

$$\pi_c = U_1/U_2, \tag{28}$$

where π_c is the consumer's price of agricultural good, the consumption subsidy being $(\phi(E) - \pi_c)/\pi_c$ per unit.

Now, consider (28). For any given L_A, the right-hand side is an increasing function of E. Further, as E tends to its lower limiting value of

$g^{-1}\{-f_M(L_M(0))\}$, U_1/U_2 tends to zero; and as E tends to its upper limiting value of $f_A(L_A)$, $U_1/U_2 \to \infty$. Hence, for any positive π_c, there exists a unique E denoted by $E(L_A, \pi_c)$ that satisfies (28). It is also clear that $\partial E(L_A, \pi_c)/\partial L_A > 0$ and $\partial E(L_A, \pi_c)/\partial \pi_c > 0$.

Substituting $E(L_A, \pi_c)$ for E in (27), we find that, for a given π_c, the left-hand side of (27) is a decreasing function of L_A while the right-hand side is an increasing function.

We have already seen (in Section 3) that when π_c equals its laissez-faire value, the graph of the two sides of (27) will intersect at a unique $L_A(0)$, satisfying $0 < L_A(0) < 1 - L_M(0)$. Furthermore, as we decrease π_c, thus increasing the rate of consumption subsidy, the graph of the left-hand side will shift to the right, while the graph of the right-hand side stays put. Hence, until π_c reaches a value $\bar{\pi}_c$, the two graphs will intersect at a feasible value of L_A; and at $\bar{\pi}_c$, they will intersect at $L_A = 1 - L_M(0)$. For any lower value of π_c, there is no equilibrium.

It is also obvious that the equilibrium value of L_A (and hence, X_A) increases as π_c decreases, i.e., $dL_A/d\pi_c < 0$ and $dX_A/d\pi_c < 0$. It can thus be shown that

$$\frac{dE}{d\pi_c} = \left[\frac{\bar{w}L_M}{(1 - L_A)^2} - \phi f_A''\right] \frac{dL_A}{d\pi_c} \Big/ f_A'\phi' > 0, \tag{29}$$

$$\frac{dU}{d\pi_c} = U_2\left[\phi f_A' \frac{dL_A}{d\pi_c} + (g' - \phi)\frac{dE}{d\pi_c}\right] < 0 \qquad (\text{since } g' < \phi). \tag{30}$$

This means that, as π_c decreases from its laissez-faire value to its full-employment value $\bar{\pi}_c$, welfare increases. Thus, the full employment subsidy is also the second-best consumption subsidy.

6. Trade Tariff (Subsidy)

Let us now consider a tariff policy. The equilibrium will now be characterized by

$$f_M' = \bar{w}, \tag{31}$$

$$\phi(E)(1 + t)f_A' = \bar{w}L_M/(1 - L_A), \tag{32}$$

$$U_1/U_2 = \phi(E)(1 + t), \tag{33}$$

where t is the ad valorem tariff rate. If the agricultural commodity is exported (imported), i.e., E is positive (negative), then t represents an export subsidy (import duty).

As earlier, L_M is uniquely determined at $L_M(0)$ by (31). From the argument of Section 3, it follows that for any given t and L_A in the feasible range $\{0, 1 - L_M(0)\}$, there exists a unique feasible $E(L_A, t)$ that satisfies (33). It is also clear that

$$\frac{\partial E}{\partial L_A} = \frac{-(\partial/\partial L_A)(U_1/U_2)}{(\partial/\partial E)(U_1/U_2) - \phi'(1+t)} > 0,$$

$$\frac{\partial E}{\partial t} = \frac{\phi}{(\partial/\partial E)(U_1/U_2) - \phi'(1+t)} > 0.$$

Substituting $E(L_A, t)$ for E in (32), we then see that the left-hand side is a decreasing function of L_A while the right-hand side is an increasing function of L_A. We know that, when $t = 0$, the graphs of the two sides intersect at a unique $L_A(0)$ in $\{0, 1 - L_M(0)\}$. As we increase t above zero, the graph of the left-hand side shifts to the right while that of the right-hand side stays put, so that the two graphs continue to intersect at an L_A in the feasible range *until* t reaches a value $\bar{t}$ when the intersection occurs at $L_A = 1 - L_M(0)$, thereby attaining full employment. For $t > \bar{t}$, there is no equilibrium.

Furthermore, as t increases, equilibrium L_A increases. It can then be shown that

$$\frac{dL_A}{dt} = \frac{\phi f_A'\,(\partial/\partial E)(U_1/U_2)}{\left[\begin{array}{l}\left\{\phi'(1+t) - \dfrac{\partial}{\partial E}\left(\dfrac{U_1}{U_2}\right)\right\}\left\{\phi(1+t)f_A'' - \dfrac{\bar{w}L_M(0)}{(1-L_A)^2}\right\} \\ \qquad\qquad + f_A'\phi'(1+t)\dfrac{\partial}{\partial L_A}\left(\dfrac{U_1}{U_2}\right)\end{array}\right]} > 0, \tag{34}$$

$$\begin{aligned}\frac{dE}{dt} &= \phi\left[-f_A'\frac{\partial}{\partial L_A}\left(\frac{U_1}{U_2}\right) + \frac{\bar{w}L_M(0)}{(1-L_A)^2} - \phi(1+t)f_A''\right] \\ &\quad \times \frac{dL_A}{dt}\Big/f_A'\frac{\partial}{\partial E}\left(\frac{U_1}{U_2}\right) > 0,\end{aligned} \tag{35}$$

$$\begin{aligned}\frac{dU}{dt} &= U_1\left\{f_A'\frac{dL_A}{dt} - \frac{dE}{dt}\right\} + U_2\left\{f_M'\frac{dL_M}{dt} + g'\frac{dE}{dt}\right\} \\ &= U_2\left[f_A'\phi(1+t)\frac{dL_A}{dt} + \{g' - \phi(1+t)\}\frac{dE}{dt}\right].\end{aligned} \tag{36}$$

Now, (36) shows clearly that the change in welfare dU/dt is the sum of two terms consisting of a production effect $U_2 f_A'\phi(1+t)(dL_A/dt)$ and a consumption and trade effect $U_2\{g' - \phi(1+t)\}(dE/dt)$. The production effect is unambiguously positive. Since $U_2 > 0$ and $dE/dt > 0$, the sign of the trade effect depends on that of $g' - \phi(1+t)$. By assumption, $g' < \phi$

and hence, $g' - \phi(1 + t) < -t\phi$. For nonnegative values of t the consumption effect is therefore negative while for negative values of t it depends on whether g' exceeds or falls short of $\phi\,(1 + t)$. Thus we cannot assert anything *in general* about the welfare effect of a tariff. However, as we said earlier, L_A and hence, total employment $L_A + L_M(0)$ increases monotonically as the tariff is increased and full employment is reached at $\bar{t}$.

7. Optimal Policy Intervention

We may now briefly state the combination of policies which would yield the first-best optimum in this model.

Thus, let t^* be the optimal tariff and s^* the optimal wage subsidy in all employment, which would obtain at the optimal equilibrium. We would then be meeting the constraints of the model as follows.

$$f_M' = \bar{w} - s^*, \tag{37}$$

$$\phi(E)(1 + t^*)f_A' = \bar{w} - s^*, \tag{38}$$

$$\phi(E)(1 + t^*) = U_1/U_2\,, \tag{39}$$

and

$$g'(E) = U_1/U_2 = f_M'/f_A'. \tag{40}$$

The diagrammatic counterpart of this optimal equilibrium is shown in Fig. 4, where the optimal wage subsidy is supposed, along with the optimal

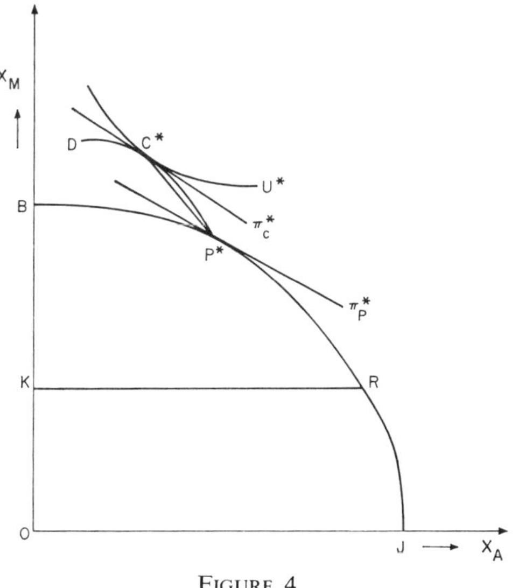

FIGURE 4

tariff, to lead to production at P^* (tangent to production price-ratio $\pi_p{}^*$), consumption at C^* (tangent to identical consumption price-ratio $\pi_c{}^* = \pi_p{}^* = \phi(E)(1 + t^*)$) and international terms of trade $\phi(E)$ equal to P^*C^*. The utility function is then maximized at value U^*.

It is readily seen, of course, that the uniform wage subsidy s^* could be given equivalently as wage subsidy to manufacturing alone, as rate s^*, *plus* a suitable production subsidy to agriculture, and so on. To derive other equivalences, the reader can refer to our earlier discussion of this subject in Section 2.

Acknowledgments

Thanks are due to the National Science Foundation for financial support of the research underlying this paper. Thanks are also due to Peter Diamond and an anonymous referee for helpful comments. To economize on space, the proofs of Theorems 5, 7, and 8 have been omitted but are available from the authors on request.

References

1. J. Bhagwati and V. K. Ramaswami, Domestic distortions, tariffs, and the theory of optimum subsidy, *J. Polit. Econ.*, February (1963).
2. J. Bhagwati, V. K. Ramaswami, and T. N. Srinivasan, Domestic distortions, tariffs and the theory of optimum subsidy: Further results, *J. Polit. Econ.*, November/December (1969).
3. J. Bhagwati and T. N. Srinivasan, The ranking of policy interventions under factor market imperfections: The case of sector-specific sticky wages and unemployment, *Sankhya Ser. B* (1973).
4. J. Bhagwati and T. N. Srinivasan, On reanalysing the Harris–Todaro model: Policy rankings in the case of sector-specific sticky wages, *Amer. Econ. Rev.*, June (1974).
5. R. Brecher, Minimum wages and the theory of international trade, *Quart. J. Econ.*, May (1973).
6. G. Haberler, Some problems in the pure theory of international trade, *Econ. J.*, June (1950).
7. E. Hagen, An economic justification of protectionism, *Quart. J. Econ.*, November (1958).
8. J. Harris and M. Todaro, Migration, unemployment and development: A two-sector analysis, *Amer. Econ. Rev.*, March (1970).
9. M. Kemp and T. Negishi, Domestic distortions, tariffs and the theory of optimum subsidy, *J. Polit. Econ.*, November/December (1969).

VII
PROJECT EVALUATION IN TRADE-DISTORTED OPEN ECONOMIES, EFFECTIVE PROTECTION, AND DOMESTIC RESOURCE COSTS

Shadow Prices for Project Selection in the Presence of Distortions: Effective Rates of Protection and Domestic Resource Costs

T. N. Srinivasan

World Bank and Indian Statistical Institute

Jagdish N. Bhagwati

Massachusetts Institute of Technology

The paper addresses the problem of deriving shadow prices for use in project evaluation when the existing allocation is characterized by ad valorem trade distortions. The analysis is used to clarify and resolve the long-standing debate among effective-rate-of-protection and domestic-resource-cost proponents as to the respective merits of their measures as methods of project evaluation. The derivation of shadow factor prices is then extended to three major factor market imperfections familiar from extensive trade-theoretic analysis.

Until recently, theorists of trade and welfare have, by and large, ignored the ever-increasing literature on project evaluation. This is puzzling since the bulk of the project evaluation literature attempts to derive shadow prices to replace the market prices that, in distorted situations, clearly will not reflect true opportunity costs whereas the major advances in the welfare theory of international trade have consisted precisely in the analysis of issues in trade and welfare when the market is characterized by a number of alternative endogenous or policy-imposed distortions.[1]

The research underlying this paper was supported by NSF grant SOC74-13210. Thanks are due to Peter Diamond for helpful conversations and to Michael Bruno, Henry Wan, Ian Little, Christopher Heady, Richard Brecher, Takashi Negishi, Koichi Hamada, Hiroshi Atsumi, Bela Balassa, and Jacob Frenkel for valuable comments on an earlier draft of this paper. The views expressed are those of the authors and should not be ascribed to the World Bank or to its affiliated institutions.

[1] See Bhagwati and Ramaswami 1963; Johnson 1965; Bhagwati, Ramaswami, and Srinivasan 1969; Bhagwati 1971; and the numerous writings of Kemp, Findlay, Corden, Magee, Brecher, and several trade theorists.

[*Journal of Political Economy*, 1978, vol. 86, no. 1]

Trade theorists have generally considered second-best problems characterizing the nature of optimal policy intervention when the given distortions cannot be (directly) removed. Project analysis, on the other hand, poses a related, but different, question: if the given distortions defining current resource (and expenditure) allocations cannot be removed, would the introduction of a project which withdraws resources from this existing allocation for project use be welfare-improving? The solution to this latter problem naturally follows from the derivation of the shadow prices of factors and outputs for use in project evaluation.

As it happens, this problem has been posed by Findlay and Wellisz (1976) in a most elegant, recent contribution, illuminating how trade-theoretic tools can be deployed to advantage in analyzing it.[2] We follow them in Section I, essentially taking over their simple model of trade theory, with primary factors producing traded goods (including the project output), with no intermediates and with fixed international prices for the traded goods, and considering with Findlay and Wellisz the case of a trade distortion (i.e., a tariff or trade subsidy). We parallel the Findlay-Wellisz analysis, using somewhat different analytical techniques, managing therefore to both complement and correct it in critical ways.

Next, in Section II, we relate these results on the appropriate shadow prices in project evaluation to the two measures which have been proposed as project-evaluation criteria in the developmental and trade literature: the effective rate of protection (ERP) and the domestic resource cost (DRC). It is shown that the ERP is an inappropriate measure for this purpose; and that DRCs, if they must yield the correct social evaluation of a project, must use the second-best shadow prices that are derived in Section I, that is, they must be appropriately defined DRCs. Thus we succeed in casting light on the inconclusive debate among the ERP and DRC proponents—as typified, for example, by the controversy in this *Journal* among Balassa and Schydlowsky (1968, 1972), Bruno (1972), and Krueger (1972)—as to their relative merits as techniques of project appraisal.[3]

Finally, in Section III, we analyze the derivation of shadow factor prices when the given distortions arise from three alternative, polar types of factor market imperfections familiar to trade theorists, rather than from the presence of a trade tariff or subsidy.

[2] Very early and pioneering analyses by Joshi (1972) and Lal (1974) attempting to examine the Little-Mirrlees (1969) *Manual* rules along trade-theoretic lines must also be mentioned. Corden (1974) also has a discussion of these rules.

[3] For a historical review of the antecedents of the DRC concept, especially in Israel, see Bruno (1972). The use of ERP as a project criterion appears, on the other hand, to have been the subject of internal World Bank memoranda during the mid-1960s, stemming presumably from the notion that, in some sense, they reflected "comparative advantage."

I. The Model and Derivation of Shadow Prices

As stated above, we consider the usual trade-theoretic model with two primary factors, k and l, producing two traded outputs, X_1 and X_2, that enjoy fixed international prices p_1^* and p_2^*. The "small" project being considered will produce commodity X_3, at fixed international price p_3^*. It is assumed that the planner is working with a well-behaved social utility function. The problem of project analysis then is to evolve suitable prices, for the primary factors and output (X_3) in the project, which would enable the analyst to decide whether the project should be accepted or rejected.

The problem would be straightforward indeed if there were no distortions in the system: the correct valuations of the primary factors would clearly be those in the market, as reflected by the international price-ratio p_1^*/p_2^*, and the correct valuation for X_3 would be the international price p_3^*. But the situation we must now introduce is one where the domestic price-ratio between commodities X_1 and X_2 is *distorted* by a tariff and/or trade subsidy and it is further assumed that this distortion must be taken as *given*. The problem then, as noted by Findlay and Wellisz (1976, p. 545) is "an inherently second best one" in which "the criterion for acceptance of the project is whether or not it will increase the value of total production at world prices as compared with the existing situation, assuming that the distortional policy on the existing goods continues unchanged":[4] this being, of course, the procedure suggested by Little and Mirrlees (1969) in their celebrated *Manual* and also by Bruno (1962, 1967*b*) in his important analytical work on project evaluation.

In applying this criterion for a "small" project, we note first that the introduction of the project will use labor and/or capital that are withdrawn from their present use. As such, the answer to the question whether or not the project (producing X_3) will increase the value of production at world prices is the *same* as to the question whether the world price of a unit of output of the project exceeds or falls short of its cost of production as obtained by evaluating the labor and capital used in producing X_3 at their *shadow* prices, that is, at prices that equal their marginal con-

[4] Provided that inferior goods are ruled out, there is of course a monotonic relationship between welfare and the distance of the availability locus (at international prices) from the origin, given a well-behaved social utility function. Thus, provided the degree of protection, and hence the degree of consumption distortion, remains unchanged over the entire economy before and after the acceptance of the project, one can disregard without error the fact that trade distortions will also distort consumption. It follows immediately, of course, that if one is dealing with a quota restriction, rather than an ad valorem tariff, so that we have essentially a *variable* (degree of) distortion, the aforementioned monotonic relationship between welfare and the distance of the availability locus (at international prices) will break down. More on this is to be found in Bhagwati and Wan (1977).

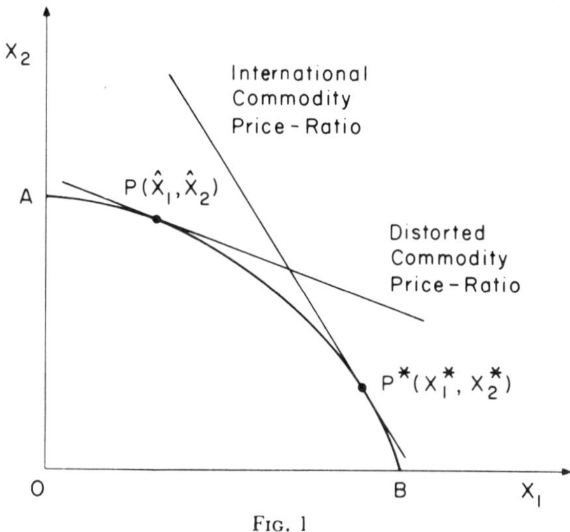

FIG. 1

tribution in their existing use to the value of total production at world prices.

Turn now to figure 1. Here AB is the production possibility curve, defined on commodities X_1 and X_2. At free trade, production would be at $P^*(X_1^*, X_2^*)$ reflecting the international commodity prices. However, with trade distortion, the commodity price-ratio is more favorable to commodity X_2 and production is at $P(\hat{X}_1, \hat{X}_2)$. Now, the planner is assumed unable to correct the situation directly, so that the commodity price-ratio, the factor price-ratio, and factor proportions for X_1 and X_2 are to be held fixed at their respective values at $P(\hat{X}_1, \hat{X}_2)$. Denote then the corresponding input coefficients as $(\hat{k}_1, \hat{l}_1)$ and $(\hat{k}_2, \hat{l}_2)$ and factor rentals as $\hat{w}$ and $\hat{r}$.

Now, as noted above, the *second-best* shadow prices of labor $(\hat{w}^*)$ and capital $(\hat{r}^*)$ in this situation must equal the change in the quantities of X_1 and X_2 output, evaluated at *international* prices p_1^* and p_2^*, resulting from a marginal change in labor and capital, respectively, starting at $P(\hat{X}_1, \hat{X}_2)$ and maintaining the distorted commodity price-ratio for production decisions.[5] Thus, defining $W = p_1^* X_1 + p_2^* X_2$ and the total availability of capital and labor as $\bar{K}$ and $\bar{L}$, respectively, it is clear that the shadow price of labor will be $dW/d\bar{L}$ and that of capital will be $dW/d\bar{K}$, where the derivatives must be evaluated for the distorted situation. This is readily done as follows. First, since capital supply is fixed $(\bar{K})$, we have: $\hat{k}_1(dX_1/d\bar{L}) + \hat{k}_2(dX_2/d\bar{L}) = 0$, and, for labor, the corresponding equation is: $\hat{l}_1(dX_1/d\bar{L}) + \hat{l}_2(dX_2/d\bar{L}) = 1$. Therefore, $dX_1/d\bar{L} = -\hat{k}_2/(\hat{k}_1\hat{l}_2 - \hat{k}_2\hat{l}_1)$ and $dX_2/d\bar{L} = \hat{k}_1/(\hat{k}_1\hat{l}_2 - \hat{k}_2\hat{l}_1)$. Hence, the shadow

[5] The notation $\hat{w}^*$, $\hat{r}^*$ is used here because the circumflex refers to the distorted situation and the asterisk to the evaluation of output change at international prices.

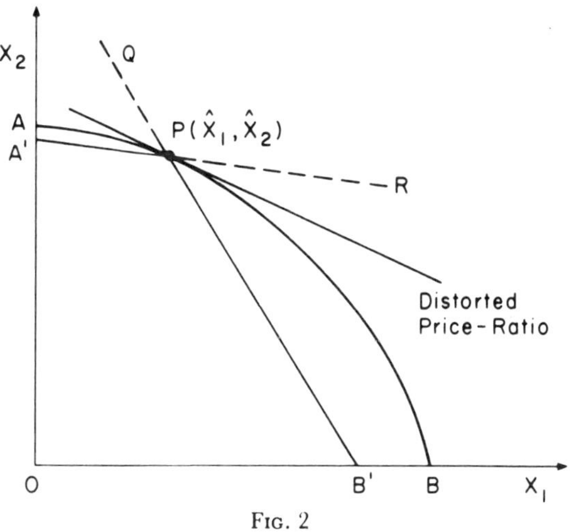

FIG. 2

price of labor, defined as: $\hat{w}^* = p_1^*(dX_1/d\bar{L}) + p_2^*(dX_2/d\bar{L})$ is seen to be equal to:

$$\hat{w}^* = \frac{p_2^*\hat{k}_1 - p_1^*\hat{k}_2}{\hat{k}_1\hat{l}_2 - \hat{k}_2\hat{l}_1}. \tag{1}$$

Similarly, we can see that the shadow price of capital is:

$$\hat{r}^* = \frac{p_1^*\hat{l}_2 - p_2^*\hat{l}_1}{\hat{k}_1\hat{l}_2 - \hat{k}_2\hat{l}_1}. \tag{2}$$

It is readily seen that these are also the values of $\hat{w}^*$ and $\hat{r}^*$ that satisfy the equations:[6]

$$p_1^* = \hat{w}^*\hat{l}_1 + \hat{r}^*\hat{k}_1 \tag{3}$$

$$p_2^* = \hat{w}^*\hat{l}_2 + \hat{r}^*\hat{k}_2. \tag{4}$$

Now, it is easy to see that the shift in outputs, as labor (capital) is withdrawn from P, maintaining the distortion and hence the distorted commodity price-ratio, is yielded by the corresponding Rybczynski line. So, assuming that X_1 is K-intensive at P (i.e., $\hat{k}_1/\hat{l}_1 > \hat{k}_2/\hat{l}_2$), one can see, in figure 2, that the economy will move from P down line PB' as

[6] This is also the procedure suggested for deriving shadow factor prices by Diamond and Mirrlees (1976) in their analysis of a similar problem. It may be noted here that, in the case where the trade distortion is not ad valorem but, say, a specific tariff (or subsidy) or a quantitative restriction, the coefficients $\hat{l}_1$, $\hat{k}_1$, $\hat{l}_2$, and $\hat{k}_2$ will change with the withdrawal of factors even for a "small" project and one cannot use this procedure for estimating shadow factor prices. Moreover, note also that, if the number of factors differs from the number of goods, then shadow factor prices may not be uniquely defined for small changes and/or may be nonstationary for large changes. On all this, see Bhagwati and Wan (1977).

labor is reduced, up line PQ as labor is increased, up PA' as capital is reduced, and down PR as capital is increased. It equally follows, from the evaluation of these shifts at the *international* (rather than the distorted) commodity price-ratio, that $\hat{w}^*$ will be negative if the international price line is steeper that PB' (i.e., $p_1^*/p_2^* > \hat{k}_1/\hat{k}_2$) and $\hat{y}^*$ will be negative if the international price line is flatter than PA' (i.e., $p_1^*/p_2^* < \hat{l}_1/\hat{l}_2$); and that nonnnegative values for $\hat{w}^*$ and $\hat{y}^*$ will obtain only when the international price-ratio is in the range spanned by PB' and PA'.

That it is possible for $\hat{w}^*$ *or* $\hat{y}^*$ to be negative would appear to be a paradox. For, it of course implies, for instance, that when (say) $\hat{w}^* < 0$, it would pay society to implement a project with zero output (X_3) and positive labor input: in other words, that if labor were withdrawn from existing production, thanks to the project, this will increase the value of such production at international prices. But then this paradox is only yet another instance of "immiserizing growth"; the presence of the marginal labor is immiserizing, given the distortion;[7] and thus the paradox is readily resolved.

In their derivation of shadow factor prices for the above problem, however, Findlay and Wellisz (1976) bypass this possibility of negative factor prices by deriving these prices instead via the solution to a programming problem which is tantamount to (see fig. 2) deriving the shadow factor prices corresponding to the international prices *but* subject to a "feasible" production possibility curve defined by $A'PB'$. These Findlay-Wellisz shadow prices ($\hat{w}^*$, $\hat{y}^*$) are clearly yielded by putting the international price-ratio tangent to $A'PB'$, in the usual way, and are illustrated to advantage in figure 3.

Figure 3 is the all-too-familiar Samuelson diagram and needs no explanation. Now, movement along the *unrestricted* production possibility curve APB in figure 2 corresponds to movement along the curve QPR in figure 3, relating the commodity price-ratio to the corresponding factor price-ratio. Similarly, movement along the *restricted* production possibility curve $A'PB'$ in figure 2 corresponds in figure 3 to following the y-axis in the fourth quadrant from ∞ up to the point S where $OS = \hat{k}_1/\hat{k}_2$, then along the curve $SPNZ$ up to Z (where N is at a distance $\hat{l}_1/\hat{l}_2$ from the x-axis) and then following a straight line parallel to the x-axis. The (restricted) curve $SPNZ$, depicting w/y as a function of p_1/p_2, can be shown to be increasing and concave, with a common tangent with the (unrestricted) curve QPR at P. Thus, the Findlay-

[7] Cf. Bhagwati (1968); Johnson (1967) who deals with the precise distortion in our model here; and Bhagwati (1971) who states the general theory of immiserizing growth that explains and ties together the different instances of immiserizing growth. The phenomenon of negative shadow factor prices, in turn, is related to the empirically important phenomenon of value subtraction at international prices: the latter requires, but does not necessarily follow from, the former; see Bhagwati, Srinivasan, and Wan (1977).

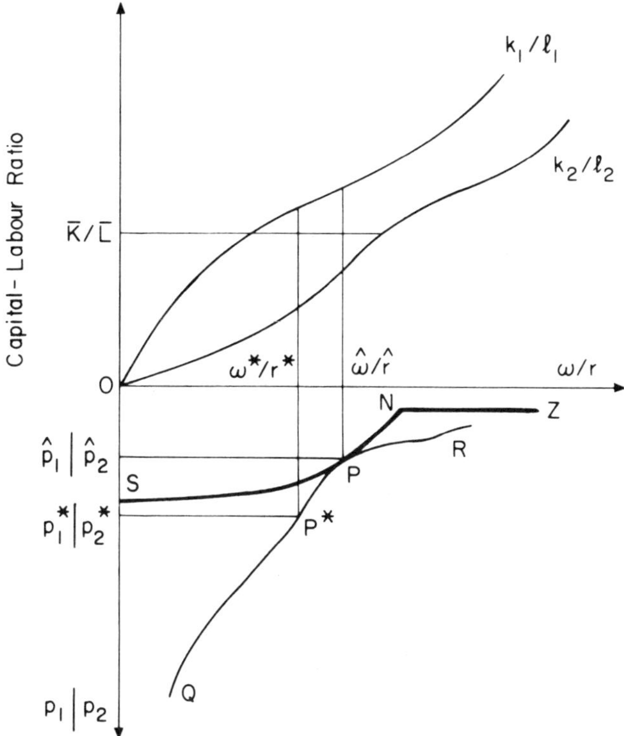

FIG. 3

Wellisz shadow price-ratio $\hat{w}^*/\hat{y}^*$ will be infinite for $p_1^*/p_2^* \geq \hat{k}_1/\hat{k}_2$ and zero for $p_1^*/p_2^* \leq \hat{l}_1\hat{l}_2$, while taking positive values in the range spanned by $\hat{k}_1/\hat{k}_2$ and $\hat{l}_1/\hat{l}_2$. This procedure therefore clearly will yield shadow prices that coincide with the correct ones yielded by our procedure only when $\hat{w}^*/\hat{y}^* \geq 0$, that is, in figures 1 and 2, only for the parametric case where the international price-ratio lies in the range spanned by PA' and PB'. For the parametric cases where the international price-ratio lies outside of this range, the Findlay-Wellisz procedure will incorrectly yield, not negative shadow factor prices, but a shadow factor price-ratio, $\hat{w}^*/\hat{y}^* = 0$ or ∞, according to whether the production specialization, corresponding to the international price-ratio, occurred in figure 2 at B' (on X_1) or A' (on X_2).[8]

II. ERPs, DRCs, et Al.

We have thus deduced, in the preceding section, the precise shadow prices that must be used, in a distorted situation, for project appraisal. We are

[8] An alternative analysis of the inappropriateness of the Findlay-Wellisz procedure, in programming terms, is available from the authors, on request.

therefore now in a position to decide on the competing claims of the ERP and DRC proponents as to their relative merits as techniques of project appraisal. As careful reading of this debate in this *Journal* (1972), already cited, will unmistakably reveal, the first priority in this area is to define one's concepts unambiguously.

Since these and other economists distinguish between direct and indirect use of factors, thus including intermediates which were not included in the analysis in Section I above, we should first state that our project-acceptance criterion, suitably amended, is the following:

$$p_3^* \geq k_3\hat{\gamma}^* + l_3\hat{w}^* + f_1 p_1^* \tag{5}$$

where it is now assumed that X_1 is used in project (X_3) with coefficient f_1 per unit output of X_3 and where k_3, l_3, and f_1 are assumed fixed so that one is essentially treating each process as a project. What the criterion says, of course, is that the project, to be accepted, must produce output which, when evaluated at international prices, exceeds or equals the cost of production evaluated at the (second-best) shadow factor prices. Now, note that the right-hand side of (5) is written in a form that includes the primary and intermediate inputs. But, it can *equivalently* be written in the form including direct *plus* indirect primary factors, that is, by decomposing intermediates into primary factors:

$$p_3^* \geq (k_3 + f_1\hat{k}_1)\hat{\gamma}^* + (l_3 + f_1\hat{l}_1)\hat{w}^*. \tag{6}$$

Now, noting that the DRC concept implies that one is measuring the domestic resources used in an activity to produce a unit of foreign exchange, we can distinguish sharply among the following, alternative concepts that correspond, in one way or another, to the concepts that are often apparently used indistinguishably in the literature.

Note, initially, that by first best we will refer to factor valuations (w^*, γ^*) corresponding to the *first-best* optimal situation at $P^*(X_1^*, X_2^*)$ in figure 1. By second best, we will denote instead the factor valuations ($\hat{w}^*$, $\hat{\gamma}^*$) that reflect the second-best optimal situation, given the distortion. Finally, by "private" we will denote the factor valuations ($\hat{w}$, $\hat{\gamma}$) that actually obtain in the distorted situation at P.

Next, we should also note that the debate includes additionally a distinction among measures working with intermediates or alternatively with the intermediates decomposed into the primary factors producing them. Hence, we will distinguish also between decomposed-intermediates and direct-intermediates measures.[9] We will thus have altogether six measures of DRCs and one for ERP. We may therefore now state these alternative concepts/measures in regard to the project producing X_3, with

[9] We could also, in principle, have distinguished between "gross" and "net" values, as explained in the text presently. However, there is no evidence that gross measures have been computed so that we confine ourselves in the text to only the net measures.

brevity, noting that, in the denominator of all the measures set out below, commodities (X_1, X_2, and X_3) are always valued at their international prices.[10]

DRC_I: First-best, Direct-Intermediates Measure

Here, we have the evaluation of the primary factors at first-best shadow wage and rental (w^*, γ^*), corresponding to the situation where the international commodity prices obtain domestically and therefore the distortions have been eliminated. These are also the shadow prices suggested by Bacha and Taylor (1971). In this case, we define:

$$\text{DRC}_\text{I} = \frac{k_3\gamma^* + l_3 w^*}{p_3^* - f_1 p_1^*} \tag{7}$$

for the project, using the "direct" formulation: $f_1 p_1^*$ in the denominator, rather than decomposing that into $[(f_1 k_1^*)\gamma^* + (f_1 l_1^*)w^*]$ as in the next measure DRC_II (where k_1^* and l_1^* are the coefficients corresponding to first-best shadow prices).

DRC_{II}: First-best, Decomposed-Intermediates Measure

Here, DRC_I modifies equivalently therefore to:

$$\text{DRC}_\text{II} = \frac{k_3\gamma^* + l_3 w^*}{p_3^* - [(f_1 k_1^*)\gamma^* + (f_1 l_1^*)w^*]} \tag{8}$$

(Now, note that we have been referring *only* to formulations that deal with *value added* in the denominator. These DRC measures are therefore "net" measures. Alternatively, we could have also chosen "gross" measures, rewriting DRC_I, for example, as $[k_3\gamma^* + l_3 w^* + f_1 p_1^*]/p_3^*$, and DRC_II, for example, as $[(k_3 + f_1 k_1^*)\gamma^* + (l_3 + f_1 l_1^*)w^*]/p_3^*$. But, as already remarked earlier, none of the DRC practitioners have used gross measures; hence they are not added here.)

DRC_{III}: Second-best, Direct-Intermediates Measure

Here, we replace the first-best shadow factor prices with the second-best shadow prices, to alter DRC_I to:

$$\text{DRC}_\text{III} = \frac{k_3\hat{\gamma}^* + l_3\hat{w}^*}{p_3^* - f_1 p_1^*}\,. \tag{9}$$

[10] While the DRCs are conceptually stated below for the project X_3, they can be readily adapted for the existing activities as well.

DRC_{IV}: Second-best, Decomposed-Intermediates Measure

Similarly, we alter $\mathrm{DRC_{II}}$ here to:

$$\mathrm{DRC_{IV}} = \frac{k_3\hat{r}^* + l_3\hat{w}^*}{p_3^* - [(f_1\hat{k}_1)\hat{r}^* + (f_1\hat{l}_1)\hat{w}^*]} \tag{10}$$

which is equivalent to $\mathrm{DRC_{III}}$.

DRC_V: Private, Direct-Intermediates Measure

Here, we use the market prices and hence get a "private" DRC measure:

$$\mathrm{DRC_V} = \frac{k_3\hat{r} + l_3\hat{w}}{p_3^* - f_1p_1^*}\,. \tag{11}$$

DRC_{VI}: Private, Decomposed-Intermediates Measure

Here, we get:

$$\mathrm{DRC_{VI}} = \frac{k_3\hat{r} + l_3\hat{w}}{p_3^* - [(f_1\hat{k}_1)\hat{r} + (f_1\hat{l}_1)\hat{w}]} \tag{12}$$

which is clearly *not* equivalent to $\mathrm{DRC_V}$ since the factor quantities yielded by the decomposition are being evaluated at the distorted, actual factor prices whereas the intermediates in $\mathrm{DRC_V}$ are directly being evaluated at the undistorted, international prices.

ERP

Then, finally, we have the well-known ERP measure:

$$\mathrm{ERP} = \left[\frac{\hat{p}_3 - f_1\hat{p}_1}{p_3^* - f_1p_1^*}\right] - 1 \tag{13}$$

where $\hat{p}_3$ is chosen such that $(\hat{p}_3 - f_1\hat{p}_1) = (\hat{k}_3\hat{r} + \hat{l}_3\hat{w})$. Note that, in consequence, the numerator in the bracketed part of the ERP measure refers to the evaluation of domestic primary factors via the valuation of output and intermediates at actual (rather than shadow) prices; the numerators of (the bracketed term in) ERP and $\mathrm{DRC_V}$ *as also* $\mathrm{DRC_{VI}}$ are therefore identical. However, the denominator in the ERP measure represents value added at international prices and is identical with the denominator of $\mathrm{DRC_V}$ *but not* $\mathrm{DRC_{VI}}$.

Now, the relevant question before us is whether, if a project is accepted by our (correctly derived) criterion, it will also be accepted if we were instead to compute the ERP or DRC for it and for the existing activities and then rank it correspondingly vis-à-vis these other activities. In short, would the ERP, and the DRC, be less for an acceptable project (X_3) than for the existing activities (X_1 and X_2)?

To answer this question, note first the fact that, for the existing activities (X_1 and X_2) at first-best *or* second-best *shadow* factor prices, the DRCs must necessarily be unity.[11] It is equally evident that the DRCs at the *private* factor prices will differ from unity. Thus we have DRC_I to $DRC_{IV} = 1$, but DRC_V and DRC_{VI} are not necessarily unity.

By comparing the above with our project acceptance criterion, we then see right away that, if we do have to take the distorted situation as given, the measures DRC_{III} and DRC_{IV} will be unity for the existing activities and less than unity for the project if the project is acceptable. Hence, the DRCs using appropriately derived second-best shadow factor prices (and international-price valuation of the traded commodities) will lead to a correct acceptance/rejection of a project.

However, it is equally evident that neither the DRCs using the first-best shadow factor prices (i.e., DRC_I and DRC_{II}) nor those using private, market prices of factors (i.e., DRC_V and DRC_{VI}) can, as a general rule, lead to the correct acceptance/rejection of the project.[12] In particular, it is clear that the ERP measure, which corresponds to DRC_V, will identically therefore be quite inappropriate to the task.[13]

While therefore ERP is an inappropriate measure to use for project analysis, it may be suggested that it be replaced by a so-called social ERP measure. The only operational implication of such a suggestion would be to convert ERP into (the *correct* criterion) DRC_{III}, that is, to replace the incorrect numerator $(\hat{p}_3 - f_1\hat{p}_1)$ in the bracketed term in ERP by the correct numerator $(k_3\hat{r}^* + l_3\hat{w}^*)$. But this implies revaluing domestic factors *directly* at the second-best prices, in the manner set out in Section I, whereas the essence of the ERP approach (which was developed in the context of the quite different, "positive," problem of predicting resource-allocational effects of a tariff structure) has always been to arrive at the numerator *indirectly* as the difference between the domestic values of inputs and outputs (yielding equivalently value added at domestic, "private," prices, of course). To derive DRCs, by estimating (as must be

[11] For complexities that arise in this regard, however, when the number of primary factors is less than the number of traded goods, see Bhagwati and Wan (1977).

[12] For an interesting analysis of the problem as to when a project accepted (rejected) by the incorrect use of first-best factor prices would be rejected (accepted) by the correct use of second-best factor prices, see Findlay-Wellisz (1976).

[13] Of course, the choice of a project on the basis of ERP rankings may nonetheless, in specific cases, be a correct choice. In fact, the interested reader may well analyze the conditions under which this will be the case, just as Findlay-Wellisz (1976) have analyzed elegantly the conditions under which the use of first-best shadow factor prices à la Bacha-Taylor (1971) will nonetheless result in a correct choice/rejection of a project.

done) the correct shadow factor prices ($\hat{w}^*$ and $\hat{r}^*$), and then to rechristen them as "social ERPs" is therefore likely to lead to confusion; and, in our judgment, it is best therefore to drop the terminology and concept of ERPs altogether from cost-benefit analysis.

Next, it is also evident that it makes absolutely no difference whether one uses the direct-intermediates measure DRC_{III} or the measure DRC_{IV} where the intermediates are decomposed into the primary factors used up in them; *as long as* second-best shadow factor prices are used for project appraisal, as indeed they should be, the two methods are identical and equally correct. This demonstration, therefore, also seems to bear out Bruno's (1972) rejection of the Balassa-Schydlowsky (1968) contention that this distinction matters: Bruno (1966, 1967*a*) was clearly working within an institutionally (quantity-) constrained framework which therefore yielded second-best shadow prices.

Furthermore, note that if the project analyst were to use the following "hybrid" DRC measure:

$$DRC_{VII} = \frac{k_3\hat{r}^* + l_3\hat{w}^*}{p_3^* - f_1\hat{p}_1} \tag{14a}$$

$$= \frac{k_3\hat{r}^* + l_3\hat{w}^*}{p_3^* - (f_1\hat{k}_1\hat{r} + f_1\hat{l}_1\hat{w})} \tag{14b}$$

then clearly the numerator is correct but the denominator is erroneous; but this clearly is *not* what Bruno (1972) proposes. In fact, this would be precisely the opposite kind of error to that which ERP would imply as a project criterion: for, with ERP, the denominator is correct but the numerator is not.

Finally, the question has been raised in this ERP versus DRC debate: what if the introduction of the garment project *leads* (via a rule for example which requires that domestic fabrics *must* be used) to the licensing and creation of a tariff-protected fabric industry?[14] If such is indeed the case, we should naturally wish to redefine and consider, as a project, the *vertically integrated* project involving *both* the garments and the fabrics that are produced for the garments. And then, the correct project appraisal would be along exactly the same lines as before, with DRC_{III} and DRC_{IV},

[14] Such a rule (or variations thereof) can be found in the context of import-substituting industrialization in many less developed countries. See Bhagwati and Desai (1970) and Bhagwati and Srinivasan (1975) for India, and Bhagwati (1977) for more extended discussion of such rules and the associated policies of "automatic" protection. An early and correct analysis of the implications of such a rule on cost-benefit analysis is in Little-Mirrlees (1969). In fact, Bruno (1962, pp. 112–13, 147) appears to have had the earliest analysis of this "fabric-garment" example!

all using second-best shadow factor prices, providing the correct method for doing project appraisal for this redefined project.

III. Alternative Factor Market Distortions and Second-best Shadow Factor Prices

In this section, we briefly extend our analysis to three standard factor market distortions which trade theorists have analyzed in great depth, deriving second-best shadow prices in each case in the manner set out in Section I. The three distortions are: (*a*) a sector-specific sticky wage;[15] (*b*) a generalized sticky wage;[16] and (*c*) a wage differential between sectors.[17]

Sector-specific Sticky Wage

Consider a typical two-sector model of the Harris-Todaro variety.[18] Here, the minimum wage is set in the manufacturing sector, producing X_2, in terms of X_2 at $\bar{w}$. The workers from the agricultural sector, producing X_1, migrate to the manufacturing sector until the agricultural wage equals the *expected* manufacturing wage. The expected wage is defined as the sticky manufacturing wage, $\bar{w}$, multiplied by the probability of a worker in the manufacturing sector obtaining employment therein. This probability, in turn, is assumed equal to the ratio of actual employment (L_2) in manufacturing to the total labor force there, (i.e., $\bar{L} - L_1$).

Assuming perfect competition and the production functions in the two sectors to be strictly concave functions of employment, and denoting the latter by F_1 and F_2 and the international price-ratio as p_1^*/p_2^* as before, we can now write the Harris-Todaro equilibrium as:

$$F_2'(L_2) = \bar{w} \tag{15}$$

$$\frac{p_1^*}{p_2^*} \cdot F_1'(L_1) = \bar{w} \cdot \frac{L_2}{\bar{L} - L_1}. \tag{16}$$

[15] This distortion was brought into analytical discussion by Harris and Todaro (1970); the "sector specificity" and its critical importance were noted and analyzed in Bhagwati and Srinivasan (1974) and in Srinivasan and Bhagwati (1975).

[16] This is the distortion where the sticky, actual wage exceeds the shadow wage but the sticky wage applies universally across sectors. The major papers on this distortion, initially analyzed by Haberler (1950), are by Lefeber (1971) and Brecher (1974*a*, 1974*b*).

[17] Among the principal positive analyses of the distortion when the same factor must be paid for differentially by different sectors are those by Hagen (1958), Johnson (1966), Bhagwati and Srinivasan (1971), Herberg and Kemp (1971), Jones (1971*a*), and Magee (1976); the welfare analyses are by Hagen (1958) and Bhagwati and Ramaswami (1963). Pearce and Mundlak have made valuable contributions also.

[18] The model as set out in Harris and Todaro (1970) is misspecified on the demand side. See therefore the correct specification, as set out in Bhagwati and Srinivasan (1974) and followed here.

Since the availability of foreign exchange in this model is given by $Z = F_2 + (p_1^*/p_2^*) \cdot F_1$, the second-best shadow price of labor is clearly:

$$\hat{w}^* = \frac{dZ}{d\bar{L}} = \frac{p_1^*}{p_2^*} \cdot F_1' \left[\frac{F_1'}{F_1' - (\bar{L} - L_1)F_1''}\right]. \tag{17}$$

With $F_1'' < 0$ by strict concavity of F_1, and $\bar{L} > L_1$, we then see that the second-best shadow wage for labor is less than the agricultural wage which, in turn, is less than the manufacturing wage. Note also that the shadow wage is positive, instead of zero, despite the unemployed labor; this is because any withdrawal of labor from the labor force ($\bar{L}$), while initially reducing unemployment, will simultaneously raise the expected wage in manufacturing and hence result in reduction of agricultural employment and output.

The foregoing analysis assumes that the employment (at whatever wage rate) in the project has no impact on the expected wage in the manufacturing sector except insofar as it affects the manufacturing labor force. Thus writing ε as the employment in the project and η as the resulting migration from agriculture, the expected wage in the manufacturing sector after migration is $\bar{w}L_2/(\bar{L} - \varepsilon) - (L_1 - \eta)$ which is equated in turn to the agricultural wage $p_1^*F_1'(L_1 - \eta)$. However, if we were to assume that the project laborers are employed at some wage, w^p, and that project employment at this wage affects the expected wage in the manufacturing sector, the latter would be $wL_2 + w^p\varepsilon/\bar{L} - (L_1 - \eta)$ which again is equated to $p_1^*F_1'(L_1 - \eta)$. Solving the latter for η and noting that the shadow wage is the loss in agricultural output per unit of project employment, that is, $p_1^*F_1'(\eta/\varepsilon)$, we get shadow wage $= (w^p \cdot F_1')/[F_1' - F_1''(\bar{L} - L_1)]$. In the case where $F_1'' = 0$, this reduces to w^p, the wage paid to the project laborer. If we make the further assumption that $w^p = \bar{w}$, that is, the project employs labor at the manufacturing wage, the shadow wage equals the manufacturing wage: a highly special case, as we have just shown, but one which has been focused upon in the standard cost-benefit analysis of the Harris-Todaro model.

Generalized Sticky Wage

Shift now to the model where the wage is sticky across the two sectors at the level $\bar{w}$. Assuming then that commodity X_2 is capital-intensive, that is, $(K_2/L_2 > K_1/L_1)$, we now get:

$$\frac{F_2}{L_2} - \frac{K_2}{L_2} \cdot F_2^K \geq \bar{w} \tag{18}$$

$$\frac{F_2}{L_2F_2^K} - \frac{K_2}{L_2} = \frac{F_1}{L_1F_1^K} - \frac{K_1}{L_1} \tag{19}$$

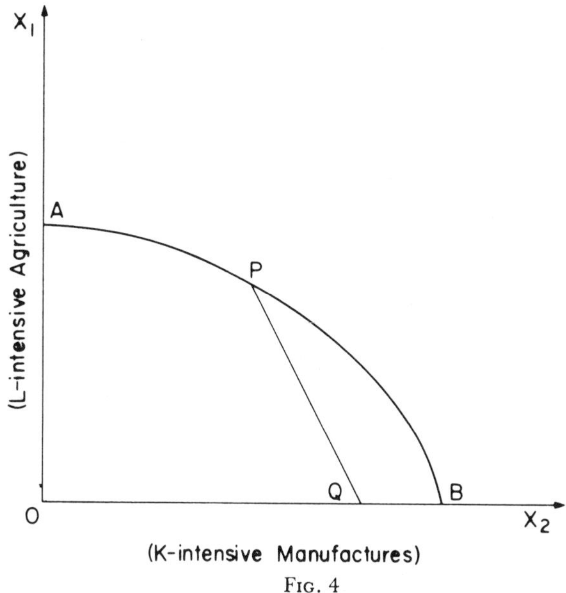

FIG. 4

where F_1^K, F_2^K, F_1^L, and F_2^L are the partial derivatives with respect to K and L, respectively; that is, they are marginal products of capital and labor; and F_2/L_2 and F_1/L_1 are the average products of labor in production of X_2 and X_1, respectively.

We can then see that, in terms of figure 4, the production possibility curve is APB, P representing the point at which $(F_2/L_2 - K_2/L_2 \cdot F_2^K) = \bar{w}$. At points to the left [right] of P, $(F_2/L_2 - K_2/L_2 \cdot F_2^K) > [<] \bar{w}$. It is evident then that, with the minimum wage constraint, the feasible production possibility curve will be APQ where PQ is the Rybczynski line (for variations in labor) and, at points on PQ other than P, there is unemployed labor. Let the capital-labor ratios at P then be $\bar{K}_2/\bar{L}_2$ and $\bar{K}_1/\bar{L}_1$.

Now, when the international price-ratio p_1^*/p_2^* yields tangency along AP, the market and shadow wages will be naturally identical, and will exceed $\bar{w}$ if the tangency is off P. For the price-ratio tangent to APB at P, the production equilibrium however may be anywhere between P and Q, the different production equilibria implying different labor availabilities. Therefore, for this tangential price-ratio, the shadow and actual wages will be $\bar{w}$ for production at P, whereas the actual wage will be $\bar{w}$ but the shadow wage will be zero for points other than P on PQ.[19] Finally, for all commodity price-ratios steeper than the price-ratio tangent at P, there

[19] At points other than P on PQ, furthermore, the shadow rental of capital will be the *average* product of capital in X_2 at P along the curve APB, rather than its market value which will equal the marginal product.

will be complete specialization on X_2 at Q and the corresponding actual wage will be $\bar{w}$ while the shadow wage will be zero.[20]

Hence, unlike in the sector-specific wage stickiness case, the unemployment of labor can indeed be taken to imply a zero shadow wage for labor. However, associated with this, the shadow rental of capital will exceed its market rental, so that the standard prescription of putting the wage of unemployed labor equal to zero but using the market rental of capital is wrong.

The Wage-Differential Case

Take, finally, the distortion where the wage in X_2 is a multiple λ of that in X_1. In this case, it is well known that the production possibility curve will shrink to AQB, in figure 5. Furthermore, AQB need not be concave to the origin, the market equilibrium need not be unique for any commodity price-ratio, and the commodity price-ratio will not equal the marginal rate of transformation along AQB.[21]

Let the market equilibrium in the initial, distorted situation be at Q. Then, we can derive the two Rybczynski lines, QB' (for variations in labor availability) and QA' (for variations in capital availability), assuming as earlier that X_2 is capital intensive.

Now, the international price-ratio equals the ratio of *marginal* products of capital in producing X_2 and X_1 with the techniques corresponding to Q (i.e., $p_1^*/p_2^* = F_K^2/F_K^1$, the latter derivatives as at Q). On the other hand, the slope of QB' (measured against the vertical axis) will equal the ratio of the corresponding *average* products.

It follows then that the international price-line would be flatter than QB' and steeper than QA', given the capital intensity of X_2 relative to X_1, provided there were no wage differential λ. However, in the presence of the wage differential, the international price-line may well be steeper (flatter) than $QB'(QA')$, with the wage in X_2 exceeding that in X_1 by factor $\lambda(>1)$, the condition for this "reversal" of relative slopes of the price-ratio and the Rybczynski line being that X_2 ceases to be capital intensive relative to X_1 if the factor intensities are compared on a *differential-weighted* basis.[22]

It is then easy to see that, as in Section I, the second-best shadow wage of labor, that is, $[p_1^*(\bar{K}_2/F_2) - p_2^*(\bar{K}_1/F_1)]/[(\bar{K}_2/F_2)(\bar{L}_1/F_1) - (\bar{K}_1/F_1)(\bar{L}_2/F_2)]$, or the shadow rental on capital, that is, $[p_2^*(\bar{L}_1/F_1) -$

[20] At Q also, the shadow price of capital will continue to be the average product of capital in manufacturing at point P, since at Q only the manufactured good, X_2, is produced using all the available capital and the same technique as at P.

[21] For these and other pathologies, see Bhagwati and Srinivasan (1971) and Magee's excellent survey (1976).

[22] Jones (1971*a*) calls the differential-weighted intensities the "value" as against the Samuelsonian "physical" factor-intensities.

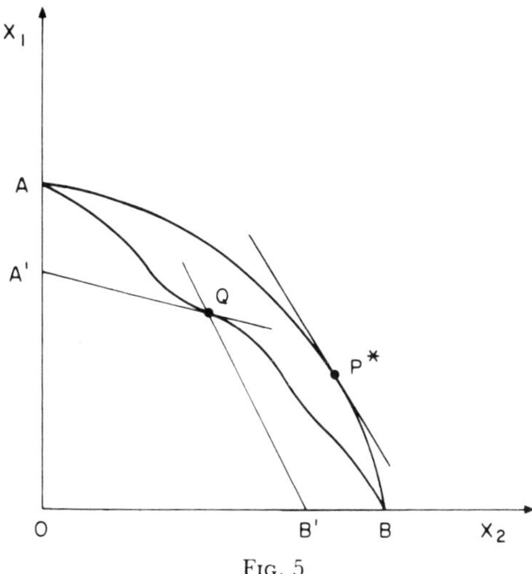

FIG. 5

$p_1^*(\bar{L}_2/F_2)]/[(\bar{K}_2/F_2)(\bar{L}_1/F_1) - (\bar{K}_1/F_1)(\bar{L}_2/F_2)]$, will be negative when such reversal of relative slopes exists; and, once again, the Findlay-Wellisz procedure of deriving shadow prices would yield an incorrect zero wage (rental).

IV. Concluding Remarks

A few concluding observations are in order. First, while our results on project appraisal have been shown to be successfully convertible into appropriately defined DRCs, this is not the same thing of course as having shown that these were precisely the DRC definitions (as against the many others that we have distinguished) that one or more of the DRC proponents, in the project-appraisal debate among the DRC and ERP proponents, had in mind.

Second, while we have confined our analysis to "small" projects, drawing infinitesimal resources away from the existing distorted situation, it is equally clear from our analysis that the results will hold also for "large" projects. Given the Rybczynski-line properties of the different models, the shadow prices of factors will be identical for small and large shifts of factors into the project.[23]

Third, we might as well note explicitly that our analysis could be extended to models involving nontraded goods; this would permit the introduction of the real exchange rate in a meaningful manner into the

[23] On the analysis of the possibility of such "stationarity" of the "marginal-variational" shadow factor prices, in more general models with many goods and factors, see Bhagwati and Wan (1977).

analysis. The extension to models with sector-specific factors is not merely readily done;[24] it will however introduce no special insights that qualify what has been learned from the present paper.

Fourth, note that we are implicitly assuming that, in respect of projects which will be chosen under shadow prices but *not* under actual market prices, the resulting losses are covered in some nondistortionary way. However, if the losses can be covered only by some form of distortionary taxation, then the shadow prices (for both inputs and outputs) have to be calculated reflecting this fact. *Alternatively*, our analysis can be held to apply without modification to the case where the planning authorities are investigating the social profitability of a private project which is commercially viable at market prices. In this instance, if social profitability is absent, the planning authorities can decide to eliminate the activity by prohibiting it, and the revenue problem does not arise.

Fifth, note also that we evaluated the project at a given technique. Thus, if a project can exploit alternative techniques, from which entrepreneurs would choose the cost-minimizing one, then the revenue problem will arise *also* because a suitable factor-use tax-cum-subsidy will have to be provided so that the "correct" technique (i.e., that using coefficients k_3, l_3, and f_1 if the project X_3 has been shown to be socially profitable) is chosen.

Finally, it is also clear that implicit in our analysis is the assumption that problems of income distribution and savings can be tackled through deployment of appropriate nondistortionary instruments. Obviously, if this is not possible, the shadow prices will have to be calculated afresh by introducing additional constraints which reflect the feasible set of public policy instruments.

References

Bacha, Edmar, and Taylor, Lance. "Foreign Exchange Shadow Prices: A Critical Review of Current Theories." *Q.J.E.* 85 (May 1971): 197–224.

Balassa, Bela, and Schydlowsky, Daniel M. "Effective Tariffs, Domestic Cost of Foreign Exchange, and the Equilibrium Exchange Rate." *J.P.E.* 76 (May/June 1968): 348–60.

———. "Domestic Resource Costs and Effective Protection Once Again." *J.P.E.* 80 (January/February 1972): 63–69.

Bhagwati, Jagdish N. "Immiserizing Growth: A Geometrical Note." *Rev. Econ. Studies* 25 (June 1958): 201–5.

———. "Distortions and Immiserizing Growth: A Generalization." *Rev. Econ. Studies* 35 (October 1968): 481–85.

———. "The Generalized Theory of Distortions and Welfare." In *Trade, Balance*

[24] For example, the latter is done readily, using the Jones (1971*b*) model where each of two sectors has a specific factor. The project (X_3) can then be thought of as drawing one or both of these specific factors and/or the mobile, nonspecific factor(s) from the existing, distorted situation.

of Payments, and Growth, edited by J. N. Bhagwati et al. Amsterdam: North-Holland, 1971.

———. *Anatomy and Consequences of Exchange Control Regimes.* New York: Nat. Bur. Econ. Res., 1977 (forthcoming).

Bhagwati, J. N., and Desai, Padma. *India: Planning for Industrialization: Industrialization and Trade Policies since 1951.* London: Oxford Univ. Press, for OECD Development Centre, 1970.

Bhagwati, J. N., and Ramaswami, V. K. "Domestic Distortions, Tariffs and the Theory of Optimum Subsidy." *J.P.E.* 71, no. 1 (February 1963): 44–50.

Bhagwati, J. N.; Ramaswami, V. K.; and Srinivasan, T. N. "Domestic Distortions, Tariffs, and the Theory of Optimum Subsidy: Some Further Results." *J.P.E.* 77, no. 6 (November/December 1969): 1005–10.

Bhagwati, J. N., and Srinivasan, T. N. "The Theory of Wage Differentials: Production Response and Factor Price Equalisation," *J. Internat. Econ.* 1 (February 1971): 19–35.

———. "On Reanalyzing the Harris-Todaro Model: Policy Rankings in the Case of Sector-Specific Sticky Wages." *A.E.R.* 64 (June 1974): 502–8.

———. *Foreign Trade Regimes and Economic Development: India.* New York: Nat. Bur. Econ. Res., 1975.

Bhagwati, J. N.; Srinivasan, T. N.; and Wan, Henry, Jr. "Value Subtracted, Negative Shadow Prices of Factors in Project Evaluations, and Immiserizing Growth: Three Paradoxes in the Presence of Trade Distortions." *Econ. J.*, 1977 (forthcoming).

Bhagwati, J. N., and Wan, Henry, Jr. "Shadow Prices in Project Evaluation, with and without Distortions, and with Many Goods and Factors." Mimeographed. Massachusetts Inst. Tech., January 1977.

Brecher, Richard A. "Minimum Wage Rates and the Pure Theory of International Trade," *Q.J.E.* 88 (February 1974): 98–116. (*a*)

———. "Optimum Commercial Policy for a Minimum Wage Economy." *J. Internat. Econ.* 4 (May 1974): 139–50. (*b*)

Bruno, Michael. *Interdependence, Resource Use and Structural Change in Israel.* Jerusalem: Bank of Israel, 1962.

———. "A Programming Model for Israel." In *The Theory and Design of Economic Development*, edited by I. Adelman and E. Thorbecke. Baltimore: Johns Hopkins Univ. Press, 1966.

———. "Optimal Patterns of Trade and Development." *Rev. Econ. and Statis.* 49 (November 1967): 545–54. (*a*)

———. "The Optimal Selection of Import-substituting and Export-promoting Projects." In *Planning the External Sector: Techniques, Problems and Policies.* New York: United Nations (ST/TAO/SER. C/91), 1967. (*b*)

———. "Domestic Resource Costs and Effective Protection: Clarification and Synthesis." *J.P.E.* 80, no. 1 (January/February 1972): 16–33.

Corden, W. M. *Trade Policy and Economic Welfare.* London: Oxford Univ. Press, 1974.

Diamond, Peter A., and Mirrlees, James A. "Private Constant Returns and Public Shadow Prices." *Rev. Econ. Studies* 43 (February 1976): 41–48.

Findlay, Ronald, and Wellisz, Stanislaw. "Project Evaluation, Shadow Prices, and Trade Policy." *J.P.E.* 84, no. 3 (June 1976): 543–52.

Haberler, Gottfried. "Some Problems in the Pure Theory of International Trade." *Econ. J.* 60 (June 1950): 223–40.

Hagen, Everett E. "An Economic Justification of Protectionism." *Q.J.E.* 72 (November 1958): 496–514.

Harris, John R., and Todaro, Michael. "Migration, Unemployment and Development: A Two-Sector Analysis." *A.E.R.* 60 (March 1970): 126–42.

Herberg, Horst, and Kemp, Murray C. "Factor Market Distortions, the Shape of the Locus of Competitive Outputs, and the Relation between Product Prices and Equilibrium Outputs." In *Trade, Balance of Payments, and Growth*, edited by J. N. Bhagwati et al. Amsterdam: North-Holland, 1971.

Johnson, Harry G. "Optimal Trade Intervention in the Presence of Domestic Distortions." In *Trade, Growth, and the Balance of Payments*, edited by R. E. Caves et al. Amsterdam: North-Holland, 1965.

———. "Factor Market Distortions and the Shape of the Transformation Curve." *Econometrica* 34 (July 1966): 686–98.

———. "The Possibility of Income Losses from Increased Efficiency or Factor Accumulation in the Presence of Tariffs." *Econ. J.* 77 (March 1967): 151–54.

Jones, Ronald W. "Distortions in Factor Markets and the General Equilibrium Model of Production." *J.P.E.* 79, no. 3 (May/June 1971): 437–59. (*a*)

———. "A Three-Factor Model in Theory, Trade, and History." In *Trade, Balance of Payments, and Growth*, edited by J. N. Bhagwati et al. Amsterdam: North-Holland, 1971. (*b*)

Joshi, V. "The Rationale and Relevance of the Little-Mirrlees Criterion." *Bull. Oxford Inst. Econ. and Statis.* 34 (February 1972): 3–33.

Krueger, Anne O. "Evaluating Restrictionist Trade Regimes: Theory and Measurement." *J.P.E.* 80, no. 1 (January/February 1972): 48–62.

Lal, Deepak. "Methods of Project Analysis: A Review." World Bank Occasional Paper no. 16, Washington, D.C., 1974. Distributed by Johns Hopkins Press, Baltimore.

Lefeber, Louis. "Trade and Minimum Wage Rates." In *Trade, Balance of Payments, and Growth*, edited by J. N. Bhagwati et al. Amsterdam: North-Holland, 1971.

Little, I. M. D., and Mirrlees, James A. *Manual of Industrial Project Analysis in Developing Countries*. Vol. 2. Paris: Org. Econ. Cooperation and Development, 1969.

Magee, Stephen. *International Trade and Distortions in Factor Markets*. New York: Marcel Dekker, 1976.

Srinivasan, T. N., and Bhagwati, Jagdish N. "Alternative Policy Rankings in a Large Open Economy with Sector-Specific Minimum Wages." *J. Econ. Theory* 1, no. 3 (December 1975): 356–71.

Erratum

Page 102, line 3 from bottom: "w/γ" should read "w/r".

INTERNATIONAL ECONOMIC REVIEW
Vol. 22, No. 2, June, 1981

THE EVALUATION OF PROJECTS AT WORLD PRICES UNDER TRADE DISTORTIONS: QUANTITATIVE RESTRICTIONS, MONOPOLY POWER IN TRADE AND NONTRADED GOODS*

BY JAGDISH N. BHAGWATI AND T. N. SRINIVASAN[1]

The recent literature[2] on project evaluation has explored the analytical soundness of the so called Little-Mirrlees (LM) rule by which a project is deemed acceptable if it results in an increase in national production valued at world prices. This exploration has been mainly in terms of models characterized by primary factors producing only tradeables, the "small-country" assumption of given world prices for the tradeable goods, and distortionary *ad valorem* tariffs rather than quantitative restrictions.

While there have been numerous discussions of how the complexities avoided by these simplifying assumptions can be accommodated into the practical application of this rule of project evaluation,[3] a rigorous analytical examination of the *precise* manner in which the LM rule may, or why it cannot, continue to be applicable in the presence of these complexities appears to be necessary. With this objective in view, Section 1 sets out the basic framework and concepts central to our analysis, building them around the familiar case of the *ad valorem* tariff. Quantitative restrictions are then analyzed in Section 2. Monopoly power in trade is treated in Section 3. Nontraded goods are considered in Section 4. Concluding observations are offered in Section 5.

1. DELINEATION OF BASIC CONCEPTS USING THE AD VALOREM TARIFF CASE

Consider a simple model with two primary factors, K and L, producing two

* Manuscript received August 30, 1979; revised September 29, 1980.

[1] Our thanks are due to Peter Diamond, Partha Dasgupta, Ronald Findlay, Peter Hammond, Joseph Stiglitz, Lance Taylor and Henry Wan, Jr., for helpful conversations and/or comments. The comments of Trent Bertrand and two other referees of this Review were very valuable. Comments at seminars at Johns Hopkins, Columbia and Yale Universities were also helpful in simplifying parts of the analysis. Partial support under National Science Foundation Grant SOC79-07541 is gratefully acknowledged. The views expressed here are personal and not necessarily of the institutions to which the authors are affiliated.

[2] Among the recent analytical papers to have addressed this specific issue are Findlay and Wellisz [1976], Diamond and Mirrlees [1976], Srinivasan and Bhagwati [1978] and Bhagwati and Wan [1979]. Of importance are also the papers by Bertrand [1974] and [1979]. The earlier literature on the Little-Mirrlees [1969] criterion, of course, is quite extensive and we should particularly mention Joshi [1972] and Lal [1974].

[3] We should note that the earlier writings of Bruno [1962, 1966] on cost-benefit analysis also essentially reflected what we call here the LM rule.

tradeable goods 1 and 2 using constant returns to scale and concave production functions. The economy is a price-taker in world markets in which good 2 sells at a price p^* in terms of good 1, the *numeraire* good. Throughout this section, there is an *ad valorem* tariff at the rate t on imports of good 2. Tariff revenue is redistributed to consumers in a lump sum fashion and, indeed, the government is presumed to undertake the lump sum transfers implicit in the use of a social utility function defined in terms of aggregate consumption of the two goods. Competition is assumed in the markets for goods and factors.[4]

With the tariff-inclusive domestic price p^d $(\equiv p^*(1+t))$ given, the factor prices $\hat{w}$, $\hat{r}$ (for labor and capital respectively), output $\hat{X}_i$, as well as the factor input coefficients $(\hat{k}_i, \hat{l}_i)$ in the production of good i $(i=1, 2)$ are determined. Now consider a project with factor input coefficients $(\hat{k}_3, \hat{l}_3)$ and producing an output with a world price of p_3^*.

1.1. *The LM Rule.* The LM rule then requires the social cost of a unit of project output to be computed as the world-price valuation of the changes in outputs, $d\hat{X}_1$ and $d\hat{X}_2$, caused by the withdrawal of the two factors in amounts $(\hat{k}_3, \hat{l}_3)$ from the production of goods 1 and 2, i.e., as $(d\hat{X}_1+p^*d\hat{X}_2)$. Valuing the unit project output also at its world price, p_3^*, we can then define the net social gain or loss from the acceptance of the project to be:

$$p_3^* - (d\hat{X}_1 + p^*d\hat{X}_2). \tag{1}$$

Hence, if this expression is positive, i.e., at world prices the value of national production (income) increases, the project will increase welfare and should be accepted. The theoretical basis for this rule is that, by a well-known theorem of welfare economics, as long as the degree of distortion in consumption is fixed, an outward shift in the social availability locus will necessarily improve social utility.[5]

1.2. *Defining and Deriving Two Alternative Shadow Factor Prices.* While therefore the LM rule writes the social cost of the project as $(d\hat{X}_1+p^*d\hat{X}_2)$, it is evidently possible also to write it as the valuation of the factors used in the project at their shadow prices: $\hat{w}^*$ and $\hat{r}^*$. We must distinguish then between these LM shadow prices, $\hat{w}^*$ and $\hat{r}^*$, which reflect world-price-valued changes in national

[4] The tariff, as also some other features (e.g., absence of nontraded goods or of monopoly power in trade), will of course be modified as necessary in later sections.

[5] A well-behaved social utility function is presumed here. If both goods are normal, a unique consumption vector exists corresponding to each position of the availability locus. The presence of inferior goods can lead to multiple equilibria, requiring us to interpret the proposition in the text as implying that social utility "can be improved," i.e., a "superior" equilibrium will necessarily exist.

It should also be noted that in using a social utility function (and the implied lump sum transfers among consumers) we have pushed income distributional issues behind the scene. We could have worked instead with a social *welfare* function defined as a function of the utility of individual consumers and modeled distributional considerations explicitly. However, this would have complicated the analysis without significant additional insights.

production/income as factors are marginally varied; and the shadow prices $\hat{w}^{**}$ and $\hat{r}^{**}$, which reflect rather the *utility* impact of such variation (via impact on *consumption*).[6]

Thus $\hat{w}^*$ equals the value at world prices of the changes in equilibrium output $(\partial\hat{X}_i/\partial\bar{L})$ caused by a marginal variation in labor endowment while the capital endowment remains unchanged. Thus, $\hat{w}^*=(\partial\hat{X}_1/\partial\bar{L}+P^*\,\partial\hat{X}_2/\partial\bar{L})$; and similarly, we can derive: $\hat{r}^*=(\partial\hat{X}_1/\partial\bar{K}+p^*\,\partial\hat{X}_2/\partial\bar{K})$.

Similarly $\hat{w}^{**}$ equals the value at *domestic* prices of changes in equilibrium consumption $(\partial\hat{C}_i/\partial\bar{L})$ induced by the same marginal variation in labor endowment. The reason is that the change in social utility $\partial\hat{U}/\partial\bar{L}$ equals $(U_1\,\partial\hat{C}_1/\partial\bar{L}+U_2\,\partial\hat{C}_2/\partial\bar{L})$. Given that at equilibrium consumers equate the marginal rate of substitution U_2/U_1 to the market prices p^d, we get $\partial\hat{U}/\partial\bar{L}=U_1(\partial\hat{C}_1/\partial\bar{L}+p^d\,\partial\hat{C}_2/\partial\bar{L})$ and converting this welfare change to a price in terms of the numeraire good 1 by dividing through by U_1 we get $\hat{w}^{**}=(\partial\hat{C}_1/\partial\bar{L}+p^d\,\partial\hat{C}_2/\partial\bar{L})$; and similarly, we can derive: $\hat{r}^{**}=(\partial\hat{C}_1/\partial\bar{K}+p^d\,\partial\hat{C}_2/\partial\bar{K})$.

Since $(\hat{k}_i, \hat{l}_i)$ are constant through the analysis (given the constancy of p^d thanks to the *ad valorem* tariff: an assumption which will be invalid under a quota), we can derive the output changes $(\partial\hat{X}_i/\partial\bar{K}$ and $\partial\hat{X}_i/\partial\bar{L})$ by differentiating the two full-utilization-of-capital-and-labor equations. We then get the well-known results (Srinivasan and Bhagwati [1978]):

$$\hat{w}^*=\frac{p^*\hat{k}_1-\hat{k}_2}{\hat{k}_1\hat{l}_2-\hat{k}_2\hat{l}_1} \tag{2}$$

$$\hat{r}^*=\frac{\hat{l}_2-p^*\hat{l}_1}{\hat{k}_1\hat{l}_2-\hat{k}_2\hat{l}_1}\,. \tag{3}$$

Again, it may be noted from (2) and (3) that, valued at $(\hat{w}^*, \hat{r}^*)$, the cost of the factors used in producing good i equals its world price — a fact which itself can be used to calculate $\hat{w}^*$ and $\hat{r}^*$; e.g., Srinivasan and Bhagwati [1978].

Next, the "true" shadow prices, reflecting the impact on utility, can be derived as:

$$\begin{aligned}\hat{w}^{**} &= \frac{\partial}{\partial\bar{L}}[\hat{C}_1+p^d\hat{C}_2] = (1+\theta p^d)(1+\theta p^*)^{-1}\frac{\partial}{\partial\bar{L}}(X_1+p^*X_2)\\ &= (1+\theta p^d)(1+\theta p^*)^{-1}\hat{r}^*\\ &= \lambda\hat{r}^*\end{aligned} \tag{4}$$

$$\hat{r}^{**} = \frac{\partial}{\partial\bar{K}}[\hat{C}_1+p^d\hat{C}_2] = (1+\theta p^d)(1+\theta p^*)^{-1}\frac{\partial}{\partial\bar{K}}(X_1+p^*X_2) \tag{5}$$

[6] The 'hat' refers to the fact that the shadow prices are calculated with reference to factor-withdrawal in the (tariff) distorted situation and the 'stars' refer to the corresponding second-best optimization. Two stars are used to distinguish these utility-change shadow prices from the corresponding LM shadow prices, $\hat{w}^*$ and $\hat{r}^*$. The distorted market prices of the factors are denoted simply then by $\hat{w}$ and $\hat{r}$.

$$= (1 + \theta p^d)(1 + \theta p^*)^{-1}\hat{w}^*$$

$$= \lambda \hat{w}^*$$

where we write:

$$\lambda = (1+\theta p^d)(1+\theta p^*)^{-1} \quad \text{and} \quad \theta = \left[\frac{U_1U_{21} - U_2U_{11}}{U_2U_{12} - U_1U_{22}}\right] > 0$$

under normalcy of both goods.

Two observations are now in order. First, it should be noted that λ is nothing but the shadow price of "foreign exchange" in the model. To see this, note that, at given world prices and domestic consumer prices, social utility U could also be written as a function: $U = W(p^d, Z)$ where $Z = (C_1 + p^*C_2)$; i.e., Z is the world price valuation of total consumption (and hence of production, with balanced trade, in our model), or "foreign exchange" in short. If p^d were constant throughout the analysis, say because of given *ad valorem* tariffs (or, as we shall see later, because a quota's consumption distortion is being offset), then the shadow price of foreign exchange in terms of the *numeraire* good 1 is $[(1/U_1)(\partial W/\partial Z)]$ and the shadow price of labor, $\hat{w}^{**}$, is equal to: $[(1/U_1)(\partial W/\partial Z)\cdot(\partial Z/\partial \bar{L})]$. However, $\partial Z/\partial \bar{L}$ is nothing but $[(\partial X_1 + p^*X_2)/\partial \bar{L}]$ and hence it follows from (4) that $[(1/U_1)(\partial W/\partial Z)]$ will equal λ. Thus λ is indeed the shadow price of "foreign exchange" in terms of the *numeraire* good 1.

Second, it is easily seen that in the present instance, the LM rule using $(\hat{w}^*, \hat{r}^*)$ is identical to the correct project acceptance criterion using $(\hat{w}^{**}, \hat{r}^{**})$. Under LM, the criterion for acceptance is:

$$p_3^* \geq \hat{l}_3\hat{w}^* + \hat{k}_3\hat{r}^*$$

whereas, under the latter, it is:

$$\lambda p_3^* \geq \hat{l}_3\hat{w}^{**} + \hat{k}_3\hat{r}^{**};$$

and the latter reduces to the LM criterion in view of (4) and (5) and since $\lambda > 0$.

2. QUANTITATIVE RESTRICTIONS

For the case of an import quota, however, the above analysis needs serious modification. For the singular case where the post-factor-withdrawal equilibrium leads to the same import level as before, the implicit tariff remains unchanged and the quota case reduces to the *ad valorem* tariff case which has been analyzed above. Where the quota ceases to be binding, furthermore, the LM rule will clearly overstate the social cost of factors since added consumption gain will accrue from the elimination of the trade constraint. Where, however, the quota remains binding and the implicit tariff is changed, the prices facing consumers will change with the introduction of the project and the LM rule will again evaluate incorrectly the social cost of the factors: the change in consumption distortion will have been ignored.

This is seen by considering first the case of a (hypothetical) trade quota that is met by adjusting *only* production to the implicit tariff and fully offsetting the consumption distortion, a case in which the LM rule continues to apply, and then considering the case of a (normal) quota where consumption and production are equally distorted by the implicit tariff and therefore the LM rule is shown to break down. Interestingly, we also demonstrate the paradoxical result that, for a well-defined possible case of binding import quotas, the shadow factor prices $\hat{w}^{**}$ and $\hat{r}^{**}$ are the market factor prices, $\hat{w}$ and $\hat{r}$: the Invisible Hand works again!

Case I: *Consumption Distortion Offset*; *Production Adjusting to the Implicit Tariff.* If consumption is allowed to occur at world prices, the LM rule will continue to apply despite the quota. The continued applicability of the LM shadow prices and rule is now demonstrated with the aid of the following model, by showing that the "true" shadow prices are identical to the LM shadow prices. This model, used with necessary modifications in the subsequent analysis of monopoly power and nontraded goods as well, simplifies by assuming that the project good enters the social utility function but that it is wholly imported prior to the project. Then we have the following:

(6) $\hat{C}_1 = \hat{X}_1 - \hat{E}_1, \quad \hat{C}_2 = \hat{X}_2 + \overline{M}_2, \quad \hat{C}_3 = \hat{M}_3$

(supply-demand balance equations)

(7) $\hat{X}_1 = F(\hat{X}_2, \overline{K}, \overline{L})$ (transformation curve)

(8) $\hat{C}_1 + p^*\hat{C}_2 + p_3^*\hat{C}_3 = \hat{X}_1 + p^*\hat{X}_2$ (social availability locus)

(9) $\dfrac{U_2}{U_1} = p^*, \quad \dfrac{U_3}{U_1} = p_3^*$

where E_1 is the export of good 1, $\overline{M}_2$ is the quota-determined level of imports of good 2 and the rates of substitution in consumption equal the world prices (eqns. (9)) because the consumption distortion is assumed to be offset. Then, the true shadow price, $\hat{w}^{**}$ is readily defined as follows:

(10) $$\hat{w}^{**} = \frac{\partial \hat{C}_1}{\partial \overline{L}} + \frac{U_2}{U_1} \cdot \frac{\partial \hat{C}_2}{\partial \overline{L}} + \frac{U_3}{U_1} \cdot \frac{\partial \hat{C}_3}{\partial \overline{L}}$$

and similarly also $\hat{r}^{**}$. Using (8) and (9), we can see that:

(11) $$\hat{w}^{**} = \frac{\partial \hat{X}_1}{\partial \overline{L}} + p^* \frac{\partial \hat{X}_2}{\partial \overline{L}} = \hat{w}^*$$

and similarly:

(12) $$\hat{r}^{**} = \frac{\partial \hat{X}_1}{\partial \overline{K}} + p^* \frac{\partial \hat{X}_2}{\partial \overline{K}} = \hat{r}^*$$

i.e., the LM shadow prices are appropriate and, for a tradeable unit project output of good 3, the corresponding project acceptance criterion can be validly written as $p_3^* \geq (\hat{l}_3 \hat{w}^* + \hat{k}_3 \hat{r}^*)$ along strict LM lines.[7]

Case II: *Consumption Distortion Not Offset*; *The Full Quota Case.* Consider now, however, the case of a standard quota, such that the implicit tariff on good 2 results in identical prices to producers and consumers. Now, while it is possible to conduct the analysis of the reason why the LM rule will break down in the perfectly general case where good 3 is freely imported, we proceed first with the rather special case where good 3 is restrained by a quota to level $\overline{M}_3$ since this special case has the interesting property that the shadow prices of factors turn out paradoxically to be their *market* prices!

For this special case, the system of equations (5)–(9) needs now to be modified such that U_2/U_1 equals the domestic rate of transformation rather than the world price p^*, i.e., $U_2/U_1 = -F_1$. Then it is readily seen that

$$\hat{w}^{**} = \frac{\partial \hat{C}_1}{\partial \bar{L}} + \frac{U_2}{U_1}\frac{\partial \hat{C}_2}{\partial \bar{L}} + \frac{U_3}{U_1}\frac{\partial \hat{C}_3}{\partial \bar{L}} \quad \text{(by definition)}$$

$$= \frac{\partial \hat{X}_1}{\partial \bar{L}} - \frac{\partial \hat{E}_1}{\partial \bar{L}} - F_1\left(\frac{\partial \hat{X}_2}{\partial \bar{L}} + \frac{\partial \overline{M}_2}{\partial \bar{L}}\right) + \frac{U_3}{U_1}\frac{\partial \overline{M}_3}{\partial \bar{L}}$$

But, given that the quotas are fixed and binding, we have: $\partial \hat{E}_1/\partial \bar{L} = \partial \overline{M}_2/\partial \bar{L} = \partial \overline{M}_3/\partial \bar{L} = 0$; further, from (7), $\partial \hat{X}_1/\partial \bar{L} = F_1\, \partial \hat{X}_2/\partial \bar{L} + F_3$, so that

$$\hat{w}^{**} = F_3. \tag{13}$$

Similarly, we can show that

$$\hat{r}^{**} = F_2. \tag{14}$$

Evidently, therefore, the true shadow factor prices now are the *market* prices and the LM shadow factor prices are inappropriate. The paradox is intuitively resolved if one notices that the quotas, when binding, reduce the economy at the margin to a closed economy.[8]

Leaving this *special* case aside, we can now argue directly the inappropriateness of the LM rule in the *general* case from yet another illuminating angle. Thus, recall that, with all goods traded at given world prices, the social utility

[7] We should emphasize that, even though the definitions of $\hat{w}^*$ and $\hat{r}^*$ are the same in the quota and the tariff cases, the procedure of obtaining them through differentiating the system of full-resource-use conditions $\Sigma \hat{X}_i \hat{k}_i = \bar{K}$, $\Sigma \hat{X}_i \hat{l}_i = \bar{L}$ with respect to K and L separately has to take into account that $(\hat{k}_i, \hat{l}_i)$ can change as we vary $\bar{L}$ or $\bar{K}$ under the quota. Thus, for instance, instead of $\Sigma k_i \partial \hat{X}_i/\partial \bar{K}$ and $\Sigma \hat{l}_i \partial \hat{X}_i/\partial \bar{L}$ being 1 and zero respectively as in the fixed tariff case, they are $[1 - \Sigma \hat{X}_i(\partial \hat{k}_i/\partial \bar{K})]$ and $[\Sigma \hat{X}_i(\partial \hat{l}_i/\partial \bar{L})]$, respectively in the *QR* case.

[8] An alternative explanation, which we owe to Trent Bertrand, is that in a situation of trade distortions, shadow and market prices differ by terms that involve price distortions weighted by changes in trade flows due, in our case, to the withdrawal of factors used in the project being evaluated. With all trade flows held constant, these terms vanish. We also owe to Bertrand the comment that we do not therefore need to assume that the domestic price of good 3 is kept at its world price through an appropriate policy to derive our results.

function $U=U[C_1, C_2, C_3]$ can be written as $W[p^d, p_3^d, Z]$, where Z is the foreign exchange available for spending on the three goods. In the case of a tariff or of a quota whose consumption distortion is offset (either fully or so as to maintain consumer prices at unchanged levels), the constancy of p^d, p_3^d ensures that the marginal change in utility (U) due to a marginal change in the availability of a primary factor, say L, (i.e., $\hat{w}^{**}U_1$), equals $(\partial W/\partial Z)(\partial Z/\partial \bar{L})$ (=(marginal utility of "foreign exchange") × (change in "foreign exchange" availability)), and $\partial Z/\partial \bar{L}$ is indeed the shadow price of labor that would be obtained by applying the LM rule. Evidently $[(1/U_1)(\partial W/\partial Z)]$ is the shadow price of foreign exchange in terms of the *numeraire* good and will equal unity, of course, if consumption takes place at world prices as when the consumption distortion of a quota is offset. If however the consumption distortion exists, as for the standard quota case, then the effect of the change in factor availability on p^d and p_3^d will *also* enter the determination of the shadow factor prices and one cannot make inferences about project acceptability by reference to LM-style world-price evaluations. More formally, this is seen by noting that:

$$\hat{w}^{**} = \frac{1}{U_1}\left(\frac{\partial W}{\partial p_1^d}\cdot\frac{\partial p^d}{\partial \bar{L}} + \frac{\partial W}{\partial p_3^d}\cdot\frac{\partial p_3^d}{\partial \bar{L}} + \frac{\partial W}{\partial Z}\cdot\frac{\partial Z}{\partial \bar{L}}\right). \tag{15}$$

Clearly, in the two cases of a tariff and of a quota on good 2 with consumption distortion offset, $\partial p^d/\partial \bar{L}=\partial p_3^d/\partial \bar{L}=0$. On the other hand, for the case where goods 2 and 3 are imported and consumed at distorted prices under a binding quota, the resulting consumption distortion leads to $\partial p^d/\partial \bar{L}\neq 0$ and $\partial p_3^d/\partial \bar{L}\neq 0$. Therefore the LM rule is clearly inappropriate in the *general* quota case; and we have already shown that market prices of factors would become the shadow prices in the special case leading to (13) and (14).[9]

3. MONOPOLY POWER IN TRADE

Next, we must consider the presence of monopoly power in trade (in the presence of atomistic firms which are ignorant of this power). Little and Mirrlees [1972, p. 161] explicitly note that the LM rule will not hold now. Instead they propose: "The general rule for traded goods is as follows: the accounting price is the border price, or, in cases where the border price is believed to vary significantly

[9] The correct project acceptance criterion in the *general* case can be written as:

$$p_3^* \frac{\partial W}{\partial Z} \geq (\hat{l}_3\hat{w}^{**}+\hat{k}_3\hat{r}^{**})U_1$$

where the term on the left represents the increase in welfare brought about by increase in the foreign exchange represented by unit project output of good 3 whereas the term on the right represents the welfare cost of factors used in producing the unit project output. For the *special* case considered above, however, the project acceptance criterion becomes the market criterion:

$$p_3^d \geq (\hat{l}_3\hat{w}+\hat{k}_3\hat{r})$$

The reason is that, with binding quotas on imports of good 3, domestic production of a unit of good 3 has to be *consumed* domestically at price p_3^d.

with the amount bought or sold, the marginal import cost, or marginal export revenue, as appropriate."

Equally, M. F. G. Scott [1974, p. 176] has argued that "The existence of a less than perfectly elastic demand for exports, or supply of imports, has to be taken into account in estimating the accounting ratios for particular traded goods" and goes on to recommend that, in this instance, the marginal revenue (rather than world price) ought to be used by the project analyst.[10]

However, if it is implied that the shadow prices of factors in the presence of (a foreign distortion caused by laissez faire in the presence of)[11] monopoly power in trade can be derived merely by adjusting the LM rule so as to write marginal revenue (in foreign exchange) rather than world (average) prices, this cannot be valid. For the foreign distortion implies that consumption is at distorted prices; and the proposed "fixing" of the LM rule so as to take the "true" shift in the social budget constraint will not get around the additional difficulty introduced by the presence of the consumption distortion.

To see this, we consider again the earlier model of Section 2, with goods 1 and 2 produced in the initial situation and 3, the project good, being only imported initially for consumption. Then, using the notation already introduced, we can write:

$$\hat{C}_1 + \hat{E}_1 = \hat{X}_1 = F(\hat{X}_2, \bar{K}, \bar{L}) \tag{16}$$

$$\hat{C}_2 - \hat{M}_2 = \hat{X}_2 \tag{17}$$

$$\hat{E}_1 = \phi(\hat{M}_2 + p_3^* \hat{M}_3) \tag{18}$$

where (18) is the foreign transformation function. The foreign transformation function is written such that in world markets the relative good 3 in terms of good 2 is constant at p_3^*. In other words, even though the home country has monopoly power in its export market, it has no market power to determine the relative price of its two imports in terms of each other. The derivative ϕ_1 of the transformation function could be termed the marginal cost of "foreign exchange" in terms of good 1; the average cost is $\hat{E}_1/\phi^{-1}(\hat{E}_1)$.

The equilibrium values of eight variables $\hat{C}_1$, $\hat{C}_2$, $\hat{C}_3$ $\hat{X}_1$, $\hat{X}_2$, $\hat{E}_1$, $\hat{M}_2$, and $\hat{M}_3$ are derived by solving (16)–(18), [adding up to four equations when the part $\hat{X}_1 = F(\hat{X}_2, K, L)$ of (15) is counted as a separate equation] and the following four equations:

$$\frac{U_3}{U_2} = p_3^*; \tag{19}$$

[10] Scott's analysis (pp. 176–178) is couched entirely in terms of the orthodox terms-of-trade argument for an optimal tariff and he seems to imply that the use of marginal revenue is all that is involved in fixing up the LM rule in the presence of monopoly power in trade.

[11] The sub-optimality of *laissez faire* in the presence of monopoly power in trade is well known. Designation of it as a "foreign distortion" is in Bhagwati's [1971] synthesis of the trade-theoretic literature on distortions and welfare.

(20) $$\frac{U_2}{U_1} = -F_1;$$

(21) $$-F_1 = \hat{E}_1/\phi^{-1}(\hat{E}_1);$$

(22) $$\hat{C}_3 = \hat{M}_3.$$

Equation (19) implies that consumers face the same price for good 3 relative to good 2 as the price in world markets, and eqns. (20)–(21) that the domestic consumer and producer price p^d is the average cost of importing good 2 in terms of the export good 1 in world markets, i.e., $\hat{E}_1/\phi^{-1}(\hat{E}_1)$. Given these assumptions, we can show that the true shadow prices are:

(23) $$\hat{w}^{**} = \left(\frac{\partial \hat{X}_1}{\partial \bar{L}} + \phi_1 \frac{\partial \hat{X}_2}{\partial \bar{L}}\right) + (p^d - \phi_1)\left(\frac{\partial \hat{X}_2}{\partial \bar{L}} + \frac{1}{\phi_1}\frac{\partial \hat{E}_1}{\partial \bar{L}}\right)$$

and

(24) $$\hat{r}^{**} = \left(\frac{\partial \hat{X}_1}{\partial \bar{K}} + \phi_1 \frac{\partial \hat{X}_2}{\partial \bar{K}}\right) + (p^d - \phi_1)\left(\frac{\partial \hat{X}_2}{\partial \bar{K}} + \frac{1}{\phi_1}\frac{\partial \hat{E}_1}{\partial \bar{K}}\right)$$

Now, it is evident that fixing up the LM shadow prices, $\hat{w}^*$ and $\hat{r}^*$, such that marginal cost rather than average world prices get utilized, will yield only $(\partial \hat{X}_1/\partial \bar{L} + \phi_1\, \partial \hat{X}_2/\partial \bar{L})$ and $(\partial \hat{X}_1/\partial \bar{K} + \phi_1\, \partial \hat{X}_2/\partial \bar{K})$ respectively. But it will not reckon with the two terms on the R. H. S. in (23) and (24).

At the same time, it is easy to see that if the initial situation were an optimal tariff situation, such that $p^d = \phi_1$, then the marginal-revenue-adjusted LM prices *would* turn out to be appropriate. However, when the tariff is optimally set to exploit monopoly power, these adjusted LM prices obviously become market prices: and the *raison d'être* for social cost-benefit analysis disappears anyway!

4. NONTRADED GOODS

Finally, we consider the appropriateness of the LM rule when nontraded goods are present. The problem here is obvious: since the LM rule requires goods to be evaluated at world prices, and primary factors to be evaluated in turn at their opportunity cost in terms of output valued at world prices, the presence of nontraded goods raises the difficulty that world prices apply only to tradeables and not to nontraded goods.[12]

If we consult the cost-benefit literature on the subject, we find again recommendations regarding how to deal with the problem. Thus, Balassa [1974, p. 158] argues that the nontraded goods be decomposed into traded inputs and primary factors, the former to be valued at world prices and the latter at their shadow prices. But how precisely these shadow prices should be derived, and

[12] Of course, at *some* price, presumably all goods may be traded. By nontraded goods, therefore, we mean those goods which will not enter trade at the prices that pertain to the equilibria being discussed in the model.

whether the LM rule continues to apply in some modified sense, are the two critical questions that are not fully clarified for the reader since no formal model is set up to analyze these questions directly. More or less the same may be said of the Little-Mirrlees [1972, pp. 162–166, 216–219] analysis, which is fairly detailed but does not fully assist the reader who seeks a formally clear resolution of the two issues above. We therefore proceed to address these questions, as also the related third question which has often been raised in the trade-theoretic and cost-benefit literature: i.e., what is the appropriate shadow "exchange rate" in the model?

In answering these questions, we note that there are two classes of models with nontraded goods that one can use: (1) where the number of primary factors equals the number of traded goods, and (2) where they do not.[13] In the former case, provided the coefficients matrix is of full rank, the given world prices of the traded goods will determine the primary factor prices and these, in turn, will determine the techniques and prices of the nontraded goods, with demand for the nontraded goods determining then their quantities (but *not* prices) in equilibrium.[14] In the latter model, however, the overall factor endowments will generally affect the price-formation in the nontraded goods sector. For reasons which will become evident below, the LM rule (suitably modified to accommodate the nontraded goods) will continue to apply in the former but not necessarily in the latter case: and so we shall analyze fully only a model belonging to the former class.

Consider now the following amendment of the simple model analyzed in the preceding sections. As before, there are two (nonproject) tradeables, and two primary factors. For simplicity, however, the (tradeable) project output is now assumed to be *exported* and not domestically consumed: it therefore does not enter the utility function. Offsetting the simplification is the introduction of the nontraded good, 4, which enters consumption. Intermediate use of any of the commodities is assumed away: but the analysis is readily extended to this case without any modification.

Given the domestic tariff-inclusive price p^d $(=p^*(1+t))$ of good 2, the import coefficients $(\hat{k}_i, \hat{l}_i)$ for the tradeables $(i=1, 2)$ and the market wage $\hat{w}$ and rental $\hat{r}$ are determined. And given $(\hat{w}, \hat{r})$, the input coefficients $(\hat{k}_4, \hat{l}_4)$ as well as the unit cost of production equalling the price $\hat{p}_4$ of the non-tradeable are determined also.

[13] The former model was used analytically by Komiya [1967] in a seminal paper; the latter class of models is considered by Suzuki [1979], who distinguishes these two classes of models in an illuminating manner.

[14] This argument assumes that the primary factor endowments lie within the McKenzie-Chipman diversification cone, as discussed in Bhagwati and Wan [1979]. Stated in this way, it is valid even when the number of traded goods (n) exceeds the number (m) of primary factors. In other words, as we vary each factor endowment, if the set of *produced* traded goods includes the same subset of m traded goods, the market and also the shadow prices of factors and hence of non-traded goods will remain unchanged.

It is possible in this model to derive a "world price" valuation of a unit of non-traded good independently of demand conditions by exploiting the fact that the market price of the non-traded good and hence the input coefficients in its production are unaffected by changes in output levels that do not take the equilibrium outside the McKenzie-Chipman diversification cone. Let us therefore define the "world price" $\hat{p}_4^*$ of a unit of non-traded good as the value of the change in the output of traded goods at world prices brought about by producing one less unit of the non-traded good. Since such a reduction releases $\hat{k}_4$ units of capital and $\hat{l}_4$ units of labor, the changes $d\hat{X}_1$, $d\hat{X}_2$ in the output of the traded goods are to be solved from:

$$(\hat{k}_1 d\hat{X}_1 + \hat{k}_2 d\hat{X}_2) = \hat{k}_4; \; (\hat{l}_1 d\hat{X}_1 + \hat{l}_2 d\hat{X}_2) = \hat{l}_4. \tag{25}$$

And $\hat{p}_4^*$ then would be $(d\hat{X}_1 + \hat{p}^* d\hat{X}_2)$. It is easily seen from (25) that:

$$\hat{p}_4^* = (\hat{l}_4 \hat{w}^* + \hat{k}_4 \hat{r}^*) \tag{26}$$

where $\hat{w}^*$, $\hat{r}^*$ are obtained by solving, as before, the following:

$$(\hat{l}_1 \hat{w}^* + \hat{k}_1 \hat{r}^*) = 1; \; (\hat{l}_2 \hat{w}^* + \hat{k}_2 \hat{r}^*) = p^* \tag{27}$$

i.e., by using information on the traded goods sector alone.

Now, $(\hat{w}^*, \hat{r}^*)$ are the LM shadow factor prices; and $(p^*, \hat{p}_4^*)$ are the associated shadow goods prices in the sense that $\hat{w}^*(\hat{r}^*)$ represents the sum of the value of all output changes induced by a variation in the $L(K)$ endowment, the valuation being at world prices for traded goods 1 and 2 and at the shadow price $\hat{p}_4^*$ for the non-traded good. To see this, consider varying the labor endowment. The induced changes in outputs satisfy:

$$\Sigma \hat{l}_i \frac{\partial \hat{X}_i}{\partial L} = 1, \quad \Sigma \hat{k}_i \frac{\partial \hat{X}_i}{\partial L} = 0. \tag{28}$$

Now we multiply the first equation in (28) by $\hat{w}^*$, the second by $\hat{r}^*$, and add them. Using (26) and (27) we then get, as asserted above:

$$\hat{w}^* = \frac{\partial \hat{X}_1}{\partial L} + p^* \frac{\partial \hat{X}_2}{\partial L} + \hat{p}_4^* \frac{\partial \hat{X}_4}{\partial L}. \tag{29}$$

Now, the true shadow wage $\hat{w}^{**}$ may be derived, and related to $\hat{w}^*$, by first noting that:

$$\begin{aligned} \hat{w}^{**} &= \frac{\partial \hat{C}_1}{\partial L} + \frac{U_2}{U_1} \frac{\partial \hat{C}_2}{\partial L} + \frac{U_4}{U_1} \frac{\partial \hat{C}_4}{\partial L} \\ &= \frac{\partial \hat{C}_1}{\partial L} + p^d \frac{\partial \hat{C}_2}{\partial L} + \hat{p}_4 \frac{\partial \hat{C}_4}{\partial L} \\ &= \hat{w}^* + p^* t \frac{\partial \hat{C}_2}{\partial L} + (\hat{p}_4 - \hat{p}_4^*) \frac{\partial \hat{C}_4}{\partial L}. \end{aligned} \tag{30}$$

Now, define $(\hat{p}_4-\hat{p}_4^*)/\hat{p}_4^*=t_4$ as the "tariff" on the non-traded good.[15] Also let

$$(31) \qquad Y^* \equiv (\hat{X}_1 + p^*\hat{X}_2 + \hat{p}_4^*\hat{X}_4)$$

be the "world price" valued national income. Then, by the balanced trade assumption and the fact the consumption of non-tradeable equals its output, we have:

$$(32) \qquad \hat{C}_1 + p^*\hat{C}_2 + \hat{p}_4^*\hat{C}_4 = Y^*.$$

Hence,

$$(33) \qquad \frac{\partial \hat{C}_1}{\partial Y^*} + p^*\frac{\partial \hat{C}_2}{\partial Y^*} + \hat{p}_4^*\frac{\partial \hat{C}_4}{\partial Y^*} = 1$$

and $\partial\hat{Y}/\partial\bar{L}=\hat{w}^*$ by (29). Hence (30) can be rewritten as:

$$(34) \qquad \hat{w}^{**} \equiv \mu w^*$$

where $\mu=(1+\Sigma t_i\, \partial C_i/\partial Y^*)$. Similarly:

$$(35) \qquad \hat{r}^{**} = \mu\hat{r}^*.$$

To demonstrate now the validity of the LM rule in this model, by showing that the project acceptance criteria using LM and the true shadow prices are equivalent, we proceed as follows. First we note that the factor of proportionality μ between $\hat{w}^{**}$ and $\hat{w}^*$ has a natural interpretation, similar to that given to factor λ which was viewed as the shadow price of foreign exchange in the model of Section 1 in which all goods were tradeable. Given that $\hat{C}_1$, $\hat{C}_2$, $\hat{C}_4$ lie on the social availability locus $(\hat{C}_1+\hat{p}^*C_2+p_4\hat{C}_4)=Y^*$ and that $U_2/U_1=p^d$, $U_4/U_2=\hat{p}_4$, the social welfare $U(C_1, C_2, C_4)$ can be written as $W(Y^*, p^d, \hat{p}_4)$. Since p^d, $\hat{p}_4$ remain fixed thanks to the unchanging tariff, we have:

$\hat{w}^{**}=[(1/U_1)(\partial U/\partial\bar{L})]=[(1/U_1)(\partial W/\partial Y^*)(\partial Y^*/\partial\bar{L})]=[(1/U_1)(\partial W/\partial Y^*)]\hat{w}^*$. Hence μ is nothing but $[(1/U_1)(\partial W/\partial Y^*)]$, i.e., the utility-based shadow price of national income at world prices.

Next we define a shadow price of foreign exchange in terms of income Y^* as follows. Now the change in income due to a change in L is $\partial Y^*/\partial\bar{L}$ whereas the change in foreign exchange proper, i.e., $(\hat{X}_1+p^*\hat{X}_2)$, due to a change in L is $[(\partial\hat{X}_1/\partial\bar{L})+p^*(\partial\hat{X}_2/\partial\bar{L})]$. Thus the ratio of the two, namely $(\partial Y^*/\partial\bar{L})/[(\partial\hat{X}_1/\partial\bar{L})+p^*(\partial\hat{X}_2/\partial\bar{L})]$ is the desired shadow price of foreign exchange in terms of Y^*.[16]

Finally, denoting this shadow prices as δ, we can write the project acceptance criterion as: $\delta p_3^*\geq\hat{l}_3\hat{w}^*+\hat{k}_3\hat{r}^*$. Equivalently, we could have written it as $(\mu\delta)p_3^*\geq\hat{l}_3\hat{w}^{**}+\hat{k}_3\hat{r}^{**}$ since $\hat{w}^{**}=\mu\hat{w}^*$ and $\hat{r}^{**}=\mu\hat{r}^*$ and $(\mu\delta)$ is the true utility-

[15] This approach leading to equations (34) and (35) for $\hat{w}^{**}$ and r^{**} was suggested by Trent Bertrand.

[16] Of course, one gets the same value of this shadow price by using the ratio $\partial Y^*/\partial\bar{K}(\partial\hat{X}_1/\partial\bar{K}+p^*\partial\hat{X}_2/\partial\bar{K})$.

based shadow price of foreign exchange. Hence the validity of the LM rule is established.

A few concluding remarks are in order. First, $\hat{p}_4^*/\hat{p}_4$, the ratio of the shadow to the actual market price of the nontraded good, may be regarded as the "shadow exchange rate" insofar as the shadow price $\hat{p}_4^*$ corresponds to the appropriate "world-price" valuation of the nontraded good, 4.

Second, such a shadow exchange rate will evidently exist, and generally will differ, for *each* nontraded good. This is perfectly compatible with the assertion that a unique shadow exchange rate can be defined quite simply as an *average*: once the individual ratios are known, the average shadow price of all nontraded goods can obviously be defined such that the aggregate valuation using it is identical with that obtained by using individual shadow prices on each nontraded good separately.[17]

Third, for situations where a shadow price for a nontraded good is not available, owing to lack of information, it has been recommended that a *Standard Conversion Factor* (SCF) be used. The SCF would be an average of the shadow exchange rates which the analyst has been able to compute. Little and Mirrlees [1974, pp. 218–219], who propose this, actually suggest that the average be based on *both* nontraded goods (i.e., $\hat{p}_4^*/\hat{p}_4$) *and* the traded goods (i.e., p_i^*/p_i^d). While there are obvious objections that one might raise to this suggestion as the way of securing the "best estimate" of an unknown shadow price on a nontraded good, there is a more subtle point involved here. In our model, if the world prices of tradeables are known and technology is known on tradeables, the only additional information necessary to derive the shadow price of a nontraded good is its technology. And the shadow price of each nontraded good is independent of that of others. Therefore, it is possible to maintain that, owing to lack of knowledge of production techniques, a nontraded good's shadow price may be guessed as the "best" estimate inferred from shadow prices of other nontraded goods. However, in other production models (e.g., the second type of nontraded goods model distinguished above) this independence need not obtain and therefore it would not be valid to claim that the analyst can estimate shadow prices for one set of nontraded goods independently of those for the other set.

Finally, note that the validity of the LM rule in our model follows because of the constancy of the nontraded good's price throughout the analysis, resulting from the postulated structure of the model. Therefore, the world-price valuation procedure works to yield the correct acceptance criterion. In the other class of models where the nontraded good's price will vary with a marginal variation of factors, however, this will no longer be so, as already discussed before. And the resurrection of the LM rule would then require that the nontraded good's price be held constant by suitable policy intervention.

[17] For controversy on this issue, see Balassa [1974, p. 158].

5. CONCLUDING OBSERVATIONS

This paper has therefore considered, for the case of trade-distorted economies, the *precise* relationship between the true shadow factor prices based on the *utility*-impact of factor withdrawal of a project and the LM shadow factor prices based on the impact instead on *production* valued at world prices. We are thus able to show *exactly* why the LM criterion for project acceptance, and associated shadow prices, are inappropriate when *QR*s are present and how the *QR*s, in turn, can be modified so as to resurrect the applicability of the LM shadow prices (by eliminating with offsetting subsidies the changes in the consumption distortion that *QR*s generally entail). We have also managed to clarify the prevailing analytical ambiguities concerning the prescriptions on how to "fix up" the LM rule to allow for monopoly power in trade and for nontraded goods.

Does our analysis have any bearing on the question whether the LM shadow prices are applicable when the economy is in "foreign exchange difficulties"? In fact, it does, and in an immediate fashion. If the analyst has in mind a "foreign exchange bottleneck," which is an *ex ante* planning concept, then it is now fairly well understood that this is tantamount to saying that the economy has monopoly power in trade: this prevents the economy from transforming what it has into what it needs.[18] In this instance the analysis of Section 3 clearly shows the inapplicability of the LM rule, even when "fixed up" by substituting marginal revenues for average international prices. Where, however, the analyst has in mind a payments regime which is characterized by deficits suppressed by exchange or import controls, the project must be considered in a framework where *QR*s operate and hence (even if all goods are tradeables at fixed international prices) the consumption distortion will generally change with the project. In this instance, as our analysis in Section 2 demonstrates, the LM shadow prices will be inappropriate. Finally, if the analyst has in mind an open deficit, an economy with all tradeables and fixed international prices will evidently be characterized by the applicability of the LM rule, since the consumption distortion will remain invariant under alternative levels of payments deficit.[19]

Columbia University, U.S.A.
Yale University, U.S.A.

[18] This is spelled out in detail in Desai and Bhagwati [1979] where the concept of "foreign exchange bottleneck" has been sharply distinguished from the concepts of open and suppressed payments deficits. These confusions are widespread in both popular and scientific discussions of "foreign exchange difficulties" in the literature on both developing and centrally planned countries, as also in the cost-benefit literature. Several trade theorists have noted these confusions earlier; cf. Bhagwati [1966] and Findlay [1971].

[19] In the case of both suppressed and open payments deficits, we have, of course, to assume that the degree of borrowing, whether zero or positive, is optimal. Otherwise, the effect of the project on the level of borrowing would itself make the unadjusted use of LM shadow prices inapplicable in the open payments deficit case, for example.

REFERENCES

BALASSA, BELA, "Estimating the Shadow Price of Foreign Exchange in Project Appraisal," *Oxford Economic Papers*, 26 (July, 1974), 147–168.

BERTRAND, TRENT J., "The Shadow Exchange Rate in an Economy with Trade Restrictions," *Oxford Economic Papers*, 26 (July, 1974), 185–191.

———, "Shadow Pricing in Distorted Economies," *American Economic Review*, 69 (December, 1979), 902–914.

BHAGWATI, JAGDISH, "The Nature of Balance of Payments Difficulties in Developing Countries," in *Measure for Trade Expansion of Developing Countries*, Japan Economic Research Center, Paper No. 5 (1966).

———, "The Generalized Theory of Distortions and Welfare," in, J. Bhagwati *et al*, eds, *Trade, Balance of Payments and Growth* (Amsterdam: North Holland Co., 1971), 69–90.

——— AND HENRY WAN, "The 'Stationarity' of Shadow Prices of Factors in Project Evaluation, with and without Distortions," *American Economic Review*, 69 (June, 1979), 261–273.

BRUNO, MICHAEL, *Interdependence, Resource Use and Structural Change in Israel* (Jerusalem: Bank of Israel, 1962).

———, "A Programming Model for Israel," in, I. Adelman and E. Thorbecke, eds., *The Theory and Design of Economic Development* (Baltimore: John Hopkins Univ. Press, 1966), 327–354.

DESAI, PADMA AND JAGDISH BHAGWATI, "Three Alternative Concepts of Foreign Exchange Difficulties in Centrally Planned Economies," *Oxford Economic Papers*, 31 (November, 1979), 358–368.

DIAMOND, PETER AND JAMES MIRRLEES, "Optimal Taxation and Public Production," *American Economic Review*, 61 (March/June, 1971), 8–27 and 261–278.

——— AND ———, "Private Constant Returns and Public Shadow Prices," *Review of Economic Studies*, 22 (February, 1976), 41–48.

FINDLAY, RONALD, "The Foreign Exchange Gap and Growth in Developing Economies," J. Bhagwati, *et al.* eds., *Trade, Balance of Payments and Growth* (Amsterdam: North Holland, 1971), 168–182.

——— AND STANISLAW WELLISZ, "Project Evaluation, Shadow Prices, and Trade Policy," *Journal of Political Economy*, 84 (June, 1976), 543–552

JOSHI, VIJAY, "The Rationale and the Relevance of the Little-Mirrlees Criterion," *Bulletin of Oxford University Institute of Statistics*, 34 (February, 1972), 3–33.

KOMIYA, RYUTARO, "Nontraded Goods and the Pure Theory of International Trade," *International Economic Review*, 8 (June, 1967), 132–152.

LAL, DEEPAK, *Methods of Project Analysis: A Review*, World Bank Occasional Paper No. 16, Washington, D. C. (1974). Distributed by Johns Hopkins University Press, Baltimore.

LITTLE, IAN AND JAMES MIRRLEES, *Project Appraisal and Planning for Developing Countries* (London: Heinemann, 1974).

SCOTT, MAURICE F. C., "How to Use and Estimate Shadow Exchange Rates," *Oxford Economic Papers*, 26 (July, 1974), 169–184.

SRINIVASAN, T. N. AND J. BHAGWATI, "Shadow Prices for Project Selection in the Presence of Distrortions: Effective Rates of Protection and Domestic Resource Costs," *Journal of Political Economy*, 88 (February, 1980), 97–116.

SUZUKI, KATSUHIKO, "Nontraded Inputs and the Effective Rate of Protection," mimeographed (1979).

Errata

Page 387, lines 2 and 3 from bottom: "$\hat{r}^*$" should read "$\hat{w}^*$".

Page 388, lines 1 and 2: "$\hat{w}^*$" should read "$\hat{r}^*$".

The "Stationarity" of Shadow Prices of Factors in Project Evaluation, with and without Distortions

By JAGDISH N. BHAGWATI AND HENRY WAN, JR.*

Until recently, the literature on cost-benefit analysis for projects has been largely within the domain of research on "public monopoly," literature currently reviewed by Jacques Lesourne, (ch. 3), and the work of public finance theorists as typified in the celebrated practical work of Ian Little and James Mirrlees in their *Manual*, and in the recent theoretical contribution of Peter Diamond and Mirrlees. International trade theorists have, however, turned now to the analysis of these problems, starting with the early work of Vijay Joshi and Deepak Lal, then that of W. M. Corden, and most recently culminating in the contributions of Ronald Findlay and Stanislaw Wellisz, and T. N. Srinivasan and Bhagwati.

The work of Findlay-Wellisz and Srinivasan-Bhagwati (F-W-S-B) explicitly deploys the tools, insights and ideas of general equilibrium international trade theory. In particular, their analyses have been addressed to the question of deriving the shadow prices for primary factors for the purpose of project evaluation in the presence of distortions: Findlay-Wellisz (F-W) considering product-market and trade distortions and Srinivasan-Bhagwati (S-B) also extending their analysis to a number of factor-market distortions.

Their analyses has been conducted essentially within the framework of the two-by-two small-country model of traditional international trade theory. An important consequence is what might be called the "stationariness" of the "marginal variational" shadow prices of factors (derived by marginal, i.e., infinitesimal, variation) such that, as S-B phrased it,

> [W]hile we have confined our analysis to 'small' projects, drawing infinitesimal resources away from the existing distorted situation, it is equally clear from our analysis that the results will also hold for 'large' projects. Given the Rybczynski-line properties of the different models, the shadow prices of factors will be identical for small and large shifts of factors into the project. [p. 113]

When the Rybczynski-line properties no longer hold, the marginal variational shadow prices applicable for single projects with infinitesimal factor withdrawals will indeed vary as the factor endowment vector varies. Similarly, for a project withdrawing finite amounts of factors[1] the marginal variational shadow prices computed *before* the withdrawal will then differ from those computed *after* the withdrawal. Moreover, shadow prices computed by marginal variations from the "residual factor vector" (after the withdrawal) will depend upon the size and composition of the factors withdrawn.[2]

The "stationarity" of the marginal varia-

*Professor of economics, Massachusetts Institute of Technology, and professor of economics, Cornell University, respectively. Our thanks are due to Trent Bertrand, Simone Clemhout, Peter Diamond, Ronald Findlay, Earl Grinols, T. N. Srinivasan, Lance Taylor, the managing editor of this *Review*, and an anonymous referee for helpful suggestions. Comments at seminars at Columbia, Yale, Johns Hopkins, and the World Bank also helped greatly. Partial support under National Science Foundation Grant SOC77-07188 is gratefully acknowledged.

[1]Equally, for a successive sequence of "small" projects, collectively withdrawing finite amounts of factors in the aggregate.

[2]As a matter of pure formality, "true" shadow prices can be defined, a posteriori, for projects withdrawing finite factor dosages (see the authors, Appendix I). Such shadow prices, used for project evaluation, *will* tautologically yield the opportunity cost. However, these prices will vary from project to project and their derivation will require each time the solution of a full programming problem for project selection. Such shadow price computation will therefore become a purely academic exercise: the projects having been selected in the programming problem already. A similar point has been made by Bhagwati and Srinivasan in relation to estimating the

tional shadow prices, in the presence of *non-infinitesimal* factor withdrawals, such that the valuation of these factors in project use at the marginal variational shadow prices nonetheless equals their true social opportunity cost, is therefore a critical question.[3] This is precisely the issue, effectively skirted in the standard analyses of shadow prices in project evaluation by the convenient assumption of "small" projects, that we propose to examine in the present paper. Towards this end, we propose to relax the two-by-two property of the F-W-S-B model to allow for many goods and factors: it is shown that uniqueness and stationarity of the marginal variational shadow prices are not always guaranteed once the number of goods differs from that of factors.

Section I recapitulates the basic F-W-S-B analysis, retaining the two-by-two model but distinguishing between the with-distortion and the no-distortion cases. Section II examines the many-goods-and-factors cases:

Case 1: *Goods equal factors, no distortion.*

Case 2: *Goods equal factors, with distortion.*

Case 3: *Goods outnumber factors, no distortion.*

Case 4: *Goods outnumber factors, with distortion.*

Case 5: *Factors outnumber goods, no distortion.*

Case 6: *Factors outnumber goods, with distortion.*

Section III offers concluding observations, indicating the applicability of our analysis to other problems in trade theory (for example, the transfer problem and the welfare effects of labor mobility) and the relationship of our results to mathematical programming. Owing to lack of space, we do not report here: 1) how the replacement of the ad valorem tariff distortion by a *quantitative* quota distortion would destroy the stationarity of shadow prices in the F-W-S-B model; nor 2) how the major propositions in Section II can be proved with rigor, and generalized to cover the cases of (i) joint outputs, (ii) traded inputs, (iii) nontraded, domestically produced inputs unfit for consumption, (iv) primary inputs with variable supply, and (v) consumable nontraded domestic products. Interested readers may refer to the authors (Section II; Appendices I, II).

I. Recapitulating and Completing Analysis within the F-W-S-B Model

The F-W-S-B model is characterized by three key features: constant-returns-to-scale production functions;[4] two primary factors producing two traded goods; and fixed foreign prices for the two traded goods (the Samuelson "small-country" assumption). The problem of deriving shadow factor prices for a project producing a third traded good then is tantamount to deriving the changes in outputs of the two traded goods (x_1 and x_2) that follow from the withdrawal of factors (v_1 and v_2) from existing allocations and then evaluating these output changes at (the fixed) *international* prices. According to the Little-Mirrlees "rule," the shadow price of a factor is precisely the value of output foregone when this factor is marginally, that is, infinitesi-

effective rate of protection (*ERP*) index for resource allocation prediction in the case of generalized factor substitution. They argue that, in general, to compute the "correct" *ERP* index, we must solve the general equilibrium system for the tariff change; but if we have done that, we already know the total resource allocation change and we do not need the *ERP* index to tell us the direction of such change.

[3]For an extremely scathing and articulate critique of cost-benefit analysts by a programmer-planner who argues that shadow prices which apply to negligible (i.e., infinitesimal) projects are of negligible interest, see Asok Rudra. He is clearly assuming what we christen here the "nonstationarity" of the marginal variational shadow factor prices and therefore his critique, while fundamentally sound in principle, goes too far in failing to show awareness of possible stationarity of shadow prices.

[4]F-W and S-B do not explicitly rule out factor-intensity reversals. On what happens when they are present, see our analysis below.

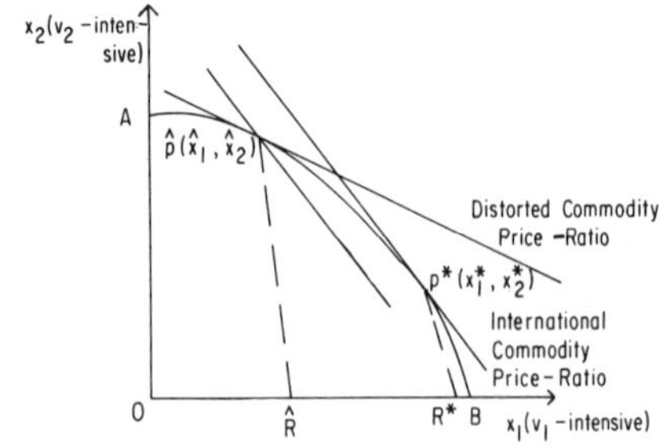

FIGURE 1

mally, withdrawn at the distorted market prices, with the valuation itself being carried out at the international prices.[5]

Thus, take Figure 1 which depicts the usual production possibility curve for the two traded goods, x_1 and x_2. Distinguish now two cases: 1) no distortion; and 2) a (given) product-market or trade distortion.[6] For the former case, production will take place at P^*; for the latter case, it will occur at $\hat{P}$. In the former case, the withdrawal of factor v_2, assumed to be intensively used in commodity x_2, will successively reduce the output of x_2 and increase it for x_1 along the Rybczynski line P^*R^* whereas a similar withdrawal of factor v_2 will define, in the latter case, a similar (nonparallel) Rybczynski line $\hat{P}\hat{R}$.[7] In each case, the commodity price ratio is clearly held constant as the factor is withdrawn for use in the project producing commodity x_3; in the no-distortion case this is the international price ratio whereas, in the distortion case, it is the distorted commodity price ratio. The *evaluation* of the changes in outputs along the relevant Rybczynski line, however, is at the *international* prices in *both* cases.[8]

An important consequence is that, as long as the withdrawal of factors, no matter how large, permits the small economy to remain on the Rybczynski line in Figure 1, whether there is a given distortion or none, the shadow factor prices will be "stationary."[9] What happens if factors are withdrawn such that the economy moves off the Rybczynski line?

First, focusing on the *no-distortion* case, assume that the withdrawal of primary factor v_2 leads the economy finally to complete specialization on commodity x_1 at the bottom of P^*R^* at R^*. If then another unit of v_2 is withdrawn, it is evident that the economy will move towards the origin along the horizontal axis and that, as it does so, the real rental of factor v_2 will rise in terms of *both* of the traded goods, x_1 and x_2. Essentially, one has slipped out of the "linearity" property of the system and diminishing returns to varying proportions are now taking over. The net result therefore is that, for any withdrawals of the primary factor v_2 beyond those that lead from P^* to R^*, the shadow prices of the

[5]Given the small-country assumption, this rule leads to the correct choice of a project because if the social cost of factors used therein, so derived, is below the international valuation of the project's output, the acceptance of the project will increase the international valuation of total output in the economy. When that happens, as long as the degree of consumption distortion remains unchanged (as when a tariff is in place), the analyst can infer that social welfare (as conventionally defined) will have increased as well (except in the presence of inferior goods when multiple equilibria can arise and society may be at an inferior equilibrium although a superior equilibrium is always available if the international valuation of total output has increased). For a full discussion of these issues, and the relationship between the Little-Mirrlees rule and the Diamond-Mirrlees technique for deriving identical shadow prices, see Srinivasan and Bhagwati.

[6]A product-market distortion essentially implies that the domestic producers face production tax-cum-subsidy-inclusive prices or tariff-inclusive prices, rather than the international prices for the two goods. If we invoke a tariff, there will be a consumption distortion as well. But this creates no difficulties for our analysis, so that our analysis holds equally for trade distortions.

[7]The slope of the Rybczynski lines reflects the average productivity of the primary factors whereas the slope of the commodity price ratio at which the Rybczynski line is defined reflects, of course, the marginal productivity of the factors. On this, as also on the relationship between the Rybczynski lines at different points on the production-possibility curve (as at P^* and $\hat{P}$), see Trent Bertrand and Frank Flatters, and Richard Brecher in particular.

[8]For simplicity, Figure 1 has been drawn such that the possibility of a negative shadow factor price is ruled out. On this paradoxical possibility, see Srinivasan and Bhagwati, and Bhagwati, Srinivasan, and Wan.

[9]S-B do not consider what happens beyond the Rybczynski line. Rather they consider other questions such as the relationship of their results on shadow factor prices to the use of domestic resource costs and effective rate of protection as project evaluation criteria.

factors are no longer stationary and can be shown to increase (for the factor withdrawn) for successive withdrawals of the factor for utilization in the project in question. This also implies that, for these ranges of increasing cost withdrawal of factor v_2, the use of the shadow prices for marginal variation at P^* would yield an *understatement* of the true shadow cost of the factor. Alternatively, one may phrase this to say that the use of marginal variational shadow prices, when stationariness does not obtain, ignores the "secondary cost" that must be added to the "primary cost" as measured at the marginal variational shadow prices.

All this can be seen perfectly generally, for withdrawals of *both* factors, in terms of the McKenzie-Chipman diversification cone in Figure 2. Assuming that q_1 and q_2 define the v_1/v_2 ratios chosen at the prevailing commodity price ratio (i.e., at P^* in Figure 1) and the associated factor-price ratio which is the slope of the line q_1q_2, note that the overall factor endowment ratio must be a weighted sum of the two sectoral factor proportions.[10] It is evident then that $q_1 0 q_2$ defines a diversification cone: as long as the factor-endowment vector lies strictly *within* the cone, both goods will be produced at the postulated commodity and associated factor-price ratios. Hence the aggregate endowment vector $(\bar{v}_1, \bar{v}_2)$ is shown to lie within the cone $q_1 0 q_2$, indicating production of both goods at levels x_1^* and x_2^* (corresponding to P^* in Figure 1). Note that the aggregate endowment vector $(\bar{v}_1, \bar{v}_2)$ is shown by the *parallelogram* in Figure 2 to be a weighted vector sum of the factor proportions in the two goods, the actual outputs being read off from the isoquants x_1^* and x_2^*.

It follows immediately that (given the commodity price ratio) as long as the *residual* factor vector, left over after successive withdrawals of the factors for project use, continues to lie within the cone $q_1 0 q_2$, the equilibrium factor-price ratio need not change from

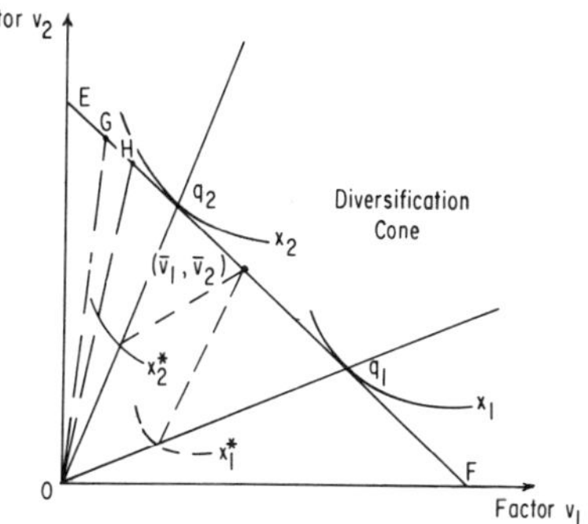

FIGURE 2

q_1q_2 and all changes in factor endowments will be accommodated merely by changes in the composition of outputs. Hence, the McKenzie-Chipman diversification cone *in the present case* is identical to what we shall refer to as the *Rybczynski cone*: the latter being the set of residual factor vectors for which marginal variational shadow factor prices will remain stationary at the slope of the price line q_1q_2. This stationarity of these shadow factor prices will disappear, however, as soon as the residual factor vector slips out of this cone.[11] Note also the following:

(i) As must be evident, the slope of the line q_1q_2 represents the ratio of the marginal variational shadow factor prices, these being the prices corresponding to infinitesimal factor withdrawal.

(ii) The secondary cost of withdrawn factors that leave the residual factor vector outside the Rybczynski cone may be defined as the excess of their true shadow cost over their cost if measured at the marginal variational prices. The *proportionate* secondary cost, defined as the ratio of the secondary cost to the cost at the marginal variational prices, will be an increasing function of the extent to

[10]Thus, denoting the overall endowments as $\bar{v}_1$ and $\bar{v}_2$, we must have (assuming full employment) $\bar{v}_1/\bar{v}_2$ as the v_2 share-weighted sum of the v_1/v_2 ratios in the production of the two goods.

[11]Reverting to Figure 1, note then that all withdrawals of factor v_1 resulting in moves along P^*R^* leave the residual factor vector in the diversification cone whereas further withdrawals of v_1, leading to moves along R^*0, imply that the residual factor vector has slipped out of the cone.

which the residual factor vector slips out of the Rybczynski cone.[12]

(iii) Finally, note that the unique Rybczynski cone in Figure 2 implicitly rules out factor-intensity reversals. If we had allowed for such reversals, however, we would have had more than one diversification cone. In this case, even if production were no longer specialized, secondary cost would emerge. Moreover, as before, the more the residual factor vector slips out of the Rybczynski cone, the higher will be the share of secondary cost in the entire project cost.

Second, for the *with-distortion* case, the preceding analysis for the no-distortion case holds qualitatively with one exception: the secondary cost can be a secondary gain. Returning to Figure 2, note that in the distortion-free case, for residual factor vectors that take the economy outside the Rybczynski cone $q_2 0 q_1$, the true social cost of factors in project use will be understated because valuing, say, a residual endowment at H at the marginal variational prices overstates its true value and hence understates the difference between the preproject and the postproject valuation of the quantities of commodities x_1 and x_2 that are being produced: this being the secondary cost noted above. But suppose now there is an export tax on x_2 so that its price is lower on the domestic market than on the world market. Guided by the domestic prices, firms collectively will produce more x_1 and less x_2 than what it takes to maximize the national output at international prices. Now assume a withdrawal of inputs which causes the residual factor vector to leave the diversification-cum-Rybczynski cone, so that good x_2 alone is produced. This change of the output mix improves on the original distortion-caused misallocation and hence increases the internationally valued national output. Conceivably, this effect may outweigh the secondary cost from the law of variable proportions and result in a net secondary gain.[13]

[12]Thus, for residual factor endowments lying on the ray OG in Figure 2, the proportionate secondary cost will be higher than for those lying on the ray OH.

II. Many Goods and Factors, with and without Distortions

The uniqueness and stationarity of the marginal variational shadow factor prices in the two-by-two F-W-S-B model, with and without the specified distortions, do not necessarily carry over to the cases with unequal numbers of goods and factors that need to be analyzed as soon as we consider many goods and factors. The analysis of these cases is simply developed in this section, at a qualitatively insightful level.[14]

The precise questions that are addressed for the six possible cases discussed here are noted best by recalling that the shadow price of factors withdrawn for project use is the sum of the resulting changes in outputs valued at *international* prices. Write this shadow cost as

$$c_k = -p^* \Delta_k x$$

where c_k denotes the shadow factor cost of a project (program) k, p^* is the vector of international prices, and $\Delta_k x$ is the vector of changes in nonproject production in the country as a result of the withdrawal of factors for project use. (Here x, p, and p^* represent m-dimensional vectors denoting output quantities, (domestic) output prices facing the firms, and international prices, respectively. Also v, w, and w^* will be n-dimensional vectors representing factor quantities and factor prices related to domestic and international prices, respectively.) Noting that

$$c_k (= -p^* \Delta_k x) = -w^* \Delta_k v$$

for preproject marginal variational shadow factor prices w^* and infinitesimal factor withdrawal for project use, we can then pose three questions of principal importance in this

[13]The secondary gain in fact may turn the social cost of the factors withdrawn for project use into a net gain, resurrecting the paradox of negative shadow prices of factors noted in Bhagwati, Srinivasan, and Wan.

[14]The algebraic analysis, necessary for general formulations, is in Appendix I of our working paper; available from the authors on request.

section:

(i) Can the social opportunity cost c_k be *uniquely* defined?

(ii) Will the shadow factor prices be stationary for finite factor withdrawals in the perfectly general sense that $-w^*\Delta_k v$ will equal $(c_k=)\ -\ p^*\Delta_k x$, i.e., the valuation of the withdrawn factors at the preproject marginal variational shadow prices will equal the social opportunity cost of the foregone output?

(iii) Will the use of marginal variational shadow factor prices, when inappropriate, necessarily understate the social cost of the project?[15]

The results of our analysis are summarized in advance for the reader's convenience in Table 1.

TABLE 1—SIX ALTERNATIVE CASES: OUTCOMES REGARDING MARGINAL VARIATIONAL SHADOW FACTOR PRICES[a]

Cases	No Distortion	With Distortion
Goods Equal Factors	I. Stationarity	II. Stationarity
Goods Outnumber Factors	III. Stationarity	IV. Shadow Prices May be Undefined
Factors Outnumber Goods	V. Possible Nonstation-arity	VI. Possible Nonstation-arity

[a]"Extreme" cases noted in fn. 15 are excluded. For the no-distortion cases, the use of marginal variational shadow factor prices will necessarily underestimate the true social cost of a project; not so for the with-distortion cases.

A. *Cases 1 and 2: Equal Numbers of Goods and Factors, with and without Distortions*

The introduction of more than two goods and factors, as long as goods are equal in number to factors, changes the results of the two-by-two F-W-S-B model in no essential manner. As before, a diversification cone can be defined and, since it is also the Rybczynski cone, the marginal variational shadow factor prices are unique and also stationary as long as the residual factor endowment leaves the economy within this cone.

When the residual factor endowment takes the economy into the nonstationarity zone, the use of marginal variational shadow factor prices will necessarily understate the true social cost of the factors used in the project if distortions are absent; but it may overstate the true cost (i.e., the secondary cost may turn into a secondary gain) when distortions are present.

B. *Case 3: Goods Outnumber Factors, No Distortions*

It is equally evident that, where goods outnumber factors and there is no distortion, there will be no problem with uniqueness and stationarity in general. A diversification-cum-Rybczynski cone can again be defined and, within it, the marginal variational shadow factor prices will be unique and stationary. The product mix will be indeterminate of course, but this does not affect the shadow factor prices, as should be evident by redrawing the Lerner-Findlay-Grubert diagram (Figure 2) for more than two goods by merely putting in more isoquants tangent to the linear segment q_2q_1.

The use of marginal variational shadow factor prices for evaluating the social cost of

[15]In answering these questions, we will generally ignore the "extreme" cases which provide exceptions to our propositions and analysis, so that we can avoid frequent repetition of caveats regarding them. Such extreme cases are reviewed readily for the two-by-two model. Thus (a) certain projects will cause difficulties. For instance, consider a project using up resources of magnitude and proportions such that the residual vector is no longer in the same diversification cone as the initial vector. Either complete specialization will occur, or the residual vector may now be in another diversification cone (as may happen when factor intensity is reversible), and shadow prices will change. (b) Certain projects almost surely will cause no difficulty. Thus, consider the case where the diverted resources, and hence the residual resources, are proportional to the initial resources. (c) Certain circumstances almost surely will cause difficulties. For instance, take the case where the two unit-output isoquants, one for each project, are tangential to a common tangent at the same point. (d) Certain circumstances almost surely will cause no difficulties. For instance, consider the case where, over some relevant range, the two inputs are "perfect substitutes" in the sense that a linear segment of the unit-output isoquant of at least one product prevails.

the factors used in the project, when the residual factor endowment leaves the economy outside this cone, will necessarily understate their true social cost: that is, secondary cost will necessarily arise.

C. *Case 4: Goods Outnumber Factors, with Distortions*

While, however, there is no problem as long as goods outnumber factors in the absence of distortions, the introduction of distortions leads to difficulties. Intuitively, it is easy to see why. For the diversification cone is defined with respect to p, the *domestic* output prices. Hence, within the cone, the indeterminacy of the output mix is still compatible with unique opportunity cost and hence with unique and stationary factor valuations as long as the marginal variational changes in outputs from factor withdrawals are evaluated at the *domestic* prices. However, the shadow factor prices require these output changes to be evaluated at the *international* goods prices p^*. When $p = p^*$ (i.e., Case 3), shadow factor prices will also be unique and stationary within the diversification cone.

But when $p \neq p^*$, the social opportunity cost of the withdrawn factors, even when the residual vector remains in the diversification cone, may not be unique but will reflect the particular product mix happening to obtain out of the indeterminate many. Hence the associated shadow factor prices may be undefined.

Suppose, however, that a "planner" *chooses* for each residual vector that particular output mix whose value, evaluated at international prices p^*, is *maximal*. Could we then argue that in this event the shadow factor prices will be stationary within the diversification cone? The answer unfortunately is again in the negative, generally speaking. Note that even if it were in the affirmative, to use such shadow prices for project evaluation, we would have to assume that these maximal-value product mixes were *in fact* the equilibrium output mixes obtaining in the economy before and after the factor withdrawals for the projects in question. Otherwise, the "true" opportunity costs of the withdrawn factors would not correspond to the "shadow" opportunity costs as calculated with the maximal-value procedure.

All this should be perfectly intuitive, once the difference between p and p^* under the specified distortion is grasped. It can be established more formally[16] but may rather be illustrated to great advantage with the aid of the "micro-theoretic" diagrams, Figures 3A–E. Figures 3A–C introduce the basic technique, while Figures 3D–E illustrate our basic propositions with this technique by using a three-good, two-factor, with-distortion depiction.

In Figure 3A, two inputs v_1 and v_2 are used to produce output x, which is depicted along the vertical axis $0x$. At the initial endowment v, height $v\bar{v}$ of the production surface $0CD$ shows the output value before factor withdrawal for project use. A project using both factors in proportion to the initial endowments will leave a residual vector $0B$ within the ray $0\bar{v}$. The difference in height between $B\bar{B}$ and $v\bar{v}$ reflects then the project cost. The unique tangent plane $0PP'$ to surface $0CD$ at $\bar{v}$ represents clearly the marginal variational valuation of any residual factor vector.[17] Since $\bar{B}$ lies both on $0C\bar{v}D$ and on its tangent plane $0PP'$, such valuation incurs no secondary cost for the project in question. By contrast, a project using factors *not* proportional to the initial endowments will leave a residual vector $0A$ off the $0v$ ray (which is of course the Rybczynski cone in the present case). The maximum output producible at A is the height of the $0CD$ surface $A\tilde{A}$, which is less than the marginal variational valuation $A\bar{A}$ for $0A$. The overvaluation of the residual vector thus causes an understatement of the true opportunity cost of (the factors used in) the project.

Figure 3B extends this construction to incorporate two goods x_1 and x_2. If we select units such that the output prices are unity for both goods, the surface $0C\bar{q}_1$ and $0D\bar{q}_2$ reflect what is producible if all inputs are used to

[16] Mathematical proofs are contained in the unpublished Appendix I in our working paper.

[17] The directional cosines at v reflect the marginal products of the two inputs. Their ratio is the slope of line CD in plane $v_1 0 v_2$, while $PP'//CD$.

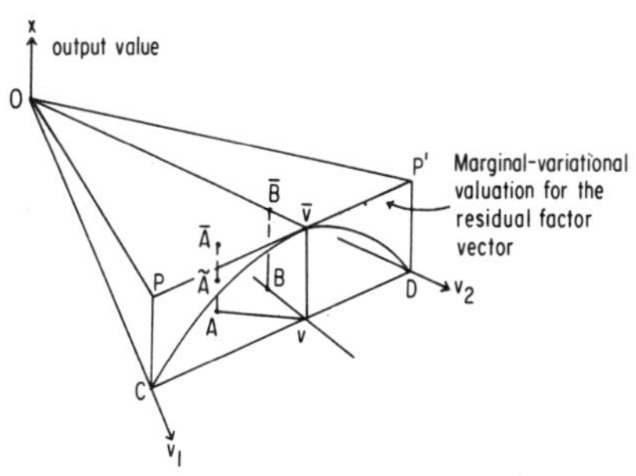

FIGURE 3A

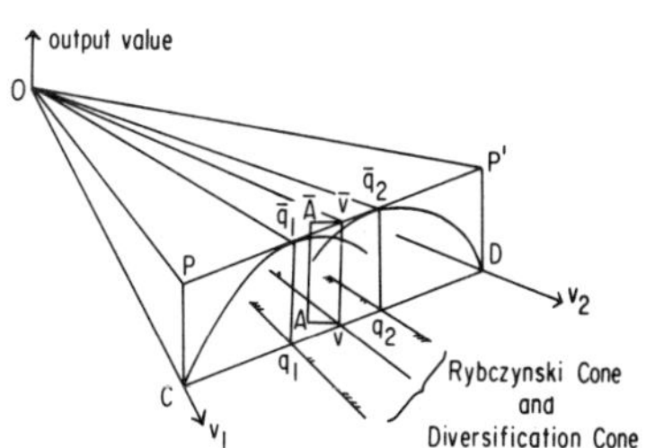

FIGURE 3B

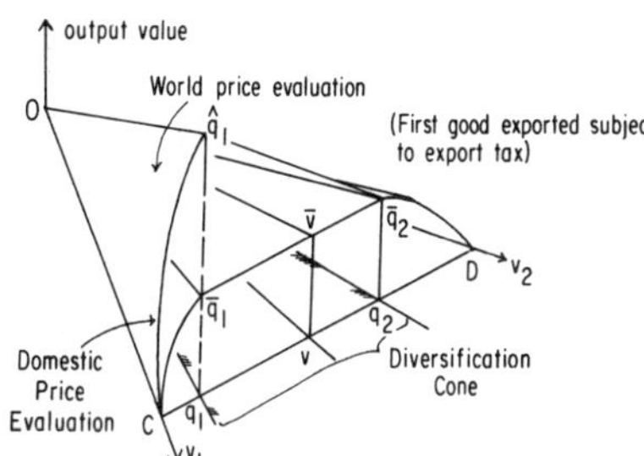

FIGURE 3C

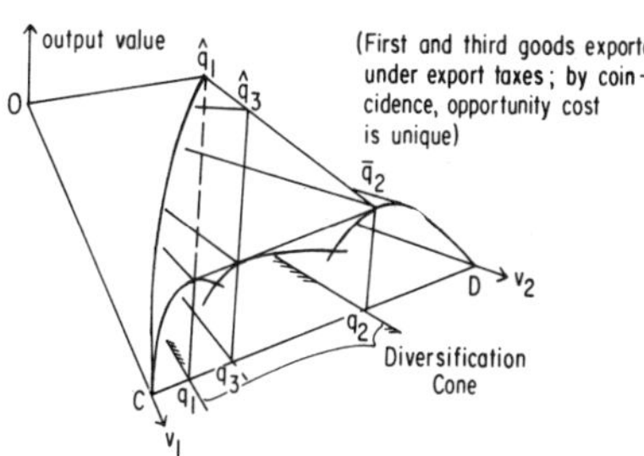

FIGURE 3D

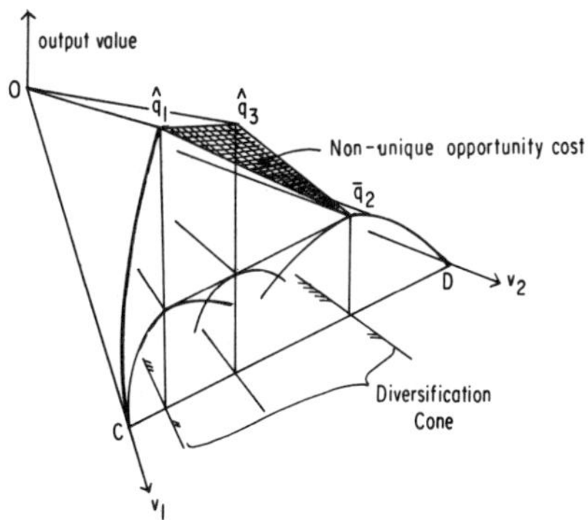

FIGURE 3E

produce only x_1 and x_2, respectively, and their convex hull therefore has surface $0CD$ and tangent plane $0PP'$ reflecting the marginal variational valuation of all residual factor vectors. The factor proportions producing good x_1 (x_2) under the prevailing factor prices before the project are reflected by ray $0q_1$ ($0q_2$). If a project leaves a residual factor vector $0A$ within the Rybczynski cone $q_1 0 q_2$, then the marginal variational valuation $A\bar{A}$, thereof, agrees with the true maximum output value producible therewith: there is therefore no overvaluation for $0A$ and thus no understatement of the project cost.

Figure 3C modifies Figure 3B to allow international prices to differ from domestic prices, illustrating the distortion. Thus, it portrays an export tax on commodity x_1. Consequently, the world market value of any output mix is higher than the domestic market value if and only if some x_1 is produced. The $0C\hat{q}_1\bar{q}_2D$ surface is constructed to reflect this fact. The $0\hat{q}_1\bar{q}_2$ planar segment reflects therefore the true social value of any residual factor vector falling within the diversification cone $q_1 0 q_2$.

We can now proceed to our full illustration of the three-good, two-factor, with-distortion case. Thus Figures 3D–E additionally portray output of x_3 which is also assumed (like x_1) to be exported under an export tax. It is further assumed that the factor intensity of good x_3 lies between that of the other two goods. Clearly the construction of the $0C\hat{q}_1\hat{q}_3\bar{q}_2D$ surface is similar to that of the $0C\hat{q}_1\bar{q}_2D$ surface in Figure 3C.

Figure 3D then shows the case where, by coincidence, $\hat{q}_1\hat{q}_3\bar{q}_2$ fall on one line such that $0\hat{q}_1\hat{q}_3\bar{q}_2$ constitutes a single planar segment whose height at any residual factor vector within the diversification cone $0q_1q_2$ then reflects the true social (i.e., international) value of that vector. Hence also the difference between that height and the height $v\bar{v}$ (corresponding to the preproject endowment vector) represents the true opportunity cost of the factors withdrawn for project use. Clearly, because of the planar segment, this opportunity cost is unique even within the diversification cone.

By contrast, the general case is depicted in Figure 3E. Here the planar segment disappears and instead one gets indeterminate, social opportunity cost for the project within the diversification cone.[18] Depending on the output mix, we can see that the (social) value producible by a residual factor vector can vary from the "optimistic surface" $0\hat{q}_1\hat{q}_3\bar{q}_2$ to the "pessimistic surface" $0\hat{q}_1\bar{q}_2$; and the project evaluator cannot predict what will happen and therefore which opportunity cost will prevail.[19]

Finally, note that the indeterminacy of the marginal variational shadow prices in this case renders somewhat academic the question whether their use outside the diversification cone would understate or overstate the true opportunity cost of factors withdrawn for project use.

D. *Case 5: Factors Outnumber Goods, No Distortion*

We now turn to the case where factors outnumber goods and there is no distortion. As one would expect from the well-known work of Paul Samuelson (1953) and other writers in the theory of international trade, even this distortion-free world will present problems, because in general primary factor prices will vary with the factor endowments so that the withdrawal of factors for project use will generally imply varying factor prices and hence the absence of a set of stationary shadow factor prices, except for a negligible set of residual factor vectors. More precisely, we will argue the following propositions concerning the implications of the case where factors outnumber goods:[20]

PROPOSITION 1: *Marginal variational shadow factor prices will be stationary if and only if the residual factor proportions belong to that negligible set of all possible propor-*

[18] The cone $q_1 0 q_2$ is no longer a Rybczynski cone since shadow factor prices are not stationary within it any more because of the distortion.

[19] On the other hand, note that the uniqueness of opportunity cost will return once we leave the diversification cone.

[20] The formal proofs are to be found in the unpublished Appendix I in our working paper.

tions[21] *where the residual factors can be absorbed into industries at preproject factor intensities.*

PROPOSITION 2: *If the condition in Proposition 1 is violated, the Law of Variable Proportions will cause the opportunity cost for the project to differ from the marginal variational value of the factors withdrawn for use in the project, and to exceed the latter by a secondary cost.*

PROPOSITION 3: *This secondary cost will bear a proportional relation to the marginal variational value of the residual factors: a proportion rising steadily from zero at a nondecreasing rate as the residual factor proportions deviate progressively from the "negligible set" cited in Proposition 1.*

PROPOSITION 4: *There is a continuum of diversification subcones, each of them polyhedral in form and corresponding to a unique domestic factor-price vector. If that domestic factor-price vector deviates from the preproject factor-price vector, then all residual factor vectors in that subcone will be overvalued under (preproject) marginal variational valuation by the same proportion. Each diversification subcone is a Rybczynski cone (defined on some domestic factor-price vector) and the totality of all such diversification cones, not necessarily convex, forms the McKenzie-Chipman diversification cone.*

Propositions 1–3 can be visualized immediately by reference to a two-factor, one-good model. In Figure 4A, if the residual factor vector lies (as at *A*) on the ray *OR* from the origin, which is the ray on which the preproject factor endowment ratio lies, clearly there will be no project-induced change in the factor prices. For projects that leave the residual factor-endowment ratios elsewhere (as at *B* and *C*, for example, on the rays *OB* and *OC*), on the other hand, there will be corresponding changes in factor prices, and

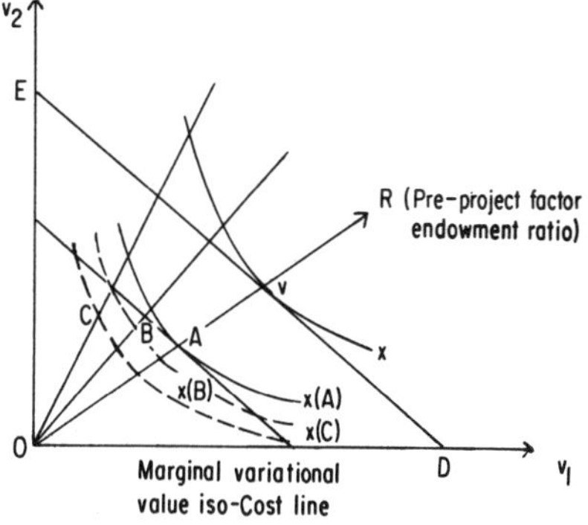

FIGURE 4A

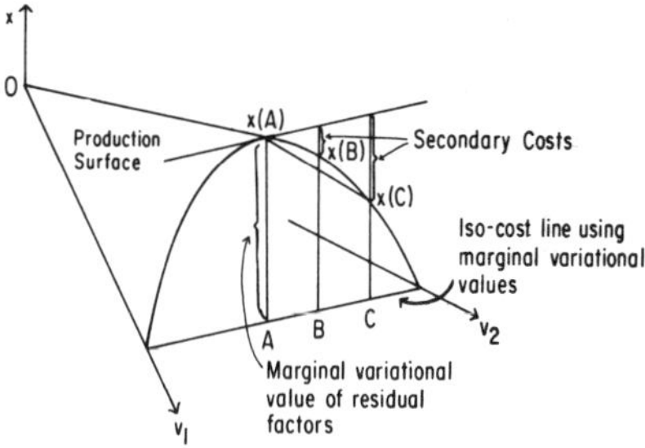

FIGURE 4B

the secondary cost that results may be illustrated in the now familiar construction (see Figure 3A) in Figure 4B. Note in particular that the values of the outputs for the isoquants passing through *A*, *B*, *C* and indeed all points along the *ABC* line in Figure 4A can be plotted as the concave curve in Figure 4B and this at once illustrates Proposition 3 above.[22] At the same time, note that the residual factor proportions must lie on the ray *OR* if stationarity of shadow factor prices is to be maintained, thus clearly demonstrating the "negligible" character of such stationarity-

[21]This set is the lower-dimension cone of the nonnegatively weighted sums of the preproject factor proportions for various industries.

[22]Recall that the curve $x(A)$ $x(B)$ $x(C)$ in Figure 4B is actually the vertical cross section of the production surface along the line *ABC* in Figure 4A.

preserving projects in our two-dimensional world, as argued in Propositions 1 and 2 above.

Turn now to the three-factor, two-good world where Proposition 4 is also admissible and hence demonstrable. (Since the formal proof is in Appendix I of our working paper, a few words of intuitive explanation should suffice here.) Corresponding to the initial preproject factor endowments, assume that the factor prices are determined such that all goods are produced (i.e., "diversification" obtains). Now, if for a finite project the postproject residual factor-endowment vector can be accommodated by suitable reweighting of the initial factor-proportions vectors, this is fine and stationarity obtains: though, as stated in Proposition 1, this set of possibilities is negligible. Suppose now that the residual factor-endowment vector requires new factor prices and hence new factor-proportion vectors in the production of the different goods. We can then immediately see both that there is now secondary cost and that, assuming continuing diversification, generally speaking there will be again a negligible set of factor-withdrawal possibilities at which the new factor prices and proportions, and hence the proportionate secondary cost vis-à-vis the old (marginal variational) factor prices, will remain unchanged. Therefore, clearly Proposition 4 is intuitively established.

E. *Case 6: Factors Outnumber Goods, with Distortion*

Here, as in Case 5, except for a negligible set of residual factor vectors, the marginal variational shadow factor prices may be nonstationary. The presence of the distortion, however, makes it impossible to assert that the use of marginal variational shadow factor prices outside of the diversification subcone to which they pertain will necessarily overstate or understate the true opportunity cost of the factors withdrawn for project use.

III. Concluding Remarks

Our analysis leads to many observations. First, as a quick perusal of the summary of Table 1 will show, the relative numbering of factors and goods is of significance. Project evaluation by shadow price computation is possible in the happy world of equal numbers of goods and factors, but lies between the Scylla of indeterminacy where goods exceed factors and the Charybdis of nonstationarity where factors exceed goods. The presence of distortions, in turn, is seen to be of significance in two ways: (i) unlike the distortion-free case, it creates nonuniqueness of shadow factor prices when goods outnumber factors; and (ii) while the distortion-free cases are characterized by secondary cost when marginal variational shadow factor prices are used outside of the zone of stationarity, the distortionary cases can be characterized instead by secondary gain as well.

Second, our analysis has clear applicability to the transfer problem, conceived *not* as a transfer of purchasing power, but rather as a transfer of factors of production as may be the case when reparations payments have to be made in barter (for example, Soviet Union transferring factories from Germany after World War II). By contrast with the purchasing power shift variety of transfers analyzed in the standard trade-theoretic literature (for example by Samuelson, 1952, 1954; Harry Johnson, 1956; and others), we must now contend with the possible existence of secondary costs (or gains, when distortions are present) even when the small-country assumption is made.

Third, our analysis also has applicability therefore to the theory of international factor mobility. Thus, the existing theoretical analyses, by Herbert Grubel and A. Scott, Albert Berry and Ronald Soligo, Johnson (1968), and Peter Kenen, of the welfare effects of brain drain on "those left behind," as reviewed and synthesized in Bhagwati and Carlos Rodriguez, relate to two-factor models with one or two products, with focus mainly on one-factor emigration. Our present analysis leads, however, to the following generalization: For a small country without distortions, and with each individual possessing the same factor endowment, any finite level of emigration of factors, singly or in combination, will harm (or have no effect on) those left behind, if the residual factor vector falls outside (or is left inside) the preemigration Rybczynski cone. The harmful effect will almost always obtain when factors outnumber goods.

Fourth, for a small country without distortion, the welfare impact of finite factor increases (for example labor immigration, capital inflow) on those originally present is completely symmetrical. If every individual has an identical endowment, there is no effect *or* there is a beneficial effect (in the absence of distortions), depending upon whether the "augmented factor vector" is inside *or* outside the Rybczynski cone, and the latter possibility will almost always arise with factors outnumbering goods.

Fifth, the *locus classicus* of shadow prices is mathematical programming. It appears desirable to relate our findings with the programming framework, cross-referencing the economic assumptions, the programming formulation, and the implications for the shadow cost of a project. All these are tabulated in Table 2. Recall that, inside the Rybczynski cone, the Law of Variable Proportions is held at bay for the small-country, constant returns situation; hence stationarity of marginal variational shadow factor cost obtains.

TABLE 2—RELATIONSHIP OF ANALYSIS TO MATHEMATICAL PROGRAMMING

Set of Economic Assumptions	Programming Framework	Secondary Cost[a]
1) Large country, decreasing returns to scale	Non-linear programming	Ubiquitous
2) Small country, constant returns to scale, variable coefficients	Generalized linear programming of Dantzig-Wolfe[b]	Absent if residual factor vector stays inside the Rybczynski cone
3) Small country, fixed coefficients	Linear programming	Absent if residual factor vector stays inside the Rybczynski cone

[a]The tabulation is based upon the distortion-free cases. With distortion, the secondary cost can be a secondary gain.
[b]See and compare George Dantzig.

REFERENCES

A. Berry and R. Soligo, "Some Welfare Aspects of International Migration," *J. Polit. Econ.*, Sept./Oct. 1969, *77*, 778–94.

T. Bertrand and F. Flatters, "Tariffs, Capital Accumulation and Immiserizing Growth," *J. Int. Econ.*, Nov. 1971, *1*, 453–60.

J. Bhagwati and T. N. Srinivasan, "The General Equilibrium Theory of Effective Protection and Resource Allocation," *J. Int. Econ.*, Aug. 1973, *3*, 259–82.

——— **and C. Rodriquez,** "Welfare-Theoretical Analyses of the Brain Drain," *J. Develop. Econ.*, Sept. 1974, *2*, 195–221; reprinted in Jagdish Bhagwati, ed., *The Brain Drain and Taxation: Theory and Empirical Analysis*, Amsterdam 1975.

———**, T. N. Srinivasan, and H. Wan, Jr.,** "Value Subtracted, Negative Shadow Prices of Factors in Project Evaluation, and Immiserizing Growth: Three Paradoxes in the Presence of Trade Distortions," *Econ. J.*, Mar. 1978, *88*, 121–25.

——— **and H. Wan, Jr.,** "Shadow Prices in Project Evaluation with and without Distortions and with Many Goods and Factors," econ. work. paper no. 205, M.I.T., July 1977.

R. Brecher, "Optimum Commercial Policy for a Minimum Wage Economy," *J. Int. Econ.*, May 1974, *4*, 139–50.

W. M. Corden, *Trade Policy and Economic Welfare*, London 1974.

George Dantzig, *Linear Programming and its Extensions*, Princeton 1963.

P. Diamond and J. Mirrlees, "Private Constant Returns and Public Shadow Prices," *Rev. Econ. Stud.*, Feb. 1976, *43*, 41–48.

R. Findlay and S. Wellisz, "Project Evaluation, Shadow Prices and Trade Policy," *J. Polit. Econ.*, June 1976, *84*, 543–52.

D. Gale and H. Nikaido, "The Jacobian Matrix and Global Univalence of Mappings," *Mathematische Annalen*, 1965, *159*.

H. Grubel and A. Scott, "The International Flow of Human Capital," *Amer. Econ. Rev. Proc.*, May 1966, *56*, 268–74.

H. Johnson, "The Transfer Problem and Exchange Stability," *J. Polit. Econ.*, June 1956, *64*, 212–25.

______, "Some Economic Aspects of Brain Drain," *Pakistan Develop. Rev.*, No. 3, 1967, *7*, 379–411.

V. Joshi, "The Rationale and Relevance of the Little-Mirrlees Criterion," *Bull. Oxford Univ. Inst. Econ. Statist.*, Feb. 1972, *34*, 3–33.

P. Kenen, "Migration, the Terms of Trade and Welfare in the Source Country," in Jagdish Bhagwati et al., eds., *Trade, Balance of Payments and Growth*, Amsterdam 1971.

D. Lal, "Methods of Project Analysis: A Review," occas. paper no. 16, World Bank, Washington 1974.

Jacques Lesourne, *Cost-Benefit Analysis and Economic Theory*, Amsterdam 1975.

Ian Little and James Mirrlees, *Manual of Industrial Project Analysis in Developing Countries*, Vol. 2, Paris 1969.

A. Rudra, "Use of Shadow Prices in Project Evaluation," *Indian Econ. Rev.*, Apr. 1972, *7*, 1–15.

P. Samuelson, "The Transfer Problem and Transport Costs: The Terms of Trade when Impediments are Absent," *Econ. J.*, June 1952, *62*, 278–304.

______, "Prices of Factors and Goods in General Equilibrium," *Rev. Econ. Stud.*, No. 1, 1953, *21*, 1–20.

______, "The Transfer Problem and Transport Costs, II: Analysis of Effects of Trade Impediments," *Econ. J.*, June 1954, *64*, 264–89.

T. N. Srinivasan and J. Bhagwati, "Shadow Prices for Project Selection in the Presence of Distortions: Effective Rates of Protection and Domestic Resource Costs," *J. Polit. Econ.*, Feb. 1978, *86*, 97–116.

DOMESTIC RESOURCE COSTS, EFFECTIVE RATES OF PROTECTION, AND PROJECT ANALYSIS IN TARIFF-DISTORTED ECONOMIES*

JAGDISH N. BHAGWATI AND T. N. SRINIVASAN

For atomistic economies (i.e., those facing fixed world prices of traded goods) and ad valorem tariff distortions and only tradable goods, it has been known since the early work of Bruno and (independently) of Little and Mirrlees [1969] that a small project should be considered acceptable if, in consequence of its implementation, the value of project plus nonproject output increases when evaluated at the world prices.[1]

APPROPRIATE DRC CRITERION

This criterion can further be translated into an equivalent criterion couched in the terminology of Domestic Resource Costs, as demonstrated by Srinivasan and Bhagwati [1978].

Thus, consider a simple model with three tradable goods and two primary factors, where two goods, 1 and 2, are being produced at a tariff-distorted equilibrium. In this context, consider the acceptability of a project that produces a unit of good 3, with the trade distortion continuing unchanged. The project will involve withdrawal (for project use) of the two primary factors, 1 and 2, from the trade-distorted equilibrium production of goods 1 and 2. However, with the tariff in place, the domestic goods price vector and hence the choice of technique in goods 1 and 2 will remain the same as before the project. Let $\hat{b}_{11}$, $\hat{b}_{21}$ be the fixed coefficients of factors 1 and 2 used per unit of output of good 1, reflecting the choice of technique at the distorted goods prices; and let $\hat{b}_{21}$, $\hat{b}_{22}$ be the corresponding coefficients in good 2. Let the project have unit coefficients b_{13}^p and b_{23}^p in the use of factors 1 and 2. Let p_1^*, p_2^*, and p_3^* represent the world prices

* Thanks are due to the National Science Foundation, Grant NO. SOC 77-07188 for financial support of the first author's research. The views expressed here do not necessarily reflect those of the institutions to which the authors are affiliated. Thanks are due to Henry Wan, Robert Dorfman, and two anonymous referees for helpful comments on an earlier draft of this paper.

1. For, in this case, an increase in the value of national income at world prices implies an increase in national welfare, given a well-behaved social utility function. The argument does not carry over to quotas which generally imply a *changing* trade distortion, rather than a *given* ad valorem trade distortion, but it can be extended to include nontraded goods under appropriate restrictions. On all this see Bhagwati and Srinivasan [1978].

The Quarterly Journal of Economics, February 1980 0033-5533/80/0094-0205$01.00

of the three goods; X_1 and X_2 represent the output levels of goods 1 and 2, respectively.

Then the Little-Mirrlees rule for project acceptance, stated above, requires that the project should be accepted if

$$p_3^* > dX_1p_1^* + dX_2p_2^*; \tag{1}$$

i.e., if the value of total production (of goods 1, 2, and 3), measured at *world* prices, increases. But we may, for small projects, also write

$$dX_1p_1^* + dX_2p_2^* = b_{13}^p\hat{w}_1^* + b_{23}^p\hat{w}_2^*; \tag{2}$$

i.e., derive the shadow "second-best" prices ($\hat{w}$*s) of the factors used in the project such that the corresponding social cost equals the loss in output of goods 1 and 2 (i.e., dX_1 and dX_2) evaluated at world prices.

Solving for dX_1 and dX_2, given the fixed $\hat{b}_{ki}$s owing to the assumption of unchanged trade distortion, the reader will find that the shadow prices of the factors ($\hat{w}_1^*$ and $\hat{w}_2^*$) are nothing but the solutions to the two equations:

$$p_1^* = \hat{b}_{11}\hat{w}_1^* + \hat{b}_{21}w_2^* \tag{3}$$

$$p_2^* = \hat{b}_{12}\hat{w}_1^* + \hat{b}_{22}\hat{w}_2^* \tag{4}$$

as is evident from Diamond-Mirrlees [1976], Srinivasan and Bhagwati [1978], and Findlay and Wellisz [1976]. Note that the second-best shadow prices, $\hat{w}_1^*$ and $\hat{w}_2^*$, so derived reflect the fact that the goods prices continue to be distorted and hence do not change as primary factors are withdrawn (from the distorted equilibrium) for the project: this, in turn, implies that the associated market prices of factors ($\hat{w}_1$ and $\hat{w}_2$) are also fixed and hence the unit requirements of factors in the production of the two goods remain fixed at $\hat{b}_{11}$, $\hat{b}_{21}$, $\hat{b}_{12}$, and $\hat{b}_{22}$.

But, (1) and (2) on the one hand, and (3) and (4) on the other, imply that

$$DRC_p = (b_{13}^p\hat{w}_1^* + b_{23}^p\hat{w}_2^*)/p_3^* < 1 \tag{5}$$

$$DRC_1 = (\hat{b}_{11}\hat{w}_1^* + \hat{b}_{21}\hat{w}_2^*)/p_1^* = 1 \tag{6}$$

and

$$DRC_2 = (\hat{b}_{12}\hat{w}_1^* + \hat{b}_{22}\hat{w}_2^*)/p_2^* = 1, \tag{7}$$

where *DRC* (domestic resource cost) of each of the three goods is clearly the *shadow*-price-weighted domestic (primary) factor cost expended per unit of foreign exchange earned therewith. It is then immediately evident that the Little-Mirrlees criterion for acceptance of small project translates into the equivalent criterion that the DRC in the project be less than that in existing activities at the trade-distorted equilibrium. For (5)–(7) imply that, writing generally for n goods produced in the distorted equilibrium,[2] the project is acceptable if

(8) $$DRC_{i=1,\ldots,n} = 1 > DRC_p.$$

Effective Rates of Protection

An examination of the *DRC* criterion for project-acceptance (8) shows that we need to value tradable *goods* at world prices and domestic (primary) factors at the appropriately derived (second-best, distortion-reflecting) Diamond-Mirrlees-Findlay-Wellisz-Srinivasan-Bhagwati shadow *factor* prices.

By inference, the use of the effective rate of protection (*ERP*) ranking at the distorted equilibrium will be an inappropriate project choice criterion for it uses *market* prices for factors, while using world prices for goods.[3]

But consider now an interesting question of the policy relevance. This question is suggested by the fact that, in a world where all goods are tradables (as in our analysis above), *ERP* calculation in the distorted equilbrium involves our knowing only the world prices of all goods, whereas the appropriate *DRC* calculation requires additionally the computation of the shadow prices of the primary factors. Now, suppose that the policy maker does not have the resources to calculate the shadow factor prices. In this "limited information" situation, we may ask the interesting question: When will the use of *ERP* ranking, inappropriate as it is, nonetheless yield the correct decision that appropriate-defined *DRC* rankings invariably yield?[4]

2. For complications that can arise if factors and goods are unequal in number at the distorted equilibrium, see Bhagwati and Wan [1977].

3. ERP is nothing but

$$\left[\frac{\text{value added at domestic prices}}{\text{value added at world prices}}\right] - 1,$$

and the ratio in the bracket is evidently the reciprocal of a *DRC* if the domestic resources are valued at market, rather than shadow, prices.

4. It should be noted, of course, that the shadow factor prices can be calculated from equations (3) and (4) in the text as soon as we know the world prices of the goods and the techniques in the activities at the distorted equilibrium, both items necessary for calculating *ERP*.

Findlay and Wellisz [1975] consider a similar problem, e.g., where the analyst uses first-best shadow factor prices, rather than the correct second-best shadow factor prices, and nonetheless the project choice is correct. This, however, is an academic exercise, though of great interest. For, informationally, the analyst must have greater information to derive the first-best factor prices than to derive the second-best factor prices: knowledge of the production functions, or of the resulting implicit transformation function, would be necessary for the former, but not the latter!

In regard to this question, it may be useful to note that we can establish two sufficiency theorems about conditions when the inappropriate *ERP* rankings will nonetheless yield the correct evaluation of a small project. Thus, consider the three-good model again, with the project producing a unit of good 3 and resulting in changes in output (dX_1 and dX_2) of goods 1 and 2. Assume that

$$ERP_1 \leq ERP_2 \quad \text{i.e.,} \quad \hat{p}_1/p_1^* \leq \hat{p}_2/p_2^*,$$

where $\hat{p}_1$ and $\hat{p}_2$ are the tariff-inclusive domestic goods prices, since intermediate use is *not* allowed. Then, we can demonstrate the following two propositions:

PROPOSITION I. If $ERP_p > ERP_2$, and $dX_1 \geq 0$, then $DRC_p > 1$, and the project should be rejected. Thus, the rank-ordering by *ERP*'s, i.e., $ERP_p > ERP_2 \geq ERP_1$, will yield in this case the correct project evaluation.

PROPOSITION II. If $ERP_p < ERP_1$ and $dX_2 \geq 0$, then $DRC_p < 1$, and the project should be accepted. Thus, the rank-ordering by *ERP*'s, i.e., $ERP_p < ERP_1 \leq ERP_2$, will yield in this case the correct project evaluation.

Proof I. By hypothesis[5]

$$ERP_p = (\hat{p}_1 dX_1 + \hat{p}_2 dX_2)/p_3^* > ERP_2.$$

Now

$$\begin{aligned}\hat{p}_1 dX_1 + \hat{p}_2 dX_2 &= p_1^* ERP_1 dX_1 + p_2^* ERP_2 dX_2 \\ &\leq ERP_2[p_1^* dX_1 + p_2^* dX_2]\end{aligned}$$

if $dX_1 \geq 0$, and $ERP_1 \leq ERP_2$. Therefore

$$\begin{aligned}ERP_2 &< \frac{\hat{p}_1 dX_1 + \hat{p}_2 dX_2}{p_3^*} \\ &\leq ERP_2 \left[\frac{p_1^* dX_1 + p_2^* dX_2}{p_3^*}\right] = ERP_2 \cdot DRC_p.\end{aligned}$$

Since $ERP_2 > 0$, $DRC_p > 1$; i.e., the project should be rejected.

The proof of Proposition II is almost exactly the same.

Of course, these propositions can be readily generalized to many goods, as was pointed out to us by Henry Wan. Thus, if n goods are

5. Of course,

$$ERP_p = (\hat{p}_1 dX_1 + \hat{p}_2 dX_2)/p_3^* - 1;$$

but the unity term is omitted for simplicity throughout the analysis.

numbered so that $ERP_i \leq ERP_{i+1}, \quad i = 1, 2, \ldots, n-1,$
our propositions can be rewritten as

PROPOSITION I. If, for the project $ERP_p > ERP_n$ and $dX_i \geq 0$ for $i > 1$, then $DRC_p > 1$, and the project should be rejected.

PROPOSITION II. If, for the project, $ERP_p < ERP_1$ and $dX_i \geq 0$ for $i < n$, then $DRC_p < 1$ and the project should be accepted.

Two remarks are worth making about these two propositions. First, they enable one to determine ex post facto whether a correct project decision has been made, using only the *ERP* index and actual changes in outputs of the existing activities. To the extent that correct *predictions* or *forecasts* can be made as to which activities will lose or gain in output, the analysis could also be ex ante.[6] Second, in a world of fixed-coefficient intermediate inputs (tradables) and substitutable factor inputs, while the calculation of second-best shadow prices would require information on *factor* and *intermediate input* coefficients, the *ERP* index is calculated on the basis of *intermediate input* coefficients alone. To this extent, our theorems on the usability of *ERP* indices for project evaluation go some way toward meeting the demand that useful cost-benefit analysis should be founded on "limited information" situations.

MASSACHUSETTS INSTITUTE OF TECHNOLOGY
WORLD BANK AND INDIAN STATISTICAL INSTITUTE

REFERENCES

Bhagwati, Jagdish, and Henry Wan, Jr., "Shadow Prices in Project Evaluation, with and without Distortions, and with Many Goods and Factors," *American Economic Review*, forthcoming (June 1979), (M.I.T. Economics Department Working Paper No. 205, July, 1977).

Bhagwati, Jagdish, and T. N. Srinivasan, "The Evaluation of Projects at World Prices under Trade Distortions: *QRs,* Monopoly Power in Trade, and Non-Traded Goods," M.I.T. (mimeo), June, 1978.

Diamond, Peter, and James Mirrlees, "Private Constant Returns and Public Shadow Prices," *Review of Economic Studies,* XLIII (Feb. 1976), 41–48.

Findlay, Ronald, and Stanislaw Wellisz, "Project Evaluation, Shadow Prices, and Trade Policy," *Journal of Political Economy,* LXXXIV (June 1976), 543–52.

Little, Ian, and James Mirrlees, *Manual of Industrial Project Analysis in Developing Countries,* Vol. 2 (Paris: O.E.C.D., 1969).

Srinivasan, T. N., and Jagdish Bhagwati, "Shadow Prices for Project Selection in the Presence of Distortions: Effective Rates of Protection and Domestic Resource Costs," *Journal of Political Economy,* LXXXVI (Feb. 1978), 97–114.

6. It may be useful to note that all we need is the direction of the changes in output, rather than the magnitude of these changes, as in Little and Mirrlees [1969].

Editor's Note

Proposition I (p. 208) can be extended to "$dX_1 \geq 0$ or $dX_2 \leq 0$" as well as "$dX_1 \geq 0$". The case $dX_2 \leq 0$ can be proved by establishing

$$\hat{p}_1\, dX_1 + \hat{p}_2\, dX_2 \leq ERP_1(p_1^*\, dX_1 + p_2^*\, dX_2).$$

since $dX_2 \leq 0$ and $ERP_1 \leq ERP_2$. Therefore

$$\begin{aligned} ERP_1 < ERP_p &= (\hat{p}_1\, dX_1 + \hat{p}_2\, dX_2)/p_3^* \\ &\leq ERP_1(p_1^*\, dX_1 + p_2^*\, dX_2)/p_3^* \\ &= ERP_1 \cdot DRC_p. \end{aligned}$$

Since $ERP_1 > 0$, $DRC_p > 1$, as desired. Similarly, Proposition II (p. 208) can be extended to "$dX_1 \leq 0$ or $dX_2 \geq 0$".

Proposition I (p. 209) can be corrected and generalized to "$dX_1 \geq 0$ for $i < m$ and $dX_j \leq 0$ for $j > n$, for any m $(1 \leq m \leq n)$". Similarly, Proposition II (p. 209) can be corrected and generalized to "$dX_i \leq 0$ for $i < m$ and $dX_j \geq 0$ for $j > m$, for any m $(1 \leq m \leq n)$".

The Economic Journal, **88** (*March* 1978), 121–125
Printed in Great Britain

VALUE SUBTRACTED, NEGATIVE SHADOW PRICES OF FACTORS IN PROJECT EVALUATION, AND IMMISERISING GROWTH: THREE PARADOXES IN THE PRESENCE OF TRADE DISTORTIONS*

I

The literature on trade distortions has now turned up three, seemingly unrelated, paradoxes:

(1) *Value Subtraction:* If inputs and outputs are evaluated at *international*, rather than (distorted) domestic, prices, the resulting value added at international prices may show value subtraction – as observed in the early empirical studies in Pakistan by Soligo and Stern (1965) and in India by Bhagwati (1968*b*) and Bhagwati and Desai (1970).

(2) *Negative Shadow Prices for Primary Factors in Project Evaluation:* Srinivasan and Bhagwati (1977) have shown that, if primary factors are withdrawn for use in a project, from existing activities which are subject to trade distortions, then their shadow prices for evaluating the project may well be negative. Thus, paradoxically, it pays the economy to withdraw factors for use in projects that produce nothing!

(3) *Immiserising Growth:* Finally, Bhagwati (1958) and Johnson (1967) have produced cases where growth may be immiserising, rather than welfare-improving, for a country with trade distortions.

These three paradoxes, however, are related in an essential manner in the following way:

Proposition I: (i) Value subtraction necessarily implies that *some* factors will carry negative shadow prices for project evaluation in the presence of the given trade distortions. (ii) The presence of negative shadow factor prices, however, does not necessarily imply value subtraction.

Proposition II: Negative shadow prices for factors in project evaluation are yet another manifestation of immiserising growth. These propositions are established in the rest of the paper. Note that, in the following analysis, drawing upon the earlier work of Findlay and Wellisz (1976) and Srinivasan and Bhagwati (1977) we consider only the effects of the production distortion implied by the trade distortion, and do not explicitly bring into the analysis the consumption distortion. However, this does not affect the essence of our analysis, as discussed in depth in Appendix II of Bhagwati and Wan (1977).

* Thanks are due to Lance Taylor and John Black for helpful comments. Research support by the National Science Foundation is gratefully acknowledged. The views expressed here do not represent those of the World Bank or any affiliated organisations.

II

Consider the following model where intermediates are explicitly introduced, permitting us to analyse the phenomenon of value subtraction: a phenomenon that obviously cannot arise when there are no intermediates. It is then easily shown, by exploring the relevant dualities, that (some) negative shadow factor prices so derived are necessarily implied by value subtraction but that value subtraction is not necessarily implied by negative shadow prices.

Thus, let $\mathbf{q}$, $\mathbf{x}$, $\mathbf{p}$ and $\mathbf{p}^*$ be n-dimensional vectors representing gross outputs, net outputs, (distorted) domestic output prices and world prices, respectively. Also let $\mathbf{y}$, $\mathbf{w}$, and $\mathbf{w}^*$ be n-dimensional vectors representing (primary) factor quantities and factor shadow prices based on domestic and world prices, respectively. Let then the isoquant producing one unit of output j be:

$$F_j(a_{1j}, \ldots, a_{nj}, b_{1j}, \ldots, b_{nj}) = 1, \tag{1}$$

where a_{ij} is the unit usage of primary factor i for output j and b_{kj} is the unit usage of intermediate input k for output j. Constant returns and cost minimisation will make

$$a_{ij} = a_{ij}(\mathbf{w}, \mathbf{p}), \quad b_{kj} = b_{kj}(\mathbf{w}, \mathbf{p}), \quad i = 1, \ldots, n; j, k = 1, \ldots, n \tag{2}$$

under the assumption of strictly convex isoquant surfaces. The matrix equations

$$\mathbf{A}(\mathbf{w}, \mathbf{p})\mathbf{q} = \mathbf{y}, \quad \mathbf{B}(\mathbf{w}, \mathbf{p})\,\mathbf{q}+\mathbf{x} = \mathbf{q}; \quad \mathbf{A} = [a_{ij}], \mathbf{B} = [b_{kj}] \tag{3}$$

now reflect competitive resource allocation, with $\mathbf{q}$ and $\mathbf{x}$ representing respectively the gross and net output vectors. Note that $\mathbf{q}$ is non-negative, while $\mathbf{x}$ need not be.

Assuming then that the Leontief inverse $[\mathbf{I}-\mathbf{B}(\mathbf{w}, \mathbf{p})]^{-1}$ exists, (3) may be written as:

$$\mathbf{A}(\mathbf{w}, \mathbf{p})\,[\mathbf{I}-\mathbf{B}(\mathbf{w}, \mathbf{p})]^{-1}\mathbf{x} = \mathbf{y}, \tag{4}$$

with its distorted and non-distorted duals:

$$\mathbf{w}'\mathbf{A}(\mathbf{w}, \mathbf{p})\,[\mathbf{I}-\mathbf{B}(\mathbf{w}, \mathbf{p})]^{-1} = \mathbf{p}', \tag{5}$$

$$\mathbf{w}^{*\prime}\mathbf{A}(\mathbf{w}, \mathbf{p})\,[\mathbf{I}-\mathbf{B}(\mathbf{w}, \mathbf{p})]^{-1} = \mathbf{p}^{*\prime} \tag{6}$$

respectively. Denoting $\mathbf{v}$ and $\mathbf{v}^*$ as value added with and without distortion respectively, we then get:

$$\mathbf{p}'[\mathbf{I}-\mathbf{B}(\mathbf{w}, \mathbf{p})] = \mathbf{v}' = \mathbf{w}'\mathbf{A}(\mathbf{w}, \mathbf{p}) \geqq \mathbf{o}', \tag{7}$$

$$\mathbf{p}^{*\prime}[\mathbf{I}-\mathbf{B}(\mathbf{w}, \mathbf{p})] = \mathbf{v}^{*\prime} = \mathbf{w}^{*\prime}\mathbf{A}(\mathbf{w}, \mathbf{p}). \tag{8}$$

Now, from (8), we observe that, due to the distortion of intermediate input usage coefficients (reflecting cost minimisation in response to the distorted domestic prices), $[\mathbf{I}-\mathbf{B}(\mathbf{w}, \mathbf{p})]$ may be such that v_j^* may be negative for some output j. Now, since

$$\mathbf{A}(\mathbf{w}, \mathbf{p}) \geqq \mathbf{o},$$

it is clear from (8) that, if the value added for output j, v_j^*, is negative, then there must be *some* w_i^* negative since

$$v_j^* = \sum_{i=1}^{n} a_{ij}(\mathbf{w}, \mathbf{p}) w_i^*$$

is a non-negatively weighted sum of the w_i^*'s. On the other hand, some negative w_i^*'s are compatible with value addition rather than subtraction. Hence, the value subtracted phenomenon implies, but is not implied by, (some) negative shadow factor prices. Therefore Proposition I is established.

III

The shadow factor prices were obtained in the analysis above as the solutions to the matrix equations (6). This is the procedure stated in Diamond and Mirrlees (1976) and Srinivasan and Bhagwati (1977) and is *equivalent* to the Little and Mirrlees (1969) rule for shadow-pricing factors under which the changes in the outputs of traded goods, resulting from the change in factor supplies, should be evaluated at international prices. [However, for problems that arise with either of the two techniques when the numbers of factors and goods are unequal, as also for "stationarity" of the "marginal-variational" shadow factor prices that may be computed, see Bhagwati and Wan (1977).]

But as soon as this equivalence is appreciated, it is readily seen that the phenomenon of negative shadow factor prices under trade distortions in project analysis is but the mirror image of the phenomenon of the immiserising growth of a trade-distorted small country, as analysed by Johnson (1967), Bertrand and Flatters (1971) and Martin (1977). For a negative shadow factor price implies, as per the Little and Mirrlees (1969) version, that the change of national output of tradeables from the trade-distorted situation, as a factor *decumulates*, is *positive* at the given international prices whereas the Johnson (1967) case of immiserising growth shows that the change of output of the economy (producing only the tradeables), as resources *accumulate* or technology improves, is *negative*. Proposition II is thus established.

IV

For the applied economist, the baring of the underlying relationship among the three paradoxes is of importance since they are not just *curiosa* but are likely to be encountered in the real world with its heavy incidence of trade distortions. Thus, for example, the phenomenon of value subtraction has been encountered in several empirical studies of protection. [Note, however, two things. (i) There may be alternative, statistical and economic, explanations of why value subtraction may be found in practice. These are examined in depth in Bhagwati and Desai (1970, ch. 17, Appendix I). (ii) Moreover, even if the explanation above is the correct one, as is often the case, the reader should not infer that the situation is *necessarily* welfare reducing and the activity with value subtraction may well be worth maintaining for dynamic reasons.

Thus, there may be dynamic advantages, as for example in the analyses of learning effects in Clemhout and Wan (1970), Bardhan (1971) and Kemp (1976, ch. 17); and of a putty-clay model in Findlay (1973, ch. 8); and corresponding advantages owing to uncertainty endogenous to first period trade levels, as with the case of an oil embargo depending on current import dependence, as analysed in Bhagwati and Srinivasan (1976).] Moreover, the phenomenon of immiserising growth, in the presence of a tariff distortion, is also a matter of some empirical relevance: Little *et al.* (1970) have argued that the growth rates of highly protected developing countries are seriously overstated by evaluation at domestic, rather than international, prices; and that the latter could show negative rates of growth. [Again, the question as to whether growth rates should be measured at international prices is rather more complex. This issue has been explored in depth in Bhagwati and Hansen (1972).] Finally, while we are not aware of any project analysts actually having calculated negative shadow prices, it is not at all heroic to imagine that, if the shadow prices were calculated with enough sophistication and accuracy in the real world of highly protected developing countries, the project analyst would find some negative shadow factor prices.

Massachusetts Institute of Technology JAGDISH N. BHAGWATI
Indian Statistical Institute and World Bank T. N. SRINIVASAN
Cornell and Boston Universities HENRY WAN, JR.

Date of receipt of final typescript: June 1977

References

Bardhan, P. K. (1970). *Economic Growth, Development and Foreign Trade.* New York: Wiley & Sons.

Bertrand, T. and Flatters, F. (1971). "Tariffs, Capital Accumulation, and Immiserising Growth." *Journal of International Economics*, vol. 1 (November).

Bhagwati, J. (1958). "Immiserising Growth: A Geometrical Note." *Review of Economic Studies*, vol. 25 (June).

—— (1968*a*). "Distortions and Immiserising Growth: A Generalization." *Review of Economic Studies* (November).

—— (1968*b*). *The Theory and Practice of Commercial Policy.* Frank Graham Memorial Lecture, Princeton University (1967), International Finance Section, Princeton.

—— and Desai, P. (1970). *India: Planning for Industrialization.* OECD Development Centre, Paris. London: Oxford University Press.

—— and Hansen, B. (1972). "Should Growth Rates be Evaluated at International Prices?" In *Development and Planning* (eds. J. Bhagwati and R. S. Eckaus). Essays in Honour of P. N. Rosenstein-Rodan. London: Allen & Unwin Ltd.

—— and Srinivasan, T. N. (1976). "Optimal Trade Policy and Compensation under Endogenous Uncertainty: The Phenomenon of Market Disruption." *Journal of International Economics*, vol. 6 (November).

—— and Wan, H. Jr. (1977). "Shadow Prices in Project Evaluation, with and without Distortions, and with Many Goods and Factors." January, Mimeographed, M.I.T.

Clemhout, S. and Wan, H. Jr. (1970). "Learning-by-Doing and Infant Industry Protection." *Review of Economic Studies*, vol. 37 (1).

Diamond, P. A. and Mirrlees, J. (1976). "Private Constant Returns and Public Shadow Prices." *Review of Economic Studies*, vol. 43.

Findlay, R. (1973). *International Trade and Development Theory*, chapter 8. New York: Columbia University Press.

Findlay, R. and Wellisz, S. (1976). "Project Evaluation, Shadow Prices and Trade Policy." *Journal of Political Economy* (June).

Johnson, H. G. (1967). "The Possibility of Income Losses from Increased Efficiency or Factor Accumulation in the Presence of Tariffs." ECONOMIC JOURNAL, vol. 77 (March).

Kemp, M. (1976). *Three Topics in the Theory of International Trade: Distribution, Welfare and Uncertainty*, Series in International Economics, vol. 2. Amsterdam: North Holland Co.

Little, I. M. D. and Mirrlees, J. A. (1969). *Manual of Industrial Project Analysis in Developing Countries*, vol. 2. Paris: OECD.

——, Scitovsky, T. and Scott, M. Fg. (1970). *Industry and Trade in Some Developing Countries.* London: Oxford University Press.

Martin, R. (1977). "Immiserising Growth for a Tariff-Distorted, Small Economy: Further Analysis." *Journal of International Economics* (November).

Soligo, R. and Stern, J. (1965). "Tariff Protection, Import Substitution, and Investment Efficiency." *Pakistan Development Review* (summer).

Srinivasan, T. N. and Bhagwati, J. (1977). "Shadow Prices for Project Selection in the Presence of Distortions: Effective Rates of Protection and Domestic Resource Costs." *Journal of Political Economy* (forthcoming).

On Inferring Resource-Allocational Implications from DRC Calculations in Trade-Distorted Small Open Economies

JAGDISH N. BHAGWATI and T.N. SRINIVASAN

Massachusetts Institute of Technology, USA & I.S.I., New Delhi

Introduction

Trade-distorted economies are generally characterized by resource misallocation. Trade ana developmental theorists and policy analysts (e.g. Krueger [1966, 1972], Bruno [1972], Balassa and Schydlowsky [1972], Behrman [1977], and Leith [1976] have utilized the concept of Domestic Resource Costs (DRC) to make inferences about the resource-allocational impact of such trade distortions.

However, the current literature is not clear on what *exact* resource-allocational inferences can be made by calculating DRCs among different activities at the trade-distorted equilibrium.

This paper is addressed initially (Section I) therefore to distinguishing sharply among two alternative types of resource-allocational inferences that could be, and indeed have been, attempted for trade-distorted economies by making DRC calculations: (1) where the analyst is inferring whether production of different activities has expanded or contracted in the trade-distorted, observed equilibrium vis-a-vis the optimal, free trade equilibrium in a competitive, "small" economy; and (2) where the analyst is inferring instead whether a small, marginal shift in resources from one activity to another, starting from the trade-distorted equilibrium, would be welfare-improving. In each case, the inference is related to the calculated DRCs in the activities at the observed trade-distorted equilibrium: the lower-DRC activity, in a 2-activity model, being considered the one that will expand in optimal free trade equilibrium and also the one whose expansion at the margin would bring welfare-improvement.

We summarize very briefly, in Section II, the obvious conclusion that the DRC concept, DRC^I, that corresponds to the earning of foreign exchange per unit of domestic resource cost where the primary resources/factors are valued at the (distorted) market prices and which therefore corresponds to the effective rate of protection (ERP) concept, is appropriate to the former of these two alternative inferences. We take the opportunity, however, to analyse the assertion that, if factor market imperfections are present in addition to trade distortions, an amended DRC^I concept that adjusts primary factor costs by using some shadow factor prices (rather than their market prices) is required.

We proceed then, in Section III, to analyse the role of DRC^{I} (or, equivalently, ERP) in making the *latter* of the two resource-allocational inferences distinguished in Section I. We show that DRC^{I} will fail generally to help the analyst make such an inference. However, we extend the analysis in this case to show that not all is lost and to categorize the possible outcomes into two sets, one where the DRC^{I} concept will yield the correct answer and the other where it will not. At the same time, we show how a suitable redefinition of DRC, DRC^{II}, exists in this problem whereby we can *always* make the correct resource-allocational inference of this second type. We further relate our analysis to the prescription that governments in trade-distorted economies ought to expand the low-DRC activities and contract the high-DRC activities: distinguishing among alternative ways in which this prescription may be followed and analysing the welfare consequences of these alternative methods.

I. Two Alternative Resource-Allocational Inferences

Take Figure 1, with AB as the production possibility curve, the world goods price-ratio for this competitive, "small" country implying production at P^* and a tariff-distorted goods price-ratio taking production instead to $\hat{P}$.

Suppose then that, as below in Section II, we were to calculate (some measure of) DRC_1 and DRC_2 in goods 1 and 2 production at $\hat{P}$, as is in fact done in several empirical studies such as Behrman (1977) for Chile, Bhagwati and Srinivasan (1976) for India, and Leith (1976) for Ghana. Suppose then that $DRC_1 < DRC_2$.

The first resource-allocational inference that may be made then is that, in optimal (free trade) equilibrium, good 1 will have expanded relative to good 2 in production: i.e., at P^*, relative to $\hat{P}$, relative production of good 1 will be higher. Call this free-trade versus trade-distorted equilibrium type of inference: *Resource-Allocational Inference* (1).

Alternatively, we may deduce that a small, "marginal" shift of resources out of good 2 into good 1, illustrated as a move from $\hat{P}$ to $\hat{\hat{P}}$ in Figure 1, will *improve* welfare.[1] This inference needs to be carefully stated, however. For we must distinguish between the inference that *some* welfare-improving marginal shift of resources out of good 2 into good 1 will exist if $DRC_1 < DRC_2$ at $\hat{P}$ and the inference that *any* marginal shift of resources out of good 2 into good 1 will be welfare-improving if $DRC_1 < DRC_2$. Call this marginal change from trade-distorted equilibrium type of inference: *Resource-Allocational Inference* (2).

1. The move from $\hat{P}$ to $\hat{\hat{P}}$ "is small" but necessarily shown geometrically as "large".

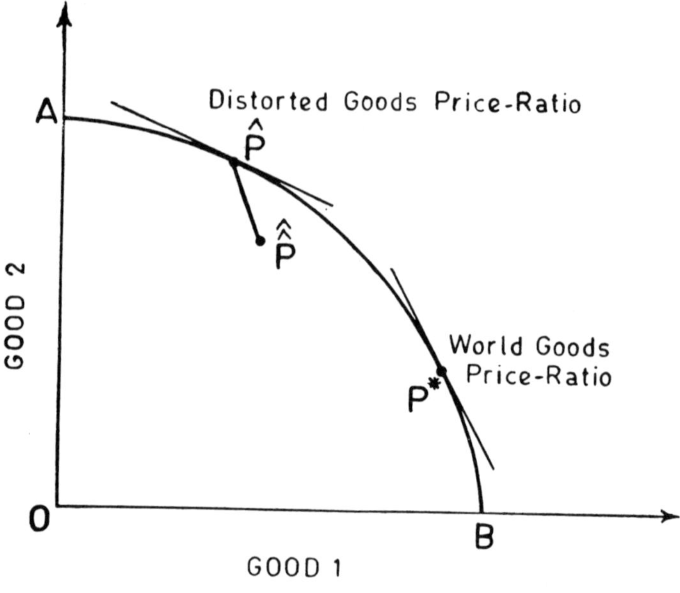

Figure 1

II. Resource-Allocational Inference (1): Trade-Distorted versus Free-Trade Optimal Equilibrium

For the free trade versus trade-distorted equilibrium comparisons, the appropriate concept to deploy at $\hat{P}$, the observable trade-distorted equilibrium, is the domestic resource cost (DRC^{I}) defined with world prices for traded goods and distorted (i.e. with tariffs in place) market prices for primary factors:

$$\text{DRC}_i^I = \frac{\hat{p}_i - \sum_{k=1}^{n} \hat{a}_{ki}\hat{p}_k^*}{\hat{p}_i^* - \sum_{k=1}^{n} \hat{a}_{ki}p_k^*} \qquad i = k = 1, \ldots, n \tag{1a}$$

$$= \frac{\sum_{j=1}^{n} \hat{b}_{ji}\hat{w}_j^*}{\hat{p}_i^* - \sum_{k=1}^{n} \hat{a}_{ki}p_k^*} \qquad i = 1, \ldots, n \tag{1b}$$

where there are n tradeable goods ($k = i = 1, \ldots, n$); n primary factors which are fixed in domestic endowment ($j = 1, \ldots, n$); the $\hat{a}_{ki}$s are the intermediate-use coefficients on tradeables in the distorted equilibrium; $\hat{b}_{ji}$s are the unit-primary-factor-use requirements in the distorted equilibrium; $\hat{p}_i^*$s are the given *world* prices of the tradeables; $\hat{p}_i$s are the trade-distorted *domestic* prices of the tradeables; and $\hat{w}_j$s are the corresponding (equilibrium-associated) trade-distorted domestic prices of the primary factors. (Notation to be used below will also include $\hat{w}_j^*$s as the "second-best" shadow factor prices, associated with p_i^*s *and* the distorted factor-use and intermediate-use coefficients.)

Note, to begin with, that ranking of the activities in the distorted equilibrium by DRC^{I} will be identical with their ranking by ERP (effective rate of protection) since ERP is the distortion-caused increment in value added divided by the value added at world prices, so that:

$$\text{ERP} = \text{DRC}^{I} - 1 \tag{2}$$

To see the appropriateness of DRC^{I} (ERP) for making the resource-allocational inference (1), consider now the simplified 2-tradeables, 2-primary-factors model of trade theory.

Thus, in Figure 1, there are two tradeables, 1 and 2, with equilibrium production at $\overset{*}{P}$ under free trade (at the given world prices $\overset{*}{p}_1/\overset{*}{p}_2$) and at $\hat{P}$ under the distorted domestic price ratio $\hat{p}_1/\hat{p}_2$. With no intermediate usage and with only two primary factors, 1 and 2, we then note immediately that, in the distorted equilibrium at $\hat{P}$

$$\text{DRC}_1^{I} = \frac{\hat{b}_{11}\hat{w}_1 + \hat{b}_{21}\hat{w}_2}{p_1^*} \tag{3}$$

$$\text{DRC}_2^{I} = \frac{\hat{b}_{12}\hat{w}_1 + \hat{b}_{22}\hat{w}_2}{p^*} \tag{4}$$

In our highly-simplified diagrammatic model, therefore, $\text{DRC}_1^{I} < \text{DRC}_2^{I}$ implies that:

$$\frac{\overset{*}{p}_1}{\overset{*}{p}_2} < \frac{\hat{b}_{11}\hat{w}_1 + \hat{b}_{21}\hat{w}_2}{\hat{b}_{12}\hat{w}_1 + \hat{b}_{22}\hat{w}_2} \tag{5}$$

$$\text{i.e. } \frac{\overset{*}{p}_1}{\overset{*}{p}_2} < \frac{\hat{p}_1}{\hat{p}_2} \tag{6}$$

since the factor-cost ratio equals the goods price-ratio in the distorted equilibrium at $\hat{P}$: the absence of intermediate usage in either activity leads to this neat result for, otherwise, the numerators and denominators in (3) and (4) would show value-added rather than output values. Thus, $DRC_1^I < DRC_2^I$ implies that the distorted goods price-ratio has a lower (relative) price of good 1 and a protected, higher (relative) price of good 2.

Now, it is easy to see that, given the convexity of the production possibility curve, and the competitive pricing assumptions which require tangency of the domestic price-ratio with the production possibility curve, $DRC_1^I < DRC_2^I$, i.e. $ERP_1 < ERP_2$, will indeed ensure that the optimal free-trade production point will be characterized by a higher output of good 1 and lower output of good 2. While, however, in the highly simplified model of trade theory in Figure 1, this inference is valid for output and for value-added (which are identical because of the absence of intermediates), we now know that the inference can be made only under particularly stringent restrictions on either production functions *or* the tariff structure under more general models permitting the use of intermediates and allowing for generalized substitution among inputs.[2]

DRC^Is, used in this way, are therefore really in the territory defined by traditional ERP theory: and this territory is not highly productive of sufficiency conditions for correct free-trade versus distorted-equilibrium type resource-allocational inferences from the DRC^I (or ERP, equivalently) rankings of the activities in the trade-distorted equilibrium.

But if this is indeed the resource-allocational use of DRC^I rankings that is intended, it is clear that the argument occasionally made by DRC^I proponents that, in the presence of factor market imperfections (*in addition* to the ad valorem trade distortions) the DRC^Is must be adjusted such that shadow-price factor valuations are utilized [in the numerator of (1b)] becomes somewhat puzzling.[3] For, what, *are* these shadow prices to be? And, are the re-defined DRC^Is, using such shadow prices, to indicate the direction of gross output or value added change (when free trade is restored) with the factor market imperfection *or* without it?

Thus, take the case of a factor wage differential imperfection. This will result in a shrinking in of the production possibility curve from $A\overset{*}{P}B$ to $A\hat{P}B$ in Figure 2 and a non-tangency between the goods price-ratio and the production possibility

2. The investigation of these sufficiency restrictions, for both gross output changes and value added changes in very general models is to be found in Bruno (1973), Bhagwati and Srinivasan (1973), Sendo (1974) and Uekawa (1978). There is a great body of literature on this subject, preceding these writings, but it is in partial-equilibrium models or deals with general-equilibrium models with simplifying restrictions on the tariff structure or on the production functions, thus reaching conclusions which were dependent on the simplifying assumptions whose general implications were not sufficiently appreciated.
3. Cf. Krueger (1972).

curve. Now, $\hat{P}$ is the observed trade-distorted equilibrium in this case. If free trade were allowed with the wage differential in place, equilibrium production would shift to $\hat{P}^*$. However, if we eliminated the wage differential as well, production would shift to P^*. Now, $\hat{P}$ is to the south-east of $\hat{P}$ but P^* is to the north-west of $\hat{P}$ in the case illustrated in Figure 2. Which directional inference is the redefined DRC^I, using the shadow prices, supposed to enable one to make?[4] And, even if we were to choose $\hat{P}^*$, for convenience, and look for an appropriately adjusted DRC^I index which *could* predict accurately the direction of change from $\hat{P}$ to $\hat{P}^*$, it is unclear what that modification would have to be.

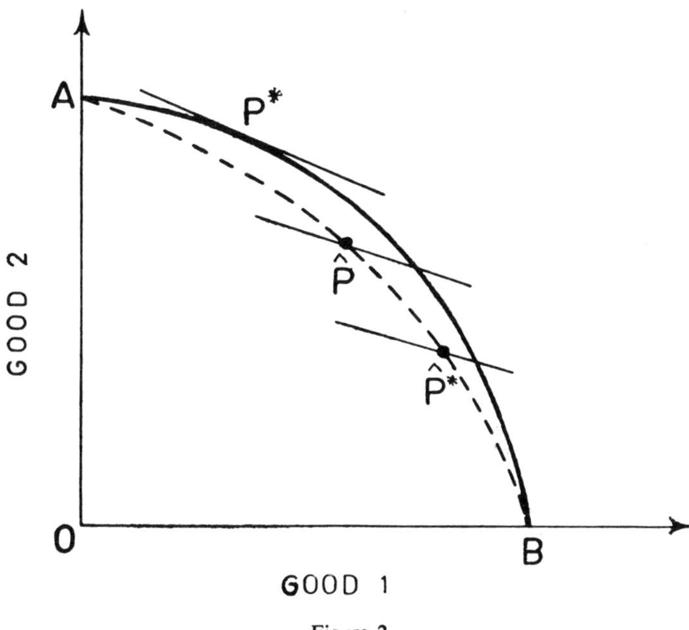

Figure 2

ERP theory, which has been worked out for models where the only "imperfection" arises in the form of tariffs, has had such limited success that one's first reaction might be that, in a factor-market-imperfection model, ERP theory may break down altogether in the sense that no ERP-DRC^I type index may be devis-

4. Besides, as Bhagwati and Srinivasan (1971) and Herberg and Kemp (1971) have noted multiple equilibria may result, so that another $\hat{P}^*$ may exist to the left of $\hat{P}$ on $A\hat{P}B$ as well.

able which could predict resource-allocational changes vis-a-vis the free trade outcome on gross outputs or value added, whether with or without the factor market distortion. What *is* clear is that there is (in the absence of theoretical analysis centering on the above questions) little meaning to be attached to the recommendation to use "shadow-price"-adjusted DRC^I's when factor market distortions are present if the objective is to predict the direction of change in resource-allocation that would occur under restoration of free trade through elimination of the ad valorem trade distortion.

III. Resource-Allocational Inference (2): Marginal Change from Trade-Distorted Equilibrium

Consider now the alternative resource-allocational inference: i.e. that $DRC_1^I < DRC_2^I$ implies that a marginal shift to the lower-DRC activity 1 would be welfare-improving.

This inference, however, needs to be carefully stated. For, as we will presently argue, it is correct that *some* welfare-improving expansion of the lower-DRC^I activity and reduction of the higher DRC^I activity does exist; but *any* expansion of the lower-DRC^I activity and reduction of the higher DRC^I activity is not necessarily welfare-improving.

For simplicity, we will consider only the simplified model with 2 tradeables, 2 primary factors and no intermediate usage, as underlying Figures 1 and 2. Thus, in turn to Figure 3.

With trade-distorted production at $\hat{P}$, and therefore $DRC_1^I < DRC_2^I$, it is evident that a policy that manages to raise the output of good 1 and lower that of good 2, *but* at a rate less favourable than the world price-ratio $\hat{P}R$, will *not* improve welfare but worsen it. The range of such possibilities is defined by "welfare-deterioration" cone $Q\hat{P}R$. Any policy that moves the production point strictly into this cone will result in a reduced value of national production measured at the world prices, thus implying, a la Bruno (1972), Little-Mirrlees (1969) and well-known trade-theoretic arguments, a deterioration of welfare.[5] By contrast, $R\hat{P}S$ defines a welfare-improving cone: any policy that moves the production point into this cone will result in an increased value of production at international prices and hence in improved welfare. [We will see below how a "policy" of introducing a public sector project, producing either good 1 or 2, at a technique different from private sector production at $\hat{P}$, may lead the economy into one cone or the

5. With an ad valorem distortion in consumption, there is a monotonic relationship between shifts in the availability locus at given world prices and the change in social utility, given a well-behaved social utility function.

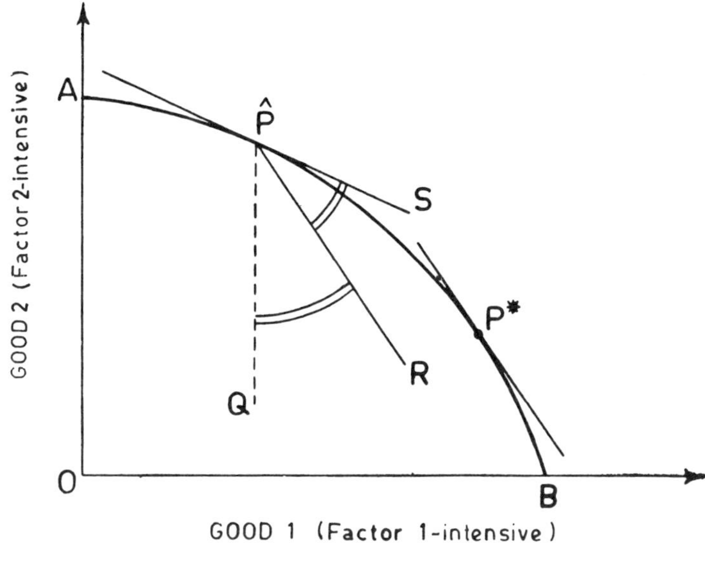

Figure 3

other; and, in particular, how a technique will necessarily exist for entering the welfare-improving cone and will reflect the cost-minimizing choice of technique appropriate to the (second-best) shadow factor prices ($\hat{w}_1^*$ and $\hat{w}_2^*$) which we will presently derive.]

The moral is evident. The DRC[I] rankings of the activities at $\hat{P}$ do *not*, in themselves, make it possible for us to infer that *any* marginal change from the higher to the lower DRC activities will improve welfare. The answer depends critically on the *actual* rate of this transformation in domestic production at the margin: and this obviously depends on the policy defining the transformation. Evidently, the customary argumentation implicitly presumes that the policy will necessarily move the economy outside of the welfare-deterioration cone; but this need not be the case.

On the other hand, if the fact that DRC_i^{I}s are different among activities in the trade-distorted equilibrium is used to argue a *weaker* proposition, namely, that *some* marginal reallocation of resources will necessarily exist at this trade-distorted equilibrium which will improve welfare, this would be a valid inference indeed. In the two-activity model of Figures 1-3, the inference could be made that such welfare-improving marginal reallocation would necessarily imply increasing the lower DRC[I] activity and contracting in the higher DRC[I] activity. (For the many-activity case, however, it is evident that the chain formed by ranking activities in the trade-distorted equilibrium by their DRC^Is can indeed be criss-crossed by a welfare-improving marginal reallocation of primary factors.)

We are then led inevitably to the question: is there then some way of measuring DRCs at the trade-distorted equilibrium that *will* provide a suitable criterion for determining whether a marginal shift from the trade-distorted equilibrium is welfare improving? i.e., can suitable DRCs be defined at the trade-distorted equilibrium such that, in the two-activity model of Figure 3, for example, the intended marginal shift of resources will take the economy into the welfare-improving cone $R\hat{P}S$ or into the welfare-deteriorating cone $Q\hat{P}R$, depending on the relative rankings of the suitably defined DRCs?

Thus, assume quite generally that the marginal shift in resources from the trade-distorted equilibrium at $\hat{P}$ in Figure 3 arises from the introduction of a small project producing a third tradeable good. (As argued below, the case where the project produces either of the two goods at $\hat{P}$, so that there are only two goods in the analysis, is only a special case: but this simple case is indeed what analysts of resource allocational inefficiencies under trade distortions have in mind.) The policy that defines the marginal shift, for the present argument, therefore, is the introduction of a small public sector project, which produces good 3.[6] And the relevant question evidently is whether one can define suitable DRCs such that, when measured for goods 1 and 2 at the trade-distorted equilibrium (in the private sector) at $\hat{P}$, *and* for the (public sector) project, welfare improvement will follow if the DRC in the project is below the DRCs in goods 1 and 2 in the private sector.

Such a suitable DRC concept can indeed be defined and has been put forth in the context of project analysis for trade-distorted economies by Srinivasan and Bhagwati (1978). Following them, this alternative, suitable concept, DRC^{II}, is defined quite simply as the following:

$$DRC_i^{II} = \frac{\sum_{j=1}^{n} \hat{b}_{ji} \hat{w}_j^*}{p_i^* - \sum_{k=1}^{n} \hat{a}_{ki} p_k^*} \qquad i = 1, 2, \ldots, n \tag{7}$$

where $\hat{w}_j^*$s are the appropriately derived second-best factor prices.[7] In fact, these shadow prices are derived (as below) by putting the numerator equal to the deno-

6. Evidently, with the trade distortion assumed fixed, we cannot assume the marginal shift in resource allocation to arise from a trade policy change (e.g. tariff reduction).

7. While this explicit DRC formulation is, to our knowledge, first put down in Srinivasan-Bhagwati (1978), the notion of appropriate second-best factor prices is of course to be found in the analyses of project evaluation.

minator for the activities at the trade-distorted equilibrium ($\hat{P}$ in Figures 1-3) so that, at this observed equilibrium, DRC^{II}s are equal to unity and hence to one another. Thus if $\mathrm{DRC}_p^{\mathrm{II}}$ for the project is less than unity, we will have the rank-ordering:

$$\mathrm{DRC}_i^{\mathrm{II}} \equiv 1 > \mathrm{DRC}_p^{\mathrm{II}} \qquad i = 1, \ldots, n \tag{8}$$

and it can be shown that the project should indeed be accepted.

Thus, revert to the simple model underlying Figure 3, with two goods, 1 and 2, being produced at the distorted equilibrium $\hat{P}$ and consider now a project producing a unit of good 3, with the trade distortion (and hence the unit coefficients in production at $\hat{P}$) continuing *unchanged.* Let the project have unit coefficients b_{13}^p and b_{23}^p, in the use of the two factors, 1 and 2. Then, according to well-known Little-Mirrlees (1969) rule, the project would be accepted as welfare-improving if:

$$p_3^* > \mathrm{d}X_1\, p_1^* + \mathrm{d}X_2\, p_2^* \tag{9}$$

i.e. if the value of total production (of goods 1, 2 and 3), measured at *world* prices, increases. But we may, for small projects, also write:

$$\mathrm{d}X_1\, p_1^* + \mathrm{d}X_2\, p_2^* = b_{13}^p\, \hat{w}_1^* + b_{23}^p\, \hat{w}_2^* \tag{10}$$

i.e. derive the shadow "second-best" prices ($\hat{w}^*$s) of the factors used in the project such that the corresponding social cost equals the loss in output of goods 1 and 2 (i.e. $\mathrm{d}X_1$ and $\mathrm{d}X_2$) evaluated at world prices.

Solving for $\mathrm{d}X_1$ and $\mathrm{d}X_2$, given the fixed $\hat{b}_{ki}$s at $\hat{P}$ owing to the assumption of unchanged trade distortion, the reader will find that the shadow prices of the factors ($\hat{w}_1^*$ and $\hat{w}_2^*$) are nothing but the solutions to the two equations:

$$p_2^* = \hat{b}_{11}\hat{w}_1^* + \hat{b}_{21}\hat{w}_2^* \tag{11}$$

$$p_2^* = \hat{b}_{12}\hat{w}_1^* + \hat{b}_{22}\hat{w}_2^* \tag{12}$$

as is evident from Diamond-Mirrlees (1976), Srinivasan and Bhagwati (1978), Findlay and Wellisz (1976) and Bhagwati and Wan (1979). Note that the second-best shadow prices, $\hat{w}_1^*$ and $\hat{w}_2^*$, so derived reflect the fact that the goods prices continue to be distorted and hence do not change as primary factors are withdrawn (from $\hat{P}$) for the project: this, in turn, implying that the associated market prices of factors ($\hat{w}_1$ and $\hat{w}_2$) are also fixed and hence the unit requirements of factors in the production of the two goods remain fixed at $\hat{b}_{11}$, $\hat{b}_{21}$, $\hat{b}_{12}$ and $\hat{b}_{22}$.

But, (9) and (10) on the one hand, and (11) and (12) on the other, imply that:

$$\text{DRC}_p^{\text{II}} = \frac{b_{13}^p \hat{w}_1^* + b_{23}^p \hat{w}_2^*}{p_3^*} < 1 \tag{13}$$

$$\text{DRC}_1^{\text{II}} = \frac{\hat{b}_{11}\hat{w}_1^* + \hat{b}_{21}\hat{w}_2^*}{p_1^*} = 1 \tag{14}$$

and

$$\text{DRC}_2^{\text{II}} = \frac{\hat{b}_{12}\hat{w}_1^* + \hat{b}_{22}\hat{w}_2^*}{p_2^*} = 1 \tag{15}$$

Therefore, evidently the acceptability of the project on criterion (9) is identical to its acceptance on criterion (8) and the rank-ordering by DRC^{II}s will indeed lead to the correct resource-allocational implications.

We may now revert to the 2-good case where the project is for producing either good 1 or good 2 or both, in the public sector. Thus, the model reduces to having only the two tradeable goods, 1 and 2, whether one takes the private sector production (initially at $\hat{P}$ in Figure 3, prior to the introduction of the project) or the public sector production. Now, it is clear that if the public sector produces good 1 or 2 at the *same* techniques as at $\hat{P}$ in the private sector, the economy will stay put at $\hat{P}$, with the public sector production marginally replacing private sector production of the good(s) in question. The interesting question, therefore, is whether the public sector choice of technique to produce either good 1 or 2, when *different* from that in the private sector at $\hat{P}$, as it well can be, will result in welfare deterioration (i.e. a *net* move into the cone $Q\hat{P}R$) or in welfare improvement (i.e. a move into the cone $R\hat{P}S$). Needless to say, as long as there is some private production, the net result of the public sector project at different techniques from the private sector production of the same good will imply that aggregate production efficiency will not be satisfied and the net move from $\hat{P}$ will be to a point inside the production possibility curve AB.

First, we should note that in this model with only two goods, our $\mathrm{DRC}^{\mathrm{II}}$-ranking criterion will naturally continue to hold, i.e. for welfare-improvement, the $\mathrm{DRC}^{\mathrm{II}}$ of the project-produced good (whether 1 or 2) ought to be less than unity while it is unity at $\hat{P}$ for private production. Geometrically, the economy ought to move in Figure 3 into the cone $R\hat{P}S$ if $\mathrm{DRC}^{\mathrm{II}}$ criterion for welfare-improvement is satisfied. This is seen readily by noting that for a project producing a unit of good 1, its acceptability i.e. $\mathrm{DRC}_p^{\mathrm{II}} < 1$ for the project, implies that:

$$p_1^* > b_{11}^p \hat{w}_1^* + b_{21}^p \hat{w}_2^*$$

$$\text{i.e.} \quad p_1^* > dx_1 p_1^* + dx_2 p_2^*$$

$$\text{i.e.} \quad p_1^*(1 - dx_1) > dx_2 p_2^*$$

$$\text{i.e.} \quad p_1^*/p_2^* > dx_2/(1 - dx_1) \tag{16}$$

where the R.H.S. defines the effective, *net* rate of transformation between the output of goods 1 and 2 at the trade-distorted equilibrium. It is immediately evident then that the satisfaction of the inequality in (16) would, in Figure 3, move the economy from $\hat{P}$ to outside of the welfare-deterioration cone $Q\hat{P}R$.

Next, we can show that there will necessarily exist (public sector) project activities that improve welfare, that is, activities that will take the economy into the welfare improving cone $R\hat{P}S$ in Figure 3. This is seen easily in the case where both shadow factor prices $\hat{w}_1^*$ and $\hat{w}_2^*$ are positive. Then any project which produces either good 1 or good 2, but using cost-minimizing technique appropriate to the shadow prices $\hat{w}_1^*$ and $\hat{w}_2^*$ at $\hat{P}$, will necessarily move the economy into the welfare-improving cone, but inside the production possibility curve. This is evident since $p_1^* = (\hat{b}_{11}\hat{w}_1^* + \hat{b}_{21}\hat{w}_2^*)$ from eq. (11). And $(\hat{b}_{11}\hat{w}_1^* + \hat{b}_{21}\hat{w}_2^*) > (b_{11}^{p*}\hat{w}_1^* + b_2^{p*}\hat{w}_2^*)$ where b_{11}^{p*} and b_2^{p*} reflect the cost-minimizing choice of technique for the *shadow* factor prices $\hat{w}_1^*$ and $\hat{w}_2^*$ whereas $\hat{b}_{11}$ and $\hat{b}_{21}$ are sub-optimal in reflecting instead the cost-minimizing choice of technique for the *market* factor prices $\hat{w}_1$ and $\hat{w}_2$. Therefore, it follows that $p_1^* > (b_{11}^p{}^*w_1^* + b_{21}^p{}^*w_2^*)$, i.e. $\mathrm{DRC}_{p*}^{\mathrm{II}} < 1$ for the project producing good 1 and hence such a project would be welfare-improving. The argument holds equally, of course, for a small project producing good 2 with cost-minimizing techniques reflecting the shadow factor prices.[8]

At the same time, it is clear that the net move within the welfare-improving cone will lie inside the production possibility curve $A\hat{P}B$ since aggregate production efficiency does not obtain: for, as we saw earlier, the relative evaluation of one good in terms of the other is not the same in private and public production.

Moreover, it should be evident that starting from $\hat{P}$ in Figure 3, while the small project which produces good 1 (or 2) with techniques that cost-minimize with respect to the shadow factor prices, $\hat{w}_1^*$ and $\hat{w}_2^*$ will necessarily improve welfare (as shown above), other welfare-improving techniques will also obtain, generally speaking. Thus *any* (b_{11}^p, b_{21}^p) technique that yields $p_1^* > b_{11}^p\hat{w}_1^* + b_{21}^p\hat{w}_2^*$ will land the economy into the welfare-improving cone $R\hat{P}S$ in Figure 3; the b_{11}^{p*}, b_{21}^{p*} technique that minimizes cost with respect to $\hat{w}_1^*$ and $\hat{w}_2^*$ is only the *best* among these techniques. Furthermore, all other techniques for producing the project output will yield a welfare loss since they will take the economy into the cone $Q\hat{P}R$. These ranges of techniques, falling into the welfare-improving and welfare-worsening classes, can be illustrated through Figure 4. Given constant returns to scale, an arbitrarily-chosen isoquant $\bar{X}_1$ will illustrate the technique in good 1 in the distorted equilibrium (corresponding to $\hat{P}$ in Figure 3) at Q as $(\hat{b}_{11}^{p*}, \hat{b}_{21}^{p*})$. However, $(b_{11}^{p*}, b_{21}^{p*})$ at R represents the cost-minimizing technique at the shadow factor prices $(\hat{w}_1^*, \hat{w}_2^*)$. It follows that the range of techniques spanned by JT, i.e. all to the left of the ray $0QN$, will yield welfare improvement if deployed in the project, by leading to a net move in Figure 3 from P into the welfare-improvement cone $R\hat{P}S$. And all techniques to the right of $0QN$ will lead into the welfare-deteriorating cone $Q\hat{P}R$. It may, of course, be emphasized that there is no reason why the choice of a public sector project to produce good 1 or 2 need *necessarily* be characterized by a technique that falls into one zone or the other in Figure 4.

Again, note that our analysis so far has viewed the choice of technique in the public sector project production of either good 1 or 2 as being essentially arbitrarily specified. This procedure is fine if we view the planners/authorities as choosing a technique for producing the project production arbitrarily from a menu of techniques (as along an isoquant in Figure 4). This view makes sense if we think

8. When one of the shadow prices is negative, a public sector activity that simply withdraws the factor from private use even if it does not produce any output is welfare-improving. If, however, the production functions are such that positive output can be produced using positive amount of either factor and none of the other, then through such a production activity using the factor (with the negative shadow price) withdrawn from private use, public production can improve welfare even further. For a discussion of negative shadow factor prices, see Srinivasan and Bhagwati (1978).

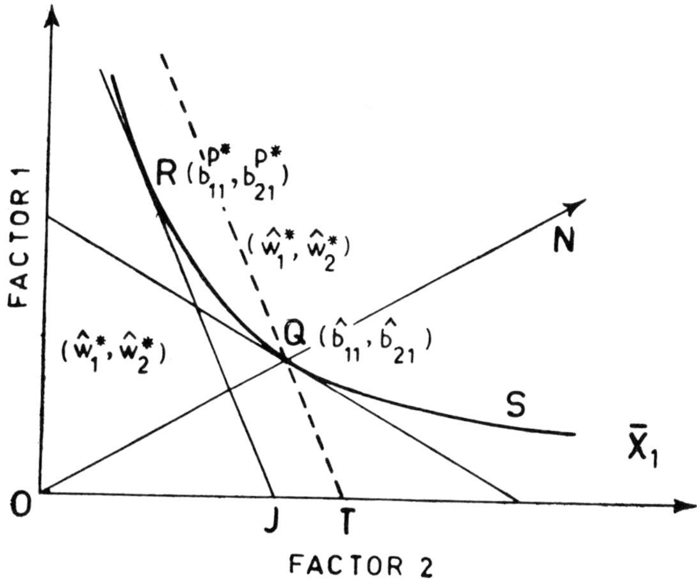

Figure 4

of the authorities starting from a trade-distorted position such as $\hat{P}$ in Figure 3, being told by analysts that the fact that DRC^{I} in good 1 is lower than DRC^{I} in good 2 requires the expansion of good 1, and then proceeding to start a public sector project for producing good 1 by using whatever technique the public sector can lay its hands on. This is not a far-fetched scenario, of course. And our analysis demonstrates (i) that the impact on the net production of goods 1 and 2 (i.e. public sector production *plus* the adjusted private sector production of goods 1 and 2) and hence the net welfare impact depends critically on the choice of technique in the public sector project, (ii) that welfare-improving techniques for public sector production of either good will necessarily exist, (iii) that the *best* such technique for public sector production will be that which minimizes cost with respect to the second-best shadow prices at the distorted equilibrium, and (iv) that the projects using any welfare-improving technique will necessarily have DRC^{II} less than unity and hence less than DRC^{II}s in private sector production of goods 1 and 2 (which are necessarily set at unity) so that the project-acceptance criterion defined in terms of DRC^{II} rankings of the private sector and project activities will be satisfied.

However, an alternative view of the public sector project decisions may be taken. We may consider rather that the public sector withdraws a marginal bundle of both primary factors from the trade-distorted equilibrium and now has to choose the optimal fashion in which to deploy them for producing either good 1 or good 2. In this problem, the public sector's choice of technique in either good as also the combination of the two goods produced are determined optimally. The public sector's choice then will clearly lead to the result that the outputs and techniques chosen will reflect maximization of the value of public sector output at world prices. In the absence of specialization, this will clearly mean the use by the public sector of techniques associated with the first-best optimum at P^* in Figure 3. Furthermore, if the public sector progressively withdraws resources from the private sector, and follows this optimal policy for deploying them, net production will necessarily wind up eventually at P^*, since all resources will then be employed in the public sector so as to maximize the value of output at world prices as if free trade were fully applicable.

In conclusion, we may address a few pertinent remarks to DRC^{II} rankings, which have been shown to be appropriate for marginal resource-allocational decisions. First, while it is possible evidently to compute shadow factor prices such that DRC^{II} rankings, using those, can yield in turn the correct resource-allocational inference, this possibility is confined to those cases where the trade distortion is in place and marginal moves, subject to this constraint, are being considered. The technique clearly cannot be extended to marginal changes which change the trade distortion itself: e.g. the evaluation of a marginal shift in resource allocation in the presence of *quantitative* trade restrictions (which will generally imply, even for small changes, varying implicit tariffs). Second, our analysis shows that the DRC^{II} measure, when appropriately used, implies the use of second-best shadow price valuations of factors even when the factor markets are perfect; the DRC^{I} measure is inappropriate even when only tariffs define the distortion. Third, if factor market imperfections are also present, the DRC^{II}-ranking will still work, though the second-best factor prices will now reflect these imperfections as well.[9]

9. Shadow factor prices in the presence of three different types of factor market imperfections have been considered in Srinivasan and Bhagwati (1978).

[Thanks are due to the National Science Foundation, Grant No. SOC 77-07188 for financial support of the first author's research. The views expressed do not necessarily reflect those of the institutions to which the authors are affiliated. The authors are Ford International Professor of Economics at M.I.T., and Professor of Economics at I.S.I. and Senior Adviser, World Bank, respectively.]

References

Balassa, Bela and Daniel Schydlowsky (1972): "Domestic Resource Costs and Effective Protection Once Again", *Journal of Political Economy*, January.

Behrman, Jere (1977): *Foreign Trade Regimes and Economic Development: Chile* (N.B.E.R., Columbia University Press, New York).

Bhagwati, Jagdish and T.N. Srinivasan (1971): "The Theory of Wage Differentials: Production Response and Factor Price Equalization", *Journal of International Economics*, April.

Bhagwati, Jagdish and T.N. Srinivasan (1973): "The General Equilibrium Theory of Effective Protection and Resource Allocation", *Journal of International Economics*, August.

Bhagwati, Jagdish and Henry Wan, Jr. (1979): "Shadow Prices in Project Evaluation, with and without Distortions, and with Many Goods and Factors", *American Economic Review*, June (M.I.T. Economic Department Working Paper No. 205, July, 1977).

Bruno, Michael (1972): "Domestic Resource Costs and Effective Protection: Clarification and Synthesis", *Journal of Political Economy*, January.

Bruno, Michael (1973): "Protection and Tariff Change under General Equilibrium", *Journal o, International Economics*, August.

Diamond, Peter and James Mirrlees (1976): "Private Constant Returns and Public Shadow Prices", *Review of Economic Studies*, February.

Findlay, Ronald and Stanislaw Wellisz (1976): "Project Evaluation, Shadow Prices, and Trade Policy", *Journal of Political Economy*, June.

Herberg, Horst and Murray Kemp (1971): "Factor Market Distortions, the Shape of the Locus of Competitive Outputs, and the Relation Between Product Prices and Equilibrium Outputs", in J. Bhagwati *et al.* (ed.), *Trade Balance of Payments and Growth* (North-Holland, Amsterdam).

Krueger, Anne (1966): "Some Economic Costs of Exchange Control: The Turkish Case", *Journal of Political Economy*, October.

Leith, Clark (1976): *Foreign Trade Regimes and Economic Development: Ghana* (N.B.E.R., Columbia University Press, New York).

Little, Ian and James Mirrlees (1969): *Manual of Industrial Project Analysis in Developing Countries*, Vol. 2 (O.E.C.D., Paris).

Sendo, Yoshiki (1974): "The Theory of Effective Protection in General Equilibrium", *Journal of International Economics*, May.

Srinivasan, T.N. and Jagdish Bhagwati (1978): "Shadow Prices for Project Selection in the Presence of Distortions: Effective Rates of Protection and Domestic Resource Costs", *Journal of Political Economy*, February (M.I.T. Economics Department Working Paper No. 180, July 1976).

Errata

Page 12, lines 6 and 7 from bottom: "$\hat{b}_2^{p}*$" should read "$\hat{b}_{21}^{p}*$".

Page 14: The zones in figure 4 correspond to those in figure 3 (page 8) if the lettering "R,Q,S" in figure 4 is replaced by "S,R,Q", respectively. The text on page 13 would then have to be modified accordingly.

Should Growth Rates be Evaluated at International Prices?[1]

J. BHAGWATI AND B. HANSEN

I THE PROBLEM

It is sometimes argued that growth rates of value-added, income, or GDP as measured by standard methods tend to be misleading when domestic market prices and factor costs are 'distorted' by tariffs, quotas, trade and price controls, and overvalued currencies.

For developing countries in particular, it has been argued that standard methods should tend to exaggerate growth rates because it is the fast-growing sectors, usually manufacturing industry, that are protected and hence 'overpriced' and 'overweighted'. Intuition suggests a simple method of adjusting the conventionally measured growth rates by weights equal to the shares of sectoral value-added in total value-added, estimated at international prices.[2] Thus the conventional formula for a two-sector economy, X and Y denoting sectors,

$$g = g_X w_X + g_Y w_Y$$

where g denotes growth rates, w denotes weights equal to the

[1] We are grateful for comments from, and discussions with, Maurice Scott and Tibor Scitovsky. They helped us much in understanding the methods of I. Little, T. Scitovsky, and M. Scott, *Industry and Trade in Some Developing Countries* (Oxford University Press, 1970) but we are, of course, responsible for the exposition and interpretation given in this paper. We had the opportunity of discussing the paper at Scitovsky's seminar at Stanford and acknowledge a number of valuable comments from the participants. Bhagwati's research has been supported by the National Science Foundation and the National Bureau of Economic Research.

[2] B. Hansen, *Economic Development in Egypt*, Rand Corporation and Resources for the Future, RM-5961-FF (October 1969), p. 16, n. 2; also suggested independently by Tibor Scitovsky in a public lecture at Berkeley in 1969.

sectoral shares in value added, $w_X + w_Y = 1$, all measured conventionally at domestic market prices, is replaced by

$$g' = g_X w'_X + g_Y w'_Y$$

where g' is the adjusted overall growth rate and w'_X and w'_Y are the sectoral shares measured at international prices, $w'_X + w'_Y = 1$.

The growth rate thus adjusted is of course a hybrid in the sense that it uses observed sectoral growth rates of value-added at domestic prices but weights them at shares in international prices. At constant prices, as generally assumed in this paper (to avoid the discussion of standard index-number problems and instead to focus on the new issues raised here), this Hansen-Scitovsky method is clearly equivalent to evaluation at international prices.

Another method for re-valuing value-added and growth contributions has been suggested by Little, Scitovsky and Scott[3] in an important, recent study of import substitution in semi-industrialized LDCs. Disregarding non-traded goods which give rise to special problems (see Section 4, below), their operational procedures imply in effect that growth rates be measured at international prices although the reader is not likely to grasp this implication of their methodology. They take it that 'the relative prices of the industry's product measure their relative marginal values to society . . .' (p. 411), and they '. . . want to measure the social *value* of the output, and not its social *costs*' (p. 411, no. 1). Efficiency considerations, on the other hand, seem to require evaluation at international prices because they represent, through foreign trade and the balance of payments (pp. 72–3 and 411–14), the true opportunity costs in production.

As a way out of this dilemma, Little, Scitovsky and Scott apparently (p. 73) first calculate value-added for all sectors at international prices, and then convert the value-added of each individual sector (thus calculated) to domestic values through a common 'multiplicative factor', ϕ, which expresses the average relation between international prices and domestic prices and (in the simplest case without non-traded goods) is taken as the ratio between aggregate value-added for all sectors at domestic market prices and at international prices (p. 416). The method thus consists of an evaluation of each individual sector's contribution to value-added and value-added growth at international opportunity costs, adjusted upwards to be

[3] Little, Scitovsky and Scott, op. cit., chap. 2 and Appendix to chap. 2, pp. 70–6 and 410–21.

expressed in terms of the average purchasing power (marginal utility) of the consumers' money (income) at domestic market prices.

Clearly this procedure, *as contrasted with the standard evaluation at domestic market prices*, implies that both the absolute and relative contributions (to value-added as also to change in welfare) of the relatively more highly protected sectors will become smaller, while the sum of *all* the sectors' contributions will remain equal to the value-added increase at *domestic* market prices.

At the same time, the relative contribution to value-added, by each sector, under this procedure, is readily seen to be independent of ϕ (which multiplies into *each* sector's value-added at international prices) and hence to be, in effect, measured purely at international prices. Furthermore, when we calculate a growth *rate* as the ratio between the sum of all sectoral value-added increments at international prices, each one multiplied by the common ϕ, and the sum of all sectoral value-added in a base year, at the same international prices and multiplied by ϕ (p. 417),[4] the common factor ϕ divides out, of course. This procedure therefore implies that relative sector shares, sectoral growth rates as also the total growth rate are measured exclusively at international prices, as with the Hansen-Scitovsky method.[5]

[4] For non-traded goods, Little, Scitovsky and Scott propose to multiply the value at domestic market prices by ϕ determined on the basis of the trading sectors.

[5] Our interpretation of the Little–Scitovsky–Scott methods is accurate in describing the *actual* method underlying their empirical estimates of growth rates in the countries these authors have studied. In terms of Figure 3.1 below, for example, their procedure is to estimate the increment in value-added at international prices (that is, JK), divide it by the base-year value of expenditure at domestic prices (that is, OH), and then multiply this ratio into ϕ which is estimated as the base-year ratio of expenditure valued at domestic prices to expenditure valued at international prices (that is, OH/OK), which yields a growth rate at *international* prices (that is, a negative growth rate: JK/OK). This result, of course, is to be expected as their procedure amounts then merely to dividing incremental value-added at international prices by base-year value-added (converted back) at international prices: which is the same thing as taking the same ratio and multiplying both the numerator and the denominator thereof by the same ϕ, which of course then cancels out no matter how ϕ is defined.

Maurice Scott has, however, pointed out that their desired *ideal* method (as distinct from their actual method, underlying their estimates) was to evaluate growth rates at *domestic* prices. According to him, the ratio JK/OH was to be multiplied into a ϕ which was to be estimated, *not* as the base-year ratio of expenditure at market prices to expenditure at international prices (that is, OH/OK), but as the *marginal* ratio of expenditure at market prices to expenditure at international prices (that is, GH/JK), thus yielding a growth rate at *domestic prices* (that is, a negative growth rate: GH/OK).

The two methods distinguished by Scott, in correspondence, as the actual and

Conventional methods, on the other hand, require measurement of growth rates at either domestic market prices or domestic factor cost. In addition, therefore, we now have measurement at international prices. Measurement at international prices certainly takes into account opportunity costs in international trade but with 'distortions' they do not express domestic consumer preferences. Measurement at domestic market prices expresses (by assumption) consumer or community preferences but seems to ignore international opportunity costs. It is clear also that we cannot evaluate at both international and domestic market prices at the same time (although this is, indeed, what the two methods described above appear to make a vain attempt to do). What shall we do then? Is there one method of evaluating growth that is preferable to all other methods? Or should all methods be applied because they illuminate different aspects of growth?

We shall examine this issue for the case of growth subject to a given tariff in the framework of the simplest conceivable model: the value-theoretic model of traditional international trade theory, with two traded goods, X and Y, produced by non-traded primary factors with exogenously determined terms of trade and a given, well-behaved community preference map. We then examine the same model for the case of growth subject to a given production subsidy. Finally, we discuss briefly complications implied by the existence of traded inputs, monopoly power in trade and non-traded goods.

II THE WELFARE CRITERION

Assume that the economy, before growth, has a production possi-

the ideal Little–Scott–Scitovsky methods, thus lead to quite different estimates of growth rates. It may be useful to discuss more clearly why this is so. Thus, note that ϕ is different for the before-growth and after-growth situations; let therefore ϕ^b and ϕ^a represent the former and the latter respectively. Under the *ideal* method, these authors would divide the incremental value-added at international prices (that is, JK) by the before-growth expenditure at market prices (that is, $OH = OK.\phi^b$); then they would multiply it into what they call the marginal ϕ, whose definition is the incremental expenditure at market prices divided by the incremental value-added at international prices (and which therefore is: $\left(\frac{OJ.\phi^a - OK.\phi^b}{JK}\right)$. This then yields: $\left(\frac{OJ.\phi^a - OK.\phi^b}{OK.\phi^b}\right)$. This can then be rewritten as $\left\{-\frac{JK}{OK}+\frac{OJ}{OK}\left(\frac{\phi^a}{\phi^b}-1\right)\right\}$.

If we now evaluate ϕ^b and ϕ^a correctly as OH/OK and OG/OJ respectively, it is easy to see that the growth rate will then reduce to $-GH/OH$. However, if a single, common ϕ is assumed, then $\phi^b = \phi^a$ and the growth rate reduces to $-JK/OK$.

bility curve, AB, while after growth it is CD; see Figure 3.1. In each situation there is a given, common tariff. In the pre-growth equilibrium, production, consumption, and welfare are at P_b, C_b and U_b, respectively. In the post-growth situation, equilibrium is at P_a, C_a and U_a. In each equilibrium situation we assume that tariff revenue is redistributed as an income subsidy to consumers; in the pre-growth equilibrium it is equivalent to EH units of X and after growth it is FG.

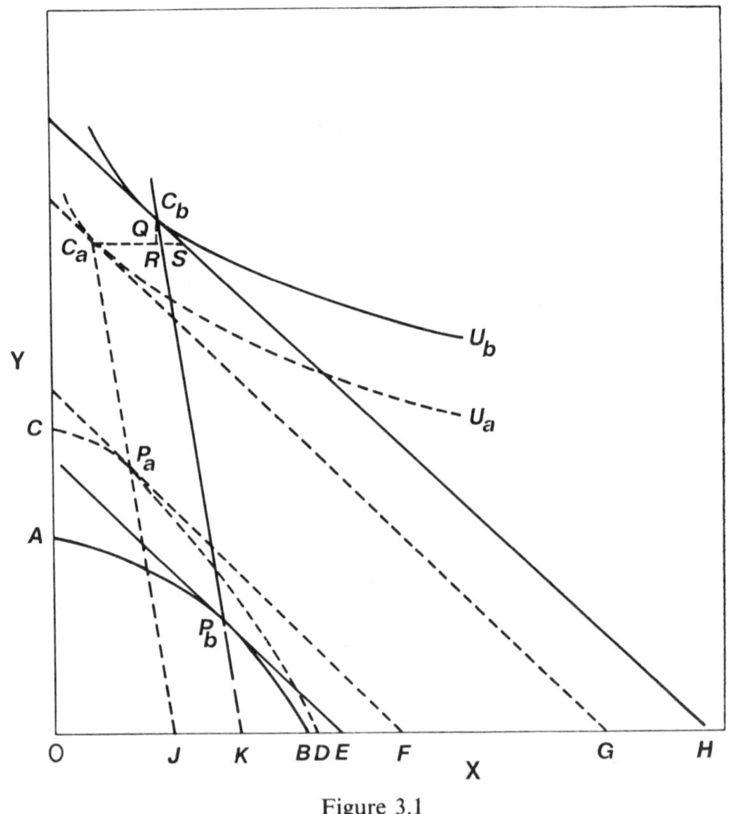

Figure 3.1

Note, first, that in this simple case with balanced trade and no factor payments to other countries, we need not distinguish between national and domestic product; and national expenditure and product (value-added, national income) are equal in size, provided that both are evaluated at either domestic factor cost or domestic factor prices or international prices. The difference between national expenditure (= national product) at domestic market prices and domestic factor cost represents clearly the total revenue from tariffs.

This is the standard national accounting terminology which we shall apply in what follows. In moving from pre-growth to post-growth equilibrium we may thus distinguish between three measures of the resulting change in national expenditure and product and ask which of these measures, if any, can measure (or at least indicate the direction of) the accompanying change in the level of welfare:

1. The change in national product (expenditure) at *domestic factor cost* (that is, evaluated at domestic, tariff-inclusive market prices excluding the value of total tariff revenue): measured in terms of commodity X, the absolute change in national product (expenditure) at factor cost is EF; and the rate of change is EF/OE. Clearly, to use this measure as an indicator of the change of welfare is wrong when we actually have immiseration ($U_a < U_b$) as we have drawn Figure 3.1.[6]

2. The change in national expenditure (product) *at market prices* (that is, evaluated at domestic, tariff-inclusive prices, including the value of tariff revenue): the absolute change, measured in terms of commodity X, in national expenditure (product) at market prices is *minus* GH, and the rate of change is *minus* GH/OH. This measure, showing a reduction in welfare, is consistent with the immiseration that has occurred. Besides, it is a 'natural' measure of the actual change in welfare because it may be construed in the Hicksian compensating-variational sense: if domestic expenditure worth GH units of X were given to the country after growth, it would restore welfare to the same level as before growth occurred.

3. The change in national product (expenditure) *revalued at international prices*: the absolute change in national product (expenditure), revalued at international prices, would show a decline (in terms of X) of JK; and the rate of change would be *minus* JK/OK. This measure would again be consistent with the actual immiseration ($U_a < U_b$). However, note two things:

i. This measure would generally have a different magnitude than the change in national expenditure (product) at market prices. In Figure 3.1, $JK \neq GH$ and $JK/OK \neq GH/OH$; hence it is *not* a

[6] The discussion here centres, of course, upon the 'odd' cases. For if both the production point and the expenditure point move to the north-east there is no doubt that both production and expenditure have increased. No matter what constant prices we use for evaluating the growth rate of production and/or expenditure, we come out with a positive growth rate. Although the measured growth rates will depend upon the prices, their signs will always be positive. It is when one or both of the expenditure and production points have moved to the north-west or south-east that problems of sign appear.

matter of indifference as to which measure is adopted for measuring either absolute growth or growth rates.

ii. Furthermore, this measure, at international prices, makes sense in the following way. If a net transfer (say, aid flow) equal to $C_aR = JK$ units of X were made to this country, starting out from the after-growth situation, the economy would clearly move from C_a to C_b, that is, from U_a to U_b, with C_aO units of the inflow held in the form of X and QR units transformed into QC_b units of Y. But, note that national expenditure would have increased by C_aR units of the transfer and RS units of tariff revenue. It follows that $C_aR = JK$ units of X represent the net transfer from abroad that would take the tariff-ridden economy back to the pre-growth level of welfare (U_b); it is thus a compensating-variational measure of the inflow of resources from abroad that would be required to restore the economy to its pre-growth level of welfare. Note that this measure is fully consistent conceptually with the preceding measure in terms of change in national expenditure at market prices: given the tariff, national expenditure must necessarily increase, to the extent that tariff revenue increases, by more than the net transfer. Hence, both measures are different evaluations of the same measure (that is, of the Hicksian compensating variation) and both would therefore seem 'natural' measures of the actual change in economic welfare.

We may therefore be tempted to conclude that the change in national product (expenditure) either at market price or revalued at international prices would correctly indicate the shift in *actual* welfare and that the choice between the two is essentially arbitrary.

However, we can conclude something a little stronger. Thus, take Figure 3.2 where we have a case, based on recent analysis of tariffs by Bhagwati, Kemp and Vanek,[7] where the growth leads to an improvement in the availabilities-locus from P_bC_b to P_aC_a but immiseration nonetheless occurs ($U_b > U_a$).[8] This case requires inferiority in social consumption of the exportable good; and the Pareto-superiority of the availability-locus P_aC_a over P_bC_b implies that a superior equilibrium exists in the after-growth situation which, if chosen, would lead to $U_a > U_b$.

[7] See J. Bhagwati, 'The Gains from Trade Once Again', *Oxford Economic Papers*, vol. 20 (1968), pp. 137–48; M. Kemp, 'Some Issues in the Analysis of Trade Gains', *Oxford Economic Papers*, vol. 20 (1968), pp. 149–61; J. Vanek, *General Equilibrium of International Discrimination* (Harvard University Press, 1965).

[8] An analogous case with a deterioration of availability and increase of welfare may also occur, but the implications are, of course, the same.

Now, in this situation, our analysis of Figure 3.1 goes through but with a new twist. We see that, starting from the after-growth situation, a *net transfer out*, worth RC_a units of X, will lead to a net increase in national expenditure of C_aS units of X (the tariff-revenue increase being RS, the transfer outflow being RC_a, the difference then being C_aS). Thus, we have the paradox: the measure in terms

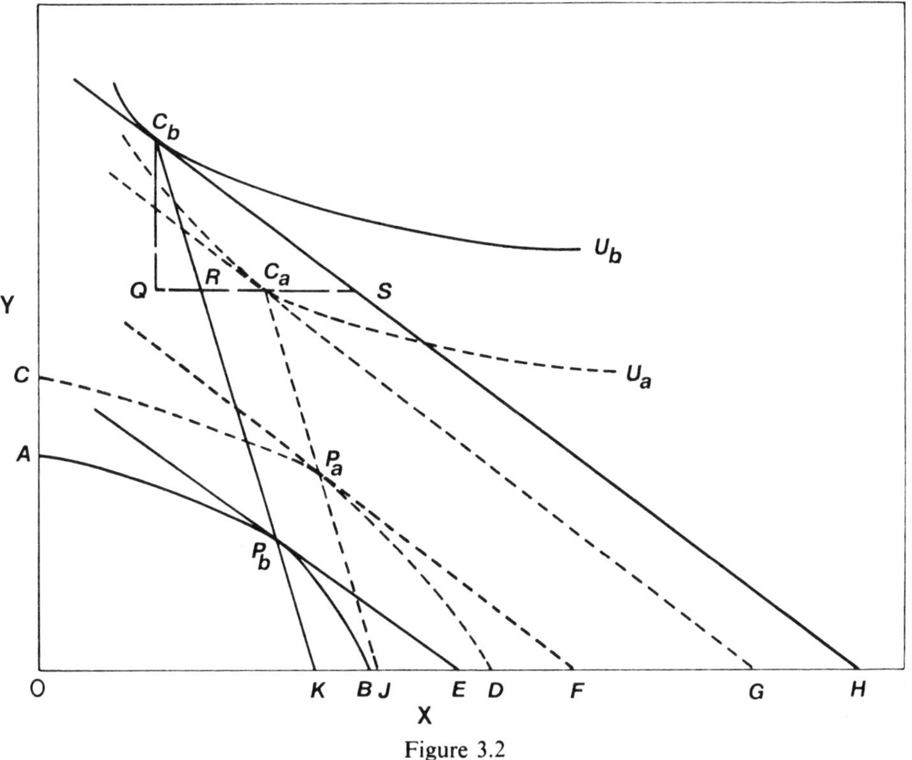

Figure 3.2

of market prices will show a *negative* growth rate of GH/OH, which is consistent with the *actual* immiseration; the measure in terms of international prices will show, on the other hand, a *positive* growth rate of JK/OK, which would contradict the fact of the immiseration that has actually occurred.

We can thus conclude that:

1. As an index of the direction of change in *actual* welfare, the conventional measure of expenditure (product) at market prices will be correct invariably; the measure at international prices will work in the absence of inferiority in social consumption; and the measure

at factor cost is both conceptually unsuitable and would be treacherous (in the presence of immiseration).

On the other hand, noting that in Figure 3.2 the availability-locus P_aC_a dominates P_bC_b and therefore potential or feasible welfare at the actual production vector will have improved even though actual welfare has reduced after growth, we can conclude that:

2. As an index of *potential* or *feasible* welfare at the *actual* production vector, the measure of national product (expenditure) at international prices will be correct invariably; the measure at market prices will work in so far as, if inferiority in consumption is present, it does not lead to choice of 'inferior' equilibria in the Pareto-superior situation;[9] and the measure at factor cost would again be both conceptually inappropriate and treacherous (in the presence of immiseration).

III THE 'PRODUCTIVE CAPACITY' CRITERION

So far we have chosen to evaluate the different national product (expenditure) measures by reference to whether they suitably indicate welfare-change. Suppose instead that we are interested in measuring changes in 'productive capacity'. Would the revaluation of actual production at international prices be correct in that case? Unfortunately, it fails here; and the correct measure (in a sense to be shortly defined) would be national product (expenditure) at factor cost – that is, the production vector evaluated at the domestic, tariff-inclusive price ratios but excluding tariff revenue.

For, if we aim to measure changes in 'productive capacity', we are essentially measuring the shift, in Figures 3.1 and 3.2, in either the production possibility curve from AB to CD or the availability-locus defined inclusive of the trade possibility.

1. In the former case, it only makes sense to measure the shift in the production possibility curve by positing a price-ratio and competitively choosing the production vector by reference to it: measuring the change in national product at domestic factor cost would do precisely this. Both production vector and price ratio would then be observable. Evaluating the production vector, which has been chosen by reference to the tariff-inclusive price ratio, at the international

[9] As Kemp (op. cit.) has shown, plausible stability conditions can be established which rule out the 'inferior' equilibria as unstable. Hence, the distinction between actual and potential welfare may not be terribly important in practice; in which case, the two measures, at international prices and at market prices, are both equally 'legitimate'.

price ratio would for this purpose be a meaningless hybrid and could, indeed, show a decline in productive capacity, as in Figure 3.1, when in fact the productive capacity has increased (that is, the production possibility curve has been pushed outwards).

2. In the latter case, where the shift in the availability-locus, inclusive of the trade opportunity, is sought to be measured, however, the international price vector does become relevant: but it should be used to evaluate a production vector which is chosen by reference to it – in Figures 3.1 and 3.2, the production bundles must be chosen, in our competitive economy, by putting the international price-ratio tangent to AB and to CD successively. In that case, evaluation at international prices measures both productive capacity and *maximal* feasible welfare; but this production point is not directly observable. When the production possibility curve has shifted outward, implying increase in productive capacity in the trade-augmented sense as well, the measure of increment in national product at factor cost will, however, be directionally correct as it must show an increase in productive capacity.[10] On the other hand, a measure which merely revalues the given production vector (chosen by reference to the tariff-inclusive prices) could, as we have just argued via Figure 3.1, show a reduction in 'productive capacity' and hence be directionally incorrect as well.

IV GROWTH SUBJECT TO A PRODUCTION SUBSIDY

If, however, we consider the case of a production subsidy – which differs from the tariff in not causing a consumption distortion as well – then the revaluation at international prices yields a measure of welfare-change which is identical with that yielded by evaluation at domestic market prices; both, therefore, indicate correctly the actual and potential change in welfare resulting from growth. (The inappropriateness of either for measuring the change in 'productive capacity', however, continues.)

Thus, in Figure 3.3, assume that commodity Y enjoys a subsidy on production at rate RS/QR. Production is therefore at P_b before growth, and at P_a after growth, at the subsidy-inclusive price-ratio equal to the slope of P_aW or P_bS. RS is the subsidy actually paid out, measured in terms of commodity X, in the situation before growth: it is assumed that it is collected by lump-sum taxation from the earnings

[10] Assuming, of course, that the old and the new production possibility curves do not intersect. This could happen if natural resources upon which the production of one of the commodities depends were exhausted, for instance.

at factor cost. The measure of national product (expenditure) at factor cost is therefore *OS* and *OW*, before and after growth, respectively.

Clearly, therefore, the increment in national product at factor cost is an erroneous measure of welfare change: it shows positive increment at rate *SW*/*OS*, whereas immiseration has occurred ($U_b > U_a$).

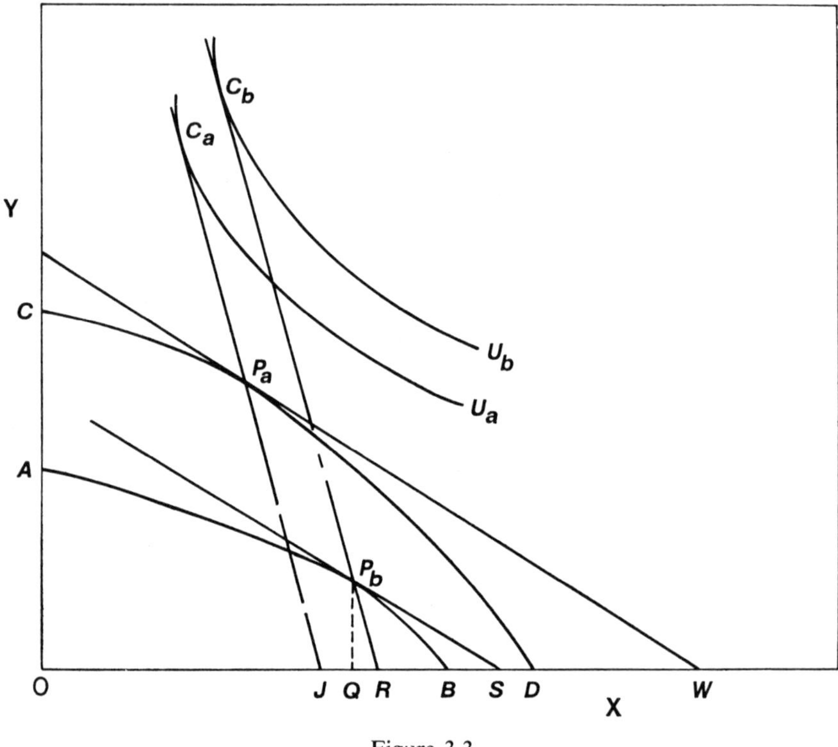

Figure 3.3

But the increment at market price correctly shows immiseration at rate *JR*/*OR*; and so does valuation at international prices. Thus the revaluation at international prices yields the correct measure of welfare-change: but note that it reduces, in view of the equality between the domestic prices at which consumption occurs and the international price vector, to the same measure as the measure in terms of domestic market prices.

V SOME COMPLICATIONS

Our analysis clarifies the issues in relation to a highly simplified value-theoretic, trade model. This simplicity of the model helps us to focus on the important issues. At the same time, however, it masks a number of difficulties.

Some of these difficulties are well known and common to all methods of evaluating growth rates: for example, price changes between the pre-growth and the post-growth situations, the presence of externalities and non-marketed output such as government services, the treatment of investment goods, and so on. We focus now rather on the problems, if any, arising from introducing multiple goods and intermediates; and the differential effect on our different measures of the presence of monopoly power in trade and of non-traded goods.

Multiple goods. Clearly our analysis is not conditional on the assumption of only two goods; it would readily carry over into a multi-good model, holding the other features of the model unchanged.

Intermediates. Our model disregards the use of produced or imported inputs in production, but abandoning this simplification does not really upset our conclusions. For such commodities are either used by both consumers and industries (for example, gasoline) or they are only used by industry (aluminium). Unless there are special consumer taxes that industry does not pay, produced or imported inputs are indeed evaluated at domestic market (consumer) prices in the first case. In the second case there is no direct consumer evaluation; the value of the inputs to the consumer is then equal to the value of the marginal product of the input at domestic market prices for the output. Profit maximization should make sure that in equilibrium the value of the marginal product is equal to the domestic market price of the input. Thus produced inputs do not present us with any new problems as far as measuring the growth rate is concerned.

Monopoly power in trade. Falling demand and rising supply curves abroad (monopoly) imply that export and import prices do not express marginal opportunity costs. The marginal revenues and costs that should be substituted for prices in such circumstances are not directly observable, and this fact immediately deprives international price evaluation of one of its major advantages. Little, Scitovsky and Scott[11] mention this possibility in the case of exports but express the hope that export taxes may have been optimal.

[11] Little, Scitovsky and Scott, op. cit., p. 418.

Should this hope be fulfilled, market prices would clearly be identical with marginal revenues, and evaluation of production at 'international opportunity costs' would be identical with evaluation of production at factor cost. On the other hand, evaluation at domestic market prices would remain the correct method if an index of actual welfare is sought.

To assume that actual export taxes are optimal would, of course, be to beg the question of measuring marginal revenues (and costs) in foreign trade. But quite apart from whether tariffs actually are optimal or not, there are a number of problems when we attempt to measure at international prices, making it necessary to take a careful look at our criteria when monopoly power in trade obtains.

i. Our first criterion was actual welfare. Given our general assumptions, the introduction of monopoly power in trade is consistent with the existence of a unique expenditure point with an associated utility level in each situation before and after growth, whether actual tariffs are optimal or not; and the change of this point is still to be measured in terms of domestic market prices to obtain a measure of the change in actual welfare.

ii. But our second criterion, feasible or potential welfare *at given production*, may break down. Feasible expenditure at given production can no longer be expressed uniquely at the observed, given international price because the price itself depends upon the volume of trade. And, in any case, international prices no longer measure opportunity costs. Hence we may shift to evaluation at marginal revenue. But generally speaking, marginal revenue also depends upon the volume of trade. Feasible expenditure at given production now takes place along a non-linear offer curve superimposed à la Baldwin[12] on the production point. Evaluating each point of the offer curve at the corresponding marginal revenue (the slope of the offer curve at that point), we find now that the value of expenditure in terms of the exportable good in the simple two-good model will be larger the larger is the volume of trade. And there is no one-to-one correspondence between the value of expenditure thus evaluated and the utility level obtained. As trade increases along the offer curve from the production point, utility will increase up to a point and then decrease while the value of expenditure in terms of X will continue increasing. We could then ask if there is any particular point on the offer curve which could be singled out. If we are looking for feasible

[12] R. E. Baldwin, 'The New Welfare Economics and Gains in International Trade', *Quarterly Journal of Economics*, vol. 64 (1952), pp. 99–101.

welfare, this point would naturally be the point of highest utility – that is, the point of tangency between the offer curve and the utility curves. Should the tariffs happen to be at optimum, this point will be identical with actual expenditure and what we measure is identical with expenditure at domestic market prices. If tariffs are not at optimum, evaluation of expenditure at marginal revenue in trade *at the highest utility level* (as defined here) is indeed an independent measure, but to make this evaluation we would have to work with quantities and marginal revenues, neither of which is directly observed and would require knowledge not only of the offer curve but also of the preference map for their (econometric) estimation.

iii. Our third criterion, 'production capacity', may now be interpreted as either the production possibility curve or the efficient Baldwin-envelope. What we said in Section II about the production possibility curve applies here, too, *mutatis mutandis*: only one set of related prices and quantities can be directly observed, viz., actual production and factor costs, and measurement at factor cost is a correct solution. Concerning the Baldwin-envelope, on the other hand, the actual expenditure point (the only directly observable point) will be on the Baldwin-envelope only if tariffs are optimal, and we are then back to evaluation at domestic market prices. If tariffs are not optimal, however, no point on the Baldwin-envelope (with the corresponding marginal revenue) will be directly observable. And even if the envelope could be econometrically estimated, we would have to evaluate the 'capacity' with respect to the preference map if we wish to come out with econometrically meaningful *single* numbers.

Thus, the existence of monopoly in trade seems to imply that evaluation at the 'correct' quantities and related *international* 'prices' (that is, marginal revenues) is generally impossible without resort to econometric estimation of the foreign offer curve – and not just of marginal revenue around the observed trade point alone – and specification of the country's own preference map. In the very special case of optimal tariffs, evaluation of international 'prices' simply coincides with one of the conventional methods, evaluation at market prices or at factor costs. The *conventional* methods, on the other hand, make sense in the same way as they did in the case where the country had no monopoly power in trade.

Non-traded goods. Conceptually, we may further modify the model to allow for non-traded goods by *either* introducing a sector which is non-tradable (for example, services) *or* assuming that all 'goods' are in principle tradable but that each good has an f.o.b. and a c.i.f. price and that, in equilibrium, one or more goods may become non-traded (with their prices lying between the c.i.f. and the f.o.b. price).

In either conceptualization, the measure of change in domestic expenditure at market prices should continue to provide an idea of the change in actual welfare. However, serious difficulties arise in revaluation of the production vector at international prices. In the former model, the non-*tradable* sector has no 'international' price by assumption; whereas, in the latter case, the equilibrium allocation of resources is likely to involve the presence of non-*traded* goods whose price is between the c.i.f. and the f.o.b. prices and hence which do not have a single, identifiable 'international' price.[13] Hence, these non-traded goods have to be perforce evaluated at other-than-international prices and the international-price-valuation approach is just not applicable in the presence of non-traded goods – as literally stated.

These problems can be fairly serious in practice. Two examples may suffice as illustrations. In Egypt, the c.i.f. price for fertilizer (15·5 calcium nitrate) was LE 18·53 per hkg in 1960 at an f.o.b. price of LE 14·95. In Afghanistan (average for 1964/5 – 67/8), at a wheat price of 7·3 USc/kg f.o.b. US port, the price c.i.f. Kabul was 10·9 USc/kg, implying a hypothetical price f.o.b. Kabul for shipment to US port of 3·7 USc/kg. Similarly, the proportion of non-tradable services in LDCs is often a large fraction of total GNP and cannot be dismissed lightheartedly.

VI CONCLUSIONS

Not surprisingly we come out with the result that the answer depends upon the question. It is best to try to specify what is meant by growth and then to look around for adequate yardsticks. We find then that:

1. If we are looking for an indicator of the development of actual welfare, granted the existence of a well-behaved community preference map, the correct measure is the conventional growth rate at domestic market prices.

2. If we seek, however, an indicator of feasible, potential welfare

[13] We may also note that no matter which method of evaluation is used, a commodity that is exported or non-traded in the pre-growth situation may be imported in the post-growth situation even at given c.i.f. and f.o.b. prices and tariffs; this will also generally lead to price changes and hence index number problems.

at actual production, the growth rate of national product or expenditure evaluated at international prices is the correct measure. But in the latter case there are serious problems arising from the existence of non-traded tradables and non-tradables; and with monopoly power in trade, the measure at international prices breaks down (in the sense discussed earlier).

3. In either case, the measures are at best ordinal; thus we cannot tell whether a particular measure 'exaggerates' the growth rate – this is an issue that seems intractable.

4. If we are interested, however, in productive capacity, the growth rate as conventionally evaluated at factor cost is a correct ordinal measure and the only one that is based on directly observable quantities and prices. If we allow for the possibility of using non-observable, estimated production, international prices may be used for obtaining a measure of capacity at optimal production, and maximum feasible welfare; but when monopoly power in trade prevails, the 'correct' quantities and 'prices' (that is, marginal revenues) have to be estimated, and this would require knowledge not only about the production possibility and offer curves, but also about the social preference map.

We do not exclude the possibility, finally, that growth may be defined in ways other than those discussed here; other measures may then be the correct ones.

Contents

Volume 2
International Factor Mobility

V
Surveys and Controversies in International Trade and Comparative Advantage

VI
Aid, Trade, and Payments

ACKNOWLEDGMENTS

The author, editor, and The MIT Press wish to thank the publishers of the following essays for permission to reprint them here.

1 *The Theory and Practice of Commercial Policy: Departures from Unified Exchange Rates,* Special Papers in International Economics No. 8, January 1968. Copyright 1968 by International Finance Section of Princeton University.

2 "The Generalized Theory of Distortions and Welfare," in J. N. Bhagwati, R. A. Mundell, R. W. Jones, and J. Vanek, eds., *Trade, Balance of Payments and Growth: Papers in International Economics in Honor of Charles P. Kindleberger,* Amsterdam: North-Holland, 1971, chapter 4, pp. 69–90. Copyright 1971 by North-Holland Publishing Company.

3 "International Trade and Economic Expansion," *American Economic Review* 48(5) (December 1958):941–953. Copyright 1958 by The American Economic Association.

4 "Immiserizing Growth: A Geometrical Note," *Review of Economic Studies* 25(3) (June 1958):201–205. Copyright 1958 by University of Essex.

5 "Distortions and Immiserizing Growth: A Generalization," *Review of Economic Studies* 35(104) (October 1968):481–485. Copyright 1968 by University of Essex.

6 "The Theory of Immiserizing Growth: Further Applications," in M. Connolly and A. Swoboda, eds., *International Trade and Money,* Toronto: University of Toronto Press, 1973, chapter 3, pp. 45–54. Copyright 1973 by University of Toronto Press; reverted to George Allen and Unwin Ltd.

7 "Optimal Policies and Immiserizing Growth," *American Economic Review* 59(5) (December 1969):967–970. Copyright 1969 by The American Economic Association.

9 "Trade and Welfare in a Steady State" (with T. N. Srinivasan), in J. S. Chipman and C. P. Kindleberger, eds., *Flexible Exchange Rates and the Balance of Payments: Essays in Memory of Egon Sohmen,* Studies in International Economics Vol. 7, Amsterdam: North-Holland, 1980, chapter 18, pp. 341–353. Copyright 1980 by North-Holland Publishing Company.

10 "Protection, Real Wages and Real Incomes," *Economic Journal* 69 (December 1959):733–748. Copyright 1959 by Macmillan and Co. Ltd.

11 "A Generalized Theory of the Effects of Tariffs on the Terms of Trade" (with H. G. Johnson), *Oxford Economic Papers* 13(3) (N.S.) (October 1961):225–253. Copyright 1961 by Oxford University Press.

12 "On the Equivalence of Tariffs and Quotas," in J. N. Bhagwati, *Trade, Tariffs and Growth,* Cambridge, MA: MIT Press, 1969, chapter 9, pp. 248–265. Copyright 1969 by Jagdish Bhagwati. [First printed, in unrevised form, under the same title in R. E. Caves, H. G. Johnson, and P. B. Kenen, *Trade, Growth, and the Balance of payments: Essays in Honor of Gottfried Haberler,* Chicago: Rand McNally, 1965, pp. 53–67.]

13 "The General Equilibrium Theory of Effective Protection and Resource Allocation" (with T. N. Srinivasan), *Journal of International Economics* 3 (1973):259–281. Copyright 1973 by North-Holland Publishing Company.

14 "Domestic Distortions, Tariffs and the Theory of Optimum Subsidy" (with V. K. Ramaswami), *Journal of Political Economy* 71(1) (February 1963):44–50. Copyright 1963 by The University of Chicago Press.

15 "Domestic Distortions, Tariffs, and the Theory of Optimum Subsidy: Some Further Results" (with V. K. Ramaswami and T. N. Srinivasan), *Journal of Political Economy* 77(6) (November/December 1969):1005–1010. Copyright 1969 by The University of Chicago Press.

16 "Ranking of Tariffs under Monopoly Power in Trade" (with Murray C. Kemp), *Quarterly Journal of Economics* 83 (May 1969):330–335. Copyright 1969 by the President and Fellows of Harvard College.

17 "Directly Unproductive Profit-Seeking (DUP) Activities," *Journal of Political Economy* 90(5) (October 1982):988–1002. Copyright 1982 by The University of Chicago Press.

18 "The Welfare Consequences of Directly-Unproductive Profit-Seeking (DUP) Lobbying Activities: Price versus Quantity Distortions" (with T. N. Srinivasan), *Journal of International Economics* 13 (1982):33–44. Copyright 1982 by North-Holland Publishing Company.

19 "A Theoretical Analysis of Smuggling" (with Bent Hansen), *Quarterly Journal of Economics* 87 (May 1973):172–187. Copyright 1973 by the President and Fellows of Harvard College.

20 "Smuggling and Trade Policy" (with T. N. Srinivasan), *Journal of Public Economics* 2 (1973):377–389. Copyright 1973 by North-Holland Publishing Company.

21 "On the Underinvoicing of Imports," *Bulletin of Oxford University Institute of Economics and Statistics* 26(4) (November 1964):389–397. Copyright 1964 by Oxford University Institute of Economics and Statistics. [Reprinted in J. N. Bhagwati, ed., *Illegal Transactions in International Trade: Theory and Measurement,* Studies in International Economics Vol. 1, Amsterdam: North-Holland, 1974, chapter 9, pp. 138–147.]

22 "Alternative Theories of Illegal Trade: Economic Consequences and Statistical Detection," *Weltwirtschaftliches Archiv: Review of World Economics* 117(3) (1981):409–426. Copyright 1981 by J. C. B. Mohr (Paul Siebeck) Tübingen.

23 "Revenue Seeking: A Generalization of the Theory of Tariffs" (with T. N. Srinivasan), *Journal of Political Economy* 88(6) (December 1980):1069–1087. Copyright 1980 by The University of Chicago Press.

24 "Revenue Seeking: A Generalization of the Theory of Tariffs—a Correction" (with T. N. Srinivasan), *Journal of Political Economy* 90(1) (February 1981):188–190. Copyright 1982 by The University of Chicago Press.

25 "Lobbying and Welfare," *Journal of Public Economics* 14 (1980):355–363. Copyright 1980 by North-Holland Publishing Company.

26 "Lobbying, DUP Activities, and Welfare: A Response to Tullock," *Journal of Public Economics* 19 (1982):395–401. Copyright 1982 by North-Holland Publishing Company.

27 "Tariff Seeking and the Efficient Tariff" (with Robert C. Feenstra), in J. N. Bhagwati, ed., *Import Competition and Response,* Chicago: University of Chicago Press, 1982, chapter 9, pp. 245–258. Copyright 1982 by The National Bureau of Economic Research.

28 "Optimal Intervention to Achieve Non-Economic Objectives" (with T. N. Srinivasan), *Review of Economic Studies* 36(1) (January 1969):27–38. Copyright 1969 by University of Essex.

29 "Trade Liberalization among LDCs, Trade Theory, and Gatt Rules," in J. N. Wolfe, ed., *Value, Capital and Growth: Papers in Honour of Sir John Hicks,* Edinburgh: Edinburgh University Press, 1968, chapter 2, pp. 21–43. Copyright 1968 by Edinburgh University Press.

30 "Optimal Trade Policy and Compensation under Endogenous Uncertainty: The Phenomenon of Market Disruption" (with T. N. Srinivasan), *Journal of International Economics* 6 (1976):317–336. Copyright 1976 by North-Holland Publishing Company.

31 "Market Disruption, Export Market Disruption, Compensation, and GATT Reform," in J. N. Bhagwati, ed., *The New International Economic Order: The North-South Debate,* Cambridge, MA: MIT Press, 1977, chapter 6, pp. 159–181. Copyright 1977 by The Massachusetts Institute of Technology.

32 "The Theory of Wage Differentials: Production Response and Factor Price Equalisation" (with T. N. Srinivasan), *Journal of International Economics* 1 (1971):19–35. Copyright 1971 by North-Holland Publishing Company.

33 "On Reanalyzing the Harris-Todaro Model: Policy Rankings in the Case of Sector-Specific Sticky Wages" (with T. N. Srinivasan), *American Economic Review* 64(3) (June 1974):502–508. Copyright 1974 by The American Economic Association.

34 "Alternative Policy Rankings in a Large, Open Economy with Sector-Specific, Minimum Wages" (with T. N. Srinivasan), *Journal of Economic Theory* 11(3) (December 1975):356–371. Copyright 1975 by Academic Press.

35 "Shadow Prices for Project Selection in the Presence of Distortions: Effective Rates of Protection and Domestic Resource Costs" (with T. N. Srinivasan), *Journal of Political Economy* 86(1) (February 1978):97–116. Copyright 1978 by The University of Chicago Press.

36 "The Evaluation of Projects at World Prices under Trade Distortions: Quantitative Restrictions, Monopoly Power in Trade and Nontraded Goods" (with T. N. Srinivasan), *International Economic Review* 22(2) (June 1981):385–399. Copyright 1981 by University of Pennsylvania.

37 "The 'Stationarity' of Shadow Prices of Factors in Project Evaluation, with and without Distortions" (with Henry Wan, Jr.), *American Economic Review* 69(3) (June 1979):261–273. Copyright 1979 by The American Economic Association.

38 "Domestic Resource Costs, Effective Rates of Protection, and Project Analysis in Tariff-Distorted Economies" (with T. N. Srinivasan), *Quarterly Journal of Economics* 96 (February 1980):205–209. Copyright 1980 by the President and Fellows of Harvard College.

39 "Value Subtracted, Negative Shadow Prices of Factors in Project Evaluation, and Immiserizing Growth: Three Paradoxes in the Presence of Trade Distortions" (with T. N. Srinivasan and Henry Wan, Jr.), *Economic Journal* 88 (March 1978):121–125. Copyright 1978 by Macmillan and Co. Ltd.

40 "On Inferring Resource-Allocational Implications from DRC Calculations in Trade-Distorted Small Open Economies" (with T. N. Srinivasan), *Indian Economic Review* 14(1) (NLSL) (April 1979):1–16. Copyright 1979 by Allied Publishers.

41 "Should Growth Rates Be Evaluated at International Prices?" (with B. Hansen), in J. N. Bhagwati and R. S. Eckaus, eds., *Development and Planning,* Cambridge, MA: MIT Press, 1973, chapter 3, pp. 53–68. Copyright 1973 by George Allen & Unwin, Ltd.

AUTHOR INDEX

SUBJECT INDEX